THE COMMON LAW LIBRARY

CHITTY
ON
CONTRACTS

Second Cumulative Supplement
to the
Thirty-Second Edition

Up-to-date to July 31, 2017

SWEET & MAXWELL  THOMSON REUTERS

Published in 2017 by Thomson Reuters
trading as Sweet & Maxwell.
Registered in England & Wales, Company No 1679046.
Registered Office and address for service:
5 Canada Square, Canary Wharf, London E14 5AQ.
For further information on our products and services,
visit *www.sweetandmaxwell.co.uk*

Computerset by Wright & Round Ltd, Gloucester
Printed and bound in the UK by CPI Group (UK) Ltd, Croydon, CR0 4YY

No natural forests were destroyed to make this product;
only farmed timber was used and replanted

A CIP catalogue record for this book is available from the British Library

ISBN Main Work (full set)   9780414050679

ISBN Supplement   9780414064805

GENERAL EDITOR

H. G. BEALE, Q.C. (Hon.), B.A., F.B.A.
Honorary Bencher of Lincoln's Inn; Professor of Law,
University of Warwick; Senior Research Fellow of Harris Manchester College
and Visiting Professor in the University of Oxford

EDITORS

A. S. BURROWS, Q.C. (Hon.), D.C.L., LL.M., M.A., F.B.A.
of the Middle Temple, Honorary Bencher; Fellow of All Souls College and
Professor of the Law of England, University of Oxford

MINDY CHEN-WISHART, BA (Hons), LL.B., LL.M. (Otago), MA (Oxon)
Fellow of Merton College and Professor of the Law of Contract,
University of Oxford

M. R. FREEDLAND, Q.C, (Hon.), LL.B., M.A., D.Phil., F.B.A.
Bencher of Gray's Inn; Emeritus Research Fellow of St John's College and
Emeritus Professor of Employment Law, University of Oxford

R. J. A. HOOLEY, M.A. (Cantab.)
of the Middle Temple, Barrister; Fellow of Fitzwilliam College and
University Lecturer, University of Cambridge

EVA LOMNICKA, M.A. (Cantab.), LL.B. (Cantab.)
Bencher of the Middle Temple; Professor of Law, King's College London

DAVID McCLEAN, C.B.E., Q.C. (Hon.), D.C.L., Hon.Litt.D., F.B.A.
Bencher of Gray's Inn; Emeritus Professor of Law, University of Sheffield

P. J. S. MACDONALD EGGERS, Q.C., LL.B. (Syd.), LL.M. (Cantab.)
of the Middle Temple, Barrister; Visiting Professor, University College London

E. G. McKENDRICK, Q.C. (Hon.), LL.B., B.C.L., M.A.
Bencher of Gray's Inn; Fellow of Lady Margaret Hall, Registrar and Professor
of English Private Law, University of Oxford

L. MERRETT, M.A., Ph.D. (Cantab.)
of Gray's Inn, Barrister; Fellow of Trinity College and
Reader in International Commercial Law, University of Cambridge

P. P. MITCHELL, B.A., D.Phil. (Oxon)
Professor of Laws, University College London

[iii]

HOW TO USE THIS SUPPLEMENT

This is the Second Cumulative Supplement to the Thirty-Second Edition of *Chitty on Contracts*, and has been compiled according to the structure of the two main work volumes.

At the beginning of each chapter of this Supplement the mini table of contents from the main volume has been included. Where a heading in this table of contents has been marked with a square pointer, this indicates that there is relevant information in the Supplement to which the reader should refer. Material that is new to the Cumulative Supplement is indicated by the symbol □. Material that has been included from the previous supplement is indicated by the symbol ■

Within each chapter, updating information is referenced to the relevant paragraph in the main volume.

It should be noted that for this Supplement there is no material for chapter 10.

This Supplement has been prepared on the premise that, despite the referendum result in favour of "Brexit", the UK remains a member of the EU and that the status of EU law in UK law remains unchanged. See below, paras 1–013A—1–013E.

TABLE OF CONTENTS

VOLUME I

VOLUME II

TABLE OF STATUTES

Where a reference indicates significant discussion of the statute in the text, it is in **bold**. Where a reference is to a footnote, it is *italic*.

TABLE OF STATUTORY INSTRUMENTS

Where a reference indicates significant discussion of the statute in the text, it is in **bold**. Where a reference is to a footnote, it is *italic*.

TABLE OF EUROPEAN UNION LEGISLATION

Where a reference indicates significant discussion of the statute in the text, it is in **bold**. Where a reference is to a footnote, it is *italic*.

TABLE OF INTERNATIONAL STATUTORY MATERIAL

Where a reference indicates significant discussion of the statute in the text, it is in **bold**. Where a reference is to a footnote, it is *italic*.

[xxiii]

TABLE OF CASES

Where a reference indicates significant discussion of the case in the text, it is in **bold**. Where a reference is to a footnote, it is *italic*.

TABLE OF EUROPEAN CASES

Where a reference indicates significant discussion of the case in the text, it is in **bold**. Where a reference is to a footnote, it is *italic*.

VOLUME I

GENERAL PRINCIPLES

Part One

INTRODUCTION

CHAPTER 1

INTRODUCTORY

[1]

1. SOURCES OF ENGLISH CONTRACT LAW

Contract law

1–001   [*Add to note 2, line 4, after* "unfair contract terms)": *page* [4]]
and see Whittaker (2017) 133 L.Q.R. 47 esp. at 66–72.

(a) *The Common Law of Contract*

The common law's dominance of the general law

1–003   [*Add to note 5, at the end: page* [5]]
See, however, Burrows, *A Restatement of the English Law of Contract* (2016), whose aim (p.x) is "to provide the best interpretation of the present English law of contract".

(b) *Statute*

Consumer contracts

1–008   [*Add new note 51a, line 31, after* "statutory or common law": *page* [8]]
    [51a] On the distinctive features of modern consumer contract law see Whittaker (2017) 133 L.Q.R. 47.

(d) *EU Law*

[*Insert new sub-heading before para.1–011: page* [9]]

(i) *The Current Position*

EU law governing contracts: the Union *acquis*

1–011   [*Add to note 63, line 15, after* "[1990] O.J. L158/59": *page* [9]]
(itself repealed and replaced by Directive (EU) 2015/2302 on package travel and linked travel arrangements [2015] O.J. L326/1 as from July 1, 2018 (arts 28 and 29))

[*Add to note 63, at the end: page* [9]]
; Directive 2014/17/EU on credit agreements for consumers relating to residential immovable property [2014] O.J. L2014/34 on which see Main Work, Vol.II, paras 39–003 and 39–531.

[*In note 65, line 3, delete* "Law Payment" *and substitute: page* [10]]
Late Payment

[*Add to note 66, last line, after* "[2004] O.J. L134/1.": *page* [10]]
The two 2004 directives were repealed and replaced as from April 18, 2016 by Directive 2014/24/EU on public procurement and repealing Directive 2004/18/EC [2014] O.J. L94/65 (see esp. art.91) and Directive 2014/25/EU on procurement by entities operating in the water, energy, transport and postal services sectors and repealing Directive 2004/17/EC [2014] O.J. L94/243 (see esp. art.107), which were supplemented by Directive 2014/23/EU on the award of concession contracts [2014] O.J. L94/1.

The Proposed Common European Sales Law (CESL)

[*Add to note 88, at the end: page* [12]]   1–013
This strategy has led, inter alia, to a Proposal for a Directive of the European Parliament and of the Council on certain aspects concerning contracts for the online and other distance sales of goods COM(2015) 635 final and a Proposal for a Directive of the European Parliament and of the Council on certain aspects concerning contracts for the supply of digital content COM(2015) 634.

[*Add new sub-heading and new paras 1–013A—1–013E: page* [13]]

(ii) *United Kingdom's Exit from the EU ("Brexit")*

A note on "Brexit". After a national referendum held on June 23, 2016 at which   1–013A
a majority voted in favour of the UK leaving the EU, the UK Conservative Government formed on July 16, 2016 declared its intention to end the UK's membership of the EU ("Brexit") and on March 29, 2017 the Prime Minister, the Right Hon. Mrs Theresa May MP, set in motion the process of doing so under art.50 of the Treaty of the European Union (TEU).[92a] The Conservative Government set out its intentions as to the position of existing EU law in the UK in two white papers, *The United Kingdom's exit from and new partnership with the European Union*[92b] and *Legislating for the United Kingdom's withdrawal from the European Union.*[92c]

[92a] The Prime Minister's authority to do so was given by the European Union (Notification of Withdrawal) Act 2017 s.1.
[92b] Department for Exiting the European Union, Cm.9417 (February 2017).
[92c] Department for Exiting the European Union, Cm.9446 (March 2017).

European Union (Withdrawal) Bill 2017. After a general election held on June   1–013B
8, 2017, the Conservative Government earlier formed by Mrs May remained in government. On July 13, 2017 the European Union (Withdrawal) Bill ("the 2017 Bill" or "the Bill") received its first reading in the House of Commons, its

second reading being held on September 7 and 11, 2017[92d]; the 2017 Bill is accompanied by Explanatory Notes ("Explanatory Notes to 2017 Bill"). For the purposes of the likely impact of Brexit on English contract law, the following points arise from the terms of the Bill as presently drafted.

[92d] See *http://services.parliament.uk/bills/2017-19/europeanunionwithdrawal.html.*

1–013C **The general preservation of the UK's EU legislative** *acquis.* The Bill would repeal the European Communities Act 1972 on "exit day",[92e] defined as "such day as a Minister of the Crown may be regulations appoint",[92f] but clearly intended to be the day on which the UK leaves the EU. Despite this repeal, the Bill would in principle retain the EU *legislative acquis* as part of UK law. First, in principle "EU-derived domestic legislation, as it has effect in domestic law immediately before exit day, continues to have effect in domestic law on and after exit day".[92g] This provision would preserve much of the UK legislation governing contract law, which has been enacted as secondary legislation under the European Communities Act 1972, as in the case of the Consumer Contracts (Information, Cancellation and Additional Charges) Regulations 2013[92h] and the Timeshare Regulations 2010[92i] in the field of consumer contracts or the Commercial Agents (Council Directive) Regulations 1993 in the field of commercial agency.[92j] Secondly, "[d]irect EU legislation, so far as operative immediately before exit day, forms part of domestic law on or after exit day".[92k] Such direct EU legislation includes EU regulations[92l] and would therefore concern such instruments affecting contract law as the Brussels I*bis* Regulation[92m] or the Rome I Regulation[92n] in the area of private international law, and the Denied Boarding Regulation in the area of consumer protection[92o]). Thirdly, the 2017 Bill contains provision for the preservation of UK primary legislation enacted for the purpose of implementing EU obligations (such as the Consumer Rights Act 2015[92p]) or secondary legislation with the same purpose but made under statutory powers other than those contained in s.2(2) of the 1972 Act.[92q] Taken together, these laws are referred to as "retained EU law" by the Bill.[92r] There are, however, two types of qualifications on the resulting preservation in UK law of the EU legislative *acquis* as the Bill itself sets out certain exceptions for this purpose, and also provides for the later amendment or repeal of legislation (primary or secondary) whose source is in EU legislation either by secondary legislation made by a Minister of the Crown or by a devolved authority (such as the Scottish Ministers), this being referred to as "dealing with deficiencies arising from withdrawal".[92s]

[92e] European Union (Withdrawal) Bill 2017 ("2017 Bill") cl.1.

[92f] 2017 Bill cl.14(1) "exit day", itself referring to cl.14(2) as regards the time of day.

[92g] 2017 Bill cl.2(1). Clause 2(2) defines "EU-derived domestic legislation" to include, in particular, any enactment made under s.2(2) of the European Communities Act 1972. The exceptions to this general position are set out by cl.5 and Sch.1.

[92h] SI 2013/3134 implementing Directive 2011/83/EU on consumer rights [2011] O.J. L304/64 on which see Main Work, Vol.I, paras 38–057 et seq.

[92i] Timeshare, Holiday Products, Resale and Exchange Contracts Regulations 2010 (SI 2010/2960) implementing Directive 2008/122/EC on the protection of consumers in respect of certain aspects of timeshare, long-term holiday product, resale and exchange contracts [2009] O.J. L33/30, on which see Vol.II, paras 38–136—38–142.

[92j] SI 1993/3053 implementing Directive 86/653 on the co-ordination of the laws of the Member States relating to self-employed commercial agents [1986] O.J. L382/17, on which see Main Work, Vol.II, paras 31–017—31–020.

[92k] 2017 Bill cl.3(1).

[92l] 2017 Bill cl.3(2).

[92m] Regulation (EU) 1215/2012 of December 12, 2012 on jurisdiction and the recognition and enforcement of judgments in civil and commercial matters (recast) [2012] O.J. L351/1.

[92n] Regulation 593/2008 on the law applicable to contractual obligations ("Rome I") [2008] O.J. L177/6, on which see Main Work, Vol.I, paras 30–129 et seq.

[92o] Regulation (EC) 261/2004 establishing common rules on compensation and assistance to passengers in the event of denied boarding and of cancellation or long delay of flights [2004] O.J. L46/1 on which see Main Work, Vol.II, paras 35–071—35–073.

[92p] The 2015 Act implements Directive 1999/44/EC on certain aspects of the sale of consumer goods and associated guarantees [1999] O.J. L171/12 (principally in Pt 1, Ch.2 of the Act); the Directive 93/13/EEC of April 5, 1993 on unfair terms in consumer contracts [1993] O.J. L95/29 (principally in Pt 2 of the Act) and certain aspects of Directive 2011/83/EU on consumer rights [2011] O.J. L304/64 (ss.11(4)–(6), 12; ss.36(3)–(4) and 37; and s.50(3)–(4) of the Act). On this see Main Work, Vol.II, paras 38–345 et seq. and 38–402, 38–431 et seq.

[92q] 2017 Bill cl.2(2) and see Explanatory Memorandum para.74, which gives as an example domestic health and safety law implementing EU obligations made under powers in the Health and Safety at Work etc. Act 1974 rather than the European Communities Act 1972.

[92r] 2017 Bill cl.6(7) defining "retained EU law" by reference to "anything which, on or after exit day, continues to be, or forms part of, domestic law by virtue of" cls 2, 3, 4 or 6(3) or (6) of the Bill, "as that body of law is added to or otherwise modified by or under [the Bill] or by other domestic law from time to time".

[92s] 2017 Bill heading of cl.7 and Sch.2 Pt 1; Cm.9446 (March 2017) paras 1.14–1.16. and Ch.3. The definition of "devolved authority" is contained in cl.14(1) of the 2017 Bill.

Further issues arising from Brexit. Three further issues in particular should be noted. First, the 2017 Bill makes provision to ensure that any remaining EU rights and obligations which are not preserved in the way just explained[92t] continue to be recognised and available in domestic law after the UK leaves the EU and these include directly effective rights contained in the European Treaties themselves.[92u] Secondly, on leaving the EU, the 2017 Bill would end the general supremacy of EU law, but this would take effect only prospectively in the sense that any conflict between two pre-exit laws (one EU-derived, one not) would be resolved in favour of the EU-derived law.[92v] Thirdly, provision is made for the future authoritative interpretation of the UK legislation whose source is EU legislation before and after the UK has left the EU ("exit day"). For this purpose a distinction is drawn between the case-law of, or principles laid down by, the Court of Justice of the EU *before* and *after* the UK's leaving the EU. As regards the former, "retained EU law"[92w] is in principle to be interpreted "in accordance with any retained case law and any retained general principles of EU law,[92x] and, having regard (among other things) to the limits, immediately before exit day, of EU competences".[92y] However, the Bill then provides that "the Supreme Court is not bound by any retained EU case law"[92z] and then explains that "[i]n deciding whether to depart from any retained EU case law, the Supreme Court . . . must apply the same test as it would apply in deciding whether to depart from its own case law".[92aa] As the Government's second white paper earlier foresaw, this would therefore treat "retained EU case law" as "normally binding" but it would allow the Supreme Court to depart from it "when it appears right to do so".[92ab] As regards the position of EU case law and principles *after* the UK has left the EU, the Bill provides that "[a] court or tribunal . . . is not bound by any principles laid down, or any decisions made, on or after exit day by the European Court"[92ac] and adds that "[a] court or tribunal need not have regard to anything done on or after exit day by the European Court, another EU entity or the EU but may do so if it considers it appropriate to do so".[92ad] This

1–013D

position would therefore mean that UK courts would not be required even to *consider* case law of the Court of Justice made after exit day, though they may do so if they consider it appropriate.[92ae] In this respect, the position would differ from the duty of UK courts under the Human Rights Act 1998 s.2(1) of which provides that in determining a question which has arisen in connection with a right under the European Convention on Human Rights a court "must take into account any ... judgment, decision, declaration or advisory opinion of the European Court of Human Rights".

[92t] Above, para.1–013C.
[92u] 2017 Bill cl.4 and Explanatory Notes to 2017 Bill, paras 87 et seq.
[92v] 2017 Bill cl.5; Cm 9446 (March 2017) paras 2.19–2.20.
[92w] See above, n.92.
[92x] Defined in terms of temporal origin by cl.6(7) of the 2017 Bill as those which are made or laid down immediately before exit day: cl.6(7) "retained EU case law" and "retained general principles of EU law".
[92y] 2017 Bill cl.6(3).
[92z] 2017 Bill cl.6(4)(a). Further provision is made as regards the (Scottish) High Court of Justiciary.
[92aa] 2017 Bill cl.6(5).
[92ab] Cm 9446 (March 2017) para.2.16 quoting the House of Lords Practice Statement (Judicial Precedent) of 1966, [1966] 1 W.L.R. 1234; and see also Explanatory Notes to 2017 Bill, para.107.
[92ac] 2017 Bill cl.6(1)(a).
[92ad] 2017 Bill cl.6(2).
[92ae] Explanatory Notes to 2017 Bill, paras 103–104.

1–013E **Present position.** However, until the UK leaves the EU (whether two years after March 29, 2017 when the Prime Minister gave the EU notice under art.50 TEU or at some later date with the agreement of the European Council), the UK remains a full member of the EU and the status of EU law remains the same as it has been since the UK's becoming a Member State in 1972 and the enactment of the European Communities Act.[92af] The text of this Supplement continues, therefore, to be written on the premise that the UK is a Member of the EU and that the status of EU law in the UK remains the same until such time as the European Union (Withdrawal) Bill is enacted, the UK leaves the EU and a Minister of the Crown therefore designates "exit day" as presently foreseen by the Bill.

[92af] This follows from the remaining in force of the European Communities Act 1972 and is acknowledged by Cm.9446 (March 2017) para.1.10.

2. DEFINITIONS OF CONTRACT

Competing definitions of contract

1–014 [*In note 96, delete* "13th edn (2011), para.1–001" *and substitute: page* [13]] 14th edn (2015), para.1–001. cf. Burrows, *A Restatement of the English Law of Contract* (2016), para.2 which defines "contract" as an agreement that is legally binding because it is supported by consideration or made by deed, certain and complete, made with the intention to create legal relations, and complies with any formal requirement needed for the agreement to be legally binding; and see the commentary at pp.44–55.

Difficulties with "contract as promise"

[*Add to note 104, at the end: page* [14]]
See also *MWB Business Exchange Centres Ltd v Rock Advertising Ltd* [2016] EWCA Civ 553, [2017] Q.B. 604 (appeal to SC pending) on which see below, para.4–119A.

1–015

Difficulties with "contract as agreement"

[*In note 112, delete* "13th edn (2011), para.3–170" *and substitute: page* [15]]
14th edn (2015), para.3–170. cf. Burrows, *A Restatement of the English Law of Contract* (2016), paras 2 and 8(1), commentary on pp.63–64, which includes agreements supported by a deed within its definition of contract, but distinguishes deeds which contain agreements and those which do not (deeds poll).

1–016

EU private international law

[*Add to note 147, line 2, after* "July 18, 2013 at para.33"*: page* [19]]
; *Brogsitter v Fabrication de Montres Normandes EURL* (C-548/12) March 13, 2014 at para.18; *ERGO Insurance SE v If P&C Insurance AS* (Joined Cases C-359/14 and C-475/14) January 21, 2016 at para.43; *Kolassa v Barclays Bank Plc* (C-375/13) January 28, 2015 at para.43; *Granarolo SpA v Ambrosi Emmi France SA* (C-196/15) July 14, 2016 at para.19.

1–021

[*Add to paragraph, at the end: page* [19]]
For this purpose, the Court of Justice of the EU has held that "the concept of 'contractual obligation' [under the Rome I Regulation] designates a legal obligation freely consented to by one person towards another".[152a]

[152a] *ERGO Insurance SE v If P&C Insurance AS* (Joined Cases C-359/14 and C-475/14) January 21, 2016 para.44; *Verein für Konsumenteninformation v Amazon EU Sàrl* (C-191/15) July 28, 2016 esp. at para.60 (action for cessation of use of unfair contract terms falls under Rome II as concerning a non-contractual obligation, though the assessment of the terms falls under Rome I as concerning a contractual obligation following the nature of these terms whether this arises in an action for cessation or in an individual action between a trader and a consumer); *Committeri v Club Mediterranee SA* [2016] EWHC 1510 (QB) at [45]–[48].

"Contract" in EU public procurement law

[*Add to note 163, at the end: page* [21]]
The conclusion of public contracts between entities in the public sector (which forms the context of this case-law) has been the subject of regulation by the Public Contracts Directive 2014: Directive 2014/24/EU on public procurement and repealing Directive 2004/18/EC [2014] O.J. L94/65 art.12 and recitals 31 and 32.

1–024

3. Fundamental Principles of Contract Law

(a) *Freedom of Contract*

Freedom of contract in the modern common law

1–027   [*Add to note 179, at the end: page* [23]]
; *Prime Sight Ltd v Lavarello* [2013] UKPC 22, [2014] A.C. 436 at [47] (contractual recital of fact known by both parties to be untrue enforceable in principle); *MWB Business Exchange Centres Ltd v Rock Advertising Ltd* [2016] EWCA Civ 553, [2017] Q.B. 604 at [31] and [34], following dicta in *Globe Motors Inc v TRW Lucas Varity Electric Steering Ltd* [2016] EWCA Civ 396, [2017] 1 All E.R. (Comm) 601 esp. at [100] and [119] (the general principle that parties are free to agree whatever terms they choose to undertake allows them to vary by contract an earlier contract containing an "anti-oral variation" clause); *Transocean Drilling UK Ltd v Providence Resources Plc* [2016] EWCA Civ 372, [2016] 2 All E.R. (Comm) 606 at [28] ("the principle of freedom of contract is still fundamental to [English] commercial law").

[*Add to note 181, line 2, after* "[1986] A.C. 80, 104–105": *page* [23]]
; *Marks & Spencer Plc v BNP Paribas Securities Services Trust Co (Jersey) Ltd* [2015] UKSC 72, [2015] 3 W.L.R. 1843 at [14]–[21] and [77].

[*Add to note 183, at the end: page* [23]]
On the views of the Supreme Court on Lord Hoffmann's approach to implied terms, see *Marks & Spencer Plc v BNP Paribas Securities Services Trust Co (Jersey) Ltd* [2015] UKSC 72, [2015] 3 W.L.R. 1843.

[*Add to paragraph, at the end: page* [24]]
Even where the common law recognises an exception to freedom of contract, as in the case of the law controlling penalty clauses,[185a] the courts have distinguished between the nature of this control and wider controls of contracts on the ground of fairness. According to Lord Neuberger P.S.C. and Lord Sumption J.S.C. (with whom Lord Carnwath J.S.C. agreed) in *Cavendish Square Holding BV v Makdessi, ParkingEye Ltd v Beavis*:

> "There is a fundamental difference between a jurisdiction to review the fairness of a contractual obligation and a jurisdiction to regulate the remedy for its breach. Leaving aside challenges going to the reality of consent, such as those based on fraud, duress or undue influence, the courts do not review the fairness of men's bargains either at law or in equity. The penalty rule regulates only the remedies available for breach of a party's primary obligations, not the primary obligations themselves."[185b]

In the view of the Supreme Court, the true test whether a contract term imposes a "penalty" on the party in default is whether "it imposes a detriment on the contract-breaker out of all proportion to any legitimate interest of the innocent party in the enforcement of the primary obligation".[185c] For this purpose,

> "the circumstances in which the contract was made are not entirely irrelevant. In a negotiated contract between properly advised parties of comparable bargaining power, the strong initial presumption must be that the parties themselves are the best

judges of what is legitimate in a provision dealing with the consequences of breach."[185d]

And the bargaining position of the parties more generally may be relevant.[185e]

[185a] *Cavendish Square Holding BV v Makdessi, ParkingEye Ltd v Beavis* [2015] UKSC 67, [2015] 3 W.L.R. 1373 at [33] ("[t]he penalty rule is an interference with freedom of contract", per Lord Neuberger and Lord Sumption); at [257] per Lord Hodge. On this decision see below, paras 26–178 et seq.
[185b] [2015] UKSC 67, [2015] 3 W.L.R. 1373 at [13]; and see similarly at [73].
[185c] [2015] UKSC 67 at [32] per Lord Neuberger P.S.C. and Lord Sumption J.S.C. (with whom Lord Carnwath J.S.C. and Lord Clarke J.S.C. agreed. See similarly per Lord Mance J.S.C. at [152] per Lord Mance J.S.C. and [249] and [255] per Lord Hodge J.S.C.
[185d] [2015] UKSC 67 at [35] Lord Neuberger P.S.C. and Lord Sumption J.S.C. (with whom Lord Carnwath J.S.C. and Lord Clarke J.S.C. agreed. See similarly at [75]. For discussion of this point, see below, para.26–214.
[185e] [2015] UKSC 67 at [35].

Freedom of contract in EU law

[Add to paragraph, at the end: page [24]]   **1–028**
The principle of "party autonomy" is also important in EU private international law.[190a]

[190a] See Regulation (EC) 593/2008 on the law applicable to contractual obligations (Rome I) [2008] O.J. L177/6, art.3 and Main Work, Vol.I, paras 30–169 et seq.; Regulation (EU) 1215/2012 of 12 December 2012 on jurisdiction and the recognition and enforcement of judgments in civil and commercial matters (recast) ("the Brussels I*bis* Regulation") art.23 (on jurisdiction agreements) and recital 14, on which see Dicey, Morris and Collins, *The Conflict of Laws*, 15th edn (2014), paras 12–099 et seq.

(iii) Restricted freedom as to terms

[Add to note 227, at the end: page [28]]   **1–034**
A legislative regime governing a particular category of contracts may require the implication of an appropriate term by the courts: see, e.g. contracts governed by the Housing Grants, Construction and Regeneration Act 1996 and the Scheme for Construction Contracts (England and Wales) Regulations 1998 (SI 1998/649) and *Aspect Contracts (Asbestos) Ltd v Higgins Construction Plc* [2015] UKSC 38, [2015] 1 W.L.R. 2961 esp. at [23].

(b) *The Binding Force of Contract*

General significance

[Add to note 251, at the end: page [31]]   **1–036**
As from October 1, 2016 the provisions in the French Civil Code governing general contract law are reformed: *Ordonnance* No.2016/131 of February 10, 2016. The equivalent provision of art.1134.1 of the Civil Code as promulgated appears in art.1103 of the Civil Code as reformed; the latter's provisions on penalty clauses are contained in art.1231-5 of the Civil Code as reformed.

Limits on binding force of contracts

1–038 [*In paragraph, lines 5–10, delete from* "As regards . . . " *up to and including note 281 and substitute: page* [33]]

As regards the latter, the Supreme Court has recently clarified the limits of the law which renders a contract term unenforceable as a penalty, holding that a contract term which stipulates the payment of a sum of money on breach of contract will be classed as a penalty clause (and so unenforceable) only if it "imposes a detriment on the contract-breaker out of all proportion to any legitimate interest of the innocent party in the enforcement of the primary obligation".[280–281]

[280–281] *Cavendish Square Holding BV v Makdessi, ParkingEye Ltd v Beavis* [2015] UKSC 67, [2015] 3 W.L.R. 1373 at [32] per Lord Neuberger of Abbotsbury P.S.C. and Lord Sumption J.S.C. (with whom Lord Carnwath and Lord Clarke of Stone-cum-Ebony JJ.S.C. (at [291] agreed); and see similarly at [152] (Lord Mance J.S.C.) and [255] (Lord Hodge J.S.C., with whom Lord Toulson J.S.C. at [292] agreed on this issue). On this decision see paras 26–178 et seq.

[*Add to paragraph, at the end: page* [35]]

According to the Supreme Court, this provision "is deliberately framed in wide terms with very little in the way of guidance about the criteria for its application . . . It is not possible to state a precise or universal test for its application, which must depend on the court's judgment of all relevant facts", though the Supreme Court offered some general points which courts should take into account for this purpose.[293a]

[293a] *Plevin v Paragon Personal Finance Ltd* [2014] UKSC 61, [2014] 1 W.L.R. 4222 at [10] per Lord Sumption J.S.C. (with whom Baroness Hale of Richmond D.P.S.C., Lord Clarke of Stone-cum-Ebony, Lord Carnwath and Lord Hodge J.J.S.C. agreed).

(c) *A Principle of Good Faith or of Contractual Fairness?*

No general principle of good faith

1–039 [*Add to note 299, at the end: page* [35]]

Burrows, *A Restatement of the English Law of Contract* (2016) considers that it remains clear that there is no free-standing rule imposing a duty to perform in good faith in English law, though notes that English law sometimes comes to the same result by implying a term: commentary to s.5, p.50; commentary to ss.15(3)–(4), p.93; on the latter, see Main Work, Vol.I, paras 1–052—1–054A.

[*Add to note 305, line 5, after* "[2013] B.L.R. 265 at [105]"*: page* [36]]

; *MSC Mediterranean Shipping Co SA v Cottonex Anstalt* [2016] EWCA Civ 789, [2017] 1 All E.R. (Comm) 483 at [45].

[*Add to paragraph, after note 305: page* [36]]

And, very recently, Moore-Bick L.J. has observed that:

"the better course is for the law to develop along established lines rather than to encourage judges to look for what the judge in this case called some 'general organising principle' drawn from cases of disparate kinds . . . There is . . . a real danger that if a general principle of good faith were established it would be invoked as often to undermine as to support the terms in which the parties have reached agreement." [305a]

[305a] *MSC Mediterranean Shipping Co SA v Cottonex Anstalt* [2016] EWCA Civ 789 at [45]. The judge at trial was Leggatt J., who had earlier given judgment in *Yam Seng Pte Ltd v International Trade Corp Ltd* [2013] EWHC 111 (QB), [2013] 1 Lloyd's Rep. 526, discussed in the Main Work, Vol.I, para.1–053.

[*Add to paragraph, at the end: page* [38]]   **1–040**

Moreover, the courts do not generally allow a party to a contract to rely on public law defences (such as one based on its legitimate expectation) against its contractual partner where the latter's claim is fundamentally for the enforcement of a commercial bargain, even if that partner was a public authority acting under statutory powers, though it has been accepted that they could do so where "a true public law defence vitiates a contractual claim". [314a] For this purpose, in the view of Lewison L.J., it cannot "usually be an abuse of power [in a public body] to exercise contractual rights freely conferred, even if the result may appear to be a harsh one". [314b]

[314a] *Dudley Muslim Association v Dudley MBC* [2015] EWCA Civ 1123, [2016] 1 P. & C.R. 10 at [29] per Lewison L.J. (with whom Treacy and Gloster L.JJ. agreed) (local authority able to enforce covenant in lease as to re-conveyance of freehold transferred under option on the failure of a condition as to obtain timely planning permission).
[314b] *Dudley Muslim Association v Dudley MBC* [2015] EWCA Civ 1123 at [49], who noted (at [50]) that in the case before the court, private law mechanisms which preclude a person from relying on his strict legal rights such as promissory estoppel had not been pleaded.

"Good faith" and "good faith and fair dealing" in EU law

[*Delete last sentence of the paragraph and note 344,* "While the proposed . . .   **1–043**
modified proposal [344]" *and substitute: page* [42]]

However, the CESL Proposal was withdrawn by the Commission in 2014, [344] and the legislative proposals put forward by the EU Commission instead are of much narrower scope than the CESL and do not refer to the concept of good faith. [344a]

[344] European Commission, Annex 2 to the Commission Work Programme 2015 Com(2014) 910 final, p.12. See also the Communication from the Commission, *A Digital Single Market Strategy for Europe*, 2015 COM(2015) 192 final, pp.4–5.
[344a] Proposal for a Directive of the European Parliament and of the Council on certain aspects concerning contracts for the online and other distance sales of goods COM(2015) 635 final and Proposal for a Directive of the European Parliament and of the Council on certain aspects concerning contracts for the supply of digital content COM(2015) 634.

(i) Duties to consider other party's interest

[*Add to note 350, at the end: page* [43]]   **1–045**
; *Alpstream AG v PK Airfinance Sarl* [2015] EWCA Civ 1318, [2016] 2 P. & C.R. 2 at [115].

[11]

(ii) Express terms as to good faith or fairness

Express term to act in good faith

1–048   [*Add to note 366, at the end: page* [46]]
See also *Astor Management AG v Atalaya Mining Plc* [2017] EWHC 425
(Comm), [2017] 1 Lloyd's Rep. 476 at [62]–[72] (Leggatt J.) (express contractual obligation to use all reasonable endeavours to achieve particular result
held enforceable, though not broken on the facts).

[*Add to note 372, at the end: page* [47]]
See also *BP Gas Marketing Ltd v La Societe Sonatrach* [2016] EWHC 2461
(Comm), 169 Con. L.R. 141 at [401] per Simon Bryan QC ("good faith does not
normally require a party to surrender contractual rights").

[*Add to note 377, at the end: page* [48]]
See also *BP Gas Marketing Ltd v La Societe Sonatrach* [2016] EWHC 2461
(Comm), 169 Con. L.R. 141 at [379]–[382].

1–049   [*Add to note 381, at the end: page* [49]]
See also *BP Gas Marketing Ltd v La Societe Sonatrach* [2016] EWHC 2461
(Comm), 169 Con. L.R. 141 (express term requiring one party to act in good faith
while performing its contractual obligations requires other party to prove the
identification of one or more such obligations and their breach by not acting in
good faith in a particular way at a particular time or times; there was no "free-
standing obligation of good faith" (at [403] per Simon Bryan QC); and on the
facts no such breach was established: at [409]).

(iii) Contractual interpretation

1–051   [*In paragraph, after note 392, delete* "Furthermore," *and substitute: page* [51]]
Furthermore, while the Supreme Court in *Arnold v Britton* recently reaffirmed
that the meaning of words in a contract must be seen in their "documentary,
factual and commercial context", including "commercial common sense",[392a]
the latter and the surrounding circumstances "should not be invoked to undervalue the importance of the language of the provision which is to be construed"[392b]: "[t]he purpose of interpretation is to identify what the parties have
agreed, not what the court thinks that they should have agreed".[392c] On the other
hand,

[392a] [2015] UKSC 36, [2015] A.C. 1619 at [15] per Lord Neuberger of Abbotsbury P.S.C. (with
whom Lord Sumption and Lord Hughes JJ.S.C. agreed); Lord Hodge J.S.C. in a separate judgment
also agreed with Lord Neuberger, at [66]). See also *Wood v Capita Insurance Services Ltd* [2017]
UKSC 24, [2017] 2 W.L.R. 1095 at [8]–[15].
[392b] [2015] UKSC 36 at [15].
[392c] [2015] UKSC 36 at [20] per Lord Neuberger of Abbotsbury P.S.C.; *Globe Motors Inc v TRW
Lucas Varity Electric Steering Ltd* [2016] EWCA Civ 396, [2017] 1 All E.R. (Comm) 601 at [62].

(iv) Implied terms

1–052   [*Add to paragraph, at the end: page* [53]]
Moreover, even in those types of contract which involve "a high degree of
communication, co-operation and predictable performance based on mutual trust

and confidence and expectations of loyalty", in which the courts may be willing to imply a duty of good faith, this will depend on the terms of the particular contract[405a]: "an implication of a duty of good faith will only be possible where the language of the contract, viewed against its context, permits it".[405b]

[405a] *Globe Motors Inc v TRW Lucas Varity Electric Steering Ltd* [2016] EWCA Civ 396, [2017] 1 All E.R. (Comm) 601 at [67].
[405b] *Globe Motors Inc v TRW Lucas Varity Electric Steering Ltd* [2016] EWCA Civ 396, [2017] 1 All E.R. (Comm) 601 at [68] per Beatson L.J.

A general implied term to perform in good faith?

[*In note 406, lines 2–3, delete* "See also *MSC Mediterranean* . . . [97] (Leggatt J.)"*:* **1–053** *page* [53]]

[*Add to note 411, at the end: page* [54]]
cf. *Astor Management AG v Atalaya Mining Plc* [2017] EWHC 425 (Comm), [2017] 1 Lloyd's Rep. 476 in which Leggatt J. observed (at [98]) that "[a] duty to act in good faith, where it exists, is a modest requirement. It does no more than reflect the expectation that a contracting party will act honestly towards the other party and will not conduct itself in a way which is calculated to frustrate the purpose of the contract or which would be regarded as commercially unacceptable by reasonable and honest people", considering it therefore a "lesser duty" than an express contractual "positive obligation to use all reasonable endeavours to achieve a specified result".

[*Add to note 413, at the end: page* [54]]
; *Acer Investment Management Ltd v Mansion Group Ltd* [2014] EWHC 3011 (QB) at [101]–[109]; *Globe Motors Inc v TRW Lucas Varity Electric Steering Ltd* [2016] EWCA Civ 396, [2017] 1 All E.R. (Comm) 601 at [67]; *Monde Petroleum SA v WesternZagros Ltd* [2016] EWHC 1472 (Comm), [2017] 1 All E.R. (Comm) 1009 at [249]–[259]; *Apollo Window Blinds Ltd v McNeil* [2016] EWHC 2307 (QB) (no implied term in contract of franchise requiring one party (the franchisor) to inform the other (the franchisee) of its contractual rights); *National Private Air Transport Services Co (National Air Services) Ltd v Creditrade LLP* [2016] EWHC 2144 (Comm) at [132]–[136] (no implied term in aircraft lease as not a "relational" contract and lessor was entitled to redelivery in compliance with contract terms (obiter)). See also *MSC Mediterranean Shipping Co SA v Cottonex Anstalt* [2016] EWCA Civ 789, [2017] 1 All E.R. (Comm) 483 at [45] (disapproving of the establishment of a general principle of good faith, contrary to the suggestion by Leggatt J. at trial).

[*Add to note 414, at the end: page* [54]]
; *Property Alliance Group Ltd v Royal Bank of Scotland Plc* [2016] EWHC 3342 (Ch) at [250] and [276] (where in addition an implied term requiring good faith would have been inconsistent with express terms excluding equitable or fiduciary duties).

[*Add to note 415, at the end: page* [54]]
cf. *Hockin v Royal Bank of Scotland* [2016] EWHC 925 (Ch) at [44]–[47] (no strike out of claim for breach of implied term as to the exercise of a right/

discretion under a contract in the absence of factual matrix to be established at trial).

[Add to paragraph, at the end: page [54]]

Moreover, the approach of the Supreme Court to the implication of terms in *Marks & Spencer Plc v BNP Paribas Securities Services Trust Co (Jersey) Ltd*[415a] may lead to a greater reluctance in the courts to imply terms requiring good faith in at least some commercial contracts: as Lord Neuberger of Abbotsbury P.S.C. there observed, "a term should not be implied into a detailed commercial contract merely because it appears fair".[415b]

[415a] [2015] UKSC 72, [2015] 3 W.L.R. 1843.
[415b] [2015] UKSC 72 at [21] and see for an example of this approach being adopted in the context of good faith: *Hockin v Royal Bank of Scotland* [2016] EWHC 925 (Ch) at [46] (high threshold for the implication of a term in a standard commercial contract). On the decision of the SC in *Marks & Spencers Plc* generally, see below, para.14–007.

Implied restrictions on broad contractual powers

1–054
[Add to note 432, line 16, after "at [110]–[112]": *page* [56]]
; *Monde Petroleum SA v WesternZagros Ltd* [2016] EWHC 1472 (Comm), [2017] 1 All E.R. (Comm) 1009 at [261]–[275]. In *British Telecommunications Plc v Telefónica O2 UK Ltd* [2014] UKSC 42, [2014] 4 All E.R. 907 at [37] Lord Sumption J.S.C. observed that, although the matter remains a matter of construction, it is "well established that in the absence of very clear language to the contrary, a contractual discretion must be exercised in good faith and not arbitrarily or capriciously".

[Add to note 433, at the end: page [57]]
See also *Abu Dhabi National Tanker Co v Product Star Shipping Ltd (The "Product Star")* [1993] 1 Lloyd's Rep. 397 esp. at 404; *Horkulak v Cantor Fitzgerald International* [2004] EWCA Civ 1287, [2005] I.C.R. 402 at [66]; *JML Direct Ltd v Freesat UK Ltd* [2010] EWCA Civ 34 at [14].

[Add to note 437, at the end: page [57]]
; applied in *Monde Petroleum SA v WesternZagros Ltd* [2016] EWHC 1472 (Comm) at [261]–[275], [2017] 1 All E.R. (Comm) 1009 (contractual right to terminate a contract not a discretion and may be exercised irrespective of the party's reasons for doing so); *Monk v Largo Foods Ltd* [2016] EWHC 1837 (Comm) at [52]–[60].

1–054A
[Add to note 437h, at the end: page [58]]
cf. *Patural v DB Services (UK) Ltd* [2015] EWHC 3659 (QB), [2016] I.R.L.R. 286 at [61].

[Add new note 437j, at end of paragraph: page [58]]
[437j] *Watson v Watchfinder.co.UK Ltd* [2017] EWHC 1275 (Comm), concerned a contractual option to purchase shares in a company which formed part of a wider commercial relationship between the parties and which was contingent on the consent of that company's board. The High Court held that the company board had a discretion as to the consent which must be exercised in a way which was not arbitrary, capricious or irrational, following the SC's decision in *Braganza*: [2017] UKSC 1275 at [102]–[103] and [116] et seq. cf. *Property Alliance Group Ltd v Royal Bank of Scotland* [2016] EWHC 3342 (Ch) at [277], where it was explained that a discretion "requires the contracting party to make some kind of assessment or to choose from a range of options" and this exercise of power

justifies the implication of a term as to its exercise arbitrarily, etc.; no such discretions were found in the contract between bank and its commercial customer (at [272]–[280]).

(v) Reasonableness and legitimate interest in relation to remedies for breach

[*In note 441, lines 1–4, delete* "This law . . . [2015] 1 Lloyd's Rep. 359 at [97]" **1–055**
and substitute: page [59]]
While this law was seen by Leggatt J. in *MSC Mediterranean Shipping Co SA v Cottonex Anstalt* [2015] EWHC 283 (Comm), [2015] 1 Lloyd's Rep. 359 at [97] as reflecting an "increasing recognition in the common law world of the need for good faith in contractual dealings" as it implies "some constraint on the decision-maker's freedom to act purely in its own self-interest", on appeal the CA (which did not see the *White & Carter* principle as applicable on the facts) did not encourage judges to recognise a "general organising principle" drawn from cases of disparate kinds in this way: [2016] EWCA Civ 789 at [43] and [45] respectively.

[*Add to paragraph, after note 441: page* [59]]
And the Supreme Court has held that a contract term stipulating payment of a sum of money on breach of contract will be a penalty clause at common law (and so unenforceable) only if the term does not serve a legitimate interest and if in the circumstances its amount is extravagant, exorbitant or unconscionable.[441a]

[441a] *Cavendish Square Holding BV v Makdessi, ParkingEye Ltd v Beavis* [2015] UKSC 67, [2015] 3 W.L.R. 1373 at [32] and [152] and see, below, paras 26–178 et seq.

[*In paragraph, line 9, delete* "And" *and substitute: page* [59]]
Finally,

4. The Human Rights Act 1998 and Contracts

(a) *Contracts made before October 2, 2000*

(ii) *Contracts made by "Public Authorities"*

Effect of any unlawful performance by a public authority

[*In note 489, update reference to Treitel on The Law of Contract to: page* [65]] **1–063**
14th edn (2015)

(b) *Contracts made on or after October 2, 2000*

(i) *The Construction and Review of Legislation Governing Contracts*

Sections 3 and 4 of the 1998 Act: primary or secondary legislation governing the contract and Convention rights

[*Add to note 500, at the end: page* [66]] **1–066**
This approach was applied in *Winstanley v Sleeman* [2013] EWHC 4792 (QB) at [58]–[59] (rule against scrutiny of academic judgments in claims for breach of contract does not bar access to the courts).

[15]

Examples of other Convention rights

1–072   *[Add to note 546, at the end: page* [72]]
See also *McDonald v McDonald* [2016] UKSC 28, [2017] A.C. 273 at [61]–[70], noted below, para.1–091.

(ii) *Contracts made by "Public Authorities"*

"Hybrid bodies" and "functions of a public nature"

1–074   *[Add to note 557, at the end: page* [73]]
The approach taken by the HL was applied in *TH v Chapter of Worcester Cathedral* [2016] EWHC 1117 (Admin) (decision by the Chapter of a cathedral affecting the claimant's ability to perform his hobby of bell-ringing was held not to be an act of a "hybrid" public authority within s.6(3) of the Human Rights Act 1998).

Unlawful manner of performance of contract

1–078   *[Add to note 595, at the end: page* [78]]
and *McDonald v McDonald* [2016] UKSC 28, [2017] A.C. 273.

(iii) *The Duty of Courts as "Public Authorities" in Relation to Contracts*

Introduction

1–082   *[Add new note 617a, line 7, after* "a 'public authority'.": *page* [81]]
        [617a] See, however, *McDonald v McDonald* [2016] UKSC 28, [2017] A.C. 273 (below para.1–091) where the SC observed that, while a court is a public authority for the purposes of the 1998 Act, when it makes an order for possession against a private sector tenant it does so "merely as the forum for determination of the civil right in dispute between the parties" and that "once it concludes that the landlord is entitled to possession, there is nothing further to investigate": at [44], quoting Lord Millett in *Harrow LBC v Qazi* [2003] UKHL 43, [2004] 1 A.C. 983 at [108].

New implied terms

1–088   *[In paragraph, line 5, delete* "even under a" *and substitute: page* [85]]
under the established

        [Add to note 641, at the end: page [85]]
; *Marks & Spencer Plc v BNP Paribas Securities Services Trust Co (Jersey) Ltd* [2015] UKSC 72, [2015] 3 W.L.R. 1843 at [14]–[21] and [77].

        [In paragraph, line 8, delete "And since" *and substitute: page* [85]]
And under

        [In paragraph, line 9, delete "of asking" *and substitute: page* [85]]
which asks

[*Add to note 643, line 2, before* "and see below"*: page* [85]]
. In *Marks & Spencer Plc v BNP Paribas Securities Services Trust Co (Jersey)
Ltd* [2015] UKSC 72, [2015] 3 W.L.R. 1843 a majority of the SC considered that
Lord Hoffmann's guidance on implied terms in the *Belize* case should not be seen
as "authoritative guidance on the law of implied terms": [2015] 3 W.L.R. 1843
at [31];

Private sector possession orders and article 8 of the Convention

[*Add to note 659, at the end: page* [87]]   **1–091**
And see Main Work, Vol.I, para.1–078.

[*Delete second paragraph (including footnotes) and substitute: page* [87]]
However, in *McDonald v McDonald*[663] the Supreme Court held that, although it
may well be that art.8 of the Convention is engaged when a court makes an order
for possession of a tenant's home at the suit of a private sector landlord under
s.21(4) of the Housing Act 1988, art.8 cannot:

> "justify a different order from that which is mandated by the contractual relationship
> between the parties, at least where, as here, there are legislative provisions which the
> democratically elected legislature has decided properly balance the competing inter-
> est of private sector landlords and residential tenants."[664]

A court considering whether to make such an order is therefore not required to
assess the proportionality of evicting the occupier in the light of s.6 of the Human
Rights Act 1998 and art.8 of the Convention.[665] In the view of the Supreme
Court,

> "[t]o hold otherwise would involve the Convention effectively being directly
> enforceable as between private citizens so as to alter their contractual rights and
> obligations, whereas the purpose of the Convention is . . . to protect citizens from
> having their rights infringed by the State. To hold otherwise would also mean that the
> Convention could be invoked to interfere with the A1P1 [art.1, 1st Protocol] rights
> of the landlord, and in a way which was unpredictable."[666]

The Supreme Court contrasted this situation where there are "legislative provisions which the democratically elected legislature has decided properly balance
the competing interests of private sector landlords and residential tenants"[666a]
with situations where the relationship between two private parties is "tortious or
quasi-tortious" rather than contractual and where the legislature has "expressly,
impliedly or through inaction, left it to the courts to carry out the balancing
exercise", for example, where a person is seeking to rely on her art.8 rights to
restrain a newspaper from publishing an article in breach of her privacy and
where the newspaper relies on art.10 of the Convention.[666b]

[663] [2016] UKSC 28, [2017] A.C. 273.
[664] [2016] UKSC 28 at [40]. The SC expressed these views conditionally on there being no
Strasbourg jurisprudence to the contrary, which it later held was the case: see [2016] UKSC 28 at
[48]–[59].
[665] [2016] UKSC 28 at [40]–[46], [59] and [76]. The SC also held, obiter, that if a proportionality
assessment were required, it would not be possible to read this into s.21(4) of the 1988 Act by way
of application of s.3(1) of the 1998 Act, the only remedy therefore being a declaration of incompati-
bility under s.4 of the 1998 Act: [2016] UKSC 28 at [69]–[70]; and that, even were a proportionality
assessment required, the claimant tenant's circumstances were not such as to justify refusing an order

for possession and thereby postponing indefinitely the right of the landlord's mortgagee/lender (acting through appointed receivers): [2016] UKSC 28 at [71], [74]–[75].

⁶⁶⁶ [2016] UKSC 28 at [41] per Lord Neuberger of Abbotsbury P.S.C. and Baroness Hale of Richmond D.P.S.C. (with whom Lord Kerr of Tonaghmore, Lord Reed and Lord Carnwath JJ.S.C. agreed). See further at [42]–[47]. The SC held that there was no support in the case law of the European Court of Human Rights for the proposition that a court must consider the proportionality of the order in the context of claims for possession by private sector landlords: see at [48]–[59] (where the relevant case-law was reviewed).

⁶⁶⁶ᵃ [2016] UKSC 28 at [40] per Lord Neuberger of Abbotsbury P.S.C. and Baroness Hale of Richmond D.P.S.C.

⁶⁶⁶ᵇ [2016] UKSC 28 at [46] per Lord Neuberger of Abbotsbury P.S.C. and Baroness Hale of Richmond D.P.S.C. See further Main Work, Vol.I, para.1–092.

5. CLASSIFICATION OF CONTRACTS

(a) Classification of Contracts According to their Subject Matter

General

1–096   [*Add to note 688, at the end: page* [90]]
(as promulgated); art.1101 C.civ. (as inserted by *Ordonnance* No.2016/131 of February 10, 2016).

(c) Classification of Contracts According to their Form or Means of Formation

Express and implied contracts

1–104   [*Add to note 731, line 2, after* "per Mance L.J.".: *page* [95]]
; *Heis v MF (Global) Services Ltd* [2016] EWCA Civ 569 at [36]–[47]

[*Add to paragraph, at the end: page* [95]]
The recognition of implied contracts in the sense explained in the present paragraph does not mean that a court should imply terms in an oral agreement so as to enable it to be sufficiently complete to amount to a binding contract. As Lewison L.J. has recently observed,

> "[i]t is of course the case that the court may imply terms into a concluded contract. But that assumes that there is a concluded contract into which terms can be implied. It is not legitimate, under the guise of implying terms, to make a contract for the parties".⁷³¹ᵃ

⁷³¹ᵃ *Devani v Wells* [2016] EWCA Civ 1106, [2017] 2 W.L.R. 1391 at [19] (with whom McCombe L.J. agreed at [79]), referring to *Scancarriers A/S v Aotearoa International Ltd* [1985] 2 Lloyd's Rep. 419, 422 per Lord Roskill.

(d) Classification of Contracts According to their Effect

Unilateral and bilateral contracts

1–107   [*Add to note 739, at the beginning: page* [96]]
For an unusual example of a unilateral contract see *Rollerteam Ltd v Riley* [2016] EWCA Civ 1291, [2017] Ch. 109 esp. at [45], where the description in the text

of unilateral contracts was cited with approval. On this case see below, para.5–017.

6. Contracts Contained in Deeds

(a) General

General abolition of the requirement of sealing

[*Add to note 769, at the end: page* [99]]   **1–114**
The recognition of "electronic seals" by Regulation (EU) 910/2014 of 23 July 2014 on electronic identification and trust services for electronic transactions in the internal market and repealing Directive 1999/93/EC [2014] O.J. L257/73 (the "eIDAS Regulation"), see esp. arts 2(25), 35–40, does not affect the law described in the text of the Main Work, as art.2(3) provides that the Regulation does not affect national or Union law related to the conclusion and validity of contracts or other legal or procedural obligations relating to form: see further below, para.5–008.

Electronic documents and deeds

[*Add new note 780a at the end of the title of this paragraph: page* [101]]   **1–116**
[780a] "Electronic documents and deeds" for the purposes of the Land Registration Act 2002 (which are the subject of the present paragraph) are to be distinguished from "electronic seals" recognised by Regulation (EU) 910/2014 of 23 July 2014 on electronic identification and trust services for electronic transactions in the internal market and repealing Directive 1999/93/EC [2014] O.J. L257/73 (the "eIDAS Regulation"), see below, para.5–008.

[*Delete text of note 783 and substitute: page* [101]]
The relevant dispositions are specified by the Land Registration Act 2002 s.91(2).

[*Add to note 785, at the end: page* [101]]
See further Law Commission, *Updating the Land Registration Act 2002, A Consultation Paper* (Consultation Paper No.227, 2016), Pt 8, which notes (at para.20.6) that the electronic system provided for by Pt 8 of the 2002 Act which would have implemented the model which it had earlier recommended has not been developed, and instead makes recommendations for a "new vision for electronic conveyancing" (at para.20.11).

(b) *Intention, Form and Delivery*

(i) *Deeds executed on or after July 31, 1989 and before or on September 14, 2005*

Deeds executed by an individual

[*Add to note 791, at the end: page* [102]]   **1–118**
The question whether the requirement of signature may be satisfied other than by a party writing his or her name or mark with his or her own hand remains unclear.

There is authority for the purposes of s.2 of the 1989 Act that requires such writing (*Firstpost Homes Ltd v Johnson* [1995] 1 W.L.R. 1567, on which see Main Work, Vol.I, para.5–037), but a more liberal position has been taken for the purposes of the (less demanding) formalities of s.4 of the Statute of Frauds: *J Pereira Fernandes SA v Mehta* [2006] EWHC 813 (Ch), [2006] 2 All E.R. 881 at [31]; *Golden Ocean Group Ltd v Salgaocar Mining Industries Pvt Ltd* [2012] EWCA Civ 265, [2012] 1 Lloyd's Rep. 542 at [32] (on which see Main Work, Vol.II, para.45–057). In *Ramsay v Love* [2015] EWHC 65 (Ch) at [7], Morgan J. observed (in the context of s.1(3) of the 1989 Act, obiter) that the position in *Firstpost Homes Ltd v Johnson* (which requires signature by an executing party with a pen in his own hand) was not designed to distinguish between signing in such a way and by use of a signature writing machine. For further discussion of the significance of "signature" see *Emmet & Farrand on Title* (looseleaf and electronic version updated to June 2016) paras 2–041— 2 041.06. For the possibility that an "electronic signature" may satisfy this requirement by way of s.7 of the Electronic Communications Act 2000 see below, para.5–008.

(ii) *Documents Executed on or after September 15, 2005*

"Valid execution": companies and corporations aggregate

1–128   [*Add to note 843, at the end: page* [108]]
It has been held that a requirement of the "execution" of a deed in a consent order must equally be understood as requiring delivery as well as signature of a document: *Arrowgame Ltd v Wildsmith* [2016] EWHC 3608 (Ch).

(iii) *Common Aspects*

Estoppel preventing reliance on formal invalidity

1–132   [*Add to note 859, at the end: page* [110]]
; *Bank of Scotland Plc v Waugh* [2014] EWHC 2117 (Ch), [2015] 1 P. & C.R. DG3 at [68]–[79].

Delivery of deed as an escrow

1–133   [*In note 863, update reference to Treitel on The Law of Contract to: page* [110]]
14th edn (2015), para.3–173

(c) *Consideration*

No consideration required

1–136   [*Add to paragraph, at the end: page* [112]]
Where a promise or agreement unsupported by consideration is enforceable by reason of its being contained in a deed, it may be avoided on the ground of

special equitable rules of mistake which are distinct from the rules of mistake applicable to contracts.[881a]

[881a] *Pitt v Holt* [2013] UKSC 26, [2013] 2 A.C. 108 esp. at [115]; applied in *Van der Merwe v Goldman* [2016] EWHC 790 (Ch), [2016] 4 W.L.R. 71 at [26]–[32]. On the common law rules applicable to mistakes in contracts, see Main Work, Vol.I, Chs 3 and 6.

(d) *Other Aspects*

Non est factum

[Delete title of paragraph and substitute: page [114]]   **1–139**

Non est factum and mistake

[Add to paragraph, at the end: page [114]]
This position is to be contrasted with mistakes made in making gifts or other voluntary dispositions (including those made by deed), where equitable rules apply which differ from the common law rules applicable to mistake in contracts (whether or not contained in deeds).[899a]

[899a] *Pitt v Holt* [2013] UKSC 26, [2013] 2 A.C. 108 esp. at [115]; applied in *Van der Merwe v Goldman* [2016] EWHC 790 (Ch), [2016] 4 W.L.R. 71 at [26]–[32]. On the common law rules applicable to mistakes in contracts, see Main Work, Vol.I, Chs 3 and 6.

Variation or discharge

[Add to note 918, at the end: page [116]]   **1–143**
The parties to a contract contained in a deed (as in the case of a simple contract) may vary or discharge that contract by simple contract despite its containing an "anti-oral variation clause" by which, for example, any variation may be effected only by deed or only in signed writing: *MWB Business Exchange Centres Ltd v Rock Advertising Ltd* [2016] EWCA Civ 553, [2017] Q.B. 604 at [19]–[34], following dicta in *Globe Motors Inc v TRW Lucas Varity Electric Steering Ltd* [2016] EWCA Civ 396, [2017] 1 All E.R. (Comm) 601 esp. at [100] and [119], and reviewing earlier conflicting authorities.

7. The Relationship between Contract and Tort

(b) *Differences of Substance between Contract and Tort*

General

[In note 963 update reference to Treitel on The Law of Contract: page [120]]   **1–148**
14th edn (2015), para.20–021

Differences of regime between contract and tort: damages

[Add to note 972, line 3, after "[1991] 1 W.L.R. 461*": page* [121]]   **1–150**
; *OMV Petrom SA v Glencore International AG* [2016] EWCA Civ 778, [2017] 3 All E.R. 157

(c) *Concurrence of Actions in Contract and Tort*

(i) *Pre-contractual Liability*

Damages for misrepresentation

1–161 [*Add to note 1034, line 3, after* "[2001] Q.B. 488": *page* [129]]
; *OMV Petrom SA v Glencore International AG* [2016] EWCA Civ 778, [2017]
3 All E.R. 157

[*In note 1036, update reference to Treitel on The Law of Contract to: page* [129]]
14th edn (2015), paras 9–050—9–058

(ii) *Torts Committed in the Course of Performance of a Contract*

Fair, just and reasonable

1–171 [*Add to paragraph, line 36, after* "the conduct and management of litigation.": *page*
[138]]
Rather, as Hamblen L.J. (with whom Gloster V.P. and Irwin L.J. agreed) observed
in *Burgess v Lejonvarn*, in cases of assumption of responsibility,

> "[w]hilst there is no need to make a further inquiry into whether it would be fair, just
> and reasonable to impose liability, that is because such considerations will have been
> taken into account in determining whether there has been an assumption of res-
> ponsibility."[1111a]

[1111a] [2017] EWCA Civ 254, [2017] P.N.L.R. 24 at [64] referring in particular to Lord Hoffman's
speech in *Customs and Excise Commissioners v Barclays Bank Plc* [2006] UKHL 28, [2006] 3
W.L.R. 1 at [35]–[36].

Effect of broad liability in tort

1–172 [*Add new note 1112a after* "paid for or not" *in line 8: page* [139]]
[1112a] See, e.g. *Burgess v Lejonvarn* [2017] EWCA Civ 254, [2017] P.N.L.R. 24 esp. at [86]–[87]
in which the claimants' friend who had provided project management services in a professional
context to them not under a contract (for lack of agreement as to terms, intention to create legal
relations and consideration) was held to a duty of care in tort based on an assumption of responsibility. The CA emphasised that the duty thereby imposed was "not a duty to provide [the] services. It
is a duty to exercise reasonable skill and care in providing the professional services which [the
defendant] did in fact provide", adding that "[a] duty expressed in these terms does not trespass on
the realm of contract": at [88] and [89] per Hamblen L.J.

Contractual exclusion of liability in tort

1–181 [*In paragraph, line 7, delete* "contra proferentum" *and substitute*: *page* [145]]
contra proferentem

Legal immunities for contractors

[*In note 1200, delete from* "[2014] EWHC 3957 (QB)" *in line 2 to the end and*   **1–185**
substitute: page [150]]
[2016] EWCA Civ 408, [2016] 1 W.L.R. 4487 (impact of absence of implied
term for duty of care in the tort of negligence), on which see below
para.1–190A.

Contractual silence and "assumption of responsibility"

[*Add to note 1206, at the end: page* [151]]   **1–188**
and *Greenway v Johnson Matthey Plc* [2016] EWCA Civ 408, [2016] 1 W.L.R.
4487 (appeal to SC pending) (below para.1–190A), which was itself seen the CA
as an analogous case to *Reid v Rush & Tompkins Group Plc*: [2016] EWCA Civ
408 at [41].

Scope of duty in tort reflected in scope of contractual implied term

[*Add to paragraph, at the end: page* [155]]   **1–190A**
Subsequently, the Court of Appeal upheld the High Court's decision in *Greenway
v Johnson Matthey Plc*,[1227f] agreeing that the claimants had not suffered any
actionable physical injury, but only pure economic losses.[1227g] The Court of
Appeal considered that the "classic formulation of the duty owed by an employer
to an employee is focussed on protection of the employee from physical injury,
not protection from economic harm ... and this is true both in contract and in
tort".[1227h] Moreover, "having regard to the general policy reasons which inform
the analysis of whether a standard term or duty of care should be implied into a
contract of employment, ... the proposed term or duty to hold the employee
harmless from economic loss should not be taken to be implied".[1227i] First, it was
not possible for a term to be implied in the claimants' contracts of employment,
"either as a usual feature of employment contracts in general or in these
particular contracts in their commercial setting", especially as the terms of the
collective agreement incorporated into the individual employment contracts had
made specific provision as to the extent of the defendant employer's responsibility as regards the financial welfare of employees affected by the possibility of
developing platinum sensitisation.[1227j] Echoing the language of the famous
approach of Lord Bridge of Harwich to the existence of a duty of care in the tort
of negligence in *Caparo Industries Plc v Dickman*,[1227k] the Court of Appeal
added that it would not be "fair, just or reasonable" to hold that the defendant's
contractual duty extended to protecting the claimants against the financial consequences of losing their jobs, etc. beyond the protection provided by those
collective agreements (notably, the receipt of special termination payments).[1227l]
Finally, the Court of Appeal held that no duty of care should be imposed in the
tort of negligence in respect of the claimants' pure economic losses, seeing such
an imposition on an employer as being recognised only in very specific situations.[1227m] Moreover, where it had been recognised, as in *Spring v Guardian
Assurance Plc*,[1227n] "[t]he policy arguments relevant to implication of the duty in
contract and the imposition of a duty of care in tort were closely similar".[1227o]

According to the Sales L.J. (with whom Davis L.J. and Lord Dyson M.R. agreed):

> "This is significant. Where the nexus between parties is founded in a contractual relationship, as here, it is the contract which they have made with each other which is the primary source and reference point for the rights they have and the obligations they owe each other. Although a duty of care in tort may run in parallel with the contractual duty and have the same content, it is difficult to see how the law of tort could impose obligations in this area which are more extensive than those given by interpretation of the contract which the parties have made for themselves. The usual rule is that freedom of contract is paramount, and if the parties have agreed terms to govern their relationship which do not involve the assumption of responsibility by the employer for some particular risk, the general law of tort will not operate to impose on the employer an obligation which is more extensive than that which they agreed."[1227p]

As a result, since there is no implied contractual term according to which the defendant employer is obliged to protect the claimants in relation to their financial losses arising in the circumstances of this case, nor could there be a duty in tort to protect them in relation to pure economic loss suffered by reason of those financial losses.[1227q] It will be seen, therefore, that while the High Court started with the restricted scope of a relevant duty of care in the tort of negligence (not extending to pure economic loss) and then held that any implied contractual duty could not differ in scope, the Court of Appeal instead held that the lack of any relevant implied contract term meant that no duty of care in tort should go any further. At the time of writing this Supplement, permission to appeal by the claimants in this case has been granted by the Supreme Court.

[1227f] [2016] EWCA Civ 408, [2016] 1 W.L.R. 4487 (appeal to SC pending).
[1227g] [2016] EWCA Civ 408 at [29]–[33].
[1227h] [2016] EWCA Civ 408 at [37] per Sales L.J. (with whom Davis L.J. and Lord Dyson M.R. agreed).
[1227i] [2016] EWCA Civ 408 at [37] per Sales L.J.
[1227j] [2016] EWCA Civ 408 at [39]–[40].
[1227k] [1990] 2 A.C. 605, 618.
[1227l] [2016] EWCA Civ 408 at [40] and [45].
[1227m] [2016] EWCA Civ 408 at [47].
[1227n] [1995] 2 A.C. 296.
[1227o] [2016] EWCA Civ 408 at [48] per Sales L.J.
[1227p] [2016] EWCA Civ 408 at [49], referring to *Scally v Southern Health and Social Services Board* [1992] 1 A.C. 294 at 303.
[1227q] [2016] EWCA Civ 408 at [51].

Damages

1–194   [*Add to note 1248, line 5, after* "para.26–031.": *page* [157]]
See also *Hughes-Holland v BPE Solicitors* [2017] UKSC 21, [2017] 2 W.L.R. 1029.

Remoteness of damage

1–195   [*Add to note 1262, line 1, after* "cf. at 413": *page* [158]]
; *Wellesley Partners LLP v Withers LLP* [2015] EWCA Civ 1146, [2016] 2 W.L.R. 1351 at [74] and [146]

*[In note 1275, delete "and cf. Greenway ... [2015] P.I.Q.R. P10, above,
para.1–190A" and substitute: page [160]]*
and cf. *Greenway v Johnson Matthey Plc* [2016] EWCA Civ 408, [2016] 1
W.L.R. 4487 (above, para.1–190A).

[In note 1274, delete from "See also ... " in line 4 to the end: page [160]]

[Add new paragraph 1–195A: page [160]]
However, in *Wellesley Partners LLP v Withers LLP*[1276a] the Court of Appeal **1–195A**
expressed the opposite view as to the proper approach to remoteness of damage
in cases of concurrence of liability in contract and tort from the one which that
court (differently constituted[1276b]) had expressed in *Yapp v Foreign and Commonwealth Office*,[1276c] which was not discussed in *Wellesley Partners LLP*. In
Wellesley Partners LLP, the claimants were a partnership of executive recruitment consultants which had instructed the defendant firm of solicitors to draft
amendments to their partnership agreement so as to allow a third party investor
to gain an interest in the partnership. The amendments which were drafted (and
agreed) allowed the investor to withdraw half its funds *within* a period of 41
months from its formation, rather than (as instructed by the partnership) only
outside such a period: this failure was held to constitute negligence in the
solicitors.[1276d] One issue before the Court of Appeal was whether the claimants
could recover a percentage of the profits which might have been made if the
investment had remained in place until the end of 41 months, in particular in
relation to a recruitment handling contract or contracts with a major bank. In this
respect, it held that where a claimant is able to sue either for breach of contract
or for pure economic loss in the tort of negligence based on an assumption of
responsibility which is assumed under a contract, the contract law test for
remoteness of damage applies even if the claim is brought in tort: "[i]t would be
anomalous . . . if the party pursuing the remedy in tort in these circumstances
were able to assert that the other party has assumed a responsibility for a wider
range of damage than he would be taken to have assumed under the contract".[1276e] In so holding, the Court of Appeal related the remoteness of damage
rule for breach of contract (as reformulated by Lord Hoffmann in *The Achilleas*
in terms of assumption of responsibility[1276f]) to the basis of liability in tort in the
context (assumption of responsibility as explained by *Henderson v Merrett
Syndicates Ltd*[1276g]). The Court of Appeal therefore disagreed with the judge at
trial on the remoteness test applicable, though it held that the application of the
contract test rather than the tort test did not make any difference on the facts as
the damage claimed by the partnership was of a kind for which the solicitors had
assumed responsibility under their contract and was in the reasonable contemplation of the parties as not unlikely to result from a breach.[1276h] The Court of
Appeal in *Wellesley Partners LLP* therefore took a different view on the question
as to the proper test of remoteness applicable to a claim in the tort of negligence
concurrent with a claim for breach of contract from the one which it had taken
in *Yapp*.[1276i] In neither case were these views necessary for the courts' decisions
on the facts before them, as in both cases they held that the two tests of
remoteness (in tort and in contract) would have led to the same result.[1276j]
Moreover, the two approaches to the proper test of remoteness, while apparently
opposing, may be reconciled by reference to their contexts. In *Yapp,* the claim
was for damages by an employee against his employer for psychiatric injury

suffered as a result of withdrawing him from his post without informing him of the case against him for doing so (which was held to have been unfair)[1276k] and the Court of Appeal held (summarising the authorities in that context) that in such a claim "for breach of the common law duty of care" it is immaterial that the duty arises in contract as well as tort.[1276l] In such a context, therefore, the defendant's liability in the tort in respect of psychiatric injury (which did not rest on any assumption of responsibility) could be seen as primary as compared with its contractual liability arising from breach of the term implied in law on the employer to take reasonable care of the employee's health and safety.[1276m] By contrast, in *Wellesley Partners LLP* the defendant's liability in contract was for breach of an express term of the contract (that is, to follow their client's instructions as to the terms of the amendment agreement) whereas its liability in tort was for pure economic loss based on an assumption of responsibility where the assumption stemmed from the contract itself: indeed, the judges in the Court of Appeal restricted their decision on the test of remoteness to the situation where the tort was based on such a contractual assumption of responsibility.[1276n] A distinction between claims for psychiatric injury (and, it is submitted, other harms, such as personal injury and damage to property) where liability in tort in the defendant does not rest on an assumption of responsibility (*Yapp*) and claims for pure economic loss where it does (*Wellesley Partners LLP*) would echo the approach of Lord Denning M.R. in his minority reasoning in *H Parsons (Livestock) Ltd v Uttley Ingham & Co Ltd* (who distinguished between concurrent claims for physical damage and pure economic loss[1276o]) with the difference that under *Wellesley Partners LLP* the contract test of remoteness would apply to a claim for pure economic loss in tort only where it is based (as would normally be the case) on an assumption of responsibility. More generally, while the Court of Appeal in *Wellesley Partners LLP* acknowledged that the House of Lords in *Henderson v Merrett Syndicates Ltd* treated liability in the tort of negligence that is based on a "broad principle" of assumption of responsibility in *Hedley Byrne* as independent from any liability in contract,[1276p] its own decision treats the liability of the defendant solicitors in tort for negligence as dependent on their liability for breach of the contract of retainer.[1276q] However, a better approach would be to hold that the contract test should apply whenever one party has had the opportunity to alert the other to the type of loss of which he is at risk, and that such an opportunity should be assumed (or perhaps presumed) where the parties are in a contractual relationship.[1276r] Most recently, in *Wright v Lewis Silkin LLP*[1276s] the Court of Appeal noted its earlier judgment in *Wellesley Partners LLP*, seeing the two cases as having in common that they both involved claims for negligence against solicitors by their clients in which there was concurrent liability and describing the decision in *Wellesley Partners LLP* as being that "where there were contractual and tortious duties to take care in carrying out instructions, the test for recoverability of damage should be the same, and it should be the contractual one".[1276t] It was, however, common ground between the parties in *Wright v Lewis Silkin LLP* that *Wellesley Partners LLP* bound the court in *Wright v Lewis Silkin LLP*, no reference being made either by the parties or the court in the latter case to the contrasting approach of the Court of Appeal in *Yapp v Foreign and Commonwealth Office*.[1276u] In *Wright v Lewis Silkin LLP* the Court of Appeal held that the main element of the loss claimed by the claimant (a 20 per cent chance of recovering the voluntary payment of a severance sum from his former Indian employers) caused by his solicitor's failure to advise him in relation to an exclusive jurisdiction clause was too remote, not being of a kind that either party at the time would have had in mind as not unlikely to result from this negligence.[1276v] On the other hand, the claimant's additional litigation costs were not too remote, being "exactly the kind of loss to be expected".[1276w]

[1276a] [2015] EWCA Civ 1146, [2016] 2 W.L.R. 1351.

[1276b] The Court of Appeal in *Yapp* consisted of Underhill, Davis and Patten L.JJ; the Court of Appeal in *Wellesley Partners LLP* consisted of Longmore and Floyd L.JJ. and Roth J.

[1276c] [2014] EWCA Civ 1512, [2015] I.R.L.R. 112 (discussed in Main Work, Vol.I, para.1–195).

[1276d] [2015] EWCA Civ 1146 at [41], [54] and [58]–[59] (decision at trial not appealed on this point).

[1276e] [2015] EWCA Civ 1146 at [68] per Floyd L.J. and see also at [75], explicitly approving the position proposed by *McGregor on Damages* at n.1265, para.22–009 that was rejected by the CA in *Yapp* [2014] EWCA Civ 1512, [2015] I.R.L.R. 112 at [119] n.8 and at [80]. See similarly, at [151] (approving the view of Burrows in Burrows and Peel (eds), *Commercial Remedies* (2003) 27 at 35), [157] and [163] (Roth J.); [183]–[186] (Longmore L.J.).

[1276f] *Transfield Shipping Inc v Mercator Shipping Inc (The Achilleas)* [2009] 1 A.C. 61. In this respect, the CA in *Wellesley Partners LLP* adopted a similar approach to Akenhead J. in *How Engineering Services Ltd v Southern Insulation (Medway) Ltd* [2010] EWHC 1878 (TCC), [2010] B.L.R. 537 (noted in the Main Work, Vol.I, para.1–195), though the earlier decision was not discussed by the CA.

[1276g] [1995] 2 A.C. 145. See [2015] EWCA Civ 1146 at [69], [74], [80]–[83] (Floyd L.J.) and [155] (Roth J.). In this respect, the CA in *Wellesley Partners LLP* adopted a similar approach to Akenhead J. in *How Engineering Services Ltd v Southern Insulation (Medway) Ltd* [2010] EWHC 1878 (TCC), [2010] B.L.R. 537 (noted in the Main Work, Vol.I, para.1–195), though the earlier decision was not discussed.

[1276h] [2015] EWCA Civ 1146 at [81]–[89] (Floyd L.J.); [179] (Roth L.J.) and [188] (Longmore L.J.).

[1276i] [2014] EWCA Civ 1512 and see Main Work, Vol.I, para.1–195.

[1276j] In *Yapp* the CA held that the claimant's depressive illness was not reasonably foreseeable under the *tort* test (seen as more favourable to the claimant), and therefore was also too remote in his claim for breach of contract: [2014] EWCA Civ 1512 at [121]–[124], [133]. In *Wellesley Partners LLP* the partnerships losses were held not too remote under the contract test thereby leading to the CA affirming the result at trial which had held them not too remote under the tort test: [2015] EWCA Civ 1146 at [81] (Floyd L.J.); [179] (Roth L.J.) and [188] (Longmore L.J.).

[1276k] [2014] EWCA Civ 1512 at [60] and [67].

[1276l] [2014] EWCA Civ 1512 at [119].

[1276m] [2014] EWCA Civ 1512 at [42]–[43]. The CA also referred to breach of the implied term of mutual trust and confidence, but this was not seen as paralleled with any breach of duty at common law.

[1276n] [2015] EWCA Civ 1146 at [80] and [151].

[1276o] [1978] Q.B. 791 at 802–804 noted in Main Work, Vol.I, para.1–195 n.1265.

[1276p] [2015] EWCA Civ 1146 at [68].

[1276q] cf. the discussion in the Main Work, Vol.I, paras 1–188—1–190 on the question whether one party to a contract can be held to have "assumed responsibility" to the other contracting party under the *Hedley Byrne* principle even where the contract contained no express or implied term as to the claimed subject-matter of such an assumption of responsibility. See also Main Work, Vol.I, paras 1–169—1–172 on assumption of responsibility under *Hedley Byrne* more generally.

[1276r] Peel (ed.), *Treitel on The Law of Contract*, 14th edn (2015) para.20–112 and see similarly *McGregor on Damages* 19th edn (2014) para.22–009.

[1276s] [2016] EWCA Civ 1308, [2017] P.N.L.R. 16.

[1276t] [2016] EWCA Civ 1308 at [60] per Jackson L.J. (with whom Patten L.J. agreed).

[1276u] [2014] EWCA Civ 1512, [2015] I.R.L.R. 112 and see Main Work, Vol.I, para.1–196.

[1276v] [2016] EWCA Civ 1308 at [65] and [66]. The CA further held that this loss was outside the scope of the solicitor's duty to advise about the possibility of including an exclusive jurisdiction

clause: at [73]–[74]. On the importance of scope of duty in relation to a solicitor's liability for negligence see *Hughes-Holland v BPE Solicitors* [2017] UKSC 21, [2017] 2 W.L.R. 1029.

[1276w] [2016] EWCA Civ 1308 at [63] per Jackson L.J.

The conflict of laws: jurisdiction

1–199 [*Add to paragraph, at the end: page* [164]]
In a series of recent cases, the Court of Justice of the EU has confirmed its approach to the relationship of the contract and tort provisions in the Brussels Regulation taken in *Kalfelis v Schröder* in relation to the Brussels Convention[1301a] and has therefore made clear that the question whether a particular claim falls within "matters relating to contract" or "matters relating to tort, delict or quasi-delict" must be judged by reference to autonomous EU law understandings of these concepts; and that for this purpose the latter concept "covers all actions which seek to establish the liability of the defendant and do not concern 'matters relating to a contract' within the meaning of Article 5(1)(a)" of the Brussels Regulation.[1301b] As a result, where a national court finds that a claim is a "matter relating to a contract", a national court does not enjoy jurisdiction on the basis that the claim could be viewed as relating to tort as a matter of national law.[1301c]

[1301a] C-189/87 [1988] E.C.R. 5565 at para.17, discussed in this paragraph of the Main Work.

[1301b] *Brogsitter v Fabrication de Montres Normandes EURL* (C-548/12) March 13, 2014 at para.20; *ERGO Insurance SE v If P&C Insurance AS* (Joined Cases C-359/14 and C-475/14) January 21, 2016 paras 43–45; *Kolassa v Barclays Bank Plc* (C-375/13) January 28, 2015 at para.44; *Granarolo SpA v Ambrosi Emmi France SA* (C-196/15) July 14, 2016 at para.20.

[1301c] *Granarolo SpA v Ambrosi Emmi France SA* (C-196/15) July 14, 2016 at para.28.

Conflict of laws: applicable law

1–200 [*Add to note 1306, at the beginning: page* [164]]
ERGO Insurance SE v If P&C Insurance AS (Joined Cases C-359/14 and C-475/14) January 21, 2016 paras 43–45; *Verein für Konsumenteninformation v Amazon EU Sàrl* (C-191/15) July 28, 2016 paras 36–53 and 58. See also *Committeri v Club Mediterranee SA* [2016] EWHC 1510 (QB) at [49]–[53].

(d) *The Influence of Contract on Tort beyond Privity*

Subsequent cases

1–215 [*Add to note 1398, at the end: page* [176]]
; *Summit Advances Ltd v Bush* [2015] EWHC 665 (QB), [2015] P.N.L.R. 18.

[*Add to note 1412, at the end: page* [178]]
See also *Playboy Club London Ltd v Banca Nazionale del Lavoro SpA* [2016] EWCA Civ 457, [2016] 1 W.L.R. 3169 (appeal pending to SC) (no assumption of responsibility in bank in giving a credit reference about one of its customers to a named company (A Co) where (unknown to the bank) the reference was to be used by another company (B Co, a casino) in the same group; nor was it "fair, just and reasonable" to impose liability on the bank in these circumstances).

8. CONTRACT AND OTHER LEGAL CATEGORIES

Contract and trust

[*Add to note 1425, line 4, after* "[1993] 3 W.L.R. 126, 147–148": *page* [180]]   **1–219**
(though *Tinsley v Milligan* was disapproved on other grounds by *Patel v Mirza*
[2016] UKSC 42, [2016] 3 W.L.R. 399, see below, para.16–198).

[*In note 1432, line 5, delete* "cf. also *Tinsley v Milligan* [1993] 3 W.L.R. 126":   **1–220**
page [181]]

CPR Pt 54

[*Add to note 1484, line 2, after* "(P. Craig).": *page* [187]]   **1–228**
cf. *R. (Holmcroft Properties Ltd) v KPMG LLP* [2016] EWHC 323 (Admin),
[2017] Bus. L.R. 932 esp. at [23] et seq. applying *R. v Panel on Takeovers and
Mergers, Ex p. Datafin Plc* [1987] Q.B. 815 (the mere fact that the source of a
body's powers is contract does not necessarily mean that public law principles do
not apply, though it remains important: [2016] EWHC 323 (Admin) at [43]).

Part Two

FORMATION OF CONTRACT

Chapter 2

THE AGREEMENT

1. Preliminary

The objective test

2–002   [*Add to note 9, at the end: page* [192]]
; *Newbury v Sun Microsystems Ltd* [2013] EWHC 2180 (QB) where Lewis J. held that it is neither legitimate nor helpful to take into account subsequent communications to determine whether documents gave rise to a binding agreement.

2. The Offer

Inactivity as an offer

[In note 35, delete "Contrast, Trunk Flooring . . . This was not a case of inactivity." **2–006**
in line 6 to the end and substitute: page [196]]
In *Trunk Flooring Ltd v HSBC Asset Finance (UK) Ltd, Costi Righi SpA* [2015]
NICA 68, the Court of Appeal held that the parties had not abandoned the
contract, as there was no evidence by way of conduct or correspondence, or of
inactivity, to support such a finding; both parties were incontrovertibly actively
engaged in the arbitration process until an impasse was created by the costs issue;
and the respondent who contributed to the situation whereby the costs of the
reference were increased, could not benefit from this action. Although the
reference to arbitration had been terminated this was distinct from the underlying
arbitration agreement.

3. The Acceptance

(a) *Definition*

Acceptance defined

[Add to paragraph, after note 142: page [208]] **2–026**
Where a prospective buyer of a home wanted to know what would happen if
there were snagging defect, and the builder replied that he had an obligation
under the NHBC scheme to remedy defects, there was no contract to repair any
defects.[142a]

[142a] *Secker v Fairhill Property Services Ltd* [2017] EWHC 69 (QB).

Negotiation after apparent agreement

[Add to note 150, at the end: page [210]] **2–028**
Contrast *Global Asset Capital Inc v Aabar Block Sarl* [2017] EWCA Civ 37,
where no contract was found because acceptance of an offer letter that was
"subject to contract" would not remove the subject to contract condition, and
subsequent communications by both parties were materially inconsistent with the
existence of a contract.

Acceptance by conduct

[Add to note 154, at the end: page [210]] **2–029**
(decision to grant summary judgment overturned on appeal on other grounds,
[2015] EWCA Civ 715).

[*Add to paragraph, after note 161: page* [211]]

Nor is a managing director's proposal of an employment contract accepted by the company paying him at the stated rate, if there is doubt over whether the company accepted the other terms.[161a]

[161a] *Arley Homes North West Ltd v Cosgrave* Unreported April 14, 2016 EAT.

(d) *Prescribed Mode of Acceptance*

Other equally efficacious mode

2–065   [*Add to note 335, at the end: page* [232]]
; *A Ltd v B Ltd* [2015] EWHC 137 (Comm).

Method of acceptance waived

2–066   [*Add new note 335a, after* "no doubt be bound by," *in line 2: page* [232]]
[335a] *A Ltd v B Ltd* [2015] EWHC 137 (Comm).

Terms of offer drawn up by offeree

2–067   [*Add to paragraph, at the end: page* [233]]
In another case,[339a] the Court of Appeal, approving this and the previous paragraphs of the 32nd edition of the Main Work, set out the rules in play here[339b] and found a concluded contract despite the contract document remaining unsigned by the offeree as required by the contract, because[339c]: the contract was on the offeree's standard form and the signature requirement was for its benefit; the requirement was waived by the offeree performing the contract as contemplated; there was no prejudice to the offeror, who had benefitted from and had actively facilitated the offeree's performance; subsequent conduct on both sides confirmed the existence of the contract; and finding a contract "accords with what would be the reasonable expectations of Lord Steyn's honest, sensible business people". Nevertheless, the Court acknowledged that the offeree's failure to sign "was at the expense of certainty as to the precise date the contract was formed", although this was not significant on the facts.[339d]

[339a] *Reveille Independent LLC v Anotech International (UK) Ltd* [2016] EWCA Civ 443.
[339b] [2016] EWCA Civ 443 at [40]–[41].
[339c] [2016] EWCA Civ 443 at [53].
[339d] [2016] EWCA Civ 443 at [53].

5. SPECIAL CASES

Difficulty of offer and acceptance analysis in certain cases

2–118   [*Add to note 573, line 4, after* "[1999] S.T.C. 821": *page* [264]]
; *Assuranceforeningen Gard Gjensidig v International Oil Pollution Compensation Fund* [2014] EWHC 3369 (Comm); *Price v Euro Car Parks Ltd* [2015]

EWHC 3253 (QB); and *Burgess v Lejonvarn* [2016] EWHC 40 (TCC); [2016] T.C.L.R. 3.

6. INCOMPLETE AGREEMENT

Agreement in principle only

[*Add to paragraph, after note 585: page* [265]]   **2–119**
In *Wells v Devani*[585a] an oral contract for an estate agent to find a buyer for a property was incomplete where the parties had failed to specify the event which would trigger the agent's entitlement to commission since such contracts do not follow a single pattern.[585b] Moreover, a court cannot turn an incomplete contract into a legally binding contract by adding expressly agreed terms and implied terms together.[585c] In *Teekay Tankers Ltd v STX Offshore and Shipbuilding Co Ltd*[585d] an option agreement for the building of oil tankers was unenforceable because the delivery dates were left to be mutually agreed. The inclusion of a "best efforts" clause in respect of delivery date implicitly recognised that both sides could have regard to their own interests and so precludes fixing a delivery date by reference to what would be "reasonable".[585e]

[585a] [2016] EWCA Civ 1106.
[585b] [2016] EWCA Civ 1106 at [21]–[24].
[585c] [2016] EWCA Civ 1106 at [19], [32] citing *Luxor (Eastbourne) Ltd v Cooper* [1941] A.C. 108 and *Scancarriers A/S v Aotearoa International Ltd* [1985] 2 Lloyd's Rep. 419.
[585d] [2017] EWHC 253 (Comm).
[585e] [2017] EWHC 253 at [175]–[210].

Agreement complete despite lack of detail

[*Add to note 592, at the end: page* [266]]   **2–120**
In *Hughes v Pendragon Sabre Ltd (t/a Porche Centre Bolton)* [2016] EWCA Civ 18 the Court of Appeal held that a customer had entered into a binding contract with a car dealership to buy a limited edition Porsche, even though the contract did not stipulate the price, specification or delivery date of the vehicle. These could be resolved by reference to the Sale of Goods Act 1979.

Stipulation for the execution of a formal document

[*Add to note 614, at the end: page* [269]]   **2–123**
Crabbe v Townsend [2016] EWHC 2450 (Ch), where the contemplated additional documents were "matters of machinery only, whose contents are sufficiently defined by the terms of the 2006 Letter and which were intended to give effect to an existing agreement, not to create one", and *Ely v Robson* [2016] EWCA Civ 774, where separating cohabitees had orally agreed their respective beneficial interests in the family home, recorded it a letter, and had acted in reliance upon it; the anticipated formal written agreement was merely the "mechanics necessary to achieve their stated objectives".

[*Add to note 617, line 3, before* "contrast ... ": *page* [270]]
Reveille Independent LLC v Anotech International (UK) Ltd [2016] EWCA Civ
443, where the respondent had clearly and unequivocally represented by its
conduct that it was bound by the deal memorandum and had waived the requirement to sign;

[*Add to paragraph, after note 617: page* [270]]
An oral agreement for the sale of land is enforceable in equity under a constructive trust despite not being in writing where both parties had considered it
to be immediately binding upon them, and where the prospective buyer had then
acted to his detriment in reliance upon it.[617a]

[617a] *Matchmove Ltd v Dowding* [2016] EWCA Civ 1233; see below, paras 4–142 and 5–040.

Letters of intent; letters of comfort

2–132   [*Add to note 679, at the end: page* [277]]
Spartafield Ltd v Penten Group Ltd [2016] EWHC 2295 (TCC), 168 Con. L.R.
221 (letter of intent displaced by contract when the key principles for the contract
were agreed and it was agreed that the terms would be those contained in the JCT
ICD form; the contemplated execution of a formal contract was not a pre-
condition to the existence of the contract).

Machinery laid down in the agreement

2–138   [*Add to paragraph, at the end: page* [284]]
However, where the designated machinery that fails is regarded as "essential",
the agreement will be unenforceable. Thus, where one party agreed to pay
compensation to the other for increased water-flow rates from flooding incidents,
and the parties failed to identify a site at which water-flow rates could be gauged
via their engineers or via arbitration, the court refused to substitute other machinery, and refused to allow the gauging site to be determined retrospectively by the
engineers or arbitration.[744a]

[744a] *Manchester Ship Canal Co Ltd v Environment Agency* [2017] EWHC 1340 (QB).

Duty to negotiate outstanding details?

2–146   [*Add to paragraph, at the end: page* [290]]
Similarly, a dispute resolution clause in an existing and enforceable contract
which requires the parties to seek to resolve a dispute by friendly discussions in
good faith and within a limited period of time before the dispute may be referred
to arbitration is enforceable. It is not incomplete; not uncertain (it has an
identifiable standard, namely, fair, honest and genuine discussions aimed at
resolving a dispute, the difficulty of proving a breach in some cases does not
mean that the clause lacks certainty); and not inconsistent with the position of a
negotiating party since the parties voluntarily accepted a restriction upon their
freedom not to negotiate. Moreover, it is in the public interest, since courts
should enforce freely agreed obligations and because it may avoid expensive and
time-consuming arbitration.[783a]

[783a] *Emirates Trading Agency v Prime Mineral Exports Private Ltd* [2014] EWHC 2104 (Comm), [2015] 1 W.L.R. 1145 at [63]–[64].

7. CERTAINTY OF TERMS

Requirement of certainty

[*Add to note 784, last line, before* "and below, para.2–149 at nn.790–792": *page* [290]]
Kunicki v Hayward [2016] EWHC 3199 (Ch) at [152] (citing this paragraph) and [154];

2–147

9. CONTRACTUAL INTENTION

Burden of proof: agreements inferred from conduct

[*Add to paragraph, at the end: page* [305]]
Likewise, in *Re MF Global UK Ltd (In Special Administration)*[879a] the court implied a contract between two companies in administration, pursuant to which one company paid the expenses of staff seconded to a second company within the same group. The established relationship between the companies was only explicable in the particular circumstances on the basis that it had a contractual foundation. In contrast, the burden of proof was not discharged in *Assuranceforeningen Gard Gjensidig v International Oil Pollution Compensation Fund*[879b] where, following a serious oil spill from an insured ship, the insurer asserted a contract with an international fund, set up to compensate for damage caused by oil pollution, to indemnify the insurer in respect of aspects of its liability. On the facts, it was impossible to construe the international fund's communications as making the offer alleged expressly or impliedly, let alone clearly and unequivocally.[879c]

2–169

[879a] [2016] EWCA Civ 569.
[879b] [2014] EWHC 3369 (Comm).
[879c] [2014] EWHC 3369 at [102], [110], [114] and [123].

Intention judged objectively

[*Add to paragraph, line 10, after* "her pupil masters.": *page* [306]]
In *New Media Holding Co LLC v Kuznetsov*[884a] the court found an intention to create legal relations in respect of a "Term Sheet" signed by both parties. On the one hand: the language of the document was brief and did not mention consideration; the document was prepared in a casual and informal way; further formalities were required; and the rights transferred were not capable of immediate enforcement. On the other hand: the parties were experienced and sophisticated businessmen; the document contained clear express terms; the language was consistent with a legally binding agreement; and the "Term Sheet" was consistent with an intention that this be part of a package agreement (with other

2–170

terms, including the consideration, to be dealt with elsewhere) and with the parties' pre-existing relationship, which itself raised a strong presumption that the parties intended to be legally bound. Where there has been substantial performance, courts are especially reluctant to reach the unrealistic conclusion that the parties lacked intention to be legally bound.[884b]

[884a] [2016] EWHC 360 (QB).
[884b] *Purton (t/a Richwood Interiors) v Kilker Projects Ltd* [2015] EWHC 2624 (TCC) at [7].

[Add to note 885, at the end: page [306]]
In contrast, no intention to be bound was concluded in *Price v Euro Car Parks Ltd* [2015] EWHC 3253 (QB) where the claimant put a business proposal, and sent an "In Principle Heads of Agreement" that neither signed, to the defendant. The defendant never accepted any offer made by the claimant; it merely allowed the claimant to go ahead (at his own risk) to research his business proposal. Moreover, the "In Principle Heads of Agreement" was too indefinite. Nor was there intention to be bound in *Burgess v Lejonvarn* [2016] EWHC 40 (TCC), [2016] T.C.L.R. 3 (affirmed [2017] EWCA Civ 254: see below, para.4–199), where an architect, for no fee, had found a contractor to landscape her friends' garden with a view to her providing subsequent design input for consideration. There was no contract to project manage the landscaping because the written discussions were simply too inchoate, there was no intention to be legally bound and there had been no consideration.

10. LIABILITY WHEN NEGOTIATIONS DO NOT PRODUCE A CONTRACT

(c) *Negotiations Broken Off Without Preliminary Agreements*

Constructive trust

2–219   *[Add to paragraph, at the beginning: page* [335]]
An oral agreement for the sale of land is enforceable in equity under a constructive trust despite not being in writing where both parties had considered it to be immediately binding upon them, and where the prospective buyer had then acted to his detriment in reliance upon it.[1151a]

[1151a] *Matchmove Ltd v Dowding* [2016] EWCA Civ 1233; see below, paras 4–142 and 5–040.

CHAPTER 3

MISTAKES AS TO THE TERMS OR AS TO IDENTITY

[*In note 1, update reference to Cartwright, Misrepresentation, Mistake and Non-disclosure to: page* [339]]
4th edn (2016)

1. INTRODUCTION TO MISTAKE

Types of mistake

[*In note 6, update reference to Anson's Law of Contract, 29th edn to: page* [340]]   **3–001**
30th edn (2015), Ch.8

Mistakes as to terms and mistakes as to facts

[*In note 12, update reference to Anson's Law of Contract to: page* [340]]   **3–002**
30th edn (2015), p.300

"Mistake" implies a positive belief

[*In note 20, update reference to Cartwright, Misrepresentation, Mistake and Non-disclosure to: page* [342]]   **3–007**
4th edn (2016), para.12-03

Mistakes that are not legally relevant

3–008 [*In note 26, delete* "29th edition by Beatson, Burrows and Cartwright (eds) (2010)" *and substitute: page* [342]]
30th edition by Beatson, Burrows and Cartwright (eds) (2015)

[*In note 26, delete* "pp.277–278" *and substitute: page* [342]]
p.300

2. MISTAKES AS TO TERMS OR IDENTITY

(a) *Underlying Principles*

Lack of agreement or agreement ambiguous

3–014 [*In note 55, update reference to Cartwright, Misrepresentation, Mistake and Non-disclosure to: page* [346]]
4th edn (2016), para.13-10

[*In note 58, update reference to Cartwright, Misrepresentation, Mistake and Non-disclosure to: page* [347]]
4th edn (2016), para.13-18

Older "subjective" notions

3–017 [*In note 63, update reference to Anson's Law of Contract to: page* [347]]
30th edn (2015), p.270

Test not wholly objective

3–018 [*In note 65, update reference to Cartwright, Misrepresentation, Mistake and Non-disclosure to: page* [347]]
4th edn (2016), paras 13-07–13-19

(c) *Unilateral Mistake as to Terms*

(i) *When Mistake will Affect Contract*

Mistake known to the other party

3–022 [*In note 83, update reference to Cartwright, Misrepresentation, Mistake and Non-disclosure to: page* [350]]
4th edn (2016), paras 13-24–13-26

Mistakes which ought to have been apparent

3–023 [*In note 92, update reference to Cartwright, Misrepresentation, Mistake and Non-disclosure to: page* [351]]
4th edn (2016), para.13-22

(ii) *Effect on Contract*

Effect of mistake as to terms: mistaken party's intention known to other

[*In note 125, update reference to Anson to: page* [355]]   **3–029**
Beatson, Burrows and Cartwright (eds), *Anson's Law of Contract*, 30th edn
(2015), p.278

[*In note 125, update reference to Treitel on The Law of Contract to: page* [355]]
14th edn (2015), para.8–053

[*In note 125, update reference to Cartwright, Misrepresentation, Mistake and Non-
disclosure to: page* [355]]
4th edn (2016), para.13-28

(d) *Mistaken Identity*

Offer to B cannot be accepted by C

[*In note 148, update reference to Anson to: page* [359]]   **3–038**
Beatson, Burrows and Cartwright (eds), *Anson's Law of Contract*, 30th edn
(2015), p.290

Identity and attributes

[*In note 194, update reference to Treitel on The Law of Contract to: page* [365]]   **3–045**
14th edn (2015), para.8–037

4. Rectification of Written Agreements

[*In note 232, update reference to Cartwright, Misrepresentation, Mistake and Non-
disclosure to: page* [370]]
4th edn (2016), paras13-38–13-54

(b) *Common Mistake*

Issue may be solved by construction

[*Add to note 247, at the end: page* [372]]   **3–060**
Compare *LSREF III Wight Ltd v Millvalley Ltd* [2016] EWHC 466 (Comm), 165
Con. L.R. 58 ("no ambiguity, no syntactical difficulty in construing the language
used and the reference to the 1992 form of ISDA Agreement cannot be said to
be such a commercial nonsense as to make it absurd for the parties to refer to it":
at [62]).

Parol evidence

[*Add to note 257, at the end: page* [374]]   **3–061**
See also *Procter and Gamble Co v Svenska Cellulosa Aktiebolaget SCA* [2012]
EWHC 498 (Ch) at [104]–[106]; *DS-Rendite-Fonds Nr.106 VLCC Titan Glory*

GmbH & Co Tankschiff KG v Titan Maritime SA [2013] EWHC 3492 (Comm) at [48]; *LSREF III Wight Ltd v Millvalley Ltd* [2016] EWHC 466 (Comm), 165 Con. L.R. 58 at [121]–[123]; *Milton Keynes BC v Viridor (Community Recycling MK) Ltd* [2017] EWHC 239 (TCC), [2017] B.L.R. 216 at [77].

Outward expression of accord

3–064   *[Add to note 274, at the end: page* [376]]
In *Prowting 1968 Trustee One Ltd v Amos-Yeo* [2015] EWHC 2480 (Ch), [2015] B.T.C. 33 rectification was ordered when an agreement did not reflect the parties' intention to transfer enough shares to entitle the claimants to tax relief, although the parties had left the number to be determined by a trustee, who had miscalculated the number (see at [37]–[38]).

Unexpressed but shared intentions

3–065   *[In note 279, update reference to Cartwright, Misrepresentation, Mistake and Non-disclosure to: page* [378]]
4th edn (2016), para.13-40

Continuing intention

3–066   *[Add to note 280, at the end: page* [378]]
It has been said that the word "continuing" in Peter Gibson L.J.'s first requirement in the *Swainland Builders* case seems to be superfluous: it is more accurate to say that there needs to be a common intention (requirement 1) which was continuing at the time that the contract was executed (requirement 3): *Milton Keynes BC v Viridor (Community Recycling MK) Ltd* [2017] EWHC 239 (TCC), [2017] B.L.R. 216 at [48] (Coulson J.). If the parties have altered their agreement extensively before the document was executed, rectification will not be appropriate because their initial intention on the point at issue may well have changed also (as in *Pindos Shipping Corp v Raven ("The Mata Hari")* [1983] 2 Lloyd's Rep. 449), but the fact that there have been minor changes to other aspects of the agreement does not prevent rectification: [2017] EWHC 239 (TCC) at [62]–[63], citing *Dunlop Haywards Ltd v Erinaceous Insurance Services Ltd* [2009] EWCA Civ 354 at [82].

(c) *Unilateral Mistake*

Inequity

3–072   *[Add to paragraph, at the end: page* [383]]
A party with little experience or few bargaining resources who has noticed a possible mistake made by a much stronger party may be entitled to assume that the stronger party "knew what it was doing".[332a] This may be explained in terms of whether the weaker party was acting unconscionably[332b]; but it can equally be seen as a question of whether the weaker party had the requisite degree of knowledge—a party who did not actually know a mistake had been made but

who shut his eyes to the obvious or failed to make enquiries is treated as "knowing of it" only if he acted dishonestly.[332c]

[332a] See *George Wimpey UK Ltd v VI Construction Ltd* [2005] EWCA Civ 77, [2005] B.L.R. 135 at [65]–[67] (Sedley L.J.).

[332b] *NHS Commissioning Board v Silovsky* [2015] EWHC 3141 (Comm) at [42]–[43].

[332c] As by the majority in *George Wimpey UK Ltd v VI Construction Ltd* [2005] EWCA Civ 77, [2005] B.L.R. 135, see at [47] and [79]; see Main Work, Vol.I, para.3–070.

(d) *The Extended Notion of Common Mistake*

Criticism of the *Chartbrook* decision

[*Add to note 367, at the end: page* [388]]   **3–081**
In *NHS Commissioning Board v Silovsky* [2015] EWHC 3141 (Comm), Leggatt J. respectfully agreed with Lord Neuberger MR but held that he was bound to apply Lord Hoffmann's "strong" objective approach: at [31]. See also *Magellan Spirit ApS v Vitol SA (The Magellan Spirit)* [2016] EWHC 454 (Comm), [2016] 2 Lloyd's Rep. 1 at [42].

"Objective" meaning known not to be party's intention

[*In note 389, update reference to Cartwright, Misrepresentation, Mistake and Non-   **3–086**
disclosure to: page* [391]]
4th edn (2016), para.13-40

(e) *General Principles*

A discretionary remedy

[*Add to note 422, at the end: page* [395]]   **3–093**
See also *Equity Syndicate Management Ltd v Glaxosmithkline Plc* [2015] EWHC 2163 (Comm), [2016] Lloyd's Rep. I.R. 155 at [46]–[47] (on the facts it would have been inequitable to withhold the remedy).

CHAPTER 4

CONSIDERATION

1. INTRODUCTION

Informal gratuitous promises

4–002   [*Add to note 10, at the end: page* [400]]
For legislation giving effect to the similar policy of protecting creditors of a gratuitous transferee of property, see Insolvency Act 1986 s.242, applied in *Joint*

Administrators of Oceancrown Ltd v Stonegale Ltd [2016] UKSC 30, 2016 SC (UKSC) 91 at [17] ("received nothing whatsoever"), approving the judgment in the Court below, quoted in [2016] UKSC 30 at [13] ("no party paid anything" for the transfer).

3. ADEQUACY OF CONSIDERATION

Courts generally will not judge adequacy

[*Add to note 81, at the end: page* [409]]   **4–014**
For the possible legal status, after the completion of "Brexit", of UK legislation which has been passed to implement EU legal requirements, see above, paras 1–013A—1–013E.

Nominal consideration

[*Add to note 122, line 11, after* "[2001] 1 W.L.R. 143;"*: page* [414]]   **4–019**
Bataillon v Shone [2016] EWHC 1174 (QB), [2016] B.P.I.R. 829 (transfers from husband to wife at an undervalue set aside as having been made for "no consideration" within s.429(1)(a) of the Insolvency Act 1986).

4. THE CONCEPT OF "VALUABLE" CONSIDERATION

Discretionary promise

[*Add to note 152, at the end: page* [418]]   **4–025**
; *Simpkin v Berkeley Group Holdings PLC* [2016] EWHC 1619 (QB), where it was not disputed that a contract had come into existence and held that an employer's discretion to decide that an employee had been a "good leaver" (and so was to receive benefits under a bonus scheme operated by the employer) must be exercised in good faith and without being "arbitrary, capricious or irrational . . . " at [327]. Such restrictions on the exercise of the discretion would also have satisfied the requirement of consideration if an issue of consideration had arisen.

5. PAST CONSIDERATION

Bills of exchange

[*Add new note 225a, line 4, after* "for the debt"*: page* [427]]   **4–035**
[225a] See *Banque Cantonale de Genève v Sanomi* [2016] EWHC 3353 (Comm), where forbearance to sue, "both promised and actual" (at [62]) was held to be consideration for two promissory notes. No reliance was placed on Bills of Exchange Act s.27(1)(b) though this provision applies, by virtue of s.89(1) of the 1882 Act, to promissory notes "with the necessary modifications".

Acknowledgement of statute-barred debts

4-036   *[Add new note 227a, line 4, after* "a debt,"*: page* [428]]
[227a] Section 29(5) is expressed to apply also to "any ... other liquidated claim" (s.29(5)(a)). In *Barnett v Creggy* [2016] EWCA Civ 1004, [2017] P.N.L.R. 4 a majority of the Court of Appeal held that the words here quoted could include a claim against a trustee for money paid away in breach of his fiduciary duty, but (unanimously) that these words did not apply to the claim for "equitable compensation" since this was "equivalent to a claim for damages" (at [37]) and so not a "liquidated claim" within s.29(5)(a), (at [40], [54], [55]).

7. COMPROMISE AND FORBEARANCE TO SUE

(c) *Actual Forbearance*

Actual forbearance may be consideration

4-058   *[Add to note 313, at the end: page* [438]]
; *cf. Banque Cantonale de Genève v Sanomi* [2016] EWHC 3353 (Comm) at [62], quoted above, para.4–035.

Express or implied request of debtor necessary

4-061   *[Add to note 326, at the end: page* [439]]
For the sufficiency of an implied request from the debtor for the creditor's forbearance, see also *Banque Cantonale de Genève v Sanomi* [2016] EWHC 3353 (Comm) at [60].

8. EXISTING DUTIES AS CONSIDERATION

(b) *Duty Imposed by Contract with Promisor*

Factual benefit to promisor

4-069   *[Add to note 369, line 5, after* "[1998] 2 Lloyd's Rep. 428 at 435"*: page* [445]]
; *Stevensdrake Ltd v Hunt* [2016] EWHC 1111 (Ch) at [61]; *MWB Business Exchange Centres Ltd v Rock Advertising Ltd* [2016] EWCA Civ 553, [2017] Q.B. 604, discussed below, para.4–119A.

4-070   *[Add to note 377, at the end: page* [446]]
A passage in the judgment of Arden L.J. in *MWB Business Exchange Centres Ltd v Rock Advertising Ltd* [2016] EWCA Civ 553, [2017] Q.B. 604 at [79] could be said to support the view that the decision in *Stilk v Myrick* (1809) 2 Camp. 317, Main Work, para.4–067, might now go the other way on the ground that the master of the ship had obtained a "practical benefit" which would constitute consideration within the reasoning of the *Williams* case [1991] 1 Q.B. 1, see

Main Work, Vol.I, para.4–069; but there is no express reference to *Stilk v Myrick* (above) in the *MWB* case, above.

[Add a new note 378a at the end of the paragraph: page [447]]
378a The above sentence in the Main Work is cited with apparent approval by Arden L.J. in *MWB Business Exchange Centres Ltd v Rock Advertising Ltd* [2016] EWCA Civ 553, [2017] Q.B. 604 at [80]. The question whether in that case the requirement of consideration was satisfied is discussed below, para.4–119A.

Increase in promisee's performance

[Add to note 390, at the end: page [448]]   **4–072**
See also *Amey Wye Valley Ltd v Hertfordshire DC* [2016] EWHC 2368 (TCC), [2016] B.L.R. 698 (contract for highway maintenance providing for inflation-linked increases in contractor's charges. The case was concerned with the interpretation of this provision; there was no reference in the judgment to the requirement of consideration).

9. DISCHARGE AND VARIATION OF CONTRACTUAL DUTIES

(b) *Variation*

(iii) *Equitable Mitigations*

Requirement of pre-existing legal relationship

[Add to note 467, line 5, after "[1995] 1 Lloyd's Rep. 599;"*: page* [460]]   **4–089**
Pacol Ltd v Trade Lines Ltd (The Henrik Sif) [1982] 1 Lloyd's Rep. 456 and *The Stolt Loyalty* [1993] 2 Lloyd's Rep. 281 were cited without adverse comment in *Costain Ltd v Tarmac Holdings Ltd* [2017] EWHC 319 (TCC), [2017] 1 Lloyd's Rep. 331 at [103]–[104], but that discussion is concerned with the scope of the circumstances in which a person may be estopped (by representation or by convention) on the ground of having failed to perform a "duty to speak": see below, para.4–092. There is no reference in the *Costain* case to the question discussed in Main Work, Vol.I, para.4–089, i.e. whether promissory estoppel can operate where there is no pre-existing legal relationship between the parties and so give rise to a cause of action, as opposed to a defence (on this point, see Main Work Vol.I, para.4–099);

The promise or representation must be "clear" or "unequivocal"

[Add to note 473, at the end: page [461]]   **4–091**
The requirement that, for the purpose of an estoppel by representation, the representation must be "clear or unequivocal" or "precise and unambiguous" is stated by Carr J. in *Spliethoff's Bevrachtingskantoor BV v Bank of China* [2015] EWHC 999 (Comm), [2015] 2 Lloyd's Rep. 123 at [156] citing, with apparent approval, para.3–090 of the 31st edition of the Main Work, replaced by para.4–091 of the 32nd (present) edition.

[*Add to note 475 at the end: page* [461]]
; *MWB Business Exchange Centres Ltd v Rock Advertising Ltd* [2016] EWCA
Civ 553, [2017] Q.B. 604 at [51], [52] and *passim;* as the promise in this case
was supported by consideration (see below, para.4–119A) it was not strictly
necessary to decide the estoppel issue: see at [50].

Conduct contrasted with inactivity

4–093   [*Add to note 503, at the end: page* [464]]
Contrast *Costain Ltd v Tarmac Holdings Ltd* [2017] EWHC 319 (TCC), [2017]
1 Lloyd's Rep. 331 where the defendant was under no "duty to speak out" (at
[102]) as it had not been guilty of any "sharp practice" (at [113] and see at [112])
in failing to do so. In that case, the estoppels alleged to operate against the
defendant were estoppel by representation and estoppel by convention and *both*
these allegations were rejected by the court (see at [126]). In relation to estoppel
by convention, which can arise without any representation (Main Work, Vol.I,
para.4–108 and below, para.4–108), Coulson J. said in the *Costain* case (above)
that the duty to speak "would extend to a positive obligation on the part of the
defendant to correct a false assumption obviously being made by the claimant
. . . " ([2017] EWHC 319 (TCC) at [124]). In such circumstances a "duty to
speak" was held to have arisen in *Process Components Ltd v Kason Kek-Gardner
Ltd* [2016] EWHC 2198 (Ch) at [129], [132].

Whether "detriment" required

4–095   [*Add to note 513, at the end: page* [465]]
; *MWB Business Exchange Centres Ltd v Rock Advertising Ltd* [2016] EWCA
Civ 553, [2017] Q.B. 604 at [54]; for this case (so far as it relates to estoppel) see
also above, para.4–091 n.475.

Effect of the doctrine generally suspensive

4–097   [*Add to note 526, line 13, after* "no promissory estoppel had arisen"*: page* [467]]
; *MWB Business Exchange Centres Ltd v Rock Advertising Ltd* [2016] EWCA
Civ 553, [2017] Q.B. 604 at [56] ("may only be suspensive"). No promissory
estoppel would have arisen in this case as reasonable notice had been given to
terminate the "variation agreement" (described below, see para.4–119A); for this
point see at [63], [67] and [92].

[*Add to note 526, at the end: page* [467]]
Notice is not required to bring an end to the suspension where, on the true
construction of the representation, the circumstances in which it was intended to
apply had come to an end: see *Dunbar Assets plc v Butler* [2015] EWHC 2546
(Ch) at [50]; or where notice of termination was not necessary "to allow a
reasonable period for the party to whom notice is given to make alternative
arrangements" (*ibid.*, at [51]).

Defensive nature of the doctrine

[*Add to note 550, at the end: page* [470]]   **4–099**
A dictum in *Dixon v Blindley Heath Investments Ltd* [2015] EWCA Civ 1023,
[2017] 3 W.L.R. 166 at [73] (quoted in para.4–114 n.684 below) seems to suggest
that promissory estoppel can "provide a cause of action". But the point does not
seem to have been argued in that case and no reference is made in the *Dixon* case
to any of the authorities which are cited in Main Work, Vol.I, para.4–089 in
support of the view that, in English law, promissory estoppel does *not* create a
cause of action; and it is respectfully submitted that the above dictum in the
Dixon case, so far as it departs from that view, should be treated as having been
made *per incuriam*.

Analogy with estoppel

[*Add to note 573, at the end: page* [474]]   **4–104**
Millett L.J.'s statement in *First National Bank plc v Thompson* [1996] Ch. 231,
236, to the effect that "the attempt to demonstrate that all estoppels ... are now
governed by the same principle ... has never won general acceptance" (quoted
in Main Work, Vol.I, para.4–104) is cited with apparent approval in *Monde
Petroleum SA v WesternZagros Ltd* [2016] EWHC 1472 (Comm), [2016] 2
Lloyd's Rep. 229 at [227], though it appears to be qualified by the point made in
the latter judgment that "a representation followed by reliance" is "a fundamental requirement of estoppel by representation and promissory estoppel"
([*ibid.*]). This is, with respect, true, but the *kinds* of representation capable of
giving rise to these two forms of estoppel are not the same, a representation as
to the future (or a promise) being capable of giving rise to promissory estoppel
but not to estoppel by representation (see Main Work, Vol.I, para.4–104). The
judgment in the *Monde Petroleum* case also accepts that estoppel by convention
(Main Work, Vol.I, paras 4–108—4–109) "does not depend on any representation or promise" ([2016] EWHC 1472 (Comm) at [227]), though it does depend
on "communications to pass across the line between the parties": *ibid.* and see
Main Work, para.4–110. The latter requirement seems to be regarded as a sort of
functional equivalent of the requirement of a representation in cases of estoppel
by representation or promissory estoppel. It is, however, less exacting than those
requirements, especially if the recent judicial suggestion that the existence of the
"common assumption" on which estoppel by convention is based (Main Work,
Vol.I, para.4–108) may be "inferred from conduct, or even silence": *Dixon v
Blindley Heath Investments Ltd* [2015] EWCA Civ 1023, [2017] 3 W.L.R. 166 at
[92]; and see below, para.4–108 n.630.

[*Add to note 583, line 9, after* "[1994] 2 A.C. 224, 235;": *page* [476]]
; in *Glencore International AG v MSC Mediterranean Shipping Co SA* [2015]
EWHC 1989 (Comm), [2015] 2 Lloyd's Rep. 508, Andrew Smith J. rejected the
submission that the facts of that case gave rise to an estoppel which "might be
characterised as an estoppel by representation or an equitable estoppel" (at [33]);
he did so on the ground that the claimant had made no relevant representation or
so conducted itself as to give rise to the alleged estoppel (*ibid.*). It seems that
"equitable estoppel" here refers to promissory estoppel;

Analogy with waiver

4-105   [*Add to note 595, line 13, after* "and promissory estoppel");"*: page* [477]]
MWB Business Exchange Centres Ltd v Rock Advertising Ltd [2016] EWCA Civ
553, [2017] Q.B. 604 at [64], describing "waiver" in the context of para.4–015
of the Main Work, Vol.I, as "akin to promissory estoppel";

Distinguished from estoppel by convention

4-108   [*Add to note 620, penultimate line, after* "without further reference to estoppel."*:
page* [481]]
F G Wilson (Engineering) Ltd v John Holt & Co (Liverpool) Ltd [2013] EWCA
Civ 1232, [2014] 1 W.L.R. 2365 is doubted in *PST Energy 7 Shipping LLC v O
W Bunker Malta Ltd (The Res Cogitans)* [2016] UKSC 23, [2016] 2 W.L.R.
1193, but not on the estoppel point for which it is cited in this footnote in the
Main Work.

[*Add to note 620, at the end: page* [481]]
The requirements of estoppel by convention are summarised in *Spliethoff's
Bevrachtingskantoor BV v Bank of China* [2015] EWHC 999 (Comm), [2015] 2
Lloyd's Rep. 123 at [159], citing "paras. 3–107 [of the 31st edition of the Main
Work] and following" with apparent approval; the corresponding paragraphs in
the present, 32nd edition are paras 4–108 *et seq.* Carr J. would have held those
requirements to have been satisfied but it was "strictly unnecessary" (at [154])
to decide the point since his "primary conclusion" (at [170]) was that the facts
which the claimant sought to estop the defendant from denying had been
established by the evidence (see at [147]–[154]). This was also the position in
Crabbe v Townsend [2016] EWHC 2450 (Ch), [2017] W.T.L.R. 13 where an
agreement between the Claimant and the Defendant (her brother) was held to
have contractual force (see above, para.2–123) and the defendant further argued
that the claimant was estopped by convention from enforcing that agreement.
The requirements of this form of estoppel were stated at [2016] EWHC 2450
(Ch) at [7] but were held not to have been satisfied on the ground that the parties
had not made any "common assumption" (at [18]) and on the further grounds
that there had been no reliance on any such assumption (at [19]), nor would it
have been "unjust or unconscionable" (at [20]) for the Claimant to enforce the
agreement, so that the requirement stated in Main Work, Vol.I, para.4–108 at
n.621 would also not have been satisfied, since no detriment had been suffered
by the defendant nor any benefit obtained by the claimant (*ibid.*).

[*Add to note 622, at the end: page* [482]]
For discussions of estoppel by convention, see also *Mitchell v Watkinson* [2014]
EWCA Civ 1472, [2015] L. & T.R. 22 at [51], where para.3–107 of the 31st
edition of the Main Work (para.4–108 of the present, 32nd, edition) is cited with
apparent approval; in that case the defence of estoppel by convention failed for
want of a common assumption (at [60]—but the appeal was dismissed on other
grounds: at [95]); *Edray Ltd v Canning* [2015] EWHC 2744 (Ch), where the two
requirements of estoppel by convention stated at notes 620 and 621 of the Main
Work (that there must be a common assumption and that it must be unjust to

allow the party alleged to be estopped to resile from that assumption (at [38]) were held to have been satisfied (at [48]); and *Roundlistic Ltd v Jones* [2016] UKUT 325 where the requirements of estoppel are stated at [47] and [48] and no such estoppel was held to have arisen as the parties had not made any "common assumption" (at [50] and [56]). See also *Preedy v Dunne* [2016] EWCA Civ 805, [2016] C.P. Rep. 44, where, after the claim based on proprietary estoppel had been rejected at first instance, an alternative claim was made on appeal that the facts had given rise to an estoppel by convention. This claim, too, was rejected on the grounds that the parties had not made any "common assumption" ([2016] EWCA Civ 805 at [64]) and that, even if there had been such an assumption, there had been no reliance on it by the party claiming the benefit of the estoppel (*ibid.*).

[*Add to note 624, at the end: page* [482]]
; *Dixon v Blindley Heath Investments Ltd* [2015] EWCA Civ 1023, [2017] 3 W.L.R. 166 at [73] ("not founded on a unilateral representation"); *Monde Petroleum SA v WesternZagros Ltd* [2016] EWHC 1472 (Comm), [2016] 2 Lloyd's Rep. 229 at [227] ("does not depend on any representation or promise"); *Process Components Ltd v Kason Kek-Gardner Ltd* [2016] EWHC 2198 (Ch) at [116], [117], distinguishing between estoppel by convention and estoppel by representation (in this case the requirements of both these forms of estoppel were satisfied: see at [135]). See also *Costain Ltd v Tarmac Holdings Ltd* [2017] EWHC 319 (TCC), [2017] 1 Lloyd's Rep. 331 at [101], where the statement that "Estoppel by convention depends on a shared assumption, not a representation . . . " forms part of Coulson J.'s discussion of the "ingredients of estoppel by convention". In that case the attempt to invoke estoppel by convention failed on the ground that there was no "common understanding" (at [111]), no "sharp practice" (at [113]) by the party alleged to be estopped, nor any detriment suffered by the other party (at [118]) so that it would not be unconscionable for the former party to act inconsistently with any assumption, had it been made (see Main Work, Vol.I, para.4–108 at n.421).

[*Add new note 624a, line 12, after* "by the other party.": *page* [482]]
[624a] The passage running from Main Work, Vol.I, para.4–108 after n.619 to n.624a is quoted with apparent approval by the Court of Appeal in *Dixon v Blindley Heath Investments Ltd* [2015] EWCA Civ 1023, [2017] 3 W.L.R. 166 at [74] quoting from the judgment of the Court below [2014] EWHC 1366 (Ch), where the quotation was taken from para.3–107 of the 31st edition of the Main Work. In the *Dixon* case, it was further held that such an estoppel was not "confined to cases of mistake" but could extend to cases in which the common assumption of the parties had arisen simply because they had forgotten the true facts" since "a mistaken recollection [was] not . . . legally different from a state of forgetfulness" (at [79]). In this case the erroneous common assumption of parties to a share transfer arose because they had forgotten that valid rights of pre-emption existed in relation to the shares.

[*Add to note 630, at the end: page* [483]]
In *Dixon v Blindley Heath Investments Ltd* [2015] EWCA Civ 1023, [2017] 3 W.L.R. 166 the Court of Appeal did "not think that there must be expression of accord" and that the common assumption could be "inferred from conduct, or even silence . . . " (at [92]), though this view did not dispense with the requirement, discussed in Main Work, Vol.I, para.4–110, that "something must be shown to have 'crossed the line' to manifest an assent to the assumption" (at [92]). "Silence", could it seems, only satisfy this requirement in cases where the

party alleged to be estopped was under a "duty to speak", as, for example in *Process Components Ltd v Kason Kek-Gardner Ltd* [2016] EWHC 2198 (Ch) : see at [129]–[132].

Assumption of law

4–111   [*Add to note 645, at the end: page* [485]]
and [2015] EWCA Civ 751, [2016] 2 All E.R. (Comm) 333 at [43]; *Dixon v Blindley Heath Investments Ltd* [2015] EWCA Civ 1023, [2017] 3 W.L.R. 166 at [73].

[*Add new note 647a, line 8, after* "this kind.": *page* [485]]
647a For a recent case in which estoppel by convention arose from a shared mistaken assumption as to the true construction of a contract, see *Zvi Construction Co LLC v Notre Dame University (USA) in England* [2016] EWHC 1924 (TCC), [2016] B.L.R. 604 at [64]. For earlier cases in which a shared assumption as to the construction of the contract gave rise to an estoppel by convention, see Main Work, Vol.I, para.4–109.

Estoppel by convention does not operate prospectively

4–113   [*Add to note 664, at the end: page* [487]]
; *Zvi Construction Co LLC v Notre Dame University (USA) in England* [2016] EWHC 1924, [2016] B.L.R. 604 where it was said (at [64]) that the estoppel which operated in relation to the dispute before the Court did not apply to any future disputes, presumably because by the time they arose the truth would have been revealed in the instant proceedings. But where the common assumption was that intellectual property was vested in one of the parties sharing that assumption it was held that the other party was "permanently (like a tenant or bailee) estopped from denying" that the property was so vested and that a licence agreement relating to it had been terminated: *Process Components Ltd v Kason Kek-Gardner Ltd* [2016] EWHC 2198 (Ch) at [136], apparently cross referring to *ibid.* at [128].

Whether estoppel by convention creates new rights

4–114   [*Add to note 676, at the end: page* [488]]
In this case the Court of Appeal allowed the appeal: see [2015] EWCA Civ 751, [2016] 2 All E.R. (Comm) 333 at [59]. The Court held that the judge below had been wrong to conclude that the contract contained the term giving effect to the allegedly shared assumption (at [50]); and that he had also been wrong in holding that, if there was no "relevant contractual term," then the lender in that case was "estopped on the basis of some sort of contractual estoppel, estoppel by convention or estoppel by representation" from denying that the borrower was protected as if there had been some such term (at [56]); but the Court further held that the lender's representations gave rise to liability (1) under the Misrepresentation Act 1967 and (2) as "contractual warranties" (at [57]), presumably collateral to the main contract.

[*Add to note 682, at the end: page* [489]]
See also *Rivertrade Ltd v EMG Finance Ltd* [2015] EWCA Civ 1295, where estoppel by convention did not "create an enforceable right" but was relied upon

"to bind the parties to [the] agreement to an interpretation that would not otherwise be correct" (at [50]).

[Add to paragraph, after note 683: page [489]]

In *Rivertrade Ltd v EMG Finance Ltd*[683a] Kitchin L.J., with whose judgment Moore-Bick and Ryder L.JJ. agreed, said that the case was not one "in which an estoppel [was] relied upon to create an enforceable right where none previously existed. It is instead one of those cases in which the estoppel is relied upon to bind the parties to an agreement to an interpretation which it would not otherwise bear"[683b]; and that, where this was the position, an estoppel by convention could "enlarge the effect of an agreement."[683c] The view that estoppel by convention may have such an effect can, where the common assumption on which the estoppel is based *increases* the obligation of the party alleged to be estopped, give rise to the same difficulty as that discussed in the context of promissory estoppel in Main Work, Vol.I, para.4–100: it could, for example, if applied in circumstances resembling those of *Stilk v Myrick*[683d] have the effect of allowing the claim that was there dismissed. It is respectfully submitted that the *Rivertrade* case[683e] should not be regarded as concluding the point. In that case, counsel for the defendant conceded the point; and although the Court approved of this concession,[683f] it also seemed to attach importance to the fact that the estoppel in that case did *not* "create an enforceable right where none previously existed."[683g] The tension between these two positions should, it is respectfully submitted, not be regarded as having been finally resolved in the *Rivertrade* case; in particular the question whether there are limits to the extent to which estoppel by convention can "enlarge the effect of an agreement" remains an open one. The answer to this question requires fuller argument[683h] than it received in the *Rivertrade* case.

[683a] [2015] EWCA Civ 1295.
[683b] At [50].
[683c] At [48].
[683d] (1809) 2 Camp. 317, 6 Esp. 129, Main Work, Vol.I, para.4–067.
[683e] Above, at note 683a.
[683f] [2016] EWCA Civ 1295 at [48].
[683g] At [50], quoted above at note 683b.
[683h] The concession referred to at note 683f had the effect that the point was not fully argued.

[Add to note 684, at the end: page [490]]

See also *Dixon v Blindley Heath Investments Ltd* [2015] EWCA Civ 1023, [2017] 3 W.L.R. 166 at [73], where it is said that the effect of estoppel by convention "is to bind the parties to their shared, even though mistaken understanding or assumption of law or facts on which their rights are to be determined (as in the case of estoppel by representation) rather than to provide a cause of action (as in the case of promissory estoppel and proprietary estoppel)". Insofar as this passage supports the view that the effect of promissory estoppel gives rise to a cause of action, it is, with respect, inconsistent with the authorities discussed in para.4–099 of the Main Work which on balance support the view that promissory estoppel does *not* of itself give rise to a cause of action; though (as is pointed out in n.550 to that paragraph) this position has given rise to some judicial "unease": *Newport City Council v Charles* [2008] EWCA Civ 1541, [2009] 1 W.L.R. 1884 at [28].

"Contractual estoppel"

4–116   [*Add to note 693, at the end: page* [491]]
The Court of Appeal allowed the appeal in the *NRAM* case: see [2015] EWCA Civ 751, [2016] 2 All E.R. (Comm) 333 at [59]. The judgment of the Court of Appeal contains two references to "estoppel by convention and/or contractual estoppel" (at [52] and [56]). Neither of these passages refers to any requirement that the statement or common assumption must relate to a "past" state of affairs to be capable of giving rise (in cases of alleged "contractual estoppel") to a cause of action.

10. Part Payment of a Debt

(a) *General Rule*

Effects of the rule

[*Add new paragraph 4–119A: page* [494]]
4–119A   The discussion in para.4–119 of the Main Work of the likely relationship between, on the one hand, the general rule stated in *Pinnel's*[714a] case and in *Foakes v Beer*,[714b] and, on the other, the more recently developed view stated in *Williams v Roffey Brothers & Nicholls (Contractors) Ltd*[714c] now calls for further discussion in the light of the decision of the Court of Appeal in *MWB Business Exchange Centres Ltd v Rock Advertising Ltd*[714d] ("the *MWB* case"). In that case, office premises managed by the claimants were occupied by the defendants under a licence agreement between themselves and the claimants. The defendants having fallen into arrears with payments due from them to the claimants, the parties agreed on February 27, 2012 to vary their original licence agreement by "re-scheduling" the payments due from the defendants to the claimants (so as in effect to give the defendants extra time to pay). One of the re-scheduled payments (of £3,500) was made on that day, but on March 30, 2012 the claimants exercised their right under the original contract to lock the defendants out of the premises.[714e] On March 30, 2012 the claimants gave notice terminating the (original) agreement[714f]; they then sued for arrears of licence fees and damages. The defendants relied on the variation agreement (re-scheduling their payments); and one of the issues before the Court of Appeal was whether the claimants' promise to (in effect) give the defendants extra time to pay was supported by consideration. In answering this question in the affirmative,[714g] the Court applied the reasoning of the *Williams* case[714h]: that is, it held that the requirement of consideration was satisfied because the variation agreement had conferred "practical benefits"[714i] on the claimants. *Foakes v Beer*[714j] and *Re Selectmove*[714k] were distinguished on the ground that they applied only where the sole benefit accruing to the creditor from the performance of the variation agreement took the form of receiving part payment of a debt already legally due to him, instead of insisting on payment of the whole.[714l] Indeed, this view is supported, as Arden L.J. points out in the *MWB* case, by the well known statement in *Pinnel's* case that the rule there laid down, and approved in *Foakes v Beer*, is subject to the

[52]

"rider" that "the gift of a horse, hawk or robe etc. shall be good satisfaction . . . ".[714m] It is sometimes assumed that the provision of such benefits satisfies the requirement of consideration because the debtor was not bound by the original contract to provide them[714n]; but the ensuing discussion will show that the requirement of consideration may (though it will not necessarily) be satisfied where the debtor's performance which confers the "practical benefit" on the creditor was already due from the debtor to the creditor under the original contract between these parties before that contract was varied by agreement between them; indeed that was the position in the *Williams* case[714o] itself. It is convenient here to begin the discussion of the consideration issue in the *MWB* case by reference to the way in which Arden L.J. there discusses this question. Her starting point is to refer to the way in which the judge in the Court below had dealt with the point: he had found that the "variation agreement conferred on [the claimant] the practical benefit of continuing occupation by" the defendant and thus (in Arden L.J.'s own words) that "of avoiding a void", the noun "void" being here used "in the sense in which it is used in property management to refer to unoccupied and therefore unproductive property, which may cause loss in the form of loss of rent *and in other ways.*"[714p] Substantially the same point is made by Kitchin L.J.,[714q] who in addition agreed with Arden L.J. on this issue[714r]; while McCombe L.J. agreed with both of the other judgments.[714s] Both these judgments also identify a second "practical benefit" obtained by the claimants. This was the benefit which they obtained by reason of the facts that, in performance of the variation agreement they had received a payment of £3,500 and that they would, under that agreement, be "likely to recover more than [they] would by enforcing the terms of the original agreement."[714t] This second "practical benefit" seems closely to resemble the benefit described by Lord Blackburn in *Foakes v Beer*,[714u] but reluctantly there regarded by him as *not* amounting to consideration, a point on which that case was followed in *Re Selectmove*.[714v] It is therefore hard to accept that the second "practical benefit" identified in the *MWB* case would, on its own, have satisfied the requirement of consideration. That benefit differs, or may differ, from the benefit that a debtor may provide by way of a horse, a hawk or a robe[714w] in that those benefits are assumed to be of a kind that the debtor is *not* obliged under the original contract to provide[714x]; and it is not clear from the report of the Court of Appeal's decision in the *MWB* case whether the original contract in that case imposed any obligation on the defendants to continue to occupy the premises for the term of the licence.[714y] The *Anangel Atlas* case[714z] supports the view that a benefit may satisfy the requirement of consideration even though it takes the form of an act which the debtor *was* bound under the contract to do, in that case taking delivery of the contractual subject-matter. This benefited the creditor in that the debtor's refusal to take delivery might have prejudiced the creditor's relations with other actual or potential customers; and from a commercial point of view this resembled the benefit that the claimants in the *MWB* case obtained from "avoiding a void."[714aa] The only situation in which a "practical benefit" conferred by the debtor on the creditor will *not* satisfy the requirement of consideration because the debtor was already bound by the contract to confer that benefit on the creditor is that in which the benefit consists of part payment (or the promise of part payment) of a debt already due. In the *MWB* case, this was said to be the only situation squarely covered by *Foakes v Beer* and *Re Select-move*.[714ab] Where the benefit is of a different kind, the *MWB* case recognises that it can constitute consideration for the creditor's promise and it can do so whether or not the debtor was already bound by the original contract to confer that benefit on the creditor. The remaining puzzle arising from this part of the reasoning of the *MWB* case is that the defendants' continuing in occupation was regarded as a benefit to the claimants in spite of the fact that, by locking the defendants out of the premises, the claimants had shown that they did not themselves so regard it.[714ac]

[714a] (1602) 5 Co. Rep. 117a; Main Work, Vol.I, para.4–117.

[714b] (1884) 9 App. Cas. 605; Main Work, Vol.I, para.4–117.

[714c] [1991] 1 Q.B. 1; Main Work, Vol.I, paras 4–069, 4–070.

[714d] [2016] EWCA Civ 553; [2017] Q.B. 604. Leave to appeal to the Supreme Court was granted on January 31, 2017.

[714e] At [4].

[714f] *ibid.*

[714g] [2016] EWCA Civ 553 at [49], [66], [67], [87].

[714h] Above, at note 714c.

[714i] [2016] EWCA Civ 553 at [42].

[714j] (1884) 9 App. Cas. 605; Main Work para.4–117.

[714k] [1995] 1 W.L.R. 474; Main Work para.4–119 n.713.

[714l] See [2016] EWCA Civ 553 at [39], [85]–[87].

[714m] At [85].

[714n] *e.g.* at [41] ("some other act that he was not bound by the contract to perform"); *cf.* at [84], explaining *Re Selectmove* (above, n.714k) on the ground that there was no "extra" benefit to the promisor.

[714o] [1991] 1 Q.B. 1, Main Work paras 4–069, 4–070.

[714p] [2016] EWCA Civ 553 at [72], italics supplied; *e.g.*, perhaps by reducing the rental value of other units in the same building.

[714q] At [48] ("would retain [the defendant] as licensee").

[714r] At [49].

[714s] At [67].

[714t] At [48].

[714u] (1884) 9 App. Cas. 605 at 622, quoted in the *MWB* case [2016] EWCA Civ 553 at [39].

[714v] [1995] 1 W.L.R. 474, Main Work, para.4–119 n.713.

[714w] See above, at note 714m.

[714x] See above at note 714n.

[714y] *Cf.*, for example, *Co-operative Insurance Society Ltd v Argyll Stores (Holdings) Ltd,* Main Work, Vol.I, para.27–031, for a clause of this kind. No issue of consideration arose in this case.

[714z] [1990] 2 Lloyd's Rep. 526, 544, discussed in the Main Work, Vol.I, para.4–125.

[714aa] [2016] EWCA Civ 553 at [72].

[714ab] See [2016] EWCA Civ 553 at [48], [49], [67] and [82]–[87].

[714ac] Perhaps the resolution of the above reasoning may be sought by reasoning similar to that of para.4–024 of the Main Work.

(c) *Limitations in Equity*

Equitable forbearance

4–130   [*Add new note 759a, after* "had come to an end." *in line 18: page* [500]]

[759a] For similar reasoning, see *Dunbar Assets plc v Butler* [2015] EWHC 2546 (Ch) where the issue was not one of part payment of a debt, but was one of the postponement of a liability. In that case A had lent money to two companies, in the management of which a "prominent part" (at [2]) was played by B for whom and whose family most of the shares in the companies were held in trust and who, without charging any fees, managed development properties owned by the companies (at [11]). B had guaranteed debts of the companies, and in an action to enforce these guarantees, B relied on the defence of promissory estoppel; such an estoppel was alleged to have arisen from a representation or promise by A that any such enforcement would be "postponed indefinitely" for so long as B continued with his (unpaid) work for the companies (at [18]). B's defence of promissory estoppel was

rejected on the ground that A's statement was intended to affect the rights of the parties "only for the intended duration of the arrangement" (at [49]), *i.e.* for so long as B continued to provide the (unpaid) management work "with the concurrence of" A (*ibid.*). It no longer applied after A had made it clear that B's work was no longer required; and, once B had ceased to do the work, his reliance on A's representation, and hence the suspension of B's liability, had come to an end (at [50]).

Suspensive nature of the doctrine

[Add to note 775, at the end: page [501]]   **4–131**
In *Stevensdrake Ltd v Hunt* [2016] EWHC 1111 (Ch), at [65], it was held that, where the creditor's "agreement permanently to forego rights" was "clear and unequivocal", and the other requirements of promissory estoppel were satisfied it would be wrong to treat the agreement as "merely suspensory", with the result that "the doctrine of promissory estoppel [was] engaged" and made it "inequitable" for the creditor to pursue its claim against the debtor. In treating the issue of the extinctive (as opposed to the "suspensory") effect of the doctrine as a matter of construction, this conclusion, though it may in the circumstance have been desirable as a matter of policy, is not easy to reconcile with earlier authorities (for example *Foakes v Beer* (1884) 9 App. Cas. 605, Main Work, Vol.I, para.4–117) cited in the *Stevensdrake* case (above) at [42].

11. PROPRIETARY ESTOPPEL

(a) *Nature of the Doctrine*

Scope of proprietary estoppel

[Add new note 825a, after "can be divided broadly" *in line 3: page* [507]]   **4–140**
825a A proprietary estoppel does not "have to fit neatly" into the "pigeon holes" of the "pure acquiescence" or "assurance" (or "encouragement") categories discussed in para.4–140 of Vol.I of the Main Work: *Hoyl Group Ltd v Cromer Town Council* [2015] EWCA Civ 782, [2015] H.L.R. 43 at [72]. In this case a finding that the claimant company was entitled to a right of way on the basis of proprietary estoppel, partly by reason of the defendant's encouragement and partly by its acquiescence in allowing use of the right of way for three years, was accordingly upheld by the Court of Appeal: see at [71]–[78]. It was further held that a party (A) could be found to have encouraged the other's (B) belief in the existence of the right claimed even though A was not aware of that belief: it sufficed for A's conduct to be consistent only with B's having the right in question (at [73]). See also *Caldwell v Bryson* [2017] NICh 9 where the proprietary estoppel was based on both "acquiescence" (at [10(ii)]) and "encouragement" (at [18(a)]).

(b) *Bases of Liability*

Expenditure on another's land in reliance on a promise

[Add to note 836, line 2, after "[1994] E.G.C.S. 134;":* page* [509]]   **4–141**
cf. *Arif v Anwar* [2015] EWHC 124 (Fam), [2016] 1 F.L.R. 359, where the person claiming to be entitled to the benefit of the proprietary estoppel had allowed money to which he was entitled to be used in improving the property; and this fact was held to be sufficient detrimental reliance (at [68]) to give rise to the

proprietary estoppel (at [69]); for this requirement, see Main Work, Vol.I, para.4–158);

Proprietary estoppel and constructive trust

4–142 *[Add to note 842, line 4, after* "and [37]"*: page* [510]]
; see also *Matchmove Ltd v Dowding and Church* [2016] EWCA Civ 1233, [2017] 1 W.L.R. 749 at [29] ("common intention constructive trust").

[Add to note 849, at the end: page [510]]
Conversely, in *Matchmove Ltd v Dowding and Church* [2016] EWCA Civ 1233, [2017] 1 W.L.R. 749 relief was given at first instance to buyers of land which they had bought without complying with the formal requirement of Law of Property (Miscellaneous Provisions) Act 1989 s.2(1) (Main Work, Vol.I, para.5–011) on the ground of "both proprietary estoppel and constructive trust" ([2016] EWCA Civ 1233 at [28]), but on appeal counsel for the buyers "was content to rely solely upon constructive trust" (*ibid.*) so that the Court of Appeal, in upholding the decision below, was able to avoid "the issue whether section 2(5) of the 1989 Act can apply to claims based upon proprietary estoppel as distinct from constructive trust" [2016] EWCA Civ 1233 at [28]. For this problem, see Main Work, Vol.I, para.4–115 n.686, para.4–160 n.981 and paras 5–044 to 5–048.

[Add to paragraph, after note 849: page [510]]
It is also possible, in cases of the first kind described in para.4–142 of the Main Work[849a] for relief to be given on the ground of proprietary estoppel[849b] even though the facts do *not,* for want of a sufficiently "clear agreement", give rise to any constructive trust.[849c]

[849a] At note 847.
[849b] *Arif v Anwar* [2015] EWHC 124 (Fam) at [69].
[849c] At [47], [68].

(c) *Conditions giving rise to Liability*

Main elements of proprietary estoppel

4–146 *[Add to note 880, line 2, after* "[2012] 2 All E.R. 754 at [114];"*: page* [514]]
Burton v Liden [2016] EWCA Civ 275, [2017] 1 F.L.R. 310 at [16];

[Add to note 880, line 6, after "or overlap with each other;"*: page* [514]]
see also *Davies v Davies* [2016] EWCA Civ 463, [2016] 2 P. & C.R. 10, restating the main elements of proprietary estoppel and repeating the point that they could not be divided into "watertight compartments" (at [38]);

[Add to note 880, at the end: page [514]]
For a case in which a daughter's claim against her mother's estate, based on proprietary estoppel, was rejected because none of the three requirements stated in para.4–146 of Vol.I of the Main Work had been satisfied, see *Wright v Waters*

[2014] EWHC 3614, [2015] W.T.L.R. 353. See also *MWB Business Exchange Centres Ltd v Rock Advertising Ltd* [2016] EWCA Civ 553, [2017] Q.B. 604, where the "three main elements" of proprietary estoppel are stated at [65] but it was held that no such estoppel arose because (1) the right claimed by the person relying on the estoppel was not "a proprietary right" and (2) that person had not "suffered any detriment." For a further statement of the requirements of proprietary estoppel, see *Moore v Moore* [2016] EWHC 2202 (Ch), where the requirements were held to have been satisfied. At [16], this form of estoppel is referred to as "equitable" estoppel; but it is clear from the authorities cited that the reference is to proprietary estoppel; see also the use of the expression "proprietary" at (*e.g.*) [16], [18], [184], [194]. The reference to "promissory" estoppel at [174] may be a misprint; in any event it is clear from the remedy granted by the Court in *Moore v Moore* (see below, para.4–169) that the outcome was not affected by the restriction on the effect of the estoppel discussed in Main Work, Vol.I, para.4–101.

Kinds of promises capable of giving rise to a proprietary estoppel

[Add to note 891, at the end: page [516]]   **4–147**
But where an oral agreement for the sale of land was intended to be legally binding by the parties to it as soon as it was made it was arguable that the agreement could give rise to a proprietary estoppel even though *later* correspondence between solicitors instructed by the contracting parties "was headed 'subject to contract'". This was the position in *Matchmove Ltd v Dowding and Church* [2016] EWCA Civ 1233, [2017] 1 W.L.R. 749 where relief was granted at first instance "on the basis of proprietary estoppel and constructive trust" (at [21]). On appeal, the decision below was affirmed (at [46]), though on the basis of constructive trust only: at [28], [48]; above, para.4–142 n.849.

[Add to paragraph, at the end: page [516]]
Where the property in question was held in trust by two trustees, it was held that the promise of only one of the trustees, who had no authority to bind the other, did not give rise to a proprietary estoppel on which the promisee sought to rely by way of defence to a claim for possession of the property, that claim having been made by both trustees.[897a] On appeal, the appellant also put forward a new claim based on estoppel by convention,[897b] but this claim failed on the ground stated above, para.4–108.

[897a] *Preedy v Dunne* [2015] EWHC 2713 (Ch), [2015] W.T.L.R. 1795.
[897b] [2016] EWCA Civ 805, [2016] C.P. Rep. 44 at [61].

"Clear enough" in context

[Add to note 918, at the end: page [518]]   **4–150**
See also *Burton v Liden* [2016] EWCA Civ 275, [2017] 1 F.L.R. 310 at [24], where the context in which the representation was made was said to be "hugely important" and Lord Walker's test of reasonable clarity in that context (stated in

Thorner v Major [2009] UKHL 18, [2009] 1 W.L.R. 776 at [56], quoted in para.4–150 of Vol.I of the Main Work) was held to have been satisfied.

Unconscionable conduct by promisor

4–164   [*Add to note 1018, at the end: page* [531]]
For further discussion of the passage of Arden L.J.'s judgment in *Herbert v Doyle* [2010] EWCA Civ 1095, [2015] W.T.L.R. 1573, see *Matchmove Ltd v Dowding and Church* [2016] EWCA Civ 1233, [2017] 1 W.L.R. 749 at [30]–[32]. The latter case differed from the *Cobbe* case [2008] UKHL 55, [2008] 1 W.L.R. 1752 in that in the *Matchmove* case the parties did intend their agreement "to be immediately binding" ([2016] EWCA Civ 1095 at [36]) even though it was oral and so did not satisfy the requirement of Law of Property (Miscellaneous Provisions) Act 1989, while in the *Cobbe* case the parties did *not* "expect their agreement to be immediately binding" (see Arden L.J. in *Herbert v Doyle* [2010] EWCA Civ 1095 at [57]).

(d) *Effects of the Doctrine*

Operation of proprietary estoppel

4–169   [*Add new note 1061a, line 3, after* "an 'equity'": *page* [535]]
[1061a] *Cf. Moore v Moore* [2016] EWHC 2202 (Ch) at [194] ("an equitable interest" in the farm which was the subject-matter of a promise (made by a father to his son) that the farm "would be his [*i.e.*, his son's] one day" (at [13], [168]).

Estoppel may operate conditionally

4–172   [*Add to note 1086, line 3, after* "the property": *page* [537]]
; *cf. Moore v Moore* [2016] EWHC 2202 (Ch) where the promisee's "equitable interest" in the farm which was the subject matter of the promise (see above, para.4–169 n.1061a) was held to be subject to the right of the promisor (who was the promisee's father) and the promisor's wife (who was the promisee's mother) to continue to reside in a house on the farm "for so long as that meets their needs", with the promisee being "responsible for maintaining and repairing it" (at [177], [193]).

Remedy: principled discretion

4–173   [*Add to note 1094, line 4, after* "reliance: above, para.4–158;": *page* [538]]
For the importance of "proportionality" in assessing the amount of monetary relief available to the promisee, see also *Davies v Davies* [2016] EWCA Civ 463, [2016] 2 P. & C.R. 10 at [38], quoting from the Court below. On appeal, it was no longer disputed that compensation in money was in this case the appropriate form of relief.

12. SPECIAL CASES

Gratuitous services

[Add to paragraph, after note 1285: page [559]]   **4–199**

Where an architect (A) had provided professional services as such for friends (B) free of charge, one reason[1285a] why there was no contract between A and B was that the requirement of consideration had not been satisfied.[1285b]

[1285a] For other reasons why there was no contract between A and B, see above, paras 1–172 and 2–170.

[1285b] *Burgess v Lejonvarn* [2017] EWCA Civ 254, [2017] B.L.R. 277 at [71], referring to the reasoning of the Court below ([2016] EWHC 40 (TCC) at [152]) and affirming the decision of that Court.

Liability in tort for negligent performance

[Add to paragraph, after note 1288: page [560]]   **4–200**

and, where the relationship between the supplier (A) of the gratuitous services and their recipient (B) was not contractual for the reasons stated in para.4–199 above, A was held liable to B in tort for having failed to exercise reasonable care in performing the services which A had in fact rendered.[1288a]

[1288a] *Burgess v Lejonvarn* [2017] EWCA Civ 254, [2017] B.L.R. 277 at [88], [128].

CHAPTER 5

FORM

1. IN GENERAL

Duties of information as requirements of form

5–003   [*Add to note 18, at the end: page* [565]]
The 1990 directive is repealed by Directive (EU) 2015/2302 on package travel and linked travel arrangements [2015] O.J. L326/1, art.4 of which sets a general principle of full harmonisation and must be implemented by January 1, 2018.

Electronic signatures

5–008   [*Delete text of paragraph including footnotes and substitute: pages* [568]–[569]]
In 1999, the EU legislator enacted the Electronic Signatures Directive,[51] whose purposes were to facilitate the use of "electronic signatures" and to contribute to their legal recognition, and to establish a legal framework for electronic signatures and certain certification-services: it expressly did not cover aspects relating to the conclusion or validity of contracts or other legal obligations where there are requirements as regards form imposed by national or Community law, nor the rules and limits governing the use of documents.[52] An "electronic signature" was defined by the Directive as "data in electronic form which are attached to or logically associated with other electronic data and which serve as a method of authentication".[52a] The United Kingdom implemented the Electronic

Signatures Directive 1999 by two instruments. First, s.7 of the Electronic Communications Act 2000 provided for the admissibility in evidence of electronic signatures and certification by any person of such a signature "in relation to any question as to the authenticity of the communication or data or as to the integrity of the communication or data, and followed for this purpose the definition of "electronic signature" in the Directive.[52b] On its terms, this provision is broad enough to include evidence for the purposes of formal requirements of a contract (such as s.2 of the Law of Property (Miscellaneous Provisions) Act 1989[52c]), but, if it were so interpreted, it would go beyond the scope of the requirements of the 1999 Directive. Secondly, the Electronic Signatures Regulations 2002 provided for the supervision and liability of "certification-service-providers" (i.e. persons who issue certificates or provide other services related to electronic signatures) and for consequential matters relating to data protection.[52d] However, the Electronic Signatures Directive 1999 was repealed and replaced by the EU Electronic Identification and Electronic Trust Services Regulation 2014 (the "eIDAS Regulation", applicable in general from July 1, 2016),[52e] which lays down the conditions under which Member States mutually recognise "electronic identification means of natural persons and legal persons falling under a notified electronic identification scheme of another Member State", and "rules for trust services, in particular for electronic transactions"; and which establishes "a legal framework for electronic signatures, electronic seals, electronic time stamps, electronic documents, electronic registered delivery services and certificate services for website authentication".[52f] Following the pattern of the 1999 Directive, the eIDAS Regulation provides expressly that it "does not affect national or Union law related to the conclusion and validity of contracts or other legal or procedural obligations relating to form".[52g] Instead, its main purpose is to ensure that businesses and individuals can use their own national electronic identification schemes (eIDs) to access public services in other EU countries where electronic identification schemes are available; it also aims to create a European internal market for electronic trust services—electronic signatures, electronic seals, time stamps etc.—by ensuring that they will work across borders and have the same legal status as traditional paper-based processes.[52h] By way of implementation of some aspects of the eIDAS Regulation, the UK revoked and replaced the Electronic Signature Regulations 2002 by the Electronic Identification and Trust Services for Electronic Transactions Regulations 2016, which came into force on July 22, 2016.[52i] The 2016 Regulations also amended s.7 of the Electronic Communications Act 2000 so as to follow the simplified definition of "electronic signature" in the eIDAS Regulation as:

> "so much of anything in electronic form as–
>> (a) is incorporated into or otherwise logically associated with any electronic communication or electronic data; and
>> (b) purports to be used by the individual creating it to sign."[52j]

The main import of s.7 remains the same, viz. to make general provision for the recognition of electronic signatures as evidence in legal proceedings.[52k] The 2016 Regulations also make new provision for electronic seals and related certificates, electronic time stamps and related certificates, electronic documents and related certificates and electronic registered delivery service and related certificates.[521] However, the eIDAS Regulation itself (as earlier noted[52m]) does not affect the law governing the definitions of signature for the purposes of formal requirements of English contract law[52n]; nor does its provision for "electronic seals" affect the common law or statutory requirements for the execution of a deed.[52o] It is submitted that the uncertainty as to the impact of s.7 of the Electronic Communications Act 2000 in relation to these same formalities remains after its amendment by the 2016 Regulations.[52p]

[51] Directive 1999/93 on a Community framework for electronic signatures [2000] O.J. L13/12.

[52] Directive 1999/93 art.1.

[52a] Directive 1999/93 art.2(1).

[52b] Electronic Communications Act 2000 s.7(2) (as enacted).

[52c] On which see Main Work, Vol.I, paras 5–010 et seq.

[52d] SI 2002/318.

[52e] Regulation (EU) 910/2014 of 23 July 2014 on electronic identification and trust services for electronic transactions in the internal market and repealing Directive 1999/93/EC [2014] O.J. L 257/73 art.52(2) (with the exceptions there noted).

[52f] Regulation (EU) 910/2014 art.1.

[52g] Regulation (EU) 910/2014 art.2(3) and recital 21.

[52h] See EU Commission, *https://ec.europa.eu/digital-single-market/en/trust-services-and-eid*.

[52i] SI 2016/696.

[52j] SI 2016/696 reg.5, Sch.3 para.1(2). The definition of certification of such an electronic signature was amended to similar effect: SI 2016/696 reg.5, Sch.3 para.1(3).

[52k] Electronic Communications Act 2000 s.7(1).

[52l] Electronic Communications Act 2000 ss.7A–7D (as inserted by SI 2016/696 reg.5, Sch.3 para.1(4)).

[52m] Regulation (EU) 910/2014 art.2(3). Later general statements, such as the statement in art.25(2) that "[a] qualified electronic signature shall have the equivalent legal effect of a handwritten signature" must be read subject to the general definition of the scope of the Regulation in art.2(3).

[52n] "Signature" is relevant to the formal requirements imposed, inter alia, by the Law of Property (Miscellaneous Provisions) Act 1989 s.1 in relation to deeds (on which see Main Work, Vol.I, para.1–118); by s.2 of the same Act in relation to contracts for the sale or other disposition of an interest in land (on which see Main Work, Vol.I, paras 5–010 et seq. and esp. para.5–037); and by the Statute of Frauds s.4 in relation to contracts of guarantee (on which see Main Work, Vol.II, paras 45–042 et seq. and esp. para.45–057). The position as regards the so-called rule in *L'Estrange v F Graucob Ltd* [1934] 2 K.B. 394 which governs the incorporation of written terms by signature (on which see Main Work, Vol.I, para.13–002) is more arguable as it is not clear that the incorporation of contract terms relates to the "conclusion and validity of contracts or other legal or procedural obligations relating to form" within the exclusion from the scope of the eIDAS Regulation reg.2(3).

[52o] See Main Work, Vol.I, paras 1–113 et seq.

[52p] For further discussion of "signature" and electronic communications see *Emmet & Farrand on Title* (updated to June 2017), paras 2–041—2–041.06.

Electronic documents and deeds

5–009   *[Add to paragraph, at the end: page* [569]]

However, the system of electronic conveyancing which these legislation provisions envisaged has not been brought into being and the Law Commission has consulted on a different scheme.[54a]

[54a] See further Law Commission, *Updating the Land Registration Act 2002, A Consultation Paper* (Consultation Paper No.227, 2016) Ch.20.

2. Contracts for the Sale or Other Disposition of an Interest in Land

(a) *Contracts within s.2 of the Law of Property (Miscellaneous Provisions) Act 1989*

"Sale or other disposition of an interest in land"

[*Add new note 70a at the end of paragraph: page* [571]]
70a Thus, e.g. a contract which would create an option the exercise of which would release a charge on land falls within s.2: *Tuscola (110) Ltd v Y2K Co Ltd* [2016] EWHC 1124 (Ch) at [205]–[213] (though it was held that no such contract had been concluded).

5–014

"Contracts for the disposition of an interest" and "contracts of disposition"

[*Add to note 87, at the end: page* [573]]
See further *Keay v Morris Homes (West Midlands) Ltd* [2012] EWCA Civ 900, [2012] 1 W.L.R. 2855 at [8].

5–017

[*Add to paragraph, at the end: page* [573]]
Similarly, in *Rollerteam Ltd v Riley*, under the terms of a settlement agreement A agreed to pay B and C certain sums of money if B executed declarations of trust by deed over two London properties in favour of A and D. B executed the declarations of trust, but A paid only a much lesser sum, arguing that the settlement agreement was for the disposition of interests in land and did not satisfy the formal requirements in s.2 of the 1989 Act. The Court of Appeal observed that "section 2 of the 1989 Act applies only to executory contracts for the future sale or other disposition of an interest in land, and does not apply to a contract which itself effects such a disposition".[89a] The contract before the court was construed as being a unilateral contract, A agreeing to pay the money to B and C in exchange for the "performance" in the shape of the execution of the two declarations of trust.[89b] As a result, at no point did B undertake an executory or future obligation to execute the two deeds and so the agreement included an immediate disposition of interests in land rather than being a contract for the disposition of interests in land and fell outside the scope of s.2.[89c]

[89a] [2016] EWCA Civ 1291, [2017] Ch. 109 at [38] (Henderson L.J. with whom David Richards and Tomlinson L.JJ. agreed).
[89b] [2016] EWCA Civ 1291 at [44]–[45].
[89c] [2016] EWCA Civ 1291 at [45].

Boundary agreements between neighbours

[*Add to note 98, at the end: page* [574]]
These observations should not be interpreted as meaning that s.2 applies where the parties intended the contract to effect an immediate disposition of an interest in land, as it applies only to executory contracts: *Rollerteam Ltd v Riley* [2016] EWCA Civ 1291, [2017] Ch. 109 at [40]–[42], as noted above, para.5–017.

5–019

(b) *Formal Requirements*

"All the terms which the parties have expressly agreed in one document": generally

5–033   [*In note 184, line 5, delete* "and [91(f)]" *and substitute: page* [584]]
and [91] (one of joined cases reversed on other grounds sub nom. *Marlbray Ltd v Laditi* [2016] EWCA Civ 476)

"Exchange of contracts"

5–035   [*Add to note 203, at the end: page* [587]]
While the judgment in *Rabiu v Marlbray Ltd* was the subject of considerable criticism (and was reversed in part) by the CA sub nom. *Marlbray Ltd v Laditi* [2016] EWCA Civ 476, [2016] 1 W.L.R. 5147 (on which see below, para.5–038), the point in the text of the Main Work was not subject to appeal.

[*Add to note 204, at the end: page* [587]]
While the judgment in *Rabiu v Marlbray Ltd* was the subject of considerable criticism (and was reversed in part) by the CA sub nom. *Marlbray Ltd v Laditi* [2016] EWCA Civ 476, [2016] 1 W.L.R. 5147 (on which see below, para.5–038), the point in the text of the Main Work was not subject to appeal.

Meaning of "signature"

5–037   [*Add to note 211, at the end: page* [588]]
For criticism of this view of "signature" for the purposes of s.2 of the 1989 Act see *Emmet & Farrand on Title* (updated to June 2017), paras 2–041—2–041.06. Nevertheless, *Emmet & Farrand on Title* concludes that "conveyancers should be as cautious as practicable and prefer in practice 'wet ink' signatures for contracts for the sale of land": *Emmet & Farrand on Title* at para.2.041.05, not following the view expressed by the Law Society in its practice note, *Execution of documents at virtual signings or closings* (February 16, 2010) (available at *http://www.lawsociety.org.uk*) . In *Ramsay v Love* [2015] EWHC 65 (Ch) at [7], Morgan J. observed (obiter and in the context of s.1(3) of the 1989 Act rather than s.2 of the same Act) that the statements in *Firstpost Homes Ltd v Johnson* which require signature by an executing party to be made with a pen in his own hand were not designed to distinguish between signing in such a way and by the use of a signature writing machine.

Signature by agent

5–038   [*In note 216, delete from* "Rabiu v Marlbray Ltd" *in line 9 to the end and substitute: page* [589]]
Simpole v Chee [2013] EWHC 4444 (Ch) at [8]–[10]. Where A signs a document setting out a contract of sale with B in respect of obligations expressed as joint and several, not only on his own behalf but also on behalf of C in respect of her joint and several obligations but without her authority, in principle the contract is valid between A and B as long as it is, on an objective interpretation, not

conditional on C's having authorised him to sign on her behalf, as the joint and several provision of the contract make it clear that A and C do not constitute a "composite" purchaser: *Marlbray Ltd v Laditi* (on appeal from sub nom. *Rabiu v Marlbray Ltd*) [2016] EWCA Civ 476, [2016] 1 W.L.R. 5147 at [56] and [68]. If in these circumstances the document signed by A and B contains all the terms of the several contract, then it satisfies the requirements of s.2 of the 1989 Act, it being irrelevant that A did not sign identifying the precise capacity in which he did so, i.e. as principal obligor under his several contract: [2016] EWCA Civ 476 at [71]. A is therefore bound under his contract with B, even though C is not.

[*Add to note 217, line 4, after* "Companies Act 1985": *page* [589]]
(now s.51 of the Companies Act 2006)

[*Add to note 217, at the end: page* [589]]
; *Royal Mail Estates Ltd v Maple Teesdale (a firm)* [2015] EWHC 1890 (Ch), [2016] 1 W.L.R. 942.

(c) *The Effect of Failure to Comply with the Formal Requirements*

Constructive trust

[*Add to note 244, line 2, after* "[2007] 1 F.L.R. 1123 at [56]": *page* [592]]   **5–040**
; *Ely v Robson* [2016] EWCA Civ 774, [2017] 1 P. & C.R. DG1. See also *Dowding v Matchmove Ltd* [2016] EWCA Civ 1233, [2017] 1 W.L.R. 749 esp. at [35]–[36] (oral agreement complete in all essential terms intended by both parties to be binding immediately, relied upon by claimants to their detriment).

Promissory estoppel ("forbearance in equity")

[*Add to paragraph, at the end: page* [594]]   **5–042**
Moreover, as Lewison L.J. has observed, "it would be surprising if one could do by promissory estoppel what one could not do by informal contract"[259a] and, moreover, in the case of promissory estoppel, "there is no question of a constructive trust of land arising" so as to fall within the exception to the formality requirements provided by the 1989 Act s.2(5).[259b]

[259a] *Dudley Muslim Association v Dudley MBC* [2015] EWCA Civ 1123, [2016] 1 P. & C.R. 10 at [33].
[259b] [2015] EWCA Civ 1123 at [33].

Cobbe v Yeoman's Row Management Ltd

[*Add to note 284, line 1, after* "[2008] UKHL 55 at [29]": *page* [597]]   **5–046**
; *Dudley Muslim Association v Dudley MBC* [2015] EWCA Civ 1123, [2016] 1 P. & C.R. 10 at [33] (doubting the law as expressed in *Yaxley v Gotts* [2000] Ch. 162 noted in the Main Work, Vol.I, para.5–045) by reference to Lord Scott of Foscote's view).

Herbert v Doyle

5–048   [*Add to note 288, at the end: page* [598]]
; *Ghazaani v Rowshan* [2015] EWHC 1922 (Ch) at [192] and [197] (allowing the possibility of proprietary estoppel/constructive trust in the "exceptional circumstances" of the case); *Muhammad v ARY Properties Ltd* [2016] EWHC 1698 (Ch) at [32]–[50]; *Pinisetty v Manikonda* [2017] EWHC 838 (QB) at [39]–[42] (agreement not sufficiently certain to be enforced).

[*Add to note 290, line 1, after* "1095 at [57].".: *page* [598]]
According to the CA in *Dowding v Matchmove Ltd* [2016] EWCA Civ 1233, [2017] 1 W.L.R. 749 at [32], Arden L.J. was not intending to describe three different situations in which s.2(5) would not apply, but rather to describe the *Cobbe* case in three different ways, which taken together meant that the party "never expected to acquire an interest in the property otherwise than under a legally enforceable contract" (quoting Lord Scott in *Cobbe* [2008] UKHL 55 at [37]).

Effects of proprietary estoppel

5–049   [*Add to note 295, line 4, after* "[2007] All E.R. (D) 71 (Dec);".: *page* [599]]
Davies v Davies [2016] EWCA Civ 463, [2016] 2 P. & C.R. 10 esp. at [39]–[42];

Restitution: recovery of money paid by purchaser on a failure of consideration

5–050   [*In note 296, update reference to Goff and Jones, The Law of Unjust Enrichment to: page* [599]]
9th edn (2016), Ch.12

5–051   [*In note 300, update reference to Goff and Jones, The Law of Unjust Enrichment to: page* [599]]
9th edn (2016), para.12-003.

[*Add to note 307, at the end: page* [600]]
Sharma v Simposh was applied by the CA in *Marlbray Ltd v Laditi* (on appeal from sub nom. *Rabiu v Marlbray Ltd*) [2016] EWCA Civ 476, [2016] 1 W.L.R. 5147 at [81]–[93], [96], esp. at [92] where it was held that a deposit paid by a joint and several purchaser off-plan of a long lease of a flat in a large block should not be returned on the basis of a failure of consideration, even if the contract was void under s.2 of the 1989 Act (which it was held not to be), as the purchaser had the benefit of the specific unit chosen being taken off the market; the flat had been secured at a specific price; the developer had (apparently) completed the works with the deposit as collateral; and the purchaser had become entitled to 10 free days at a London hotel. For this purpose, it made no difference that the deposit was held by a third-party stakeholder: [2016] EWCA Civ 476 at [99].

Restitution: recovery of money paid by purchaser under a mistake of law

[In note 311, update reference to Goff and Jones, The Law of Unjust Enrichment to: **5–052**
page [601]]
9th edn (2016), paras 9-101 et seq.

[In note 318, update reference to Goff and Jones, The Law of Unjust Enrichment to:
page [602]]
9th edn (2016), para.2-21.

CHAPTER 6

COMMON MISTAKE

[*In note 1, update reference to Cartwright, Misrepresentation, Mistake and Non-disclosure to: page* [605]]
4th edn (2016)

1. INTRODUCTION TO MISTAKE

Types of mistake

6–001   [*In note 7, update reference to Anson's Law of Contract, 29th edn to: page* [606]]
30th edn (2015), Ch.8.

Mistakes as to facts and mistakes as to terms

6–002   [*In note 12, update reference to Anson's Law of Contract to: page* [606]]
30th edn (2015), p.300

"Mistake" implies a positive belief

6–004   [*In note 18, update reference to Cartwright, Misrepresentation, Mistake and Non-disclosure to: page* [607]]
4th edn (2016), para.12-03

[*Add to note 18, line 6, after* "acted as he did": *page* [607]]
; *Co-operative Bank Plc v Hayes Freehold Ltd* [2017] EWHC 1820 (Ch) at [143(i)], citing this paragraph of Chitty.

Mistakes that are not legally relevant

[*In note 23, delete* "29th edition by Beatson, Burrows and Cartwright (eds) (2010)" **6–005**
and substitute: page [607]]
30th edition by Beatson, Burrows and Cartwright (eds) (2015)

[*In note 23, delete* "pp.277–278" *and substitute: page* [607]]
p.300

[*Add to note 25, at the end: page* [608]]
; *Co-operative Bank Plc v Hayes Freehold Ltd* [2017] EWHC 1820 (Ch) at [130]–[132]; *Bainbridge v Bainbridge* [2016] EWHC 898 (Ch) at [6] (applying the remedy of rescission, as for misrepresentation, see below, para.7–126. Whether a transaction is subject to the narrower rules that apply to contracts or the wider grounds that apply to voluntary settlements depends on whether there was consideration for the transfer: *Van der Merwe v Goldman* [2016] EWHC 790 (Ch), [2016] 4 W.L.R. 71.

Underlying policy

[*In note 31, update reference to Cartwright, Misrepresentation, Mistake and Non-* **6–006**
disclosure to: page [608]]
4th edn (2016), para.15-34

Common mistake and construction of the contract

[*Add new note 66a, line 5, after* "when an agreement is concluded": *page* [612]] **6–014**
[66a] *Co-operative Bank Plc v Hayes Freehold Ltd* [2017] EWHC 1820 (Ch) at [143(ii)], citing this sentence of the paragraph.

3. Different Approaches before *Bell v Lever Bros*

Kennedy's case

[*In note 92, update references to Treitel on The Law of Contract to: page* [616]] **6–020**
14th edn (2015)
[*The paragraph numbers remain unchanged.*]

4. Mistake at Common Law

(b) *The Modern Doctrine*

(i) *Analysis after* Bell v Lever Bros

The Great Peace

6–034   [*Add to note 148, at the end: page* [624]]
In *Chancery Client Partners Ltd v MRC 957 Ltd* [2016] EWHC 2142 (Ch), [2016] Lloyd's Rep. F.C. 578 it was held that the contract was not void for common mistake because its performance was not impossible (at [37]). See also *National Private Air Transport Co v Kaki* [2017] EWHC 1496 (Comm) at [25(iii)].

(ii) *Conditions for Common Mistake to Render Contract Void*

Non-existence of the state of affairs must not be attributable to the fault of either party

6–038   [*Add to note 160, at the end: page* [626]]
In *National Private Air Transport Co v Kaki* [2017] EWHC 1496 (Comm) the state of affairs was attributable to the claimant's fault because it resulted from the claimant's non-performance of another contract (see at [25(ii)]).

[*Add to note 161, at the end: page* [626]]
Steyn L.J.'s dictum was applied in *National Private Air Transport Co v Kaki* [2017] EWHC 1496 (Comm) at [25(i)].

[*In note 165, update reference to Cartwright, Misrepresentation, Mistake and Non-disclosure to: page* [626]]
4th edn (2016), para.15-22

[*In note 165, update reference to Treitel on The Law of Contract to: page* [626]]
14th edn (2015), para.8–005

Section 6 cases

6–045   [*In note 181, update reference to Treitel on The Law of Contract to: page* [628]]
14th edn (2015), para.8–010

[*In note 182, update reference to Atiyah's Sale of Goods to: page* [629]]
Twigg-Flessner, Canavan and MacQueen (eds), *Atiyah and Adams' Sale of Goods*, 13th edn (2016), p.80

[*In note 182, update reference to Treitel on The Law of Contract to: page* [629]]
14th edn (2015), para.8–010

Impossibility of the contractual venture

[*Add to note 201, at the end: page* [631]]   **6–050**
Thus the test now seems to be whether performance of the contract or the contractual venture has turned out to be impossible. See also *Co-operative Bank Plc v Hayes Freehold Ltd* [2017] EWHC 1820 (Ch) at [143(iii)]. In *Dana Gas PJSC v Dan Gas Sukuk Ltd* [2017] EWHC 1896 (Comm) H.H. Judge Waksman QC said (at [65]) that common mistake is not confined to cases where the contract is impossible to perform, but he cited the headnote to *The Great Peace* [2003] Q.B. 679 (which speaks of the contract performance being essentially different from the performance the parties had contemplated) rather than what was said by the Court of Appeal itself (at [76], quoted in Main Work, Vol.I, para.6–035); and in any event it seems to have been arguable in the *Dana Gas* case that the contractual venture was impossible, see at [68].

What mistakes may frustrate contractual venture?

[*In note 206, update reference to Treitel on The Law of Contract to: page* [632]]   **6–051**
14th edn (2015), para.8–019

[*In note 207, update reference to Treitel on The Law of Contract to: page* [632]]
14th edn (2015), para.8–020

6. No Separate Rule in Equity

Mistake and equity after *The Great Peace*

[*In note 276, line 13, after* "[2008] UKPC 17" *add: page* [639]]   **6–060**
; *British Red Cross v Werry* [2017] EWHC 875 (Ch), [2017] W.T.L.R. 441.

7. Mistake and Construction

Contract void as a matter of construction where no common mistake

[*In note 287, update reference to Treitel on The Law of Contract to: page* [640]]   **6–063**
14th edn (2015), para.2–066

MISREPRESENTATION

[*In note 1, update reference to Cartwright, Misrepresentation, Mistake and Non-disclosure to*: page [643]]
4th edn (2016)

2. WHAT CONSTITUTES EFFECTIVE MISREPRESENTATION

(a) *False Statement of Fact*

Statements of fact

7–006   [*Add to note 25, at the end: page* [646]]
It has been said that whether the representee was entitled to rely on the representation is partly a question of reasonableness: *Monde Petroleum SA v WesternZagros Ltd* [2016] EWHC 1472 (Comm) at [219]. A party is not entitled to

rely on a statement that the party was reasonably expected to have checked by its lawyers: *Co-operative Bank Plc v Hayes Freehold Ltd* [2017] EWHC 1820 (Ch) at [119]–[122].

[*In note 26, update reference to Cartwright, Misrepresentation, Mistake and Non-disclosure to: page* [647]]
4th edn (2016), para.3-06

Statement of opinion amounts to statement of fact if not honestly held

[*In note 31, update reference to Cartwright, Misrepresentation, Mistake and Non-disclosure to: page* [648]]   **7–008**
4th edn (2016), para.3-17

Statement of opinion may carry implication that grounds for belief

[*In note 34, delete last sentence,* "While a party . . . " *and substitute: page* [648]]   **7–009**
A party who merely gives a contractual warranty does not necessarily represent that the fact warranted is true (see *Sycamore Bidco Ltd v Breslin* [2012] EWHC 3443 (Ch) at [203]–[209] and *Idemitsu Kosan Co Ltd v Sumitomo Corp* [2016] EWHC 1909 (Comm), declining to follow the unreported decision in *Invertec Ltd v De Mol Holding BV* [2009] EWHC 2471 (Ch)). Merely offering for signature a document containing the warranty is not a representation of the truth of the facts warranted: [2016] EWHC 1909 (Comm) at [28]–[30]. If there was a previous representation, followed by a warranty, the fact of the warranty does tend to imply that the party giving the warranty has reasonable grounds for believing the facts warranted: *Avrora Fine Arts Investment Ltd v Christie, Manson & Woods Ltd* [2012] EWHC 2198 (Ch) at [133].

[*In note 36, update reference to Cartwright, Misrepresentation, Mistake and Non-disclosure to: page* [649]]
4th edn (2016), para.3-16

Statement of intention not honestly held

[*Add to note 48, line 2, after* "(1991) P.&.C.R. 388": *page* [651]]   **7–012**
; *C21 London Estates Ltd v Maurice Macneill Iona Ltd* [2017] EWHC 998 (Ch) at [44], applying this paragraph (but in that case it was not shown that the representation was false).

Liability in tort for incorrect opinions and forecasts

[*In note 66, update reference to Cartwright, Misrepresentation, Mistake and Non-disclosure to: page* [653]]   **7–015**
4th edn (2016), para.6-12

Statements of law

[*In note 82, update reference to Cartwright, Misrepresentation, Mistake and Non-disclosure to: page* [654]]   **7–016**
4th edn (2016), para.3-30

[*In note 83, update reference to Cartwright, Misrepresentation, Mistake and Non-disclosure to: page* [654]]
4th edn (2016), para.3-39

Representation ceases to be true

7–021   [*Add to note 112, line 8, after "*111 L.Q.R. 385*": page* [658]]
; *Abu Dhabi Investment Company v H Clarkson and Co Ltd* [2007] EWHC 1267 (Comm) at [232] (rev'd on other grounds [2008] EWCA Civ 699).

[*Add new paragraph 7–021A: page* [658]]
7–021A   **Withdrawals and corrections.** A misrepresentation will cease to have effect if it is withdrawn or corrected before the contract is made, as then it will not have induced the contract.[113a] The burden of establishing a correction or withdrawal rests on the person making the correction and the correction must be sufficiently clear in all the circumstances of the case.[113b]

   [113a] *Cramaso LLP v Viscount Reidhaven's Trustees* [2014] UKSC 9, [2014] 2 W.L.R. 317 at [20]. On inducement see Main Work, Vol.I, paras 7–035 et seq.
   [113b] *Mortgage Express v Countrywide Surveyors Ltd* [2016] EWHC 224 (Ch) at [194], referring to *Arnison v Smith* (1889) 41 Ch. D. 348, 370, 373 and *Abu Dhabi Investment Company v H Clarkson and Co Ltd* [2007] EWHC 1267 (Comm).

(c) *Other Requirements*

The representee or person intended to act on the representation

7–031   [*In note 160, line 4, after "*[115]–[118]*": page* [664]]
; in the Court of Appeal Moore-Bick L.J. said ([2016] EWCA Civ 1262 at [11]) that "In an age when most commercial documents exist primarily in electronic form and can be made available to a wide audience at the touch of a button it is important not to allow inroads to be made too easily into the principles enunciated in cases such as *Peek v Gurney* ... In order for a representation in a document to be actionable at the suit of the recipient there has to be a connection between the maker and the recipient of a kind that enables the court to be satisfied that the maker was intending the recipient to rely on the document in a particular way". On the facts, the defendant had encouraged the party selling the investments to direct the investor to the information on the defendant's website.

[*In note 160, update reference to Gower & Davies, Principles of Modern Company Law to: page* [664]]
10th edn, 2016, para.25–32.

Intention

7–033   [*In note 171, update reference to Cartwright, Misrepresentation, Mistake and Non-disclosure to: page* [665]]
4th edn (2016), para.5-19

[*In note 173, update reference to Cartwright, Misrepresentation, Mistake and Non-disclosure to: page* [666]]
4th edn (2016), para.3-49

Inducement

[In note 186, delete from the second sentence "In Hayward v Zurich *. . . " to the end and substitute: page [667]]*

7–035

In *Hayward v Zurich Insurance Co Plc* [2016] UKSC 48 the Supreme Court, reversing the decision of the Court of Appeal ([2015] EWCA Civ 327) held that a settlement of an insurance claim could be avoided by the insurer when it discovered that the amount of loss had been exaggerated fraudulently, even though at the time the insurer had doubts over the extent of the claim. It was sufficient that the false claim influenced the insurer in the sum offered in settlement. It is not necessary that the insurer believed that the claim made was true.

[Add to note 187, at the end: page [667]]
If it would have been unreasonable of the representee to rely upon the representation, that may go to show that the representee did not in fact rely on it: *Monde Petroleum SA v WesternZagros Ltd* [2016] EWHC 1472 (Comm) at [219].

Need not be sole inducement

[Add to note 193, at the end: page [668]]
(reversed on other grounds [2016] EWCA Civ 1262).

7–037

"But for" causation normally required

[Add to note 199, line 3, after "31st edn": page [668]]
(reversed on other grounds [2016] EWCA Civ 1262).

7–038

Material misrepresentation and a presumption of inducement

[Add to note 214, at the end: page [670]]
Hayward v Zurich Insurance Co Plc [2016] UKSC 48 at [34], quoting this paragraph, and [37].

7–040

Materiality

[In note 216, update reference to Treitel on The Law of Contract to: page [670]]
14th edn (2015), para.9–020

7–041

Unforeseeable reliance

[In note 224, update reference to Treitel on The Law of Contract to: page [672]]
14th edn (2015), para.9–020

7–042

Representee could have discovered truth: rescission

[In note 230, update reference to Treitel on The Law of Contract to: page [673]]
14th edn (2015), para.9–028

7–043

Representee could have discovered truth: damages

7–044   [*Add to note 235a, at the end: page* [674]]
; [2016] EWCA Civ 1262, [2017] Q.B. 633 at [51].

3. DAMAGES FOR MISREPRESENTATION

(a) *Fraudulent Misrepresentation*

Claims for damages for fraud

7–047   [*Add to note 250, at the end: page* [675]]
In *Cassa di Risparmio della Repubblica di San Marino SpA v Barclays Bank Ltd*
[2011] EWHC 484 (Comm), [2011] 1 C.L.C. 701 at [229] Hamblen J. summarised the point thus: "Where a serious allegation (such as deceit) is in issue,
this does not mean the standard of proof is higher. However, the inherent
probability or improbability of an event is itself a matter to be taken into account
when weighing the probabilities and deciding whether, on balance, the event
occurred. The more improbable the event, the stronger must be the evidence that
it did occur before, on the balance of probability, its occurrence will be established".

Definition of fraud

7–048   [*Add a new note 255a, at end of paragraph: page* [676]]

    255a "I can conceive of many cases where the fact that an alleged belief was destitute of all
    reasonable foundation would suffice of itself to convince the Court that it was not really entertained,
    and that the representation was a fraudulent one.": Lord Herschell (1889) 14 App. Cas. 337, 375,
    cited in *Mortgage Express v Countrywide Surveyors Ltd* [2016] EWHC 224 (Ch) at [164].

Principal and agent

7–053   [*Add to note 265, at the end: page* [677]]
This sentence was quoted with approval in *Greenridge Luton One Ltd v Kempton
Investments Ltd* [2016] EWHC 91 (Ch) at [77].

Measure of damages for fraudulent misrepresentation

7–055   [*Add to note 273, at the end: page* [678]]
Doyle v Olby is of general application, so it applies whether the claimant is the
buyer or the seller: *Inter Export LLC v Townley* [2017] EWHC 530 (Ch) at
[8].

    [*Add to note 274, at the end: page* [679]]
    ; *Wemyss v Karim* [2016] EWCA Civ 27 at [23].

Property worth less than paid for it

[Add to note 286, at the end: page [681]]   **7–060**
; *Wemyss v Karim* [2016] EWCA Civ 27 at [24]–[25].

[Insert new paragraph 7–060A: page [681]]
Difference in value at time of acquisition. As Lord Browne-Wilkinson states in   **7–060A**
his propositions (3) and (4),[286a] the general rule is that the claimant is entitled to
the difference between what he paid and the value of the property he received at
the date he acquired it. The court will not reduce the damages to reflect that fact
that, as it turned out, various risks that, at that date, reduced the value of the
property, did not in fact materialise.[286b] The claimant will normally recover the
difference between the price paid and the value of the property bought, and also
any consequential loss.[286c]

[286a] See Main Work, Vol.I, para.7–057.
[286b] *OMV Petrom SA v Glencore International AG* [2016] EWCA Civ 778 ("The purpose of the
flexibility of approach about the valuation date to which Lord Browne-Wilkinson referred was to
ensure that the person duped should not suffer an injustice by failing to recover full compensation in
the type of circumstances to which he referred. There is no need to adopt such an approach in order
to relieve the fraudster from the general rule as to damages, especially if to do so means that the
person defrauded ends up paying more than the cargo was worth at the time that he bought it." (at
[39]).
[286c] [2016] EWCA Civ 778 at [66].

(b) *Negligent Misrepresentation*

Misrepresentation Act s.2(1)

[Add new note 334a, after title to paragraph: page [688]]   **7–075**
[334a] Note that under s.2(4) of the Misrepresentation Act 1967 (added by Consumer Protection
(Amendment) Regulations 2014 (SI 2014/870) reg.5), a consumer who has a right to redress under
Pt 4A of the Consumer Protection from Unfair Trading Regulations 2008 (on which see Main Work,
Vol.I, para.7–002 and Vol.II, paras 38–145 et seq.) in respect of the conduct constituting misrepresentation no longer has a right to damages under s.2 of the Act: see Main Work, Vol.II,
para.38–188.

Application of rules on damages for fraud

[In note 366, update reference to Treitel on The Law of Contract to: page [691]]   **7–078**
14th edn (2015), para.9–072

Fraud rules on knowledge

[Add to note 369a, at the end: page [691]]   **7–079**
(reversed on other grounds [2016] EWCA Civ 1262).

Contributory negligence

[Add to note 379, at the end: page [692]]   **7–082**
The *Taberna* case was reversed on appeal on other grounds but Moore-Bick L.J.
appears ([2016] EWCA Civ 1262, [2017] Q.B. 633 at [51]) to agree with the first
instance judge's analysis.

Misrepresentation by third person

7–085   *[Delete text of note 390a, and substitute: page* [694]]
It has been held that s.2(1) does not apply if B is induced by a representation by C to enter a contract with A that also results in B coming into a contractual relationship with C: *Taberna Europe CDO II Plc v Selskabet* [2016] EWCA Civ 1262, [2017] Q.B. 633 at [48] (B induced by C's misrepresentation to purchase from A subordinated loan notes issued by C; effect that B came into contractual relationship with C).

Liability for negligence at common law

7–086   *[In note 392, update reference to Cartwright, Misrepresentation, Mistake and Non-*
          disclosure to: page [694]]
4th edn (2016), Ch.6

Hedley Byrne & Co Ltd v Heller & Partners Ltd

7–089   *[Add to note 403, line 3, after* "s.2(2)": *page* [695]]
or Consumer Rights Act 2015 s.62(2)

Voluntary assumption of responsibility

7–091   *[Add to paragraph, at the end: page* [697]]
or the requirement of fairness under the Consumer Rights Act 2015,[418a] as appropriate.

     [418a] s.62. See Main Work, Vol.II, paras 38–374—38–375.

Relationship between manufacturer and purchaser of goods

7–094   *[In paragraph, line 31, delete* "when it comes into force the Consumer Rights Act 2015" *and substitute: page* [700]]
(for contracts made on or after October 1, 2015) the Consumer Rights Act 2015

Other legislative provisions creating liability for negligent misrepresentations: financial services

7–098   *[In note 449, update reference to Cartwright, Misrepresentation, Mistake and Non-*
          disclosure to: page [701]]
4th edn (2016), paras 7-82–7-83

          [In note 449, delete the last sentence, "For the possibility" *and substitute: page*
          [701]]
For the possibility of a restitution order on the basis that the conduct may constitute market abuse within the Market Abuse Regulation (Regulation (EU) 596/2014) see Gower & Davies, *Principles of Modern Company Law*, 10th edn (2016), paras 30–51 and 30–55 and cf. *Securities and Investments Board Ltd v Pantell SA (No.2)* [1993] Ch. 256, decided under Financial Services Act 1986.

[*In note 450, update reference to Gower & Davies, Principles of Modern Company Law to: page* [701]]
10th edn (2016), paras 25–10 et seq.

[*In note 450, update reference to Cartwright, Misrepresentation, Mistake and Non-disclosure to: page* [701]]
4th edn (2016), paras 7-49 et seq.

[*In note 453, update reference to Gower & Davies, Principles of Modern Company Law: page* [702]]
10th edn (2016), paras 25–36—25–39

Package Travel, etc

[*In note 462, update reference to Cartwright, Misrepresentation, Mistake and Non-disclosure to: page* [702]]   **7–100**
4th edn (2016), para.7-68

[*In note 463, update reference to Cartwright to: page* [694]]
4th edn (2016), para.7-69

(c) Innocent Misrepresentation

No damages for innocent misrepresentation

[*Add to note 471, at the end: page* [703]]   **7–102**
If the statement amounts to a contractual term, the promisee need not show reliance: *Wemyss v Karim* [2016] EWCA Civ 27 at [26], citing Slade L.J. in *Harlingdon and Leinster Enterprises Ltd v Christopher Hull Fine Art Ltd* [1991] 1 Q.B. 564, 584. The measure of damages will also differ: see above, para.7–055.

Misrepresentation Act section 2(2)

[*Add new note 479a, after title to paragraph: page* [704]]   **7–104**
479a Note that under s.2(4) of the Misrepresentation Act 1967 (added by Consumer Protection (Amendment) Regulations 2014 (SI 2014/870) reg.5), a consumer who has a right to redress under Pt 4A of the Consumer Protection from Unfair Trading Regulations 2008 (on which see Main Work, Vol.I, para.7–002 and Vol.II, paras 38–145 et seq.) in respect of the conduct constituting misrepresentation no longer has a right to damages under s.2 of the Act: see Main Work, Vol.II, para.38–188.

4. Rescission for Misrepresentation

(a) General

Misrepresentation Act section 1(a)

[*Add to note 518, line 11, after* "and representations': at [202].": *page* [710]]   **7–113**
See also *Idemitsu Kosan Co Ltd v Sumitomo Corp* [2016] EWHC 1909 (Comm) (above, para.7–009).

Misrepresentation as defence to proceedings

7–117   [*In note 526, update reference to Treitel on the Law of Contract to: page* [712]]
14th edn (2015), para.9–088

Court order not required

7–119   [*Add to note 535, at the end: page* [713]]
See also Turner (2016) 132 L.Q.R. 388.

(b) Restitutio in Integrum

Common law and equity

7–124   [*Add to note 550, at the end: page* [715]]
A claimant is not entitled to recover the price paid to the defendant for shares if
the claimant is able to return the shares to the defendant but is merely unwilling
to do so: *Gamatronic (UK) Ltd v Hamilton* [2016] EWHC 2225 (QB) at [218];
to pay the value of the shares to the defendant instead of returning them would
not put the parties back into their original position or anywhere near it (at
[219]).

Partial rescission not allowed

7–126   [*Add to note 569, at the end: page* [717]]
Note that in cases in which a voluntary settlement is being set aside for mistake
(see Main Work, Vol.I, and also above, para.6–025 n.25) or misrepresentation,
partial rescission may be allowed: *Kennedy v Kennedy* [2014] EWHC 4129 at
[46]; *Bainbridge v Bainbridge* [2016] EWHC 898 (Ch) at [22].

A more flexible approach?

7–128   [*Add to note 582, at the end: page* [719]]
Neither this case nor *Cheese v Thomas* [1994] 1 W.L.R. 129 (see below,
para.8–106) is authority for allowing a claimant to recover the price paid to the
defendant for shares if he is unwilling to return the shares to the defendant:
Gamatronic (UK) Ltd v Hamilton [2016] EWHC 2225 (QB) at [218].

(c) Others Bars to Remedy of Rescission

Third-party rights

7–138   [*Delete first sentence of the paragraph and substitute: page* [724]]
The intervention of third-party rights may prevent the misrepresentee from
rescinding the contract and reclaiming property transferred under it.[615a]

[615a] But see next paragraph. The effect of insolvency of the misrepresentor is unclear. Older cases
such as *Tilley v Bowman Ltd* [1910] 1 K.B. 745 assume that the misrepresentee may still rescind and
recover any property from the misrepresentor's trustee in bankruptcy but more recent cases involving

companies have suggested that the rights of unsecured creditors have intervened to prevent recovery of the property: *Re Crown Holdings (London) Ltd* [2015] EWHC 1876 (Ch) at [37]–[45]: *Shalson v Russo* [2003] EWHC 1637 (Ch), [2005] Ch. 281 at [126]. See Goff and Jones, *The Law of Unjust Enrichment*, 9th edn (2016), para.40–027.

[*Add new paragraph 7–138A: page* [724]]

Tracing proceeds of disposition. Even though the fact that, before rescission, an innocent third party has acquired rights over the property transferred under the contract that was induced by misrepresentation will prevent the misrepresentee from recovering the property as such, the misrepresentee obtains an equity on which it may rely to trace into other property that represents the proceeds of disposition of the original property,[621a] thus giving it a proprietary claim rather than merely a personal claim against the misrepresentor.[621b]   **7–138A**

[621a] See *Shalson v Russo* [2003] EWHC 1637 (Ch), [2005] Ch. 281 at [122]–[127]; *National Crime Agency v Robb* [2015] Ch. 520 at [40]–[46] (cases of fraud); *Pearce v Beverley* [2013] EWHC 2627 (Ch) (undue influence); and *Bainbridge v Bainbridge* [2016] EWHC 898 (Ch) at [24]–[32] (voluntary settlement sought to be set aside for mistake (see Main Work, Vol.I, and also above, para.6-025 n.25)).

[621b] *Shalson v Russo* [2003] EWHC 1637 (Ch) at [122].

A "mere equity"

[*In note 622, update reference to Cartwright, Misrepresentation, Mistake and Non-disclosure to: page* [724]]   **7–139**

4th edn (2016), para.4-10

5. EXCLUSION OF LIABILITY FOR MISREPRESENTATION

Misrepresentation Act s.3

[*Delete text of note 643 and substitute: page* [728]]   **7–146**

With the coming into force of the Consumer Rights Act 2015 (for contracts made on or after October 1, 2015), s.3 of the Misrepresentation Act 1967 is amended so as to no longer apply to "a term in a consumer contract within the meaning of Pt 2 of the Consumer Rights Act 2015": see next paragraph.

[*Delete text of note 643a and substitute: page* [728]]

Although s.3 applies only to terms and not to notices, a mere declaration of non-liability by the representor cannot have the effect of preventing a representor from incurring liability for misrepresentation: see *IFE Fund SA v Goldman Sachs International* [2006] EWHC 2887 (Comm), [2007] 1 Lloyd's Rep. 264 in particular at [65]; but the notice may go to the question of whether the alleged misrepresentation was made at all (at [67]); in other words, whether he has made has made a misrepresentation on which the other was entitled to rely. See also *Taberna Europe CDO II Plc v Selskabet* [2016] EWCA Civ 1262 at [20].

Consumer cases

[*Delete first three sentences of paragraph and substitute: pages* [728]–[729]]   **7–147**

With the coming into force of the Consumer Rights Act 2015 (for contracts made on or after October 1, 2015), s.3 of the Misrepresentation Act 1967 is amended so as to no longer apply to "a term in a consumer contract within the meaning of Pt 2 of the Consumer Rights Act 2015".[646] These terms are controlled under the 2015 Act by the general test of unfairness provided by s.62.[647] This has the effect of making the application of the legislation (the Misrepresentation Act 1967 s.3 on the one hand, the Consumer Rights Act on the other) turn on the distinction between a person who contracts as a "consumer" with a "trader" within the meanings of the Act and otherwise.

[646] Consumer Rights Act 2015 s.75; Sch.4 para.1. On the effect of the Act on the law on unfair terms, see Main Work, Vol.II, paras 38–196 and 38–334 et seq. It should be noted that (with exceptions that are not relevant here) s.62 applies to any term of a consumer contract, not just terms that were not individually negotiated, as was the case under the Unfair Terms in Consumer Contracts Regulations 1999 (on which see Main Work, Vol.II, paras 38–201 et seq.).

[647] On which see Main Work, Vol.II, paras 38–359 et seq.

Section 3 and no reliance clauses

7–150   [*Add to paragraph, after note 666: page* [731]]
Christopher Clarke J. held that the same was true of a non-reliance clause in the agreement.[666a]

[666a] [2010] EWCA Civ 1221 at [182]. In *Thornbridge Ltd v Barclays Bank Plc* [2015] EWHC 3430 (QB) at [97]–[121] H.H. Judge Moulder, sitting as a judge of the High Court, said "the test is not whether the clause attempts to rewrite history or parts company with reality. The first step is to determine as a matter of construction whether the terms define the basis upon which the parties were transacting business or whether they were clauses inserted as a means of evading liability" (at [105]); and in *Sears v Minco Plc* [2016] EWHC 433 (Ch) at [74]–[84] H.H. Judge Hodge, sitting as a judge of the High Court, said "I respectfully agree with Judge Moulder's analysis and conclusions [in *Thornbridge*]" (at [80]). But in *First Tower Trustees Ltd v CDS (Superstores International) Ltd* [2017] EWHC 891 (Ch), [2017] 4 W.L.R. 73 Michael Brindle QC, sitting as a High Court judge, differed, holding that the *Springwell* case "makes it entirely clear that where a representation has been made pre-contract and relied upon, a subsequent provision in the contract which states that there has been no representation or no reliance is, although contractually valid, an attempt to exclude or restrict liability and therefore subject to the reasonableness regime" (at [32]).

[*Add to note 667, at the end: page* [731]]
Similarly, a clause has been held to prevent a duty of care arising in tort rather than excluding liability, so the clause did not fall within s.2(2) of the Unfair Contract Terms Act 1977: *Crestsign Ltd v National Westminster Bank Plc* [2014] EWHC 3043 (Ch).

[*Add to paragraph, after note 667: page* [731]]
Or, even if it had relied on a statement made by the other party, it was not "entitled to do so" as the statement was not put forward as one of fact.[667a]

[667a] cf. Main Work, Vol.I, para.7–006.

Unfair Contract Terms Act 1977 s.3(2)(b)(ii)

7–151   [*Amend the title of this paragraph and the reference in line 5 to: pages* [731]–[732]]
Unfair Contract Terms Act 1977 s.3(2)(b)(i)

Reasonableness

Add to note 673, last line, after "the particular contract.".: *page* [732]]
Thus where a "no-reliance" clause is subject to the Act (see above, n.666a) it is likely to be reasonable if it expressly permits reliance on any reply given by the landlord's or vendor's solicitors to the tenant's or purchaser's solicitors, whereas one that seeks to prevent the landlord or vendor from incurring any liability for misrepresentation other than for fraud is unlikely to be reasonable: see *FoodCo UK LLP (t/a Muffin Break) v Henry Boot Developments Ltd* [2010] EWHC 358 (Ch) at [177]; *Lloyd v Browning* [2013] EWCA Civ 1637 at [34]; *First Tower Trustees Ltd v CDS (Superstores International) Ltd* [2017] EWHC 891 (Ch), [2017] 4 W.L.R. 73 at [36]–[38] ("not a reasonable clause to put into the lease, even if the parties are of equal bargaining power and act on legal advice, because its effect would render the whole exercise of making inquiries and relying on answers thereto all but nugatory" (at [39]–[40])).

7–152

Clauses covering breach

[*In note 680, update reference to Treitel on The Law of Contract to: page* [733]]
14th edn (2015), para.9–130

7–153

[*In note 681, update reference to Treitel on The Law of Contract to: page* [733]]
14th edn (2015), para.9–131

6. Contracts where a Duty of Disclosure

Non-disclosure

[*In note 692, update reference to Cartwright, Misrepresentation, Mistake and Non-disclosure to: page* [734]]
4th edn (2016), para.17-03

7–155

Rescission but not damages

[*In note 708, update reference to Cartwright, Misrepresentation, Mistake and Non-disclosure to: page* [736]]
4th edn (2016), para.17-37

7–156

(a) *Insurance*

Insurance Act 2015 to Continuing duty

Note that the Insurance Act 2015 came into force and the Marine Insurance Act 1906 was repealed in August 2016.

**7–157 to
7–168**

(b) *Contracts to take Shares in Companies*

Companies

7–169   [*In note 766, update reference to Gower & Davies, Principles of Modern Company Law to: page* [742]]
10th edn (2016), paras 25–8 to 25–43

[*In note 766, update reference to Cartwright, Misrepresentation, Mistake and Non-disclosure to: page* [742]]
4th edn (2016), para.17-53 et seq.

[*In note 769, update reference to Gower & Davies, Principles of Modern Company Law to: page* [742]]
10th edn (2016), para.25–39

CHAPTER 8

DURESS AND UNDUE INFLUENCE

2. DURESS

[*In note 20, update reference to Goff and Jones, Law of Unjust Enrichment to: page* [751]]
9th edn (2016)

[*In note 20, update reference to Virgo, Principles of the Law of Restitution to: page* [751]]
3rd edn (2015)

(b) *Nature of Duress*

Legitimacy of the pressure or threat:

8–008   [*Add new note 50a, line 24, after* "treated as illegitimate,"*: page* [755]]
        [50a] Threats of armed force between states are non-justiciable and cannot give rise to a defence of duress in English law: *Law Debenture Trust Corp Plc v Ukraine* [2017] EWHC 655 (Comm) at [308].

(c) *Types of Illegitimate Pressure*

Types of illegitimate pressure

8–011   [*In note 60, update reference to Goff and Jones, Law of Unjust Enrichment to: page* [756]]
9th edn (2016), para.10-02.

        [*Add new note 63a, line 15, after* "may amount to duress,"*: page* [756]]
        [63a] See also *Carter v Carter* (1829) 5 Bing. 406, 130 E.R. 1118, cited by *Goff and Jones, Law of Unjust Enrichment*, 9th edn (2016), para.10-02

(i) *Duress of the Person*

Form of duress

8–012   [*Add to note 65, at the end: page* [757]]
Threats of armed force between states are non-justiciable and cannot give rise to a defence of duress in English law: *Law Debenture Trust Corp Plc v Ukraine* [2017] EWHC 655 (Comm) at [308].

        [*In note 67, update reference to Goff and Jones, Law of Unjust Enrichment to: page* [757]]
9th edn (2016), para.10-15.

(ii) *Duress of Goods*

Duress of goods

8–013   [*In note 78, update reference to Goff and Jones, Law of Unjust Enrichment to: page* [758]]
9th edn (2016), paras 10-20–10-21.

Recognition of duress of goods

8–014   [*In note 79, update reference to Goff and Jones, Law of Unjust Enrichment to: page* [758]]
9th edn (2016), paras 10-30 et seq.

(d) *Causation*

Causation in economic duress: "but for"

[*In note 119, update reference to Goff and Jones, Law of Unjust Enrichment to:*   **8–028**
page [765]]
9th edn (2016), paras 10-73–10-74

[*Add to note 119, at the end: page* [765]]
It has been suggested that a defendant who has used both duress and mis-representation will not be allowed to argue that the "but for" test is not satisfied in relation to one wrong because the claimant would still have entered the contract because of the defendant's other wrong: *Times Travel (UK) Ltd v Pakistan International Airlines Corp* [2017] EWHC 1367 (Ch) at [258].

Reasonable alternative: a matter of evidence

[*In note 135, update references to Goff and Jones, Law of Unjust Enrichment to:*   **8–033**
page [767]]
9th edn (2016), paras 10-75 and 10-77

Conclusion on causation in economic duress

[*In note 146, update reference to Virgo, Principles of the Law of Restitution to: page*   **8–037**
[768]]
3rd edn (2015), p.225

(e) *Legitimacy of the Demand*

Bad faith

[*In note 168, update reference to Goff and Jones, Law of Unjust Enrichment to:*   **8–042**
page [771]]
9th edn (2016), paras 10-62–10-63

Fairness of the demand

[*In note 175, update reference to Goff and Jones, Law of Unjust Enrichment to:*   **8–043**
page [772]]
9th edn (2016), para.10-64

A range of factors

[*In note 188, update reference to Goff and Jones, Law of Unjust Enrichment to:*   **8–045**
page [774]]
9th edn (2016), paras 10-62–10-63

(f) *Threats of Actions not in Themselves Wrongful*

Threat to commit otherwise lawful act

8–046   [*Add to note 194, at the end: page* [775]]
In *Times Travel (UK) Ltd v Pakistan International Airlines Corp* [2017] EWHC
1367 (Ch) Warren J. (at [252]) said that the words of this paragraph to this point
represented an "accurate albeit incomplete summary" of the law. In that case it
was held that even though the defendant had not threatened actions that were
unlawful, the pressure it had applied was illegitimate: at [262].

8–047   [*Add to note 198, line 1, after* "[1994] 4 All E.R. 715": *page* [775]]
; *Marsden v Barclays Bank Plc* [2016] EWHC 1601 (QB)

[*Add to note 200, at the beginning: page* [776]]
Marsden v Barclays Bank Plc [2016] EWHC 1601 (QB) at [35].

Threat not to contract

8–048   [*In note 204, update reference to Goff and Jones, Law of Unjust Enrichment to:
page* [776]]
9th edn (2016), paras 10-71–10-72

(h) *General Effect of Duress*

[*Add new paragraph 8–054A: page* [780]]
8–054A   **Right to rescind cannot be excluded.** The right to rescind an agreement reached
under duress cannot be excluded by the terms of the agreement.[237a]

[237a] *Borrelli v Ting* [2010] UKPC 21, [2010] Bus. L.R. 1718 at [40]. Compare the right to rescind
for fraud, Main Work, Vol.I, para.7–143.

3. Undue Influence

(a) *Introduction*

When the stronger party's conscience is engaged

8–059   [*In note 273, update reference to Goff and Jones, Law of Unjust Enrichment to:
page* [784]]
9th edn (2016), paras 11-08–11-11

[*Add to paragraph, at the end: page* [786]]
It is submitted, however, that in the light of the decision of the House of Lords
in *Royal Bank of Scotland v Etridge (No.2)*[284a] that there are not two classes of
undue influence, actual and presumed, but merely two methods of proving undue
influence (by direct proof or by use of a presumption that arises when there is a
relationship of trust and confidence between the parties[284b] and a transaction
between them that "requires explanation"[284c]) to insist that undue influence is

limited to cases of wicked exploitation would involve at least a substantial re-working of the authorities.[284d]

[284a] [2001] UKHL 44, [2002] 2 A.C. 773. See Main Work, Vol.I, para.8–061.

[284b] See Main Work, Vol.I, paras 8–073 et seq.

[284c] See Main Work, Vol.I, paras 8–065 and 8–090 et seq.

[284d] See Beale, "Undue Influence and Unconscionability" in Dyson, Goudkamp and Wilmot-Smith (eds), *Defences in Contract* (2017), Ch.5, where it is argued that while the primary purpose of the doctrine may be to prevent "tyranny, trickery and fraud", those are not requirements. First, exploitation may be passive. Secondly, the defendant's behaviour need not be dishonest: it can consist of a failure to ensure that the claimant was properly informed, was thinking through the consequences and was acting free of the defendant's influence. Thirdly, the transaction need not always be apparently to the claimant's disadvantage at the time.

(b) *Direct Proof of Undue Influence*

[*Add new paragraph 8–069A: page* [794]]

Bribery as a form of undue influence. It has been said that bribery may also be a form of "actual" undue influence.[350a]   **8–069A**

[350a] *Libyan Investment Authority v Goldman Sachs International* [2016] EWHC 2530 (Ch) at [167]–[168], Rose J. As bribery had not been established, the "difficult legal question" was left open.

(c) *Presumed Undue Influence*

(i) *Relationships Giving Rise to Presumption of Influence*

Solicitor and client

[*Add new note 408a in line 5, after* "transaction with the solicitor": *page* [800]]   **8–080**
[408a] *Royal Bank of Scotland v Etridge (No.2)* [2001] UKHL 44, [2002] 2 A.C. 773 at [18]; *AKB v Willerton, OH v Craven* [2016] EWHC 3146 (QB), [2017] 4 W.L.R. 25 at [30]

(ii) *Confidential Relationship Shown on Facts in earlier Decisions*

Relationships that may be confidential

[*Add to note 446, line 1, after* "[1985] A.C. 686": *page* [804]]   **8–086**
; cf. *Libyan Investment Authority v Goldman Sachs International* [2016] EWHC 2530 (Ch) at [167]–[278] and [427].

(iii) *A Transaction not Explicable by Ordinary Motives*

Examples from other contracts

[*Add to note 486, at the end: page* [810]]   **8–096**
In contrast, in *Libyan Investment Authority v Goldman Sachs International* [2016] EWHC 2530 (Ch) the profits made by Goldman Sachs were not excessive given the nature of the trades and the work that had gone in to winning them, and so no presumption was raised (at [427]).

[Add to paragraph, at the end: page [810]]
It has been held that vesting a large sum of money to which a successful personal injury claimant has recently become absolutely entitled in the settlor's solicitor upon a bare trust for the settlor (but subject to charging and other powers vested in the solicitor) cannot readily be accounted for by ordinary motives.[487a]

[487a] *AKB v Willerton, OH v Craven* [2016] EWHC 3146 (QB), [2017] 4 W.L.R. 25 at [30]. On the steps that should be taken to show the settlor was not unduly influenced, see below, para.8–100 n.504.

(d) *Rebutting the Presumption*

Adequacy of advice

8–100   *[Add to note 504, at the beginning: page* [812]]
In the context of a personal injury trust under which the claimant's solicitor is to be trustee (see above, para.8–096 n.487a), it has been said that, with a settlement of £1 million or more where its in-house trust corporation is to be a trustee, to ensure that the claimant is not unduly influenced a separate partner in the firm should instruct Chancery Counsel of not less than five years' standing to advise the claimant: *AKB v Willerton, OH v Craven* [2016] EWHC 3146 (QB), [2017] 4 W.L.R. 25 at [31].

(f) *Undue Influence by a Third Party*

Undue influence by a third person

8–108   *[Add to note 531, at the end: page* [815]]
; *Chancery Client Partners Ltd v MRC 957 Ltd* [2016] EWHC 2142 (Ch), [2016] Lloyd's Rep. F.C. 578.

Constructive notice: *Barclays Bank v O'Brien*

8–112   *[Add to note 544, line 2, after* "rev. October 2014": *page* [817]]
and September 2015

[Add to note 544, at the end: page [817]]
On July 21, 2016, the Lending Standards Board published a new Standards of Lending Practice, which come into force on October 1, 2016. The Standards of Lending Practice replace the Lending Code. The Standards of Lending Practice apply to personal customers and cover loans, credit cards and current account overdrafts. The new Standards represent a move away from the Lending Code, which was focused more on compliance with provisions than customer outcomes. New Standards of Lending Practice for Business Customers were published on March 28, 2017 and became effective on July 1, 2017. They replace the micro-enterprise provisions of the Lending Code. See further below, para.34–219. Until July 2017, the existing protections of the Lending Code continued to apply to micro-enterprises (Standards of Lending Practice, p.3). The issue of guarantees provided by individuals is dealt with in a separate document issued by the Lending Standards Board, *The Standards of Lending Practice for personal customers: Account maintenance and servicing* (September 2016), Pt 8.

Transaction not on its face to the advantage of the surety

[*In note 567, delete last sentence* "A change in . . . " *and substitute: page* [819]]   **8–117**
Nor is a bank excused from making enquiry when the wife is the husband's
partner in the business, especially if there is a change in the nature or scale of the
lending: *O'Neill v Ulster Bank Ltd* [2015] NICA 64 at [17].

4. Unconscionable Bargains and Inequality of Bargaining Power

Equitable relief against unconscionable bargains

[*Add to note 601, line 2, after* "Consumer Contracts Regulations 1999": *page* [825]]   **8–130**
or Consumer Rights Act 2015 Pt 2

Unconscionable bargains with poor and ignorant persons

[*In note 609, update reference to Treitel on The Law of Contract to: page* [826]]   **8–132**
14th edn (2015), para.10–044

An oppressive bargain

[*Add to note 628, at the end: page* [828]]   **8–134**
It is arguable that if the effect of a clause in the contract is that the bargain is
worth a great deal less to the claimant than he thought, this may make the bargain
oppressive: see Beale, "Undue Influence and Unconscionability" in Dyson,
Goudkamp and Wilmot-Smith (eds), *Defences in Contract* (2017), Ch.5.

The complainant's circumstances

[*Add to note 635, at the end: page* [829]]   **8–135**
It is arguable that relief may be given when the claimant's "bargaining weakness" took the form of not knowing of a clause in the contract he was signing,
or not appreciating its possible effect: relief can then be given if the result is that
the deal is worth a great deal less to the claimant than he thought, and if the other
party deliberately took advantage of the claimant's ignorance or lack of understanding. This form of bargaining weakness seems to fall within Fullagar J.'s
words in *Blomley v Ryan* (1956) 99 C.L.R. 362, 405, quoted in the text of the
paragraph, which included "lack of assistance or explanation where assistance or
explanation is necessary": see Beale, "Undue Influence and Unconscionability"
in Dyson, Goudkamp and Wilmot-Smith (eds), *Defences in Contract* (2017),
Ch.5.

Part Three

CAPACITY OF PARTIES

CHAPTER 9

PERSONAL INCAPACITY

2. MINORS

(b) *Contracts Binding on a Minor*

(i) *Liability for Necessaries*

Contracts for necessaries must be beneficial

9–012   [*In notes 51 and 52 delete* "(on its coming into force)" *and substitute: page* [843]] (as regards contracts made on or after October 1, 2015)

Executory contracts for necessary goods

[*In note 54, update reference to Goff and Jones, The Law of Unjust Enrichment to:* page [844]] **9–014**
9th edn (2016), paras 24-14–24-27.

[*In note 58, update reference to Treitel on The Law of Contract to:* page [844]]
14th edn (2015), para.12–008

Goods necessary when delivered, but not when sold, and vice versa

[*In note 65, update reference to Treitel on The Law of Contract to:* page [845]] **9–015**
14th edn (2015), para.12–008

Trading contracts

[*In note 103, update reference to Goff and Jones, The Law of Unjust Enrichment to:* page [847]] **9–021**
9th edn (2016), paras 19-09–19-13.

(ii) *Apprenticeship, Employment and Other Beneficial Contracts*

Statutory "apprenticeship agreements"

[*Delete text and footnotes from start of paragraph to* " . . . rule of law".^{135"} *in line* **9–029**
6 and substitute: page [850]]
The Apprenticeships, Skills, Children and Learning Act 2009 recognised a new form of apprenticeship founded on an "apprenticeship agreement", and set out rules governing, inter alia, its form and certification.¹³⁴ In 2015, the 2009 Act was amended so as to distinguish between "approved English apprenticeships"¹³⁵ and "Welsh apprenticeships".¹³⁵ᵃ Under the 2009 Act as so amended, both "approved English apprenticeships" and "Welsh apprenticeships" are to be treated as "contracts of service" and are not to be treated as "contracts of apprenticeship" for "the purposes of any enactment or rule of law".¹³⁵ᵇ

¹³⁴ Apprenticeships, Skills, Children and Learning Act 2009 Pt 1 (as enacted). The provisions on the "prescribed form" were contained in s.32(2)(b) and this form was later designated as being either "a written statement of particulars of employment" given to the employee/apprentice or "a document in writing in the form of a letter of engagement" as foreseen by the Employment Rights Act 1996: the Apprenticeships (Form of Apprenticeship Agreement) Regulations 2012 (SI 2012/844) reg.2, referring to the Employment Rights Act 1996 ss.2 and 7A respectively (with the exceptions specified by the Regulations). In 2015, s.32 was amended so as to apply only to "Welsh apprenticeships", as explained in the following text and notes.
¹³⁵ Apprenticeships, Skills, Children and Learning Act 2009, esp. Ch.A1 as inserted by the Deregulation Act 2015 Sch.1 para.1 (in force May 26, 2015).
¹³⁵ᵃ Apprenticeships, Skills, Children and Learning Act 2009 ss.2, 7–12, 18–22, 28–36 (as amended).
¹³⁵ᵇ Apprenticeships, Skills, Children and Learning Act 2009 s.A5 (approved English apprenticeships) and s.35 (Welsh apprenticeships).

(c) *Contracts Binding on a Minor Unless Repudiated*

Contracts for an interest of a permanent nature

9–037   [*In note 176, update reference to Treitel on The Law of Contract to: page* [855]]
14th edn (2015), paras 12–025—12–026

Partnerships

9–046   [*In note 213, update reference to Treitel on The Law of Contract to: page* [859]]
14th edn (2015), para.12–020 n.89

Effects of avoidance

9–047   [*In note 222, update reference to Goff and Jones, The Law of Unjust Enrichment to: page* [860]]
9th edn (2016), paras 24-21 et seq.

    [*In note 223, update reference to Goff and Jones, The Law of Unjust Enrichment to: page* [860]]
9th edn (2016), para.24-21

(f) *Liability of Minor in Tort and Contract*

Torts independent of the contract

9–054   [*In note 263, update reference to Treitel on The Law of Contract to: page* [863]]
14th edn (2015), para.12–031

(g) *Liability of Minor to Make Restitution*

At common law

9–056   [*In note 272, update reference to Goff and Jones, The Law of Unjust Enrichment to: page* [865]]
9th edn (2016), paras 34-16–34-17

Restoration of gains

9–058   [*In note 277, update reference to Goff and Jones, The Law of Unjust Enrichment to: page* [865]]
9th edn (2016), paras 34-18–34-29

    [*In note 286, update reference to Anson's Law of Contract to: page* [866]]
30th edn (2016) pp.263–264

    [*In note 286, update reference to Treitel on The Law of Contract to: page* [866]]
14th edn (2015) para.12–046

[*In note 287, update reference to Goff and Jones, The Law of Unjust Enrichment to:
page* [866]]
9th edn (2016), paras 34-29

"Property"

[*In note 298, update reference to Treitel on The Law of Contract to: page* [867]]   **9–062**
14th edn (2015) para.12–041

"Any property representing it"

[*In note 300, update reference to Goff and Jones, The Law of Unjust Enrichment to: **9–063**
page* [867]]
9th edn (2016), para.34-31

3. PERSONS LACKING MENTAL CAPACITY

(a) *The Rule in* Imperial Loan Co Ltd v Stone

(ii) *Constructive Knowledge of a Party's Mental Incapacity*

The Supreme Court's decision in *Dunhill v Burgin*

[*In note 353, update reference to Goff and Jones, The Law of Unjust Enrichment to: **9–078**
page* [873]]
9th edn (2016), para.24-09

Summary

[*Add new note 424a, at end of paragraph: page* [883]]   **9–088**
[424a] See similarly Peel (ed.), *Treitel on The Law of Contract*, 14th edn (2015) para.12–055 n.179;
Beatson, Burrows and Cartwright, *Anson's Law of Contract*, 30th edn (2016), p.267 at n.194 (stating
the rule as being that the other party needs to have been aware of the incapacity, though noting
Baroness Hale J.S.C.'s view that constructive knowledge is sufficient).

(iii) *The Nature of Mental Capacity and Establishing Incapacity*

Nature of understanding required

[*In paragraph, line 6, delete* "an understanding of" *and substitute: page* [883]]   **9–089**
the capacity to understand[426a]

[426a] What is required is an ability to understand, rather than actual understanding: *Fehily v Atkinson*
[2016] EWHC 3069 (Ch), [2017] Bus. L.R. 695 at [81] and [85], referring to *Manches v Trimborn*
(1946) 115 L.J.K.B. 305 and *Re Smith (deceased)* [2015] 4 All E.R. 329 at [27]. See also *Masterman-
Lister v Brutton & Co (Nos 1 and 2)* [2002] EWCA Civ 1889, [2003] 1 W.L.R. 1511 at [58].

[*In note 427, lines 1 to 2, delete* "Re Roberts [1978] 1 W.L.R. 653 (capacity to marry)": *page* [883]]

[*Add to note 427, at the end: page* [883]]
; *Gibbons v Wright* (1954) 91 C.L.R. 423 at 427; *Masterman-Lister v Brutton & Co (Nos 1 and 2)* [2002] EWCA Civ 1889, [2003] 1 W.L.R. 1511 at [58]. In *Fehily v Atkinson* [2016] EWHC 3069 (Ch), [2017] Bus. L.R. 695 at [87]–[103], which concerned the capacity to conclude an individual voluntary arrangement (IVA) under Pt VIII of the Insolvency Act 1986, the reference to understanding "the general nature of what he is doing" stated in the text was held to be accurate, although in so holding Stephen Jourdan QC clarified that what is required is "the capacity to absorb, retain, understand, process and weigh information about the key features and effects of the contract, and the alternatives to it, if explained in broad terms and simple language" (at [102]).

[*Add to paragraph, at the end: page* [883]]
The assessment of a person's mental capacity in relation to a contract should take into account relevant information or advice which could be available for this purpose.[428a]

[428a] *Fehily v Atkinson* [2016] EWHC 3069 (Ch), [2017] Bus. L.R. 695 at [82]–[83] and [102] (capacity to enter individual voluntary arrangement under Pt VIII of the Insolvency Act 1986). According to Stephen Jourdan QC in *Fehily* at [82], "in a case where a person needs advice to enable them to understand the transaction, the question is whether they have: (1) the insight and understanding to realise that they need advice; (2) the ability to find an appropriate adviser and instruct them with sufficient clarity to get the advice; and (3) to understand and make decisions based on that advice", referring to *Masterman-Lister v Brutton & Co (Nos 1 and 2)* [2002] EWCA Civ 1889, [2003] 1 W.L.R. 1511 at [18] and [75] (which concerned capacity for the purposes of CPR Pt 21).

[*Add to note 428, line 1, after* "Mr Martin Nourse QC": *page* [883]]
; *A County Council v MS* (2014) 17 C.C.L. Rep. 229, [2014] W.T.L.R. 931 at [64]–[72].

Relationship of common law and statutory tests of mental capacity

9–092   [*Add to note 446, at the end: page* [885]]
cf. *A County Council v MS* (2014) 17 C.C.L. Rep. 229, [2014] W.T.L.R. 931 at [64]–[72] (capacity to make gift for purposes of Mental Capacity Act 2005).

(iv) *The Effect of Mental Incapacity where operative*

Contract voidable

9–093   [*Add to note 447, line 5, after* "(not deciding the issue)": *page* [885]]
and cf. *Fehily v Atkinson* [2016] EWHC 3069 (Ch), [2017] Bus. L.R. 695 at [118]–[127] where it was said, obiter, that the approach to the effect of mental incapacity on a contract applies to an individual voluntary arrangement (IVA) made under Pt VIII of the Insolvency Act 1986, distinguishing the position as regards voluntary dispositions which are rendered void by mental incapacity.

[*In note 450, update reference to Goff and Jones, The Law of Unjust Enrichment to: page* [885]]
9th edn (2016), paras 24-10–24-11

(b) *Liability for Necessaries*

Liability for necessaries: the old law

[*In note 454, update reference to Goff and Jones, The Law of Unjust Enrichment to: page* [886]]   **9–095**
9th edn (2016), paras 24-15–24-19.

Liability for necessaries: the new law

[*Add to note 468, at the end: page* [888]]   **9–096**
; permission to appeal on the application of s.7 of the 2005 Act was refused and the provider of the services' appeal regarding the existence of the local authority's duty under the 1948 Act was rejected: [2014] EWCA Civ 1350, [2014] P.T.S.R. 1507 (note).

[*Add to paragraph, line 27, after* "were provided by"*: page* [888]]
the service provider under an arrangement with

(d) *Property and Affairs Under the Control of the Court*

Position under Mental Capacity Act 2005   **9–099**

[*In note 487, update reference to Treitel on The Law of Contract to: page* [890]]
14th edn (2015) paras 12–056—12–057

(e) *Other Matters*

Lasting powers of attorney

[*Add to note 513, at the end: page* [893]]   **9–103**
and see *TB v KJP* [2016] EWCOP 6, [2016] W.T.L.R. 687.

Chapter 11

THE CROWN, PUBLIC AUTHORITIES AND THE EUROPEAN UNION

3. Public Authorities

(a) *The Scope of Statutory Powers*

(i) *Express Powers*

Construction of statutory language

11–022   [*Delete from paragraph, lines 13–16, from* "the tax authorities' power to" *to* "inland revenue.[147] Similarly,"*: page* [961]]

[*Insert new paragraph 11–023A: page* [963]]

11–023A   **Procedural irregularity.** An authority's failure to follow its own procedures for entering a contract does not render the agreement ultra vires. As the Privy

Council put it in *Central Tenders Board v White*, "There is a difference between a case of procedural irregularity in the formation of a contract of a kind which a public body has power to enter, and a case of a public body purporting to conclude a contract of a kind which it has no power to make".[157a] In that case the authority had accepted a tender for a building project despite the tenderer failing to comply with the authority's instructions that all tenderers must state, on their form of tender, what the duration of the works would be. The authority was found not to have departed from its own procedures (since the procedures permitted non-conforming tenders to be considered), but the court went on to express the view that, assuming there had been a procedural irregularity on the facts, it would not have made the ensuing contract void. The court explained that any attempt to nullify a contract entered into following a procedural irregularity would have to be assessed in the light of "the seriousness of the breach and the degree of any injustice and public inconvenience which may be caused by invalidating the act", as well as "any alternative remedies available to a person legitimately aggrieved by the conduct of the public body".[157b] The court observed that it would be "a serious denial of [a party's] rights" to invalidate a contract because of a proce-dural defect in the contractual process,[157c] and indicated that "it would be wrong for a court to [quash an administrative decision] in such a way as to nullify a contract made between a public body pursuant to a legal power and a person acting in good faith, except possibly on terms which adequately protect that person's interest".[157d] Where a tenderer had been unfairly disadvantaged by the authority's failure to follow its own procedures, the Privy Council envisaged that recourse could be had to an implied tender process contract, of the kind recog-nised in *Blackpool and Fylde Aero Club Ltd v Blackpool Borough Council*.[157e]

[157a] [2015] UKPC 39, [2015] B.L.R. 727 at [19]. *Law Debenture Trust Corp Plc v Ukraine* [2017] EWHC 655 (Comm) at [134]. Cf. the public procurement regulatory regime, outlined at para.11–051, below.
[157b] [2015] UKPC 39, [2015] B.L.R. 727 at [22].
[157c] [2015] UKPC 39, [2015] B.L.R. 727 at [25].
[157d] [2015] UKPC 39, [2015] B.L.R. 727 at [26].
[157e] [1990] 1 W.L.R. 1195. See Main Work, Vol.I, paras 11–042 et seq.

(d) *Alternative Contracts Formed by Conduct*

Identification of alternative contract

[*In note 260, update the reference to Goff and Jones, The Law of Unjust Enrichment* **11–038**
to: page [974]]
9th edn (2016), paras 1-06–1-08

(e) *Ultra Vires and Human Rights*

Impact of human rights on ultra vires

[*In note 266, update the reference to Goff and Jones, The Law of Unjust Enrichment* **11–040**
to: page [975]]
9th edn (2016)

4. TENDER PROCESS CONTRACTS

(a) *Conditions for the Implication of a Tender Process Contract*

Factual conditions

11–044   [*Add to note 307, at the end: page* [979]]
; *Central Tenders Board v White* [2015] UKPC 39, [2015] B.L.R. 727 at [28].

6. PUBLIC PROCUREMENT

(a) *European Union Legislation*

11–051   [*Delete the text of note 352 and substitute: page* [984]]
Public Contracts Regulations 2015 (SI 2015/102) and Utilities Contracts Regulations 2016 (SI 2016/274).

Remedies for failure to follow the contract award procedure commenced after December 20, 2009

11–052   [*In paragraph, line 12, delete* "Treasury" *and substitute: page* [984]]
Minister for the Cabinet Office

[*Delete text of note 355 and substitute: page* [984]]
Public Contracts Regulations 2015 (SI 2015/102) reg.98(2)(c) and Utilities Contracts Regulations 2016 (SI 2016/274) reg.113(2)(c). See further *EnergySolutions EU Ltd v Nuclear Decommissioning Authority* [2017] UKSC 34, [2017] 1 W.L.R. 1373.

[*Delete text of note 356 and substitute: page* [984]]
Public Contracts Regulations 2015 (SI 2015/102) reg.99 and Utilities Contracts Regulations 2016 (SI 2016/274) reg.114.

[*Delete text of note 357 and substitute: page* [984]]
Public Contracts Regulations 2015 (SI 2015/102) reg.98(2)(a) and Utilities Contracts Regulations 2016 (SI 2016/274) reg.113(2)(a).

[*Delete text of note 358 and substitute: page* [984]]
Public Contracts Regulations 2015 (SI 2015/102) reg.100 and Utilities Contracts Regulations 2016 (SI 2016/274) reg.115.

[*Delete text of note 359 and substitute: page* [984]]
Public Contracts Regulations 2015 (SI 2015/102) regs 98(2)(b) and 102; Utilities Contracts Regulations 2016 (SI 2016/274) regs 113(2)(b) and 117.

[*Delete text of note 360 and substitute: page* [984]]
Public Contracts Regulations 2015 (SI 2015/102) reg.101 and Utilities Contracts Regulations 2016 (SI 2016/274) reg.116.

[*Delete text of note 361 and substitute: page* [984]]
Public Contracts Regulations 2015 (SI 2015/102) reg.102(7) and Utilities Contracts Regulations 2016 (SI 2016/274) reg.117(7).

[*Delete text of note 362 and substitute: page* [984]]
Public Contracts Regulations 2015 (SI 2015/102) reg.102(3) and Utilities Contracts Regulations 2016 (SI 2016/274) reg.117(3).

[*Delete text of note 363 and substitute: page* [985]]
Public Contracts Regulations 2015 (SI 2015/102) reg.101(4) and Utilities Contracts Regulations 2016 (SI 2016/274) reg.116(4).

CHAPTER 12

POLITICAL IMMUNITY AND INCAPACITY

1. FOREIGN STATES, SOVEREIGNS, AMBASSADORS AND INTERNATIONAL ORGANISATIONS

Foreign states and sovereigns: the common law rule

12–001   [*Add to note 1, at the end: page* [987]]
The immunity is not available to a State before its own Courts: *Iraqi Civilians v Ministry of Defence (No.2)* [2016] UKSC 25, [2016] 1 W.L.R. 2001 at [11].

Sovereign immunity and human rights

12–003   [*In note 13, line 8, delete "Al-Malki v Reyes . . . 929" and substitute: page* [988]]
Reyes v Al-Malki [2017] UKSC 61

[*Add to note 15, at the end: page* [989]]
See *Belhaj v Straw* [2017] UKSC 3, [2017] 2 W.L.R. 456, [11(v)], [108]–[109] (Lord Mance), [258]–[268] (Lord Sumption).

[*Delete final sentence and substitute: page* [989]]
In *Benkharbouche v Secretary of State for Foreign and Commonwealth Affairs*,[18] the Supreme Court, like the Court of Appeal below, preferred not to choose between the competing approaches, but noted that Lords Millett's and Bingham's views were compelling or powerfully made. In this case, the Supreme Court held that ss.4(2)(b) and 16(1)(a) of the State Immunity Act 1978 to the extent that they were relied on in the claims before the Court were incompatible with art.6 and, in the case of s.4(2)(b), art.14 of the Human Rights Convention, because they did not reflect a principle of international law.

[18] [2015] EWCA Civ 33, [2015] H.R.L.R. 3 at [16]; [2017] UKSC 62 at [30]. See also *Oge-legbanwei v President of the Federal Republic of Nigeria* [2016] EWHC 8 (QB) at [21]–[26]; *Al Attiya v Al Thani* [2016] EWHC 212 (QB) at [82]; *Reyes v Al-Malki* [2017] UKSC 61.

State Immunity Act 1978

[Add to note 20, at the end: page [990]]   **12–004**
In *Belhaj v Straw* [2017] UKSC 3, [2017] 2 W.L.R. 456 at [12]–[31] (Lord
Mance), the Supreme Court affirmed the decision of Leggatt J.

[Add to note 21, at the end: page [990]]
See also *LR Avionics Technologies Ltd v Federal Republic of Nigeria* [2016]
EWHC 1761 (Comm), [2016] 4 W.L.R. 120.

[Add to note 24, line 2, after "[1997] 4 All E.R. 108": *page* [990]]
; *Al Attiya v Al Thani* [2016] EWHC 212 (QB) (former prime minister of
Qatar)

[Add to note 25, line 9, after "[2011] EWCA Civ 616": *page* [991]]
; *Pearl Petroleum Co Ltd v Kurdistan Regional Government of Iraq* [2015]
EWHC 3361 (Comm), [2016] 4 W.L.R. 2.

[Add to note 27, penultimate line, after "[2015] EWCA Civ 835 at [39]–[48]": *page*   **12–005**
[992]]
; *Gold Reserve Inc v Bolivarian Republic of Venezuela* [2016] EWHC 153
(Comm), [2016] 1 W.L.R. 2829; *LR Avionics Technologies Ltd v Federal Republic of Nigeria* [2016] EWHC 1761 (Comm), [2016] 4 W.L.R. 120

[Add to paragraph, after note 29: page [992]]
If a State grants a lease of its premises to a privately owned company to which
the State outsources consular activities such as the handling of passport and visa
applications, the property is not being used for commercial purposes within the
meaning of s.13(4) of the 1978 Act.[29a]

[29a] *LR Avionics Technologies Ltd v Federal Republic of Nigeria* [2016] EWHC 1761 (Comm),
[2016] 4 W.L.R. 120.

[In note 31, lines 13–14, delete "Benkharbouche v Embassy... I.R.L.R. 929." *and
substitute: page* [992]]
Benkharbouche v Secretary of State for Foreign and Commonwealth Affairs
[2015] EWCA Civ 33, [2015] H.R.L.R. 3; [2017] UKSC 62; *Reyes v Al-Malki*
[2017] UKSC 61.

[Add to note 40, at the end: page [993]]
; *Gold Reserve Inc v Bolivarian Republic of Venezuela* [2016] EWHC 153
(Comm), [2016] 1 W.L.R. 2829; *LR Avionics Technologies Ltd v Federal Repub-
lic of Nigeria* [2016] EWHC 1761 (Comm), [2016] 4 W.L.R. 120.

[Add to note 42, at the end: page [994]]   **12–006**
; *Gold Reserve Inc v Bolivarian Republic of Venezuela* [2016] EWHC 153
(Comm), [2016] 1 W.L.R. 2829.

[Update note 45: page [994]]
Khurts Bat v Investigating Judge of the German Federal Court [2011] EWHC
2029 (Admin) is reported at [2013] Q.B. 349

Acts of sovereign states

12–007   [*In note 49, delete "Rahmatullah v Ministry" to the end and substitute: page* [994]]
Rahmatullah v Ministry of Defence [2017] UKSC 1, [2017] 2 W.L.R. 287.

[*Add to paragraph, after note 49: page* [994]]
In *Rahmatullah v Ministry of Defence*,[49a] the Supreme Court explained the application of the doctrine which rendered Crown Acts of State as non-justiciable, namely that (1) the act should be an exercise of sovereign power, inherently governmental in nature; (2) the act should be done outside the United Kingdom; (3) the act should be done with the prior authority or subsequent ratification of the Crown; and (4) the act should be done in the conduct of the Crown's relations with other states or their subjects.

[49a] *Rahmatullah v Ministry of Defence* [2017] UKSC 1, [2017] 2 W.L.R. 287 at [69]–[70] (Baroness Hale), [81] (Lord Sumption).

[*Add to note 50, at the end: page* [994]]
; [2017] UKSC 3, [2017] 2 W.L.R. 456.

[*Add to paragraph, after note 50: page* [994]]
The principle of non-justiciability under the "act of state" doctrine may also extend to the acts of a foreign sovereign state performed on territory other than its own territory.[50a]

[50a] *Belhaj v Straw* [2014] EWCA Civ 1394, [2015] 2 W.L.R. 1105 at [127]–[133]; [2017] UKSC 3, [2017] 2 W.L.R. 456 at [165] (Lord Neuberger), [237] (Lord Sumption); *High Commissioner for Pakistan in the United Kingdom v Prince Mukkaram Jah* [2016] EWHC 1465 (Ch) at [84]–[87]. cf. *Yukos Capital Sarl v OJSC Rosneft Oil Co (No.2)* [2012] EWCA Civ 855, [2013] 3 W.L.R. 1329 at [66].

[*Add to note 51, final line, after* "Final Court of Appeal)": *page* [995]]
; *Chugai Pharmaceutical Co Ltd v UCB Pharma SA* [2017] EWHC 1216 (Pat), [2017] Bus. L.R. 1455.

[*Add to paragraph, after note 51: page* [995]]
In *Belhaj v Straw*,[51a] the Supreme Court analysed the Act of State doctrine in the context of its application to foreign sovereign nations and, in so doing, identified separate strands or rules of the doctrine: (1) a foreign state's legislation will normally be recognised and treated as valid, so far as it affects movable or immovable property within the foreign state's jurisdiction; (2) a domestic court will not normally question the validity of any sovereign act in respect of property within the foreign state's jurisdiction, at least in times of civil disorder; (3) a domestic court will treat as non-justiciable, meaning that it would abstain or refrain from adjudicating upon or questioning, certain categories of sovereign act by a foreign state abroad, even if they occur outside the foreign state's jurisdiction. Further, the doctrine does not apply where there is no challenge to the validity or lawfulness of an act of a foreign state.[51b]

[51a] [2017] UKSC 3, [2017] 2 W.L.R. 456 at [11(iii)], [35]–[45] (Lord Mance), [120]–[124] (Lord Neuberger), [234] (Lord Sumption). It was doubted that there is a fourth rule that the doctrine may be invoked where a ruling would embarrass the United Kingdom in its international dealings: at

[11(iv)] (Lord Mance), [148]–[149] (Lord Neuberger), [240]–[241] (Lord Sumption). See *Law Debenture Trust Corp Plc v Ukraine* [2017] EWHC 655 (Comm) at [275]–[295].
[51b] *AAA v Unilever Plc* [2017] EWHC 371 (QB), [35]–[62].

[Add to note 52, line 4, after "[81]–[93]": page [995]]
; [2017] UKSC 3, [2017] 2 W.L.R. 456 at [11(v)], [85]–[107] (Lord Mance), [153]–[162] (Lord Neuberger), [249]–[280] (Lord Sumption)

[Add to note 54, at the end: page [996]]
; [2017] UKSC 3, [2017] 2 W.L.R. 456 at [11(v)], [85]–[107] (Lord Mance), [153]–[162] (Lord Neuberger), [249]–[280] (Lord Sumption); *Law Debenture Trust Corp Plc v Ukraine* [2017] EWHC 655 (Comm), [296]–[308].

[Add to paragraph, at the end: page [996]]
Unlike sovereign immunity, the principle of non-justiciability under the "act of state" doctrine is not capable of being waived, because it is a matter going to the substantive jurisdiction of the Court.[54a]

[54a] *R. v Bow Street Metropolitan Stipendiary Magistrate Ex p. Pinochet Ugarte (No.3)* [2000] 1 A.C. 61, 90; *High Commissioner for Pakistan in the United Kingdom v Prince Mukkaram Jah* [2016] EWHC 1465 (Ch) at [89]–[90].

Foreign heads of state, ambassadors and their staffs

[Update note 56: page [996]]   **12–008**
Harb v Aziz [2015] EWCA Civ 481 is reported at [2016] Ch. 308

[Add to note 56, at the end: page [996]]
See also *Al Attiya v Al Thani* [2016] EWHC 212 (QB) (civil claim against former prime minister of Qatar).

Categories of persons entitled to diplomatic immunity

[Delete the second sentence of note 60 and substitute: page [996]]   **12–010**
As a matter of customary international law and the common law, a receiving State is obliged to secure, for the duration of a special or ad hoc mission, personal inviolability and immunity from criminal jurisdiction for the members of the mission accepted as such by the receiving State: see *Khurts Bat v Investigating Judge of the German Federal Court* [2011] EWHC 2029 (Admin), [2013] Q.B. 349; *R. (on the application of the Freedom and Justice Party) v Secretary of State for Foreign and Commonwealth Affairs* [2016] EWHC 2010 (Admin) at [116]–[120].

Diplomatic agents

[Add note 64, at the end: page [997]]   **12–011**
; *Reyes v Al-Malki* [2017] UKSC 61.

[Add to paragraph, at the end: page [997]]
The Diplomatic Privileges Act 1964 applies only to permanent diplomatic missions; the status of special or ad hoc missions is a matter for the common law.[65a]

^{65a} *R. (on the application of the Freedom and Justice Party) v Secretary of State for Foreign and Commonwealth Affairs* [2016] EWHC 2010 (Admin).

Period of immunity

12–014   *[Add to note 71, at the end: page* [998]]
The immunity applies while the diplomat was in post: *Reyes v Al-Malki* [2017] UKSC 61, [18]–[19], [48]–[49], [55].

[Add to note 72, at the end: page [998]]
See also *Al Attiya v Al Thani* [2016] EWHC 212 (QB) at [48], [81].

Certificate of entitlement

12–015   *[Add to note 79, at the end: page* [998]]
Al Attiya v Al Thani [2016] EWHC 212 (QB) at [37], [59], [83]; *R. (on the application of the Freedom and Justice Party) v Secretary of State for Foreign and Commonwealth Affairs* [2016] EWHC 2010 (Admin) at [174].

Waiver of immunity: common law

12–020   *[Add to note 112, at the end: page* [1002]]
By contrast, the principle of non-justiciability under the "act of state" doctrine is not capable of being waived by a State, because it is a matter going to the Court's substantive jurisdiction, whereas sovereign immunity is no more than a procedural bar to the Court's jurisdiction: *R. v Bow Street Metropolitan Stipendiary Magistrate Ex p. Pinochet Ugarte (No.3)* [2000] 1 A.C. 61, 90; *High Commissioner for Pakistan in the United Kingdom v Prince Mukkaram Jah* [2016] EWHC 1465 (Ch), at [89]–[90].

Submission to jurisdiction

12–021   *[Add to note 121, penultimate line, after* "[2015] EWHC 55 (Ch) at [72]–[76]"*: page* [1002]]
; *Gold Reserve Inc v Bolivarian Republic of Venezuela* [2016] EWHC 153 (Comm), [2016] 1 W.L.R. 2829; *LR Avionics Technologies Ltd v Federal Republic of Nigeria* [2016] EWHC 1761 (Comm), [2016] 4 W.L.R. 120 at [20]–[23].

Part Four

THE TERMS OF CONTRACT

CHAPTER 13

EXPRESS TERMS

1. PROOF OF TERMS

Proof of terms

[*Add to note 5, line 8, after* "onerous or unusual)": *page* [1014]]   **13–002**
, on which see further *Dawson v Bell* [2016] EWCA Civ 96, [2016] 2 B.C.L.C.
59 at [102]–[103].

(a) *Contractual Undertakings and Representations*

Collateral contracts

[*Add to note 29, line 1, after* "[1976] Q.B. 801": *page* [1016]]   **13–005**
; *Times Travel (UK) Ltd v Pakistan International Airlines Corp* [2017] EWHC
1367 (Ch) at [234].

(b) *Standard Form Contracts*

Meaning of notice

13–013   [*Add to note 61, at the end: page* [1020]]
However, the court may be slower to incorporate a term into a contract where that term is to be found in a contract between two other parties or between one of the contracting parties and a third party: *Barrier Ltd v Redhall Marine Ltd* [2016] EWHC 381 (QB); *Habas Sinai Ve Tibbi Gazlar Isthisal Endustri AS v Sometal SAL* [2010] EWHC 29 (Comm), [2010] 1 Lloyd's Rep. 661; *TTMI SARL v Statoil ASA* [2011] EWHC 1150 (Comm), [2011] 2 Lloyd's Rep 220.

2. CLASSIFICATION OF TERMS

(a) *Conditions*

Conditions and other contract terms

13–026   [*Add to note 107, at the end: page* [1027]]
Where the contract uses the term "condition" once and provides that "It is a condition of the agreement . . . " that should generally suffice to constitute the term as a condition: *Personal Touch Financial Services Ltd v Simplysure Ltd* [2016] EWCA Civ 461 at [28].

(c) *Intermediate Terms*

Instances of classification

13–035   [*Add to paragraph, at the beginning: page* [1032]]
In the absence of either express classification as a condition by the parties or of statute or binding authority classifying the disputed term as a condition, modern courts seem more inclined to classify a term as intermediate rather than as a condition: "the modern approach is that a term is innominate unless a contrary intention is made clear".[156a]

[156a] *Grand China Logistics Holding (Group) Co Ltd v Spar Shipping AS* [2016] EWCA Civ 982, [2016] 2 Lloyd's Rep. 447 at [93].

Classification of time stipulations

13–037   [*Add to note 191, at the end: page* [1035]]
; *Grand China Logistics Holding (Group) Co Ltd v Spar Shipping AS* [2016] EWCA Civ 982, [2016] 2 Lloyd's Rep. 447 at [56].

[*Add to note 192, at the end: page* [1035]]
; *Grand China Logistics Holding (Group) Co Ltd v Spar Shipping AS* [2016] EWCA Civ 982, [2016] 2 Lloyd's Rep. 447.

Force majeure clauses

13–039

[*Add new note 195a, after* "right to rely on the clause." *in line 8: page* [1036]]
[195a] However, the analogy with an intermediate term may not be exact, given that it has been held that there is no rule of law according to which the consequence of a breach of a procedural requirement specified in the contract is the loss of the right to claim relief on the ground of force majeure. The inability of a party to invoke the force majeure clause in the contract arises as a consequence of the construction of the contract and would appear not to follow from the application of a rule of law: *Scottish Power UK Plc v BP Exploration Operating Co Ltd* [2015] EWHC 2658 (Comm), [2016] 1 All E.R. (Comm) 536 at [234].

Conclusion

13–040

[*Add to note 202, line 3, after* "[1987] Q.B. 527": *page* [1036]]
; *Personal Touch Financial Services Ltd v Simplysure Ltd* [2016] EWCA Civ 461 at [28]–[31]

[*Add to note 204, at the end: page* [1037]]
; *C21 London Estates Ltd v Maurice Macneill Iona Ltd* [2017] EWHC 998 (Ch) at [70]–[72].

[*Add to note 205, at the end: page* [1037]]
; *Grand China Logistics Holding (Group) Co Ltd v Spar Shipping AS* [2016] EWCA Civ 982, [2016] 2 Lloyd's Rep. 447 at [97], [99].

3. CONSTRUCTION OF TERMS

[*In note 207, update reference to Lewison, The Interpretation of Contracts to: page* [1037]]
6th edn (2015)

(a) *General Principles of Construction*

Object of construction

13–042

[*Add to paragraph, at the end: page* [1038]]
Interpretation is a "unitary" exercise which "involves an iterative process by which each suggested interpretation is checked against the provisions of the contract and its commercial consequences are investigated".[211a]

[211a] *Wood v Capita Insurance Services Ltd* [2017] UKSC 24, [2017] 2 W.L.R. 1095 at [12]. The "iterative" approach has been held to indicate "that there is no hard and fast order for the application of the various tools of interpretation, and that the Court always has the prospect of revisiting or taking an overview of the effect of the application of those tools at every and any moment before the end of the interpretative process": *125 OBS (Nominees1) v Lend Lease Construction (Europe) Ltd* [2017] EWHC 25 (TCC) at [98].

"Intention of the parties"

13–044

[*Add to note 220, last line, after* "[2015] EWHC 110 (Comm) at [24]": *page* [1039]]
; *Arnold v Britton* [2015] UKSC 36, [2015] A.C. 1619 at [77]; *Europa Plus SCA SIF v Anthracite Investments (Ireland) Plc* [2016] EWHC 437 (Comm) at [29];

Wood v Capita Insurance Services Ltd [2017] UKSC 24, [2017] 2 W.L.R. 1095 at [12].

"Striking a balance"

13–046   [*Add new note 222a, after* "uncertainty or tension in the case-law" *in line 4: page* [1040]]
²²²ᵃ In a number of cases there is agreement on the principles to be applied to the facts of the case (see, for example, *BSI Enterprises Ltd v Blue Mountain Music Ltd* [2015] EWCA Civ 1151 at [38]; *Canary Wharf Finance II Plc v Deutsche Trustee Co Ltd* [2016] EWHC 100 (Comm) at [16] and *Videocon Global Ltd v Goldman Sachs International* [2016] EWCA Civ 130 at [50]), and the disagreement relates to the application of these principles to the facts of the case and the weight to be attached to the various principles.

[*Add to note 224, at the end: page* [1040]]
The need to strike a balance between the indications given by the language and the implications of rival constructions was acknowledged by Lord Hodge in *Wood v Capita Insurance Services Ltd* [2017] UKSC 24, [2017] 2 W.L.R. 1095 at [11]–[13]. The current approach of the courts appears to give more weight to the natural and ordinary meaning of the words, at least in the case where the parties are commercially experienced and have access to skilled legal advice: *Canary Wharf Finance II Plc v Deutsche Trustee Co Ltd* [2016] EWHC 100 (Comm) at [17] and *Vitol E & P Ltd v Africa Oil and Gas Corp* [2016] EWHC 1677 (Comm); *Wood v Capita Insurance Services Ltd* [2017] UKSC 24, [2017] 2 W.L.R. 1095 at [13].

(b) *Ordinary Meaning to be Adopted*

Meaning of words

13–051   [*Add to note 246, at the end: page* [1043]]
; *Persimmon Homes Ltd v Ove Arup & Partners Ltd* [2015] EWHC 3573 (TCC), [2016] B.L.R. 112 at [21].

Adoption of the ordinary meaning of words

13–052   [*Add new note 247a, line 4, after* "is generally understood": *page* [1044]]
²⁴⁷ᵃ An emphasis on the natural and ordinary meaning of the words used by the parties is not to be equated with "an unduly literal or semantic interpretation" (*Fomento de Construcciones y Contratas SA v Black Diamond Offshore Ltd* [2016] EWCA Civ 1141, [2017] 1 B.C.L.C. 196 at [12]) nor does it permit an over-literal interpretation of one provision without regard to the whole of the document, particularly in the case of complex documents which have been put into circulation in the market (*Metlife Seguros de Retiro SA v JP Morgan Chase Bank, National Association* [2016] EWCA Civ 1248). The normal or dictionary meaning of the words used may yield to their context (*Savills (UK) Ltd v Blacker* [2017] EWCA Civ 68 at [33]), although the balance to be struck between the natural and ordinary meaning of the words and their context is not always an easy one to strike.

Absurdity, inconsistency, etc.

13–056   [*Add to note 266, at the end: page* [1047]]
; *LSREF III Wight Ltd v Millvalley Ltd* [2016] EWHC 466 (Comm); *Bouygues (UK) Ltd v Febrey Structures Ltd* [2016] EWHC 1333 (TCC); *BP Gas Marketing Ltd v La Societe Sonatrach* [2016] EWHC 2461 (Comm), 169 Con. L.R. 141 at

[281]. It is "only in exceptional cases" that commercial common sense can "drive the court to depart from the natural meaning of contractual provisions" (*Carillion Construction Ltd v Emcor Engineering Services Ltd* [2017] EWCA Civ 65, [2017] B.L.R. 203 at [46]; *Grove Developments Ltd v Balfour Beatty Regional Construction Ltd* [2016] EWCA Civ 990, [2017] 1 W.L.R. 1893 at [42]; *Arnold v Britton* [2015] UKSC 36, [2015] A.C. 1619 at [19]–[20]). For an example of such an "exceptional" case see *Sutton Housing Partnership Ltd v Rydon Maintenance Ltd* [2017] EWCA Civ 359.

[*Add to note 267, at the end: page* [1047]]
In *Credit Suisse Asset Management LLC v Titan Europe 2006-1 Plc* [2016] EWCA Civ 1293 Arden L.J. at [28] referred to the fundamental principle of English law of party autonomy, from which it follows that the court will not rewrite the bargain that the parties have freely chosen to make (see also *BP Gas Marketing Ltd v La Societe Sonatrach* [2016] EWHC 2461 (Comm), 169 Con. L.R. 141 at [274]).

[*Add to note 267a, at the end: page* [1047]]
In *Wood v Capita Insurance Services Ltd* [2017] UKSC 24, [2017] 2 W.L.R. 1095 Lord Hodge acknowledged (at [11]) that the court "must be alive to the possibility that one side may have agreed to something which with hindsight did not serve his interest".

Ambiguity

[*Add to note 268, at the end: page* [1047]]   **13–057**
But it may be going too far to state that, in a case where there is no ambiguity in the disputed contract term, considerations of commercial common sense do not need to be considered: *Liontrust Investment Partners LLP v Flanagan* [2017] EWCA Civ 985 at [39]).

[*Add to note 270, line 1, after* "[2011] 1 W.L.R. 2900 at [21] (Lord Clarke)": *page* [1047]]
; *Wood v Capita Insurance Services Ltd* [2017] UKSC 24, [2017] 2 W.L.R. 1095 at [11]. The fact that there are two possible meanings of the disputed term has been held to be the beginning of the inquiry, not its end (*Scottish Power UK Plc v BP Exploration Operating Co Ltd* [2016] EWCA Civ 1043 at [29]). It is then necessary for the court to apply "all its tools of linguistic, contextual, purposive and common sense analysis to discern what the clause really means" (per Briggs L.J. in *Nobahar-Cookson v Hut Group Ltd* [2016] EWCA Civ 128, [2016] 1 C.L.C. 573 at [19]).

Badly drafted contracts

[*Add to note 271, at the end: page* [1047]]   **13–058**
; *MT Højgaard A/S v E.ON Climate & Renewables UK Robin Rigg East Ltd* [2017] UKSC 59 at [48].

[*Add to note 272, at the end: page* [1048]]
But the mere fact that the contract does not achieve what one party subsequently states was its object does not necessarily result in the conclusion that the contract

was badly drafted: *Fairway Lakes Ltd v Revenue & Customs Commissioners* [2015] UKFTT 605 (TC). In *Wood v Capita Insurance Services Ltd* [2017] UKSC 24, [2017] 2 W.L.R. 1095 Lord Hodge acknowledged (at [13]) that in cases where the contract is one of some sophistication and complexity and has been negotiated and prepared with the assistance of skilled professionals, the agreement may be successfully interpreted principally by textual analysis. But in the case where the contract is one of some informality or has not been drafted with the benefit of skilled professional assistance it may be appropriate to place greater emphasis on the factual matrix when seeking to interpret the contract. However, Lord Hodge also acknowledged that negotiators of complex formal contracts may often not achieve a logical and coherent text because of, for example, the conflicting aims of the parties, failures of communication, differing drafting practices, or deadlines which require the parties to compromise in order to reach agreement. It is therefore important to recognise that there may be provisions in a detailed professionally drawn contract which lack clarity and the lawyer or judge in interpreting such provisions "may be particularly helped by considering the factual matrix and the purpose of similar provisions in contracts of the same type".

Mercantile contracts

13–059   [*Add to note 280, at the end: page* [1049]]
; *Credit Suisse Asset Management LLC v Titan Europe 2006-1 Plc* [2016] EWCA Civ 1293 at [28].

(c) *Whole Contract to be Considered*

The whole contract to be considered

13–065   [*Add to note 302, at the end: page* [1052]]
; *Wood v Capita Insurance Services Ltd* [2017] UKSC 24, [2017] 2 W.L.R. 1095 at [10].

Control by recitals

13–068   [*Add to note 314, at the end: page* [1053]]
; *Mr H TV Ltd v ITV2 Ltd* [2015] EWHC 2840 (Comm) at [38]. In *Russell v Stone (trading as PSP Consultants)* [2017] EWHC 1555 (TCC) Coulson J. noted that modern methods of interpretation, in which background plays a far larger part than used to be the case, may have "tempered" the traditional approach, such that recitals in a deed can be looked at as part of the surrounding circumstances of the contract "without a need to find ambiguity in the operative provisions of the contract".

Several instruments

13–069   [*Add to note 321, at the end: page* [1054]]
; and *BNY Mellon Corporate Trustee Services Ltd v LBG Capital No.1 Plc* [2016] UKSC 29 at [30], although it was acknowledged that in the case of a contract or

trust deed which governs the terms upon which a negotiable instrument is held "very considerable circumspection" is appropriate before the contents of such other documents are taken into account.

(d) *Making sense of the agreement*

Meaning of agreement

[*Add to note 334a, at the end: page* [1056]]   **13–074**
The importance of giving appropriate weight to the language of the contract, especially where the parties have access to skilled legal advice, has been recognised in more recent case law: see, for example, *Canary Wharf Finance II Plc v Deutsche Trustee Co Ltd* [2016] EWHC 100 (Comm) at [17] and *Vitol E & P Ltd v Africa Oil and Gas Corp* [2016] EWHC 1677 (Comm); *Carillion Construction Ltd v Emcor Engineering Services Ltd* [2017] EWCA Civ 65, [2017] B.L.R. 203 at [46]; *Grove Developments Ltd v Balfour Beatty Regional Construction Ltd* [2016] EWCA Civ 990, [2017] 1 W.L.R. 1893 at [42].

Modifying

[*Add to note 349, at the end: page* [1058]]   **13–077**
; *Bouygues (UK) Ltd v Febrey Structures Ltd* [2016] EWHC 1333 (TCC); *LSREF III Wight Ltd v Millvalley Ltd* [2016] EWHC 466 (Comm); *Hayfin Opal Luxco 3 SARL v Windermere VII CMBS Plc* [2016] EWHC 782 (Ch).

Inconsistent or repugnant clauses

[*Add to paragraph, line 7, after* "construction of documents"*: page* [1059]]   **13–080**
When considering how to interpret a contract in the case of alleged inconsistency, the courts distinguish between a case where the contract makes provision for the possibility of inconsistency and the case where there is no such provision. In the latter case the contract documents should as far as possible be read as complementing each other and therefore as expressing the parties' intentions in a consistent and coherent manner.[363a] However, matters are otherwise in the case where there is a term in the contract dealing with the possibility of inconsistency.[363b] In such a case court should approach the interpretation of the contract without any pre-conceived assumptions and should neither strive to avoid nor to find an inconsistency but rather should approach the documents in a "cool and objective spirit to see whether there is inconsistency or not".[363c]

[363a] *RWE Npower Renewables Ltd v JN Bentley Ltd* [2014] EWCA Civ 150.
[363b] *Pagnan SpA v Tradax Ocean Transportation SA* [1987] 2 Lloyd's Rep. 342; *Alexander (as representative of the "Property 118 Action Group") v West Bromwich Mortgage Co Ltd* [2016] EWCA Civ 496.
[363c] *Pagnan SpA v Tradax Ocean Transportation SA* [1987] 2 Lloyd's Rep. 342, 350; *Alexander (as representative of the "Property 118 Action Group") v West Bromwich Mortgage Co Ltd* [2016] EWCA Civ 496.

[*Add to note 364, at the end: page* [1059]]
; *Alexander (as representative of the "Property 118 Action Group") v West Bromwich Mortgage Co Ltd* [2016] EWCA Civ 496.

[*Add to note 365, at the end: page* [1059]]
; *Mercuria Energy Trading Pte Ltd v Citibank NA* [2015] EWHC 1481 (Comm), [2015] 1 C.L.C. 999 at [76].

[*In note 368, delete "Alexander v West Bromwich Mortgage Co Ltd* [2015] EWHC 135 (Comm), [2015] 2 All E.R. (Comm) 224" *and substitute: page* [1060]]
; *Alexander (as representative of the "Property 118 Action Group") v West Bromwich Mortgage Co Ltd* [2016] EWCA Civ 496; *MT Højgaard A/S v E.ON Climate & Renewables UK Robin Rigg East Ltd* [2017] UKSC 59. It is a question of construction for the court whether the multiple provisions cover the same or similar territory are all effective to impose the several obligations that their terms suggest, or that the effect of one or more provisions is to modify or exclude the apparent meaning of another provision of the contract: *125 OBS (Nominees1) v Lend Lease Construction (Europe) Ltd* [2017] EWHC 25 (TCC) at [99].

Unforeseen events: change of circumstances

13–081   [*Add to note 371, at the end: page* [1060]]
There are, however, no special rules of interpretation applicable to long term or relational contracts other than the need to recognise that terms in such contracts must often be phrased in broad, flexible terms to enable parties to adjust their bargain to meet changing circumstances and the courts should therefore not be too astute to declare such terms to be unenforceable on the ground of uncertainty or vagueness: *Globe Motors Inc v TRW Lucas Varity Electric Steering Ltd* [2016] EWCA Civ 396 at [64]–[68].

Clauses incorporated by reference

13–082   [*Add to note 374, at the end: page* [1061]]
When considering whether to incorporate the terms of one contract document into another contract, the first rule of interpretation is to construe the incorporating clause in order to decide on the width of the incorporation, and the second is that the court must read the incorporated wording into the host document to see if, in that setting, some parts of the incorporated wording nevertheless have to be rejected as inconsistent or insensible when read in their new context: *TJH and Sons Consultancy Ltd v CPP Group Plc* [2017] EWCA Civ 46 at [13].

Saving the document

13–084   [*Add to note 382, at the end: page* [1062]]
The maxim can only be invoked in a case where there is a genuine ambiguity: *Egon Zehnder Ltd v Tillman* [2017] EWCA Civ 1054 at [12].

Party cannot rely on his own breach

13–085   [*Add to note 389, at the end: page* [1063]]
; *Eurobank Ergasias SA v Kalliroi Navigation Co Ltd* [2015] EWHC 2377 (Comm).

(e) *Construction against Grantor*

Construction against grantor

[*Add to note 394, at the end: page* [1063]]   **13–086**
; *Impact Funding Solutions Ltd v Barrington Support Services Ltd* [2016] UKSC 57,
[2016] 3 W.L.R. 1422 at [6]; *Persimmon Homes Ltd v Ove Arup & Partners Ltd*
[2017] EWCA Civ 373, [2017] P.N.L.R. 29 at [52]–[53].

[*Add to note 395, at the end: page* [1064]]
; *Hut Group Ltd v Nobahar-Cookson* [2016] EWCA Civ 128 (although note the
difference of view between Briggs L.J. (who at [12]–[21] invoked the *contra
proferentem* rule) and Hallett L.J. and Moylan J. who did not (see paras [40] and
[41]).

[*Add to note 396, at the end: page* [1064]]
; *Transocean Drilling UK Ltd v Providence Resources Plc* [2016] EWCA Civ
372 at [20].

[*Add to note 408, at the end: page* [1065]]   **13–088**
There is a possibility that the rule in its application to exclusion clauses might
now develop separately from the *contra proferentem* rule. Instead of searching
for the *proferens* to whom the rule may be applicable, the courts may regard the
rule as a general rule of construction applicable to exclusion clauses according to
which ambiguity in an exclusion clause may have to be resolved by a narrow
construction because an exclusion clause cuts down or detracts from the ambit of
some important obligation in a contract, or a remedy conferred by the general
law: *Hut Group Ltd v Nobahar-Cookson* [2016] EWCA Civ 128 at [18].

[*Add to note 409, at the end: page* [1065]]
But note that in *Bloomberg LP v Sandberg (A Firm)* [2015] EWHC 2858 (TCC),
[2016] B.L.R. 72 at [24] Fraser J. held that the rule was of "no assistance"
because he could not identify the *proferens*.

4. ADMISSIBILITY OF EXTRINSIC EVIDENCE

(a) *The Parol Evidence Rule*

Scope of the rule

[*Add new note 458a, at the end of the paragraph: page* [1072]]   **13–101**
458a *Adibe v National Westminster Bank Plc* [2017] EWHC 1655 (Ch) at [34].

Law Commission Report

[*In note 462, update reference to Treitel on The Law of Contract to: page* [1072]]   **13–102**
14th edn (2015), para.6–014

(d) *Evidence to Interpret or Explain the Written Agreement*

Evidence of surrounding circumstances

13–121   [*Add to note 560, at the end: page* [1083]]
The court will have regard to the background knowledge reasonably available to
the person or the class of persons to whom the document is addressed (*Metlife
Seguros de Retiro SA v JP Morgan Chase Bank, National Association* [2016]
EWCA Civ 1248). The background knowledge that the neutral, reasonable
person employs when understanding a commercial document can include knowledge of the relevant law (*Gloucester Place Music Ltd v Le Bon* [2016] EWHC
3091 (Ch), [2017] F.S.R. 27 at [28]). The factual matrix takes account of facts
and circumstances known or reasonably available to both parties at the time of
entry into the contract but not a fact or circumstance known to, or reasonably
available to, only one of the parties: *Arnold v Britton* [2015] UKSC 36, [2015]
A.C. 1619 at [21] and *Jomast Accommodation Ltd v G4S Care and Justice
Services (UK) Ltd* [2017] EWHC 200 (Ch) at [122].

13–122   [*Add to note 564, penultimate line, after* "(2007) 111 Const. L.R. 48 at [150]"*:
page* [1085]]
; *Globe Motors Inc v TRW Lucas Varity Electric Steering Ltd* [2016] EWCA Civ
396 at [61].

   [*Add to note 571, line 4, after* "[2007] 1 All E.R. (Comm) 421 at [63]"*: page*
   [1085]]
; *Scottish Power UK Plc v BP Exploration Operating Co Ltd* [2015] EWHC 2658
(Comm), [2016] 1 All E.R. (Comm) 536 at [21]; *BP Gas Marketing Ltd v La
Societe Sonatrach* [2016] EWHC 2461 (Comm), 169 Con. L.R. 141 at [37].

Subsequent acts

13–129   [*Add to note 613, at the end: page* [1090]]
; *Reveille Independent LLC v Anotech International (UK) Ltd* [2016] EWCA Civ
443 at [41].

   [*Delete* "and" *in the penultimate line, and add at the end of paragraph: page*
   [1090]]
; and (viii) where the contract between the parties has been made by conduct.[616a]

   [616a] *Vivienne Westwood Ltd v Conduit Street Development Ltd* [2017] EWHC 350 (Ch) at [28].

CHAPTER 14

IMPLIED TERMS

Implication of terms

[In paragraph, delete from after note 2 to the end and substitute: pages [1095]–[1096]]
14–002

However, in *Att-Gen of Belize v Belize Telecom Ltd*[3] Lord Hoffmann challenged the validity of this difference in treatment on the ground that in both cases the court is seeking to establish what the contract would reasonably have been understood to mean having regard to the commercial purpose of the contract as a whole and the relevant available background of the transaction.[4] The extent to which the process of implication can be assimilated with the principles applicable to the interpretation of the express terms of a contract has since been the subject of much judicial comment[5] and academic controversy.[6] More recently the Supreme Court has sought to distance itself from the approach of Lord Hoffmann, with a majority describing his analysis in *Belize* as "a characteristically inspired discussion rather than authoritative guidance on the law of implied terms".[7] However, it does not follow from this that there is no relationship at all between the principles that govern the implication of terms and those which apply to the construction of express terms. While the process of interpretation precedes implication and thus may be described as "the precursor of implication",[7a] the two processes, while "logically distinct" have nevertheless been held to be "closely related" in that "both involve taking into account the words used in the contract, the surrounding circumstances known or available to the parties at the time of the contract, commercial common sense and the reasonable reader or reasonable parties".[7b]

---

[3] [2009] UKPC 10, [2009] 1 W.L.R. 1988 at [17]–[27]. For an earlier statement of Lord Hoffmann's views, expressed extra-judicially, see Lord Hoffmann (1997) 56 S.A.L.J. 656 and (1995) 29 *Law Teacher* 127.

[4] *Att-Gen of Belize v Belize Telecom Ltd* [2009] UKPC 10, [2009] 1 W.L.R. 1988 at [19]–[21].

[5] While the courts regularly applied *Belize* and recognised it for a period of time as the leading modern authority on the implication of terms into a contract, cases can be found in which the courts expressed some uncertainty about the precise scope of the decision and its relationship with earlier case-law: see, for example, *Stena Line Ltd v Merchant Navy Ratings Pension Fund Trustees Ltd* [2011] EWCA Civ 543, [2011] Pens. L.R. 22 at [44]; *Spencer v Secretary of State for Defence* [2012] EWHC 120 (Ch), [2012] 2 All E.R. (Comm) 480 at [52] and *Wuhan Ocean Economic and Technical Co-operation Co Ltd v Schiffahrts-Gesellschaft "Hansa Murcia" mbH & Co KG* [2012] EWHC 3104 (Comm), [2013] 1 All E.R. (Comm) 1277 at [15]. The reaction to *Belize* in the Commonwealth has been more mixed. Thus the courts in Singapore have declined to follow *Belize* (see *Foo Jong Peng v Phua Kiah Mai* [2012] SGCA 55, [2012] 4 S.L.R. 1267 and *Sembcorp Marine Ltd v PPL Holdings*

Pte Ltd [2013] SGCA 43, [2013] 4 S.L.R. 193) but it has been followed by the courts in New Zealand (*Dysart Timbers Ltd v Nielsen* [2009] NZSC 43, [2009] 3 N.Z.L.R. 160).

[6] See, for example, McLauchlan [2014] L.M.C.L.Q. 203; Courtney and Carter (2014) 31 J.C.L. 151; Hooley [2014] C.L.J. 315; McCaughran [2011] C.L.J. 607; Davies [2010] L.M.C.L.Q. 140; Macdonald (2009) 26 J.C.L. 97; Kramer [2004] C.L.J. 384; McMeel, *The Construction of Contracts*, 2nd edn (2011), Ch.11.

[7] *Marks & Spencer Plc v BNP Paribas Securities Services Trust Co (Jersey) Ltd* [2015] UKSC 72, [2016] A.C. 742 at [31] per Lord Neuberger. Not all members of the Supreme Court are, however, of the same view. Thus in *Marks & Spencer* Lord Carnwath (at [74]) saw no sufficient reason to question the "continuing authority" of the judgment of Lord Hoffmann in *Belize* and the judgment of Lord Clarke (at [76]) is more equivocal, as is the judgment of Lord Mance in *Trump International Golf Club Scotland Ltd v Scottish Ministers* [2015] UKSC 74, [2016] 1 W.L.R. 85 at [42]–[44]. However, the judgment of Lord Neuberger represents the majority view, so that the authority of Lord Hoffmann's judgment has now been considerably diminished. See also *Utilise TDS Ltd v Davies* [2016] EWHC 2127 (QB) at [52].

[7a] *Trump International Golf Club Scotland Ltd v Scottish Ministers* [2015] UKSC 74, [2016] 1 W.L.R. 85 at [35] per Lord Hodge.

[7b] *Europa Plus SCA SIF v Anthracite Investments (Ireland) Plc* [2016] EWHC 437 (Comm), [34] per Popplewell J. The relationship between the two may be particularly close in the case where it is alleged that something has been omitted from the contract. As was noted by Snowden J. in *Hayfin Opal Luxco 3 SARL v Windermere VII CMBS Plc* [2016] EWHC 782 (Ch) at [68], the gap in such a case can be filled either by a process of corrective interpretation or by the implication of an appropriate term in the contract. But in either case it is important to note that the test applied by the court is a strict one, so that a court will not lightly correct the contract by supplying the alleged missing term, whether by corrective interpretation or by implication.

Att-Gen of Belize v Belize Telecom Ltd

14–006   [*Delete text of paragraph from after note 23 to the end: page* [1095]]

14–007   [*Delete text of paragraph 14–007 and substitute: page* [1098]]

Marks and Spencer v BNP Paribas. Initially, Lord Hoffmann's judgment received the endorsement of both the Court of Appeal[24] and it was applied or referred to in a number of cases at first instance.[25] As a result, the traditional "tests" for the implication of terms into a contract were treated as guidelines to be applied by the courts when seeking to answer the single question: Is this what the instrument, read as a whole against the relevant background, would reasonably be understood to mean? However, in *Marks & Spencer Plc v BNP Paribas Securities Services Trust Co (Jersey) Ltd*[26] the Supreme Court re-established the traditional principles applicable to the implication of terms and "qualified"[27] the judgment of Lord Hoffmann in *Belize*. In doing so the Supreme Court emphasised that Lord Hoffmann had not diluted the requirements which must be satisfied before a term will be implied into a contract.[28] The test which must be applied by the courts when seeking to imply a term into a contract as a matter of fact is whether the term satisfies the test of "business necessity".[29] It is not enough to show that the term is a reasonable one for it to be implied into the contract.[30] Reasonableness may be a necessary requirement before a term will be implied but it is not sufficient. Thus a term should not be implied into a detailed commercial contract merely because it appears fair or because the parties might have agreed to it had it been suggested to them.[31] The test remains one of necessity, albeit not "absolute necessity" but whether, without the term, the contract would lack commercial or practical coherence or whether it is necessary to imply the term "in order to make the contract work".[32] In short, in order to imply a term into an ordinary business contract, the term must be necessary to give business efficacy to the contract; it must be so obvious that it goes without saying; it must be capable of clear expression; and it must not contradict any express term of the contract.[32a]

[24] *Mediterranean Salvage & Towage Ltd v Seamar Trading & Commerce Inc (The Reborn)* [2009] EWCA Civ 531, [2009] 2 Lloyd's Rep. 639 at [8]–[14]; *Chantry Estates (South East) Ltd v Anderson* [2010] EWCA Civ 316, 130 Con. L.R. 11; *KG Bominflot Bunkergesellschaft für Mineralöle mbh v Petroplus Marketing AG* [2010] EWCA Civ 1145, [2011] 1 Lloyd's Rep. 442 at [44]; *Beazer Homes Ltd v Durham CC* [2010] EWCA Civ 1175 at [36]; *Crema v Cenkos Securities Plc* [2010] EWCA Civ 1444, [2011] 1 W.L.R. 2066 at [36]; *Garratt v Mirror Group Newspapers Ltd* [2011] EWCA Civ 425, [2011] I.R.L.R. 591 at [46]; *Stena Line Ltd v Merchant Navy Ratings Pension Fund Trustees Ltd* [2011] EWCA Civ 543, [2011] Pens. L.R. 22 at [36]; *BDW Trading Ltd v JM Rowe (Investments) Ltd* [2011] EWCA Civ 548, [2011] 20 E.G. 113 (C.S.) at [34]; *Consolidated Finance Ltd v McCluskey* [2012] EWCA Civ 1325, [2012] C.T.L.C. 133; *Procter and Gamble Co v Svenska Cellulosa Aktiebolaget SCA* [2012] EWCA Civ 1413; *Rathbone Brothers Plc v Novae Corporate Underwriting Ltd* [2014] EWCA Civ 1464 at [84].

[25] *Durham Tees Valley Airport Ltd v BMI Baby Ltd* [2009] EWHC 852 (Ch), [2009] 2 Lloyd's Rep. 246 at [89]; *Inta Navigatiori v Ranch Investments Ltd* [2009] EWHC 1216 (Comm), [2010] 1 Lloyd's Rep. 74 at [42]; *AET Inc Ltd v Arcaola Petroleum Ltd* [2009] EWHC 2337 (Comm), [2010] 1 Lloyd's Rep. 593 at [4]; *ENE 1 Kos Ltd v Petroleo Brasileiro SA* [2009] EWHC 1843 (Comm), [2010] 1 Lloyd's Rep. 87 at [42]; *Fortis Bank SA/NV v Indian Overseas Bank* [2010] EWHC 84 (Comm), [2010] 2 Lloyd's Rep. 641 at [60]; *Redmayne Bentley Stockbrokers v Isaacs* [2010] EWHC 1504 (Comm) at [84]; *Cassa di Risparmio della Repubblica di San Marino SpA v Barclays Bank Ltd* [2011] EWHC 484 (Comm), [2011] I.C.L.C. 701 at [541]; *F & C Alternative Investments (Holdings) Ltd v Barthelemy* [2011] EWHC 1731 (Ch) at [271]; *Leander Construction Ltd v Mulalley & Co Ltd* [2011] EWHC 3449 (TCC) at [41]; *Spencer v Secretary of State for Defence* [2012] EWHC 120 (Ch); *SNCB Holding v UBS AG* [2012] EWHC 2044 (Comm); [2012] All E.R. (D) 259 (Jul); *Graiseley Properties Ltd v Barclays Bank Plc* [2012] EWHC 3093 (Comm) at [28]; *Wuhan Ocean Economic & Technical Co-operation Co Ltd v Schiffahrts-Gesellschaft "Hansa Murcia" mbH & Co KG* [2012] EWHC 3104 (Comm), [2013] 1 All E.R. (Comm) 1277 at [15]; *Greatship (India) Ltd v Oceanografia SA de CV* [2012] EWHC 3468 (Comm), [2013] 1 All E.R. (Comm) 1244 at [41]; *Yam Seng Pte Ltd v International Trade Corp Ltd* [2013] EWHC 111 (QB), [2013] 1 All E.R. (Comm) 1321 at [132]; *TSG Building Services Plc v South Anglia Housing Ltd* [2013] EWHC 1151 (TCC), [2013] B.L.R. 484 at [44]; *Lombard North Central Plc v Nugent* [2013] EWHC 1588 (QB); *Marex Financial Ltd v Creative Finance Ltd* [2013] EWHC 2155 (Comm), [2014] 1 All E.R. (Comm) 122 at [72]; *Straw v Jennings* [2013] EWHC 3290 (Ch) at [99]; *Carewatch Care Services Ltd v Focus Care Services Ltd* [2014] EWHC 2313 (Ch) at [104]; *Rosserlane Consultants Ltd v Credit Suisse International* [2015] EWHC 384 (Ch).

[26] [2015] UKSC 72, [2016] A.C. 742. See also *Ali v Petroleum Co of Trinidad and Tobago* [2017] UKPC 2, [2017] I.C.R. 531 at [5].

[27] *Walter Lilly & Co Ltd v Clin* [2016] EWHC 357 (TCC), [2016] B.L.R. 247 at [39] and *Manor Asset Ltd v Demolition Services Ltd* [2016] EWHC 222 (TCC) at [45].

[28] *Marks & Spencer Plc v BNP Paribas Securities Services Trust Co (Jersey) Ltd* [2015] UKSC 72, [2016] A.C. 742 at [24], [66] and [77].

[29] [2015] UKSC 72 at [17].

[30] [2015] UKSC 72 at [23]. See also *Rosenblatt (A Firm) v Man Oil Group SA* [2016] EWHC 1382 (QB) at [59].

[31] [2015] UKSC 72 at [21].

[32] [2015] UKSC 72 at [21] and [77]. Commercial coherence must be ascertained objectively and not simply from the perspective of one party. The fact that without the term the contract might potentially work to the disadvantage of one party in certain circumstances, in that it does not make a profit it might have made at other times, does not necessarily render the contract as a whole incoherent: *J Toomey Motors Ltd v Chevrolet UK Ltd* [2017] EWHC 276 (Comm) at [91]–[92].

[32a] *Hallman Holding Ltd v Webster* [2016] UKPC 3 at [14]. See also *Europa Plus SCA SIF v Anthracite Investments (Ireland) Plc* [2016] EWHC 437 (Comm) at [33]. Given the strict nature of the test established by the Supreme Court it is now a very difficult task to persuade a court to imply a term into a contract, particularly a written contract of some length which has been negotiated with the benefit of legal advice, and a number of cases can now be found in which the courts have applied the approach of the Supreme Court in *Marks and Spencer* and, on that basis, have declined to imply a term into the contract between the parties (see, for example, *Impact Funding Solutions Ltd v*

Barrington Support Services Ltd [2016] UKSC 57, [2016] 3 W.L.R. 1422 at [31]–[32]; *BP Gas Marketing Ltd v La Societe Sonatrach* [2016] EWHC 2461 (Comm) at [320]; *Teekay Tankers Ltd v STX Offshore & Shipbuilding Co Ltd* [2017] EWHC 253 (Comm), [2017] 1 Lloyd's Rep 387 at [190]; *J Toomey Motors Ltd v Chevrolet UK Ltd* [2017] EWHC 276 (Comm); *Law Debenture Trust Corp Plc v Ukraine* [2017] EWHC 655 (Comm) at [356]; *Gard Shipping AS v Clearlake Shipping Pte Ltd (The Zaliv Baikal)* [2017] EWHC 1091 (Comm), [2017] 2 All E.R. (Comm) 179 at [51] and *Co-operative Bank Plc v Hayes Freehold Ltd (in liquidation)* [2017] EWHC 1820 (Ch) at [99]).

Incomplete contract

14–011   [*Add to note 69, at the end: page* [1104]]
However, the implication of a term into a contract assumes that there is a concluded contract into which terms can be implied and it is not legitimate for the court, under the guise of the implying a term, to make the contract for the parties (see *Wells v Devani* [2016] EWCA Civ 1106, [2017] 2 W.L.R. 1391 at [19] and [81] and *Scancarriers A/S v Aotearoa International Ltd* [1985] 2 Lloyd's Rep. 419).

Co-operation

14–014   [*Add to note 121, last line, after* "[2014] 2 Lloyd's Rep. 50 at [32], [33]": *page* [1110]]
; *Ali v Petroleum Co of Trinidad and Tobago* [2017] UKPC 2, [2017] I.C.R. 531 at [8].

When implied from previous course of dealing

14–025   [*Add new note 166a, line 4, after* "a particular course of dealing": *page* [1115]]
[166a] It has been observed that it is "something of a misnomer to see these terms as being implied on any conventional basis. Rather, it is a question of what terms are to be incorporated as *express* terms. Implication only arises for consideration once the express terms have been identified and considered": *J Toomey Motors Ltd v Chevrolet UK Ltd* [2017] EWHC 276 (Comm) at [98].

Express terms prevail

14–026   [*Add to note 169, at the end: page* [1115]]
An inconsistency for this purpose can be either linguistic or substantive: *Irish Bank Resolution Corp Ltd v Camden Markets Holding Corp* [2017] EWCA Civ 7 at [35].

Implied restriction on contractual discretion

14–029   [*Add to note 178, at the end: page* [1117]]
; *Hockin v Royal Bank of Scotland* [2016] EWHC 925 (Ch) at [37]; *Monde Petroleum SA v WesternZagros Ltd* [2016] EWHC 1472 (Comm) at [242]–[276]; *Property Alliance Group Ltd v Royal Bank of Scotland Plc* [2016] EWHC 3342 (Ch) at [277]; *Brogden v Investec Bank Plc* [2016] EWCA Civ 1031, [2017] I.R.L.R. 90 at [20].

Implied term as to trust and confidence

[*Add to note 184, line 3, after* "[2015] EWHC 1322 (Ch)"*: page* [1117]]   **14–030**
; *Mr H TV Ltd v ITV2 Ltd* [2015] EWHC 2840 (Comm) at [43]–[51].

Implied term as to good faith

[*Add to note 188, line 4, after* "[2013] B.L.R. 484"*: page* [1118]]   **14–031**
; *Globe Motors Inc v TRW Lucas Varity Electric Steering Ltd* [2016] EWCA Civ
396 at [68].

[*Add to note 189, at the end: page* [1118]]
; *Property Alliance Group Ltd v Royal Bank of Scotland Plc* [2016] EWHC 3342
(Ch) at [276].

[*Add to note 190, at the end: page* [1118]]
See also *Monde Petroleum SA v WesternZagros Ltd* [2016] EWHC 1472 (Comm)
at [242]–[276].

[*Add to note 191, at the end: page* [1118]]
; *Apollo Window Blinds Ltd v McNeil* [2016] EWHC 2307 (QB); *T and L Sugars
Ltd v Tate and Lyle Industries Ltd* [2015] EWHC 2696 (Comm) at [152] ("while
it would be right to imply a term that the Defendant would act in good faith and
honestly in carrying out the process envisaged in clauses 3.7.1 and 3.7.3, there is
no proper basis for the implication of the very much more onerous term for which
the Claimant argues").

CHAPTER 15

EXEMPTION CLAUSES

1. In General

Generally

15–001   [*Add new note 3a, after* "expected to insure." *in line 16: page* [1128]]
    [3a] See, e.g. *Nobahar-Cookson v Hut Group Ltd* [2016] EWCA Civ 128, [2016] 1 C.L.C. 573, noted below, para.15–012.

Types of exemption clause

15–003   [*Add to paragraph, line 11, after* "rescind the agreement.": *page* [1129]]
    Similarly, an exemption clause can subject a party's liability for breach of contract to an onerous condition, such as a number of days within which the injured party must serve notice of the breach or bring proceedings.[12a]

[12a] e.g. *Nobahar-Cookson v Hut Group Ltd* [2016] EWCA Civ 128, [2016] 1 C.L.C. 573(contractual time-bar an exclusion clause for the purposes of the principle of strict construction) and see the definition of the "exclusion or restriction" of liability in the Unfair Contract Terms Act 1977 s.13 and Main Work, Vol.I, para.15–069.

[*Add to note 17, line 3, after "*[1981] C.L.J. 108*": page* [1129]]
; White [2016] J.B.L. 373

Exemption clauses distinguished from other similar clauses

[*Add to paragraph, after note 18: page* [1129]]   **15–004**
Whereas an agreed damages clause entitles the injured party to recover the sum stipulated without proof of loss, an injured party subject to a limitation clause must prove its actual loss sustained and can recover this loss up to the limitation stipulated[18a]; and an agreed damages clause (unlike a limitation clause) is for the benefit of both the injured party and the party in breach.[18b] The form of the clause is not decisive of the difference between the two: rather "it is the fact that the clause is expressed as one agreeing a figure [as a pre-estimate of damage], and not as imposing a limit".[18c]

[18a] *Suisse Atlantique Société d'Armement SA v NV Rotterdamsche Kolen Centrale* [1967] 1 A.C. 361 at 395 and 420 (demurrage clause in charterparty). As is explained below, paras 26–178 et seq., the Supreme Court has recently reframed the common law governing penalty clauses so as to reduce the significance of the distinction between "liquidated damages clauses" and penalty clauses, but this does not affect the distinction drawn in the text between agreed damages clauses and limitation clauses.

[18b] [1967] 1 A.C. 361 at 420–421.
[18c] [1967] 1 A.C. 361 at 436 per Lord Wilberforce.

Legislative control of exemption clauses

[*In paragraph, lines 33–35, delete from* "As the relevant parts . . . " *to* " . . . this   **15–005**
chapter will" *and substitute: page* [1131]]
The relevant provisions in Pts 1 and 2 of the 2015 Act affecting exemption clauses (and the resultant amendments of the 1977 Act[32a]) were brought into force so as to apply to contracts made on or after October 1, 2015, with the exception that Pt 1's provisions governing "services contracts" apply to "consumer transport services" (as specially defined) only if made on or after October 1, 2016.[32b] This chapter will therefore

[32a] These are contained in the 2015 Act s.75, Sch.4 paras 2–27; the Consumer Rights Act 2015 (Commencement No.3, Transitional Provisions, Savings and Consequential Amendments) Order 2015 (SI 2015/1630) art.3(c).

[32b] The Consumer Rights Act 2015 (Commencement No.3, Transitional Provisions, Savings and Consequential Amendments) Order 2015 (SI 2015/1630) arts 3–4 and 6(2) as amended by the Consumer Rights Act 2015 (Commencement No.3, Transitional Provisions, Savings and Consequential Amendments) (Amendment) Order 2016 (SI 2016/484) art.2. SI 2015/1630 art.6(4) provides that the Unfair Terms in Consumer Contracts Regulations 1999 continue to have effect in relation to any contract or notice relating to any contract entered into before October 1, 2015 despite their revocation by the 2015 Act Sch.4 para.34.

2. PRINCIPLES OF CONSTRUCTION

General principles

15–007   *[In note 35, lines 3–4, delete* "; *Kudos Catering (UK) Ltd* . . . 1192 (QB);": *page* [1131]]

[Add to note 37, at the end: page [1132]]
; *Persimmon Homes Ltd v Ove Arup & Partners Ltd* [2015] EWHC 3573 (TCC), [2016] B.L.R. 112 at [25]–[28].

[Add to note 41, at the end: page [1132]]:;cf. the restrictive interpretation of the decision on the construction of a clause dis-applying a statutory limitation of liability in *Clarke v Earl of Dunraven and Mount-Earl, The Satanita* [1897] A.C. 59 by the PC in *Bahamas Oil Refining Co International Ltd v Owners of the Cape Bari Tankschiffahrts GmbH & Co KG* [2016] UKPC 20 at [49], in part on the basis that the earlier case was decided "at a time when the relevant principles of construction were much less developed than they are today".

[In note 42, lines 3–4, delete "Transocean Drilling UK Ltd . . . para.7–017" *and substitute: page* [1133]]
Nobahar-Cookson v Hut Group Ltd [2016] EWCA Civ 128, [2016] 1 C.L.C. 573 esp. at [12]–[22] but cf. *Transocean Drilling UK Ltd v Providence Resources Plc* [2016] EWCA Civ 372, [2016] 2 All E.R. (Comm) 606 at [14] and [19] ("artificial approaches to construction" should not be applied to a contract by which the parties entered "mutual undertakings to accept the risk of consequential loss flowing from each other's breaches of contract"). And see Peel (ed.), *Treitel on The Law of Contract*, 14th edn (2015) para.7–016.

Clear and unambiguous expression

15–008   *[Add to note 43, line 16, after* "(ordinary rules of construction apply)": *page* [1133]]
; and cf. *Bahamas Oil Refining Co International Ltd v Owners of the Cape Bari Tankschiffahrts GmbH & Co KG* [2016] UKPC 20 at [31]–[40] (exclusion of limitation of liability arising by statute and international convention).

[Add to note 43, line 19, after "payment obligation)": *page* [1133]]
(though the CA was overruled on other grounds in *PST Energy 7 Shipping LLC v OW Bunker Malta Ltd* [2016] UKSC 23, [2016] 2 W.L.R. 1193 at [58]).

[Add to note 46, at the end: page [1133]]
; *Scottish Power UK Plc v BP Exploration Operating Co Ltd* [2016] EWCA Civ 1043 at [30].

[Add to note 47, line 3, after "2 Lloyd's Rep. 216 at [20]–[22]": *page* [1134]]
; *McGee Group Ltd v Galliford Try Building Ltd* [2017] EWHC 87 (TCC), [2017] B.T.C. 19 at [22]–[25].

[Add to paragraph, after note 47: page [1133]]
Moreover, a majority of the Supreme Court has recently observed that this strict
approach to exemption clauses should also apply to terms:

> "where they seek to prevent a liability from arising by removing, through a subsidi-
> ary provision, part of the benefit which it appears to have been the purpose of the
> contract to provide. The vice of a clause of that kind is that it can have a propensity
> to mislead, unless its language is sufficiently plain. All that said, words of exception
> may be simply a way of delineating the scope of the primary obligation."[47a]

[47a] *Impact Funding Solutions Ltd v Barrington Support Services Ltd (formerly Lawyers at Work
Ltd)* [2016] UKSC 57, [2017] A.C. 73 at [35] per Lord Toulson J.S.C. (with whom Lord Mance, Lord
Sumption and Lord Hodge JJ.S.C. agreed) (exclusion in contract of professional indemnity insurance). cf. Lord Hodge J.S.C. at [7] (with whom Lord Toulson, Lord Mance, and Lord Sumption
JJ.S.C. agreed) who considered that the established strict construction of exemption clauses does not
apply to "exclusion clauses" limiting the extent of cover in a contract of professional liability
insurance.

[In note 50, lines 3–4, delete "Kudos Catering (UK) Ltd . . . 1192 (QB)" *and
substitute: page* [1134]]
Nobahar-Cookson v Hut Group Ltd [2016] EWCA Civ 128, [2016] 1 C.L.C. 573
at [19]; *Transocean Drilling UK Ltd v Providence Resources Plc* [2016] EWCA
Civ 372, [2016] 2 All E.R. (Comm) 606 at [28] and [35]

[In note 51, lines 2–3, delete "; Transocean Drilling UK Ltd . . . [2015] B.L.R. 190
at [39]": *page* [1134]]

[Add to paragraph, at the end: page [1134]]
In an appropriate case, therefore, the existence of the presumption does not
prevent a court from finding, applying "all its tools of linguistic, contextual,
purposive and common sense analysis", that the contract intended to deprive one
of the parties of a right at law which he might otherwise have had.[51a]

[51a] *Scottish Power UK Plc v BP Exploration Operating Co Ltd* [2016] EWCA Civ 1043 at [29]
quoting Briggs L.J. in *Nobahar-Cookson v Hut Group Ltd* [2016] EWCA Civ 128, [2016] 1 C.L.C.
573 at [19].

Clause must extend to event

[Add to note 56, at the end: page [1135]]   **15–009**
However, some of these earlier cases may be decided differently today given that
the courts are now more willing to recognise that words take their meaning from
their context and that the same word or phrase may mean different things in
different documents: *Transocean Drilling UK Ltd v Providence Resources Plc*
[2016] EWCA Civ 372, [2016] 2 All E.R. (Comm) 606 at [15]. cf. *Star Polaris
LLC v HHIC-PHIL Inc* [2016] EWHC 2941 (Comm), [2017] 1 Lloyd's Rep. 203
at [11]–[18] and [39] (which noted the statement in this paragraph of the Main
Work and the doubts expressed in *Caledonia North Sea* and in *Transocean
Drilling UK Ltd* and held that in the context of the contract an exclusion of
liability for "consequential or special losses, damages or expenses" did not refer
losses, etc. falling within the second limb in *Hadley v Baxendale*, but had a wider
meaning).

Inconsistency with main purpose of contract

15–010   [*In note 62, lines 6–7, delete* "; *Transocean Drilling UK Ltd* . . . [2015] B.L.R. 190
at [167]"*: page* [1135]]
[*Add to paragraph, at the end: page* [1137]]
t1 And it has been said recently that the principle in *Tor Line A/B v Alltrans Group
of Canada Ltd*[72a] "should be seen as one of last resort" and that there is authority
that "it applies only in cases where the effect of the clause is to relieve one party
from all liability for breach of any of the obligations which he has purported to
undertake" as "[o]nly in such a case could it be said that the contract amounted to
nothing more than a mere declaration of intent".[72b]

[72a] [1984] 1 W.L.R. 48.
[72b] *Transocean Drilling UK Ltd v Providence Resources Plc* [2016] EWCA Civ 372, [2016] 2 All
E.R. (Comm) 606 at [27] per Moore-Bick L.J. (with whom McFarlane and Briggs L.JJ. agreed)
referring to *Great North Eastern Railway Ltd v Avon Insurance Plc* [2001] EWCA Civ 780, [2001]
1 Lloyd's Rep. I.R. 793 (the relevant passages are at [31]).

Construction *contra proferentem*

15–012   [*Add to note 83, line 2, after* "[1992] 2 Lloyd's Rep. 127, 134"*: page* [1138]]
; *Nobahar-Cookson v Hut Group Ltd* [2016] EWCA Civ 128, [2016] 1 C.L.C.
573 esp. at [14] and [16] (distinguishing "the *contra proferentem* rule in its
classic form", which is "a rule designed to resolve ambiguities against the party
who prepared the document", and the principle that, if necessary to resolve
ambiguity, [exclusion clauses] should be narrowly construed"); *Transocean
Drilling UK Ltd v Providence Resources Plc* [2016] EWCA Civ 372, [2016] 2
All E.R. (Comm) 606 at [20] (*contra proferentem* has no role to play where the
meaning of the words is clear or where a clause favours both parties equally);
Persimmon Homes Ltd v Ove Arup & Partners Ltd [2017] EWCA Civ 373 at
[52]–[53].

[*Add to paragraph, after note 85: page* [1138]]
For example, in *Nobahar-Cookson v Hut Group Ltd* a clause in a commercial
contract provided that the sellers of a company would not be liable for any claim
unless the buyer served notice of it within 20 business days "after becoming
aware of the matter".[85a] The Court of Appeal held that "there remains a principle
that an ambiguity" in the meaning of such a clause (which was rightly to be
treated as an exclusion clause) "may have to be resolved by a preference for the
narrower construction, if linguistic, contextual and purposive analysis do not
disclose an answer to the question with sufficient clarity".[85b] The Court recognised that the phrase "after becoming aware of the matter" could have three
possible meanings, but held that, given that the commercial purpose of the term
was to prevent the buyer from keeping claims of which it was aware "up its
sleeve", and assisted by the principle which it had stated, the phrase should be
interpreted as referring to an awareness of a claim and not merely an awareness
of facts which could give rise to a claim.[85c] However, the Court of Appeal
considered that:

> "This approach to exclusion clauses is not now regarded as a presumption, still less
> as a special rule justifying the giving of a strained meaning to a provision merely
> because it is an exclusion clause. Commercial parties are entitled to allocate between

them the risks of something going wrong in their contractual relationship in any way they choose. Nor is it to be mechanistically applied wherever an ambiguity is identified in an exclusion clause. The court must still use all its tools of linguistic, purposive and common-sense analysis to discern what the clause really means."[85d]

Rather, the principle is "essentially one of common sense; parties do not normally give up valuable rights without making it clear that they intend to do so".[85e] It will be seen, therefore, that this aspect of the construction *contra proferentem* is clearly related to the approach of the courts which requires clear and unambiguous language effectively to exclude liability for breach.[85f]

[85a] [2016] EWCA Civ 128, [2016] 1 C.L.C. 573 at [5].
[85b] [2016] EWCA Civ 128 at [21] per Briggs L.J.
[85c] [2016] EWCA Civ 128 at [36] (with whom Hallett L.J. and Moylan J. agreed, though placing greater emphasis on the commercial sense of the resulting decision: [2016] EWCA Civ 128 at [40] and [41]).
[85d] *Nobahar-Cookson v Hut Group Ltd* [2016] EWCA Civ 128, [2016] 1 C.L.C. 573 at [19] per Briggs L.J. See similarly *Persimmon Homes Ltd v Ove Arup & Partners Ltd* [2017] EWCA Civ 373 at [57] per Jackson L.J.
[85e] *Seadrill Management Services Ltd v OAO Gazprom* [2010] EWCA Civ 691, [2011] 1 All E.R. (Comm) 1077 at per Moore-Bick L.J. quoted by Briggs L.J. in *Nobahar-Cookson v Hut Group Ltd* [2016] EWCA Civ 128 at [19].
[85f] On which see Main Work, Vol.I, para.15–008.

[*Delete from paragraph, line 18,* "the makers of the document. In" *and substitute: page* [1138]]
However, while accepting the existence of the contra proferentem rule, the Court of Appeal has recently observed that "[i]n relation to commercial contracts, negotiated between parties of equal bargaining power, that rule now has a very limited role"[87a] and quoted the judgment of Lord Neuberger M.R. in *K/S Victoria Street v House of Fraser (Stores Management) Ltd* to the effect that:

"'rules' of interpretation such as contra proferentem are rarely decisive as to the meaning of any provisions in a commercial contract. The words used, commercial sense, and the documentary and factual context are, and should be, normally enough to determine the meaning of a contractual provision."[87b]

By contrast, in

[87a] *Persimmon Homes Ltd v Ove Arup & Partners Ltd* [2017] EWCA Civ 373 at [52] per Jackson L.J. (with whom Moylan and Beatson L.JJ. agreed).
[87b] [2011] EWCA Civ 904, [2012] Ch. 497 at [68], quoted at [2017] EWCA Civ 373 at [52].

Liability for negligence

[*In note 91, lines 5–6, delete* "; *Transocean Drilling UK Ltd* . . . [2015] B.L.R. 190 at [40]–[54]": *page* [1139]] **15–013**

[*Add to paragraph, at the end: page* [1140]]
Moreover, Lord Morton's observations have recently been criticised by the Court of Appeal in that they treat exemption clauses and indemnity clauses "in one single compendious passage", whereas they are more relevant to the latter than the former.[96a]

[96a] *Persimmon Homes Ltd v Ove Arup & Partners Ltd* [2017] EWCA Civ 373 at [55] and [56] per Jackson L.J. (with whom Moylan and Beatson L.JJ. agreed).

Words wide enough to cover negligence

15–014 *[Add to note 105, at the end: page* [1141]]
; *Persimmon Homes Ltd v Ove Arup & Partners Ltd* [2017] EWCA Civ 373 at
[60] ("liability for any claim in relation to asbestos is excluded").

Indemnity clauses

15–018 *[Add to note 134, line 7, after* "[2014] 1 W.L.R. 3517 at [94]"*: page* [1144]]
; *Capita (Banstead 2011) Ltd v RFIB Group Ltd* [2015] EWCA Civ 1310, [2016]
2 W.L.R. 1429 at [10].

[Add to paragraph, after note 136: page [1144]]
In the case of dishonest wrongdoing, "general words will not serve", as "the
language used must be such as will alert a commercial party to the extraordinary
bargain he is invited to make".[136a]

[136a] *HIH Casualty & General Insurance Ltd v Chase Manhattan Bank* [2003] UKHL 6, [2003] 2
Lloyd's Rep. 61 per Lord Bingham of Cornhill (exemption clause); *Capita (Banstead 2011) Ltd v
RFIB Group Ltd* [2015] EWCA Civ 1310, [2016] 2 W.L.R. 1429 at [10] (indemnity clause).

[Add to note 137, line 15, after "[2014] 1 W.L.R. 3517 at [96]"*: page* [1145]]
; *Capita (Banstead 2011) Ltd v RFIB Group Ltd* [2015] EWCA Civ 1310, [2016]
2 W.L.R. 1429.

[Add text paragraph, at the end: page [1144]]
For this purpose, the Supreme Court has recently applied its general approach to
contractual construction to an indemnity clause in a detailed and professionally
drafted contract concluded by commercially sophisticated parties, therefore holding that the wording of an "avoidably opaque" clause must be examined in detail
in the context of the contract as a whole and taking into account whether the
wider factual matrix gives guidance as which is the better of its possible
interpretations.[137a] In this context, the Supreme Court found that the proper
interpretation of the indemnity clause (there relating to the circumstances which
trigger the indemnity) was "to be found principally in a careful examination of
the language which the parties have used".[137b]

[137a] *Wood v Capita Insurance Services Ltd* [2017] UKSC 24, [2017] 2 W.L.R. 1095 at [26].
[137b] *Wood v Capita Insurance Services Ltd* [2017] UKSC 24 per Lord Hodge J.S.C. (with whom
Lord Neuberger of Abbotsbury P.S.C., Lord Mance, Lord Clarke of Stone-cum-Ebony, Lord Sumption JJ.S.C. agreed).

Deliberate breaches

15–019 *[Add to note 144, line 5, after* "[17]–[19]"*: page* [1146]]
; *Polypearl Ltd v Building Research Establishment Ltd* Unreported, July 28, 2016
(Mercantile Ct) at [83] and [88].

4. Application of Principles of Construction to Particular Contracts

Sale of goods: terms as to quality, etc.

[*Delete text of note 200 and substitute: page* [1153]]   **15–030**
The relevant provisions of the 2015 Act were brought into force so as to apply
to consumer contracts made on or after October 1, 2015: see above, para.15–005
and also below, para.38–335.

Hire purchase

[*Add to paragraph, line 1, after* "October 1, 2015 (when the": *page* [1154]]   **15–031**
relevant provisions of

Carriage of goods: deviation

[*Add to note 213, at the end: page* [1155]]   **15–032**
However, the provisions in the 2015 Act relating to the exclusion or restriction
of liability in "services contracts" do not apply to certain "consumer transport
services" (certain rail passenger services, carriage by air, and sea and inland
waterway transport, all as specially defined by the 2015 Order art.2) until
October 1, 2016: 2015 Order arts 4 and 6(2) as amended by the Consumer Rights
Act 2015 (Commencement No.3, Transitional Provisions, Savings and Consequential Amendments) (Amendment) Order 2016 (SI 2016/484) art.2. See
further below, para.38–403.

Bailment: acts inconsistent with bailment

[*Add to note 236, at the end: page* [1158]]   **15–037**
On the qualifications on the general temporal application of the relevant provisions of the 2015 Act, see above, para.15–005.

5. Exemption Clauses and Third Parties

Effect of the 1999 Act: burden

[*Add to paragraph, line 23, before* "liability for negligence": *page* [1161]]   **15–044**
business

[*Add to note 265, at the end: page* [1162]]
On the qualifications on the date of the coming into force of the relevant
provisions of the 2015 Act in the case of "consumer transport services" see
above, para.15–005.

6. Legislative Control of Exemption Clauses

(a) *Unfair Contract Terms Act 1977*

(i) *Overview*

Consumer Rights Act 2015

15–064   [*Delete text of note 351 and substitute: page* [1175]]
The relevant provisions of Pts 1 and 2 of the 2015 Act came into force (with
certain qualifications in relation to "consumer transport services") on October 1,
2015, on which see above, para.15–005 and below, para.38–335.

[*In paragraph, line 16, delete* "will be two principal legislative" *and substitute:
page* [1175]]
are two principle legislative

(ii) *The Pattern of Control: Key Definitions*

Varieties of exemption clause

15–070   [*Add to note 378, line 4, after* "[1981] C.L.J. 108": *page* [1177]]
; White (2016) J.B.L. 373

[*Add to note 386, last line, after* "see above, para.7–149": *page* [1178]]
; *Crestsign Ltd v National Westminster Bank Plc* [2014] EWHC 3043 (Ch) at
[112]–[119] (permission to appeal on other grounds: [2015] EWCA Civ 986);
Thornbridge Ltd v Barclays Bank Plc [2015] EWHC 3430 (QB) at [97]–[111]
(appeal pending) (on "basis clauses" stipulating that defendants were not providing advice in relation to interest rate "swap agreements")

The new law: "dealing as consumer" deleted from the 1977 Act

15–079   [*Add to note 410, at the end: page* [1181]]
On the qualifications on the date of the coming into force of the relevant
provisions of the 2015 Act in the case of "consumer transport services" see
above, para.15–005.

(iii) *The Controls Provided by the 1977 Act*

Negligence liability: the new law

15–083   [*Add to note 430, at the end: page* [1183]]
On the qualifications on the date of the coming into force of the relevant
provisions of the 2015 Act in the case of "consumer transport services" see
above, para.15–005.

Liability arising in contract: the old law

[*Add new note 435a, after* "reference or by course of dealing." *in line 12: page* [1183]]

[435a] See the example of use of the RIBA Form of engagement in *British Fermentation Products Ltd v Compare Reavell Ltd* [1999] 2 All E.R. (Comm) 389 at [46] (H.H.J. Bowsher QC), expressly approved in *African Export-Import Bank v Shebah Exploration and Production Co Ltd* [2017] EWCA Civ 845 at [20] (Longmore L.J.).

15–084

[*Add to paragraph, after new note 435a, line 12: page* [1183]]

The requirement that the term is part of the other party's standard terms of business has been held to mean that "it has to be shown that that other party habitually uses those terms of business" and it is not enough that a model form has, on the particular occasion, been used.[435b]

[435b] *African Export-Import Bank v Shebah Exploration and Production Co Ltd* [2017] EWCA Civ 845 at [20] per Longmore L.J. (with whom Henderson L.J. agreed).

[*Add to note 436, last line, after* "[2015] EWHC 1280 (QB) at [91]–[95]": *page* [1184]]

; *Commercial Management (Investments) Ltd v Mitchell Design & Construct Ltd* [2016] EWHC 76 (TCC) at [61]–[73] (A's standard terms incorporated only to the extent to which B's terms did not prevail over them, term held still one of A's "written standard terms of business")

[*Add to paragraph, at the end: page* [1184]]

In *African Export-Import Bank v Shebah Exploration and Production Co Ltd* Longmore L.J. observed that for this purpose:

> "it is relevant to enquire whether there have been more than insubstantial variations to the terms which may otherwise have been habitually used by the other party to the transaction. If there have been substantial variations, it is unlikely to be the case that the party relying on the Act will have discharged the burden on him to show that the contract has been made 'on the other's written standard terms of business'."[437a]

Where there is "substantial negotiation" (including the proposed amendment of the draft contract) this may be enough to demonstrate that the terms ultimately agreed were not standard business terms even though the particular term was not itself affected: "[t]here is . . . no requirement that negotiations must relate to the exclusion terms of the contract, if the Act is not to apply".[437b]

[437a] [2017] EWCA Civ 845 at [25] per Longmore L.J. (with whom Henderson L.J. agreed), approving dicta in *McCrone v Boots Farm Sales* [1981] S.L.T. 103 at 105; *Hadley Design Associates v Westminster City Council* [2003] EWHC 1617 (TCC), [2004] T.C.L.R. 1 at [78].
[437b] [2017] EWCA Civ 845 at [36] per Longmore L.J.

Liability arising in contract: the new law

[*Add to note 455, at the end: page* [1186]]

On the qualifications on the date of the coming into force of the relevant provisions of the 2015 Act in the case of "consumer transport services" see above, para.15–005.

15–087

Indemnity clauses: the new law

15–090   [*Add to note 465, at the end: page* [1187]]
On the qualifications on the date of the coming into force of the relevant provisions of the 2015 Act in the case of "consumer transport services" see above, para.15–005.

(iv) *Test of Reasonableness*

Guidelines

15–097   [*Add to note 508, at the end: page* [1192]]
cf. *Thornbridge Ltd v Barclays Bank Plc* [2015] EWHC 3430 (QB) at [116] (appeal pending) (equal bargaining power evidenced by party threatening to go elsewhere); *Polypearl Ltd v Building Research Establishment Ltd* Unreported, July 28, 2016 (Mercantile Ct) at [105]; *Halsall v Champion Consulting Ltd* [2017] EWHC 1079 (QB) at [297].

[*Add to note 510, at the end: page* [1192]]
; *Polypearl Ltd v Building Research Establishment Ltd* Unreported, July 28, 2016 (Mercantile Ct) at [105].

[*Add to note 511, at the end: page* [1193]]
; *Commercial Management (Investments) Ltd v Mitchell Design & Construct Ltd* [2016] EWHC 76 (TCC) at [86]–[88].

Limits on amount

15–099   [*Add new note 514a, line 15, after* "can be obtained,": *page* [1193]]
[514a] The statement in the text was approved by *Goodlife Foods Ltd v Hall Fire Protection Ltd* [2017] EWHC 767 (TCC), [2017] B.L.R. 389 at [76] and [80]–[87].

[*Add to note 515, at the end: page* [1194]]
; *Goodlife Foods Ltd v Hall Fire Protection Ltd* [2017] EWHC 767 (TCC), [2017] B.L.R. 389 at [76].

Powers of the court

15–112   [*Add to note 577, at the end: page* [1202]]
; *Goodlife Foods Ltd v Hall Fire Protection Ltd* [2017] EWHC 767 (TCC), [2017] B.L.R. 389 at [70].

[*Add new note 577a, at the end of paragraph: page* [1202]]
[577a] e.g. *Trolex Products Ltd v Merrol Fire Protection Engineers Ltd* Unreported, November 20, 1991 CA, (contrasting views of Staughton and Nourse L.JJ. as to whether a clause should be treated as one or more "terms" for the purposes of the Act); *Goodlife Foods Ltd v Hall Fire Protection Ltd* [2017] EWHC 767 (TCC), [2017] B.L.R. 389 at [71] (though expressly obiter).

[*In lines 5-6, delete* "it would appear that ... could nevertheless" *and substitute: page* [1202]]   **15–114**
the term, while being ineffective to exclude or restrict the former liability, may nevertheless

[*Delete text of note 580 and substitute: page* [1202]]
Trolex Products Ltd v Merrol Fire Protection Engineers Ltd Unreported, November 20, 1991 CA, (under issue B(viii)), quoting with approval the view then tentatively expressed by the equivalent paragraph to para.15-114 in 26th edn, 1989; *Goodlife Foods Ltd v Hall Fire Protection Ltd* [2017] EWHC 767 (TCC), [2017] B.L.R. 389 at [66]–[70] (distinguishing the issue of the "excision" of part of a term wholly ineffective under the 1977 Act and the issue considered in *Stewart Gill Ltd v Horatio Myer & Co Ltd* [1992] Q.B. 600 where it was held that a party had to show that the whole of a term was reasonable and not merely that part of a term on which it wished to rely).

(v) *Exclusions from the Scope of the 1977 Act or Some of its Provisions*

Specific exceptions

[*Add to note 584, after* "The Act": *page* [1203]]   **15–116**
generally

Schedule 1

[*Add to paragraph, line 5, before* "the Consumer Rights Act": *page* [1204]]   **15–118**
the relevant provisions of

[*Add to note 594, at the end: page* [1204]]
The general date of the coming into force of the 2015 Act on October 1, 2015 has an exception as regards "consumer transport services" (as specially defined) in relation to which the relevant provisions of the 2015 Act come into force only for contracts made on or after October 1, 2016: the Consumer Rights Act 2015 (Commencement No.3, Transitional Provisions, Savings and Consequential Amendments) Order 2015 (SI 2015/1630) art.4 and 6(2) as amended by the Consumer Rights Act 2015 (Commencement No.3, Transitional Provisions, Savings and Consequential Amendments) (Amendment) Order 2016 (SI 2016/484) art.2. This applies to the amendments to Sch.1 of the 1977 Act: SI 2015/1630 art.4(c) referring, inter alia, to the 2015 Act Sch.4 paras 26 and 27.

[*Add to note 600, at the end: page* [1205]]   **15–119**
For the special position of "consumer transport services" see above, para.15–118 n.594.

[*Add to paragraph, line 13, before* "coming into force of": *page* [1205]]
the relevant provisions of

International supply contracts

[*Add to note 607, at the end: page* [1205]]   **15–122**
As regards "consumer transport services" the deletion of the reference to s.4 of the 1977 Act applies only to contracts made or on after October 1, 2016: SI

2015/1630 arts 4(c) and 6(2) (as amended by the Consumer Rights Act 2015 (Commencement No.3, Transitional Provisions, Savings and Consequential Amendments) (Amendment) Order 2016 (SI 2016/484) art.2) referring to the 2015 Act Sch.4 para.23.

Contractual provisions authorised or required by statute or international agreement

15–123   [*In note 614, delete second sentence and substitute: page* [1206]]
This amendment generally comes into force as regards contracts made on or after October 1, 2015, but this finds an exception as regards "consumer transport services" where the relevant date is October 1, 2016: SI 2015/1630 arts 3(g), 4(c) and 6(2) (as amended by SI 2016/484 art.2) referring to the 2015 Act Sch.4 para.25.

Choice of English law clauses

15–125   [*Add to paragraph, line 10, before* "the Consumer Rights Act": *page* [1207]]
the relevant provisions of

[*Add new note 622a, after* "came into force" *in line 11: page* [1207]]
622a The changes noted in the text apply to "consumer transport services" where made on or after October 1, 2016: SI 2015/1630 arts 4(c) and 6(2) (as amended by SI 2016/484 art.2) referring to the 2015 Act Sch.4 para.24.

(vi) *Incidental Matters*

Anti-avoidance provisions

15–128   [*Add to note 635, at the end of first sentence: page* [1208]]
; *Times Travel (UK) Ltd v Pakistan International Airlines Corp* [2017] EWHC 1367 (Ch) at [273]–[275].

(b) *Misrepresentation Act 1967*

Liability for misrepresentation: the old law

15–130   [*Add to paragraph, line 2, before* "the Consumer Rights Act": *page* [1209]]
relevant provisions of

[*Delete text of note 639 and substitute: page* [1209]]
See below, para.15–131, n.642.

Liability for misrepresentation: the new law

15–131   [*In paragraph, line 2, delete* "the Consumer Rights Act 2015," *and substitute: page* [1209]]
of the relevant provisions of the Consumer Rights Act 2015 on October 1, 2015,

[Delete text of note 642 and substitute: page [1209]]
Consumer Rights Act 2015 (Commencement No.3, Transitional Provisions, Savings and Consequential Amendments) Order 2015 (SI 2015/1630) arts 3I and 6(1) and (4); the relevant provisions of the 2015 Act are ss.61–76 and Sch.4 para.1. For contracts made before October 1, 2015 see Main Work, Vol.II, para.38–334.

(c) *Other Legislation*

Finance

[Add new note 671a, at the end of paragraph: page [1212]]   **15–140**
671a With general effect from January 13, 2018 the substantive provisions of the Payment Services Regulations 2009 are revoked and replaced by the Payment Services Regulations 2017 (SI 2017/752) which implement in the UK Directive (EU) 2015/2366 of the European Parliament and of the Council of 25 November 2015 on payment services in the internal market [2015] O.J. L337/35 ("Second Payment Services Directive"). The 2017 Regulations reg.137 provides that "a payment service provider may not agree with a payment service user that it will not comply with any provision of these Regulations unless—(a) such agreement is permitted by these Regulations, or (b) such agreement provides for terms which are more favourable to the payment service user than the relevant provisions of these Regulations". Provisions in the 2017 Regulations allowing the exclusion of certain of their requirements include regs 40(7), 42(2)(b) and (c), 63(5) and 65(2).

Consumer protection legislation on unfair contract terms

[Add to paragraph, line 2, before "Consumer Rights Act": page [1212]]   **15–142**
relevant provisions of the

[Add to note 675, at the beginning: page [1212]]
Consumer Rights Act 2015 (Commencement No.3, Transitional Provisions, Savings and Consequential Amendments) Order 2015 (SI 2015/1630) arts 3(c), (g) and 6(4).

Mandatory character of much consumer protection legislation

[Add to note 682, line 5, before "See further Vol.II, para.38–134": page [1213]]   **15–143**
The 1990 Directive is repealed and replaced by Directive (EU) 2015/2302 on package travel and linked travel arrangements [2015] O.J. L326/1, art.23 of which provides for the "imperative nature" of its provisions.

7. COMMON LAW QUALIFICATIONS

Acknowledgements

[Add to note 703, at the end: page [1216]]   **15–147**
; *Crestsign Ltd v National Westminster Bank Plc* [2014] EWHC 3043 (Ch) at [112]–[119] (permission to appeal on other grounds: [2015] EWCA Civ 986); *Thornbridge Ltd v Barclays Bank Plc* [2015] EWHC 3430 (QB), at [97]–[111]

(appeal pending) (on "basis clauses" stipulating that defendants were not providing advice in relation to interest rate "swap agreements").

8. Force Majeure Clauses

Burden of proof

15–155   [*Add to note 739, line 12, after* "[2013] EWCA Civ 1628 at [22]"*: page* [1220]] (the application of the "prohibition clause" was not in issue before the SC [2015] UKSC 43, [2015] Bus. L.R. 987).

"Prevented" clauses

15–156   [*Add to note 748, penultimate line, after* "connection must be shown"*: page* [1222]] (the application of the "prohibition clause" was not in issue before the SC [2015] UKSC 43, [2015] Bus. L.R. 987).

15–157   [*Add to note 754, at the end: page* [1223]] (the application of the "prohibition clause" was not in issue before the SC [2015] UKSC 43, [2015] Bus. L.R. 987).

"Force majeure"

15–162   [*Add to note 776, at the end: page* [1225]]
cf. the Payment Services Regulations 2017 (SI 2017/752) (in force generally January 13, 2018) reg.96 ("Force majeure") which provides that: "(1) A person is not liable for any contravention of a requirement imposed on it by or under this Part [of the Regulations] where the contravention is due to abnormal and unforeseeable circumstances beyond the person's control, the consequences of which would have been unavoidable despite all efforts to the contrary; (2) A payment service provider is not liable for any contravention of a requirement imposed on it by or under this Part where the contravention is due to the obligations of the payment service provider under other provisions of EU or national law". Regulation 96 implements in UK law Directive (EU) 2015/2366 of the European Parliament and of the Council of 25 November 2015 on payment services in the internal market [2015] O.J. L337/35 ("Second Payment Services Directive") art.93 (which is, however, entitled "abnormal and unforeseeable circumstances" rather than "force majeure").

[*Add to note 777, at the end: page* [1225]]
The French Civil Code as promulgated did not define *cause étrangère* or force majeure but its provisions on general contract law were revised (with effect from October 1, 2016) and the new art.1218 al.1 (as enacted by *Ordonnance* No.2016-131 of February 10, 2016) provides that: "[i]n contractual matters, there is force majeure where an event beyond the control of the debtor, which could not reasonably have been foreseen at the time of the conclusion of the contract and

whose effects could not be avoided by appropriate measures, prevents performance of his obligation by the debtor" (trans. Cartwright, Fauvarque-Cosson and
Whittaker).

[*Add to note 803, line 7, after* "[2002] C.L.Y. 4043 (Cty Ct)": *page* [1228]]   **15–164**
The 1990 Directive is repealed and replaced by Directive (EU) 2015/2302 on
package travel and linked travel arrangements [2015] O.J. L326/1, which does
not use the expression "force majeure" but instead refers to "unavoidable and
extraordinary circumstances", which art.3(12) defines as "a situation beyond the
control of the party who invokes such a situation and the consequences of which
could not have been avoided even if all reasonable measures had been taken". In
addition, art.14(3)(b) of the 2015 Directive provides that the organiser does not
have to pay the traveller compensation in respect of "non-conformity" of the
package where he proves, inter alia, that this is "attributable to a third party
unconnected with the provision of the travel services included in the package
travel contract and is unforeseeable or unavoidable".

Part Five

ILLEGALITY AND PUBLIC POLICY

CHAPTER 16

ILLEGALITY AND PUBLIC POLICY

1. Introduction

Underlying principle

[*Add to paragraph, after note 2: page* [1236]]
As a result of the recent decision of the Supreme Court in *Patel v Mirza*[2a] this is now the question that the court poses in addressing the question of the effect of illegality in contractual claims.

[2a] [2016] UKSC 42, [2016] 1 W.L.R. 399.

16–001

[*In paragraph, lines 20–22, delete* "As will be seen . . . parties to illegal contracts.[4]"*: page* [1236]]

A problematic topic

[*In paragraph, line 11, delete* "*Jetivia SA v Bilta (UK) Ltd*" *and substitute: page* [1236]]
Jetivia SA v Bilta (UK) Ltd (reported sub nom. *Bilta (UK) Ltd v Nazir (No.2)*)

16–002

[*Add to paragraph, line 14, after* "as appropriately possible . . . "*: page* [1237]]
This the Supreme Court did in *Patel v Mirza*.[11a]

[11a] [2016] UKSC 42, [2016] 1 W.L.R. 399.

2. The Position At Common Law

(a) *Generally*

Scope of public policy

[*Add to note 35, at the end: page* [1240]]
: *Hounga v Allen* [2014] UKSC 47, [2014] 1 W.L.R. 2889.

16–006

(b) *Contracts involving the commission of a legal wrong*

(i) *Introduction*

Nature of the public policy when contracts involve commission of a legal wrong

[*Add to note 44, at the end: page* [1241]]
See also *Patel v Mirza* [2016] UKSC 42.

16–009

[*Add to note 46, at the end: page* [1241]]
; and *Patel v Mirza* [2016] UKSC 42.

How illegality may affect a contract

16–011   [*In paragraph, lines 29–32, delete* "The defence of illegality . . . to any particular dispute".*52" and substitute: page* [1242]]
However many of these criticisms are no longer valid in the light of the Supreme Court decision in *Patel v Mirza.*52

   52 [2016] UKSC 42, [2016] 1 W.L.R. 399; see below, para.16–014B.

A more flexible approach adopted by the Court of Appeal

16–012   [*Delete the existing title to the paragraph and add to the beginning of paragraph: page* [1242]]
Developments before *Patel v Mirza. In the light of the judgment in Patel v Mirza*53a the text in paras 16–612—16–614 is mainly of historical interest.

   53a [2016] UKSC 42, [2016] 1 W.L.R. 399.

Disagreement in the Supreme Court

16–014   [*In paragraph, lines 19–20, delete* "In the latest illegality case . . . *v Nazir (No.2)" and substitute: page* [1246]]
In *Jetivia SA v Bilta (UK) Ltd* (reported sub nom. *Bilta (UK) Ltd v Nazir (No.2)*)

   [*In paragraph, line 30, delete* "is a pressing need" *and substitute: page* [1246]]
was a pressing need

   [*In paragraph, sentence after note 89, delete* "*Jetivia*" *and substitute: page* [1246]]
Bilta (UK) Ltd

   [*Add to note 91, at the end: page* [1247]]
In *Top Brands Ltd v Sharma* [2015] EWCA Civ 1140 the Court of Appeal pointed out the different approaches and considered "that the proper approach to the defence of illegality needs to be addressed by the Supreme Court (conceivably with a panel of nine Justices) as soon as appropriately possible . . . " at [38], a view identical to that of Lord Neuberger in *Bilta (UK) Ltd* [2015] UKSC 23, [2016] A.C. 1 at [15], see Main Work, Vol.I, para.16–002.

   [*In paragraph, before note 93, delete* "*Jetivia*" *and substitute: page* [1247]]
Bilta (UK) Ltd

   [*Delete sentence of sub-paragraph beginning* "Therefore for the time being . . . " *and substitute: page* [1247]]
Therefore after the *Bilta (UK) Ltd* case it had to be assumed that the flexible approach advocated by the Law Commission and adopted by the Court of Appeal92 did not represent the law, though the issue remained open for review by the Supreme Court.

   92 See above, para.16–012.

   [*Add to note 94, at the end: page* [1247]]
, [2016] Q.B. 23, [2015] 4 All E.R. 495

[*Add new paragraphs 16–014A—16–014L: page* [1247]]

A new approach. In *Patel v Mirza*[101a] the Supreme Court fundamentally recast the doctrine of illegality in contract. The law remains that the court will not order performance or grant damages for breach of a contract if the claim should not be enforced because of illegality, but the question is to be decided on a "factors-based approach". However, the court will normally order restitution of any money or property transferred under it.[101b] The result is that much of the previous law on judicial remedies with respect to illegal contracts is mainly of historical interest.[101c]

16–014A

[101a] [2016] UKSC 42, [2016] 1 W.L.R. 399.
[101b] See paras 16–014B et seq.
[101c] This is particularly so of law set out in Main Work, Vol.I, paras 16–008—16–014.

Patel v Mirza. In *Patel v Mirza*[101d] P transferred £620,000 to M for the purchase of shares in a listed company on the basis of information from contacts in the listed company. The information from the company contacts was an anticipated government announcement which would affect the price of the shares. The agreement between P and M constituted the criminal offence of insider trading under s.52 of the Criminal Justice Act 1993. The government announcement did not materialise and P brought an action against M to recover the £620,000 he had transferred to M. The claim was put on various grounds, one of which was unjust enrichment; as the money had been transferred for a consideration that failed, P claimed to be entitled to recover it. In order to show such failure P had to disclose the illegality involving the insider trading. The Supreme Court held that the doctrine of illegality (ex turpi causa) applied to unjust enrichment actions[101e] but on the facts P was entitled to rescind the contract and recover his money. Both the first instance judge and the Court of Appeal[101f] considered that the claim for unjust enrichment was precluded by the decision in *Tinsley v Milligan*[101g] as the claimant had to rely on his illegality. However, the Court of Appeal, disagreeing with the court at first instance, held that the claimant could rely on the *locus poenitentiae* principle.[101h] In *Patel v Mirza*[101i] the Supreme Court considered that the reasoning in *Tinsley* "should no longer be followed"[101j] but the result was considered correct as it would "have been disproportionate to have prevented her from enforcing her equitable interest in the property and conversely to have left Miss Tinsley unjustly enriched."[101k]

16–014B

[101d] [2016] UKSC 42, [2016] 1 W.L.R. 399 (a panel of nine Justices).
[101e] *Patel v Mirza* [2016] UKSC 42 at [2]: "Illegality has the potential to provide a defence to civil claims of all sorts, whether relating to contract, property, tort, or unjust enrichment, and in a wide variety of circumstances".
[101f] [2015] Ch. 271. Gloster L.J. held that the claimant could recover as he did not have to rely on the illegal contract to recover his money.
[101g] [1994] 1 A.C. 340. The Supreme Court in *Patel* considered this judgment to be wrong: see below, para.16–198.
[101h] See below, paras 16–205—16–207.
[101i] [2016] UKSC 42.
[101j] [2016] UKSC 42 at [110].
[101k] [2016] UKSC 42 at [112].

A "factors-based" approach. Lord Toulson gave the majority judgment of the court in *Patel v Mirza*,[101l] which upheld the Court of Appeal's judgment in favour of recovery by the claimant but on a different basis than that of the court. The action in *Patel v Mirza* was not an action to enforce an illegal contract but

16–014C

to obtain restitution and recover money transferred under an illegal contract.[101m] However, the Court laid down a fundamentally different approach to the effect of illegality with respect to contract, tort, restitutionary and property claims. The issue before the court was "whether the policy underlying the rule which made the contract . . . illegal would be stultified"[101n] if the claim (on the facts, a claim for unjustified enrichment) were to succeed. In answering the question of whether allowing recovery for a claim tainted with illegality would be harmful to the integrity of the legal system, the court could not do so without[101o]

> "a) considering the underlying purpose of the prohibition that has been transgressed, b) considering conversely other relevant public policies which may be rendered ineffective or less effective by denial of the claim, and c) keeping in mind the possibility of overkill unless the law is applied with a due sense of proportionality."

Thus the law in illegality in contract is no longer a prescriptive, mechanical rule but rather involves a determination of whether the policy underlying a particular rule would be advanced or frustrated by the application of the rule. The court granted restitutionary recovery to prevent the unjust enrichment of the defendant.

[101l] [2016] UKSC 42 (the minority judgments also favoured recovery).
[101m] On the remedy of restitution see para.16–194.
[101n] [2016] UKSC 42 at [115].
[101o] [2016] UKSC 42 at [101].

16–014D   **Rule-based approach vs range of factors approach.** In *Patel v Mirza*[101p] Lord Toulson set out two alternative approaches in analysing the law of illegality in contract developed by Professor Burrows—the "rule-based approach" and the "range of factors approach".[101q]

[101p] [2016] UKSC 42.
[101q] Burrows, *Restatement of the English Law of Contract* (OUP, 2016) at pp.221–223.

16–014E   **Rule-based approach.** A possible example of a rule-based approach given by Burrows would be a single master rule involving reliance:

> "If the formation, purpose or performance of a contract involves conduct that is illegal (such as a crime) or contrary to public policy (such as a restraint of trade), a party cannot enforce the contract if he has to rely on that conduct to establish its claim."[101r]

Burrows then sets out a more extended analysis of the rule-based approach which goes beyond the reliance rule. This approach involved two core rules: Rule 1 refers to "illegality in formation", that is, the contract is illegal as made, and Rule 2 referring to "illegality in performance".[101s] Burrows considers that the rule-based approach is fatally flawed because it will simply be too complex, it fails to distinguish between serious and trivial illegalities, in practice it does not give rise to greater certainty, and it is well nigh impossible to formulate comprehensive rules with appropriate exceptions to cover all eventualities.[101t] The law of illegality needs to have a greater degree of flexibility than that allowed by a rule-based approach.

[101r] Burrows, *Restatement of the English Law of Contract* (2016) at p.224.
[101s] Burrows, *Restatement of the English Law of Contract* (2016) at p.225.
[101t] [2016] UKSC 42 at [87]–[92] where Lord Toulson sets out the criticisms of Burrows, *Restatement of the English Law of Contract* (2016) at pp.224–229.

Range of factors approach. A possible formulation of range of factors approach **16–014F**
is set out by Burrows as follows[101u]:

> "If the formation, purpose or performance of a contract involves conduct that is
> illegal (such as a crime) or contrary to public policy (such as a restraint of trade), the
> contract is unenforceable by one or either party if to deny enforcement would be an
> appropriate response to that conduct, taking into account where relevant–
> (a) how seriously illegal or contrary to public policy the conduct was;
> (b) whether the party seeking enforcement knew of, or intended, the conduct;
> (c) how central to the contract or its performance the conduct was;
> (d) how serious a sanction the denial of enforcement is for the party seeking
>   enforcement;
> (e) whether denying enforcement will further the purpose of the rule which the
>   conduct has infringed;
> (f) whether denying enforcement will act as a deterrent to conduct that is illegal
>   or contrary to public policy;
> (g) whether denying enforcement will ensure that the party seeking enforcement
>   does not profit from the conduct;
> (h) whether denying enforcement will avoid inconsistency in the law thereby
>   maintaining the integrity of the legal system."[101v]

Lord Toulson found the Burrows list "helpful" but that he "would not attempt to
lay down a prescriptive or definitive list because of the infinite variety of
cases".[101w]

[101u] Burrows, *Restatement of the English Law of Contract* (2016) at pp.229–230 cited in *Patel v
Mirza* [2016] UKSC 42 at [93].
[101v] Burrows notes that the final factor could be given a wider or narrower interpretation depending
on the meaning attached to inconsistency: Burrows, *Restatement of the English Law of Contract*
(2016) at p.230.
[101w] [2016] UKSC 42 at [107]. Lord Neuberger also considered that it was not "helpful to list all
the potentially relevant factors": [2016] UKSC 42 at [173].

Lord Neuberger's view. Lord Neuberger saw the issue in *Patel v Mirza*[101x] as **16–014G**
involving:

> "a claim for the return of money paid by the claimant to the defendant pursuant to
> a contract to carry out an illegal activity, and the illegal activity is not in the event
> proceeded with owing to matters beyond the control of either party."

He considered that in such a case "the general rule should . . . be that the claimant
is entitled to the return of the money which he has paid".[101y] He referred to this
as "the Rule".[101z] The Rule should apply in appropriate cases "even where the
contemplated illegal activity has been performed in part or in whole".[101aa] The
Rule required a determination of what constitutes an illegal contract. Lord
Neuberger considered that this would involve "a contract where the illegality
would result in the court (if it could otherwise do so) not being able to award
specific performance of the contract or damages for its breach",[101ab] this would
obviously apply to a contract whose whole purpose or essential ingredient was
the commission of a crime.[101ac] The application of the Rule was subject to
possible exceptions, two of which were identified by Lord Neuberger. The first
was where the criminal legislation was designed to protect one of the parties to
the contract.[101ad] The second was where the defendant was "unaware of the facts
which gave rise to the illegality"[101ae] particularly where "he had received money
and had altered his position so that it might be oppressive to expect him to repay
it".[101af] This second exception, ignorance of the facts and alteration of position,

adds considerable flexibility to the illegality principle. Lord Neuberger also addressed the criticism that the Rule would come close to enforcing the contract. He conceded that this was indeed the case and that "application of the Rule would sometimes involve the court making an order whose effect in practice is similar to performance of the illegal contract".[101ag] An example, not given by Lord Neuberger, would be an illegal lending contract where the borrower had to repay the money. He considered that there was nothing to this point that the Rule could produce an outcome equivalent to performance; if a "particular outcome is correct, then the mere fact that the same outcome could have been arrived at on a wrong basis does not make it a wrong outcome".[101ah] This view was questioned by Lord Sumption. As Lord Sumption pointed out "an order for restitution would be functionally indistinguishable from an order for enforcement, as in the case of an illegal loan or a foreign exchange contract".[101ai] Citing *Boissevain v Weil*[101aj] for the principle that "if the law will not enforce an agreement it will not give the same financial relief under a different label",[101ak] he was "inclined to think that the principle is sound"[101al] but preferred not to express a concluded view.

[101x] [2016] UKSC 42 at [145].
[101y] [2016] UKSC 42 at [146].
[101z] [2016] UKSC 42 at [146].
[101aa] [2016] UKSC 42 at [167].
[101ab] [2016] UKSC 42 at [159].
[101ac] [2016] UKSC 42 at [159].
[101ad] [2016] UKSC 42 at [162].
[101ae] [2016] UKSC 42 at [162].
[101af] [2016] UKSC 42 at [162].
[101ag] [2016] UKSC 42 at [171].
[101ah] [2016] UKSC 42 at [171].
[101ai] [2016] UKSC 42 at [255].
[101aj] [1950] A.C. 327.
[101ak] [2016] UKSC 42 at [255].
[101al] [2016] UKSC 42 at [255].

16–014H In relation to contract claims generally, Lord Neuberger favoured the approach of Lord Toulson,[101am] and although his "analysis might be slightly different" there was no difference in practice.[101an] He preferred this to the "multi-factorial" approach of Burrows as the approach of Lord Toulson was a "structured approach" and not "akin in practice to a discretion . . . ".[101ao]

[101am] [2016] UKSC 42 at [174]–[175], referring to Lord Toulson's judgment at [101].
[101an] [2016] UKSC 42 at [186]. Lord Clarke considered that Lord Neuberger "expressed some support for the approach of Lord Toulson" but he was not persuaded by his reasoning that it was appropriate: [2016] UKSC 42 at [223].
[101ao] [2016] UKSC 42 at [175].

16–014I **The minority approach: Lord Mance.** Lord Mance, agreeing with Lord Sumption,[101ap] considered that the right of a party to recover property or money transferred under an illegal transaction was a consequence of the exercise of the right of rescission and this "right should be restored to its former significance and generalised".[101aq] The principle of rescission should not be restricted, "the logic of the principle is that the illegal transaction should be disregarded, and the parties restored to the position in which they would have been, had they never entered into it".[101ar] There should be no objection to permitting rescission after part performance "by making, where possible appropriate adjustments for benefits received . . . ".[101as] He specifically dissented from the decision of Lord

Neuberger on certain points.[101at] He could not see how "an imbalance or lack of parity of delict between the parties could act as a necessary or even probable bar to rescission".[101au] More generally, Lord Mance considered that Lord Toulson and the majority had attempted to rewrite the law of illegality on the basis of the reasoning of the Canadian Supreme Court in *Hall v Hebert*[101av]; which is set out in Lord Toulson's judgment.[101aw] Lord Mance was critical of such an approach as it would "introduce not only a new era but entirely novel dimensions into an issue of illegality".[101ax] Under such an approach the[101ay]:

> "Courts would be required to make a value judgment, by reference to a widely spread, mélange of ingredients, about the overall 'merits' or strengths, in a highly unspecific non-legal sense, of the prospective claims of the public interest and of each of the parties."

[101ap] [2016] UKSC 42 at [245]–[252].
[101aq] [2016] UKSC 42 at [197].
[101ar] [2016] UKSC 42 at [197]. In his opinion this principle had considerable lineage citing Mellish L.J. in *Taylor v Bowers* [1876] 1 Q.B.D. 291 at 300.
[101as] [2016] UKSC 42 at [198].
[101at] Set out at [2016] UKSC 42 at [162] and dealt with above, para.16–014E.
[101au] [2016] UKSC 42 at [198].
[101av] [1993] 2 S.C.R. 159.
[101aw] Lord Toulson also referred to the Burrows range of factors approach: [2016] UKSC 42 at [93].
[101ax] [2016] UKSC 42 at [206].
[101ay] [2016] UKSC 42 at [206].

The minority: Lord Sumption. Lord Sumption considered that as regards the enforcement of a claim founded on an illegal act the underlying principle is that for reasons of consistency the court will not give effect, at the suit of a person who committed the illegal act (or someone claiming through him), to a right derived from that act. By "consistency", citing extensively from the judgment of McLachlin J. in *Hall v Hebert*,[101az] he meant that the law should not "allow a person to profit from illegal or wrongful conduct or would permit an evasion or rebate of a penalty prescribed by the criminal laws".[101ba] The law "cannot give with one hand what it takes away with the other".[101bb]   **16–014J**

[101az] [1993] 2 S.C.R. 159 at 169 (now Chief Justice McLachlin). Also analysed by Lord Toulson at [2016] UKSC 42 at [55]–[61].
[101ba] [2016] UKSC 42 at [230] citing the judgment of McLachlin J. in *Hall v Hebert* [1993] 2 S.C.R. 159 at 169.
[101bb] *Hounga v Allen* [2014] UKSC 47, [2014] 1 W.L.R. 2889 at [55] (a dissenting judgment but not on this point) cited in *Patel v Mirza* [2016] UKSC 42 at [232].

Lord Sumption considered that the test for determining the effect of illegality was whether a party was relying on the illegality, the "reliance test".[101bc] The reliance test was the "narrowest test of connection" between the illegality and the contract, all alternative tests would widen the application of the defence of illegality and render its application more uncertain.[101bd] The strength of the test was that (a) it gave "effect to the basic principle that a person may not derive a legal right from his own illegal act",[101be] (b) it established a direct causal link between the illegality and the claim and distinguished between collateral or background facts,[101bf] and (c) it ensured that the illegality principle would not be applied more widely than was needed to prevent legal rights from being derived from illegal acts.[101bg] In opting for the reliance test, Lord Sumption rejected the   **16–014K** test that the facts relied on should be "inextricably linked" with the illegal act on the grounds that it is "far from clear what the test means".[101bh]

[101bc] *Patel v Mirza* [2016] UKSC 42 at [239].
[101bd] [2016] UKSC 42 at [239].
[101be] [2016] UKSC 42 at [239].
[101bf] [2016] UKSC 42 at [239].
[101bg] [2016] UKSC 42 at [239].
[101bh] [2016] UKSC 42 at [240].

16–014L Lord Sumption also dealt with the "range of factors" approach[101bi] put forward by Burrows[101bj] which he considered was derived from the Law Commission Consultative Report[101bk] on illegality.[101bl] As regards the range of factors identified by the Law Commission and Professor Burrows the important issue for Lord Sumption was whether these factors are to be regarded[101bm]:

"(i) as part of the policy rationale of a legal rule and the various exceptions to that rule, or (ii) as matters to be taken into account by a judge deciding in each case whether to apply the legal rule at all."

Lord Sumption considered that the former approach represents the law. The latter would require the courts to "weigh or balance, the adverse consequences of respectively granting or refusing relief on a case by case basis"[101bn] an approach that had been rejected in *Tinsley v Milligan*.[101bo] He considered that as the principle of illegality was based on public policy, the "operation of the principle cannot depend on the evaluation of the equities as between the parties or the proportionality of its impact upon the claimant".[101bp] The range of factors approach would largely devalue the principle of consistency because it resulted in the court making an evaluative judgment as to the weights to be attributed to the various factors.[101bq] He considered that factor (g) of the Burrows schema ("whether denying enforcement will ensure that the party seeking enforcement does not profit from his conduct") was "fundamental to the principle of consistency, and not just a factor to be weighed against others".[101br]

Lord Sumption also strongly objected to factor (a) ("how seriously illegal or contrary to public policy the conduct was") as it was "difficult to reconcile with any kind of principle the notion that there may be degrees of illegality as Professor Burrows' factor (a) seems to envisage".[101bs] Such a rule would depend "on the court's view of how illegal the illegality was or how much it matters"[101bt] and there would be "no principle whatever to guide the evaluation other than the judge's gut instinct".[101bu] The adoption of the range of factors approach would discard "any requirement for an analytical connection between the illegality and the claim"[101bv] by making it one factor in a broad evaluation of the case without offering "guidance as to what sort of connection might be relevant".[101bw] Lord Sumption dissented from the conclusion of Lord Toulson[101bx] that the illegality principle should depend on the "policy factors involved and . . . and the circumstances of the illegal conduct".[101by] Lord Sumption considered that this was:

" . . . far too vague and potentially far too wide to serve as the basis on which a person may be denied his legal rights. . . . it converts a legal principle into an exercise of judicial discretion, in the process exhibiting all the vices of 'complexity, uncertainty, arbitrariness and lack of transparency'."[101bz]

He considered that the remedy of restitution would not give effect to the illegal act but "return the parties to the status quo ante where they should always have been . . . This was Gloster LJ's main reason for upholding Mr Patel's right to recover the money".[101ca]

Lord Clarke gave a brief judgment agreeing with Lord Sumption's reasons[101cb] for rejecting the "range of factors" approach.[101cc]

[101bi] [2016] UKSC 42 at [259].
[101bj] Burrows, *Restatement of the Law of Contract* (2016) at pp.229–231.
[101bk] *The Illegality Defence* (LCCP 189, 2009).
[101bl] [2016] UKSC 42 at [259].
[101bm] [2016] UKSC 42 at [261].
[101bn] [2016] UKSC 42 at [261].
[101bo] [1994] 1 A.C. 340.
[101bp] [2016] UKSC 42 at [262(i)].
[101bq] [2016] UKSC 42 at [262(ii)].
[101br] [2016] UKSC 42 at [262(ii)] Lord Sumption mistakenly refers to this as factor (f).
[101bs] [2016] UKSC 42 at [262(iii)].
[101bt] [2016] UKSC 42 at [262(iii)].
[101bu] [2016] UKSC 42 at [262(iii)].
[101bv] [2016] UKSC 42 at [262(iii)].
[101bw] [2016] UKSC 42 at [262(iii)].
[101bx] [2016] UKSC 42 at [265].
[101by] Lord Toulson at [2016] UKSC 42 at [109].
[101bz] [2016] UKSC 42 at [265].
[101ca] [2016] UKSC 42 at [268]. Lord Sumption considered that a possible objection to this is that the court should not sully itself by being involved with the illegality as not being a "reputable foundation for the law of illegality": [2016] UKSC 42 at [268].
[101cb] These are set out in para.16–014K.
[101cc] [2016] UKSC 42 at [216]. See also [223] where he disagrees with Lord Neuberger in so far as the latter supports the opinion of Lord Toulson. The criticisms of the "range of factors approach" are set out above, para.16–014L.

Illegality as to formation

[*Add to paragraph, at the beginning: page* [1248]]   **16–016**
The following paragraphs[106a] reflect "a rules based approach" to illegality as this was the basis on which the cases were decided. However, *Patel v Mirza*[106b] has adopted "a range of factors approach",[106c] although even if this had been applicable it is questionable whether the cases would have been differently decided.

[106a] Main Work, Vol.I, paras 16–016—16–027.
[106b] [2016] UKSC 42, [2016] 1 W.L.R. 399.
[106c] See above, para.16–014F.

(ii) *Acts or Objects Which are Illegal by Common Law or by Statute*

Other civil wrongs

[*Add to paragraph, at the end: page* [1257]]   **16–027**
Patel v Mirza[181a] does not discuss the law on when a court will find that a civil wrong would render a contract illegal. However, the range of factors approach could well produce a result similar to that in *Les Laboratoires Servier v Apotex Inc.*[181b]

^{181a} [2016] UKSC 42.
^{181b} [2012] EWCA Civ 593.

(c) *Objects Injurious to Good Government*

(i) *Domestic Affairs*

Procurement of honours

16–030   [*Add to paragraph, after note 189: page* [1258]]
In *Parkinson v College of Ambulance Ltd*^{189a} the plaintiff had brought an unsuccessful action to recover money from a charity to which he had made a donation on the undertaking by the charity to secure a knighthood for the plaintiff. As Lord Toulson pointed out, where the bribe had been made to a public body such as a political party or the holder of a public office, it might be regarded "as more repugnant to the public interest that the recipient should keep it than that it should be returned".^{189b} In *Patel v Mirza*^{189c} Lord Neuberger stated that he considered that *Parkinson v College of Ambulance Ltd*^{189d} had been "wrongly decided".

^{189a} [1925] 2 K.B. 1.
^{189b} [2016] UKSC 42 at [118]. See also [2016] UKSC 42 at [228].
^{189c} [2016] UKSC 42 at [150].
^{189d} [1925] 2 K.B. 1.

(ii) *Foreign Affairs*

Contract forbidden in place of performance

16–041   [*Add to note 244, at the end: page* [1264]]
In *Eurobank Ergasias SA v Kalliroi Navigation Co Ltd* [2015] EWHC 2377 (Comm) at [36] the court considered "that *Ralli* remains good law" despite the Convention on the Law Applicable to Contractual Obligations (Rome Convention): see Main Work, Vol.I, paras 30–017 et seq.

(d) *Objects Injurious to the Proper Working of Justice*

(iv) *Maintenance and Champerty*

Non-champertous agreements between solicitor and client

16–065   [*Add to note 384, at the end: page* [1277]]
; *Lexlaw Ltd v Zuberi* [2017] EWHC 1350 (Ch).

[*Add to note 385, at the end: page* [1277]]
; *Lexlaw Ltd v Zuberi* [2017] EWHC 1350 (Ch).

(f) *Contracts in Restraint of Trade*

(i) *Scope of Doctrine*

Competition Law

[*Delete the last two sentences of the paragraph, after note 518 and substitute: pages* [1291]–[1292]]
This matter is now dealt with by art.101 of the Treaty on the Functioning of the European Union.

16–086

Injunctions

[*Add to paragraph, at the end: page* [1306]]
t1b An injunction may also be refused if there has been unreasonable delay in seeking an order.[637a]

16–112

[637a] *Legends Live Ltd v Harrison* [2016] EWHC 1938 (QB).

Interlocutory injunction

[*Add to note 640, at the end: page* [1306]]
; *Egon Zehnder Ltd v Tillman* [2017] EWHC 1278 (Ch).

16–113

(ii) *Employer and Employee*

Employee's activities after determination of employment

[*Add to paragraph, line 3, after note 646: page* [1307]]
An employer is entitled to protect the "general goodwill of the business including potential clients",[646a] as the prospect of obtaining new clients from recommendations is an intrinsic part of a business.[646b]

16–114

[646a] *One Step (Support) Ltd v Morris-Garner* [2016] EWCA Civ 180, [2016] I.R.L.R. 435 at [32].
[646b] *Allied Dunbar (Frank Weisinger) Ltd v Weisinger* [1988] I.R.L.R. 60 at [26].

[*Add to paragraph, before* "Thus in *Home Counties*": *page* [1307]]
Where a covenant is capable of two constructions, one of which would lead it to being held unreasonable and the alternative producing the opposite result, the latter construction should be adopted "on the basis that the parties are to be deemed to have intended their bargain to be lawful and not to offend against the public interest".[650a]

[650a] *TFS Derivatives Ltd v Morgan* [2004] EWHC 3181 (QB) at [43], cited with approval in *Egon Zehnder Ltd v Tillman* [2017] EWHC 1278 (Ch) at [33].

[*Add new paragraph 16–114A: page* [1308]]
Relevant time. In determining reasonableness, the court does not only look "at the actual position as at the date the payment started" as to do so would result in few covenants being valid since "the employee will not have engaged fully

16–114A

enough with the business to justify it".[656a] The court has to go further and "look at what was in contemplation of both parties".[656b]

[656a] *Egon Zehnder Ltd v Tillman* [2017] EWHC 1278 (Ch) at [27].
[656b] [2017] EWHC (Ch) at [27] where the court held that such contemplation could include promotion.

Protection by general law and by covenant

16–117   [*Add to note 681, line 2, after "para.16–119)": page* [1310]]
; *Capita Plc v Darch* [2017] EWHC 1248 (Ch).

Breach

16–124   [*Add to note 756, at the end: page* [1318]]
; *Rush Hair Ltd v Gibson-Forbes* [2016] EWHC 2589 (QB).

(iii) *Vendor and Purchaser of Business*

Vendor and purchaser

16–126   [*Add to note 778, at the end: page* [1320]]
A failure by a solicitor to advise the purchaser of a business that the agreement did not contain a restraint against competition has been held to constitute negligence: see *Luffeorm Ltd v Kitsons LLP* [2015] P.N.L.R. 30 QB.

4. ENFORCEMENT OF COLLATERAL AND PROPRIETARY RIGHTS

(a) *The Maxim Ex Turpi Causa Non Oritur Actio and Related Rules*

Ex turpi causa non oritur actio

16–174   [*Add to paragraph, line 42, after " . . . which vary in different circumstances".": page* [1346]]
The "range of factors" principle applied in *Patel v Mirza*[960a] endorses this approach.[960b]

[960a] [2016] UKSC 42, [2016] 1 W.L.R. 399.
[960b] See above, para.16–014B.

Attribution and the law of illegality

16–175   [*In paragraph, lines 6–7, delete "Bilta (UK) Ltd v Nazir (No.2)" and substitute: page* [1346]]
Jetivia SA v Bilta (UK) Ltd (reported sub nom. *Bilta (UK) Ltd v Nazir (No.2)*)

[*In paragraph, line 9, delete "Jetivia SA" and substitute: page* [1346]]
Bilta (UK) Ltd

The *Stone & Rolls case*

[In paragraph, line 11, delete "Jetivia SA" and substitute: page [1348]]   **16–179**
Bilta (UK) Ltd

[In paragraph, line 2, delete "Jetivia SA" and substitute: page [1349]]   **16–180**
Bilta (UK) Ltd

[Add to paragraph, at the end: page [1349]]
The principles of attribution are not affected by the judgment in *Patel v Mirza*[1001a] as there will still need to be a determination of whether the wrongful act should be attributed to the company.

[1001a] [2016] UKSC 42. See above, paras 16–014A et seq.

Tainting

[In note 1014, delete the words "Vakante v Addey & Stanhope School" and   **16–183**
substitute: page [1351]]
V v Addey & Stanhope School

(c) *Recovery of Money Paid or Transferred under Illegal Contracts*

Non-recovery of consideration

[Delete paragraph and substitute: page [1361]]   **16–194**
    Restitution of benefits under an illegal contract. The decision in *Patel v Mirza*[1098] has changed the law governing the restitution of benefits conferred under a contract that is unenforceable because of illegality in a fundamental way. It would normally permit the recovery of any money or property transferred under the contract. As Lord Toulson stated[1099]:

> "a person who satisfied the ordinary requirements of a claim in unjust enrichment will not prima facie be debarred from recovering money paid or property transferred by reason of the fact that the consideration which has failed was an unlawful consideration".

Lord Toulson, speaking for the majority, was here applying the factors-based approach[1100]; but the minority also considered that restitution should be available, as explained earlier.[1101]

[1098] [2016] UKSC 42. See Strauss, "The Diminishing Power of the Defendant: Illegality After *Patel v Mirza*" [2016] R.L.R. 145; Burrows, *A New Dawn for the Law of Illegality*, Oxford Legal Studies Research Paper No.42 (2017). See above, paras 16–014B—16–014C.
[1099] [2016] UKSC 42 at [116].
[1100] See above, para.16–014F.
[1101] See above, paras 16–014G—16–014L.

[Insert new paragraph 16–194A: page [1361]]
Quantum meruit. It seems that the restitutionary remedies available may   **16–194A**
include a quantum meruit for services rendered under the unenforceable contract.
In *Patel v Mirza*[1102] Lord Toulson pointed out that the courts in *Hounga v Allen*[1102a] did not consider whether the claimant was "entitled to be paid for the

services she rendered on a quantum meruit". Such a claim would be independent of the illegality and a strong argument can be made that it should be available. Lord Sumption, citing *Hounga v Allen*[1102b] was of the opinion that "a claim for a quantum meruit for services performed" may well have been successful.[1102c]

[1102] [2016] UKSC 42 at [74].
[1102a] [2014] UKSC 47, [2014] 1 W.L.R. 2889. Lord Neuberger considered that there was real room for debate that the principle was applicable: [2016] UKSC 42 at [180].
[1102b] [2014] UKSC 47, [2014] 1 W.L.R. 2889 at [243]. See para.16–013 for analysis of *Hounga v Allen*.
[1102c] [2016] UKSC 42 at [243].

Determination of limited interests created by illegal transactions

16–198   *[Add to note 1124, at the end: page* [1364]]
See also *Davies v O'Kelly* [2015] 1 W.L.R. 2725 at [20].

[Add to paragraph, after note 1131: page [1365]]
It is important to note that *Tinsley v Milligan*[1131a] is exclusively about title and not the enforcement of illegal contracts, and does not "endorse ... a claim to title, where the title is dependent upon the enforceability of the illegal transaction".[1131b]

[1131a] [1994] 1 A.C. 340.
[1131b] *Shah v Greening* [2016] EWHC 548 (Ch) at [61].

[Add to paragraph, at the end: page [1365]]
In *Patel v Mirza*[1132a] Lord Neuberger considered that "it would have been disproportionate to have refused to enforce Miss Milligan's equitable interest in the relevant property on grounds of the illegal activity". Lord Toulson agreed, he considered that it "would have been disproportionate to have prevented her from enforcing her equitable interest in the property and conversely to have left Miss Tinsley unjustly enriched".[1132b] Also, as Lord Mance pointed out as the court in *Tinsley v Milligan* was reversing rather than enforcing the illegal transaction it could therefore "take into account both the objective fact of joint contributions and the parties' actual and by itself, legal purpose of joint ownership".[1132c]

[1132a] [2016] UKSC 42 at [181].
[1132b] [2016] UKSC 42 at [112]. See also Lord Neuberger [2016] UKSC 42 at [164], decision in "*Tinsley* ... is generally thought to be unsatisfactory", Lord Neuberger endorsed the judgment of Lord Toulson: [2016] UKSC 42 at [181].
[1132c] [2016] UKSC 42 at [201].

Locus poenitentiae: presumption of advancement

16–199   *[Add to note 1135, line 1, after* "[2002] B.P.I.R. 1057.".: *page* [1365]]
"It is ... now accepted on all sides that, if *Collier v Collier* [2002] BPIR 1057 came before the courts today it would be decided differently": *Patel v Mirza* [2016] UKSC 42 at [221], per Lord Clarke. This was not accepted by Lord Sumption who considered that if "*Collier v Collier* were to come before the courts today, the result should be the same ... ": *Patel v Mirza* [2016] UKSC 42 at [238].

Class-protecting statutes

[In paragraph, line 1, delete "The action for money had and received will" *and substitute: page* [1366]]   **16–202**
Quite apart from the decision in *Patel v Mirza*,[1142a] which opens the way in most cases for the recovery of benefits conferred under a contract that is unenforceable because of illegality,[1142b] the action for money had and received would

[1142a] [2016] UKSC 42, [2016] 1 W.L.R. 399.
[1142b] See above, para.16–194.

Oppression and fraud

[In paragraph, line 1, delete "A person can" *and substitute: page* [1367]]   **16–203**
Even before the decision in *Patel v Mirza*[1148a] a person could

[1148a] [2016] UKSC 42, [2016] 1 W.L.R. 399; see above, para.16–194.

Mistake

[In paragraph, line 1, delete "There is" *and substitute: page* [1368]]   **16–204**
Although in the light of *Patel v Mirza*[1156a] it may seldom be necessary to rely on it, there is

[1156a] [2016] UKSC 42, [2016] 1 W.L.R. 399; see above, para.16–194.

Locus poenitentiae: general

[Delete paragraphs 16–205—16–207 and substitute: pages [1368]–[1371]]   **16–205 to 16–207**
16–205–207

Locus poenitentiae. The *locus poenitentiae* principle enabled a party to resile from an executory contract and recover anything paid or transferred under the contract.[1158] Lord Toulson stated in *Patel v Mirza*[1159] that it was "not necessary to discuss the question of *locus poenitentiae*" as the court was permitting the claimant to recover his consideration. He added that the principle had "only acquired importance because of the strictness of the basic rule" on the effect of illegality on the enforcement of contracts, and the fact that the courts had adopted the "wrong approach" to the effect of illegality on contracts.[1160] Lord Mance was unable to accept this as the "concept behind *locus poenitentiae* is restitutionary".[1161] Lord Sumption considered that the "notion of penitence" or "the voluntary character of the plaintiff's withdrawal" were irrelevant when dealing with the consequences of an unenforceable illegal contract as the right of restitution follows from the "legal ineffectiveness of the contract".[1162] Although the minority did not set out a definitive view on the principle of *locus poenitentiae* it is clear that money or property transferred under an illegal contract is recoverable provided such recovery is not against public policy.[1163–1178]

[1158] *Bone v Ekless* (1860) 29 L.J. Ex. 438, 440; *Palaniappa Chettiar v Arunasalam Chettiar* [1962] A.C. 294, 302–303. The right to resile was subject to a number of qualifications which need not be addressed.
[1159] [2016] UKSC 42 at [116]. See also Lord Neuberger at [193].
[1160] [2016] UKSC 42 at [116].

¹¹⁶¹ [2016] UKSC 42 at [202]. He considered that "it would be desirable to avoid the moral undertones of the Latin brocard" and simply recognise the claimant's restitutionary right: [2016] UKSC 42 at [202].

¹¹⁶² [2016] UKSC 42 at [252].

^{1163–1178} See [2016] UKSC 42 at [110] where Lord Toulson considered it appropriate to refuse assistance where this would "assist the claimant in a drug trafficking operation".

6. PLEADING AND PRACTICE

Pleading of illegality

16–222   *[Add to note 1248, at the end: page* [1379]]
; *AB (by his litigation friend CD) v Royal Devon & Exeter NHS Foundation Trust* [2016] EWHC 1024 (QB) at [81].

Part Six

JOINT OBLIGATIONS, THIRD PARTIES AND ASSIGNMENT

CHAPTER 17

JOINT OBLIGATIONS

Assessment of contribution

[Add to note 100, line 2, after "(contribution)"*: page* [1395]]   **17–034**
; *Euro-Asian Oil SA v Abilo (UK) Ltd* [2016] EWHC 3340 (Comm), [2017] 1 Lloyd's Rep 287 at [365]–[368].

CHAPTER 18

THIRD PARTIES

2. The Common Law Doctrine

(a) *Parties to the Agreement*

Who are the parties?

18–004 *[Add to note 21, line 7, after* "[2015] 1 Lloyd's Rep. 216 at [68], [73]–[76];": *page* [1400]]
Navig8 Inc v South Vigour Shipping Co [2015] EWHC 32 (Comm), [2015] 1 Lloyd's Rep. 436 at [94] per Teare J. (" . . . identification of the parties to a contract is a question of fact" the answer to which is generally governed by an objective test, the subjective intentions of one party are relevant only "where such intentions are communicated to the other" (*ibid.*));

[In note 22, update reference to Carver on Bills of Lading to: page [1400]]
4th ed. (2017)

[Add to note 22, at the end: page [1400]]
The general rule that a person who is named as the consignee in a contract of carriage contained in or evidenced by a bill of lading is not, merely by reason of

[156]

being so named, "in a true sense an original party to the contract" (*Standard Chartered Bank v Dorchester LNG (2) Ltd (The Erin Schulte)* [2014] EWCA Civ 1382, [2015] 1 Lloyd's Rep. 97 at [16]), and the various qualifications of that rule, are likewise beyond the scope of this book. They are fully discussed in *Carver*, 4th ed. (2017), paras 4-001 to 4-031.

Collateral contracts

[*Add new note 25a, after* "paint would last for seven years." *in line 10: page* [1401]]

18–005

25a Contrast *Royal Bank of Scotland Plc v McCarthy* [2015] EWHC 3626 (QB), where the argument that there was a collateral contract between one of the parties to the main contract and a person who was not a party to the main contract was rejected for want of the requisite "assurance" (at [158]) from the former to the latter person. For a judicial statement of the requirements of a collateral contract, see *Secker v Fairhill Properties Ltd* [2017] EWHC 69 (QB) at [54] per Stuart-Smith J. Those requirements are further discussed in Main Work, Vol.I, paras 18–010 and 18–011. On the facts of the *Secker* case, no collateral contract arose because the relevant defendant had not agreed to "any *separate* contractual obligation" (at [57] (italics supplied); *cf.* [2017] EWHC 69 (QB) at [55]; "separate" here means an obligation additional to those arising under the main contract). The fact that the alleged collateral contract would not have imposed on that defendant any obligation beyond those already incumbent on him under the original (main) contract would tend to negative that party's intention to give the collateral undertaking contractual force: *cf. The Aramis* [1989] 1 Lloyd's Rep. 213, where similar reasoning led the Court of Appeal to refuse to *imply* a contract for want of contractual intention (see Main Work, Vol.I, para.2–109); in the *Secker* case, the Court rejected the collateral contract argument on the same ground, even though the undertaking alleged to have given rise to that contract was an *express* one (*cf.* Main Work, Vol.I, para.18–011). No third party problem arose in the *Secker* case as the main contract was between the same parties as the alleged collateral contract: see [2017] EWHC 69 (QB) at [3] and [4iii].

Collateral contracts

[*Add to note 36, at the end: page* [1402]]

18–006

Cooke J.'s decision in *British American Tobacco Switzerland SA v Exel Europe Ltd* [2012] EWHC 694 (Comm), [2013] 1 W.L.R. 397 was reversed on appeal ([2013] EWCA Civ 1319, [2014] 1 W.L.R. 4526) but restored on further appeal to the Supreme Court ([2015] UKSC 65, [2016] A.C. 262: see below, paras 36–141, 36–146).

Consideration in collateral contracts

[*Add to note 62, at the end: page* [1404]]

18–010

For another case (again not involving any third party) in which the claimant provided consideration for the defendant's promise giving rise to a collateral contract by entering into the main contract, see *Hughes v Pendragon Sabre Ltd* [2016] EWCA Civ 18, [2016] 1 Lloyd's Rep. 311 at [32], [35]. For this case, see also this Supplement paras 2–120, 44–020.

3. Scope

(a) *Liability in Negligence to Third parties*

Tort and contract damages contrasted

18–038   [*Add to note 225, at the end: page* [1427]]
The Scottish Law Commission's proposals for the reform and clarification of this branch of Scots law are contained in the Commission's *Review of Contract Law: Report on Third Party Rights*, Scot Law Com No.245 (2016), which contains, in its Ch.2, a summary of the present law on the subject. The Draft Contract (Third Party Rights) (Scotland) Bill appended to this Report differs significantly from the English Contracts (Rights of Third Parties) Act 1999 (discussed in Main Work, Vol.I, paras 18–090 et seq.). The above Report was substantially implemented when the Contract (Third Party Rights) (Scotland) Bill 2017 was passed by the Scottish Parliament, with some amendments, on September 21, 2017 (see paras 3 and 4 of the Policy Memorandum accompanying the Bill).

4. Contracts for the Benefit of Third Parties

(a) *Effects of a Contract for the Benefit of a Third Party*

(i) *Promisee's Remedies*

Whose loss?

18–050   [*Add to paragraph, after paragraph heading: page* [1437]]
The question whether loss had been suffered by the promisee arose in *Glory Wealth Shipping Pte Ltd v Flame SA*,[298a] where a contract between A and B would, if the contract had been duly performed by B, have resulted in B's making payments to A, who, because it had become insolvent and wished to "protect its monetary assets"[298b] from its creditors, directed B to make those payments to two companies (C1 and C2) which "were not acting as agents of [A] and so would not have held the [moneys] on behalf of [A]".[298c] In breach of the contract between A and B, B failed to make the stipulated payments; and Teare J. held that this breach had caused a loss to A of (as was found by the arbitrators) more than USD 3 million.[298d] The reason for this conclusion was that, but for B's breach, A would have been "entitled to receive the [payments] ... and to dispose of [them]"[298e] and the breach had "deprived [A] of the right to receive and dispose of [the payments]". Just as it would not matter to the assessment of loss if [A] had intended to give the [payments] away once it had received [them], so it matters not that [A] had previously decided that the payments should be [made to C1 and C2]".[298f]

[298a] [2016] EWHC 293 (Comm), [2016] 1 Lloyd's Rep. 571.

[298b] At [6]. There was no appeal against the arbitrator's decision that this "turpitude", being only "incidental", did not give rise to the "defence of illegality" : at [8].

²⁹⁸ᶜ [2016] EWHC 293 (Comm) at [12].
²⁹⁸ᵈ [2016] EWHC 293 (Comm) at [18], [25].
²⁹⁸ᵉ [2016] EWHC 293 (Comm) at [25].
²⁹⁸ᶠ [2016] EWHC 293 (Comm). Teare J. reached this conclusion "without enthusiasm" because of A's "dishonest concealment and turpitude" [2016] EWHC 293 (Comm) at [28] but (no doubt for the reason given in n.298b above) these matters "could not affect the court's consideration of the question of law raised by this appeal". For the formulation of this question, see [2016] EWHC 293 (Comm) at [3].

Damages in respect of third party's loss: exceptions in general

[*Add to note 339, line 3, after* "[1987] 1 Lloyd's Rep. 465;"*: page* [1441]]   **18–054**
the reasoning of *Obestain Inc v National Mineral Development Corp Ltd (The Sanix Ace)* [1987] 1 Lloyd's Rep. 465 was followed in *Titan Europe 2006-3 Plc v Colliers International UK Plc* [2015] EWCA Civ 1083, [2016] 1 All E.R. (Comm) 999 at [30] to enable an owner of property to recover damages in tort in respect of negligent valuation of property (in this case, choses in action) by virtue of his ownership of that property, even though that owner was not a party to the contract with the valuer.

[*Add to note 339, line 10, after* "[1977] C.L.J. 24."*: page* [1441]]
Albacruz (Cargo Owners) v Albazero (Owners) (The Albazero) [1977] A.C. 774 was distinguished in *Titan Europe 2006-3 Plc v Colliers International UK Plc* [2015] EWCA Civ 1083 at [32] on the ground that the loss in the latter case had been suffered by an owner in respect of property which he had retained while the claimant in the former case had, at the relevant time, parted with the property in question.

Damages in respect of third party's loss: exceptions in general

[*Add new note 340a, line 16, after* "but only to a third party."*: page* [1441]]   **18–054**
³⁴⁰ᵃ Exceptions to the general rule that a contracting party cannot recover damages in respect of loss suffered, not by himself, but by a third party (Main Work, Vol.I, para.18–051) are further discussed by the Supreme Court in *Swynson Ltd v Lowick Rose LLP* [2017] UKSC 32, [2017] 2 W.L.R. 1161 (see further para.18–057, text after n.359a, below). Lord Neuberger in that case described some of these exceptions (in particular those discussed in Main Work, paras 18–052 to 18–069) as "anomalous" (a word that perhaps carries a note of disapproval); and it is interesting to note that neither he nor any other member of the Supreme Court in that case made any reference to the judicial criticisms of the general rule discussed in Main Work, para.18–053, perhaps because these criticisms were not drawn to the attention of the Supreme Court in the *Swynson* case.

Further exceptions: building contracts

[*Add new note 343a, at the end of paragraph heading: page* [1442]]   **18–055**
³⁴³ᵃ See further para.18–057, text after n.359a, below.

[*Add to note 344, at the end: page* [1442]]
The discussion in paras 18–055 to 18–064 of the Main Work, Vol.I, is directly concerned only with the extension of the reasoning of the "*Albazero* exception"

(Main Work, para.18–054) to *building* contract cases. The view that these cases
have extended this exception to "contracts generally" (*Swynson Ltd v Lowick
Rose LLP* [2017] UKSC 32, [2017] 2 W.L.R. 1161 per Lord Sumption at [15],
and see Main Work para.18–057 line 24) does not mean that the (so extended)
exceptions necessarily apply to all contracts whatsoever: it is, for example, still
an open question whether their reasoning would apply to a contract by which A
promised B to pay a sum of money to C, as in the *Woodar* case [1980] 1 W.L.R.
277 (Main Work, para.18–052). For the scope of the *Albazero* exception in bill
of lading contracts, see also *Carver on Bills of Lading*, 4th ed. (2017) para.5–070.

The "broader ground": promisee's expense of curing the breach

18–056 [*Add new note 347a, at the end of paragraph heading: page* [1442]]
347a See further para.18–057, text after n.359a, below.

The "narrower ground": loss suffered by third party as transferee of the affected property

18–057 [*Add new note 352a, at the end of paragraph heading: page* [1443]]
352a See further para.18–057, text after n.359a, below.

[*Add to note 354, at the end: page* [1443]]
See also *Swynson Ltd v Lowick Rose LLP* [2017] UKSC 32, [2017] 2 W.L.R.
1161 at [17], quoted below, para.18–057 at n.359l.

[*Add to note 356, at the end: page* [1443]]
For the distinction between *Albacruz (Cargo Owners) v Albazero (Owners) (The
Albazero)* [1977] A.C. 774 and *Titan Europe 2006-3 Plc v Colliers International
UK Plc* [2015] EWCA Civ 1083, [2016] 1 All E.R. (Comm) 999 at [32] see
above, para.18–054.

[*Add to paragraph, at the end: page* [1444]]
The "further exceptions"359a to the general rule that a contracting party cannot
recover damages in respect of loss suffered by a third party, as well as the
"broader" and "narrower" grounds for these exceptions359b are discussed by the
Supreme Court in *Swynson Ltd v Lowick Rose LLP.*359c In that case two loans
were made by a company (A) controlled and beneficially owned by an individual
(here referred to as C) to another company (X) to finance the buy-out of a further
entity (Y). These loans were made at the instigation of C and in reliance on a
report prepared by the defendant, a firm of accountants engaged by A and X359d;
C was not a party to this contract. It was common ground that the accountants
had been negligent in preparing the report.359e The original two loans were paid
off with money lent by C to X under a refinancing agreement; and one of the
issues359f before the Supreme Court was whether A could recover damages in
respect of the loss suffered by C when this third loan remained unpaid. In support
A's claim in respect of this loss, A and C relied on the "*Albazero* exception"359g
and on the "further exceptions" referred to above.359h The Supreme Court
referred to these exceptions as being based on "the principle of transferred
loss"359i and recognised that the operation of this principle might be justified on

either a "broader" or on a "narrower" ground; these two grounds are discussed in paras 18–055 and 18–056 of the Main Work. But in the *Swynson* case the Supreme Court concluded that A's claim for damages in respect of C's loss could not succeed on either of these grounds. It could not succeed on the "narrower" ground because C "did not suffer loss in his capacity as owner of property"[359j] or because A "did not contract with [the accountants] on behalf of"[359k] C. Nor could it be supported on the "broader" ground, (though there was "much to be said for the broader principle"[359l]) since it was "no part of the object of the engagement [of the accountants by A] . . . to benefit [C]"[359m]; indeed, the latter point would defeat a claim by A in respect of C's loss based on the "narrower", no less than such a claim based on the "broader" ground.[359n]

[359a] Discussed in Main Work, para.18–055.
[359b] Discussed in Main Work, paras 18–056, 18–057.
[359c] [2017] UKSC 32, [2017] 2 W.L.R. 1161.
[359d] [2017] UKSC 32 at [4], [40], [92].
[359e] [2017] UKSC 32 at [4].
[359f] Many other issues were discussed by the Supreme Court: see below, paras 26–099B, 26–102.
[359g] [2017] UKSC at [14]; for the destination of damages so recovered by A in respect of C's loss, see Main Work, para.18–078.
[359h] Above at n.359a.
[359i] [2017] UKSC 32 at [14], [16], [52], [54], [101]; for an earlier use of the phrase "transferred loss" see *Alfred McAlpine Construction Ltd v Panatown Ltd* [2001] 1 A.C. 518 at 529. The same phrase was also used by Robert Goff L.J. in *Leigh & Sillavan Ltd v Aliakmon Shipping Co Ltd (The Aliakmon)* [1985] Q.B. 350, 399, in a passage which, when that case reached the House of Lords, drew adverse comment from Lord Brandon: see [1986] A.C. 785 at 820. But in *The Aliakmon* that passage was used in a context different from that which arose in the *Swynson* case. In *The Aliakmon*, the question arose whether C was *bound* by a term of the contract between A and B, while in the *Swynson* case the question was whether C could, at least indirectly, *benefit* from a contract between A and B. These two questions raise different issues of policy; and this may well have been the reason why, in the *Swynson* case, *The Aliakmon* was not cited to the Supreme Court.
[359j] [2017] UKSC 32 at [17], [107].
[359k] [2017] UKSC 32 at [54], [107].
[359l] [2017] UKSC 32 at [17].
[359m] [2017] UKSC 32 at [17] and see at [108].
[359n] See the use by Lord Sumption in [2017] UKSC 32 at [17] of the phrase "in either form". Lord Neuberger's reasoning at [107]–[108] seems also to apply to both the "broader" and the "narrower" forms of the principle.

No transfer of affected property from promisee to third party

[*Add to note 364, at the end: page* [1444]]   **18–058**

In *Swynson Ltd v Lowick Rose LLP* [2017] UKSC 32, [2017] 2 W.L.R. 1161 Lord Sumption, in discussing the "*Albazero* exception" (see Main Work, Vol.I, para.18–054) and its extension to "contracts generally" ([2017] UKSC 32 at [15]) said at [14] that these exceptions applied where the third party was "the intended transferee of property affected by the breach"; and Lord Neuberger similarly referred at [102] to their application "where there is a contract between A and B relating to A's property which is subsequently acquired by C . . . ". These statements may, at first sight, seem to be inconsistent with *Darlington B.C. v Wiltshier Northern Ltd* [1995] 1 W.L.R. 68 (discussed in Main Work para.18–058); but it is submitted that they should not be read in this way. They should be read rather as general statements of the scope of the "*Albazero* exception" and its extensions, and not as casting doubt on the *Darlington* case.

That case was cited without disapproval by Lord Mance in the *Swynson* case [2017] UKSC 32 at [52] and is not questioned in the other two judgments (*i.e.*, those of Lord Sumption and of Lord Neuberger) in that case. The ground for the decision that the exceptions did not apply in the *Swynson* case is stated above, para.18–057, text after n.359a.

Third party having independent contractual rights against promisor

18–060   *[Add to note 379, at the end: page* [1446]]
For the distinction between *Albacruz (Cargo Owners) v Albazero (Owners) (The Albazero)* and *Titan Europe 2006-3 Plc v Colliers International UK Plc* [2015] EWCA Civ 1083, [2016] 1 All E.R. (Comm) 999 at [32], see above, para.18–054 note 339.

Third party having independent contractual rights against promisor

18–061   *[Add to note 382, at the end: page* [1447]]
Cf. the statement in *Swynson Ltd v Lowick Rose LLP* [2017] UKSC 32, [2017] 1 W.L.R. 1161 at [16] that the "principle of transferred loss" (see above, para.18–057 at n.359i) is "not available if the third party has a direct right for the same loss, *on whatever basis*" (italics supplied). In that case, the third party had "abandoned the argument that a duty of care was owed [by the defendant] to him [the third party] personally" ([2017] UKSC 32 at [10]) but there were other reasons why the principle of transferred loss did not there apply: see above, para.18–057.

[Add to note 385 at the end: page [1477]]
For the view that the "principle of transferred loss" (see above, para.18–057 at n.359i) is "driven by legal necessity" (*i.e.*, by the necessity of avoiding a "legal black hole" of the kind described in para.18–061 of the Main Work) see *Swynson Ltd v Lowick Rose LLP* [2017] UKSC 32, [2017] 1 W.L.R. 1161 at [16].

(b) *Exceptions to the Doctrine*

(ii) *Contracts (Rights of Third Parties) Act 1999*

Express provision

18–091   *[Add to note 554, at the end: page* [1467]]
; but this provision does not apply where there is *no* "dispute" between the relevant parties : see *Milton Keynes BC v Viridor (Community Recycling MK) Ltd* [2016] EWHC 2764 (TCC), [2017] B.L.R. 47.

Term purporting to confer a benefit on third party

18–093   *[Add new note 564a, after* "to confer a benefit on him"" *in line 3: page* [1468]]
564a A term may purport to confer a benefit on C even though it is also for the benefit of B. This was held to be the position in *Cavanagh v Secretary of State for Work and Pensions* [2016] EWHC 1136 (QB), where a contract of employment contained a term by which the employer promised the

employee to make specified deductions from the employee's pay and to pay these deductions to the employee's trade union. It was held that this term was enforceable against the employer by the union: the term purported to confer a benefit on the union even though it could also be said to benefit the employee.

[Add to note 565, at the beginning: page [1468]]
See *Royal Bank of Scotland Plc v McCarthy* [2015] EWHC 3626 (QB), where an alternative ground for the decision (i.e., alternative to that stated in note 569 below) was that the fact that the third party had other remedies than enforcement of the term in the contract between A and B indicated that A and B did not intend the term in the contract between them to be enforceable by C (at [143]), so that C's claim under the Contracts (Rights of Third Parties) Act failed by virtue of s. 1(2) of that Act.

[Add to note 569, at the end: page [1468]]
See also *Royal Bank of Scotland Plc v McCarthy* [2015] EWHC 3626 (QB), where the mere fact that a benefit to the third party was an "incidental effect" (at [137]) of the performance of the contract was held not to satisfy the requirement set out in s.1(1)(b) of the 1999 Act. The question whether the contract purported to confer a benefit on the third party was one of the "construction" of the contract (at [123], [129]), and this requirement had not been satisfied. In support of this conclusion, the Court who relied on the *Dolphin Maritime* case [2009] EWHC 716 (Comm), [2009] 2 Lloyd's Rep. 123, cited in Main Work, Vol.I, para.18–093 note 568.

Third party to be "expressly" identified

[Add to note 607, at the end: page [1473]]   **18–097**
Lord Hoffmann's description in *Attorney General of Belize v Belize Telecom Ltd* [2009] UKPC 10, [2009] 1 W.L.R. 1988 of the process of implication as one of "the construction of the instrument as a whole" was extensively discussed by the Supreme Court in *Marks & Spencer Plc v BNP Paribas Security Services Trust Co (Jersey) Ltd* [2015] UKSC 72, [2016] A.C. 742. Lord Neuberger (with whose judgment Lord Sumption and Lord Hodge agreed) there said (at [26]) that Lord Hoffmann's observation (quoted above) "could obscure the fact that construing the words used and implying additional words are different processes governed by different rules" and (at [31]) that they (i.e. those observations) should "henceforth be treated as a characteristically inspired discussion rather than authoritative guidance on the law of implied terms." For the same view, see also *Globe Motors Inc v TRW Varity Electric Steering Ltd* [2016] EWCA Civ 396 at [58], following the *Marks & Spencer* case. The majority view in the *Marks & Spencer* case was not there shared by Lord Carnwath (see [2015] UKSC 72 at [74]); while Lord Clarke said at [76] that both processes (i.e. construction and implication) could "properly be said" to be "part of the construction of the contract in a broad sense." The judgments in the *Marks & Spencer* case on the present point are more fully discussed in para.14–007 above. Even before that case the scope of Lord Hoffmann's views in the *Belize* case had been narrowed by judicial statements to the effect that those views applied only to the implica-

tion of terms in fact, and not to the implication of terms in law: see *Société Générale, London Branch v Geys* [2012] UKSC 63, [2013] 1 A.C. 523 at [55] per Baroness Hale and *Yam Seng Ltd v International Trade Corp Ltd* [2013] EWHC 111 (QB), [2013] 1 Lloyd's Rep. 526 at [131], [132], per Leggatt J.; for the difference between these two types of implied terms, see Main Work, Vol.I, para.14–004.

[*In note 612, update reference to Carver on Bills of Lading to: page* [1474]]
4th ed. (2017)

The second group of exceptions

18–118   [*Add to note 684, at the end: page* [1484]]
In *Cavanagh v Secretary of State for Work and Pensions* [2016] EWHC 1136 (QB), see above, para.18–093 note 564a, enforcement of the term by the union was held not to amount to enforcement of it "against the employee" within s.6(3) of the Contracts (Rights of Third Parties) Act 1999 (see at [75]).

(iii) *Other Statutory Exceptions*

Third parties' rights against insurers

18–136   [*In note 766, delete the words from* "will be made" *in line 15 to the end and substitute: page* [1495]]
have been made by the Third Parties (Rights against Insurers) Regulations 2016 (SI 2016/570) which came into force immediately after the coming into force of the 2010 Act and of Insurance Act 2015 s.20 and Sch.2. Section 19 of the Insurance Act 2015 (which replaces s.19 of the Third Parties (Rights against Insurers) Act 2010) came into force on April 12, 2015: see s.23(3)(a) of the 2015 Act. The rest of the 2010 Act is brought into force by the Third Parties (Rights against Insurers) Act 2010 (Commencement) Order 2016 (SI 2016/550) with effect from August 1, 2016.

The Motor Insurers' Bureau

18–137   [*In note 767, line 4, delete* "1280" *and substitute: page* [1495]]
1208

[*Add to note 770, line 4, after* "[2014] R.T.R. 25": *page* [1496]]
; *Wigley-Foster v Wilson* [2016] EWCA Civ 454, [2017] 1 All E.R. (Comm) 715, citing *Jacobs v Motor Insurers' Bureau* [2010] EWCA Civ 1208, [2011] 1 W.L.R. 2609.

[*Add to note 771, line 6, after* "March 21, 1997": *page* [1496]]
; Uninsured Drivers Agreement 2015 (in force August 1, 2015).

5. Enforcement Against Third Parties

Third party's knowledge: the time factor

[*Add to note 845, at the end: page* [1505]]   **18–151**
For the defence of "justification" to the tort of inducing a breach of contract, see also *Royal Bank of Scotland Plc v McCarthy* [2015] EWHC 3626 (QB) at [107], [114], [115]. The tort claim was also rejected on the ground that there had been no "inducement" of any breach (at [105]).

ASSIGNMENT

1. ASSIGNMENT

Assignment of choses in action: at common law

19–001   [*In note 1 update the reference to Tolhurst, The Assignment of Contractual Rights to: page* [1509]]
2nd edn (2016).

(a) *Statutory Assignments*

Part of a debt

19–015   [*Add new note 56a, line12, after* "equitable assignment.": *page* [1515]]
    56a *National Bank of Abu Dhabi PJSC v BP Oil International Ltd* [2016] EWHC 2892 (Comm) at [24].

(b) *Equitable Assignments*

Enforcement of legal chose in action equitably assigned

19–039   [*Add to note 148, at the end: page* [1527]]
; *Mailbox (Birmingham) Ltd v Galliford Try Construction Ltd* [2017] EWHC 67 (TCC), [2017] B.L.R. 180 at [50].

(c) *Principles Applicable to Statutory and Equitable Assignments*

(i) *What rights are Assignable*

Rights declared by contract to be incapable of assignment

[Add to note 159, at the end: page [1529]] **19–044**

The validity of "no-assignment" clauses has been thought to be inconvenient in the context of "factoring", where a company buys up multiple debts the precise terms of which cannot be realistically checked. For this reason, s.1 of the Small Business, Employment and Enterprise Act 2015 authorises regulations invalidating some "no assignment" clauses. So s.1(1) authorises provisions for the purpose of securing that any "non-assignment of receivables term" of a relevant contract has no effect, or has no effect in relation to persons of a prescribed description, or has effect in relation to persons of a prescribed description only for such purposes as may be prescribed. By s.1(2), a "non-assignment of receivables term" of a contract is a term which prohibits or imposes a condition, or other restriction, on the assignment by a party to the contract of the right to be paid any amount under the contract or any other contract between the parties. By s.1(3), a contract is a relevant contract if it is a contract for goods, services or tangible assets which is not an excluded financial services contract and at least one of the parties has entered into it in connection with the carrying on of a business. Draft Regulations were issued in September 2017, see *http:// www.legislation.gov.uk/ukdsi/2017/9780111160305/pdfs/ukdsi_9780111160305_ en.pdf.*

[Add to note 160, line 6, after "[2008] 2 All E.R. (Comm) 264"*: page* [1529]]
; *National Bank of Abu Dhabi PJSC v BP Oil International Ltd* [2016] EWHC 2892 (Comm).

(iv) *Assignments "subject to equities"*

Assignments "subject to equities"

[Add to note 258, at the end: page [1542]] **19–071**

In *Bibby Factors Northwest Ltd v HFD Ltd* [2015] EWCA Civ 1908, [2016] 1 Lloyd's Rep 517, there was a helpful application and clarification of the passage from Templeman J.'s judgment, cited in this paragraph, in *Business Computers Ltd v Anglo-African Leasing Ltd* [1977] 1 W.L.R. 578, 585. The assignor supplied goods to customers. The customers were contractually entitled to a rebate on the money owing under those contracts. The question was whether the rebate applied—that is, whether the customers were entitled to set-off the rebate—as against the assignee (who had bought the debts as a factor). The rebate arose in respect of debts owing both before and after notice of the assignment. It was held that the customers (i.e. the debtors) could set-off the rebate against the claims brought by the assignees. It did not matter whether the debts to which the rebate related were before or after the notice of assignment. This was because the rebate fell to be set-off applying the rules of equitable set-off. By those rules, there is an equitable set-off if the monetary cross-claim is so closely connected to the claim that it would be manifestly unjust to enforce payment without taking into account the cross-claim (see *Geldof Metaalconstructie NV v Simon Carves Ltd* [2010] EWCA Civ 667, [2011] 1 Lloyd's Rep. 517). The passage from Templeman J.'s judgment in the *Business Computers* case was therefore setting out alternatives. Where equitable set-off applies, it does not matter whether the debt to which the set-off relates accrues before or after the notice of assignment because the principle being applied is that the assignment is subject to equities and the assignee cannot be in a better position than the assignor. This is distinct from the principle that the debtor cannot "take away" the rights of the assignee (referred to in the text of this paragraph), to which the timing of the accrual of the debt is relevant.

CHAPTER 20

DEATH AND BANKRUPTCY

2. BANKRUPTCY

(f) *Contracts Made After Adjudication*

After-acquired property

[*Add to paragraph, after note 263: page* [1579]]   **20–054**
The fact that the property does not automatically vest in the trustee allows the
trustee to assess whether such vesting would be in the interests of the estate and
avoids the cost of having to disclaim onerous property.[263a]

[263a] *Viscount St Davids v Lewis* [2015] EWHC 2826 (Ch) at [26].

Part Seven

PERFORMANCE AND DISCHARGE

CHAPTER 21

PERFORMANCE

1. IN GENERAL

When notice to perform is required

21–009　　　*[Add to note 39, at the beginning: page* [1590]]
Edwards v Kumarasamy [2016] UKSC 40, [2016] 3 W.L.R. 310 at [29]–[38];

[Add to note 40, at the beginning: page [1590]]
In most of these cases the obligation of the tenant to give notice operates as an implied term of the contract, so that the implication is based on the normal principles applicable to the implication of terms, namely necessity or obviousness: *Edwards v Kumarasamy* [2016] UKSC 40, [2016] 3 W.L.R. 310 at [30], [47], [57] and [63]. See also

[Add to paragraph, at the end: page [1590]]
The obligation on the tenant to give notice does not normally apply to premises which are not in the possession of the tenant.[47a] However, exceptionally, the law may imply an obligation on the part of the tenant to give notice where the property is neither in the possession of the landlord nor the tenant and the tenant, but not the landlord, is in a position to know of the disrepair.[47b]

[47a] *Edwards v Kumarasamy* [2016] UKSC 40, [2016] 3 W.L.R. 310 at [42].
[47b] *Edwards v Kumarasamy* [2016] UKSC 40, [2016] 3 W.L.R. 310 at [48]–[59]. However, as a general rule, the obligation to give notice is unlikely to apply to the common parts of a block of flats let by the landlord because the landlord would ordinarily be in possession of the common parts.

2. TIME OF PERFORMANCE

[In note 57, update reference to Treitel on The Law of Contract, to: page [1591]]
14th edn (2015), paras 18–096—18–107

Time made expressly or implicitly "of the essence"

[Add to note 82, at the end: page [1594]]   **21–013**
; *Grand China Logistics Holding (Group) Co Ltd v Spar Shipping AS* [2016]
EWCA Civ 982, [2016] 2 Lloyd's Rep. 447 at [56].

[Delete text to note 83 and substitute: page [1594]]
Grand China Logistics Holding (Group) Co Ltd v Spar Shipping AS [2016]
EWCA Civ 982, [2016] 2 Lloyd's Rep. 447, which resolved a conflict of
authority on the question whether the obligation to make punctual payment of
hire is a condition of a time charterparty by concluding that it is not a condition,
but an innominate term. In so concluding the Court of Appeal took account of a
number of factors, including the fact that the contract contained an express term
of the contract which entitled the owner of the vessel to withdraw it in the event
that hire was not made punctually, the need to strike a balance between the
promotion of certainty and the need to avoid disproportionate consequences in
the case of trivial breaches, the understanding or reaction of the market and
previous authority.

3. PARTIAL PERFORMANCE OF AN ENTIRE OBLIGATION

[In note 177, update reference to Treitel on The Law of Contract to: page [1605]]
14th edn (2015), paras 17–031—17–048

Partial performance of entire obligations

[Add to note 191, line 1, after "not a working day:"*: page* [1607]]   **21–031**
Hartley v King Edward VI College [2017] UKSC 39, [2017] 1 W.L.R. 2110 at
[31];

Substantial performance

[In note 201, update reference to Treitel on The Law of Contract, to: page [1608]]   **21–033**
14th edn (2015), para.17–040

4. PAYMENT

(a) *In General*

Place of payment

[Add to note 325, at the end: page [1620]]   **21–056**
The presumption that the debtor must seek out the creditor at his place of

business and pay him there is of long standing but it is readily displaced implicitly and not just expressly; in considering whether the presumption has been displaced the court can take account of modern ways of making commercial payment based on its daily experience: *Canyon Offshore Ltd v GDF Suez E&P Nederland BV* [2014] EWHC 3810 (Comm), [2015] Bus. L.R. 578 at [38].

(b) *Appropriation of Payments*

Rights to appropriate payments

21–061   [*Add to note 355, at the end: page* [1623]]
; *Lomas v Burlington Loan Management Ltd* [2015] EWHC 2269 (Ch), [2016] B.C.C. 239 at [40].

Appropriation as between principal and interest

21–069   [*Add to note 383, at the end: page* [1626]]
; *Lomas v Burlington Loan Management Ltd* [2015] EWHC 2269 (Ch), [2016] B.C.C. 239 at [41]; *CBRE Loan Servicing Ltd v Gemini (Eclipse 2006-3) Plc* [2015] EWHC 2769 (Ch) at [48]. The presumption is based on what is normally the commercially sensible course that a creditor would take, but it will be displaced if unusually the circumstances indicate otherwise: see *Smith v Law Guarantee & Trust Society Ltd* [1904] 2 Ch. 569.

5. TENDER

Actual production of the money

21–090   [*Add to note 483, at the end: page* [1637]]
; *Novoship (UK) Ltd v Mikhaylyuk* [2015] EWHC 992 (Comm) at [10]; *Marksans Pharma Ltd v Peter Beck & Partner VVW GmbH* [2015] EWHC 1608 (Comm).

Chapter 22

DISCHARGE BY AGREEMENT

2. RELEASE

Construction of release

[Add to note 18, penultimate line, after "[2015] EWHC 992 (Comm) at [14]"*: page*   **22–005**
[1643]]
; *Marsden v Barclays Bank Plc* [2016] EWHC 1601 (QB) at [46] (where one of
the issues before the court was whether the settlement agreement applied to a
claim in deceit and it was held that the "reference to 'all causes of action which
arise directly or indirectly . . . ' was wide enough, and was clearly intended, to
encompass an existing threat of misrepresentation claims, including those in
deceit").

[Add to note 23, at the end: page [1643]]
(affirmed by the Court of Appeal: *Leslie v News Group Newspapers Ltd* [2016]
EWCA Civ 79).

[Add to note 25, at the end: page [1644]]
(affirmed by the Court of Appeal: *Leslie v News Group Newspapers Ltd* [2016]
EWCA Civ 79).

[Add to note 26, at the end: page [1644]]
(affirmed by the Court of Appeal: *Leslie v News Group Newspapers Ltd* [2016]
EWCA Civ 79).

3. ACCORD AND SATISFACTION

Payment in different form, at earlier time, in different place

22–017   [*Add to paragraph, at the end: page* [1648]]
More generally, a court is likely to find the existence of consideration where the creditor receives a practical benefit over and above that derived merely from accommodating the debtor.[70a]

[70a] *MWB Business Exchange Centres Ltd v Rock Advertising Ltd* [2016] EWCA Civ 553 (where the practical benefit obtained by the creditor landlord as a result of the re-scheduling of the tenant's payment obligations under the licence was that the tenant would continue to occupy the property and it would not be left standing empty for some time at further loss to the tenant). On this case see further above, para.4–119A. See also *Stevensdrake Ltd v Hunt* [2016] EWHC 1111 (Ch).

4. RESCISSION

Rescission by agreement

22–025   [*Add to paragraph, after note 94: page* [1650]]
It must also be distinguished from a contractual right to rescind the contract under which the party exercising the right to rescind is entitled to forfeit and keep any deposit and accrued interest, resell the property and any chattels included in the contract and claim damages.[94a]

[94a] *Hardy v Griffiths* [2014] EWHC 3947 (Ch), [2015] 2 W.L.R. 1239 at [115].

5. VARIATION

Variation or rescission?

22–034   [*Add to note 142, at the end: page* [1655]]
; *Plevin v Paragon Personal Finance Ltd (No.2)* [2017] UKSC 23, [2017] 1 W.L.R. 1249 at [13].

6. WAIVER

Contracting out of waiver

22–045   [*Delete text of the paragraph and substitute: pages* [1661]–[1662]]
It is not uncommon for contracting parties to seek by a term of their contract to exclude or restrict the operation of the doctrine of waiver. Thus a contract term may provide that in no event shall any delay, neglect or forbearance in enforcing any term of the contract be or be deemed a waiver of that term. Another

frequently encountered term is one which provides that the contract can only be altered if the parties go through a prescribed formality (such as a written amendment, signed by both parties). Contracting parties are free to stipulate that a particular act, such as payment of a rental instalment under an equipment lease, should not be taken to waive a right to terminate for an earlier breach.[193] But the effect of such a term is not necessarily to deprive a waiver of effect. Nor does a contract term which requires that any amendment be made in writing and signed by both parties necessarily have the effect of depriving an oral variation of the contract of validity. Such terms do not deprive the parties of their freedom to vary, waive or otherwise depart from the terms of their original contract.[194] Freedom of contract, or party autonomy, does not only apply at the time of entry into the contract: it also applies to the variation and the unmaking or discharge of the contract.[195] The effect of a term which purports to restrict the ability of the parties to amend their contract or to deprive an apparent waiver of effect may be to cause the court to question whether the parties have in fact agreed to amend their contract or waive their rights when they have not gone through the pre-scribed formality,[196] but it does not formally alter the burden of proof, nor is it the case that the courts will require "strong evidence" before giving effect to an amendment or a variation which does not comply with the agreed formality.[196a] If the court is satisfied on the balance of probabilities that the contracting parties have agreed an oral variation of their contract or that one party has orally agreed to waive its rights under the contract, then the court should give effect to the variation or the waiver notwithstanding the existence of a term in the original contract which purports to deprive the amendment or waiver of validity.[196b]

[193] *State Securities Plc v Initial Industry Ltd* [2004] EWHC 3482 (Ch), [2004] All E.R. (D) 317.
[194] *Globe Motors Inc v TRW Lucas Varity Electric Steering Ltd* [2016] EWCA Civ 396; *MWB Business Exchange Centres Ltd v Rock Advertising Ltd* [2016] EWCA Civ 553. The consideration of the issue in *Globe Motors* is obiter because the case was decided on another ground, whereas in *MWB Business Exchange Centres* it was part of the *ratio* of the case. The point was previously the subject of apparently conflicting decisions of the Court of Appeal (contrast *United Bank Ltd v Asif* Unreported, February 11, 2000, in which it was held that the contract could only be altered by going through the prescribed formality, and *World Online Telecom Ltd v I-Way Ltd* [2002] EWCA Civ 413 where the Court of Appeal refused summarily to give effect to a term which provided that "no addition, amendment or modification of this Agreement shall be effective unless it is in writing and signed by or on behalf of both parties"). The relationship between these apparently conflicting decisions and their precedent value is considered by Beatson L.J. in *Globe Motors* at [110]–[114] and was followed by Kitchin L.J. in *MWB Business Exchange Centres Ltd* at [26].
[195] *Globe Motors Inc v TRW Lucas Varity Electric Steering Ltd* [2016] EWCA Civ 396 at [100] and [119] and *MWB Business Exchange Centres Ltd v Rock Advertising Ltd* [2016] EWCA Civ 553 at [34].
[196] *Globe Motors Inc v TRW Lucas Varity Electric Steering Ltd* [2016] EWCA Civ 396 at [120].
[196a] *MWB Business Exchange Centres Ltd v Rock Advertising Ltd* [2016] EWCA Civ 553 at [28] (Kitchin L.J.), following the judgment of Beatson L.J. in *Globe Motors Inc v TRW Lucas Varity Electric Steering Ltd* [2016] EWCA Civ 396 at [120] and declining to follow *Spring Finance Ltd v HS Real Co LLC* [2011] EWHC 57 (Comm) at [57] and *World Online Telecom Ltd v I-Way Ltd* [2002] EWCA Civ 413 at [33], which had adopted the "strong evidence" requirement.
[196b] *MWB Business Exchange Centres Ltd v Rock Advertising Ltd* [2016] EWCA Civ 553 at [28], following in this respect the judgment of Gloster L.J. in *Energy Venture Partners Ltd v Malabu Oil & Gas Ltd* [2013] EWHC 2118 (Comm) at [273] and Beatson L.J. in *Globe Motors Inc v TRW Lucas Varity Electric Steering Ltd* [2016] EWCA Civ 396 at [120].

Waiver of breach

22–047   [*In note 202, update reference to Treitel on The Law of Contract: page* [1663]]
14th edn (2015), para.18–082

[*In note 204, update reference to Treitel: page* [1663]]
Treitel on The Law of Contract, paras 18–079—18–088

7. PROVISION FOR DISCHARGE IN THE CONTRACT ITSELF

Relationship with right to terminate at common law

22–049   [*In note 217, line 20, after* "[2010] B.L.R. 267 at [1366]", *delete* "and": *page* [1665]]

[*Add to note 217, line 21, after* "[2014] EWHC 661 (Comm) at [49]–[54]": *page* [1665]]
; *Vinergy International (PVT) Ltd v Richmond Mercantile Ltd FZC* [2016] EWHC 525 (Comm); *Imperial Chemical Industries Ltd v Merit Merrell Technology Ltd* [2017] EWHC 1763 (TCC), [186]–[191].

[*In note 223, lines 3–6, delete* "; *Kuwait Rocks Co* . . . of Flaux J. in *The Astra*)": *page* [1666]]

CHAPTER 23

DISCHARGE BY FRUSTRATION

2. THE TEST FOR FRUSTRATION

[*In note 24, update reference to Treitel on The Law of Contract to: page* [1674]]
14th edn (2015), paras 19–114—19–123

[*In note 24, update reference to Anson's Law of Contract to: page* [1674]]
30th edn (2016), pp.509–514

[*In note 24, update reference to Cheshire, Fifoot and Furmston, Law of Contract to: page* [1674]]
17th edn (2017), pp.711–716

Application of the test

[*Add to note 62, at the end: page* [1680]]   **23–015**
; *Armchair Answercall Ltd v People in Mind Ltd* [2016] EWCA Civ 1039 at [51]
("Frustration if it occurs, is a definite event. Whether any given event is a

frustrating event is, once the facts said to constitute the event have been determined, a question of law. If it was, the fact that the parties did not immediately
treat it as such does not alter the position. What the parties did or did not do after
the event may, however, be a pointer to whether the event was in truth a
frustrating one").

Practical differences between the tests

23–018   [*In note 76, update reference to Treitel on The Law of Contract to: page* [1682]]
14th edn (2015), paras 19–114—19–123

3. ILLUSTRATIONS OF THE DOCTRINE

(b) *Common Types of Frustrating Events*

(ii) *Cancellation of an Expected Event*

Herne Bay Steamboat Co v Hutton

23–034   [*In note 144, update reference to Treitel on The Law of Contract to: page* [1690]]
14th edn (2015), paras 19–041—19–043

[*In note 144, update reference to Cheshire, Fifoot and Furmston, Law of Contract
to: page* [1690]]
17th edn (2017), pp.717–718

(c) *Application of the Doctrine to Common Types of Contracts*

(ii) *Charterparties*

[*In note 190, update reference to Scrutton on Charterparties and Bills of Lading to:
page* [1695]]
23rd edn (2015), Art.21

Examples not amounting to frustration

23–045   [*In note 206, update reference to Scrutton on Charterparties and Bills of Lading to:
page* [1698]]
23rd edn (2015) at Arts 122–135

4. THE LIMITS OF FRUSTRATION

Significance of a foreseen event

23–059   [*In note 278, update reference to Treitel on The Law of Contract to: page* [1708]]
14th edn (2015), paras 19–076—19–081

[*In note 279, update reference to Treitel on The Law of Contract to: page* [1708]]
14th edn (2015), paras 19–076—19–081

[*In note 285, update reference to Treitel on The Law of Contract to: page* [1708]]
14th edn (2015), para.19–076

Event foreseeable but not foreseen

[*Add to note 287, at the end: page* [1709]]   **23–060**
; *Armchair Answercall Ltd v People in Mind Ltd* [2016] EWCA Civ 1039 at
[30]

The Super Servant Two

[*In note 302, update reference to Treitel on The Law of Contract to: page* [1711]]   **23–063**
14th edn (2015), paras 19–086—19–088

Partial excuse at common law

[*In note 328, update reference Treitel on The Law of Contract to: page* [1714]]   **23–068**
14th edn (2015), paras 17–059 and 19–049—19–050

Limits of partial excuse

[*In note 333, update reference Treitel on The Law of Contract to: page* [1715]]   **23–069**
14th edn (2015), para.19–088

5. The Legal Consequences of Frustration

Contract discharged automatically

[*Add to note 336, at the end: page* [1716]]   **23–071**
See further McKendrick in Dyson, Goudkamp and Wilmot-Smith (eds), *Defences
in Contract* (2017), Ch.8.

Breaches before discharge

[*In note 364, update reference to Treitel on The Law of Contract to: page* [1720]]   **23–079**
14th edn (2015), para.19–105

Burden of proof

[*In note 383, update reference to Treitel on The Law of Contract to: page* [1722]]   **23–082**
14th edn (2015), paras 19–098

Destruction of the end product

23–086   [*In note 393, update reference to Treitel on The Law of Contract to: page* [1724]]
14th edn (2015), para.19–103

Contracts excluded from the Act

23–096   [*In note 415, update reference to Cheshire, Fifoot and Furmston, Law of Contract to: page* [1728]]
17th edn (2017), pp.737–738

[*In note 415, update reference to Treitel on The Law of Contract to: page* [1728]]
14th edn (2015), paras 19–111—19–113

CHAPTER 24

DISCHARGE BY BREACH

1. IN GENERAL

A middle ground

24–002

[*In note 15, update reference to Treitel on The Law of Contract to: page* [1734]]
14th edn (2015), paras 18–001—18–027

Affirmation irrevocable

24–004

[*In note 30, update reference to Treitel on The Law of Contract to: page* [1736]]
14th edn (2015), para.17–091

[*Add to note 33, at the end: page* [1736]]
In the context of an ongoing relationship such as a contract of employment it was
held in *Vairea v Reed Business Information Ltd* UKEAT/0177/15/BA at [81] that
an "entirely innocuous" act cannot "revive" a previous fundamental breach so
that it is necessary, in order to be entitled to terminate the contract on the ground
of the other party's breach, to establish that there has been a new breach entitling
the innocent party to make a second election. Where there has been a series of
breaches, followed by an affirmation of what would otherwise have been the
"last straw" entitling the innocent party to terminate the contract, the scale does
not remain loaded and ready to be tipped by adding another "straw". Rather, the
scale has been emptied by the affirmation and the new "straw" lands in an empty
scale (*Vairea* at [84]).

Effect of affirmation

24–010

[*In note 73, update reference to Treitel on The Law of Contract to: page* [1742]]
14th edn (2015), paras 21–011—21–015

[*Add to note 74, at the end: page* [1742]]
However, the Court of Appeal in *MSC Mediterranean Shipping Co SA v Cottonex Anstalt* [2016] EWCA Civ 789 at [45] did not find it necessary to invoke a duty of good faith in order to decide the outcome of the case and expressed its concern about the dangers which may follow were a general principle of good faith to be established and invoked in a case such as the present. In any event, the Court of Appeal concluded that Lord Reid's legitimate interest test was not applicable in a case where the commercial purpose of the adventure had been frustrated such that further performance had become impossible (at [42]–[43] and [61]).

[*Add to paragraph, at the end: page* [1743]]
Finally, it would appear that the innocent party cannot continue to hold the contract open in a case where the contractual purpose of the adventure has been frustrated such that further performance of the contract is either impossible or would be something radically different from what had been agreed by the parties at the time of entry into the contract.[79a]

[79a] *MSC Mediterranean Shipping Co SA v Cottonex Anstalt* [2016] EWCA Civ 789 at [41]–[44] and [61]–[64].

Acceptance of repudiation

24–013   [*Add to note 99, at the end: page* [1746]]
; *Vitol SA v Beta Renowable Group SA* [2017] EWHC 1734 (Comm).

[*Add new note 102a, after* "will be sufficiently unequivocal for this purpose" *six lines from the end: page* [1747]]
[102a] However, where the innocent party does nothing, in circumstances where it is not failing to perform a particular contractual obligation, a court is likely to conclude its inactivity is at best equivocal and so does not amount to an acceptance of the repudiation: *Alan Ramsay Sales & Marketing Ltd v Typhoo Tea Ltd* [2016] EWHC 486 (Comm), [2016] E.C.C. 12 at [79].

No reason or bad reason given

24–014   [*Add to note 108, at the end: page* [1748]]
In *C&S Associates UK Ltd v Enterprise Insurance Co Plc* [2015] EWHC 3757 (Comm) at [93] Males J. held that this exception applies only to anticipatory breaches or, to the extent that this is different, to situations where if the point had been taken steps could have been taken to avoid the party being in breach altogether, either by giving it an opportunity to perform its obligation in time or by enabling it to perform in some other valid way.

Both parties in breach

24–016   [*In note 119, update reference to Treitel on The Law of Contract to: page* [1749]]
14th edn (2015), para.18–094

2. RENUNCIATION

Renunciation

[*Add to note 122, at the end: page* [1750]]   **24–018**
; *Grand China Logistics Holding (Group) Co Ltd v Spar Shipping AS* [2016]
EWCA Civ 982, [2016] 2 Lloyd's Rep. 447 at [66]–[78]; *Teekay Tankers Ltd v
STX Offshore & Shipbuilding Co Ltd* [2017] EWHC 253 (Comm), [2017] 1
Lloyd's Rep. 387 at [217]. The question whether there has been a renunciation
depends on what a reasonable person would understand from the conduct of the
party alleged to have renounced the contract and all of the circumstances
prevailing at the time of the termination, including the history of the transaction
or relationship.

[*In note 135, lines 5–6, delete* "Spar Shipping SA v . . . (Comm) 879 at [209]" *and
substitute: page* [1751]]
Grand China Logistics Holding (Group) Co Ltd v Spar Shipping AS [2016]
EWCA Civ 982, [2016] 2 Lloyd's Rep. 447 at [73]–[76].

Reconciliation of the case-law

[*Add to note 145, at the end: page* [1753]]   **24–020**
and for a case in which it was not satisfied see *Mr H TV Ltd v ITV2 Ltd* [2015]
EWHC 2840 (Comm) at [269]–[275].

Anticipatory breach

[*Add to note 153, at the end: page* [1753]]   **24–022**
There is authority to support the proposition that a party who purports to have
accepted the renunciation as terminating the contract must also demonstrate that
it subjectively believed that the relevant words or conduct were evincing an
intention not to perform and further that, at the time of the alleged acceptance, it
actually accepted the same as terminating the contract: *SK Shipping (S) Pte Ltd
v Petroexport Ltd ("The Pro Victor")* [2009] EWHC 2974 (Comm), [2010] 2
Lloyd's Rep. 158 at [90]–[97]. However the need for a subjective belief in this
context has been criticised (see Q. Liu [2010] L.M.C.L.Q. 359) and the point was
left open by Carr J. in *Vitol SA v Beta Renowable Group SA* [2017] EWHC 1734
(Comm) at [48].

3. IMPOSSIBILITY CREATED BY ONE PARTY

Anticipatory breach

[*In note 187, update reference to Treitel on The Law of Contract to: page* [1759]]   **24–031**
14th edn (2015), para.17–077

[*In note 188, update reference to Treitel to: page* [1759]]
Treitel on The Law of Contract, paras 17–087—17–088

No anticipation of express right to terminate

24–032   [*In note 189, update reference to Treitel to: page* [1760]]
Treitel on The Law of Contract, para.17–084

4. FAILURE OF PERFORMANCE

Failure of performance: other situations

24–041   [*Add to note 226, at the end: page* [1764]]
; *Grand China Logistics Holding (Group) Co Ltd v Spar Shipping AS* [2016]
EWCA Civ 982, [2016] 2 Lloyd's Rep. 447 at [75].

[*Add to note 231, at the end: page* [1765]]
See also *C21 London Estates Ltd v Maurice Macneill Iona Ltd* [2017] EWHC
998 (Ch) at [85]–[89].

"Frustration by breach" and frustration

24–048   [*Add to note 262, at the end: page* [1769]]
; *MSC Mediterranean Shipping Co SA v Cottonex Anstalt* [2016] EWCA Civ 789
at [25].

5. CONSEQUENCES OF DISCHARGE

Obligations which survive discharge

24–050   [*Add to note 280, at the end: page* [1771]]
; *Involnert Management Inc v Aprilgrange Ltd* [2015] EWHC 2225 (Comm),
[2016] 1 All ER (Comm) 913 at [171]–[178].

Rights acquired before discharge

24–053   [*In note 297, line 2, delete* ". Contrast *Lowe v Hope* [1970] Ch. 94" *and substitute: page* [1773]]
; *Hardy v Griffiths* [2014] EWHC 3947 (Ch), [2015] 2 W.L.R. 1239. Contrast
Lowe v Hope [1970] Ch. 94, although the latter decision has been regarded as
incorrectly decided since the decision of the Court of Appeal in *Damon Compa-
nia Naviera SA v Hapag-Lloyd International SA*: see *Hardy v Griffiths* [2014]
EWHC 3947 (Ch) at [102] and [108].

[*Add to note 298, at the end: page* [1773]]
; *Hardy v Griffiths* [2014] EWHC 3947 (Ch), [2015] 2 W.L.R. 1239.

[*Add to note 299, line 7, after* "[2014] 1 All E.R. (Comm) 593;": *page* [1773]]
Hardy v Griffiths [2014] EWHC 3947 (Ch), [2015] 2 W.L.R. 1239.

CHAPTER 25

OTHER MODES OF DISCHARGE

1. MERGER

Requirements

[*Add to note 50, at the beginning: page* [1782]]   **25–012**
A decision on procedure alone is not a decision on the merits. A decision on the merits is one which establishes certain facts as proved or not in dispute, states what are the relevant principles of law applicable to such facts and expresses a conclusion with regard to the effect of applying those principles to the factual situation concerned: *DSV Silo-und Verwaltungsgesellschaft mbH v Owners of the Sennar* [1985] 1 W.L.R. 490, 499; *Saleh v Director of the Serious Fraud Office* [2017] EWCA Civ 18 at [51]–[54].

[*Add to note 52, at the end: page* [1783]]
There does not appear to be a requirement that the earlier proceedings must have been dismissed when the second proceedings were initiated. While that will normally be the case when *res judicata* is invoked, it is the pursuit of the second proceedings notwithstanding the disposal of the first which is objectionable and so if suffices that the earlier proceedings have been disposed of even if the disposal occurred subsequent to the initiation of the second proceedings: *Srivatsa v Secretary of State for Health* [2016] EWHC 2916 (QB) at [86].

Issues not raised previously

[*Add to note 64, at the end: page* [1784]]   **25–013**
See also *Dickinson v UK Acorn Finance Ltd* [2015] EWCA Civ 1194 at [20] ("the principles of abuse of process . . . are quite different from the somewhat technical doctrines of cause of action estoppel and issue estoppel").

[185]

Foreign judgment in rem

25–019   [*Add to note 108, at the end: page* [1789]]
; *Saleh v Director of the Serious Fraud Office* [2017] EWCA Civ 18 at [48] ("Whatever the appearance of the judgment it will only be regarded as a judgment *in rem* if it is made by a court with jurisdiction to determine proceedings where the function of those proceedings is to determine rights or status as against the world. Findings which are merely incidental to a determination that the court is required to make *in personam* are not binding on the world at large").

Part Eight

REMEDIES FOR BREACH OF CONTRACT

Chapter 26

DAMAGES

[187]

1. THE NATURE OF DAMAGES FOR BREACH OF CONTRACT

(a) *General*

Introduction

26–001   [*Add new note 1a, line 3, at the end of the first sentence: page* [1798]]
¹ᵃ For an example see *Scottish Power UK Plc v BP Exploration Operating Co Ltd* [2016] EWCA Civ 1043. There is a presumption that the parties do not intend to give up rights or claims which the general law gives them, and clear express words must be used in order to rebut this presumption: *Gilbert-Ash (Northern) Ltd v Modern Engineering (Bristol) Ltd* [1974] A.C. 689, 717–718 (Lord Diplock); but as the *Scottish Power* case shows, it is a matter of interpretation.

[*Add new note 7a, after* "terminated for breach" *in line 14: page* [1799]]
⁷ᵃ Thus a football club that has terminated a contract for improvements to its pitch before paying the price cannot recover the full price of employing a third party to carry out the work instead: *Gartell & Son v Yeovil Town Football & Athletic Club Ltd* [2016] EWCA Civ 62, [2016] B.L.R. 206.

[*Add to paragraph, after note 8: page* [1799]]
Where the claimant is to be compensated for loss of an income stream, a capital sum will be awarded with an appropriate discount for accelerated receipt.⁸ᵃ

^{8a} *Zodiac Maritime Agencies Ltd v Fortescue Metals Group Ltd (The Kildare)* [2010] EWHC 903 (Comm), [2011] 2 Lloyd's Rep. 360 at [73]; *Mitsui Osk Lines Ltd v Salgaocar Mining Industries Private Ltd* [2015] EWHC 565 (Comm), [2015] 2 Lloyd's Rep. 518 at [56]–[58].

[Add new paragraph 26–006A: page [1801]]

Abatement of price. The victim of a breach of contract who has not yet paid the other party may be entitled to rely on the fact that what he has received is worth less than it would have been, had the contract been performed, as a ground for abatement of the price. In *Multiplex Constructions (UK) Ltd v Cleveland Bridge UK Ltd*[43a] Jackson J. reviewed a number of authorities[43b] and said[43c]:

26–006A

> "Although there is not a complete harmony of approach to be discerned from this line of cases, I derive seven legal principles from the authorities cited:
> (i) In a contract for the provision of labour and materials, where performance has been defective, the employer is entitled at common law to maintain a defence of abatement.
> (ii) The measure of abatement is the amount by which the product of the contractor's endeavours has been diminished in value as a result of that defective performance.
> (iii) The method of assessing diminution in value will depend upon the facts and circumstances of each case.
> (iv) In some cases, diminution in value may be determined by comparing the current market value of that which has been constructed with the market value which it ought to have had. In other cases, diminution in value may be determined by reference to the cost of remedial works. In the latter situation, however, the cost of remedial works does not become the measure of abatement. It is merely a factor which may be used either in isolation or in conjunction with other factors for determining diminution in value.
> (v) The measure of abatement can never exceed the sum which would otherwise be due to the contractor as payment.
> (vi) Abatement is not available as a defence to a claim for payment in respect of professional services.
> (vii) Claims for delay, disruption or damage caused to anything other than that which the contractor has constructed cannot feature in a defence of abatement."

The fact that the innocent party has paid the price in full does not prevent a later claim for damages[43d]; nor does an abatement of the price to reflect the diminution in value of the performance preclude a later claim for other kinds of loss.[43e] Similarly, s.53 of the Sale of Goods Act 1979 provides that

> "(1) Where there is a breach of warranty by the seller, or where the buyer elects (or is compelled) to treat any breach of a condition on the part of the seller as a breach of warranty, the buyer is not by reason only of such breach of warranty entitled to reject the goods; but he may—
> (a) set up against the seller the breach of warranty in diminution or extinction of the price
> . . .
> (4) The fact that the buyer has set up the breach of warranty in diminution or extinction of the price does not prevent him from maintaining an action for the same breach of warranty if he has suffered further damage."[43f]

Under the Consumer Rights Act 2015 a consumer who has received goods, digital content or services that do not conform to the contract may have the right to a "price reduction".[43g] There are, however, certain cases in which there is no right to abatement of the price, in addition to contracts for professional services (as noted by Jackson J.). Claims in respect of cargo cannot be deducted from freight,[43h] and an employer has no right to make deductions from an employee's salary on account of bad work unless there is provision to that effect in the contract.[43i]

[43a] [2006] EWHC 1341 (TCC).

[43b] *Mondel v Steel* [1841] 8 M. & W. 858; *Davis v Hedges* [1871] L.R. 6 Q.B. 687; *H. Dakin & Co v Lee* [1916] 1 K.B. 566; *Gilbert-Ash (Northern) Ltd v Modern Engineering (Bristol) Ltd* [1974] A.C. 689; *Hutchinson v Harris* [1978] 10 B.L.R. 19; *Acsim (Southern) v Danish Contracting and Development Co* [1989] 47 B.L.R. 55; *Duquemin Ltd v Raymond Slater* [1993] 65 B.L.R. 124; *Foster Wheeler Wood Group Engineering v Chevron UK Ltd* Unreported February 29, 1996; *Mellowes Archital Ltd v Bell Projects Ltd* [1997] 87 B.L.R. 26.

[43c] [2006] EWHC 1341 (TCC) at [652].

[43d] *Davis v Hedges* [1871] L.R. 6 QB 687.

[43e] *Mondel v Steel* [1841] 8 M. & W. 858.

[43f] See Main Work, Vol.II, para.44–411.

[43g] See Consumer Rights Act 2015 ss.19(4)(b) and 24 (goods), ss.42(2)(b) and 44 (digital content) and ss.54(3)(b) and 56 (services); Main Work, Vol.II, para.38–483.

[43h] *Aries Tanker Corp v Total Transport Ltd (The Aries)* [1977] 1 W.L.R. 185 HL.

[43i] *Sagar v H Ridehalgh & Son Ltd* [1931] 1 Ch. 310 CA.

(g) *Difficulty in the Assessment of Damages*

Difficulty of assessment

26–015   [*Add new note 85a, line 7, after* "deprive the claimant of a remedy.": *page* [1806]]
[85a] The preceding sentences were quoted with apparent approval in *Wemyss v Karim* [2016] EWCA Civ 27 at [43].

[*Add to note 87, line 2, after* "Toulson L.J.": *page* [1807]]
See also *Wellesley Partners LLP v Withers LLP* [2015] EWCA Civ 1146, [2016] Ch. 529 at [95]–[96].

[*Add to note 87, at the end: page* [1807]]
The principle applies where the defendant has suppressed or failed to produce evidence to which it has access, not when the evidence is simply incomplete or involves a measure of conjecture, see *Porton Capital Technology Funds v 3M UK Holdings Ltd* [2011] EWHC 2895 (Comm) at [244]; *University of Wales v London College of Business Ltd* [2016] EWHC 888 (QB) at [10].

[*Add to paragraph, at the end: page* [1807]]
When the profit-earning capacity of a business sold was less than had been warranted by the seller and there was no evidence of either the business's actual value or the value it would have had if the warranty had been met, damages were assessed by working out the ratio between the price the buyer was willing to pay and the warranted earning capacity, and then applying that to the shortfall in earning capacity.[89a]

[89a] *Wemyss v Karim* [2016] EWCA Civ 27 at [49].

2. Compensable Heads of Loss

(b) *Expenditure Wasted as a Result of the Breach*

Damages assessed on a "no transaction" basis

[*Delete text from* "An analogous case is", *line 14, to the end, and substitute: pages* [1818]]   **26–031**

In *South Australia Asset Management Corp v York Montague Ltd*[163] the question was whether a valuer who is employed by a potential secured lender and who negligently over-values the property offered as security is liable not only for the difference between the negligent valuation of the property and its actual value at the time but for the whole loss suffered by the claimant if the property market falls so that the security becomes even less adequate. The Court of Appeal[164] distinguished between "no transaction" cases, in which the transaction would not have proceeded but for the defendant's negligence, and "successful transaction" cases in which it would have proceeded but possibly on different terms or for a different amount: once it was proved that the lender would not have made the particular loan but for the valuer's negligence, the valuer was liable for the entire loss flowing from the transaction so far as it was foreseeable. The House of Lords[165] disagreed, holding that that the distinction between "no transaction" and "successful transaction" cases should be abandoned. Lord Hoffmann, with whose reasons the other Members of the Judicial Committee agreed, said that the starting point must be the scope of the defendant's duty and the kind of loss for which the claimant is entitled to compensation.[166] The principle

> " . . . is that a person under a duty to take reasonable care to provide information on which someone else will decide upon a course of action is, if negligent, not generally regarded as responsible for all the consequences of that course of action. He is responsible only for the consequences of the information being wrong. A duty of care which imposes upon the informant responsibility for losses which would have occurred even if the information which he gave had been correct is not in my view fair and reasonable as between the parties. It is therefore inappropriate either as an implied term of a contract or as a tortious duty arising from the relationship between them. The principle thus stated distinguishes between a duty to *provide information* for the purpose of enabling someone else to decide upon a course of action and a duty to *advise* someone as to what course of action he should take. If the duty is to advise whether or not a course of action should be taken, the adviser must take reasonable care to consider all the potential consequences of that course of action. If he is negligent, he will therefore be responsible for all the foreseeable loss which is a consequence of that course of action having been taken. If his duty is only to supply information, he must take reasonable care to ensure that the information is correct and, if he is negligent, will be responsible for all the foreseeable consequences of the information being wrong."[167]

This has become known as the SAAMCo principle.[168] In *Hughes-Holland v BPE Solicitors*[169] the Supreme Court confirmed where the defendant's duty was to advise on the transaction as a whole, the claimant is in principle entitled to recover its full loss from entering the transaction; whereas where the duty was only to provide information on which the claimant was to base its decision, even if the information was critical to the claimant's decision, the defendant may be liable for the financial consequences of its being wrong but not for the financial consequences of the claimant entering into the transaction so far as these are greater. Lord Sumption, with whose judgment the President and other Justices agreed, said:

> "In cases falling within Lord Hoffmann's 'advice' category, it is left to the adviser to consider what matters should be taken into account in deciding whether to enter into the transaction. His duty is to consider all relevant matters and not only specific factors in the decision. If one of those matters is negligently ignored or misjudged, and this proves to be critical to the decision, the client will in principle be entitled to recover all loss flowing from the transaction which he should have protected his client against. The House of Lords might have said of the 'advice' cases that the client was entitled to the losses flowing from the transaction if they were not just attributable to risks within the scope of the adviser's duty but to risks which had been negligently assessed by the adviser.
>
> By comparison, in the 'information' category, a professional adviser contributes a limited part of the material on which his client will rely in deciding whether to enter into a prospective transaction, but the process of identifying the other relevant considerations and the overall assessment of the commercial merits of the transaction are exclusively matters for the client (or possibly his other advisers). In such a case, as Lord Hoffmann explained in [*Nykredit Mortgage Bank Plc v Edward Erdman Group Ltd (No.2)*[170]], the defendant's legal responsibility does not extend to the decision itself. It follows that even if the material which the defendant supplied is known to be critical to the decision to enter into the transaction, he is liable only for the financial consequences of its being wrong and not for the financial consequences of the claimant entering into the transaction so far as these are greater. Otherwise the defendant would become the underwriter of the financial fortunes of the whole transaction by virtue of having assumed a duty of care in relation to just one element of someone else's decision."[171]

So the first basis applied where a broker negligently advised the claimant to enter a transaction; he was held liable for all the losses suffered by the claimant from that entry.[172] In contrast, if the defendant's duty was only to give information on a particular aspect of the proposed transaction or, as has occurred in a number of conveyancing cases, to report to a lender on title or similar matters, the claimant should not recover the whole of the loss suffered through entering the transaction that turned out to be bad for other reasons.[172a] Thus if the defendant's duty was to advise the client on whether to enter another transaction or arrangement, because of the defendant's breach of contract the claimant entered that other transaction when it would not otherwise have done so, and the transaction turned out badly for other reasons, the claimant may be able to recover its wasted expenditure in full.[172b] However, the claimant's loss must still have been within the contemplation of the parties[172c]; and again[172d] the claimant is not put into a better position than he would have been in if the contract had been performed properly. Thus a claimant will not recover if the project would not have been viable and the claimant would have lost its investment even without the defendant's breach.[172e] It is clearly established that when the defendant fraudulently induced the claimant to enter into a transaction, even if it is not an "advice" case, damages may also be assessed on the "no transaction" basis.[172f] In fraud cases, neither the normal remoteness test nor the principle that the claimant must not be put into a better position than if the contract had been performed applies.[172g]

---

[163] [1997] A.C. 191 (below, para.26–168).
[164] sub nom. *Banque Bruxelles Lambert SA v Eagle Star Insurance Co Ltd* [1995] Q.B. 375.

¹⁶⁵ [1997] A.C. 191.

¹⁶⁶ [1997] A.C. 191, 211

¹⁶⁷ [1997] A.C. 191, 214. *Hayes v James & Charles Dodd (A Firm)* [1990] 2 All E.R. 815 CA and *County Personnel (Employment Agency) Ltd v Alan R Pulver and Co* [1987] 1 W.L.R. 916 CA were seemingly approved on the basis of the mitigation or "extrication" principle ("a reasonable attempt to cope with the consequences of the defendant's breach of duty") see [1997] A.C. 191, 219, though in *Hayes v James & Charles Dodd* the damages went beyond "extrication" and covered *all* the plaintiff's wasted expenditure from the beginning of the transaction.

¹⁶⁸ See further below, para.26–168.

¹⁶⁹ [2017] UKSC 21, [2017] 2 W.L.R. 1029.

¹⁷⁰ [2017] 1 W.L.R. 1627 HL.

¹⁷¹ *Hughes-Holland v BPE Solicitors* [2017] UKSC 21 at [40]–[41].

¹⁷² *Aneco Reinsurance Underwriting Ltd v Johnson & Higgins Ltd* [2001] 2 All E.R. (Comm) 929 HL, as explained in *Hughes-Holland v BPE Solicitors* [2017] UKSC 21 at [43]–[44].

¹⁷²ᵃ See [2017] UKSC 21 at [47]–[52], disapproving the reasoning in the *Steggles Palmer* and *Colin Bishop* cases (two of the cases brought by the *Bristol and West Building Society*, and reported in [1997] 4 All E.R. 582), and also the application of the *Steggles Palmer* case by the Court of Appeal in *Portman Building Society v Bevan Ashford* [2000] P.N.L.R. 344.

¹⁷²ᵇ The burden of proving the extent of the defendant's duty is on the claimant: [2017] UKSC 21 at [53].

¹⁷²ᶜ It is thought that if the defendant has undertaken such a duty to advise, then the loss will not be one for which the defendant could not reasonably be assumed to be taking responsibility: cf. Main Work, Vol.I, paras 26–126 et seq.

¹⁷²ᵈ cf. Main Work, Vol.I, para.26–028.

¹⁷²ᵉ As in *Hughes-Holland v BPE Solicitors* [2017] UKSC 21, see at [11], [19].

¹⁷²ᶠ *Smith New Court Securities Ltd v Scrimgeour Vickers (Asset Management) Ltd* [1997] A.C. 254; see Main Work, Vol.I, paras 7–061—7–065.

¹⁷²ᵍ See Main Work, Vol.I, paras 7–055—7–056.

3. MEASURES OF COMPENSATION

(c) *Claimant's Original Purpose Fulfilled Despite Breach*

Sale of goods cases

[Add new note 210a, after "purpose without any loss." *in line 5: page* [1824]]   **26–040**

²¹⁰ᵃ This situation must be distinguished from the case in which the claimant has been able to mitigate its loss by subsequent action that reduced or eliminated it: see Main Work, Vol.I, para.26–095. Most of the cases cited in that paragraph concern the recovery of loss beyond the value of the promised performance itself, but it is thought that mitigation may also reduce the claim below the difference in value between the promised performance and the performance in fact rendered. For example, if the buyer has the goods repaired so that they conform to the contract for less than the difference in value, the buyer will recover only the cost of repair not the difference in value between the goods as they should have been and as they were delivered.

Shortcomings in contracts for services

[Add to note 219, at the end: page [1826]]   **26–041**
But see above, para.26–040, n.210a.

[Add new paragraph 26–041A: page [1826]]
Landlord's failure to maintain or repair. A slightly different approach has   **26–041A**
been taken by the Court of Appeal in a case in which a landlord had failed to repair premises that had been flooded.²¹⁹ᵃ The Court held that the loss consists in

the impairment to the rights of amenity afforded to the lessee by the lease; discomfort, inconvenience and distress (and even the deterioration of the health of a loved one) are only symptoms. Therefore the lessee may claim for loss of amenity even though for reasons unconnected with the disrepair itself he may have chosen not to make full use, or even any use, of them during part or all of the relevant period. But the non-use of the premises may be seen as a form of mitigation of loss, and non-use of the premises for other reasons may also be taken into account, so that the lessee will not necessarily recover the full market rental for the period of disrepair. If the lessee has to rent other premises, then the cost of doing so may be the best measure of his loss and may be recoverable even if it exceeds the market rental value of the original property[219b]; conversely,

> " . . . the court is entitled and, I would say, obliged to temper the rigour of those rules which seek to implement the compensatory principle which lies at the heart of the law of damages, where particular circumstances make it just to do so".[219c]

The cases on goods and services cited in the previous paragraphs[219d] were not cited. It is not obvious why a buyer of goods or services should recover the difference between the value of the goods or services that should have been provided and the value of what was provided, but a lessee who has been deprived of the use of the property because of a failure to repair will not recover the full market rental irrespective of whether he would have used the property.

[219a] *Moorjani v Durban Estates Ltd* [2015] EWCA Civ 1252, [2016] H.L.R. 6.

[219b] [2015] EWCA Civ 1252 at [35]–[39] (Briggs L.J., with whom the other members of the court agreed).

[219c] [2015] EWCA Civ 1252 at [40]. Briggs L.J. relied in particular on *Earle v Charalambous* [2006] EWCA Civ 1090, [2007] H.L.R. 8, in which the lessee had gone to live with his parents and the Court of Appeal limited his damages to 50 per cent of the notional market rent for the period: see [2015] EWCA Civ 1252 at [37].

[219d] See Main Work, Vol.I, paras 26–040—26–041.

The "performance interest"

26–042   [*Add new note 219e, after* "benefit a third person" *in line 7: page* [1826]]

[219e] Thus a party who has been deprived by the defendant's breach of the chance to earn freight suffers a substantial loss even if the first party would have directed the money to be paid to a third party who was not the first party's agent nor bound to account for it: *Glory Wealth Shipping Pte Ltd v Flame SA* [2016] EWHC 293 (Comm), [2016] 1 Lloyd's Rep. 571.

4. MEASURES THAT ARE NOT STRICTLY COMPENSATORY

(c) *Depriving the Defendant of Part of his Profit*

Hypothetical bargain damages on the *Wrotham Park basis*

26–051   [*Add to note 276, at the end: page* [1832]]

See also *One Step (Support) Ltd v Morris-Garner* [2016] EWCA Civ 180 at [81].

> [*Add new note 281a, at the end of the paragraph: page* [1832]]
>
> [281a] However, in *Marathon Asset Management LLP v Seddon* [2017] EWHC 300 (Comm), [2017] I.C.R. 791 no award was made when the defendant had wrongfully made a copy of the claimant's

data. The claimants had not attempted to show that they had suffered any loss (at [155]) or that the defendants had made any gain (at [156]); the defendants had not benefitted from having the data (the defendant had made very little use of it and the claimant based its case solely on the making of the copy: at [243]); and the remedy must match the wrong (at [256]). Unlike the cases of wrongful use of the claimant's goods, making a copy did not deprive the claimant of anything (at [159]). Leggatt J. said that it may be appropriate to award what he termed "licence fee damages" in a mere breach of contract case if the defendant has obtained a benefit that has a market value (at [189]), or where there was an alternative way in which the defendant could have obtained the same thing; or if it was reasonable to expect that the claimant would grant a licence if a reasonable fee was paid (at [233]). But if it was not reasonable to expect this and the defendant could not obtain the same thing from elsewhere, then a hypothetical bargain makes no sense and the appropriate method of valuation is to assess the amount of profit actually made by the wrongdoer which is fairly attributable to its wrongful use of the claimant's property or other wrongful act (at [235]–[236]). As the mere copying of the files neither harmed the claimant nor benefitted the defendant, no reasonable person would charge or agree to pay more than a token sum for that right (at [260]).

Breach of contract cases

[*Add to paragraph, after note 290: page* [1833]]   **26–053**
In cases of a breach of non-competition clauses in a sale of a business, a fourth factor is whether it is doubtful that interim relief could be obtained.[290a]

[290a] Longmore L.J. in *One Step (Support) Ltd v Morris-Garner* [2016] EWCA Civ 180 at [151] (defendant's furtive conduct deprived claimant of opportunity to obtain interim relief).

[*In note 291, update reference to One Step (Support) Ltd v Morris-Garner to: page* [1834]]
[2016] EWCA Civ 180 at [126] and [149].

[*In paragraph, after note 294, delete* "However, it" *and substitute; page* [1834]]
However, in *One Step (Support) Ltd v Morris-Garner* the Court of Appeal declined to follow this dictum and held that *Wrotham Park* damages may be awarded when it will be very difficult to prove the loss that has been caused by the breach; the question is whether an award would be a just response.[294a] It

[294a] [2016] EWCA Civ 180, [2017] Q.B. 1 at [122] and [145]–[146]. In that case the defendants had made wrongful use of confidential information and broken no-solicitation covenants. The case is noted by Davies [2017] L.M.C.L.Q. 201. In *Marathon Asset Management LLP v Seddon* [2017] EWHC 300 (Comm) Leggatt J. said (at [217]) he did not find it easy to discern the principle on which the award for breach of obligations not to compete had been made in the *One Step* case. The fact that the claimant's loss would be difficult to prove or quantify might be a good reason for granting an injunction rather than leaving the claimant to seek damages, but it is not a principled reason for awarding a sum of money which does not depend on whether the claimant has suffered any loss at all. Awarding a gain-based remedy can only be a just response where compensatory damages are an inherently inadequate remedy because they would not represent adequate redress for the wrong done to the claimant even where any loss caused by the defendant's wrong can be fully identified and reversed (at [214]–[215]).

[*Add to paragraph, after note 295: page* [1834]]
; or possibly if the real loss would be suffered by a third party.[295a]

[295a] cf. *ParkingEye Ltd v Beavis* [2015] UKSC 67, [2016] A.C. 1172, below, paras 26–195 et seq.

Assessing hypothetical bargain damages

[*Add to note 301, at the end: page* [1835]]   **26–054**
See also *Marathon Asset Management LLP v Seddon* [2017] EWHC 300 (Comm), [2017] I.C.R. 791 at [245]–[252].

5. Causation and Contributory Negligence

(a) *Causation*

Requirement of a causal connection

26–058   [*Add to note 334, at the end: page* [1839]]
In *Environment Agency v Empress Car Co (Abertillery) Ltd* [1999] 2 A.C. 22, 31
Lord Hoffmann said "One cannot give a common sense answer to a question of
causation for the purpose of attributing responsibility under some rule without
knowing the purpose and scope of the rule". That was not a contract case but the
dictum is applicable to contract cases: e.g. *IG Index Ltd v Ehrentreu* [2015]
EWHC 3390 (QB) at [110] (purpose of contractual obligation considered).

Duty to prevent third party's act

26–062   [*In note 342, update reference to Treitel on The Law of Contract to: page* [1840]]
14th edn (2015), para.20–097

[*In note 344, update reference to Treitel on The Law of Contract to: page* [1840]]
14th edn (2015), para.20–097

[*Also in note 344, update reference to Clerk & Lindsell on Torts to: page* [1840]]
21st edn (2014), paras 2–107 et seq.

Intervening act or omission of the claimant

26–064   [*Add new note 350a, line 1, after* "Other contract cases"*: page* [1841]]
    [350a] See also cases on a party's decision to continue with spread betting: e.g. *IG Index Ltd v Ehrentreu* [2015] EWHC 3390 (QB) at [107]–[118]. Permission to appeal has been granted: [2017] EWCA Civ 326.

A fact-specific issue

26–065   [*Add new note 356a, at end of paragraph: page* [1842]]
    [356a] e.g. *IG Index Ltd v Ehrentreu* [2015] EWHC 3390 (QB), in which both mitigation and contributory negligence were considered. Permission to appeal has been granted: [2017] EWCA Civ 326.

The claimant's lost opportunities: hypothetical consequences

26–069   [*Add new note 364a, after* "deficient in some other way." *in line 7: page* [1843]]
    [364a] Where the defendant's negligence has allegedly led to the claimant losing an opportunity to pursue a claim in litigation or in commercial negotiation, the defendant may bear an evidential burden to prove that there is no causal link between the negligence and the loss: see *Mount v Barker Austin* [1998] P.N.L.R. 493, 510, applied in *Harding Homes (East Street) Ltd v Bircham Dyson Bell* [2015] EWHC 3329 (Ch) at [34]. Where there are multiple contingencies that are not independent, the court should make an overall assessment rather than simply multiplying the percentage chances of each one: *Tom Hoskins Plc v EMW Law* [2010] EWHC 479 (Ch), [2010] E.C.C. 20 at [133]–[134]; *Harding Homes (East Street) Ltd v Bircham Dyson Bell* [2015] EWHC 3329 (Ch) at [42].

A hypothetical action of a third party

[*Add to paragraph, line 8, after* "party's action,"*: page* [1844]]
and the loss of chance is not too remote,[368a]

26–071

[368a] As in *Wright v Lewis Silkin LLP* [2016] EWCA Civ 1308 at [62]–[66]. On remoteness see Main Work, Vol.I, paras 2–107 et seq.

[*Add to note 369, line 5, after* "out of court settlement)"*: page* [1844]]
; *Wellesley Partners LLP v Withers LLP* [2015] EWCA Civ 1146, [2016] Ch. 529 (distinguishing, at [96]–[98], the different exercise of assessing or quantifying the loss once the loss of chance has been established; on assessment, see Main Work, Vol.I, para.26–015); *Commodities Research Unit International (Holdings) Ltd v King and Wood Mallesons LLP* [2016] EWHC 727 (QB); *McGill v Sports and Entertainment Media Group* [2016] EWCA Civ 1063.

Contingency has occurred by time of trial

[*Add to note 378, line 8, after* "at [35]–[38]"*: page* [1845]]
(but for a contrary suggestion, see *OMV Petrom SA v Glencore International AG* [2016] EWCA Civ 778 at [56])

26–074

(b) *Contributory Negligence*

Contributory negligence and breach of contract

[*Add to note 396, at the end: page* [1848]]
; *IG Index Ltd v Ehrentreu* [2015] EWHC 3390 (QB), in which the judge, had he considered it to be a category 3 case, would have made a deduction of 95 per cent (at [130]). Permission to appeal has been granted: [2017] EWCA Civ 326.

26–077

6. MITIGATION OF DAMAGE

(a) *The Principles of Mitigation*

Avoidable loss

[*Add to note 405, line 2, after* "605, 608 CA"*: page* [1850]]
For a recent example, see *IG Index Ltd v Ehrentreu* [2015] EWHC 3390 (QB), quoting this passage in the 31st edn (at [120]). Permission to appeal has been granted: [2017] EWCA Civ 326.

26–081

"Reasonable steps"

[*Add to note 411, at the end: page* [1851]]
Nonetheless it requires an objective analysis that may involve more than just fact-finding, so an appellate court may interfere if the trier of fact has clearly

26–082

gone wrong: *LSREF III Wight Ltd v Gateley LLP* [2016] EWCA Civ 359, [2016] P.N.L.R. 21 at [39].

[*Add to note 412, at the end: page* [1851]]
The claimant may have to take an obvious step even if it is not part of its ordinary business: *LSREF III Wight Ltd v Gateley LLP* [2016] EWCA Civ 359, [2016] P.N.L.R. 21 (lender on security of lease should have pursued lessor's offer to remove clause providing for forfeiture on lessee-borrower's insolvency).

(c) *Timing of Mitigation and the Assessment of Damages*

The time for mitigating action

26–087   [*Add to paragraph, at the beginning: page* [1855]]
There is no duty on a party to mitigate before there has been a breach or, normally, an anticipatory repudiation that the party has accepted.[444a]

[444a] *Shindler v Northern Raincoat Co Ltd* [1960] 1 W.L.R. 1038, 1048; *Scottish Power UK Plc v BP Exploration Operating Co Ltd* [2016] EWCA Civ 1043 at [41]. On mitigation after an anticipatory breach see further, Main Work, Vol.I, para.26–092.

[*In note 445, update reference to Treitel to: page* [1855]]
Peel (ed.), *Treitel on The Law of Contract*, 14th edn (2015), para.20–072

[*In note 446, update reference to Benjamin's Sale of Goods to: page* [1855]]
9th edn (2014), paras 17–059—17–060

The relevant date for the assessment of damages

26–088   [*Add to note 452, at the end: page* [1855]]
; *Marathon Asset Management LLP v Seddon* [2017] EWHC 300 (Comm) at [250].

(e) *Savings to be Taken into Account*

Loss which is avoided cannot be recovered

26–095   [*In note 493, delete last sentence and substitute: page* [1861]]
The authorities were analysed and helpfully summarised by Popplewell J. in *Fulton Shipping Inc of Panama v Globalia Business Travel SAU* [2014] EWHC 1547 (Comm), see below, para.26–099.

Benefits independent of mitigation

26–099   [*Delete paragraph and substitute: page* [1863]]
Benefit arising from decision to sell property required in order to perform contract. A very difficult question of whether there was a sufficient link between the breach and a benefit obtained by the innocent party arose in *Fulton Shipping Inc of Panama v Globalia Business Travel SAU*.[511] The owners of a vessel that the time-charterer had, in breach of contract, redelivered early could find no

alternative employment for her and sold her for over US $23 million, whereas by the end of the charter (after the financial crisis of 2007–08) she would have been worth only US $7 million. The owners claimed for loss of net profit that would have been earned during the remaining two years of the charter. The arbitrator held that the price obtained on the sale should be taken into account, which would reduce the claim for loss of profit to nil. Popplewell J., after a detailed review and summary[512] of the authorities, held that the owner's decision to sell the vessel was independent of the breach and the sale should not be taken into account. The Court of Appeal allowed the charterer's appeal.[512a] Longmore L.J. said:

> "… if a claimant adopts by way of mitigation a measure which arises out of the consequences of the breach and is in the ordinary course of business and such measure benefits the claimant, that benefit is normally to be brought into account in assessing the claimant's loss unless the measure is wholly independent of the relationship of the claimant and the defendant. That should be a principle sufficient to guide the decision of the fact-finder in any particular case."[512b]

Where there is an available market, the innocent party is expected to make use of it, and any further profit as well as any further losses will normally be irrelevant[512c]; and where there are no such opportunities and the owner decides to sell the vessel, the resale price should equally be taken into account.[512d] The Supreme Court, however, restored the order made by Popplewell J.[512e] Lord Clarke, with whom the other members of the Supreme Court agreed, said that the owners' interest in the capital value had nothing to do with the interest injured by the charterers' repudiation, not because the benefit must be of the same kind as the loss caused by the wrongdoer, which is "too vague and potentially too arbitrary a test" but because it must have been caused either by the breach or by a successful act of mitigation.[512f] There was not a sufficient causal link between the breach and the benefit from the sale because the owners could have sold the vessel during the term of the charter party and they were making a decision at their own risk about the disposal of an interest in the vessel which was no part of the subject matter of the charterparty and had nothing to do with the charterers. If the value of the vessel had risen after it had been sold, the owners could not have claimed the difference in value, and equally they were not required to bring into account the benefit obtained by its sale. Nor was there any reason to pick on the sale price at the end of the charter period as the comparator, as the ship would not necessarily have been sold then. "The causal link fails at both ends of the transaction".[512g] Equally, Lord Clarke continued, the sale of the vessel was not a relevant act of mitigation. The measure of loss was the difference between the contract rate and what might have been earned from employing the vessel under similar or shorter charters, whereas the sale did not provide a substitute income stream and therefore was incapable of mitigating the loss.[512h] A sale of the vessel, say a year, after the repudiation might have been relevant as it would shorten the period for which there was a lost income stream to mitigate, and if such a sale had been for less than the price that would have been obtainable by selling the vessel with the benefit of the income of the remaining charter period, they might have been able to recover that loss, but neither would make the sale an act of mitigation.[512i]

[511] [2014] EWHC 1547 (Comm); [2015] EWCA Civ 1299, [2016] 1 W.L.R. 2450; [2017] UKSC 43, [2017] 1 W.L.R. 2581. The first instance decision was applied in *Thai Airways International Public Co Ltd v KI Holdings Co Ltd* [2015] EWHC 1250 (Comm) at [51].

512 [2014] EWHC 1547 (Comm) at [63]–[64], quoted in full by Lord Clarke [2017] UKSC 43 at [16].

512a [2015] EWCA Civ 1299. The CA decision was the subject of a critical note by Hooper (2016) 132 L.Q.R. 547. See also McLauchlan [2016] L.M.C.L.Q. 459.

512b [2015] EWCA Civ 1299 at [23]. For the application of a similar principle in a case of a solicitor's negligence in failing to discover a restriction on use of property the client was buying, where subsequently the client was able to get the restriction lifted at minimal cost, see *Bacciottini v Gotelee & Goldsmith* [2016] EWCA Civ 170, [2016] 4 W.L.R. 98.

512c [2015] EWCA Civ 1299 at [24] and [49].

512d [2015] EWCA Civ 1299 at [30] and [50].

512e [2017] UKSC 43, [2017] 1 W.L.R. 2581.

512f [2017] UKSC 43 at [29]–[30].

512g [2017] UKSC 43 at [32]–[33].

512h [2017] UKSC 43 at [34].

512i [2017] UKSC 43 at [35].

26–099A This decision may prove controversial. As the owners would not have sold the vessel in 2007 but for the breach, and selling then meant that they did not suffer its subsequent loss in the value, it is certainly possible to argue that the Court of Appeal was right: the benefit arose directly from the breach and wiped out any loss. It can also be argued that Lord Clarke was not correct to say that, had the market price for vessels risen between 2007 and 2009, the charterers would not have been liable for the owners' loss, as the claimant may recover damages for loss or expense incurred by him in reasonably attempting to mitigate his loss following the defendant's breach, even when the mitigating steps were unsuccessful or in fact led to greater loss.[512j] However, it is submitted that the Supreme Court's approach is correct. While the owners would not have sold in 2007 but for the breach, the fact that they could have sold the vessel (subject to the charter) at any time before 2009, and equally might have retained it after that date, suggests that the sale was a completely independent transaction. Nor is it clear that the owners would have been entitled to recover for the loss in value of the ship had prices gone up not down: again, it was not known whether they would have sold in 2009, and at least where (as on the facts of the *Fulton* case) selling the ship was not something they were required to do by way of mitigation,[512k] the loss again followed from their independent decision to sell rather than from the breach. One statement made by Lord Clarke may be questioned, however. Lord Clarke said that a sale of the vessel a year after the repudiation might have been relevant as it would shorten the period for which there was a lost income stream to mitigate, and if such a sale had been for less than the price that would have been obtainable by selling the vessel with the benefit of the income of the remaining charter period, they might have been able to recover that loss.[512l] What difference does it make that the sale is a year after the repudiation rather than immediate? It is submitted that selling the vessel after a year would no more affect the owner's loss of income than did the immediate sale. And if the owners are to be compensated for loss of the charter income, it would be wrong also to compensate them because the sale produced a lower price than a sale with the benefit of the charter would have done, as that would in effect compensate them twice for the same loss.

512j See Main Work, Vol.I, para.26–102. In the Court of Appeal, counsel for the charterers had accepted that if the sale had been in consequence of the breach and had been undertaken by way of mitigation, and the price had risen between 2007 and 2009, the charterers would have been liable for the owner's inability to take advantage of the rise: see [2017] UKSC 43 at [28].

[512k] See [2017] UKSC 43 at [20].
[512l] [2017] UKSC 43 at [35].

Act by third party. When a lender claimed damages from a valuer for   26–099B
negligence in preparing a report on a borrower, and the individual who
controlled the lender, but to whom the valuers owed no duty, personally lent
further funds to the borrower that enabled the borrower to pay off some of the
loans, that was taken into account, as it discharged the very liability which the
lenders claimed as their loss and it was a distinct transaction between different
parties.[512m] Nor was the cost recoverable as a cost of mitigation, as it was not
an act done by the claimant and was not caused by the valuer's breach of
duty.[512n]

[512m] *Swynson Ltd v Lowick Rose LLP (In Liquidation) (formerly Hurst Morrison Thomson LLP)*
[2017] UKSC 32, [2017] 2 W.L.R. 1161 at [13], [47]–[49], [97] and [99].
[512n] [2017] UKSC 32 at [13], [46] and [97]; see below, para.26–102.

(f) *Expenses of Mitigation*

Recovery of loss or expense suffered while attempting to mitigate

[Add new note 518a, line 3, after "expense incurred by him"*: page* [1866]]   26–102
[518a] The rule has no application to the cost of actions carried out by a third party, not at the
claimant's request, even though they may reduce the claimant's loss: *Swynson Ltd v Lowick Rose LLP
(In Liquidation) (formerly Hurst Morrison Thomson LLP)* [2017] UKSC 32, [2017] 2 W.L.R. 1161
at [13], [46] and [97]; see above, para.26–099B.

(g) *Choosing between Remedies*

"Legitimate interest" in performing

[Add to note 545, at the end: page [1868]]   26–106
Strictly speaking the point did not arise in *MSC Mediterranean Shipping Co SA
v Cottonex Anstalt* [2016] EWCA Civ 789 (see below, n.547), but the Court of
Appeal clearly accepted the "legitimate interest" qualification as part of the
law.

[Add to paragraph, line 12, after "accepted this qualification,"*: page* [1868]]
it has been referred to by the Supreme Court with apparent approval,[545a]

[545a] *Cavendish Square Holding BV v Makdessi* and *ParkingEye Ltd v Beavis* [2015] UKSC 67,
[2016] A.C. 1172 at [29].

[Add to note 547, at the end: page [1869]]
The Court of Appeal in that case ([2016] EWCA Civ 789, [2016] 2 Lloyd's Rep.
494) held that the issue did not arise because it was impossible to continue to
perform the contract, as the contractual adventure had been frustrated (at [41])
but agreed that had it been open to the carrier to affirm the contract, the carrier

would have had no legitimate interest in continuing to insist on performance by the shipper (at [43]).

7. REMOTENESS OF DAMAGE AND ASSUMPTION OF RESPONSIBILITY

(b) Remoteness

The type or kind of loss

26–116   [*Add to note 582, line 4, after* "[1996] 4 All E.R. 119, 126": *page* [1874]]
; *Transfield Shipping Inc v Mercator Shipping Inc (The Achilleas)* [2008] UKHL 48, [2009] 1 A.C. 61 at [21]; *Wellesley Partners LLP v Withers LLP* [2015] EWCA Civ 1146 at [74].

The degree of probability

26–118   [*In note 608, delete from* "The difference between the rules" *in line 1 to the end: page* [1877]]

[*Add new paragraph 26–118A: page* [1877]]
26–118A **Concurrent liability.** The difference between the remoteness rule in contract and the remoteness rule in tort has given rise to difficulty in cases of concurrent liability.

> "Damage may be of a kind which is reasonably foreseeable (and therefore recoverable in tort) yet highly unusual or unlikely (and therefore irrecoverable in contract).[608a]

In *Parsons (Livestock) Ltd v Uttley, Ingham & Co Ltd*[608b] Lord Denning M.R. said that in the test for remoteness of damage in contract there is a distinction between loss of profit (or only economic loss) cases, and physical damage (or expense) cases[608c]; but this distinction was not accepted by the other members of the Court of Appeal,[608d] and seemed to lack supporting authority. However, no clear answer emerged from the other judgments. Academic writers suggested that where a claimant was in previous communication with the defendant, the contract rule should apply.[608e] The question has recently been subject to apparently conflicting decisions of the Court of Appeal.[608f] In *Yapp v Foreign and Commonwealth Office*,[608g] an employment case, Underhill L.J., with whom the other members of the court agreed, held that whether psychiatric injury was too remote a consequence of a breach of the employer's duty of care was to be determined by the test applicable in tort.[608h] But in *Wellesley Partners LLP v Withers LLP*[608i] (in which *Yapp's* case was not cited) the Court accepted the academic arguments and held that in cases of concurrent liability for failure to carry out instructions the contract rule should apply.[608j] The members of the Court saw this as consistent with the decisions of the House of Lords in the *SAAMCo* case[608k] and *The Achilleas*[608l] that the extent of liability should be determined by the scope of the defendant's duty and what responsibility the defendant could reasonably be taken to have assumed.[608m] It may be necessary[608n] to distinguish the *Wellesley* case and the *Yapp* case on the ground that *Yapp's* case was concerned with a breach of the common law duty of care[608o] leading to psychiatric injury, whereas the *Wellesley* case involved economic loss, which requires an assumption of responsibility[608p]; indeed Floyd L.J's view was that "the test for recoverability of damage for economic loss should be the same, and should be the contractual one",[608q] while Roth J. referred to tort cases in which liability was based on a voluntary assumption of responsibility and Longmore L.J. to the liability of solicitors for failing to carry out their instructions—both thus seeming to refer also to economic losses for which the defendant had assumed responsibility. In *Wright v Lewis Silkin LLP*,[608r] another solicitors' negligence case, the Court of Appeal held that it was bound to follow the *Wellesley* case.

[608a] Floyd L.J. in *Wellesley Partners LLP v Withers LLP* [2015] EWCA Civ 1146 at [86].

[608b] [1978] Q.B. 791.

[608c] See at 804–805 (Orr L.J.) and at 805–806 (Scarman L.J.).

[608d] See at 804–805 (Orr L.J.) and at 805–806 (Scarman L.J.).

[608e] See A Burrows, "Limitations on Compensation" in Burrows and Peel, *Commercial Remedies* (2003), pp.27, 35; *McGregor on Damages*, 19th edn (2014), para.22–009; Peel (ed.), *Treitel on The Law of Contract*, 14th edn (2015), para.20–112.

[608f] See also above, para.1–195A.

[608g] [2014] EWCA Civ 1512.

[608h] See [2014] EWCA Civ 1512 at [119]. Underhill L.J's propositions are summarised in Main Work, Vol.I, para.26–147.

[608i] [2015] EWCA Civ 1146, [2016] 2 W.L.R. 1351, noted Balen [2016] L.M.C.L.Q. 186.

[608j] See [2015] EWCA Civ 1146, [2016] Ch. 529 at [80], [157] and [186].

[608k] *South Australia Asset Management Corp v York Montague Ltd* [1997] A.C. 191 (see Main Work, Vol.I, para.26–168).

[608l] *Transfield Shipping Inc v Mercator Shipping Inc (The Achilleas)* [2008] UKHL 48, [2009] 1 A.C. 61. See Main Work, Vol.I, paras 26–126 et seq.

[608m] See [2015] EWCA Civ 1146 at [74], [152]–[157] and [182]–[187]

[608n] While in *Yapp's* case the claim for psychiatric injury failed even on the wider tort test and in *Wellesley* the claim for loss of profit succeeded even on the narrower contract test, in each case the applicable test was discussed at length and the discussion cannot be treated as obiter.

[608o] Underhill L.J. specifically noted that he was not following the approach taken by the academics, remarking that "as regards the common law duty of care owed to employees the position seems to be the opposite" see note 8 to [119] of the judgment.

[608p] See above, para.1–195A.

[608q] [2015] EWCA Civ 1146 at [80].

[608r] [2016] EWCA Civ 1308 at [60]–[61].

Loss of a kind that is "not unusual"

[*In note 617, update reference to Treitel on The Law of Contract to: page* [1878]] **26–121**
14th edn (2015), para.20–106

(c) *Assumption of Responsibility*

Assumption of responsibility

[*In note 635, update reference to Treitel on The Law of Contract 13th edn (2011) to:* **26–126**
page [1881]]
14th edn (2015), paras 20–098 and 20–106

The Achilleas

26–128   *[Add new note 666a, at the end of paragraph: page* [1885]]
   [666a] An award of damages for loss beyond the end date of the broken charter was upheld in *Louis Dreyfus Commodities Suisse SA v MT Maritime Management BV (The MTM Hong Kong)* [2015] EWHC 2505 (Comm). It appears that no argument on assumption of responsibility had been put to the arbitrators: at [72].

8. PARTICULAR RESTRICTIONS ON RECOVERY OF DAMAGES

(a) *Non-pecuniary Losses*

Inconvenience and discomfort

26–142   *[Add to paragraph, at the end: page* [1894]]
   ; and the Court of Appeal has held that distress and inconvenience caused by disrepair are not freestanding heads of claim, but are symptomatic of interference with the lessee's enjoyment of the premises.[730a] It follows that care should be taken to ensure that any award for distress and inconvenience does not overlap with an award of loss of the market rental value of the property.[730b]

   [730a] *Earle v Charalambous* [2006] EWCA Civ 1090, [2007] H.L.R. 8 at [32], applied in *Moorjani v Durban Estates Ltd* [2015] EWCA Civ 1252, [2016] H.L.R. 6 at [31].
   [730b] See *Wallace v Manchester City Council* (1998) 30 H.L.R. 1111, 1121. On recovery of the market rental value see above, para.26–041A.

Nervous shock

26–143   *[Add to note 732, at the end: page* [1894]]
   ; *BAE Systems (Operations) Ltd v Konczak* [2017] EWCA Civ 1188, [2017] I.R.L.R. 893 (a case involving apportionment between multiple causes).

Loss of amenity

26–146   *[Add to note 744, at the end: page* [1896]]
   Causation and quantum must be pleaded: *Abbott v RCI Europe* [2016] EWHC 2602 (Ch) at [116]–[117].

Employment cases

26–147   *[Add new note 748a, after* "must have been foreseeable)." *in line 12: page* [1896]]
   [748a] But contrast above, para.26–118A.

   [Add to note 749, at the end: page [1896]]
   ; *BAE Systems (Operations) Ltd v Konczak* [2017] EWCA Civ 1188 (a case involving apportionment between multiple causes).

Loss of reputation

[*Add to note 757, at the end: page* [1897]] **26–148**
On when a specific award of stigma damages may be necessary, see *Abbey National Plc v Chagger* [2009] EWCA Civ 1202, [2010] I.C.R. 397 at [97]–[99].

9. ILLUSTRATIONS OF THE ASSESSMENT OF DAMAGES

(b) *Sale of Goods*

Delay in delivery

[*In note 800, update reference to Treitel on The Law of Contract to: page* [1902]] **26–158**
14th edn (2015), para.20–049

Delivery of defective goods

[*In note 809, update reference to Treitel on The Law of Contract to: page* [1903]] **26–159**
14th edn (2015), para.20–051

[*Add to note 809, at the end: page* [1903]]
In *OMV Petrom SA v Glencore International AG* [2016] EWCA Civ 778, [2016] 2 Lloyd's Rep. 432 Christopher Clarke L.J. seemed to think that the *Bence Graphics* case could not stand with *Slater v Hoyle Smith Ltd*, but left the matter open (at [45]–[46]).

(d) *Contracts Concerning Land*

Valuer-surveyor's report to a lender

[*Delete text of note 851 and substitute: page* [1907]] **26–168**
See however the "advice cases" recognised by the House of Lords in the *South Australia* case [1997] A.C. 191 and discussed by the Supreme Court in *Hughes-Holland v BPE Solicitors* [2017] UKSC 21, [2017] 2 W.L.R. 1029, above, para.26–031

[*Add to note 852, at the end: page* [1908]]
Although the lender may suffer a form of loss when it makes the loan, it will normally be appropriate to calculate the lender's loss at the date of trial when the amount of loss may have crystallised: *Nykredit* case [1997] 1 W.L.R. 1627, 1633; *LSREF III Wight Ltd v Gateley LLP* [2016] EWCA Civ 359, [2016] P.N.L.R. 21 at [33].

[*Add new note 854a, line 13, after* "since the loan was made": *page* [1908]]
[854a] As in *South Australia Asset Management Corp v York Montague Ltd* [1997] A.C. 191 itself: see *Hughes-Holland v BPE Solicitors* [2017] UKSC 21 at [45]–[46], where Lord Sumption defends the SAAMCo limit as "a tool for giving effect to the distinction between (i) loss flowing from the fact

that as a result of the defendant's negligence the information was wrong and (ii) loss flowing from the decision to enter into the transaction at all", even if it may be "mathematically imprecise".

10. Liquidated Damages, Deposits and Forfeiture of Sums Paid

26–178 to
26–216
[*Delete paragraphs 26–178 to 26–216 and substitute: pages* [1912]–[1941]]

(a) *Liquidated Damages or Penalty*

26–178 **Introduction.** Where the parties to a contract agree that, in the event of a breach, the contract-breaker shall pay to the other a specified sum of money, the sum fixed may be classified by the courts either as a penalty (which is irrecoverable) or as liquidated damages (which are recoverable).[891] The law on this topic has been fundamentally re-written by the decision of the Supreme Court in the cases (heard together) of *Cavendish Square Holding BV v Makdessi* and *ParkingEye Ltd v Beavis*.[892] A clause is enforceable if it meets the traditional test that it does not extravagantly exceed a genuine attempt to estimate in advance the loss which the claimant would be likely to suffer from a breach of the obligation in question,[893] but the true test is whether the party to whom the sum is payable had a legitimate interest in ensuring performance by the other party and the sum payable in the event of breach is not extravagant or unconscionable in comparison to that interest. This supersedes a number of decisions suggesting that a clause which provides for an additional payment to be made by a party who is in breach of the contract may also be enforceable, even if it was not strictly speaking a pre-estimate of the likely loss, if it was "commercially justifiable, provided always that its dominant purpose was not to deter the other party from breach".[894]

[891] A valid agreed damages clause is probably not subject to the Unfair Contract Terms Act 1977 (see Main Work, Vol.I, paras 15–062 et seq.), even if it is set at a figure below the likely loss, see below, para.26–180. cf. however, the Unfair Terms in Consumer Contracts Regulations 1999 and Consumer Rights Act 2015 (below, para.26–180).

[892] [2015] UKSC 67, [2016] A.C. 1172, noted by Conte (2016) 132 L.Q.R. 382 and Morgan [2016] C.L.J. 11. In what follows the decisions will frequently be referred to as "*Cavendish Square*" and "*ParkingEye*".

[893] See the test laid down by Lord Dunedin in *Dunlop Pneumatic Tyre Co Ltd v New Garage & Motor Co Ltd* [1915] A.C. 79, below, para.26–182. It is presumed that a party has a legitimate interest in recovering its likely loss: *Cavendish Square* [2015] UKSC 67 at [32]. cf. a performance bond, which is *not* an estimate of the damage which might be caused by a breach of contract: *Cargill International SA v Bangladesh Sugar & Food Industries Corp* [1996] 4 All E.R. 563; *Comdel Commodities Ltd v Siporex Trade SA* [1997] 1 Lloyd's Rep. 424 CA.

[894] *Lordsvale Finance Plc v Bank of Zambia* [1996] Q.B. 752, 762–764; *United International Pictures v Cine Bes Filmcilik ve Yapimcilik AS* [2003] EWCA Civ 1669 at [15]; *Euro London Appointments Ltd v Claessens International Ltd* [2006] EWCA Civ 385, [2006] 2 Lloyd's Rep. 436 at [30]; *General Trading Co (Holdings) Ltd v Richmond Corp Ltd* [2008] EWHC 1479 (Comm), [2008] 2 Lloyd's Rep. 475; *Makdessi v Cavendish Square Holdings BV* [2013] EWCA Civ 1539. See further below, paras 26–193—26–194.

26–178A **Effect of distinction.** If the clause is not void as a penalty, it is enforceable irrespective of the loss actually suffered, whether the actual loss is less or greater.[895] Courts of equity held that if the sum fixed was unenforceable as a penalty to ensure that the promise was not broken, the promisee should nevertheless receive by way of damages the sum which would compensate him for his actual loss.[896] The Court of Appeal has held that the strict legal position is that the innocent party can sue on the penal clause, but "it will not be enforced . . . beyond the sum which represents [his] actual loss".[897] Where there is provision for liquidated damages, the claimant may nevertheless, in appropriate cases, elect to ask for an injunction instead of enforcing the liquidated damages.[898]

[895] *Clydebank Engineering & Shipbuilding Co Ltd v Don Jose Ramos Yzquierdo y Castaneda* [1905] A.C. 6. This rule does not apply to deposits, though at least a deposit that it is larger than the customary amount may be a penalty: see below, paras 26–216Q and 26–216R.

[896] Story, *Equitable Jurisprudence*, para.1316. The assessment of damages is according to common law; there is no equitable rule on damages where a clause has been held to be penal: *AMEV-UDC Finance Ltd v Austin* (1986) 60 A.L.J.R. 741.

[897] *Jobson v Johnson* [1989] 1 W.L.R. 1026, 1040 (see also at 1038, 1039–1042, 1049). (cf. however, the dictum in *Scandinavian Trading Tanker Co AB v Flota Petrolera Ecuatoriana (The Scaptrade)* [1983] 2 A.C. 694, 702). ("The classic form of relief against such a penalty clause has been to refuse to give effect to it, but to award the common law measure of damages for the breach of the primary obligation instead.") In *Cavendish Square Holding BV v Makdessi* and *ParkingEye Ltd v Beavis* [2015] UKSC 67, [2016] A.C. 1172 *Jobson v Johnson* was disapproved on other grounds, see below, para.26–216K. On whether the claimant may recover more than was provided for by the invalid penalty clause, see below, para.26–216L.

[898] See the cases cited in Main Work, Vol.I, para.26–007 n.48. Agreed damages clauses do not bar the remedy of rejection of the goods: *Benjamin's Sale of Goods*, 9th edn (2014), para.13–037.

Purpose of liquidated damage clauses. The purpose[899] of the parties in fixing **26–179** a sum is to facilitate recovery of damages without the difficulty and expense of proving actual damage[900]; or to avoid the risk of under-compensation, where the rules on remoteness of damage might not cover consequential, indirect or idiosyncratic loss[901]; or to give the promisee an assurance that he may safely rely on the fulfilment of the promise[902]; or to deter a party from breaching the contract.[903] Often the parties to a contract fix a sum as liquidated damages in the event of one specific breach, and leave the claimant to sue for unliquidated damages in the ordinary way if other types of breach occur.[904]

[899] For an economic analysis of agreed damages clauses, see Goetz and Scott (1977) 77 Col. L.R. 554; Rea (1984) 13 J.Leg.Stud. 147. See also Harris, Campbell and Halson, *Remedies in Contract and Tort*, 2nd edn (2002) at Ch.9.

[900] *Clydebank Engineering & Shipbuilding Co Ltd v Don Jose Ramos Yzquierdo y Castaneda* [1905] A.C. 6, 11. Even where the consequences of a breach are precisely ascertainable after the event, a sum reserved by the contract may be intended by the parties as an agreed estimate of damage in order to avoid the expense and difficulty of assessment: *Diestal v Stevenson* [1906] 2 K.B. 345.

[901] *Robophone Facilities Ltd v Blank* [1966] 1 W.L.R. 1428, 1447–1448. See further below, para.26–186.

[902] The clause may also operate as a limitation on liability: below, para.26–180. The traditional legal test, which was restricted to expected *loss*, did not permit the promisee to justify the sum fixed as a reasonable incentive to the promisor to perform his promise, nor as a disincentive to the promisor not to commit a *deliberate* breach (see Harris, Campbell and Halson at pp.136–139); but giving an incentive to perform or deterring breach is now accepted as legitimate if the party to whom the sum must be paid has a legitimate interest is securing performance rather than relying on damages. See below, para.26–197.

[903] *Cavendish Square Holding BV v Makdessi* and *ParkingEye Ltd v Beavis* [2015] UKSC 67, [2016] A.C. 1172.

[904] e.g. *Aktieselskabet Reidar v Arcos Ltd* [1927] 1 K.B. 352.

"Underliquidated damages". In practice, liquidated damages clauses fre- **26–180** quently serve to limit one party's liability. In other words, the parties may agree that in the event of breach, the party in breach will pay a sum which is demonstrably less than a pre-estimate of the likely loss. A clause of this type is sometimes called an "underliquidated damages clause". This will not prevent it being a valid liquidated damages clause.[905] These clauses are often the basis of the insurance arrangements to be made by the parties. A clause of this type may operate as a limitation of the party's liability. For that reason it is likely to be construed in the same way as other clauses limiting liability.[906] It is possible that an underliquidated damages clause is not caught by the Unfair Contract Terms Act 1977[907] because it does not merely exclude or restrict one party's liability: the same amount is payable whether the actual loss is greater or less.[908] However, were such a clause to occur in a consumer contract, it would seem to fall within the Unfair Terms in Consumer Contract Regulations 1999 (if the contract was made before September 30, 2015 and if the term had not been individually negotiated[909]) or (if the contract was made after October 1, 2015) Pt 2 of the Consumer Rights Act 2015.[910]

[905] *Cellulose Acetate Silk Co Ltd v Widnes Foundry (1925) Ltd* [1933] A.C. 20; *Tullett Prebon Group Ltd v El-Hajjali* [2008] EWHC 1924 (QB), [2008] I.R.L.R. 760 at [83] ("a significantly smaller stipulated sum than the probable damages would be most unlikely to render a clause a penalty clause, though each case has to be decided on its own individual facts").
[906] cf. the rule that the effect of an exemption clause depends on the construction of the contract: *Suisse Atlantique Société d'Armement Maritime v NV Rotterdamsche Kolen Centrale* [1967] 1 A.C. 361; *Photo Production Ltd v Securicor Transport Ltd* [1980] A.C. 827 (see Main Work, Vol.I, paras 15–025 et seq.).
[907] See Main Work, Vol.I, paras 15–066 et seq., and in particular para.15–069.
[908] See Peel (ed.), *Treitel on The Law of Contract*, 14th edn (2015), paras 7–055 and 20–140.
[909] See Main Work, Vol.II, paras 38–201 et seq.
[910] See Main Work, Vol.II, paras 38–334 et seq.

26–181 **Similar types of clause.** In *Cavendish Square Holding BV v Makdessi*[911] a majority of the Supreme Court held that the penalty clause rules apply to provisions that would prevent a party who breaks the contract from receiving a sum to which it would otherwise be entitled,[912] and also to provisions that require a party in breach to transfer property to the other party at less than its full value.[913] The Supreme Court indicated that the penalty rules also apply to deposits[914] and forfeiture clauses[915] but not to sums that are payable on events other than a breach of contract, for example a sum that must be paid if a party exercises a right under the contract.[916]

[911] [2015] UKSC 67, [2016] A.C. 1172.
[912] See below, para.26–216.
[913] See below, para.26–216.
[914] See below, para.26–216Q.
[915] See below, paras 26–216S et seq.
[916] See below, paras 26–216C et seq.

26–181A **Reluctance to find clause penal.** The rule against penalties has often been seen as anomalous because it applies even to clauses that were negotiated between experienced parties of equal bargaining power.[917] In *Cavendish Square Holding BV v Makdessi* and *ParkingEye Ltd v Beavis*[918] Lords Neuberger and Sumption described it as "an edifice which has not weathered well".[919] The Privy Council[920] has cited with approval[921] the view of Dickson J. in the Supreme Court of Canada that:

" . . . the power to strike down a penalty clause is a blatant interference with freedom of contract and is designed for the sole purpose of providing relief against oppression for the party having to pay the stipulated sum. It has no place where there is no oppression."[922]

Therefore, where there is no suggestion of oppression, "the court should not be astute to decry a 'penalty clause'".[923] The:

" . . . courts are predisposed . . . to uphold [liquidated damages clauses]. This predisposition is even stronger in the case of commercial contracts freely entered into between parties of comparable bargaining power."[924]

However, as it was put before the doctrine was modified by the *Cavendish Square* case, the correct question is not whether one party secured the clause by the use of unequal bargaining power or oppression, but whether or not the clause is a genuine pre-estimate of the likely loss:

" . . . whether a provision is to be treated as a penalty is a matter of construction to be resolved by asking whether at the time the contract was entered into the predominant contractual function of the provision was to deter a party from breaking the contract or to compensate the innocent party for breach . . . . The question that has always had to be addressed is therefore whether the alleged penalty clause can pass muster as a genuine pre-estimate of loss."[925]

Similarly, in *Cavendish Square Holding BV v Makdessi* and *ParkingEye Ltd v Beavis* the Supreme Court emphasised that where a party has a legitimate interest in securing performance rather than damages, the test of validity is whether the amount payable if the contract is broken is extravagant and unconscionable in comparison to that interest.[926] A clause may be a penalty even though it was freely negotiated between parties of equal bargaining power.[927]

[917] For an early example see *Betts v Burch* (1859) 4 H & N 506, 509, cited by Lords Neuberger and Sumption in *Cavendish Square Holding BV v Makdessi* and *ParkingEye Ltd v Beavis* [2015] UKSC 67, [2016] A.C. 1172 at [8]. See also their judgment at [33].
[918] [2015] UKSC 67, [2016] A.C. 1172.
[919] The history of the rule in English law is summarised in the judgments of Lords Neuberger and Sumption in the *Cavendish Square* case [2015] UKSC 67 at [4]–[8] and of Mason and Wilson JJ. in the Australian case of *AMEV-UDC Finance Ltd v Austin* (1986) 162 C.L.R. 170 at [27]–[34]. See also A. Simpson, "The Penal Bond with Conditional Defeasance" (1996) 82 L.Q.R. 392; D. Ibbetson, *A Historical Introduction to the Law of Obligations* (1999), especially at pp.213 et seq. and 255 et seq. Lord Hodge gives an account of the history in Scots law at [2015] UKSC 67 at [251]–[253].
[920] *Philips Hong Kong Ltd v Att-Gen of Hong Kong* (1993) 61 Build. L.R. 49, 58.
[921] The view was also cited with approval in the High Court of Australia: *Esanda Finance Corp Ltd v Plessing* (1989) 166 C.L.R. 131, 140. See also Lord Neuberger and Lord Sumption's descriptions of the doubts as to the basis of the doctrine, *Cavendish Square Holding BV v Makdessi* [2015] UKSC 67 at [3].
[922] *Elsey v J.G. Collins Insurance Agencies Ltd* (1978) 83 D.L.R. (3d.) 1, 15.
[923] *Robophone Facilities Ltd v Blank* [1966] 1 W.L.R. 1428, 1447.
[924] *Alfred McAlpine Capital Projects Ltd v Tilebox Ltd* [2005] Build. L.R. 271 (TCC) at [48]. See also the *Cavendish Square* case [2015] UKSC 67 at [33].
[925] *Lordsvale Finance Plc v Bank of Zambia* [1996] Q.B. 752, 762–764, cited with approval in *Euro London Appointments Ltd v Claessens International Ltd* [2006] EWCA Civ 385, [2006] 2 Lloyd's Rep. 436 at [30].
[926] [2015] UKSC 67 at [32]. On the role of unconscionability in this context, see below, para.26–214.
[927] *Makdessi v Cavendish Square Holdings BV* [2013] EWCA Civ 1539; [2015] UKHL 67, esp. at [257] (Lord Hodge).

26–181B   **A question of law.** The question whether a sum stipulated for in a contract is a penalty or liquidated damages is a question of law.[928]

[928] *Sainter v Ferguson* (1849) 7 C.B. 716, 727.

26–181C   **A question of construction.** In *Cavendish Square Holding BV v Makdessi* and *ParkingEye Ltd v Beavis*[929] a majority stated that whether a clause is a penalty is a question of construction. From this it follows, Lords Neuberger and Sumption said, that the test must be applied as of the date of the agreement, not when it falls to be enforced; a penalty clause is a species of agreement that is by its nature contrary to public policy. It also follows that the application of the test does not involve a discretion, and if the clause is penal it is wholly unenforceable. These points suggest that the question is one that other courts have preferred to call one of characterisation rather than of interpretation or construction.[930] However, construction in the normal sense may also be relevant. Though it is usually accepted that the words used by the parties are not determinative,[931] if the parties' intention was to compensate rather than to deter, it seems that the validity of the clause should be judged by whether it is extravagant by comparison to a "genuine pre-estimate" test, disregarding any interest that might have justified a deterrent.

[929] [2015] UKSC 67, [2016] A.C. 1172 at [9] (Lords Neuberger and Sumption) and [243] (Lord Hodge). See particularly on the construction point Dawson [2016] L.M.C.L.Q. 207.
[930] See the two-stage process (interpretation of the agreement to ascertain the parties' rights and obligations, followed by correct characterisation of the agreement) set out by Lord Millett in *Agnew v Inland Revenue Commissioners* [2001] UKPC 28, [2008] 2 A.C. 710 at [32].
[931] See Lord Dunedin's first proposition in *Dunlop Pneumatic Tyre Co Ltd v New Garage & Motor Co Ltd* [1915] A.C. 79, 86, quoted below, para.26–182 and n.934.

(b) *Genuine Pre-estimate of the Likely Loss*

26–182   **Genuine pre-estimate test.** What has been referred to above as the "traditional" test, which for many years was considered to have been the only test applicable,[932] was summed up by Lord Dunedin in delivering his opinion in *Dunlop Pneumatic Tyre Co Ltd v New Garage & Motor Co Ltd*[933] in the following propositions:

> "(1) Though the parties to a contract who use the words 'penalty' or 'liquidated damages' may prima facie be supposed to mean what they say, yet the expression used is not conclusive. The court must find out whether the payment stipulated is in truth a penalty or liquidated damages . . . .[934]
>
> (2) The essence of a penalty is a payment of money stipulated as *in terrorem* of the offending party; the essence of liquidated damages is a genuine pre-estimate of damage.[935]
>
> (3) The question whether a sum stipulated is a penalty or liquidated damages is a question of construction to be decided upon the terms and inherent circumstances of each particular contract, judged of at the time of the making of the contract, not as at the time of the breach.[936]
>
> (4) To assist this task of construction various tests have been suggested which, if applicable to the case under consideration, may prove helpful or even conclusive.[937] Such are:
>
>> (a) It will be held to be a penalty if the sum stipulated for is extravagant and unconscionable in amount in comparison with the greatest loss which could conceivably be proved to have followed from the breach.[938]

(b) It will be held to be a penalty if the breach consists only in not paying a sum of money, and the sum stipulated is a sum greater than the sum which ought to have been paid . . . .[939]

(c) There is a presumption (but no more) that it is a penalty when 'a single lump sum is made payable by way of compensation, on the occurrence of one or more or all of several events, some of which may occasion serious and others but trifling damage.'[940]

On the other hand:

(d) It is no obstacle to the sum stipulated being a genuine pre-estimate of damage, that the consequences of the breach are such as to make precise pre-estimation almost an impossibility. On the contrary, that is just the situation when it is probable that pre-estimated damage was the true bargain between the parties."[941]

In this case, dealers in tyres had agreed not to resell any tyres bought from the manufacturers to any private customers at less than the manufacturers' current list prices, not to supply them to persons whose supplies the manufacturers had decided to suspend, not to exhibit or export them without the manufacturers' consent, and to pay £5 by way of liquidated damages for every tyre sold or offered in breach of the agreement. It was held that the £5 was not a penalty and thus was recoverable as liquidated damages.

[932] In *Cavendish Square Holding BV v Makdessi* [2015] UKSC 67 at [22] Lords Neuberger and Sumption described it as having "achieved the status of a quasi-statutory code".

[933] [1915] A.C. 79, 86–88.

[934] "But no case . . . decides that the term used by the parties themselves is to be altogether disregarded, and I should say that, where the parties themselves call the sum made payable a 'penalty,' the onus lies on those who seek to show that it is to be payable as liquidated damages": *Willson v Love* [1896] 1 Q.B. 626, 630. See *Alder v Moore* [1961] 2 Q.B. 57, 65; *Robert Stewart & Sons Ltd v Carapanayoti & Co Ltd* [1962] 1 W.L.R. 34. cf. *Workers Trust & Merchant Bank Ltd v Dojap Investments Ltd* [1993] A.C. 573, 579.

[935] *Clydebank Engineering & Shipbuilding Co Ltd v Don Jose Ramos Yzquierdo y Castaneda* [1905] A.C. 6. See also *Bridge v Campbell Discount Co Ltd* [1962] A.C. 600, 622; *Photo Production Ltd v Securicor Transport Ltd* [1980] A.C. 827, 850; *Cameron-Head v Cameron & Co* (1919) S.C. 627; the *Workers Trust* case [1993] A.C. 573. It should be noted that by s.24 of the Agricultural Holdings Act 1986 "notwithstanding any provision in a contract of tenancy of an agricultural holding making the tenant liable to pay a higher rent or other liquidated damages" for breach of covenant, etc. the landlord may not recover for any such breach any sum "in excess of the damage actually suffered".

[936] *Commissioner of Public Works v Hills* [1906] A.C. 368, 376; *Webster v Bosanquet* [1912] A.C. 394. If the contract was varied in a way that will affect the likely loss, the validity of the clause should be judged by the time of the variation: *Unaoil Ltd v Leighton Offshore Pte Ltd* [2014] EWHC 2965 (Comm) at [75].

[937] *Pye v British Automobile Commercial Syndicate Ltd* [1906] 1 K.B. 425.

[938] *Clydebank Engineering & Shipbuilding Co Ltd v Don Jose Ramos Yzquierdo y Castaneda* [1905] A.C. 6, 17; *Webster v Bosanquet* [1912] A.C. 394; *Cooden Engineering Co Ltd v Stanford* [1953] 1 Q.B. 86; cf. *Bridge v Campbell Discount Co Ltd* [1962] A.C. 600 (below, para.26–216C).

[939] *Kemble v Farren* (1829) 6 Bing. 141. See also *Astley v Weldon* (1801) 2 B. & P. 346; *Wallis v Smith* (1882) 21 Ch. D. 243, 256–257. The breach may involve more than a failure to pay: *Thos. P. Gonzales Corp v F. R. Waring (International) Pty Ltd* [1986] 2 Lloyd's Rep. 160, 163. A discount for prompt payment, however, was held not make the undiscounted sum a penalty; nor was it a penalty where a loan agreement provides for a modest increase in the rate of interest, which operates only from the date of the borrower's default: *Lordsvale Finance Plc v Bank of Zambia* [1996] Q.B. 752 (a 1 per cent increase: if, however, the increase operated retrospectively, it might be a penalty. On this case see further below, paras 26–193—26–194); cf. *Jeancharm Ltd v Barnet Football Club Ltd* [2003] EWCA Civ 58, [2003] 92 Con. L.R. 26 (interest rate for late payment of 5 per cent per week held to be a penalty).

[940] *Lord Elphinstone v Monkland Iron & Coal Co Ltd* (1886) 11 App. Cas. 332, 342. See *Kemble v Farren* (1829) 6 Bing. 141, 148; *Magee v Lavell* (1874) L.R. 9 C.P. 107, 115; *Ford Motor Co v Armstrong* (1915) 31 T.L.R. 267 (see below, para.26–189); *Michel Habib Raji Ayoub v Sheikh Suleiman* [1941] 1 All E.R. 507, 510; *Cooden Engineering Co Ltd v Stanford* [1953] 1 Q.B. 86, 98; *Interoffice Telephones Ltd v Robert Freeman Co Ltd* [1958] 1 Q.B. 190, 194. The parties, in such a case, should fix separate sums for the various possible breaches: *Imperial Tobacco Co v Parslay* [1936] 2 All E.R. 515.

[941] See *Clydebank Engineering & Shipbuilding Co Ltd v Don Jose Ramos Yzquierdo y Castaneda* [1905] A.C. 6, 11; *Webster v Bosanquet* [1912] A.C. 394, 398; *English Hop Growers Ltd v Dering* [1928] 2 K.B. 174; *Imperial Tobacco Co v Parslay* [1936] 2 All E.R. 515, 519; *Philips Hong Kong Ltd v Att-Gen of Hong Kong* (1993) 61 Build. L.R. 49, 60 PC (the impact of delay by one contractor on other contracts). Some of the clauses that were justified under this category in particular, including the *Dunlop* case itself, may now be better viewed as cases of legitimate deterrence: see below, para.26–197.

26–183 **The basis of the decision in the *Dunlop* case.** The traditional approach treated Lord Dunedin's second proposition as an exhaustive dichotomy,[942] and had thus concentrated on whether the clause was a genuine pre-estimate of the loss that the payee was likely to suffer. A clause would be regarded as in terrorem if it provided for a greater sum, or at least an extravagantly greater sum, than the loss the payee was likely to suffer.[943] In *Cavendish Square Holding BV v Makdessi* and *ParkingEye Ltd v Beavis*[944] the Supreme Court pointed out that other judges in the *Dunlop* case had decided the case on a wider basis[945]; and as the result of the Supreme Court's decision in those cases, a clause may also be justified on the basis that the party who would benefit from it has a legitimate interest in securing performance rather than damages, and the amount payable or other consequence if the contract is broken is not extravagant and unconscionable in comparison to that interest.[946] However, as Lords Neuberger and Sumption said:

> "In the case of a straightforward damages clause, that interest will rarely extend beyond compensation for the breach, and we therefore expect that Lord Dunedin's four tests would usually be perfectly adequate to determine its validity."[947]

Thus if the party cannot demonstrate a legitimate interest in securing performance rather than damages, or does not seek to do so, the clause may still be valid under the "genuine pre-estimate" test, and therefore that test is explored in more detail in this section.

[942] cf. *United International Pictures v Cine Bes Filmcilik ve Yapimcilik AS* [2003] EWCA Civ 1669 at [15].

[943] "That the contractual function is deterrent rather than compensatory can be deduced by comparing the amount that would be payable on breach with the loss that might be sustained if breach occurred". *Lordsvale Finance Plc v Bank of Zambia* [1996] Q.B. 752, 762, Colman J.

[944] [2015] UKSC 67, [2016] A.C. 1172.

[945] See below, para.26–197.

[946] See below, para.26–197.

[947] [2015] UKSC 67 at [32].

26–184 **An objective approach.** Asking whether a clause was a genuine pre-estimate of the loss might suggest a subjective approach, so that whether the clause is liquidated damages or a penalty depends on an assessment of what the parties thought they were agreeing on. However, there are clearly objective elements to a test which depends on whether the amount is "extravagant and unconscionable in comparison with the greatest loss"[948]; and it has been held that:

" . . . the test does not turn upon the genuineness or honesty of the party or parties who made the pre-estimate. The test is primarily an objective one."[949]

[948] Lord Dunedin's proposition (4)(a) above, para.26–182.
[949] *Alfred McAlpine Capital Projects Ltd v Tilebox Ltd* [2005] Build. L.R. 271 (TCC) at [48] (Jackson J.).

A substantial discrepancy. In *Murray v Leisureplay Plc*[950] the Court of Appeal **26–185** emphasised that a clause will not be a penalty merely because it is not a precise pre-estimate of the loss.[951] Arden L.J. said that a contractual provision does not become a penalty simply because it results in overpayment in particular circumstances: "The parties are allowed a generous margin".[952]

[950] [2005] EWCA Civ 963, [2005] I.R.L.R. 946.
[951] See also Jackson J. in *Alfred McAlpine Capital Projects Ltd v Tilebox Ltd* [2005] Build. L.R. 271 (TCC) at [48].
[952] [2005] EWCA Civ 963 at [43]; see too the judgments of Clarke and Buxton L.JJ. at [105] and [114] respectively. See also *Cleeve Link Ltd v Bryla* [2014] I.R.L.R. 86 EAT.

Pre-estimate of damage. The word "damage" must mean "net loss" after taking **26–186** account of the claimant's expected ability to mitigate his loss. The comparison is to be made to the loss that the innocent party would be entitled to recover by way of damages, not to the possibly greater actual loss.[953] If the clause is a genuine pre-estimate of the loss,[954] there is no scope for arguing that the claimant could in fact have mitigated the loss: the purpose of the clause is to make proof of the actual loss unnecessary and irrelevant[955]; but the mitigation principle must be taken into account in deciding whether or not the clause was a genuine pre-estimate in the first place.[956] A genuine pre-estimate may include loss that would be too remote[957] unless notice of its possibility had been given to the party in breach at the time the contract was made.[958] It has been suggested that a party may stipulate for liquidated damages in order to ensure it is compensated for some idiosyncratic loss that might not otherwise be recoverable, such as sentimental value attached to property.[959] It must be the case that a genuine pre-estimate can include damages for loss of amenity or distress when the purpose of the contract is to provide that amenity or freedom from distress[960]; it seems unlikely that such loss be a legitimate part of a pre-estimate when the loss would not be recoverable by way of unliquidated damages,[961] but a genuine concern about such loss would presumably give rise to a legitimate interest that could be protected under the alternative basis set out in *Cavendish Square Holding BV v Makdessi* and *ParkingEye Ltd v Beavis*.[962] If, as it seems, "hypothetical bargain damages" allowing the innocent party to recover a share of the profit made by the other party through his breach of contract[963] may be recoverable in addition to other damages,[964] presumably a genuine pre-estimate of the loss may include such a figure if, at the time the contract was made, it is likely that the type of breach to which the agreed damages clause applies will lead to the party in breach making a profit from it. The claimant's chance to bargain with the defendant might constitute a legitimate interest[965] but it is probably unnecessary for the claimant to show this if the amount agreed falls within a genuine pre-estimate. On the traditional account of liquidated damages, the fact that the damage is difficult to assess with precision strengthened the presumption that a sum agreed between the parties represents a genuine attempt to estimate it and to overcome the difficulties of proof at the trial.[966] It seems that the risk of this kind

[213]

of difficulty will now be treated as giving the claimant a legitimate interest in deterring breach.[967]

[953] *Lansat Shipping Co Ltd v Glencore Grain BV (The Paragon)* [2009] EWHC 551 (Comm), [2009] 1 Lloyd's Rep. 658 at [24]. See also para.26–197.

[954] Note that under the approach taken in the *Cavendish Square* and *ParkingEye* cases, a clause may be valid even if it is not a genuine pre-estimate of the loss: see below, para.26–197.

[955] *MSC Mediterranean Shipping Co SA v Cottonex Anstalt* [2015] EWHC 283 (Comm) at [70]–[71], referring to dicta in *Abrahams v Performing Rights Society Ltd* [1995] I.C.R. 1028, 1040–1041. However, in a contract in which the liquidated damages were only payable while the contract remained on foot, the innocent party was not entitled to ignore a repudiation and keep the contract alive so as to be able to continue to claim liquidated damages, as they would have no legitimate interest is doing so: at [94]–[105]. The Court of Appeal [2016] EWCA Civ 789 agreed (at [43]) though it decided the case on other grounds: see above, para.26–106.

[956] *MSC Mediterranean Shipping Co SA v Cottonex Anstalt* [2015] EWHC 283 (Comm) at [113]. If the relevant clause purported to give the innocent party an unfettered right to ignore the repudiation when it had no legitimate interest is doing so, the clause would be a penalty: [2015] EWHC 283 (Comm) at [116] (aff'd without reference to this point, [2016] EWCA Civ 789). In *Bunge SA v Nidera BV* [2015] UKSC 43 Lord Sumption said the Default Clause in a GAFTA sale contract differs from the common law paradigm in that the injured party is not required to mitigate by going into the market and buying or selling against the defaulter, but has a discretion whether to do so (at [28]). He did not discuss whether this might amount to a penalty, merely remarking that there is a difference between a clause prescribing a fixed measure of loss (such as a liquidated damages clause) and a clause providing a mechanical formula in place of the more nuanced and fact-sensitive approach of the common law (such as the GAFTA clause) (at [26]). With respect, a formula for measuring damages may also amount to a penalty if it produces results that are much greater than the damages that would be recoverable at common law: *Lombard North Central Plc v Butterworth* [1987] Q.B. 527. In contrast, Lord Toulson (with whom the other members of the Court agreed) did not think the GAFTA formula excluded the duty to mitigate (at [62]). In *Novasen SA v Alimenta SA* [2013] EWHC 345 (Comm), [2013] 1 Lloyd's Rep. 648 at [18], Popplewell J. said that the Default Clause did not constitute a penalty clause, applying his dicta in *Imam-Sadeque v Bluebay Asset Management (Services) Ltd* [2012] EWHC 3511 (QB).

[957] See Main Work, Vol.I, paras 26–107—26–134.

[958] *Robophone Facilities Ltd v Blank* [1966] 1 W.L.R. 1428, 1447–1448 (Diplock L.J.). The agreed sum may take account of loss likely to be suffered which may not fall within the normal remoteness test: *Robert Stewart & Sons Ltd v Carapanayoti & Co Ltd* [1962] 1 W.L.R. 34, 39; *Philips Hong Kong Ltd v Att-Gen of Hong Kong* (1993) 61 Build. L.R. 49, 60–61 (the agreed sum may be justified by knowledge of "special circumstances").

[959] Goetz & Scott (1977) Columbia L.R. 554, 572–573.

[960] See Main Work, Vol.I, paras 26–144—26–146.

[961] The question whether the parties may give their own meaning to "loss" is mentioned below, para.26–192, text after n.994.

[962] [2015] UKSC 67, [2016] A.C. 1172; see below, paras 26–196 et seq.

[963] See Main Work, Vol.I, paras 26–051—26–054.

[964] See Main Work, Vol.I, para.26–053, n.295.

[965] See below, para.26–197.

[966] *Dunlop Pneumatic Tyre Co Ltd v New Garage & Motor Co Ltd* [1915] A.C. 79; *English Hop Growers Ltd v Dering* [1928] 2 K.B. 174; *Imperial Tobacco Co v Parslay* [1936] 2 All E.R. 515; *Robophone Facilities Ltd v Blank* [1966] 1 W.L.R. 1428, 1447; *Philips Hong Kong Ltd v Att-Gen of Hong Kong* (1993) 61 Build. L.R. 49 (the loss to a governmental body caused by delay in construction was especially difficult to assess).

[967] See below, para.26–197.

26–187 **Fluctuating sums.** Although a valid agreed damages clause may specify a graduated scale of sums payable according to the varying extent of the expected loss,[968] a sum which is liable to fluctuate according to extraneous circumstances will not be classified as liquidated damages.[969] In a railway construction contract it was provided that in the event of a breach by the contractor he should forfeit "as and for liquidated damages" certain percentages retained by the government of money payable for work done as a guarantee fund to answer for defective work, and also certain security money lodged with the government.[970] The Judicial Committee held that this was a penalty, since it was not a definite sum, but was:

> " . . . liable to great fluctuation in amount dependent on events not connected with the fulfilment of this contract. It is obvious that the amount of retained money . . . depended entirely on the progress of those contracts, and that further, as those moneys are primarily liable to make good deficiencies in these contract works, the eventual sum available . . . could not in any way be estimated as a fixed sum."[971]

[968] See below, para.26–191, for graduated damages.
[969] *Commissioner of Public Works v Hills* [1906] A.C. 368, 376.
[970] On the question of the application of the penalty rules to this kind of clause, see below, para.26–216, esp. at n.1118m.
[971] *Commissioner of Public Works v Hills* [1906] A.C. 368, 376 (followed in *Jobson v Johnson* [1989] 1 W.L.R. 1026, 1036).

Minimum payment clause. A "minimum payment" clause in a hire-purchase or hiring agreement that applies when the hirer is in breach of the contract by refusing to continue with it,[972] will usually be held to fail the genuine pre-estimate test if it provides for the same total sum to be payable by the hirer irrespective of how long the agreement has been in force.[973]   **26–188**

[972] Compare the situation where the hirer exercises an option, below, para.26–216C.
[973] *Lamdon Trust Ltd v Hurrell* [1955] 1 W.L.R. 391; *Bridge v Campbell Discount Co Ltd* [1962] A.C. 600. ("It is a sliding scale of compensation, but a scale that slides in the wrong direction": at 623.) See also *Anglo-Auto Finance Co Ltd v James* [1963] 1 W.L.R. 1042; *United Dominions Trust (Commercial) Ltd v Ennis* [1968] 1 Q.B. 54.

Single sum payable upon different breaches. The mere fact that the same amount is made payable upon the breach of several undertakings of varying importance is by no means conclusive.[974] It may be that the amount is not disproportionate to the least important of these undertakings, and therefore represents a genuine attempt at an agreed estimate of real damage[975]; or, if the loss is hard to assess, the test seemed to be satisfied if a modest sum was used; but a clause setting a very high amount would not pass muster. Thus in *Dunlop Pneumatic Tyre Co Ltd v New Garage & Motor Co Ltd*,[976] the dealers had agreed not to resell any tyres bought from the manufacturers to any private customers at less than the manufacturers' current list prices, not to supply them to persons whose supplies the manufacturers had decided to suspend, not to exhibit or export them without the manufacturers' consent, and to pay £5 by way of liquidated damages for every tyre sold or offered in breach of the agreement. It was held that the £5 was not a penalty and thus was recoverable as liquidated damages.[977] The decision seems to fall within Lord Dunedin's last proposition: **26–189**

> " . . . the damage caused by each and every one of those events, however varying in importance, may be of such an uncertain nature that it cannot be accurately ascertained"[978]

The clause may also be a genuine pre-estimate where the stipulated sum is taken as an average or mean figure of the losses probably incurred in the different events.[979] In *Ford Motor Co v Armstrong*,[980] in contrast, the retailer in a similar case agreed to pay £250 as "the agreed damage which the manufacturer will sustain" upon the breach of any one of several covenants (similar to those in the *Dunlop* case, above), and the Court of Appeal by a majority held that this (in 1915) was a penalty, since it was an arbitrary and substantial sum, and made payable for various breaches differing in kind, some of which might cause only trifling damage. The high amount of the agreed sum in this case showed that it could not be a genuine pre-estimate of loss.

[974] See r.4(c) in Lord Dunedin's propositions, above, para.26–182. See *Makdessi v Cavendish Square Holdings BV* [2013] EWCA Civ 1539 at [64]–[74].

[975] *Wallis v Smith* (1882) 21 Ch. D. 243; *Pye v British Automobile Commercial Syndicate Ltd* [1906] 1 K.B. 425; *Dunlop Pneumatic Tyre Co Ltd v New Garage & Motor Co Ltd* [1915] A.C. 79; *Philips Hong Kong Ltd v Att-Gen of Hong Kong* (1993) 61 Build. L.R. 49, 62–63 (Privy Council refers to: " . . . the error of assuming that, because in some hypothetical situation the loss suffered will be less than the sum quantified in accordance with the liquidated damage provision, that provision must be a penalty"). This suggests that the validity of a clause should be judged by its normal operation: Peel (ed.), *Treitel on The Law of Contract*, 14th edn (2015), para.20–131.

[976] [1915] A.C. 79.

[977] The House of Lords took the view that the £5 did not apply to the second and third obligations (not to sell to prohibited person, and not to exhibit without permission).

[978] *Dunlop Pneumatic Tyre Co Ltd v New Garage & Motor Co Ltd* [1915] A.C. 79, 95–96. See also *Galsworthy v Strutt* (1848) 1 Ex. 659, 666–667. Again, in some cases of this type the claimant may now be seen as having a legitimate interest in deterring breach, see below, para.26–197.

[979] *Dunlop Pneumatic Tyre Co Ltd v New Garage & Motor Co Ltd* [1915] A.C. 79, 99; *English Hop Growers Ltd v Dering* [1928] 2 K.B. 174, 182.

[980] (1915) 31 T.L.R. 267.

26–190   **Breach may cause varying loss.** A different case is where the sum is payable for any breach of a particular term of the contract, but the loss that follows may vary significantly from case to case. This seems to fall within Lord Dunedin's heading 4(a):

> "It will be held to be penalty if the sum stipulated for is extravagant and unconscionable in amount in comparison with the greatest loss that could conceivably be proved to have followed from the breach."[981]

It is not clear that the converse proposition, that the sum will not be unconscionable if it is no more than the greatest possible loss, follows. Lord Parker said that loss caused by a breach of a non-solicitation covenant might vary according to where or not the solicitation was successful; nonetheless,

> "whatever damage there is must be the same in kind for every possible breach, and the fact that it may vary in amount for each particular breach has never been held to raise any presumption or inference that the sum agreed to be paid is a penalty, at any rate in cases where the parties have referred to it as agreed or liquidated damages."[982]

That might be taken to suggest that provided the sum stipulated is not extravagant and unconscionable in relation to the greatest loss that might follow, it will not be a penalty even though the loss might well be much less and therefore the sum could not strictly be described as a genuine pre-estimate of the likely loss.[983] On occasion Lord Dunedin's statement has been applied literally,[984] and it was repeated by Lord Hodge in *Cavendish Square Holding BV v Makdessi* and *ParkingEye Ltd v Beavis*.[985] However, in the past it has been held a clause may be penal under the "genuine pre-estimate test" even though the sum does not exceed the greatest possible loss.[986] In *Bridge v Campbell Discount Co Ltd* a clause in a hire-purchase providing for a minimum payment if the hirer defaulted in paying was held to be a penalty because the loss to the finance company would differ according to how long the hirer kept the vehicle.[987] True, in that case the amount payable under the clause would also vary according to how much of the price the hirer had already paid, so that the two situations are technically distinguishable, but it is thought that the result in the *Bridge* case would have been the same if the clause had simply stated a fixed sum that the hirer must pay however much he had paid already. So it is better to treat Lord Dunedin's and Lord Parker's statements quoted above as no more than a presumption to be used when the genuine pre-estimate test is being applied[988]; and to note that when the claimant has a legitimate interest in obtaining performance rather than damages, an agreed sum that is not extravagant and unconscionable in relation to the greatest loss that might follow is likely to be treated as valid.[989]

[981] *Dunlop Pneumatic Tyre Co Ltd v New Garage & Motor Co Ltd* [1915] A.C. 79, 87.

[982] [1915] A.C. 79, 98.

[983] The cases on covenants in restraint of trade, such as *Crisdee v Bolton* (1827) 3 C. & P. 240; *Price v Green* (1847) 16 M. & W. 346, 354; *Reynolds v Bridge* (1856) 6 E. & B. 528, 541, have generally treated the sum payable for a breach as a sum stipulated for the breach of a single obligation, although it "is capable of being broken more than once, or in more ways than one": *Dunlop Pneumatic Tyre Co Ltd v New Garage & Motor Co Ltd* [1915] A.C. 79, 98 (see also at 92–93); *Law v Redditch Local Board* [1892] 1 Q.B. 127, 136.

[984] *Cleeve Link Ltd v Bryla* [2014] I.R.L.R. 86 (EAT) (clause upheld when not extravagant in relation to maximum loss, though loss would vary significantly depending on how soon breach occurred).

[985] [2015] UKSC 67, [2016] A.C. 1172 at [255].

[986] *Makdessi v Cavendish Square Holdings BV* [2013] EWCA Civ 1539 at [73]–[74].

[987] [1962] A.C. 600. ("It is a sliding scale of compensation, but a scale that slides in the wrong direction": at 623.)

[988] See *Makdessi v Cavendish Square Holdings BV* [2013] EWCA Civ 1539 at [72], where Christopher Clarke L.J. added that "there may be some tension between" the two speeches.

[989] See further below, paras 26–196 et seq.

Graduated damages. In building contracts and other similar contracts the courts **26–191** have upheld as liquidated damages a system of graduated sums which increase in proportion to the seriousness of the breach, e.g. so much per week for delay in performance,[990] or so much according to the number of items in question.[991] If in a building contract there is no such graduation the sum fixed is less likely to be held to be a genuine pre-estimate.[992] The sum must be graduated so that it changes in the right direction. Depreciation obviously increases over time, so a sum said to be compensation for depreciation is not a genuine pre-estimate of loss if it *decreases* over time as a hirer pays more instalments.[993]

[990] *Clydebank Engineering Co v Don Jose Ramos Yzquierdo y Castaneda* [1905] A.C. 6; *Philips Hong Kong Ltd v Att-Gen of Hong Kong* (1993) 61 Build. L.R. 49, 60 (PC); *Alfred McAlpine Capital Projects Ltd v Tilebox Ltd* [2005] Build. L.R. 271 (TCC). See also *Law v Redditch Local Board* [1892] 1 Q.B. 127; *Cellulose Acetate Silk Co Ltd v Widnes Foundry (1925) Ltd* [1933] A.C. 20 (above, para.26–180). The party entitled to the benefit of a liquidated damages clause in the event of failure to complete on time cannot take advantage of it if the delay is partly due to his own fault: *Peak Construction (Liverpool) Ltd v McKinney Foundations Ltd* (1971) 69 L.G.R. 1, 11, 16. Demurrage under a charterparty is a case of graduated liquidated damages: *President of India v Lips Maritime Corp* [1988] A.C. 395, 422–423.

[991] *Lord Elphinstone v Monkland Iron and Coal Co* (1886) 11 App. Cas. 332; *Diestal v Stevenson* [1906] 2 K.B. 345.

[992] e.g. *Commissioner of Public Works v Hills* [1906] A.C. 368 (above, para.26–188). See also *Re Newman* (1876) 4 Ch. D. 724.

[993] *Bridge v Campbell Discount Co Ltd* [1962] A.C. 600. ("It is a sliding scale of compensation, but a scale that slides in the wrong direction": at 623.) If it slides in the right direction, the clause is more likely to be held valid: *Phonographic Equipment (1958) Ltd v Muslu* [1961] 1 W.L.R. 1379. cf. *Lombank Ltd v Excell* [1964] 1 Q.B. 415.

26-192 Damages following termination by the innocent party under an express term. Where the hirer has neither repudiated the hiring (or hire-purchase) agreement, nor committed a "fundamental breach" of it, but the owner terminates it in the exercise of an express power to do so conferred by the agreement, the owner's damages are limited to loss suffered through any breaches up to the date of the termination.[994] This is, in effect, the measure of loss defined by law and the parties are not free to define it otherwise. A clause that provides for a larger sum to be paid, such as a "minimum payment" clause or one providing for recovery of the amount of future payments, even with deductions for any savings made,[995] will (under the genuine pre-estimate test) be void as a penalty.[996] It should be noted, however, that this principle does not apply where the contract made the broken term into a condition, any breach of which entitled the innocent party to terminate (e.g. a clause making compliance with time "of the essence"[997]). In this case the innocent party may both terminate the contract and recover damages for the loss of the bargain (viz in respect of all the outstanding obligations of the other party).[998] A clause that makes the hirer liable for a genuine pre-estimate of the owners' full loss in such a case will be valid.

[994] *Financings Ltd v Baldock* [1963] 2 Q.B. 104. The principle stated in the text has been regularly followed by the Court of Appeal: *Brady v St Margaret's Trust Ltd* [1963] 2 Q.B. 494; *Charterhouse Credit Co Ltd v Tolly* [1963] 2 Q.B. 683; *United Dominions Trust (Commercial) Ltd v Ennis* [1968] 1 Q.B. 54; *Capital Finance Co Ltd v Donati* (1977) 121 S.J. 270; *Lombard North Central Plc v Butterworth* [1987] Q.B. 527. See also the Australian cases cited, below, para.26–216A, n.1118p.

[995] In *Lombard North Central Plc v Butterworth* [1987] Q.B. 527 the contract contained a formula under which the owner was entitled to arrears, all future instalments that would have fallen due had and agreement not been terminated less a discount for accelerated payment. It omitted an allowance for the resale value of the repossessed goods. This would have prevented it being a genuine pre-estimate of the loss, but it was held that even had it provided for an allowance, the clause would have been a penalty for the reason stated in the text.

[996] *Lombard North Central Plc v Butterworth* [1987] Q.B. 527.

[997] See Main Work, Vol.I, paras 21–011 et seq.

[998] The *Lombard* case [1987] Q.B. 527. See Treitel [1987] L.M.C.L.Q. 143; Beale (1988) 104 L.Q.R. 355.

(c) *Commercially Justified but not a Deterrent*

26-193 "Genuine pre-estimate" and "whether imposed in terrorem". Before the decision of the Supreme Court in *Cavendish Square Holding BV v Makdessi* and *ParkingEye Ltd v Beavis*[999] there were a number of dicta to the effect that a clause that was not a genuine pre-estimate at all might nonetheless be valid if it was "commercially justifiable, provided always that its dominant purpose was not to deter the other party from breach".[1000] In *Makdessi v Cavendish Square Holdings BV*[1001] Makdessi had sold shares in his advertising and marketing business to another company, with payment to be made in stages. Ultimately Cavendish was substituted for the original purchaser by a novation agreement and ended up holding 60 per cent of the shares, Makdessi retaining 40 per cent. The purchaser had an option to buy the remaining shares. Makdessi entered various non-competition covenants. Clause 5.1 provided that if Makdessi was in breach of the non-competition clauses, he would not be entitled to further instalments of the price; and clause 5.6 provided that, in the same circumstances, the purchaser could require him to transfer his remaining shares at a price that was much lower than the option price, being based on asset value alone and ignoring any element of good will. Cavendish argued that Makdessi was in breach, refused to pay the outstanding instalments of the price and demanded that he transfer the remaining shares at the reduced value. Makdessi argued that clauses 5.1 and 5.6 were penalty clauses and unenforceable. Christopher Clarke L.J., with whom the other members of the court agreed, distinguished the traditional "genuine pre-estimate" approach from the "new approach" and said that the recent cases:

> " . . . show the court adopting the broader test of whether the clause was extravagant and unconscionable with a predominant function of deterrence; and robustly declining to do so in circumstances where there was a commercial justification for the clause. That this is a reversion to the foundation of the doctrine is apparent from the observations of Lord Halsbury in *Clydebank Engineering* when he asked of the relevant clause:
> 'whether it is, what I think gave the jurisdiction to the Courts in both countries to interfere at all in an agreement between the parties, unconscionable and extravagant, and one which no Court ought to allow to be enforced'."[1002]

Christopher Clarke L.J. made it clear that in his view, deterrence is not recognised as a commercial justification.[1003] He then applied the two tests sequentially.[1004] The clauses, which would result in the seller of a business who had broken various undertakings not to compete receiving millions of dollars less in consideration, were held to be neither a genuine pre-estimate of the buyers' likely loss[1005] nor commercially justified. Although it had been argued that the clauses were part of a commercial bargain, reached after extensive negotiation, as to the price at which shares in the Company were to change hands:

> "The underlying rationale of the doctrine of penalties is that the Court will grant relief against the enforcement of provisions for payment (or the loss of rights or the compulsory transfer of property at nil or an undervalue) in the event of breach, where the amount to be paid or lost is out of all proportion to the loss attributable to the breach. If that is so, the provisions are likely to be regarded as penal because their function is to act as a deterrent.
> That seems to me the position here. The payment terms of clauses 5.1 and 5.6 do not serve to fulfil some justifiable commercial or economic function such as is exemplified in the cases—a modest extra interest in respect of a defaulting loan; a provision for the payment of the costs of earlier litigation; a generous measure of damages for wrongful dismissal; an allocation of credit risk; or the provision of capital which would be needed if a promised guarantee of a loan was not forthcoming . . . "[1006]

As will be seen in the next section, the Supreme Court[1007] reversed this decision, holding that a clause may be valid even if it clearly has a deterrent function, provided that the party to whom the sum will be paid has a legitimate interest in securing performance rather than damages, and the amount payable or other consequence if the contract is broken is not extravagant and unconscionable in comparison to that interest.[1008]

[999] [2015] UKSC 67, [2016] A.C. 1172.

[1000] *Lordsvale Finance Plc v Bank of Zambia* [1996] Q.B. 752, 762–764; *United International Pictures v Cine Bes Filmcilik ve Yapimcilik AS* [2003] EWCA Civ 1669 at [15]; and semble, Arden L.J. in *Murray v Leisureplay Plc* [2005] EWCA Civ 963, [2005] I.R.L.R. 946 (Clarke and Buxton L.JJ. preferred to decide the case on the basis that given the difficulty of forecasting the possible effect on the claimant's employability and how quickly he would be able to obtain other employment, the sum payable was not, in the words of Lord Dunedin in the Dunlop case, "extravagant and unconscionable in amount in comparison with the greatest loss that could conceivably be proved to have followed from the breach" see [2005] EWCA Civ 963 at [105] and [114]–[115]). See also *Euro London Appointments Ltd v Claessens International Ltd* [2006] EWCA Civ 385, [2006] 2 Lloyd's Rep. 436 at [30]; *General Trading Co (Holdings) Ltd v Richmond Corp Ltd* [2008] EWHC 1479 (Comm), [2008] 2 Lloyd's Rep. 475.

[1001] [2013] EWCA Civ 1539; for an account of the Supreme Court decision in this case, [2015] UKSC 67, see below, para.26–197.

[1002] [2013] EWCA Civ 1539 at [104]. The reference is to *Clydebank Engineering & Shipbuilding Co Ltd v Don Jose Ramos Yzquierdo y Castaneda* [1905] A.C. 6.

[1003] [2013] EWCA Civ 1539 at [125].

[1004] [2013] EWCA Civ 1539 at [105]–[117] and [118]–[123].

[1005] [2013] EWCA Civ 1539 at [105]–[117].

[1006] [2013] EWCA Civ 1539 at [120]–[121].

[1007] [2015] UKSC 67, [2016] A.C. 1172.

[1008] See below, para.26–197.

26–194 **"Commercial justifications" and "legitimate interests".** It seems likely that the "commercial justifications" given in the cases referred to in this section and listed by Christopher Clarke L.J. in the passage cited in the previous paragraph, would also constitute legitimate interests[1009] within the meaning of the Supreme Court's new test.[1010] If that is correct, there is no further need to refer to "commercial justification" as a test of whether an agreed damages or similar clause is valid or a penalty.

[1009] On what constitutes a legitimate interest see below, para.26–198.

[1010] Lord Hodge said that the broader approach adopted in this group of cases "involves a correct analysis of the law" (at [225]; see also at [246]).

(d) Deterrence to Protect a Legitimate Interest

26–195 **Permissible deterrence in protecting broader interests.** The first modern decision that a clause requiring a sum that is not a genuine pre-estimate of the loss that will be suffered by the other party, and which is clearly aimed at deterrence, may nonetheless be a valid liquidated damages clause was the decision of the Court of Appeal in *ParkingEye Ltd v Beavis*.[1011] The claimants operated a car park at a retail park on behalf of the owners. Motorists were allowed to park free of charge for up to two hours after which they should leave, but a "failure to comply" would result in a parking charge of £85. Moore-Bick L.J., with whom the other members of the court agreed, said the claimants would suffer no direct loss if the motorists overstayed the two hours; it had only an indirect commercial interest in that if it did not deliver the service required by the owners of the retail park it might lose its contract and its reputation.[1012] There was also a social interest,[1013] in that consumers and retailers would benefit from having free parking for limited periods.[1014] Although it was clear that the principal purpose of the parking charge was to deter motorists from overstaying, a charge designed to protect a combination of indirect commercial interests and social interests might be valid, provided that it was not manifestly excessive. The judge at first instance had taken the correct approach when he held that the charge was neither improper in its purpose nor manifestly excessive in its amount, having regard to the level of charges imposed by local authorities and others for overstaying in public car parks.[1015] While in a purely commercial context[1016] a "dominant purpose of deterrence" had been equated to extravagance and unconscionability, in the context of the case that was not the case.[1017] An appeal in the *ParkingEye* case was heard by the Supreme Court along with the appeal in the *Makdessi* case[1018]; as will be explained in the next paragraph, the Supreme Court[1019] rejected the appeal in the *ParkingEye* case, upholding the £85 charge on an even wider ground than had the Court of Appeal.

[1011] [2015] EWCA Civ 402.
[1012] [2015] EWCA Civ 402 at [25].
[1013] [2015] EWCA Civ 402 at [27].
[1014] [2015] EWCA Civ 402 at [30].
[1015] [2015] EWCA Civ 402 at [26].
[1016] Or, as Sir Timothy Lloyd put it, "where the transaction between the contracting parties can be assessed in monetary terms, as can the effects of a breach of the contract by one party or the other" (at [44]). To prohibit this provision would "fail to take account of the nature of the contract, with its gratuitous but valuable benefit of two hours' free parking, and of the entirely legitimate reason for limiting that facility to a two hour period" (at [49]).
[1017] [2015] EWCA Civ 402 at [27]. The Court also held that the term was not unfair under the Unfair Terms in Consumer Contracts Regulations 1999: see below, para.38–251A.
[1018] See above, para.26–193.
[1019] *Cavendish Square Holding BV v Makdessi* and *ParkingEye Ltd v Beavis* [2015] UKSC 67, [2016] A.C. 1172.

Penalty doctrine confirmed. The appeals from *Makdessi v Cavendish Square Holdings BV*[1020] and *ParkingEye Ltd v Beavis*[1021] were heard together by a seven-justice panel of the Supreme Court.[1022] The Court did not accept the argument made by counsel for Cavendish that the rule against penalty clauses should be abolished altogether[1023] or confined to cases in which the parties did not meet "on an equal playing field"[1024]; although consumers are protected by the statutory power to strike down terms that are unfair, the doctrine serves a useful role in business to business contracts.[1025] In particular small businesses might need the protection offered by the doctrine.[1026] To abolish the doctrine would be inconsistent with the provisional recommendations of the Law Commission and the recommendations of the Scottish Law Commissions,[1027] and out of line with other jurisdictions both elsewhere in the common law world and in Europe.[1028]

26–196

[1020] [2013] EWCA Civ 1539; for the facts, see the account of the Court of Appeal decision in this case, above, para.26–193.
[1021] [2015] EWCA Civ 402; for the facts, see above, para.26–195.
[1022] *Cavendish Square Holding BV v Makdessi* and *ParkingEye Ltd v Beavis* [2015] UKSC 67, [2016] A.C. 1172, noted by Conte (2016) 132 L.Q.R. 382, Morgan [2016] C.L.J. 11, Fisher [2016] L.M.C.L.Q. 169 and Dawson [2016] L.M.C.L.Q. 207.
[1023] See [2015] UKSC 67 at [36], [162] (Lord Mance), [218] and [256] (Lord Hodge).
[1024] See Lord Hodge [2015] UKSC 67 at [256] and [267].
[1025] [2015] UKSC 67 at [38], [260].
[1026] Lord Mance [2015] UKSC 67 at [167]; Lord Hodge at [263].
[1027] See Lord Mance [2015] UKSC 67 at [163]; Lord Hodge at [263].
[1028] See [2015] UKSC 67 at [164]–[167] (Lords Neuberger and Sumption) and [264]–[265] (Lord Hodge).

Protecting legitimate interests. However, the Supreme Court in *Cavendish Square* and *ParkingEye*[1029] was unanimous that the decision in *Dunlop Pneumatic Tyre Co Ltd v New Garage & Motor Co Ltd*,[1030] had been interpreted too

26–197

narrowly. Lord Dunedin had not intended to lay down a strict code, and the other Lords had not adopted to his reasoning in full. In particular Lord Atkinson had upheld the clause requiring payment of £5 for every tyre sold at less than the list price not because it was hard to estimate the loss from the particular breach but because Dunlop had a broader interest to protect, namely its system of price maintenance.[1031] As Lord Mance put it[1032]:

> "It is clear . . . that a concern can protect a system which it operates across its whole business by imposing an undertaking on all its counterparties to respect the system, coupled with a provision requiring payment of an agreed sum in the event of any breach of such undertaking. The impossibility of measuring loss from any particular breach is a reason for upholding, not for striking down, such a provision. The qualification and safeguard is that the agreed sum must not have been extravagant, unconscionable or incommensurate with any possible interest in the maintenance of the system, this being for the party in breach to show."

A clause may be valid even if it does not represent a genuine pre-estimate of the loss, and even though it is aimed at deterring a party from breaking the contract, provided that the other party can show a legitimate commercial interest in deterring the breach rather than simply being entitled to damages[1033] and that the clause is not extravagant or unconscionable in proportion to that interest. Lords Neuberger and Sumption said:

> "The true test is whether the impugned provision is a secondary obligation which imposes a detriment on the contract-breaker out of all proportion to any legitimate interest of the innocent party in the enforcement of the primary obligation. The innocent party can have no proper interest in simply punishing the defaulter. His interest is in performance or in some appropriate alternative to performance. In the case of a straightforward damages clause, that interest will rarely extend beyond compensation for the breach, and we therefore expect that Lord Dunedin's four tests would usually be perfectly adequate to determine its validity. But compensation is not necessarily the only legitimate interest that the innocent party may have in the performance of the defaulter's primary obligations."[1034]

Cavendish had a legitimate interest in preserving the good will for which it was paying such a large amount[1035]; it would be hard to prove the loss flowing from any breach of the non-competition covenants; the seller's loyalty was critical and indivisible[1036] and therefore it was legitimate to deter Makdessi from any breach. Likewise, in the *ParkingEye* case there was clearly a legitimate interest in ensuring that motorists did not stay longer than two hours.[1037] Therefore Cavendish's appeal succeeded but Beavis' failed.

[1029] *Cavendish Square Holding BV v Makdessi* and *ParkingEye Ltd v Beavis* [2015] UKSC 67, [2016] A.C. 1172.

[1030] [1915] A.C. 79.

[1031] [2015] UKSC 67 at [22]–[23], [135]–[139], referring to [1915] A.C. 79, 90–93. Lord Mance (at [132]–[134]) also referred to the words of Lord Robertson in *Clydebank Engineering & Shipbuilding Co Ltd v Yzquierdo y Castaneda* [1905] A.C. 6, 19.

[1032] [2015] UKSC 67 at [143].

[1033] [2015] UKSC 67 at [28]; cf. at [248]–[249] (Lord Hodge).

[1034] [2015] UKSC 67 at [32]. cf. Lord Hodge at [255], [275]. As Lord Carnwath and, on this point, Lord Clarke (see at [291]) agreed with Lords Neuberger and Sumption, this statement may be taken as the authoritative statement of the penalty rule. Lord Mance and Lord Hodge, with both of whom Lord Toulson agreed on this issue (see at [292]), each gave slightly different accounts but it is not thought that the differences between the judgments on this issue are substantial.

[1035] [2015] UKSC 67 at [75].

[1036] [2015] UKSC 67 at [75]; and see Lord Hodge at [272]. Lord Mance's analysis does not seem essentially different: he said that cl.5.1 should be judged in the light of the general interest being protected: at [179]–[180], and likewise cl.5.6 "must be viewed in nature and impact as a composite whole as well as in context".

[1037] [2015] UKSC 67 at [99] (Lords Neuberger and Sumption, with whom Lords Carnwath and, on this point, Clarke, agreed), [184] (Lord Mance) and [285]–[286] (Lord Hodge). Lord Toulson, who considered that the clause in the *ParkingEye* case was unfair within the meaning of the Unfair Terms in Consumer Contracts Regulations 1999 (see below, para.38–251A), declined to discuss whether it also amounted to a penalty at common law (at [316]).

"Legitimate interest". In *Makdessi v Cavendish Square Holdings BV* and *ParkingEye Ltd v Beavis*[1038] the Supreme Court held that an agreed damages clause or other type of clause that falls within the scope of the penalty doctrine[1039] will be valid if it is designed to protect a legitimate interest of the innocent party and the amount involved is not extravagant or unconscionable in proportion to that interest.[1040] Punishment of the party in breach is not a legitimate purpose.[1041] The Supreme Court decided that when shares in a company that has been purchased will be of little value to the buyer if the seller is not loyal, as in the *Cavendish Square* case, or if a perfectly lawful scheme will not work unless there is an effective deterrent, as in the *ParkingEye* case, and damages will not provide an adequate sanction, there is a legitimate interest in deterrence and a sum that is designed to deter will not be penal, provided that it is not extravagant or unconscionable compared to the relevant legitimate interest.[1042] What general factors are relevant to whether the claimant has a legitimate interest for this purpose? **26–198**

[1038] [2015] UKSC 67: see above, para.26–197.
[1039] See below, paras 26–216 et seq.
[1040] This test was applied in *Hayfin Opal Luxco 3 SARL v Windermere VII CMBS Plc* [2016] EWHC 782 (Ch) at [142] and in *BHL v Leumi Abl Ltd* [2017] EWHC 1871 (QB) at [44]. In *First Personnel Services Ltd v Halfords Ltd* [2016] EWHC 3220 (Ch) no evidence was given to justify a rate of interest on late payment far above both the usual commercial rate and what was payable under the Late Payment of Commercial Debts (Interest) Act 1998; it was not justified by the creditor's interest in securing punctual payment having regard to its own liability to pay employees (at [163]).
[1041] See [2015] UKSC 67 at [13] and [30] (Lords Neuberger and Sumption), [148] (Lord Mance), [243] (Lord Hodge).
[1042] See [2015] UKSC 67 at [99].

Difficulty of proving loss. Lords Neuberger and Sumption referred to a legitimate interest in obtaining performance rather than merely damages[1043]; and, in support of their argument that in fashioning the rules on remedies the law takes into account legitimate interests, referred to the rule that specific performance may be available (subject to other constraints) if the innocent party has "a legitimate interest extending beyond pecuniary compensation for the breach".[1044] In each of the cases before the court, it seems that damages would not be adequate compensation, nor be adequate as a deterrent to breach, as it would be hard to prove what loss, if any, flowed from any particular breach.[1045] The same was true in the case of in *Dunlop Pneumatic Tyre Co Ltd v New Garage & Motor Co Ltd*,[1046] in which a payment of £5 per tyre sold at below the list price was upheld. **26–199**

[1043] [2015] UKSC 67 at [28]. In *Vivienne Westwood Ltd v Conduit Street Development Ltd* [2017] EWHC 350 (Ch) Timothy Fancourt QC, sitting as a Deputy Judge of the High Court, said the test is whether the claimant has a legitimate interest beyond pecuniary compensation for any loss caused by the particular breach, so as to justify the secondary obligation (at [49]). The interest must in performance of the tenant's obligations, not merely in being able to claim the higher rent that became payable in the event of the tenant failing to comply with one of its obligations (at [52]). On the facts, the term that required the tenant, in the event of any non-trivial breach of its obligations, to pay a substantially higher rent was out of all proportion to the lessor's interest in having the tenant perform every one of its obligations rather than pay compensation for any breaches (at [63]), especially as the increased rent was payable in addition to damages for any loss caused by the breach. The increased rent was payable with retroactive effect from the start of the lease, but even if it had been purely prospective it would have been a penalty (at [65]).

[1044] [2015] UKSC 67 at [30].
[1045] cf. Main Work, Vol.I, para.27–008 (difficulty in quantifying damages may mean damages inadequate).
[1046] [1915] A.C. 79.

26–200   Difficulty in detection. A related factor is that damages for each individual breach will not be an effective remedy if it will be hard for the claimant to detect breaches by the defendant.[1047]

[1047] See Lord Mance [2015] UKSC 67 at [172].

26–201   Substitute not available. The analogy drawn with specific performance indicates that it would also suffice that the contract was for a unique piece of property, so that the claimant would be unable to purchase a substitute.[1048] The case would presumably be even stronger if the claimant might suffer consequential loss (such as a reduction in trading profits that might have been made using a unique vessel[1049]) that is again hard to prove or quantify. It is submitted that a party may also have a legitimate interest in deterring the defendant from breaching a contract to provide services if it will be difficult for the claimant to obtain the services from a replacement contractor, even though specific performance of the contract might not be granted for other reasons, such as that because it would involve personal service[1050] or because it might require the court to supervise performance.[1051]

[1048] On the "adequacy of damages" test and the availability of a substitute, see Main Work, Vol.I, paras 27–010 et seq.
[1049] cf. Main Work, Vol.I, para.27–012 n.61.
[1050] See Main Work, Vol.I, paras 27–024 et seq.
[1051] See Main Work, Vol.I, paras 27–030 et seq.

26–202   Loss suffered by third party. In the *ParkingEye* case, there was an additional reason for damages being inadequate: the loss caused by the motorist overstaying the two hours free parking would be suffered not by ParkingEye Ltd but by the operator of the retail park and by members of the public who wished to use it. It is not only the legitimate interests of the contracting party that count for this purpose.[1052] It may be added that this appears to be a form of consequential loss that would not be recoverable under the principles that exceptionally permit a party to a contract to recover damages on the basis that the promisee has not received the benefit that he contracted for,[1053] nor to be within the cases that have permitted a promisee to recover for loss that is suffered by a third party.[1054] In *Beswick v Beswick*[1055] the majority considered that the promisee could recover only nominal damages, while the third party suffered the real loss, and that therefore specific performance was an appropriate remedy. It seems the presence of similar factors will mean that the promisee has a legitimate interest in securing performance rather than relying on the remedy of damages.

[1052] [2015] UKSC 67 at [99].

[1053] The "broader principle" suggested by Lord Griffiths in *Linden Gardens Trust Ltd v Lenesta Sludge Disposals Ltd* [1994] 1 A.C. 85. Further, even the cost of performance may be recoverable by the promisee only if he would be able and likely to remedy the breach: see Main Work, Vol.I, para.18–056 and paras 18–063—18–068.

[1054] e.g. when the parties contemplated that the property would be transferred to a third party, the ground of the majority decision in *Linden Gardens Trust Ltd v Lenesta Sludge Disposals Ltd* [1994] 1 A.C. 85: see Main Work, Vol.I, paras 18–057 et seq.

[1055] [1968] A.C. 58; see Main Work, Vol.I, paras 18–022 and 18–051 et seq.

Insolvency risk. The possible insolvency of either party may also be a relevant factor, at least when it is the claimant's solvency that is at risk. A factor that has sometimes been taken into account in deciding whether to grant specific perform- ance (or, on the facts of the case, an injunction against breach) is that the defendant may not be able to pay any damages.[1056] It is not evident that the defendant's inability to pay damages can by itself[1057] give the claimant a legitimate interest in deterring breach by imposing liability for "deterrent" liquidated damages, which would mean the defendant paying even greater sums. Conversely, it has been said to be a relevant factor to specific performance that delay is likely to be encountered in securing the actual payment of any damages and that the claimant might become insolvent before they are paid.[1058] It is submitted that this may be relevant to an agreed damages clause. The claimant clearly has a legitimate interest in remaining solvent, and if the contract is sufficiently important to the claimant's financial state that non-performance by the defendant coupled with a likely delay in recovering the damages would put the claimant's solvency at serious risk, the claimant seems to have a legitimate interest in performance rather than damages.

26–203

[1056] *Evans Marshall & Co v Bertola SA (No.1)* [1973] 1 W.L.R. 349, 367 (Kerr J. at first instance) and 385 (Edmund Davies L.J.).

[1057] Insolvency of the defendant is not a ground for refusing specific performance where the remedy is normally available as a matter of course: *AMEC Properties v Planning Research & Systems* [1992] 1 E.G.L.R. 70. See Main Work, Vol.I, para.27–013.

[1058] *Thames Valley Power Ltd v Total Gas and Power Ltd* [2006] 1 Lloyd's Rep. 441 at [64]; see Main Work, Vol.I, para.27–016 at n.95.

Preference for performance. Specific performance will not be awarded merely because the claimant would prefer performance to damages, if damages would be (or are likely to be) an adequate remedy. Equally, it is submitted that, despite another analogy which will be considered in the next paragraph,[1059] the decision in the *Cavendish Square* case[1060] does not mean that a party who simply has a preference for performance (which would presumably include most contracting parties, unless they have come to regret entering the contract) has a legitimate interest in deterring breach sufficient to justify an agreed damages clause that is aimed at deterring breach rather than being a genuine pre-estimate of the loss. To put the point another way, whether the claimant has a legitimate interest in performance rather than damages seems to be an objective test.[1061] It is submitted further that the claimant would not be able to overcome this by showing that it had paid a higher price to the defendant than it would have had to pay had the clause not been included in the contract.

26–204

[1059] See below, para.26–205.

¹⁰⁶⁰ *Cavendish Square Holding BV v Makdessi* and *ParkingEye Ltd v Beavis* [2015] UKSC 67, [2016] A.C. 1172.
¹⁰⁶¹ cf. above, para.26–184.

26–205 **Continuing performance after a repudiation.** Lords Neuberger and Sumption[1062] also referred to the line of cases, starting with a dictum of Lord Reid in *White & Carter (Councils) Ltd v McGregor*,[1063] to the effect that a party faced with a wrongful repudiation by the other party may, if he is able to continue to perform his part of the contract without the repudiating party's co-operation, ignore the repudiation, perform his part and sue for the agreed price unless he has no legitimate interest in doing so. The Court of Appeal has accepted the "no legitimate interest" restriction as part of the law.[1064] But in the context of repudiation, the concept of legitimate interest operates not as a reason for allowing an additional remedy but as a restriction on the right to keep the contract in force, a restriction that allows the right to be exercised except in fairly extreme cases. Facts that have been mentioned as possibly justifying an innocent party in continuing to perform and claiming the price despite the repudiation have included that the shipowner faced with a wrongful repudiation by the charterer would, if the owner could not claim the hire, be left with the burden of re-letting the ship rather than the charterer having to find a use for it[1065]; that the charter hire might have been assigned to a bank as security for a loan[1066]; that if the innocent party had to claim damages from a repudiating party who was in financial difficulties, the defendant's funds might have been directed elsewhere before the damages were paid[1067]; and the fact that an innocent ship owner would be left "in a difficult market where a substitute time charter was impossible, and trading on the spot market very difficult".[1068] The innocent party has been held to have a legitimate interest in performing "unless maintaining the contract can be described as 'wholly unreasonable',[1069] 'extremely unreasonable' or, as Popplewell J. put it after surveying the cases, "perhaps, in my words, 'perverse'".[1070] An arbitrator's decision that the shipowner had no legitimate interest in continuing to claim the hire under a charter because the owner could re-let the ship on the spot market and claim damages from the charter was held to be a misapplication of the law.[1071] So it is not clear that the analogy of the *White & Carter* cases will provide helpful guidance on the meaning of legitimate interest in the context of the penalty rule. The Supreme Court seemed to regard a legitimate interest in obtaining performance rather than recovering damages as exceptional,[1072] not as applying unless seeking to obtaining performance would be wholly unreasonable. It is submitted that the fact that the claimant would be faced with having to go into an uncertain market in order to mitigate its loss does not give it a legitimate interest sufficient to support a clause that is aimed at deterring breach rather than being a pre-estimate of loss. However, when the amount of loss is hard to predict the claimant will no doubt still be given a "generous margin"[1073] before the pre-estimate will be treated as extravagant or unconscionable and therefore a penalty.

¹⁰⁶² [2015] UKSC 67 at [29].
¹⁰⁶³ [1962] A.C. 413, 431: see Main Work, Vol.I, para.26–106.
¹⁰⁶⁴ See Main Work, Vol.I, para.26–106.
¹⁰⁶⁵ *Gator Shipping Corp v Trans-Asiatic Oil SA (The Odenfeld)* [1978] 2 Lloyd's Rep. 357, 374. A similar point was made in respect of a landlord faced with a repudiation of a lease by a tenant: *Reichman v Beveridge* [2006] EWCA Civ 1659 at [31], though in that case the court also held it was

reasonable for the landlord to continue to claim the rent given that there was uncertainty over whether English law permits a landlord who has terminated the lease to claim damages for loss of rent (at [28]), an uncertainty that does not arise in relation to contracts in general.

[1066] *Clea Shipping Corp v Bulk Oil International (The Alaskan Trader) (No.2)* [1984] 1 All E.R. 129, 137.

[1067] *Isabella Shipowner SA v Shagang Shipping Co Ltd (The Aquafaith)* [2012] EWHC 1077 (Comm), [2012] 2 Lloyd's Rep. 61 at [47].

[1068] *Isabella Shipowner SA v Shagang Shipping Co Ltd (The Aquafaith)* [2012] EWHC 1077 (Comm), [2012] 2 Lloyd's Rep. 61 at [56].

[1069] *Gator Shipping Corp v Trans-Asiatic Oil Ltd SA (The Odenfeld)* [1978] 2 Lloyd's Rep 357, 373.

[1070] *Isabella Shipowner SA v Shagang Shipping Co Ltd (The Aquafaith)* [2012] EWHC 1077 (Comm), [2012] 2 Lloyd's Rep. 61 at [44]. In *Attica Sea Carriers Corp v Ferrostaal Poseidon Bulk Reederei GmbH (The Puerto Buitrago)* [1976] 1 Lloyd's Rep. 250 the innocent party has been held to have no legitimate interest in claiming the hire of a chartered ship until it was returned fully repaired, when the vessel was beyond economic repair; and in *MSC Mediterranean Shipping Co SA v Cottonex Anstalt* [2016] EWCA Civ 789 the court said there would be no legitimate interest in claiming the demurrage in respect of containers that were being detained by a third party with no end in sight, so that the contractual venture had become frustrated (at [43]): see above, para.26–106.

[1071] *Isabella Shipowner SA v Shagang Shipping Co Ltd (The Aquafaith)* [2012] EWHC 1077 (Comm), [2012] 2 Lloyd's Rep. 61 at [42]. Popplewell J. seemed to doubt the decision of Lloyd J. in *Clea Shipping Corp v Bulk Oil International (The Alaskan Trader) (No.2)* [1983] 2 Lloyd's Rep. 645, of which Popplewell J. said: "Lloyd J found it impossible to interfere with the decision of the experienced commercial arbitrator who could not be shown to have applied the wrong test when finding that the owners' election to maintain the time charter (which had included 10 months of service, followed by six months of off-hire repairs) for a balance of eight months following premature re-delivery was a commercial absurdity".

[1072] It is probably for the claimant to show that it has a legitimate interest, whereas in the repudiation situation it is for the party in breach to show that the innocent party has no legitimate interest in performing: *Ocean Marine Navigation Ltd v Koch Carbon Inc (The Dynamic)* [2003] EWHC 1936 (Comm), [2003] 2 Lloyd's Rep. 693 at [23].

[1073] cf. above, para.26–185.

Analogy to account of profits. A further possible analogy, though not mentioned by the Supreme Court in the *Cavendish Square* case,[1074] are the cases in which a claimant is permitted to recover an account of the profit[1075] or, at least damages on the *"Wrotham Park"* basis,[1076] in other words, a share of the profit that the defendant has made through breaking the contract. An account of profit was awarded in *Att-Gen v Blake*[1077] after Blake had written and published a book in breach of the confidentiality agreement made by him when he entered the Secret Intelligence Service. The circumstances were said to be "exceptional", but Lord Nicholls said:

26–206

> "The court will have regard to all the circumstances, including the subject matter of the contract, the purpose of the contractual provision which has been breached, the circumstances in which the breach occurred, the consequences of the breach and the circumstances in which relief is being sought. A useful general guide, although not exhaustive, is whether the plaintiff had a legitimate interest in preventing the defendant's profit-making activity and, hence, in depriving him of his profit.
> It would be difficult, and unwise, to attempt to be more specific . . . "[1078]

Presumably the government would equally have had a sufficient legitimate interest to justify a clause requiring ex-employees who broke the confidentiality agreement to pay a sum that was designed to be a deterrent. Later cases have emphasised that for an account of profits to be appropriate the circumstances must be exceptional, and this has been taken to mean that an account of profits will not normally be appropriate in a commercial case,[1079] though it is certainly possible.[1080] To date an account of profits has been awarded in commercial circumstances only in one case at first instance. In *Esso Petroleum Co Ltd v Niad Ltd*[1081] the defendant had agreed to participate in a "Price Watch" scheme under which participating petrol stations agreed not to sell at above set prices. The defendant broke the agreement by selling at higher prices. The claimants were unable to show what loss this had caused them but it was held that they had a strong interest in performance and an account of profits was ordered. Though Esso's aim was to prevent dealers from selling petrol at higher prices than permitted by the scheme, rather than to prevent sales at less than a list price, in other respects the facts are quite similar to those of *Dunlop Pneumatic Tyre Co Ltd v New Garage & Motor Co Ltd*,[1082] and it seems clear that Esso would have had a sufficient legitimate interest to justify a clause requiring dealers who broke the agreement to pay a sum that was designed to be a deterrent, provided the sum set was not extravagant or unconscionable in proportion to Esso's interest. Moreover, it seems likely that an agreed damages clause that was calculated to take away any profit that the dealer might make by selling at higher than the set price would be proportionate to Esso's legitimate interest in deterring this kind of breach of contract by dealers.[1083] Beyond this, however, it is hard to gain much guidance from a class of cases that by definition are exceptional.

[1074] *Cavendish Square Holding BV v Makdessi* and *ParkingEye Ltd v Beavis* [2015] UKSC 67, [2016] A.C. 1172.

[1075] See Main Work, Vol.I, para.26–055.

[1076] See Main Work, Vol.I, paras 26–046 et seq.

[1077] [2001] 1 A.C. 268. See Main Work, Vol.I, paras 26–055 et seq.

[1078] [2001] 1 A.C. 268, 285 (per Lord Nicholls). For a more detailed consideration of the relevant facts see Main Work, Vol.I. para.26–055.

[1079] See Main Work, Vol.I. para.26–055.

[1080] See the discussion in *Experience Hendrix LLC v PPX Enterprises Inc* [2003] EWCA Civ 323, [2003] 1 All E.R. (Comm) 830.

[1081] [2001] All E.R. (D) 324 (Nov).

[1082] [1915] A.C. 79.

[1083] See further below, para.26–208.

26–207 **Analogy to *"Wrotham Park"* damages.** In cases in which the claimant has found it impossible or difficult to show that it has suffered a loss as the result of the defendant's breach of contract, the courts have more often awarded what are often now called *"Wrotham Park"* or "hypothetical bargain" damages, in other words, damages measured by the sum that the claimant could reasonably have demanded as the price of releasing the defendant from its obligation.[1084] So where the defendant has failed to provide the services promised but the claimant cannot show a consequential loss, if damages cannot be awarded on the simple difference in value between the services promised and those provided,[1085] an award on the hypothetical bargain basis may be made instead.[1086] The facts do not have to be exceptional in the way required if an account of profits is to be ordered, nor is it necessary that to deny *Wrotham Park* damages would produce a manifest injustice; the question is whether an award would be a just response.[1087] Some of the factors taken into account in deciding whether to award *Wrotham Park* damages seem relevant to the question of whether the claimant has a legitimate interest in securing performance rather than damages.[1088] These include difficulty in showing loss, even if it would be possible for the court to make an award of general damages assessed "in a robust manner".[1089] Although it had been said that "the inability to demonstrate identifiable financial loss of the conventional sort is a pre-condition to the award of such damages",[1090] in *One Step (Support) Ltd v Morris-Garner* the Court of Appeal declined to follow this dictum and held that *Wrotham Park* damages may be awarded when it will be very difficult to prove the loss that has been caused by the breach.[1091] It may also be relevant that it would be difficult for the claimant to obtain interim relief.[1092] These factors seem to reflect similar ones that were suggested earlier. In any event, it was suggested earlier that loss of a hypothetical bargain is a kind of loss that may form part of a genuine pre-estimate of the loss.[1093] If that is correct, no further legitimate interest need be shown to justify an agreed damages clause that is designed to deter breach in circumstances in which "*Wrotham Park*" damages might be available.

[1084] See Main Work, Vol.I, paras 26–051 et seq.

[1085] See Main Work, Vol.I, para.26–041.

[1086] *Giedo van der Garde BV v Force India Formula One Team Ltd* [2010] EWHC 2373 (QB). Hamblen J. pointed out that an award was not "precluded by any of the following factors: (i) that the claimants advanced no claim for an injunction or specific performance, or the fact that there would have been no prospect of such an order being granted; (ii) the fact that damages are not claimed under Lord Cairns' Act in lieu of an injunction; (iii) the fact that the claim is not based on a breach of a restrictive covenant; and (iv) the fact that the claim is based on breach of contract rather than invasion of property rights" (at [533]). On the facts of the case, the loss assessed on this basis would be same amount as the difference in value (at [559]).

[1087] *One Step (Support) Ltd v Morris-Garner* [2016] EWCA Civ 180 at [122] and [145]–[146].

[1088] Other facts taken into account do not seem relevant. In *Experience Hendrix LLC v PPX Enterprises Inc* [2003] EWCA Civ 323, [2003] 1 All E.R. (Comm) 830 at [36], [44], [54] and [58] the Court of Appeal used some of the factors relevant to the granting of an account of profits as also relevant to their discretion to grant *Wrotham Park* damages, taking into account the fact that the defendant "did do the very thing it had contracted not to do"; that the defendant "knew that it was doing something which it had contracted not to do"; that it was a "deliberate breach", a "flagrant contravention" of the defendant's obligation. These factors do not seem relevant to whether or not the claimant had a legitimate interest in deterring the defendant from breach.

[1089] [2016] EWCA Civ 180 at [123].

[1090] *Abbar v Saudi Economic & Development Co (SEDCO) Real Estate Ltd* [2013] EWHC 1414 (Ch) at [225].

[1091] [2016] EWCA Civ 180 at [122] and [145]–[146]. It is submitted that *Wrotham Park* damages may also be awarded when the conventional measure of damages would leave the claimant under-compensated: see Main Work, Vol.I, para.26–053.

[1092] cf. Longmore L.J. in *One Step (Support) Ltd v Morris-Garner* [2016] EWCA Civ 180 at [151] (another wrongful competition case, in which the defendant's furtive conduct deprived claimant of opportunity to obtain interim relief).

[1093] See above, para.26–186.

Capturing any profit from breach. A further possible reason for including an   **26–208** agreed damages clause that fixes the sum to be paid at a sum much greater than the pre-estimated loss is that, even though damages will in other respects be an adequate remedy for the claimant's losses, the claimant considers that the defendant may break the contract in order to make a greater profit and wants to be able to claim the whole of the profit, not just a share of it as under the approach discussed in the last paragraph. If damages would be adequate,[1094] it seems unlikely that the claimant would be treated as having a legitimate interest in capturing the whole of the defendant's profit. In *Co-operative Insurance Society Ltd v Argyll Stores (Holdings) Ltd*[1095] Lord Hoffmann expressed the concern that in some circumstances an award of specific performance may allow "the plaintiff to enrich himself at the defendant's expense" by negotiating an

excessive price for releasing the defendant from performance; one that "exceeds
the value of performance to the plaintiff and approaches the cost of performance
to the defendant".[1096] A similar concern would prevent a court holding that a
claimant has a legitimate interest in a clause that is designed to capture the whole
of, or a large share in, any profit that the defendant might make.[1097]

[1094] As opposed to a case like *Esso Petroleum Co Ltd v Niad Ltd* [2001] All E.R. (D) 324 (Nov),
discussed above, para.26–206, in which the loss to the petrol supplier would be hard to prove.
[1095] [1998] A.C. 1.
[1096] [1998] A.C. 1, 15, citing Sharpe, "Specific relief for Contract breach" in Reiter and Swan
(eds), *Studies in Contract Law* (1980), 129.
[1097] It should be noted that "*Wrotham Park*" damages, though they compensate the innocent party
for its loss of opportunity to negotiate a price for releasing the defendant from the relevant contractual
obligations, do not have the same effect of allowing the claimant to hold out for a large share of the
profit, at least if the damages are fixed at a fairly modest share of the profit. In *Pell Frischmann
Engineering Ltd v Bow Valley Iran Ltd* [2009] UKPC 45, [2011] 1 W.L.R. 2370 Lord Walker said that
"Damages under this head . . . represent 'such a sum of money as might reasonably have been
demanded by [the claimant] from [the defendant] as a *quid pro quo* for [permitting the continuation
of the breach of covenant or other invasion of right]" (at [48]); the court should consider a
hypothetical negotiation between a willing buyer (the contract-breaker) and a willing seller (the party
claiming damages), both parties to be assumed to act reasonably, so that the fact that one or other
would have refused to make a deal is to be ignored. But the fact that the alternative project could not
proceed unless the negative rights were bought out can properly be taken into account (at [53]). See
Main Work, Vol.I, paras 26–052—26–054.

26–209 **Part of a legitimate scheme.** The decision in the *ParkingEye* case[1098] may also
be explained, without having to show that a breach of the contract would cause
the claimant to suffer a loss that would not be compensable (or indeed, any loss
at all) on the basis that the charge was an essential part of a lawful
scheme.[1099]

[1098] *ParkingEye Ltd v Beavis* [2015] UKSC 67, [2016] A.C. 1172.
[1099] See [2015] UKSC 67 at [99], [199].

26–210 **Conclusion on legitimate interest.** It is submitted that a claimant will have a
sufficient legitimate interest in obtaining performance rather than damages to
justify an agreed damages clause that is intended to deter breach, rather than as
a pre-estimate of loss, in the following situations:

- if the claimant would face serious difficulties in proving what loss, if any,
flowed from the breach[1100];
- if the claimant would face serious difficulties in detecting whether there
has been a breach[1101];
- if damages will not be an adequate remedy because, if the defendant fails
to perform, the claimant will not be able to obtain substitute goods, other
property or services (irrespective of the fact that specific performance of
the contract might not be available for other reasons)[1102];
- if loss will be suffered by a third party rather than by, or in addition to,
the claimant[1103];
- if having to claim damages from the defendant would put the claimant's
solvency at risk[1104];
- if that even though neither the claimant nor a third party will suffer any
loss through the defendant's breach but the claimant has an exceptional
interest in ensuring that defendant performs such that the court would
award an account of profits, as in *Att-Gen v Blake*[1105]; or

– more generally, if deterrence is an essential element of a lawful scheme.[1106]

In contrast, the claimant does not have a legitimate interest in obtaining more than damages, or agreed damages that are substantially more than a genuine pre-estimate of the likely loss, merely because the claimant would have to incur time and expense in arranging a substitute transaction, or simply would prefer performance to claiming damages[1107]; nor because it hopes to secure a large share of any profit the defendant might make through breaking the contract, when damages would otherwise be an adequate remedy.[1108]

[1100] See above, para.26–199.
[1101] See above, para.26–200.
[1102] See above, para.26–201.
[1103] See above, para.26–202.
[1104] See above, para.26–203.
[1105] See above, para.26–206.
[1106] As in the *ParkingEye* case, see above, para.26–197.
[1107] See above, para.26–205.
[1108] See above, para.26–208.

"Not extravagant or unconscionable". Even if the claimant can show that it has a legitimate interest in obtaining actual performance instead of damages in lieu of performance, an agreed damages clause or other clause that is within the penalty clause rules will not be valid if it is extravagant or unconscionable compared to the legitimate interest. Lord Mance's reference to the sum being "not . . . incommensurate"[1109] and Lord Hodge's to whether it is "wholly disproportionate"[1110] to the interest to be protected are helpful to show what is meant.   **26–211**

[1109] [2015] UKSC 67 at [143].
[1110] [2015] UKSC 67 at [226]–[227], [255].

Proportionate. "Not extravagant or unconscionable compared to the legitimate interest", and "not incommensurate" or "not disproportionate", appears to mean that a sum agreed to be payable upon breach must not be substantially more than is required in order to deter the defendant from breach. How is this to be determined? Since the decision in *ParkingEye Ltd v Beavis*,[1111] there have been anecdotal reports[1112] of parking companies charging motorists who overstay the period of "free parking" as much as £300. Is that unconscionable or disproportionate? It does not seem to matter that the loss may vary from breach to breach. Though there is no necessary connection between deterrence and the amount of the loss caused by a breach, a motorist who overstays by ten minutes presumably causes less loss to the landowner and less inconvenience to the public, and is therefore less of a threat to the claimant's "legitimate interests" than one who overstays by six hours, but there is no suggestion in the case that the agreed sum needs to be gradated according to the length of the overstay in order to avoid being classed as a penalty.[1113] Some motorists will be more attentive than others to notices setting out charges for overstaying and other breaches of the rules, and some will be deterred more readily than others. Will a charge remain "proportionate" unless it is higher than is needed to make even the most inattentive motorist sufficiently aware of the charges to "stop and think" and to deter even   **26–212**

the most thoughtless or perverse? This was not discussed in the *ParkingEye* case. Rather, there were references to proportionality in another sense, their Lordships pointing out that the £85 charge was not much greater than the fine for over-staying in many car parks operated by local authorities, and the latter do not usually allow a period of free parking.[1114] The difficulty of deciding what is not unconscionable or wholly disproportionate seems greater still when the breaches that will trigger the agreed damages or other clause[1115] may be quite various in nature. A seller of a business might breach a non-competition covenant by no more than continuing to make a few small transactions with no intent to compete further, which would probably pose no real threat to the buyer of the business; yet in the *Cavendish Square* case it was not treated as disproportionate to impose a price reduction of millions of dollars for any breach of the covenants. The Supreme Court's decision in *Cavendish Square* case may suggest that deterrent sums will only be disproportionate if they are excessive even for the "worst case scenario". However, it is submitted that the decision may be explained on the basis that the parties were of equal bargaining power and would not have agreed on a more draconian clause than was reasonably necessary to protect the buyer's interests.[1116] Had the parties been less equal, the "not extravagant or unconscionable" test might have been applied in a less generous way. If the sum is payable for any one of many different possible breaches, some of which may be comparatively minor, it is likely to be disproportionate.[1116a]

[1111] [2015] UKSC 67.

[1112] Information received during seminars on the case at the Judicial College.

[1113] Nor, according to the majority, to avoid it being unfair within the meaning of the Unfair Terms in Consumer Contracts Regulations 1999 (and now the Consumer Rights Act 2015), but see the dissent on this point by Lord Toulson. This aspect of the case is discussed below, para.38–251A.

[1114] [2015] UKSC 67 at [100].

[1115] For the kinds of clause that are within the penalty rule, see below, paras 26–215 et seq.

[1116] See below, para.26–214.

[1116a] *Vivienne Westwood Ltd v Conduit Street Development Ltd* [2017] EWHC 350 (Ch).

26–213   **"Not … extravagant".** The word "extravagant" can be taken to mean that disproportion will not be judged harshly; as in "pre-estimate" cases,[1117] the parties will be allowed "a generous margin of error". But otherwise it seems "usually to amount to the same thing" as "unconscionable".[1118]

[1117] See above, para.26–185.

[1118] Lords Neuberger and Sumption [2015] UKSC 67 at [31].

26–214   **"Not … unconscionable".** It is not clear whether the word "unconscionable", which recurs in all the judgments, was intended to have any independent effect. Lord Toulson clearly thought "unconscionable" added nothing to "extravagant",[1118a] but Lord Hodge twice refers to it as a separate requirement.[1118b] Lords Neuberger and Sumption said[1118c]

"the circumstances in which the contract was made are not entirely irrelevant. In a negotiated contract between properly advised parties of comparable bargaining power, the strong initial presumption must be that the parties themselves are the best judges of what is legitimate in a provision dealing with the consequences of breach."

Lord Mance also said that[1118d]

" . . . the extent to which the parties were negotiating at arm's length on the basis of legal advice and had every opportunity to appreciate what they were agreeing must at least be a relevant factor."

These statements do not appear to mean that there is a separate requirement of procedural fairness. It seems more likely that all Lords Neuberger, Sumption and Mance meant was that if the parties meet on more-or-less equal terms, the non-breaching party is less likely to get away with a provision that is disproportionate to what it needs if there is no effective bargaining pressure from the other party. This may well be one reason[1118e] why the court did not question whether the provisions in the *Cavendish Square* case were proportionate to the buyer's legitimate interest.[1118f]

[1118a] [2015] UKSC 67 at [293].
[1118b] Lord Hodge does not seem to have been referring to the general doctrine of unconscionable bargains, which normally requires claimants to show they were suffering from an identifiable bargaining weakness: see Main Work, Vol.I, paras 8–133 and 8–135. The possible application of the doctrine in cases like *Cavendish Square* is considered above, para.8–135.
[1118c] [2015] UKSC 67 at [35].
[1118d] [2015] UKSC 67 at [152].
[1118e] Lords Neuberger and Sumption's approach may also have been affected by their view that the clauses were not subject to the penalty rules at all because they were "primary obligations": see below, para.26–216H.
[1118f] See above, para.26–212.

(e) *Scope of the Law of Penalties*

Sums payable on and other consequences of breach. The penalty rules apply   **26–215**
to sums that are payable on breach of contract by the defendant and to a variety of other clauses that will have an adverse consequence for a defendant who is in breach the contract, such as a clause that disentitles a defendant who is in breach from receiving the full amount of the price that would otherwise be paid.[1118g] The law on penalties is not applicable to many sums of money payable under a contract. Thus, it is not relevant where the claimant claims an agreed sum (a debt) which is due from the defendant in return for the claimant's performance of his obligations,[1118h] or which is due upon the occurrence of an event other than a breach of the defendant's contractual duty owed to the claimant,[1118i] though there have been suggestions that some such clauses may be "disguised penalties" that do fall within the rules.[1118j] It has also been said that some clauses, though "triggered" by a breach by the defendant, are exempt from the rules because they reflect the "primary obligations" of the defendant, whereas the penalty rules are said to apply only to "secondary obligations".[1118k]

[1118g] See below, para.26–216.
[1118h] *White & Carter (Councils) Ltd v McGregor* [1962] A.C. 413 (above, para.26–104). However, in a contract in which the liquidated damages were only payable while the contract remained on foot, the innocent party was not entitled to ignore a repudiation and keep the contract alive so as to be able to continue to claim liquidated damages, as they would have no legitimate interest in doing so: *MSC Mediterranean Shipping Co SA v Cottonex Anstalt* [2015] EWHC 283 (Comm) at [94]–[105]; the Court of Appeal [2016] EWCA Civ 789 agreed that there was no legitimate interest in continuing to perform but because the contractual venture had been frustrated: see above, para.26–106. The contrast between a debt and liquidated damages is drawn by the House of Lords in *President of India v Lips Maritime Corp* [1988] A.C. 395, 422–423, 424.
[1118i] See below, para.26–216C.
[1118j] See below, para.26–216G.
[1118k] See below, para.26–216H.

(i) Types of Clause within the Penalty Doctrine

26–216 **Types of clause within the penalty rules.** In *Cavendish Square Holding BV v Makdessi*[1118l] the Supreme Court held that the penalty clause rules apply not only to agreed damages clauses but also to provisions that would prevent a party who breaks the contract from receiving a sum to which it would otherwise be entitled,[1118m] and also provisions that require a party in breach to transfer property to the other party at less than its full value.[1118n] The Supreme Court also stated that the penalty rules also apply to deposits and forfeiture clauses; these will be considered in a separate section.[1118o]

[1118l] [2015] UKSC 67, [2016] A.C. 1172.

[1118m] See [2015] UKSC 67 at [170] (Lord Mance); [226] (Lord Hodge); Lord Toulson agreed with both of them (at [292]). Lords Neuberger and Sumption were prepared to assume this without deciding it (at [73]); they considered that cl.5.1 of the agreement in the *Cavendish Square* case was part of the parties' primary obligations and therefore altogether outside the penalty rules: see below, para.26–216H. However, Lord Clarke preferred to leave this question open; he must therefore have held that the penalty rules do apply to clauses of this type. In *Gilbert Ash (Northern) Ltd v Modern Engineering (Bristol) Ltd* [1974] A.C. 689 the House of Lords had considered a clause entitling the contractor to "suspend or withhold" the payment of money due to the subcontractor on any breach of contract. It had been conceded that the clause fell within the doctrine, but a majority of the House appeared to consider that the concession was correct: see [2015] UKSC 67 at [70], [154] and [226].

[1118n] See at [170] and [183] (Lord Mance); [230] and [280] (Lord Hodge). On this point Lord Clarke (at [291]) agreed with Lord Hodge and Lord Toulson (at [292]) with both Lord Mance and Lord Hodge.

[1118o] See below, paras 26–216N et seq.

26–216A **Acceleration clauses.** An "acceleration" clause is often found in contracts providing for payment by instalments: on default in paying one instalment, all future instalments become immediately payable as one sum. Although the operation of these clauses produces results which may be "penal", the courts have usually enforced them on the ground that they do not increase the contract-breaker's overall obligation.[1118p] The Court of Appeal has held that it is not a penalty for an acceleration clause in a contract of loan to provide that, upon failure to pay an agreed instalment, the whole capital of the loan becomes immediately due and repayable.[1118q] But it might be held to be a penalty if it provided that, upon such failure, future interest (viz on payments not yet due) should be payable immediately.[1118r]

[1118p] *Protector Endowment Loan Co v Grice* (1880) 5 Q.B.D. 592 (a loan case); *Wallingford v Mutual Society* (1880) 5 App. Cas. 685. See Goode [1982] J. Bus. L. 148; cf. *Wadham Stringer Finance Ltd v Meaney* [1981] 1 W.L.R. 39, 48 (see Main Work, Vol.II, para.39–272); *Edgeworth Capital (Luxembourg) Sarl v Ramblas Investments BV* [2015] EWHC 150 (Comm) at [67], citing this paragraph as it appeared in the 31st edition; the Court of Appeal, [2016] EWCA Civ 412, did not comment on this point. The High Court of Australia has sometimes upheld acceleration clauses (*IAC (Leasing) Ltd v Humphrey* (1972) 126 C.L.R. 131 (see also Main Work, Vol.II, para.39–353)) but sometimes not (holding them to be penalties): *O'Dea v Allstates Leasing Systems (WA) Pty Ltd* (1983) 152 C.L.R. 359; Muir (1985) 10 Sydney L.R. 503; *AMEV-UDC Finance Ltd v Austin* (1986) 162 C.L.R. 170; cf. *Esanda Finance Corp Ltd v Plessing* (1989) 166 C.L.R. 131.

[1118q] *The Angelic Star* [1988] 1 Lloyd's Rep. 122, 125, 127.

[1118r] *The Angelic Star* [1988] 1 Lloyd's Rep. 122. cf. *Lordsvale Finance Plc v Bank of Zambia* [1996] Q.B. 752 (see above, para.26–193).

26–216B **Termination for breach of condition.** As explained earlier,[1118s] where the hirer has neither repudiated the hiring (or hire-purchase) agreement, nor committed a "fundamental breach" of it, but the owner terminates it in the exercise of an express power to do so conferred by the agreement, the owner's damages are limited to loss suffered through any breaches up to the date of the termination.[1118t] It was noted, however, that this principle does not apply where the contract made the broken term into a condition, any breach of which entitled the innocent party to terminate (e.g. a clause making compliance with time "of the essence"[1118u]). In this case the innocent party may both terminate the contract and recover damages for the loss of the bargain (viz in respect of all the outstanding obligations of the other party).[1118v] A clause that makes the hirer liable for a genuine pre-estimate of the owners' full loss in such a case will be valid. The Court of Appeal decided that the clause making prompt payment "of the essence" when it would not be so otherwise[1118w] is not itself subject to the law on penalties.[1118x] The difference between the two types of clause (viz an express power to terminate, and a clause making time of the essence) is "one of drafting form and wholly without substance".[1118y] The result is that the position of the parties may be changed by a simple, small change in the terminology of the contract which makes every term a "condition" in the sense of a term any breach of which entitles the promisee to terminate.[1118z] This follows, however, not from the law on penalties but from the firmly established rule that the parties are free to agree that any term of the contract is a condition.[1118aa]

[1118s] See above, para.26–192.

[1118t] *Financings Ltd v Baldock* [1963] 2 Q.B. 104. (A "minimum payment" clause specifying a larger sum will be held to be a penalty: see above, para.26–192.) The principle stated in the text has been regularly followed by the Court of Appeal: *Brady v St Margaret's Trust Ltd* [1963] 2 Q.B. 494; *Charterhouse Credit Co Ltd v Tolly* [1963] 2 Q.B. 683; *United Dominions Trust (Commercial) Ltd v Ennis* [1968] 1 Q.B. 54; *Capital Finance Co Ltd v Donati* (1977) 121 S.J. 270; *Lombard North Central Plc v Butterworth* [1987] Q.B. 527. See also the Australian cases cited, above, para.26–216A, n.1118p.

[1118u] See Main Work, paras 21–011 et seq.

[1118v] The *Lombard* case [1987] Q.B. 527. See Treitel [1987] L.M.C.L.Q. 143; Beale (1988) 104 L.Q.R. 355.

[1118w] In the *Lombard* case [1987] Q.B. 527, it was held that, according to common law principles, the hirer had not committed a repudiatory breach of the contract: at 543–545. The court nevertheless awarded as damages at common law almost the same sum which it had previously found not to be a genuine pre-estimate of loss (a penalty).

[1118x] The *Lombard* case [1987] Q.B. 527, 536–537.

[1118y] The *Lombard* case [1987] Q.B. 527, 546.

[1118z] Would the law uphold a clause providing expressly that for any breach, however trivial, the damages shall be assessed on the basis that the whole benefit of the contract has been lost by the other party? cf. decisions on mitigation, such as *The Solholt* [1983] 1 Lloyd's Rep. 605 (Main Work, Vol.I, para.26–093).

[1118aa] See Main Work, Vol.I, para.13–026.

(ii) *Events other than Breach*

Sum payable on event other than breach. In *Cavendish Square Holding BV v Makdessi* and *ParkingEye Ltd v Beavis*[1118ab] the Supreme Court endorsed the view that the penalty clause rules apply only to sums payable, and equivalent consequences,[1118ac] that follow from a breach of contract. Previous authority was not wholly clear. In *Campbell Discount Co Ltd v Bridge*,[1118ad] a hire-purchase agreement permitted the hirer at his option to terminate the hiring during the period of the agreement, and provided that the hirer should thereupon pay a sum   **26–216C**

by way of agreed compensation for the depreciation of the chattel; the Court of Appeal held that the owner could recover the agreed sum, since being payable upon an event not constituting a breach of the agreement, it fell outside the scope of the law as to penalties. In the House of Lords[1118ae] the decision was based on a different view of the facts,[1118af] but four of their Lordships expressed obiter their views on the ruling of the Court of Appeal; two agreed that the law as to penalties was inapplicable, but two were prepared to hold that the hirer was entitled to some relief. The later decision of the House of Lords in the *Export Credits Guarantee* case[1118ag] appeared to support the restriction of the scope of the law on penalties to payments[1118ah] triggered by a breach of contract. The House held that the law did not apply to a clause providing for the contract-breaker (the defendant) to pay a specified sum to the plaintiff upon the happening of a certain event which was *not* the breach of a contractual duty owed by the defendant to the plaintiff. So it could not be a penalty where the defendant had agreed to reimburse the plaintiff the amount paid by the plaintiff to third parties under a guarantee (even where the plaintiff's obligation to meet the guarantee arose on the occasion of the defendant's breach of his contractual duties owed to other parties).[1118ai] Although the case concerned a guarantee in a complex commercial arrangement and the plaintiff was claiming only the sum it had actually lost, their Lordships' limitation on the scope of the law on penalties was expressed in such wide terms that it would prevent many other clauses from being subject to that law, for example a sum payable by one party should it exercise an option as to perform at a later date than anticipated (but not required).[1118aj] Although statutory protection is available in some cases[1118ak] the common law position has been thought unsatisfactory; for instance, an honest business hirer, who terminates his hire-purchase agreement when he finds that he cannot keep up the instalments, is in a worse position than the hirer who simply breaks his agreement by failing to pay the instalments.[1118al] The High Court of Australia had not followed the *Export Credits Guarantee* case,[1118am] holding that a clause may be a penalty:

> "if, as a matter of substance, it is collateral (or accessory) to a primary stipulation in favour of a second party and this collateral stipulation, upon the failure of the primary stipulation, imposes upon the first party an additional detriment, the penalty, to the benefit of the second party."[1118an]

However in *Cavendish Square Holding BV v Makdessi* and *ParkingEye Ltd v Beavis*[1118ao] the Supreme Court[1118ap] rejected this approach, which in any event they regarded as unworkable,[1118aq] and said that the penalty rules only come into play when a clause is triggered by a breach.[1118ar]

[1118ab] [2015] UKSC 67, [2016] A.C. 1172.

[1118ac] See above, para.26–216.

[1118ad] [1961] 1 Q.B. 445 (following *Associated Distributors Ltd v Hall* [1938] 2 K.B. 83); see Main Work, Vol.II, paras 39–349—39–354. The decision is based on the non-statutory law. For statutory regulation of hire-purchase agreements, see Main Work, Vol.II, paras 39–356 et seq.

[1118ae] [1962] A.C. 600.

[1118af] viz that the hirer had committed a breach. The law on penalties applies to a minimum payment clause if the agreement is in fact terminated on the ground of the hirer's breach: *Cooden Engineering Co Ltd v Stanford* [1953] 1 Q.B. 86; *Lamdon Trust Ltd v Hurrell* [1955] 1 W.L.R. 391. See Main Work, Vol.II, paras 39–349—39–354.

[1118ag] *Export Credits Guarantee Department v Universal Oil Products Co* [1983] 1 W.L.R. 399. It is unfortunate that the short speech in this case made no attempt to discuss the opinions expressed in

the *Campbell Discount* case [1962] A.C. 600. See also *Euro London Appointments Ltd v Claessens International Ltd* [2006] EWCA Civ 385, [2006] 2 Lloyd's Rep. 436 (a condition precedent imposing no obligation).

[1118ah] And similar events: see above, para.26–216 and below, paras 26–216N et seq.

[1118ai] *Export Credits Guarantee Department v Universal Oil Products Co* [1983] 1 W.L.R. 399.

[1118aj] See also *Edgeworth Capital (Luxembourg) Sarl v Ramblas Investments BV* [2015] EWHC 150 (Comm); [2016] EWCA Civ 412. In *Berg v Blackburn Rovers Football Club & Athletic Plc* [2013] EWHC 1070 (Ch), [2013] I.R.L.R. 537 it was held that the penalty rules did not apply to a payment due when one party to a fixed-term employment contract exercised a right to terminate it early. In *M&J Polymers Ltd v Imerys Minerals Ltd* [2008] EWHC 344 (Comm), [2008] All E.R. (D) 445 (Feb) it was held that a "take or pay" clause is subject to the penalty rules (though it was held on the facts not to be a penalty). It is submitted that this will depend on the form of the clause. It will not be subject to the penalty rules if the buyer is simply obliged to pay for a minimum quantity with an option whether or not to take delivery of all the goods. On the facts of the case, however, it was held that the buyer was in breach of an obligation to order a certain quantity (at [41]). See also *E-Nik Ltd v Secretary of State for Communities and Local Government* [2012] EWHC 3027 (Comm) at [25] (clause requiring a customer to pay for a minimum amount of services was treated as being subject to the penalty rules but nonetheless upheld). In *Associated British Ports v Ferryways NV* [2008] EWHC 1265 (Comm), [2008] 2 Lloyd's Rep. 353 (affirmed on other grounds [2009] EWCA Civ 189, [2009] 1 Lloyd's Rep. 595) it was held that the penalty rules did not apply to sums due under a "minimum through-put" clause.

[1118ak] In particular under the Unfair Terms in Consumer Contracts Regulations 1999 or Consumer Rights Act 2015 s.62: see below, Main Work, Vol.II, paras 38–201 et seq. and 38–334 et seq. When the term provides for the forfeiture of a deposit or other sum, see below, paras 26–216N et seq.

[1118al] See the Law Commission's Working Paper No.61 (1975), paras 17–26; *Edgeworth Capital (Luxembourg) Sarl v Ramblas Investments BV* [2015] EWHC 150 (Comm) at [59] (rev'd on other grounds [2016] EWCA Civ 412).

[1118am] *Export Credits Guarantee Department v Universal Oil Products Co* [1983] 1 W.L.R. 399. It is unfortunate that the short speech in this case made no attempt to discuss the opinions expressed in the *Campbell Discount* case [1962] A.C. 600. See also *Euro London Appointments Ltd v Claessens International Ltd* [2006] EWCA Civ 385, [2006] 2 Lloyd's Rep. 436 (a condition precedent imposing no obligation); *Jervis v Harris* [1996] Ch. 195, 206–207.

[1118an] *Andrews v Australia and New Zealand Banking Group Ltd* (2012) 247 C.L.R. 205 at [10].

[1118ao] [2015] UKSC 67, [2016] A.C. 1172.

[1118ap] Lords Neuberger and Sumption (with whom Lord Carnwath and, seemingly on this point, Lord Clarke agreed) [2015] UKSC 67 at [42]–[43]; Lord Hodge (with whom Lord Toulson agreed) at [241]. Note however the suggestion that a clause may be "a disguised penalty", discussed below, para.26–216G. Lord Mance said that the point concerning clauses that operate on events other than breach was not up for decision but the distinction is "not without rational or logical underpinning": at [130].

[1118aq] Lords Neuberger and Sumption [2015] UKSC 67 at [42].

[1118ar] If the sum is payable on one of several events, some of which are breaches and others are not, the penalty rule will apply if the event that in fact triggered the payment was a breach, but not otherwise, nor if, as on the facts of the case, it was a breach of a different contract by another party: *Edgeworth Capital (Luxembourg) Sarl v Ramblas Investments BV* [2015] EWHC 150 (Comm) at [60], [69]; the Court of Appeal confirmed that the penalty rule did not apply, [2016] EWCA Civ 412 at [7]. The death or bankruptcy of a party might be another event, not constituting a breach, upon which money is to be paid. cf. *Mount v Oldham Corp* [1973] Q.B. 309 (claim for a term's school fees in lieu of notice withdrawing a pupil).

Sums payable on exercise of an option under the contract. Thus the law does not apply where one party to the contract is given an option to choose a particular method of performance, subject to his making a stipulated payment to the other[1118as]; or where a member of a pooling agreement failed to pay his levy to finance litigation and was excluded from sharing in the proceeds of the litigation.[1118at] It does not apply to an employee's loss of contingent future interests in fund units to which he would have been entitled had his employment continued.[1118au] In the Court of Appeal in the *ParkingEye* case it was said that the   **26–216D**

penalty rules would not apply to an £85 charge for overstaying in an otherwise free parking facility if the arrangement were expressed in terms of a licence to use the car park subject to conditions coupled with an agreement to pay the charge if the conditions are not adhered to.[1118av]

[1118as] *Fratelli Moretti SpA v Nidera Handelscompagnie BV* [1981] 2 Lloyd's Rep. 47, 53; for another example see *BHL v Leumi Abl Ltd* [2017] EWHC 1871 (QB) at [44].
[1118at] *Nutting v Baldwin* [1995] 1 W.L.R. 201.
[1118au] *Imam-Sadeque v Bluebay Asset Management (Services) Ltd* [2012] EWHC 3511 (QB), citing the Australian case of *Interstar Wholesale Finance Pty Ltd v Integral Home Loans Pty Ltd* (2008) 257 A.L.R. 292. The provision was in any event commercially justifiable and not penal when read in the light of the contract as a whole: [2012] EWHC 3511 (QB) at [223]–[234].
[1118av] *ParkingEye Ltd v Beavis* [2015] EWCA Civ 402 at [23].

26–216E **Reimbursement is not a penalty.** If a contract provides that in a certain event a sum of money paid under the contract is to be repaid to the original payer, the reimbursement cannot be a penalty.[1118aw] So where the defendant received an insurance payment on the basis of his permanent disablement the insurers were able to enforce his undertaking to pay them "a penalty" of the same amount if he took part in a specified sport in future.[1118ax]

[1118aw] *Alder v Moore* [1961] 2 Q.B. 57 (approving *Re Apex Supply Co Ltd* [1942] Ch. 108).
[1118ax] *Alder v Moore* [1961] 2 Q.B. 57. Although the defendant had agreed not to take part again in professional football, the majority considered that this was not a case in which the defendant was in breach by so doing but of a condition on the defendant retaining the insurance payment: see at 65 and 77.

26–216F **Incentive payments.** The reverse of an agreed damages clause is an incentive payment such as an extra payment for early completion. The law on penalties does not apply to a clause providing for an *increase* in the price if certain targets in the contract are bettered or if costs are reduced; similarly, the price for a specially-manufactured machine may be graduated according to its efficiency in operation. A Government report has recommended that in building contracts incentive payments should be preferred to agreed damages clauses.[1118ay]

[1118ay] Banwell Report (Report of the Committee on Placing and Management of Contracts for Building and Civil Engineering Work) (HMSO, 1964), para.9.22.

26–216G **Disguised penalties.** Some doubt is thrown on the division between sums payable upon breach and sums payable on other events by the suggestion by some of their Lordships in *Cavendish Square Holding BV v Makdessi* and *ParkingEye Ltd v Beavis*[1118az] that certain clauses may amount to "disguised penalties". This follows a suggestion by Bingham L.J. in *Interfoto Picture Library Ltd v Stiletto Visual Programmes Ltd*[1118ba] that the clause in that case, which required a party who had hired photographic slides to pay a much higher charge if the slides were not returned within a fixed period, might be a "disguised penalty".[1118bb] It is hard to find any support for such a concept in earlier cases, and it is unclear how a disguised penalty differs from other sums payable if the party exercises an option under the contract. The only possible distinction seems to be that the amount of the payment is out of proportion to the claimant's interest in obtaining performance—in which case the "disguised penalty" rule would have the effect that the penalty clause rules (including the new "legitimate deterrent rule") would after all apply to a clause setting a price on an option that the defendant has chosen to exercise.

¹¹¹⁸ᵃᶻ [2015] UKSC 67, [2016] A.C. 1172 at [77] (Lords Neuberger and Sumption) and [258] (Lord Hodge).

¹¹¹⁸ᵇᵃ [1989] Q.B. 433.

¹¹¹⁸ᵇᵇ [1989] Q.B. 433, 439. The decision rested on the ground that the clause was not incorporated into the contract: see Main Work, Vol.I, para.13–015.

(iii) *"Primary Obligations"*

Primary obligations. In *Cavendish Square Holding BV v Makdessi*¹¹¹⁸ᵇᶜ Lords   **26–216H**
Neuberger and Sumption (with whom Lord Carnwath agreed) held that the
clauses which provided that the seller of the business, if he was in breach of the
non-competition covenants, would not receive the outstanding instalments of the
price, and would require him to transfer further shares to the buyers at a much
reduced value, were not subject to the penalty rules at all. Even if they were
triggered by the seller's breach, clause 5.1 bore no relation to damages; it
represented the reduced price that the buyer was prepared to pay for the business
if it could not count on the loyalty of the seller, and so formed part of the
"primary obligations" of the parties.¹¹¹⁸ᵇᵈ The analysis of clause 5.6 was essentially similar: it represented the reduced price that the purchaser was prepared to
pay when it could not count on the loyalty of Makdessi.¹¹¹⁸ᵇᵉ The law places
controls over only the parties' secondary obligations, not their primary obligations,¹¹¹⁸ᵇᶠ and both clauses belong among the primary obligations, even if the
occasion of their operation was a breach of contract.¹¹¹⁸ᵇᵍ In any event, both
clauses were justified by the same legitimate interest in matching the price to the
value that the seller was providing.¹¹¹⁸ᵇʰ Unlike an agreed damages clause, if the
clauses did not stand there is no scale by which the court could make an award.
The other members of the Supreme Court either decided the case on the ground
that the clauses did not amount to penalties or preferred to leave the matter
open.¹¹¹⁸ᵇⁱ With respect, it is unclear how a payment (or other obligation that is
within the doctrine¹¹¹⁸ᵇʲ) that is "triggered" by a breach of contract by the
defendant but which is a primary obligation is to is to be distinguished from an
agreed damages clause. The fact that the clause is in the form of a price reduction
seems to emphasise form over substance; and while it is true that ex ante there
is no alternative scale by which the court could fix appropriate prices, when an
agreed damages clause is held to be unenforceable the court makes an ex post
assessment of the actual loss suffered by the claimant. It seems that a court could
equally assess damages in terms of the reduction in value in the shares caused by
a breach by the seller of a non-competition covenant, and the valuation could
include an element for the risk that the seller who had been disloyal once may be
disloyal again.

¹¹¹⁸ᵇᶜ [2015] UKSC 67, [2016] A.C. 1172.

¹¹¹⁸ᵇᵈ [2015] UKSC 67 at [74]–[75]. Compare *Vivienne Westwood Ltd v Conduit Street Development Ltd* [2017] EWHC 350 (Ch), in which an increased rent became payable in the event of any
breach of its obligations by the tenant: the court held that the increased rent was a secondary
obligation that was capable of being a penalty (at [49]).

¹¹¹⁸ᵇᵉ [2015] UKSC 67 at [81].

¹¹¹⁸ᵇᶠ [2015] UKSC 67 at [14] and [32].

¹¹¹⁸ᵇᵍ [2015] UKSC 67 at [83].

¹¹¹⁸ᵇʰ [2015] UKSC 67 at [82].

¹¹¹⁸ᵇⁱ Lord Mance said that cl.5.1 had the effect of revising the price payable for the shares but he
clearly considered the clause to be subject to the penalty doctrine: see [2015] UKSC 67 at [181];

similarly, though cl.5.6 had the effect of reshaping of the parties' primary relationship (at [183]), it was valid because it was neither exorbitant or unconscionable (at [185]). Lord Hodge agreed that there were "strong arguments" for regarding each clause as primary obligations to which the doctrine does not apply: at [270] and [280]; but he decided the validity of cl.5.1 by applying the penalty doctrine, and held that cl.5.6 was a secondary obligation, adding that "if all such clauses were treated as primary obligations, there would be considerable scope for abuse". Lord Toulson agreed with the relevant parts of both Lord Mance's and Lord Hodge's judgments. Lord Clarke agreed with Lord Hodge rather than with Lords Neuberger and Sumption on these points: at [291].

[1118bj] See above, para.26–216.

26–216I **"Core" obligations rather than primary obligations.** One can understand the reluctance of judges to relieve a party from an obligation, whether it is correctly analysed as primary or secondary, that was negotiated with the assistance of experts and presumably agreed to in full knowledge of its possible implications, especially one that must have been seen as a central element of the agreement. Possibly a more useful distinction might be based on an approach suggested by Lord Toulson during argument, as a possible substitute for the penalty clause doctrine (which the Court had been invited to abandon[1118bk]). This was to borrow from the Directive on Unfair Terms in Consumer Contracts[1118bl] and ask whether the provision was a "core term".[1118bm] "Core" terms are likely to have been considered carefully by each party, even if the parties were not of equal sophistication or bargaining power, and therefore there is less reason to interfere than with more peripheral clauses that may not have been fully taken into account by both parties. The suggestion seems to be that if the change in price is so central to the deal that the party agreeing to it must have had it in mind, it would be exempt from control as a penalty. Lord Toulson did not, however, repeat this suggestion in his judgment.

[1118bk] See above, para.26–196.

[1118bl] 93/13/EC: see Main Work, Vol.II, paras 38–199 et seq.

[1118bm] In other words, it is the main subject matter or concerns the adequacy of the price or other remuneration and is therefore exempt from assessment for fairness provided that it is in plain and intelligible language, see art.4(2).

(iv) *"Invoicing back" Clauses*

26–216J **"Invoicing back" clauses.** The express terms of the contract may not only exclude or limit the innocent party's right to claim damages for breach of contract,[1118bn] but may also provide other provisions intended to apply in the event of a breach. Subject to the law as to penalties,[1118bo] and to the effect of the Unfair Contract Terms Act 1977[1118bp] or (if applicable) the Consumer Rights Act 2015,[1118bq] the courts will enforce these terms, despite the unexpected results which may occur. In one case,[1118br] a clause in a contract for the sale of goods provided that if the sellers made default in shipping, the contract should "be closed by invoicing back the goods" at the closing price fixed by the London Corn Trade Association. The sellers failed to ship, and the Association declared a closing price, which, because of a fall in market price, was lower than the contract price, so that a balance was due in favour of the sellers. Nevertheless, the Court of Appeal enforced the clause, despite the fact that the sellers were the party in default.[1118bs] An "invoicing back" clause may not be interpreted as the exclusive remedy,[1118bt] e.g. the clause may not prevent the buyer obtaining damages for his loss of profits,[1118bu] and judges have interpreted such clauses restrictively.[1118bv] An "invoicing back" clause may also allow a percentage of the market price to be added to, or deducted from, the price, which if reasonable, will be upheld as liquidated damages covering items of loss not covered by the price alone.[1118bw]

[1118bn] On exemption clauses, see Main Work, Vol.I, Ch.15, above.

[1118bo] Above, paras 26–178 et seq.

[1118bp] See Main Work, Vol.I, paras 15–066 et seq.

[1118bq] See Main Work, Vol.II, paras 38–334 et seq.

[1118br] *Lancaster v J.F. Turner & Co Ltd* [1924] 2 K.B. 222 (Scrutton L.J. dissenting); followed in *J.F. Adair & Co Ltd v Birnbaum* [1939] 2 K.B. 149 (and the earlier case noted, 173); *Podar Trading Co Ltd v Tagher* [1949] 2 K.B. 277. cf. *James Laing, Son & Co Ltd v Eastcheap Dried Fruit Co Ltd* [1961] 2 Lloyd's Rep. 277.

[1118bs] Some clauses are drafted differently and avoid this difficulty, e.g. the clause may apply only to the defaulting buyer, and only if the market price has fallen: *Alexandria Cotton and Trading Co (Sudan) Ltd v Cotton Co of Ethiopia Ltd* [1963] 1 Lloyd's Rep. 576.

[1118bt] *Roth, Schmidt & Co v D. Nagase & Co Ltd* (1920) 2 Ll. L. Rep. 36 CA (the clause did not expressly exclude the right to reject the goods or to recover damages upon rejection).

[1118bu] *Re Bourgeois and Wilson Holgate & Co* (1920) 25 Com. Cas. 260 (the Court of Appeal decided in this case that the seller in these circumstances could not enforce the clause against the buyer).

[1118bv] One judge has held that the interpretation of a clause which requires damages to be paid *to* the defaulting party is contrary to "natural justice": *Cassir, Moore & Co Ltd v Eastcheap Dried Fruit Co* [1962] 1 Lloyd's Rep. 400, 402. See also the qualifications suggested in *Lancaster v J.F. Turner & Co Ltd* [1924] 2 K.B. 222, 231; *J.F. Adair & Co Ltd v Birnbaum* [1939] 2 K.B. 149, 169.

[1118bw] *Robert Stewart & Sons Ltd v Carapanayoti & Co Ltd* [1962] 1 W.L.R. 34.

(f) *Effect of Clause if a Penalty*

Penalty clause is not enforceable. As mentioned earlier,[1118bx] if a clause is penal because it passes neither the "genuine pre-estimate" test[1118by] nor the "legitimate deterrent test,"[1118bz] the clause will be wholly unenforceable.[1118ca] The court has no power to re-write the clause in order to make it valid.[1118cb]   **26–216K**

[1118bx] See above, para.26–178A.

[1118by] See above, para.26–182.

[1118bz] See above, para.26–196.

[1118ca] *Cavendish Square Holding BV v Makdessi* and *ParkingEye Ltd v Beavis* [2015] UKSC 67, [2016] A.C. 1172 at [9] and at [291], where Lord Clarke expressed his agreement with this part of the Lords Neuberger and Sumption's judgment.

[1118cb] [2015] UKSC 67 at [84]–[86], [283] and [292], disapproving *Jobson v Johnson* [1989] 1 W.L.R. 1026 on this point. Lord Mance preferred to leave this point for further argument (at [186]). In *Vivienne Westwood Ltd v Conduit Street Development Ltd* [2017] EWHC 350 (Ch) at [66]–[71] Timothy Fancourt QC, sitting as a Deputy Judge of the High Court, expressed the view that it is possible to sever part of a clause that makes the clause penal if the offending part can be removed without adding to or modifying the rest, the remaining terms are supported by consideration, the change does not alter the character of the contract and severance does not conflict with the public policy making the offending part unenforceable. However, the authorities cited in support are cases on restraint of trade and, with respect, it is not clear that severance can be applied to penalty clauses.

Can damages exceed the sum fixed in penal clause? A clause which is not a genuine pre-estimate, e.g. because it stipulates for more than the likely loss, and which is therefore a penalty, may be ignored if it is for less than the actual damage suffered. Where a charterparty contained the following clause: "[p]enalty for non-performance of this agreement proved damages, not exceeding   **26–216L**

estimated amount of freight", it was held that the clause provided a penalty and not a limitation of liability, so that the party complaining of non-performance was entitled to recover damages for his actual loss although it exceeded the estimated amount of freight.[1118cc] It is unsettled whether this principle applies to penalty clauses in other types of contract, so as to entitle the claimant to ignore the sum stipulated as a penalty (where it was clearly not intended to limit liability) and to sue for damages for a greater amount to compensate him for his actual loss.[1118cd]

[1118cc] *Wall v Rederiaktiebolaget Luggude* [1915] 3 K.B. 66 (approved by the House of Lords in *Watts, Watts & Co Ltd v Mitsui & Co Ltd* [1917] A.C. 227). But this case may require reconsideration in the light of the *Suisse Atlantique* case [1967] 1 A.C. 361 (where a demurrage clause was held to be an agreed damages clause) and the *Photo Production* case [1980] A.C. 827.

[1118cd] In *Cellulose Acetate Silk Co Ltd v Widnes Foundry (1925) Ltd* [1933] A.C. 20, 26, the House left: " . . . open the question whether, where a penalty is plainly less in amount than the prospective damages, there is any legal objection to suing on it or, in a suitable case, ignoring it and suing for damages". cf. dicta to the effect that the penalty fixes the maximum recoverable: *Wilbeam v Ashton* (1807) 1 Camp. 78; *Elphinstone v Monkland Iron & Coal Co* (1886) L.R. 11 App. Cas. 332, 346; *Elsley v J.G. Collins Insurance Agencies Ltd* (1978) 83 D.L.R. (3d) 1, 14–16; *W.&J. Investments Ltd v Bunting* [1984] 1 N.S.W.L.R. 331, 335–336. See also Hudson (1974) 90 L.Q.R. 31; Gordon (1974) 90 L.Q.R. 296; Hudson (1975) 91 L.Q.R. 25; Barton (1976) 92 L.Q.R. 20; Hudson (1985) 101 L.Q.R. 480; Peel (ed.), *Treitel on The Law of Contract*, 14th edn (2016), para.20–140.

(g) *Consumer Contracts*

26–216M **Sums payable on breach in consumer contracts.**[1118ce] The Unfair Terms in Consumer Contracts Regulations 1999 provided that in a contract between a business and a consumer an "unfair term" that was not individually negotiated was not be binding on the consumer. For consumer contracts made after October 1, 2015, Pt 2 of the Consumer Rights Act 2015 provides that an unfair term[1118cf] in a consumer contract will not be binding on the consumer. The Regulations and the Act give illustrations of terms which may be regarded as unfair: relevant to clauses fixing damages is "requiring any consumer who fails to fulfil his obligation to pay a disproportionately high sum in compensation".[1118cg] So a consumer will be able to appeal to this standard, as well as to the common law on penalties; and it has been held that a term may be unfair even though on the facts it did not amount to a penalty at common law.[1118ch]

[1118ce] SI 1999/2083.
[1118cf] Whether negotiated or not: s.62. See Main Work, Vol.II, para.38–358.
[1118cg] 1999 Regulations Sch.2 para.1(e); 2015 Act Sch.2 Pt 1 para.(6).
[1118ch] *Munkenbeck & Marshall v Harold* [2005] EWHC 356 (TCC), [2005] All E.R. (D) 227; see below, Vol.II, para.38–280. For clauses requiring a consumer to make a payment on some event that is not a breach of contract, see above, para.26–216C.

(h) *Deposits and Forfeiture of Sums Paid*

26–216N **Deposits and forfeiture of sums paid.**[1118ci] A contract may, instead of fixing a sum to be paid upon breach, provide that a sum already paid shall be forfeited[1118cj] upon breach by the party who paid it.[1118ck] Alternatively, a sum may be paid as a deposit, in which case the sum is forfeited if the payer breaks the contract.[1118cl] If the deposit has not been paid when the contract is terminated, but it was payable, it may be recovered as a debt[1118cm]; if the contract was repudiated and terminated before the deposit became payable, the innocent party may recover the amount of the deposit by way of damages.[1118cn] In *Cavendish Square Holding BV v Makdessi* and *ParkingEye Ltd v Beavis*[1118co] the Supreme Court said that both deposits and forfeiture clauses are subject to the penalty rules (though it will be submitted that to some extent the rules still differ[1118cp]). Many deposits and forfeiture provisions will also fall within the Law of Property Act 1925 s.49(2), the Consumer Credit Act 1974[1118cq] and the Consumer Rights Act 2015.[1118cr]

[1118ci] See Goff and Jones, *The Law of Unjust Enrichment*, 9th edn (2016), Ch.14; *McGregor on Damages*, 19th edn (2014), paras 15–096 et seq.; the Law Commission, Working Paper No.61 (1975) ("Penalty Clauses and Forfeiture of Moneys Paid"), paras 50, 65, 66; Smith [2001] C.L.J. 178; cf. *Commissioner of Public Works v Hills* [1906] A.C. 368 (recovery of amount deposited as "security" in a building contract; above, para.26–187).
[1118cj] The payee "forfeits" the sum where he retains it for his own beneficial use, having freed himself of any further obligations under the contract by terminating the contract on account of the payer's breach. It is then up to the payer to challenge the forfeiture if he has any legal ground for doing so.
[1118ck] If the sum is a deposit paid by the buyer (viz a sum intended to be received by the seller as a security for the completion of the purchase by the buyer) it will be assumed that it is intended to be forfeited to the seller if the buyer defaults: *Howe v Smith* (1884) 27 Ch. D. 89, 97–98 (Main Work, Vol.I, para.29–068); *Stockloser v Johnson* [1954] 1 Q.B. 476, 490 ("or the money is expressly paid as a deposit (which is equivalent to a forfeiture clause)"). The court has power to order the return of a deposit paid under a contract for the sale of land.
[1118cl] *Howe v Smith* (1889) 27 Ch. D. 89. If the payee claims damages from the payer, he must give credit for the amount of the deposit: see the dictum of Fry L.J. at 104 and *Ng v Ashley King (Developments) Ltd* [2010] EWHC 456 (Ch).
[1118cm] See above, Main Work, Vol.I, paras 24–053 and 26–008.
[1118cn] *Damon Compagnia Naviera SA v Hapag-Lloyd International SA* [1985] 1 W.L.R. 435 (see above, para.24–053); *Griffon Shipping LLC v Firodi Shipping Ltd (The Griffon)* [2013] EWCA Civ 1567, [2014] 1 C.L.C. 1. The contrary decision in *Lowe v Hope* [1970] Ch. 94 is no longer good law: see *Hardy v Griffiths* [2014] EWHC 3947 (Ch) at [102].
[1118co] [2015] UKSC 67, [2016] A.C. 1172.
[1118cp] See below, para.26–216R.
[1118cq] See below, para.26–216AA.
[1118cr] See below, para.26–216AB.

Recovery of prepayments where no provision for forfeiture. If in a contract of sale there is no express requirement that the buyer must pay a deposit or will, in the event of breach, forfeit sums paid, and the seller terminates the contract upon the buyer's default, the buyer may recover any prepayment or instalments paid in part payment of the price, subject to a cross-claim by the seller for damages for the breach of contract.[1118cs] Thus, in *Dies v British and International Mining and Finance Corp Ltd*,[1118ct] where a buyer repudiated his contract to purchase goods, he was nevertheless held to be entitled to recover a substantial prepayment (not in the nature of a deposit) made by him, subject to a deduction in respect of the actual damage suffered by the seller through the breach of contract: the court held that if it permitted the whole prepayment to be retained by the seller, it would be permitting the retention of a penalty, not liquidated damages.[1118cu] This decision has been distinguished by two of their Lordships in the House of Lords[1118cv] on the ground that it concerned a sale of existing goods where no expenditure was intended to be incurred by the seller in reliance on the advance payment. It has been persuasively argued[1118cw] that the question should depend on the construction of the clause in the contract requiring the advance payment: was the right to retain the payment intended to be conditional upon

26–216O

performance by the payee of his obligations, or was it intended to be a security for performance of the payer's obligations?

[1118cs] *Palmer v Temple* (1839) 9 A. & E. 508; *Mayson v Clouet* [1924] A.C. 980; *Dies v British and International Mining and Finance Corp Ltd* [1939] 1 K.B. 724; *Stockloser v Johnson* [1954] 1 Q.B. 476, 483, 489–490; Williams, *Vendor and Purchaser*, 4th edn (1936), p.1006.

[1118ct] [1939] 1 K.B. 724 (followed in *Rover International Ltd v Cannon Film Sales Ltd* [1989] 1 W.L.R. 912).

[1118cu] See also *RV Ward Ltd v Bignall* [1967] 1 Q.B. 534 (Main Work, Vol.II, para.44–358). It has been noted that the *Dies* case was decided on the basis that the buyer's payment of the price was conditional, but that now the case might be decided on the ground that there had been a total failure of consideration: *Cadogan Petroleum Holdings Ltd v Global Process Systems LLC* [2013] EWHC 214 (Comm) at [23]. On either approach, the payment is not recoverable if the contract provides otherwise: [2013] EWHC 214 (Comm) at [18] and [27].

[1118cv] *Hyundai Heavy Industries Co Ltd v Papadopoulos* [1980] 1 W.L.R. 1129, 1142–1143, 1147–1148. (The contract in this case was for work and material supplied in the course of building a ship, and so it was treated as analogous to a building contract: see Beatson (1981) 97 L.Q.R. 389, 401–404; *Stocznia Gdanska SA v Latvian Shipping Co* [1998] 1 W.L.R. 574 HL.) The *Dies* [1939] 1 K.B. 724 case was also distinguished in the *Hyundai* case 1134–1136, on the ground that there was a total failure of consideration in *Dies*: see Main Work, Vol.I, paras 29–057 et seq.

[1118cw] Beatson (1981) 97 L.Q.R. 389, 391–401. See also Dixon J. in *McDonald v Dennys Lascelles Ltd* (1933) 48 C.L.R. 457, 477 (following termination of the contract "rights are not divested or discharged which have already been *unconditionally* acquired" (italics supplied)); and the *Fibrosa* case [1943] A.C. 32, 65 ("[t]he condition of retaining it [the advance payment] is eventual performance"; cf. at 75).

(i) *Deposits*

26–216P Law of Property Act 1925 s.49(2). Perhaps the most common use of provisions for a deposit is in contracts for the sale of land, which normally fall within Law of Property Act 1925 s.49(2); this may account for the relative paucity of case law on deposits at common law. Section 49(2) provides:

> "Where the court refuses to grant specific performance of a contract, or in any action for the return of a deposit, the court may, if it thinks fit, order the repayment of any deposit."

This provision is restricted to contracts for the sale or exchange of any interest in land.[1118cx] Apart from this provision, the vendor would be obliged to return the deposit only where he was in breach of contract[1118cy]; the statutory discretion conferred on the court by s.49(2) enables the court to make an order where the justice of the case requires it.[1118cz] The scope of application of this section was for a time thought to be narrow. It was said that it:

> " . . . was passed to remove the former hardship which existed where a defendant had a good defence in equity to a claim for specific performance but no defence in law, and, therefore, the deposit was forfeited . . . outside that ambit [the jurisdiction] should only be exercised, if at all, sparingly and with caution."[1118da]

It now seems to be accepted that "repayment must be ordered in any circumstances which make this the fairest course between the two parties".[1118db] But an order will not be made in every case in which the purchaser defaults, even if the vendor does not suffer any loss: rather, the case must be somehow exceptional for an order to be made for the return of a standard 10 per cent deposit.[1118dc] The court's jurisdiction cannot be excluded by the parties.[1118dd]

[1118cx] Law of Property Act 1925 s.49(3).

[1118cy] *Best v Hamand* (1879) 12 Ch. D. 1; *Re Scott and Alvarez's Contract* [1895] 2 Ch. 603; *Beyfus v Lodge* [1925] Ch. 350; *James Macara Ltd v Barclay* [1945] K.B. 148, 156.

[1118cz] *Finkeilkraut v Monohan* [1949] 2 All E.R. 235, 237–238. (cf. *James Macara Ltd v Barclay* [1945] K.B. 148, 156).

[1118da] *Michael Richards Properties Ltd v Corp of Wardens of St Saviour's Parish, Southwark* [1975] 3 All E.R. 416, 424 (Goff J.).

[1118db] *Universal Corp v Five Ways Properties Ltd* [1979] 1 All E.R. 553, 555 (Buckley L.J.). See also *Schindler v Pigault* [1975] 30 P. C.R. 328; *County & Metropolitan Homes Survey Ltd v Topclaim Ltd* [1997] 1 All E.R. 254 (effect of exclusion of Law of Property Act 1925 s.49(2)); *Omar v El-Wakil* [2001] EWCA Civ 1090.

[1118dc] See *Omar v El-Wakil* [2001] EWCA Civ 1090, [2002] 2 P. & C.R. 3 at [37], [49] and [55]; *Tennaro Ltd v Majorarch Ltd* [2003] EWHC 2601 (Ch), [2003] 47 E.G. 154 (C.S.) at [84]; *Aribisala v St James Homes (Grosvenor Dock) Ltd* [2008] EWHC 456 (Ch), [2008] All E.R. (D) 201 (Mar); *Midill (97PL) Ltd v Park Lane Estates Ltd* [2008] EWCA Civ 1227, [2009] 2 P. & C.R. 6, citing the Privy Council case of *Bidaisee v Sampath* [1995] N.P.C. 59; *Cohen v Teseo Properties Ltd* [2014] EWHC 2442 at [57]; *Solid Rock Investments UK Ltd v Reddy* [2016] EWHC 3043 (Ch). In the *Midill* case Carnwath L.J. said that "The critical point . . . is that the deposit is 'an earnest for the performance of the contract', which can be retained by the seller if the buyer defaults, without any necessary regard to the question of actual loss or its amount": [2008] EWCA Civ 1227 at [52].

[1118dd] *Aribisala v St James Homes (Grosvenor Dock) Ltd* [2007] EWHC 1694 (Ch), [2007] 37 E.G. 234, [2007] 2 P. & C.R. DG25.

Penalty rules and deposits. If the contract provides for one party to pay a deposit, and a breach of contract by the payor leads the payee justifiably to terminate the contract, then subject to the Law of Property Act 1925 s.49(2)[1118de] and what is said in the following paragraphs[1118df] the payee may retain the deposit provided that it does not exceed the amount that is customary (in contracts for the sale of land, normally 10 per cent of the purchase price). English courts have traditionally treated such deposits as somewhat different from a sum payable upon breach and have not required the seller to show that the amount is a genuine pre-estimate of the loss.[1118dg] In *Workers Trust & Merchant Bank Ltd v Dojap Investments Ltd* the Privy Council said, in general terms, that the law on penalties applies to:

26–216Q

> " . . . a contractual provision which requires one party in the event of his breach of the contract to pay or forfeit a sum of money to the other party."[1118dh]

In that case a contract for the sale of land required a 25 per cent deposit. The Privy Council held that a larger deposit than the customary 10 per cent would be valid only if the seller could show that it was reasonable to demand one; and in the absence of that the whole deposit was invalid and must be repaid, subject to a cross-claim for any loss suffered by the seller. However, the Privy Council accepted that a customary 10 per cent deposit may be forfeited by the seller on the buyer's default, irrespective of the amount of the seller's loss. In *Cavendish Square Holding BV v Makdessi* and *ParkingEye Ltd v Beavis*[1118di] the Supreme Court again said that the penalty rules apply to deposits,[1118dj] but either explained the right to keep a customary 10 per cent deposit either on the grounds that this is to be seen as "earnest money" that is not subject to the penalty doctrine[1118dk] or, it is thought, on the basis of a legitimate interest of the seller in deterring breach by the buyer. This seems to rest on the fact that each piece of land is treated as unique, so that damages are not considered an adequate remedy. That justifies ordering specific performance[1118dl] and so it gives the either party a legitimate interest for the purposes of the penalty rules.[1118dm] A deposit in other types of contract, such as a deposit paid when goods are ordered, may not be treated in the same way[1118dn]: a seller of goods does not seem to have a legitimate interest in obtaining performance by the buyer rather than damages,[1118do] at least when the goods are readily re-saleable, so the deposit may be valid only if meets the genuine pre-estimate test.[1118dp]

[1118de] See above, para.26–216P.

[1118df] Especially para.26–216AB.

[1118dg] See *Cadogan Petroleum Holdings Ltd v Global Process Systems LLC* [2013] EWHC 214 (Comm) at [34].

[1118dh] [1993] A.C. 573, 578. Law of Property Act 1925 s.49(2) did not apply.

[1118di] [2015] UKSC 67, [2016] A.C. 1172.

[1118dj] See [2015] UKSC 67 at [16] (Lords Neuberger and Sumption; see also at [35]); [238] (Lord Hodge; this was one of the paragraphs with which Lord Toulson (at [292]) said that he agreed); Lord Mance cited the *Workers Trust* case with apparent approval at [156] but left the application of the penalty rules to deposits open: at [170]). Lord Clarke referred to forfeiture clauses but not specifically to deposits.

[1118dk] Lord Hodge [2015] UKSC 67 at [238]. cf. above, para.26–216P n.1118dc.

[1118dl] See Main Work, Vol.I, para.27–007.

[1118dm] See above, para.26–198.

[1118dn] If the sale is to a consumer, the deposit might be challenged under the Unfair Terms in Consumer Contract Regulations 1999 or the Consumer Rights Act 2015 s.62, see below, para.26–216AB.

[1118do] See above, para.26–204.

[1118dp] See above, para.26–182.

26–216R **Damages in addition to forfeiture of deposit.** Although in *Cavendish Square Holding BV v Makdessi* and *ParkingEye Ltd v Beavis*[1118dq] the majority of the Supreme Court[1118dr] said that deposits are subject to the penalty rules, it is submitted that this is not so entirely. A valid agreed damages clause gives the claimant a right to the agreed sum, no less but also no more.[1118ds] In contrast it is well established that in contracts for a sale of land, a vendor who validly terminates the contract because of a breach by the purchaser may both forfeit the deposit and recover damages, giving due allowance for the amount of the deposit.[1118dt] It is not thought that the Supreme Court intended that this rule should be affected by its decision.

[1118dq] [2015] UKSC 67, [2016] A.C. 1172.

[1118dr] Lord Hodge said that the customary 10 per cent deposit was exempt as "earnest money": see above, para.26–216Q. If this is the correct explanation, the issue discussed in the present paragraph does not arise.

[1118ds] See above, para.26–178.

[1118dt] *Lock v Bell* [1931] 1 Ch. 35. (In that case a separate clause requiring either party to pay the sum of £200 if it failed to perform any part of the contract. This was held to be a penalty clause and the court ordered an inquiry into the damages, if any, suffered by the vendor beyond the amount of the deposit: see [1931] 1 Ch. 35, 46.) See also *Behzadi v Shaftesbury Hotels Ltd* [1992] Ch. 1, 10.

(ii) *Forfeiture of Sums Paid*

26–216S **Forfeiture provisions.** As noted earlier, a contract may, instead of fixing a sum to be paid upon breach, provide that a sum already paid shall be forfeited[1118du] upon breach by the party who paid it. There has been considerable doubt over whether, or to what extent, the penalty rules apply to provisions of this type and of the relationship between the penalty rules and the court's jurisdiction to give relief against forfeiture. In *Cavendish Square Holding BV v Makdessi* and *ParkingEye Ltd v Beavis*[1118dv] the Supreme Court said that the penalty rules do apply to forfeiture provisions of this type, and may render the provision invalid. Even if the provision is valid (as a genuine pre-estimate of the innocent party's loss or as a "legitimate deterrent"), in an appropriate case the court may still be able to grant relief against forfeiture.[1118dw]

[1118du] The payee "forfeits" the sum where he retains it for his own beneficial use, having freed himself of any further obligations under the contract by terminating the contract on account of the payer's breach. It is then up to the payer to challenge the forfeiture if he has any legal ground for doing so.
[1118dv] [2015] UKSC 67, [2016] A.C. 1172.
[1118dw] Lord Mance [2015] UKSC 67 at [160].

Purchase by instalments and pre-payment of price. Traditionally, the courts were willing to grant relief against "forfeiture" clauses in only two situations; and, as will be seen below,[1118dx] the relief was of a limited form, which if the payee was entitled to terminate the contract, did not include ordering a return of the sums paid. The first type of case is of landlord and tenant. There has been a long history of equitable relief against forfeiture of leasehold interests, viz where a clause in the lease entitled the landlord to repossess the premises if the tenant failed to pay an instalment of the rent.[1118dy] The second situation was where the contract-breaker has been purchasing land by paying the price by instalments: it is clearly established that if, under a contract to purchase land by instalment payments, the purchaser defaults in payment of an instalment of the price, the court has jurisdiction in a proper case to relieve him against a clause providing for forfeiture of the instalments already paid, by granting him an extension of time within which he could pay the instalment now due.[1118dz] It is implicit in these cases that payment within the extended period would preserve the purchaser's contractual rights in the same way as payment by the time originally agreed would have done. In what follows it is primarily the second situation that will be addressed, as it is thought that this is what the Supreme Court had in mind. Lords Neuberger and Sumption stated that

26–216T

> "Where a proprietary interest or a 'proprietary or possessory right' (such as a patent or a lease) is granted or transferred subject to revocation or determination on breach, the clause providing for determination or revocation is a forfeiture and cannot be a penalty."[1118ea]

Moreover, the first situation is equivalent termination of the contract by the landlord because of the tenant's breach of contract, and there is no sign that the Supreme Court intended to place any restrictions on the right to terminate, even when the right would not exist at common law and arises only because of an express term of the contract.[1118eb] The Court's remarks might apply, however, if the tenant has paid a premium that would not be returnable, so that in effect the tenant ends up paying in advance for occupation rights that he will not be able to exercise.[1118ec]

[1118dx] Below, paras 26–216V—26–216W.
[1118dy] See also the Law of Property Act 1925 s.146. See also n.1118ed, below.
[1118dz] *Re Dagenham (Thames) Dock Co* (1972-73) L.R. 8 Ch. App. 1022; *Kilmer v British Columbia Orchard Lands Ltd* [1913] A.C. 319; *Steedman v Drinkle* [1916] 1 A.C. 275; *Mussen v Van Diemen's Land Co* [1938] Ch. 253; *Starside Properties Ltd v Mustapha* [1974] 1 W.L.R. 816. (Time

was not made "of the essence" in this contract: cf. above, para.26–216B.) The Privy Council has refused to extend this principle: *Union Eagle Ltd v Golden Achievement Ltd* [1997] A.C. 514 (see the comments by Heydon (1997) 113 L.Q.R. 385; and Stevens (1998) 61 M.L.R. 255). See Lang (1984) 100 L.Q.R. 427; Harpum [1984] C.L.J. 134.

[1118ea] [2015] UKSC 67 at [17]; relief against forfeiture is available (at [17]), though relief against forfeiture of leases may now be governed exclusively by the Law of Property Act 1925 s.146 (at [10], referring to *Official Custodian for Charities v Parway Estates Departments Ltd* [1985] Ch. 151).

[1118eb] See above, para.26–216B.

[1118ec] See below, para.26–216Z, n.1118fg.

26–216U　　It is only relatively recently that the courts began to grant a limited type of relief against forfeiture in a wider range of situations. A condition said to be necessary before equitable relief may be granted is that the forfeiture clause was inserted in order:

> " . . . to secure a stated result which can effectively be attained when the matter comes before the court, and where the forfeiture provision is added by way of security for the production of that result."[1118ed]

The wider development began in 1954 with *Stockloser v Johnson*[1118ee]: there was a provision, in a contract to purchase plant and machinery by instalment payments, that upon default by the buyer, the seller might terminate the contract and forfeit the instalments already paid. The majority of the Court of Appeal held that the court has an equitable jurisdiction to relieve against forfeiture of such instalments, even after termination of the contract, if in the actual circumstances of the case the clause was penal and it would be oppressive and unconscionable for the seller to retain all the instalments. In 1983, the House of Lords upheld the jurisdiction to relieve against forfeiture, but limited it to contracts concerning the transfer or creation of proprietary or possessory rights.[1118ef] Thus it did not apply to the facts of the case before the House, where a shipowner withdrew his ship (chartered under a time charter[1118eg]) on the ground of the charterer's failure to make punctual payment of an instalment of hire. Similarly, the House of Lords has refused relief against the forfeiture of "mere contractual licences" to use certain names and trade marks.[1118eh] But the principle is not limited to real property, so the Privy Council has granted relief in the case of a charge over shares.[1118ei] The Court of Appeal granted relief (in the form of an extension of time in which a payment could be made by the defendant) in a commercial contract which provided that his failure to pay a sum on time would entitle the plaintiff to claim an assignment of patent rights held by the defendant.[1118ej] The House of Lords[1118ek] has granted relief to the lessee of chattels from their forfeiture: the House held that the court's power to make an interim order for the sale of chattels (which formed the subject matter of the proceedings) did not prejudice the lessee's right to seek relief from forfeiture. The proceeds of sale stood in the place of the chattels and relief could be given by an order deciding the proportions in which the parties were entitled to the money; it did not matter that the lessee could not be restored to possession.

[1118ed] *Shiloh Spinners Ltd v Harding* [1973] A.C. 691, 723. (The case concerned the right to forfeit (re-enter upon) leasehold property for failure to repair fences and to maintain works for the protection of adjoining property.)

[1118ee] [1954] 1 Q.B. 476. (See also Main Work, Vol.II, para.39–343.)

[1118ef] *Scandinavian Trading Tanker Co AB v Flota Petrolera Ecuatoriana (The Scaptrade)* [1983] 2 A.C. 694 (followed in *Union Eagle Ltd v Golden Achievement Ltd* [1997] A.C. 514 PC, failure by 10 minutes to pay balance of purchase price on time, when time was "of the essence": see Heydon

(1997) 113 L.Q.R. 385; Stevens (1998) 61 M.L.R. 255). See also *The Laconia* [1977] A.C. 850, 869–870, 873–874, 878, 887; cf. the High Court of Australia in *Legione v Hateley* (1983) 46 A.L.R. 1; *Ciavarella v Balmer* (1983) 153 C.L.R. 438; and in *Stern v McArthur* (1988) 165 C.L.R. 489.

[1118eg] A charter by demise would have given the charterer a possessory interest in the ship.

[1118eh] *Sport Internationaal Bussum BV v Inter-Footwear Ltd* [1984] 1 W.L.R. 776 (followed in *Crittall Windows Ltd v Stormseal (UPVC) Window Systems Ltd* [1991] R.P.C. 265). But it is not a purely contractual right where a hirer is entitled to indefinite possession of chattels so long as he makes hire payments: hence relief against forfeiture is available: *On Demand Information Plc v Michael Gerson (Finance) Plc* [2002] UKHL 13, [2003] 1 A.C. 368 at [29]. In *General Motors UK Ltd v Manchester Ship Canal Co Ltd* [2016] EWHC 2960 (Ch) relief was given in respect of a right to discharge surface water into a canal.

[1118ei] *Çukurova Finance International Ltd v Alfa Telecom Turkey Ltd* [2013] UKPC 2.

[1118ej] *BICC Plc v Burndy Corp* [1985] Ch. 232, 251–252. (The line drawn between this and the *Sport Internationaal* case [1984] 1 W.L.R. 776 is not justifiable in commercial terms.)

[1118ek] *On Demand Information Plc v Michael Gerson (Finance) Plc* [2002] UKHL 13.

Form of relief: additional time to pay. Under this equitable principle, the courts will seldom do more than give the contract-breaker more time in which to pay the sum he had failed to pay on time. This relief has the effect that the contract-breaker does not forfeit the rights which he had under the contract, provided he pays within the time fixed by the court. 26–216V

Return of payments subject to forfeiture clause. If the contract-breaker is unable to pay, or if the contract has already been terminated, the position is less clear. Traditionally, the courts have been more reluctant[1118el] to allow recovery of money already paid by the contract-breaker (i.e. to grant affirmative relief)[1118em] than to deny recovery of a sum (a penalty) agreed to be payable upon breach by the contract-breaker (i.e. to grant negative relief) or to give more time to him to make a payment. In one case, the House of Lords directed the relief at the proceeds of sale where the court had made an interim order for sale pending the outcome of the litigation.[1118en] On the facts of *Stockloser v Johnson*, above, although the majority of the court were prepared to order that money paid be returned if it would be unconscionable for the seller to keep it, they did not think that the seller's conduct in retaining £4,750 out of the £11,000 price in one contract, and £3,500 out of the £11,000 price on another, was unconscionable, because the buyer had already received substantial benefits in the form of royalties.[1118eo] In any event, subsequent cases tended to follow the view of the third judge, Romer L.J., that there could be relief only if there had been fraud, sharp practice or unconscionable conduct on the part of the seller.[1118ep] In a Privy Council case in 1906, the contract-breaker obtained an order that the deposit he had paid in advance to the innocent party should, despite a forfeiture clause, be repaid to him (subject to his paying damages for the actual loss caused to the innocent party by the breach of contract),[1118eq] but this case has not to date been followed in England.[1118er] In *Cadogan Petroleum Holdings Ltd v Global Process Systems LLC* Eder J. held that it was unnecessary to resolve that debate because counsel accepted that in the circumstances the court did have jurisdiction to grant relief against forfeiture and that such jurisdiction went beyond simply giving the buyer more time to pay.[1118es] However, as the goods were of no use to the seller and their value was very uncertain, the court refused to order repayment of the sums already paid or that sums due before the date of termination should cease to be payable.[1118et] 26–216W

[1118el] *Dies v British and International Mining and Finance Corp Ltd* [1939] 1 K.B. 724 (sale of goods); *Stockloser v Johnson* [1954] 1 Q.B. 476, 483, 489–490; *Mayson v Clouet* [1924] A.C. 980 (sale of land); *Galbraith v Mitchenall Estates Ltd* [1965] 2 Q.B. 473.

[1118em] cf. above, para.26–216Q.

[1118en] *On Demand Information Plc v Michael Gerson (Finance) Plc* [2002] UKHL 13.

[1118eo] [1954] 1 Q.B. 476, 484, 492.

[1118ep] See *Galbraith v Mitchenall Estates Ltd* [1965] 2 Q.B. 473.

[1118eq] *Commissioner of Public Works v Hills* [1906] A.C. 368 (above, para.26–187).

[1118er] Though the penalty rules were assumed to apply to a sum paid by way of deposit in *Pye v British Automobile Commercial Syndicate Ltd* [1906] 1 K.B. 425 (held not penal).

[1118es] [2013] EWHC 214 (Comm) at [38].

[1118et] [2013] EWHC 214 (Comm) at [41].

26–216X **Provision for forfeiture may be a penalty.** The Supreme Court has now expressed at least the provisional view that a clause providing for the forfeiture of sums already paid is subject to the penalty rules[1118eu]; and similarly[1118ev] a clause requiring the contract-breaker, upon breach, to re-transfer some property to the innocent party.[1118ew] Thus if the provision does not pass either the genuine pre-estimate test[1118ex] or the legitimate deterrent test,[1118ey] the sum that was to be forfeited will be subject to the normal rules on the repayment of sums already paid and the requirement to transfer the property at a reduced price will unenforceable.[1118ez]

[1118eu] *Cavendish Square Holding BV v Makdessi* and *ParkingEye Ltd v Beavis* [2015] UKSC 67, [2016] A.C. 1172. Lord Mance said that it is "both logical and correct in principle under the current law" that a clause may both be subject to the penalty doctrine and the power of the court to give relief for forfeiture (at [160]) but said the application of the penalty doctrine to deposits and the forfeiture of money paid must await decision in due course (at [170]). Lord Hodge said that the court should determine whether a forfeiture clause was a penalty: at [227]. Lord Toulson agreed with what Lord Mance had said at [160] and with the relevant paragraphs of Lord Hodge's judgment; Lord Clarke was inclined to agree with them also. Lords Neuberger and Sumption said they could see the force in the arguments of Lords Mance and Hodge: at [18].

[1118ev] Lord Mance at [160]–[161], Lord Hodge at [230], [233]. Lords Neuberger and Sumption said there is no reason in principle "why an obligation to transfer assets (either for nothing or at an undervalue) should not be capable of constituting a penalty" (at [16]). At [84] they said that it was not necessary to decide whether it was open to the purchaser in *Jobson v Johnson* to argue that the obligation to transfer back shares he had received was a penalty: it may be subject only to the forfeiture rules but not the penalty rules, referring back to [18] of their judgment.

[1118ew] As in *Jobson v Johnson* [1989] 1 W.L.R. 1026. The order made in that case was disapproved: see below, para.26–216K.

[1118ex] See above, para.26–182.

[1118ey] See above, para.26–196.

[1118ez] See above, para.26–216.

26–216Y **Relief against forfeiture may also be given.** In the *Cavendish Square* case[1118fa] Lords Mance and Hodge said[1118fb] that even if the clause providing for the forfeiture of sums already paid is not void as a penalty from the outset, if the party who will be prejudiced by the clause defaults, the court may grant relief against forfeiture. The Supreme Court seemed to envisage this relief normally taking the form of giving the defaulting party extra time in which to pay,[1118fc] but Lord Hodge at least indicated that it might also involve the purchaser recovering the payments made.[1118fd]

[1118fa] *Cavendish Square Holding BV v Makdessi* and *ParkingEye Ltd v Beavis* [2015] UKSC 67, [2016] A.C. 1172.

[1118fb] *Cavendish Square Holding BV v Makdessi* and *ParkingEye Ltd v Beavis* [2015] UKSC 67 at [160] (Lord Mance) and [227], [230] (Lord Hodge): Lord Toulson agreed, Lord Clarke was inclined

to agree (see at [291]). Lords Neuberger and Sumption saw force in the argument but preferred not to express a view.

[1118fc] See Lord Mance [2015] UKSC 67 at [160], quoting the Privy Council in *Çukurova Finance International Ltd v Alfa Telecom Turkey Ltd (No.4)* [2013] UKPC 25, [2015] 2 W.L.R. 875 at [13] ("relief in equity will only be granted on the basis of conditions requiring performance, albeit late, of the contract in accordance with its terms as to principal, interest and costs"). This would not preclude relief in the form granted in *On Demand Information Plc v Michael Gerson (Finance) Plc* [2002] UKHL 13, [2003] 1 A.C. 368, see above, para.26–216U.

[1118fd] [2015] UKSC 67 at [229].

Forfeiture of leases and relief against termination clauses. As stated ear- lier,[1118fe] a common situation in which relief against forfeiture may be given is where a lease entitles the landlord to repossess the premises because the tenant has failed to pay an instalment of the rent. It is not thought that the Supreme Court's statements in *Cavendish Square Holding BV v Makdessi* and *ParkingEye Ltd v Beavis*[1118ff] that forfeiture provisions are subject to the penalty rules were intended to address this situation. The tenant will normally not suffer the same "double loss"—loss of both their property rights and the money they have so far paid—as in, for example, cases in which the contract-breaker has been purchasing land by paying the price by instalments and the agreement provides that if he defaults in a payment, he will lose both the land and the sums he has paid.[1118fg] A similar situation occurs when a contract may provide that it may be terminated because of a default that at common law would not be sufficiently serious to justify termination. Although some such clauses have been held to confer only a right to terminate and not the further right to damages for non-performance,[1118fh] it has been held that the penalty rules are not relevant to this situation.[1118fi] There is nothing in the *Cavendish Square* case to indicate that the Supreme Court intended to change this position.

26–216Z

[1118fe] See above, para.26–216T.
[1118ff] [2015] UKSC 67, [2016] A.C. 1172.
[1118fg] See above, para.26–216T. Possibly the penalty rule will apply if the tenant has paid a substantial premium in advance and will lose the benefit of that as well as losing the premises, but this suggestion is speculative.
[1118fh] See above, para.26–216T.
[1118fi] See above, para.26–216B.

(iii) *Deposits and Forfeiture of Money Paid in Consumer Contracts*

The Consumer Credit Act 1974. Some of the problems created by contractual provisions requiring payments on the occurrence of specified events will be governed by the Consumer Credit Act 1974.[1118fj] For instance, s.100(1) provides that where a debtor under a regulated hire-purchase (or a regulated conditional sale) agreement[1118fk] has prematurely terminated the agreement, he shall be liable to pay the difference between the sums already paid or payable by him and one-half of the total price; but by s.100(3) the court may order payment of a smaller sum if that would be equal to the loss sustained by the creditor.[1118fl] The court is also empowered to intervene if it determines that the relationship between the creditor and the debtor is "unfair".[1118fm] It may determine that the relationship is unfair because of one or more of the following:

26–216AA

(a) any of the terms of the agreement or of any related agreement;

(b) the way in which the creditor has exercised or enforced any of his rights under the agreement or any related agreement;

(c) any other thing done (or not done) by, or on behalf of, the creditor (either before or after the making of the agreement or any related agreement).[1118fn]

The court may, for example, require the creditor, or any associate of his, to repay (in whole or in part) any sum paid by the debtor or by a surety, reduce or discharge any sum payable by the debtor or by a surety by virtue of the agreement, or alter the terms of the agreement or of any related agreement.[1118fo] The Act will therefore cover many of the situations which arise in practice, and the common law and equitable rules will not need to be applied. Thus, it is uncertain how far the principle discussed in paras 26–209—26–213, above, applies to hire-purchase[1118fp] or hiring[1118fq] agreements that fall within the Act so as to permit the court to grant relief to a hirer against a clause providing for the forfeiture of instalments already paid or for a "minimum payment" by the hirer upon his termination of the agreement.[1118fr] When a hire-purchase agreement is terminated by the owner upon the hirer's default, the common law as to penalties[1118fs] and the provisions of the Act will often protect the hirer against clauses requiring further payments, e.g. for "depreciation"; the common law rules apply to similar clauses in hiring agreements.[1118ft] The question whether a depreciation clause is a penalty or not depends on the construction of the clause in the light of all the circumstances surrounding the particular agreement.[1118fu]

[1118fj] See Main Work, Vol.II, paras 33–085 et seq. deal with hiring agreements, while paras 39–005 et seq. deal with the other agreements within the scope of the Act.

[1118fk] Definitions of these agreements are examined in Main Work, Vol.II, paras 39–356 et seq.

[1118fl] See Main Work, Vol.II, paras 39–368—39–369; cf. the similar power conferred on the court by s.132 in the case of a regulated consumer hire agreement.

[1118fm] Consumer Credit Act 1974 ss.140A–140C, inserted by Consumer Credit Act 2006 ss.19–22. These provisions replace ss.137–140 on "extortionate credit bargains", which are repealed by s.70 and Sch.4 of the 2006 Act. See further Main Work, Vol.II, paras 39–212 et seq.

[1118fn] s.140A(1).

[1118fo] s.140B(1). These powers can be exercised in relation to any credit agreement where the debtor is an individual (as defined in s.189(1), as amended: see Main Work, Vol.II, paras 39–016 et seq.) or any related agreement (as defined in s.140C(4)). The fact that the agreement is an exempt, and not a regulated, agreement is immaterial, except that no order can be made in connection with a credit agreement which is an exempt agreement by virtue of s.16(6C). These provisions came into force on April 6, 2007 (SI 2007/123 (c.6)).

[1118fp] *Campbell Discount Co Ltd v Bridge* [1961] 1 Q.B. 445 CA (on appeal, the case was decided on another point: [1962] A.C. 600); see Main Work, Vol.II, paras 39–349—39–353; Diamond (1956) 19 M.L.R. 498 and (1958) 21 M.L.R. 199; Prince (1957) 20 M.L.R. 620.

[1118fq] *Galbraith v Mitchenall Estates Ltd* [1965] 2 Q.B. 473; *Barton Thompson & Co Ltd v Stapling Machines Co* [1966] Ch. 499.

[1118fr] See the proposals for reform in the Law Commission's Working Paper No.61, *Penalty Clauses and Forfeiture of Moneys Paid* (1975).

[1118fs] *Bridge v Campbell Discount Co Ltd* [1962] A.C. 600, upholding the decision of the Court of Appeal in *Cooden Engineering Co Ltd v Stanford* [1953] 1 Q.B. 86; *Anglo Auto Finance Co Ltd v James* [1963] 1 W.L.R. 1042, 1049.

[1118ft] *Robophone Facilities Ltd v Blank* [1966] 1 W.L.R. 1428.

[1118fu] *Lombank Ltd v Excell* [1964] 1 Q.B. 415 (interpreting *Phonographic Equipment (1958) Ltd v Muslu* [1961] 1 W.L.R. 1379).

26–216AB Unfair Terms in Consumer Contracts Regulations 1999 and Consumer Rights Act 2015.[1118fv] The Unfair Terms in Consumer Contracts Regulations

1999 provided that in a contract between a business and a consumer an "unfair term" will not be binding on the consumer.[1118fv] For contracts made after October 1, 2015, the Consumer Rights Act 2015 replaces the Regulations. The Regulations and the Act give illustrations of terms which will, prima facie, be regarded as unfair: relevant to clauses fixing damages is "requiring any consumer who fails to fulfil his obligation to pay a disproportionately high sum in compensation".[1118fx] This does not in so many words cover the case of a deposit or provision for forfeiture, but there seems no doubt that such a term may be declared to be unfair in an appropriate case.

[1118fv] SI 1999/2083.
[1118fw] See Main Work, Vol.II, paras 38–201 et seq.
[1118fx] cf. Main Work, Vol.II, para.38–280.

12. INTEREST

(b) Damages for Loss of Interest at Common Law

Loss of interest compensable if pleaded and proved

[*Add to note 1198, at the end: page* [1950]]   26–230
It has been held that "general evidence" that the claimant suffered loss from the delay will suffice: *Equitas Ltd v Walsham Bros & Co Ltd* [2013] EWHC 3264 (Comm) at [123], [2014] Lloyd's Rep. I.R. 398; *Sainsbury's Supermarkets Ltd v Mastercard Inc* [2016] CAT 11 at [521].

(d) Statutory Rights to Interest

Interest on commercial debts

[*Add to text, line 1, before note 1203: page* [1950]]   26–232
    "created by virtue of an obligation under a contract . . . to pay the whole or any part of the contract price"

[*Add to note 1203, at the start: page* [1950]]
s.3(1), Late Payment of Commercial Debts (Interest) Act 1998.

[*Add to note 1203, line 4, after* "at [7]–[8]": *page* [1950]]
; *Mailbox (Birmingham) Ltd v Galliford Try Construction Ltd* [2017] EWHC 67 (TCC) at [56].

Period of statutory interest: where a date for payment has been agreed

[*In paragraph, line 4, delete* "two" *and substitute: page* [1951]]   26–233
three

[*Add to note 1218a, at the end: page* [1952]]
The Late Payment of Commercial Debts Regulations 2002 (SI 2002/1674) reg.3, allow representative bodies to bring proceedings in the High Court on behalf of

small and medium-sized enterprises to obtain an injunction preventing other businesses using terms purporting to oust or vary the right to statutory interest in relation to qualifying debts created by those contracts. The Department of Business, Innovations and Skills has consulted on amendments to this regime: *Late Payment: challenging "grossly unfair" terms and practices: Consultation Paper* (2015).

When interest ceases to run

26–235   [*Add to note 1224, at the end: page* [1952]]
See also *First Personnel Services Ltd v Halfords Ltd* [2016] EWHC 3220 (Ch) at [164]–[169], applying the principles stated by Jackson J. in *Claymore Services Ltd v Nautilus Properties Ltd* [2007] EWHC 805 (TCC) at [55], a case involving a statutory discretion to award interest, see below, para.26–238 n.1261.

(e) *Statutory Discretion to Award Interest*

Period of interest

26–238   [*Add to note 1261, at the end: page* [1955]]
In *Claymore Services Ltd v Nautilus Properties Ltd* [2007] EWHC 805 (TCC) Jackson J. reviewed the authorities and concluded that "(1) Where a claimant has delayed unreasonably in commencing or prosecuting proceedings, the court may exercise its discretion either to disallow interest for a period or to reduce the rate of interest; (2) In exercising that discretion the court must take a realistic view of delay. In the case of business disputes, litigation is for all parties an unwelcome distraction from their proper business. It is not reasonable to expect any party to take every litigious step at the first possible moment, or to concentrate on litigation to the exclusion of all else. Delay should only be characterised as unreasonable for present purposes when, after making due allowance for the circumstances, it can be seen that the claimant has neglected or declined to pursue his claim for a significant period; (3) When determining what disallowance or reduction of interest should be made to mark a period of unreasonable delay, the court should bear in mind that the defendant has had the use of the money during that period of delay" (at [55]).

CHAPTER 27

SPECIFIC PEFORMANCE AND INJUNCTION

1. INTRODUCTION

Scope of the remedy

[*Add to paragraph, after note 14: page* [1962]]   **27–003**
, and the court can, in principle, direct the defendant to take steps before the date of performance in order to meet its obligations on that date.[14a]

[14a] *Airport Industrial GP Ltd v Heathrow Airport Ltd* [2015] EWHC 3753 (Ch) at [113]. Morgan J. recognised that this would be applicable to many cases of anticipatory breach.

2. THE "ADEQUACY" OF DAMAGES

Damages nominal, not recoverable, or excluded

[*Add to paragraph, at the end: page* [1967]]   **27–009**
Damages may also be inadequate where the infringement of the interest that a party is trying to protect by way of an injunction is a person's privacy or reputation.[51a]

[51a] *PJS v News Group Newspapers* [2016] UKSC 26 at [43]; *Kent Community Health NHS Foundation Trust v NHS Swale Clinical Commissioning Group* [2016] EWHC 1393 (TCC) at [15].

Discretion as to appropriate remedy to consumers

27–022   [*Delete heading, text and footnotes of paragraph and substitute: pages* [1976]–[1978]]

Discretion and consumer's choice between repair and replacement. The 2015 Act places restrictions on the consumer's rights of "repair or replacement" relating to goods and digital content.[144] It also places restrictions on the consumer's right to "repeat performance" which applies to services,[145] but the restrictions are different. In the case of goods and digital content, ss.23(3) and 43(3) of the 2015 Act provide that the consumer cannot require the trader to repair or replace the goods or digital content if "that remedy" is (a) "impossible" or (b) "disproportionate compared to the other of those remedies", i.e. if it "imposes costs on the trader which, compared to those imposed by the other, are unreasonable".[146] It seems from the wording of these provisions that "repair" and "replacement" are here treated as separate rights or remedies and that these provisions are concerned with the power of the court to choose *between them*. By contrast, where services do not conform to the contract, the consumer's right or remedy that corresponds to "repair or replacement" is "the right to require repeat performance"[147]; and since this is a single right there can be no question of its being "disproportionate" to anything else. However, repeat performance cannot be required where completing performance would be impossible.[148]

[144] Consumer Rights Act 2015 s.23(3) applies to goods and s.43(9) applies to digital content.
[145] Consumer Rights Act 2015 s.53(3).
[146] Taking into account a list of factors specified in the Consumer Rights Act 2015 ss.23(4) and 43(4).
[147] Consumer Rights Act 2015 ss.54(3)(a), 55(1).
[148] Consumer Rights Act 2015 s.55(3).

[*Insert new paragraphs 27–022A and 27–022B: page* [1978]]

27–022A   **Discretion to award price reduction: digital content and services.** Where ordering either repair or replacement (in the case of digital content[149]) or repeat performance (in the case of services) would be disproportionate or even cause severe hardship to the defendant,[150] the court can instead award a price reduction.[151] This is provided under s.58. When the customer claims to exercise any of the above "rights"[152] (or "remedies"),[153] "on the application of the consumer, the court may make an order requiring specific performance of"[154] the trader's obligation to repair or replace goods[155] or digital content[156] or to repeat performances of services.[157] Further, s.58(3) and (4) provide that "if the exercise of another right is appropriate"[158] then "the court may proceed as if the consumer had exercised that other right"[159]; and the other rights are defined so as to include, in each case, price reduction.[160] The effect is that if the consumer claims repair or replacement, the court may instead order (if it is more appropriate than either repair or replacement) another of the remedies provided by the Act. In respect of digital content and services, that can only be a price reduction.[161] These provisions differ from those discussed in the previous paragraph[162] by which the consumer cannot require (for example) repair if that is "impossible" or "disproportionate"[163] because it imposes unreasonable costs on the trader or because the "other remedy" would cause "significant inconvenience to the consumer". The choice that the consumer is required to make under those provisions is between repair and replacement. In contrast, the "powers of the court"[164] are wider: under s.58 the court could, for example, refuse to order repair or replacement or repeat performance and instead order a price reduction.[164a] There is also no requirement under s.58[164b] that the remedy sought by the consumer must be "disproportionate", but it is hard to see on what other ground it would be appropriate for the court to do so. It would not be appropriate for the court to refuse to order repair or replacement or repeat performance, and instead order a price reduction, simply on the ground that damages would be an adequate remedy. That would render the provisions giving the consumer the right to repair or replacement or repeat performance nugatory.

[149] But not in the case of goods: see below, para.27–022B.
[150] cf. below, para.27–036.
[151] To which the consumer is entitled under ss.19(3)(c) (goods), 42(2)(b) (digital content) and 54(3)(b) (services) under the Consumer Rights Act 2015.
[152] i.e. "the right to repair or replacement of goods (s.19(3)(b)) or of digital content (s.42(2)(a)) or the "right to require repeat performance" of a service (s.54(3)(a)) Consumer Rights Act 2015. In addition, "specific performance" is listed among "other remedies" (ss.19(10), 42(7) and 54(7)) which the consumer may seek. In those situations, the word "other" suggests that the reference to "specific performance" is not to the right to repair or replacement, or repeat performance but is to cover the (unlikely) possibility that specific performance might be available under the normal principles governing that remedy.
[153] A term used in this context to mean the same thing as rights: see, for example, the use of the phrase "other remedies" in the Consumer Rights Act 2015 ss.19(10), 42(7) and 54(7).
[154] Consumer Rights Act 2015 s.58(2).
[155] Consumer Rights Act 2015 s.23.
[156] Consumer Rights Act 2015 s.43.
[157] Consumer Rights Act 2015 s.55.
[158] Consumer Rights Act 2015 s.58(3).
[159] Consumer Rights Act 2015 s.58(4). See below, paras 38–485, Main Work, Vol.II, paras 38–520, 38–543.
[160] Consumer Rights Act 2015 s.58(8).
[161] There is no right to treat a contract for digital content as at an end for non-conformity: s.42(8) (contrast the right to reject goods and treat the contract as at an end: see ss.19(3) and s.20(4)). In contracts for services the consumer's right to treat the contract as at an end is preserved, and in both contracts for digital content and for services so too is the right to damages (see ss.42(7) and 54(7)), but these are not "right[s] under the relevant remedies provisions" within s.58(3) and so cannot be ordered by the court instead of specific performance. See Main Work, Vol.II, para.38–486.
[162] Above, para.27–020.
[163] Consumer Rights Act 2015 ss.23(3) and (4), 43(3) and (4).
[164] Heading before Consumer Rights Act 2015 s.58.
[164a] See the references to Consumer Rights Act 2015 ss.24, 44 and 56 in s.58(8).
[164b] As there is under Consumer Rights Act 2015 ss.23(3)(b) and 43(3)(b).

No discretion to award price reduction: goods. In the case of goods, for the court to exercise its discretion under s.58 to order price reduction[164c] on the grounds that it is more appropriate than either repair or replacement would be inconsistent with the requirements of Directive 1999/44/EC,[164d] which Ch.2 of the Consumer Rights Act is designed to implement.[164e] The consumer's right to repair or replacement of goods under the Consumer Rights Act must be interpreted in the light of the interpretation of the Directive in *Weber and Putz*[164f] by the Court of Justice of the EU, at least while the United Kingdom remains in the EU.[164g] The Court's assumption that the consumer's specific rights under the Directive were enforceable in kind against the seller has three consequences. First, on the facts of the case, it was decided that national law should not allow   **27–022B**

the trader to refuse replacement on the ground of disproportionality with the value of conforming goods and with the significance of the non-conformity, even though it meant that the trader had to bear the costs of the removing the goods installed by the consumer and the reinstallation of the replacement goods. Second, it suggests that English courts should not refuse specific performance in support of the consumer's right to repair or replacement because damages would be an adequate remedy, since this would then replace the consumer's "European rights" and so render them ineffective. Third, it suggests that, in the case of "sales contracts", use of the court's powers to substitute another "appropriate right" under s.58 is incompatible with the 1999 Directive except in the two situations referred to in the Directive: where the choice is between repair or replacement or where neither repair nor replacement is possible.[164h] The corollary is that courts should not apply other "bars" to specific performance not mentioned in the Directive itself.

[164c] Or equally to make an order as if the consumer had claimed to reject the goods and treat the contract as at an end, see s.19(3) and s.20(4).

[164d] Directive on certain aspects of the sale of consumer goods and associated guarantees [1999] O.J. L171/99, p.12, art.3(2). See Main Work, Vol.II, paras 44–006—44–013.

[164e] See below, para.38–485. And see Whittaker (2017) 133 L.Q.R. (forthcoming). On the Consumer Sales Directive 1999 generally, see Main Work, Vol.II, para.38–400. On "sales contracts" see Main Work, Vol.II, paras 38–452—38–454.

[164f] *Gebr Weber GmbH v Wittmer, Putz v Medianess Electronics GmbH* (C-65/09 and C-87/09) [2011] 3 C.M.L.R. 27, [63]–[78].

[164g] See above, paras 1–013A et seq.

[164h] The Directive only mentions impossibility and disproportionality compared to the other specific remedy. Directive 1999/44/EC art.3(3) is reflected in 2015 Act s.23(3)–(4) and see Main Work, Vol.II, para.38–482.

4. Other Grounds for Refusing Specific Performance

Severe hardship to defendant

27–036

[Add to paragraph, after note 264: page [1990]]
, and even where the death of the vendor's husband resulted in the vendor's inability to work from anxiety and depression.[264a]

[264a] *Shah v Greening* [2016] EWHC 548 (Ch).

[Add to paragraph, at the end: page [1990]]
, or the loss of its entire interest in a joint venture.[265a]

[265a] *Man UK Properties Ltd v Falcon Investments Ltd* [2015] EWHC 1324 (Ch).

[Add new paragraph 27–036A: page [1990]]

27–036A **Adjustments to mitigate harshness.** The court may, instead of denying specific performance, make adjustments to the specific performance order to mitigate its harshness, taking into account the proportionality between the adverse consequences of specific performance without adjustment, the defendant's degree of fault, and the adequacy of damages to compensate the claimant for any variation to its entitlement. In *Airport Industrial GP Ltd v Heathrow Airport Ltd*[265b] Morgan J. permitted a two-year delay on the time of performance in the context of an obligation of 999 years duration, subject to damages being paid to the claimant for the delay, to allow the defendant time to implement a method of performance that was more advantageous for it but would take longer compared with a more immediate method which was likely to render it insolvent. However,

> "the court's order should seek to specify milestones to be achieved with provision for a default position [i.e. an obligation to revert to the immediate method] to apply if the defendant does not achieve a milestone."[265c]

[265b] [2015] EWHC 3753 (Ch) at [133]–[134].
[265c] [2015] EWHC 3753 (Ch) at [133].

8. INJUNCTION

Interim injunctions

[*Add to note 443, at the end: page* [2009]]   **27–066**
And see *Kent Community Health NHS Foundation Trust v NHS Swale Clinical Commissioning Group* [2016] EWHC 1393 (TCC) on what is meant by the adequacy of damages for a not-for-profit organisation and on the role of the public interest in assessing the balance of convenience; *Allfiled UK Ltd v Eltis* [2015] EWHC 1300 (Ch) on the effect of the claimant's delay.

[*Add to paragraph, at the end: page* [2010]]
Damages may also be inadequate where the infringement of the interest that a party is trying to protect by way of an injunction is a person's privacy or reputation.[447a]

[447a] *PJS v News Group Newspapers Ltd* [2016] UKSC 26 at [43]; *Kent Community Health NHS Foundation Trust v NHS Swale Clinical Commissioning Group* [2016] EWHC 1393 (TCC) at [15].

[*Add to note 449, at the end: page* [2010]]   **27–067**
See also *RSM International Ltd v Harrison* [2015] EWHC 2252 (QB).

Restraint of trade

[*Add to paragraph, at the end: page* [2016]]   **27–074**
Moreover, an injunction to enforce a valid restraint of trade may be denied if the claimant's delay has induced the defendant's detrimental reliance.[495a] A short delay (even of two months) may make it inequitable to grant an injunction where it was deliberately timed to cause avoidable loss to third parties.[495b]

[495a] *Lindsay Petroleum Co v Hurd* (1874) L.R. 5 P.C. 221 and *Fisher v Brooker* [2009] UKHL 41, [2009] 1 W.L.R. 1764.
[495b] *Legends Live Ltd v Harrison* [2016] EWHC 1938 (QB) at [90]–[110] (claimant's delay of two months meant the defendant had become an integral part of a competing show and an injunction would affect the livelihoods of other performers).

Injunction against refusal to contract

27–079   [*Add to paragraph, line 2, after* "refusing to contract with another": *page* [2020]]
, particularly if it would force an entity to engage in a long-term contract with another[524a]

[524a] Although it may do so exceptionally: *Woods Building Services v Milton Keynes Council* [2015] EWHC 2172 (TCC) at [9]–[11].

CHAPTER 28

LIMITATION OF ACTIONS

1. PERIODS OF LIMITATION

Latent damage in actions in the tort of negligence

[*Add to note 59, at the end: page* [2035]]   **28–011**
; *Schumann v Veale Wasbrough* [2015] EWCA Civ 441, [2015] P.N.L.R. 25.

Carriage by sea

[*In note 99, delete last sentence, starting "In Feest . . . " and substitute: page*   **28–023**
[2039]]
In *Feest v South West Strategic Health Authority* [2015] EWCA Civ 708, [2016] Q.B. 503 it was held that the two-year limitation period under the Athens Convention does not bar a claim by an alleged tortfeasor for contribution against the carrier, under the Civil Liability (Contribution) Act 1978, in respect of personal injury to a passenger.

2. ACCRUAL OF THE CAUSE OF ACTION

Successive and continuing breaches

[*Add to note 159, at the end: page* [2046]]   **28–035**
Although not involving any question of limitation, as regards the apparent conflict regarding whether there was a continuing breach of contract between

Midland Bank Trust Co Ltd v Hett, Stubbs and Kemp [1979] Ch. 384 and *Bell v Peter Browne & Co* [1990] 2 Q.B. 495, the majority of the Court of Appeal in *Capita (Banstead 2011) Ltd v RFIB Group Ltd* [2015] EWCA Civ 1310, [2016] P.N.L.R. 17, indicated that they preferred (and indeed, as a matter of precedent, were bound to apply) the latter case rather than the former.

Money lent

28–036   [*Add to note 164, at the end: page* [2046]]
; *Goldsmith v Chittell* [2016] EWHC 630 (Ch).

Civil Liability (Contribution) Act 1978

28–051   [*Add to note 211, at the end: page* [2050]]
Similarly, an interim payment does not start the two-year limitation period running: *Jellett v Brooke* [2016] EWHC 2828 (QB), [2017] 1 W.L.R. 1177.

5. EXTENSION OF THE PERIOD

(b) *Fraud, Concealment or Mistake*

Concealment

28–087   [*Add to note 333, at the end: page* [2063]]
See also *Gresport Finance Ltd v Battaglia* [2016] EWHC 964 (Ch) (s.32(1)(b) was applied in the context of breach of contract and breach of fiduciary duty by the defendant who had concealed his lack of authority).

7. COMMENCEMENT OF PROCEEDINGS

Legal proceedings

28–117   [*In note 461, delete the second sentence, starting* "See also ... " *and substitute: page* [2075]]
On the relevance, to the commencement of proceedings for limitation purposes, of the non-payment of the correct court fee, see *Page v Hewetts Solicitors* [2012] EWCA Civ 805; *Bhatti v Ashgar* [2016] EWHC 1049 (QB); *Glenluce Fishing Co Ltd v Watermota Ltd* [2016] EWHC 1807 (TCC).

Defence, set-off and counterclaim

28–123   [*Add new note 490a, line 10, after* "the original action.": *page* [2078]]
490a *Al-Rawas v Hassan Khan and Co* [2017] EWCA Civ 42, [2017] P.N.L.R. 13.

Part Nine

RESTITUTION

CHAPTER 29

RESTITUTION

1. INTRODUCTION

[In note 1, line 2, update reference to Goff and Jones, The Law of Unjust Enrichment to: page [2093]]
9th edn (2016)

(a) *Nature of Restitution*

The essence of restitution

[Add to note 3, at the end: page [2094]]   **29–001**
In *Revenue and Customs Commissioners v Investment Trust Companies* [2017]
UKSC 29, [2017] 2 W.L.R. 1200 at [59], Lord Reed recognised that the purpose

of restitution is to reverse a defective transfer and not to compensate for loss suffered.

Common Law

29–002   [*Add to note 7, at the end: page* [2095]]
In *Co-operative Bank Plc v Hayes Freehold Ltd* [2017] EWHC 1820 (Ch) at [149] Henry Carr J. recognised that the doctrine of unjust enrichment could not be used to relieve a party of the consequences of the bargain which he or she had made.

Classification

29–004   [*Add to note 17, at the end: page* [2096]]
and Havelock (2016) L.Q.R. 470.

(c) *The Theoretical Basis of the Law of Restitution*

Two main theories

29–010   [*Add to note 46, line 2, after* "[2013] Ch. 156.": *page* [2101]]
See also *Bank of Cyprus UK Ltd v Menelaou* [2015] UKSC 66, [2016] A.C. 176 at [37] (Lord Clarke); [98] (Lord Neuberger); [108] (Lord Carnwath).

[*Add to paragraph, at the end: page* [2101]]
In *Lowick Rose LLP v Swynson Ltd*[48a] Lord Sumption recognised that there was no universal theory in English law to explain all the cases where restitution is available.

[48a] [2017] UKSC 32, [2017] 2 W.L.R. 1161 at [22].

The principle of unjust enrichment

29–011   [*Add to note 50, penultimate line, after* "[2013] UKSC 50, [2014] A.C. 938": *page* [2101]]
Bank of Cyprus UK Ltd v Menelaou [2015] UKSC 66, [2016] A.C. 176; *Patel v Mirza* [2016] UKSC 42, [2017] A.C. 467.

Judicial recognition

29–013   [*Add to note 60, at the end: page* [2102]]
In *Revenue and Customs Commissioners v Investment Trust Companies* [2017] UKSC 29, [2017] 2 W.L.R. 1200 at [39] Lord Reed recognised that a claim based on unjust enrichment does not create judicial licence to reach a fair result on a case-by-case basis. Rather, legal rights which arise from unjust enrichment should be determined by rules of law which are ascertainable and consistent. See also *Lowick Rose LLP v Swynson Ltd* [2017] UKSC 32, [2017] 2 W.L.R. 1161 at [22] (Lord Sumption).

[*Add new note 60a, line 8, after* "from those precedents.".: *page* [2103]]
[60a] See *Revenue and Customs Commissioners v Investment Trust Companies* [2017] UKSC 29, [2017] 2 W.L.R. 1200 at [40] (Lord Reed): "the wisdom of our predecessors is a valuable resource".

The state of the unjust enrichment principle

[*Add to note 77, at the end: page* [2104]]   **29–015**
Also in Malaysia: *Dream Property v Atlas Housing* [2015] 2 M.L.J. 441.

[*Add to paragraph, at the end: page* [2104]]
In *Revenue and Customs Commissioners v Investment Trust Companies*[81a] Lord Reed recognised that law of unjust enrichment is founded on the principle of corrective justice and that its purpose is to "correct normatively defective transfers of value" typically by restoring the parties to their pre-transfer positions; with "normative" referring to a defect recognised by the law of unjust enrichment.

[81a] [2017] UKSC 29, [2017] 2 W.L.R. 1200 at [42]–[43].

Different claims within the law of restitution

[*Add to note 85, line 3, after* "[2013] Ch. 156": *page* [2105]]   **29–016**
However, in *Bank of Cyprus UK Ltd v Menelaou* [2015] UKSC 66, [2016] A.C. 176 a majority of the Supreme Court recognised that the proprietary remedy of subrogation could be awarded to reverse the defendant's unjust enrichment. See Watterson [2016] C.L.J. 209. See generally Salmons (2017) 76 C.L.J. 399.

2. Unjust Enrichment

(a) *The Content of the Unjust Enrichment Principle*

The elements of unjust enrichment

[*Add to note 87, penultimate line, after* "[2014] EWCA Civ 361, [52] (Etherton   **29–017**
C.).": *page* [2105]]
See also *Bank of Cyprus UK Ltd v Menelaou* [2015] UKSC 66, [2016] A.C. 176 at [80] where Lord Neuberger described the remedy as "financial compensation".

[*Add to note 87, at the end: page* [2105]]
In *Revenue and Customs Commissioners v Investment Trust Companies* [2017] UKSC 29, [2017] 2 W.L.R. 1200 at [45], Lord Reed recognised that the loss suffered by the claimant to establish a claim in unjust enrichment need not be a loss in the same sense as in the law of damages and he emphasised that a restitutionary remedy is not compensatory. The relevant loss could, for example, be established if the claimant had provided a service without payment, since the claimant would have given up something of economic value.

[*Add to note 89, penultimate line, after* "if they had statutory force": *page* [2106]]
This was confirmed by Lord Clarke in *Bank of Cyprus UK Ltd v Menelaou* [2015] UKSC 66, [2016] A.C. 176 at [19]. But failing to consider the distinct elements of the unjust enrichment claim will result in a loss of rigour in the analysis and application of the law. This was recognised by Lord Reed in *Revenue and Customs Commissioners v Investment Trust Companies* [2017] UKSC 29, [2017] 2 W.L.R. 1200 at [41], although he emphasised that the elements do not involve legal tests the meaning of which can be discerned as if by statutory interpretation; rather, they are signposts towards areas of inquiry which involve distinct legal requirements. See also *Lowick Rose LLP v Swynson Ltd* [2017] UKSC 32, [2017] 2 W.L.R. 1161 at [112] (Lord Neuberger).

[*Add to note 90, at the end: page* [2106]]
See also *Patel v Mirza* [2016] UKSC 42, [2017] A.C. 467 at [246] (Lord Sumption).

Defences and denials

29–018   [*Add to note 98, at the end: page* [2107]]
In *Universal Advance Technology Ltd v Lloyds Bank Plc* [2016] EWCA Civ 933 a claim in debt in respect of goods supplied failed because the goods had not been supplied and, consequently, if the claim had succeeded the claimant would have become unjustly enriched at the expense of the defendant. See also *Lowick Rose LLP v Swynson Ltd* [2017] UKSC 32, [2017] 2 W.L.R. 1161 at [119] (Lord Neuberger).

[*Add to note 100, at the end: page* [2107]]
; *Erith Holdings Ltd v Murphy* [2017] EWHC 1364 (TCC), [102] (O'Farrell J.).

(b) *Enrichment*

The nature of the enrichment

29–019   [*Add to note 108, at the end: page* [2108]]
See also *Richards v Worcestershire County Council* [2016] EWHC 1954 (Ch) (discharge of defendant's statutory liabilities).

[*In paragraph, lines 9–11, delete from* "In *Menelaou*" *to* "belonging to the defendant." *and substitute: page* [2108]]
In *Bank of Cyprus UK Ltd v Menelaou*[112] the Supreme Court recognised that the transfer of freehold property without a charge, when the property should have been subject to a valid charge, constituted an enrichment to the extent of the amount with which the property should have been charged. In *Lowick Rose LLP v Swynson Ltd*[112a] Lord Mance recognised that an enrichment included the reduction of a loss which would otherwise have been recoverable by a claim for damages for breach of contract or breach of a duty.

[112] [2015] UKSC 66, [2016] A.C. 176.
[112a] [2017] UKSC 32, [2017] 2 W.L.R. 1161 at [57]. See also Lord Neuberger at [113].

[Add to note 114, at the end: page [2108]]
See also *Revenue and Customs Commissioners v Investment Trust Companies*
[2017] UKSC 29, [2017] 2 W.L.R. 1200 at [30] (Lord Reed).

Non-monetary benefits

[In note 119, update reference to Goff and Jones: page [2109]] **29–020**
Goff and Jones at paras 4-43–4-50

Use value of money

[Add to paragraph, at the end: page [2111]] **29–023**
In *Ipswich Town Football Club Co Ltd v Chief Constable of Suffolk*[132a] it was
recognised that, where there was no evidence that the defendant had benefited
from the receipt and possession of the payment, and also that the claimant had
suffered no loss from being deprived of the time value of the money, only simple
and not compound interest would be awarded. This is consistent with the
subsequent decision of the Supreme Court in *Revenue and Customs Commissioners v Investment Trust Companies*[132b] that the defendant's enrichment must
be directly obtained at the expense of the claimant, who must have incurred a loss
as a result of providing the benefit. Whilst the Supreme Court did not consider
the impact of this principle on the decision in *Sempra Metals*, it is certainly the
case that the use of compound interest as the measure of the defendant's use
value of the money received could only be justified if the claimant had suffered
a loss as a result of paying the money.

[132a] [2017] EWHC 375 (QB).
[132b] [2017] UKSC 29, [2017] 2 W.L.R. 1200. See below, paras 29-028 and 29-029.

Valuing enrichment

[Add to note 134, at the end: page [2112]] **29–024**
See also *MacInnes v Gross* [2017] EWHC 46 (QB) at [162]–[166] (Coulson
J.).

[Add to paragraph, at the end: page [2112]] **29–025**
In *Bank of Cyprus UK Ltd v Menelaou*[136a] Lord Neuberger suggested that if the
valuation of the enrichment resulted in a sum which was "unfair or oppressive"
it was open to the court to adjust it, although he identified no basis for the court
to make such an adjustment.

[136a] [2015] UKSC 66, [2016] A.C. 176 at [81].

(c) *At the Expense of the Claimant*
Enrichment at the claimant's expense

[Add to note 138, at the end: page [2112]] **29–026**
In *Revenue and Customs Commissioners v Investment Trust Companies* [2017]
UKSC 29, [2017] 2 W.L.R. 1200 at [43], Lord Reed recognised that the reversal

of unjust enrichment is premised on the defendant having received a benefit from the claimant such that the claimant has incurred a loss as a result of the provision of the benefit.

Direct and indirect enrichment

29–028   *[Delete text of paragraph and substitute: pages* [2113]–[2115]*]*
In establishing whether the enrichment was obtained at the claimant's expense, the question whether the enrichment must have been received directly by the claimant from the defendant or whether indirect enrichment, via a third party, suffices, has proved controversial. In *Investment Trust Companies v Revenue and Customs Commissioners*[146] the Court of Appeal had affirmed the analysis of Henderson J.[147] that, although there is no rule excluding unjust enrichment claims against indirect recipients, there is a general requirement of direct enrichment to which there are limited exceptions, including where the defendant's enrichment can be considered to have been obtained at the expense of the claimant with reference to the economic realities of the case to determine where the economic burden has fallen. This approach was reversed in the Supreme Court on the ground that it was too vague.[148] Likewise, in *Bank of Cyprus UK Ltd v Menelaou*[149] Lord Clarke had held that establishing that the defendant had been enriched at the claimant's expense required consideration of whether there was a sufficient causal connection between the claimant's loss and the defendant's benefit. This was criticised by the Supreme Court in the *ITC* case on the ground that it left unanswered what degree of connection was sufficient.[150] In the *ITC* case the suppliers of investment management services to customers were thought to be liable to pay VAT to the Commissioners. The customers bore a contractual liability to pay the full amount of VAT to the suppliers. Once it was discovered that the VAT was not lawfully due, because the services were exempt, and the suppliers were unable to recover all that had been paid, the customers sought restitution of the remaining amount from the Commissioners. This claim failed because the Commissioners had not been directly enriched at the expense of the customers, since no payment was made by the customers to the Commissioners; in other words, there was no direct dealing between the parties. The key test is whether the defendant had received a benefit from the claimant and the claimant had incurred a loss through the provision of that benefit. Whilst Lord Reed, with whom the other Justices agreed, recognised a number of scenarios which the law treated as equivalent to a direct transfer of value, none of these applied on the facts of the case. These scenarios are: (i) where an agent is interposed between the claimant and the defendant; (ii) where the right to restitution is assigned, so that the claimant stands in the shoes of the assignor; (iii) where an intervening transaction is a sham which is created to conceal the connection between the claimant and defendant; (iv) where a set of co-ordinated transactions is treated as forming a single scheme or transaction; (v) where the claimant can trace into property received by the defendant from a third party; (vi) where the claimant discharges a debt owed by the defendant to a third party whereby the defendant is directly enriched by the discharge of the debt rather than by the receipt of the money.[151] Lord Reed acknowledged that this list was not necessarily complete. One further scenario should have been recognised, namely where the defendant has intercepted an enrichment which would otherwise have been transferred to

the claimant by a third party: this will be treated as an enrichment at the expense of the claimant.[152]

[146] [2015] EWCA Civ 82, [2015] S.T.C. 1280.
[147] [2012] EWHC 458 (Ch), [2012] S.T.C. 1150 at [67]. See also *Uren v First National Home Finance Ltd* [2005] EWHC 2529 (Ch) at [23] (Mann J.).
[148] [2017] UKSC 29, [2017] 2 W.L.R. 1200.
[149] [2015] UKSC 66, [2016] A.C. 176 at [27].
[150] [2017] UKSC 29, [2017] 2 W.L.R. 1200 at [37] (Lord Reed).
[151] See below, para.29–105.
[152] See *Official Custodian for Charities v Mackey (No.2)* [1985] 1 W.L.R. 1308. See Virgo at pp.111–114. cf. Burrows at pp.79–85; Smith (1991) O.J.L.S. 481.

Lord Reed considered that his decision explained a number of earlier decisions. So, for example, in *MacDonald Dickens and Macklin v Costello*[153] Etherton L.J. had recognised that the defendants who were directors and shareholders of a company could not be considered to have been enriched at the claimant's expense where the claimant had provided a service to the company, because the enrichment to the defendant would only have been provided indirectly by the claimant. In *Relfo Ltd v Varsani*[154] it was possible to look behind the various accounts via which money had been transferred and conclude that the true nature of the transaction involved a direct payment from the claimant to the defendant. This was because a director of the claimant company had intended from the start that money would be transferred from the claimant to the defendant via various intermediaries, which was characterised by Floyd L.J. as an "elaborate façade" since it was designed to conceal the true nature of the transaction. Treating co-ordinated transactions as a single transaction involving the direct transfer of an enrichment from the claimant to the defendant was also considered to explain the unjust enrichment claim in *Banque Financière de la Cité SA v Parc (Battersea) Ltd*,[155] and *Bank of Cyprus UK Ltd v Menelaou*[156] On the facts of the latter case there was a direct transfer of value from the respondent bank to the appellant, since the bank had agreed to release £785,000 of the sum which it was owed on one property to enable another property to be purchased, but subject to a charge in favour of the bank on that property. In the end that property was received by the appellant without a valid charge, and she was consequently enriched to the extent that the property had not been charged. Lords Clarke and Neuberger[156a] considered this to involve one single scheme which directly benefited the appellant.

29–028A

[153] [2011] EWCA Civ 930, [2012] Q.B. 244 at [20].
[154] [2014] EWCA Civ 360, [2015] 1 B.C.L.C. 14.
[155] [1999] 1 A.C. 221; see below para.29–180.
[156] [2015] UKSC 66, [2016] A.C. 176. See Leung and Wong [2016] L.M.C.L.Q. 337 and see generally Winterton [2016] R.L.R. 164.
[156a] [2015] UKSC 66 at [25] and [73].

Incidental benefits

[Delete text of paragraph and substitute: pages [2115]–[2116]] **29–029**
In *TFL Management Ltd v Lloyds Bank Plc*[157] the Court of Appeal recognised that the defendant will be considered to be enriched at the claimant's expense even if the claimant was acting primarily out of self-interest to benefit himself but, in doing so, the defendant was incidentally benefited. This was, however, rejected by the Supreme Court in *Revenue and Customs Commissioners v*

Mistaken voluntary dispositions

29–052   [*Add to note 308, at the end: page* [2133]]
; *Freedman v Freedman* [2015] EWHC 1457 (Ch); *Van der Merwe v Goldman* [2016] EWHC 790 (Ch), [2016] 4 W.L.R. 71; *Bainbridge v Bainbridge* [2016] EWHC 898 (Ch), [2016] W.T.L.R. 943. In *Co-operative Bank Plc v Hayes Freehold Ltd* [2017] EWHC 1820 (Ch) at [130] Carr J. recognised that the jurisdiction to rescind did not apply where the transaction was neither a gift nor a voluntary disposition. In that case a deed of release from a landlord's covenants was not characterised as a voluntary disposition because in return an underlease was surrendered and so consideration was provided.

[*Add to note 310, at the end: page* [2133]]
In *Gresh v RBC Trust Co (Guernsey) Ltd* (2016) 18 I.T.E.L.R. 753 the Royal Court of Guernsey held that a request by a member of a pension fund to be paid a lump sum distribution in the mistaken belief that it was not subject to tax, did not constitute an equitable mistake because there was nothing which rendered the retention of the distribution unconscionable as between the member and the pension fund.

[*Add to note 311, at the end: page* [2133]]
See further Dodds [2016] R.L.R. 129.

(f) *Failure of Basis*

General principles

29–057   [*Add to note 328, line 8, after* "endeavour between the parties.".: *page* [2136]]
cf. *Bank of Cyprus UK Ltd v Menelaou* [2015] UKSC 66, [2016] A.C. 176 where it was accepted that the ground of total failure of consideration applied (Lord Clarke at [21]) without analysis of whether there was a joint endeavour between respondent and appellant, which could not have been established because the appellant was unaware of the basis for the transfer of the enrichment. In *Lowick Rose LLP v Swynson Ltd* [2017] UKSC 32, [2017] 2 W.L.R. 1161 at [30] Lord Sumption recognised that the basis had to be mutually shared by the claimant and the defendant, save where the remedy of subrogation is sought. See below, para.29–180.

Illustrations of total failure of basis

29–059   [*In note 350, update reference to Goff and Jones to: page* [2139]]
Goff and Jones, para.13-30.

Artificiality of distinctions

29–060   [*Add to note 351, at the end: page* [2143]]
See *Marsfield Automotive Inc v Siddiqi* [2017] EWHC 187 (Comm) at [24] (Teare J.).

Contract discharged or ineffective

[In note 363, update reference to Goff and Jones to: page [2140]]
Goff and Jones at paras 15-51–15-57

29–061

Recovery of deposits

[Add to note 420, at the end: *page* [2147]]
This also applies where no contract was made due to lack of authority: *Rabiu v Marlbray Ltd* [2016] EWCA Civ 476, [2016] 1 W.L.R. 5147, although Gloster L.J. acknowledged (at [90]) that restitution of the deposit might lie despite there not being a total failure of basis if the bargain was unconscionable or the defendant's behaviour was overbearing.

29–068

[In note 424, update reference to Goff and Jones to: page [2147]]
Goff and Jones at paras 14-25–14-29

Relevance of the contract price

[In note 472, update reference to Goff and Jones to: page [2154]]
Goff and Jones at paras 3-47–3-51

29–075

[Add new note 476a, line 29, after "the best evidence.": *page* [2154]]
476a In *MacInnes v Gross* [2017] EWHC 46 (QB) Coulson J. recognised (at [166]) that an agreement as to remuneration for services may unusually be the best evidence of the objective market value of the services provided, but usually other objective evidence would be required, such as expert evidence.

Payments made under a void contract

[Add to note 505, at the end: page [2157]]
See also *Marlbray Ltd v Laditi* [2016] EWCA Civ 476 (no recovery of deposit where no failure of consideration).

29–080

Services rendered or goods supplied under a void contract

[In note 515, update reference to Goff and Jones to: page [2158]]
Goff and Jones at para.4-35

29–082

Money paid under illegal contracts

[Delete text of paragraph and substitute: page [2159]]
If money is paid under a contract which is illegal it has been recognised that restitution should not be awarded because of the taint of illegality.[518] However, following the decision of the Supreme Court in *Patel v Mirza*,[519] as a general rule restitution will be awarded if the elements of the unjust enrichment claim can be established, which will usually be possible because an illegal transaction will always involve a failure of consideration since the basis for the transaction will be void, save where the court considers that the taint of illegality should defeat

29–083

the claim for restitution. In determining whether the defence of illegality should operate the court should have regard to a "trio of considerations", namely examination of the reason for making the conduct illegal; identification of the policies which would be adversely affected by denying the claim; and proportionality.[520] Lord Toulson recognised that various factors will be relevant to determine whether it is disproportionate to refuse relief, although he did not consider that it was possible to produce a definitive list because of the infinite variety of cases which might raise illegality. Factors he identified include the seriousness of the conduct, its centrality to any contract, whether the conduct was intentional and whether there was a marked disparity in the parties' respective culpability.[521]

[518] e.g. *Parkinson v College of Ambulance Ltd* [1925] 2 K.B. 1.
[519] [2016] UKSC 42, [2017] A.C. 467. See also above, paras 16–014A et seq. See Grabiner (2017) 76 C.L.J. 168; Goudkamp (2017) 133 L.Q.R. 14; Strauss [2016] R.L.R. 145.
[520] [2016] UKSC 42 at [101].
[521] [2016] UKSC 42 at [107].

[Add new paragraph 29–083A: page [2159]*]*

29–083A In *Patel v Mirza*[521a] itself the respondent had transferred £620,000 to the appellant to be used by the latter to bet on share price movements based on inside information. Such insider dealing is a crime under Pt V of the Criminal Justice Act 1993. The inside information was not forthcoming and so the agreement was not carried out. The respondent sought restitution of the money paid on the ground that the appellant had been unjustly enriched at his expense, the ground of restitution being that the basis for the transfer had failed totally. In the Supreme Court the nine Justices unanimously held that the respondent should recover the money he had paid to the appellant. The general approach of the Supreme Court was that it was appropriate to return the parties to the status quo ante despite the illegality of the transaction because, as Lord Sumption recognised,[521b] "an order for restitution would not give effect to the illegal act or to any right derived from it". It follows that there is only a very limited role for the defence of illegality in the law of restitution, since the courts will be willing to unwind the transaction because the claimant will not profit from it, save perhaps where the illegality is considered to be particularly serious.[521c] The old rule[521d] that the defence of illegality would apply whenever the claimant needs to rely on the illegality to establish a claim was rejected by the Supreme Court in *Patel v Mirza*.[521e] The majority did not examine the old doctrine of *locus poenitentiae*, by virtue of which a claim will not be defeated by illegality if the claimant has voluntarily withdrawn from the transaction before any part of the illegal purpose has been achieved,[521f] but it is likely that this doctrine will be considered to have been subsumed into the new "trio of considerations" approach of the majority.[521g]

[521a] [2016] UKSC 42, [2017] A.C. 467. See also above, paras 16–014A et seq.
[521b] [2016] UKSC 42 at [268].
[521c] [2016] UKSC 42 at [116] (Lord Toulson).
[521d] See *Tinsley v Milligan* [1994] 1 A.C. 340.
[521e] [2016] UKSC 42, [2017] A.C. 467 at [110] (Lord Toulson).
[521f] See *Tribe v Tribe* [1996] Ch. 107.
[521g] [2016] UKSC 42 at [101]; see above, para.29–083.

Services provided under illegal contracts

[*Add to note 522, at the end: page* [2159]]
This was confirmed in *Patel v Mirza* [2016] UKSC 42, [2017] A.C. 467 at [119]
(Lord Toulson).

29–084

Minors' contracts

[*In note 532, update reference to Goff and Jones to: page* [2161]]
Goff and Jones at paras 24-20–24-23

29–087

[*Add to note 532, at the end: page* [2161]]
See Häcker in *Defences in Unjust Enrichment* (ed. Dyson, Goudkamp and
Wilmot-Smith) (2016), Ch.9.

(g) *Ultra vires Receipts by the Revenue and Public Authorities*

Scope of right

[*Add to note 569, line 16, after* "restitution against public bodies.": *page* [2165]]
In *Richards v Worcestershire County Council* [2016] EWHC 1954 (Ch) the
claimant was allowed to pursue a private law claim for restitution arising from
the claimant discharging the defendant's statutory obligations, even though this
raised questions as to whether the defendant had performed public law duties.
This conclusion was reached both because the claimant only sought financial
redress rather than any other relief and because the strict time limit for judicial
review proceedings was inappropriate for a private law claim for restitution.

29–091

[*Add to note 558, at the end: page* [2164]]
See further on the former provision *Jazztel Plc v Revenue and Customs Commissioners* [2017] EWHC 677 (Ch), [2017] S.T.C. 1422 at [100(vi)] where the
provision was disapplied for the recovery of overpaid taxes where the right had
accrued before the statute came into force, but this right was only discovered
subsequently: so called "hidden retrospectivity".

[*Add new note 564a, line 31, after* "and valid demand.": *page* [2165]]
564a In *Ipswich Town Football Club Co Ltd v Chief Constable of Suffolk* [2017] EWHC 375 (QB)
the *Woolwich* principle applied even though the demand for payment was not backed by legal
compulsion, save that the defendant, the Police, had an economic power through monopoly to compel
payment. Compulsion was considered (at [73]) to be a trait of a *Woolwich* claim but was not a
requisite part of the test.

[*Add to note 566, at the end: page* [2165]]
In *Ipswich Town Football Club Co Ltd v Chief Constable of Suffolk* [2017]
EWHC 375 (QB) the *Woolwich* principle applied to recover payments for
services provided by the police, for which payment was not lawfully due, even
though the charges could not be characterised as fiscal.

Statutory provisions

29–092   [*In note 570, line 5, delete reference to Investment Trust Companies and substitute:* page [2166]]
Revenue and Customs Commissioners v Investment Trust Companies [2017] UKSC 29, [2017] 2 W.L.R. 1200, [88] (Lord Reed);

[*In note 570, lines 6-8 delete the sentence* "Whether this exclusion ... S.T.C. 1714" *and substitute:* page [2166]]
In *Revenue and Customs Commissioners v Investment Trust Companies* [2017] UKSC 29, [2017] 2 W.L.R. 1200 at [94] Lord Reed held that the statutory exclusion of the common law claim for restitution was compatible with EU law.

Defences

29–093   [*Add to note 579, at the end:* page [2167]]
For consideration of evidence relating to the establishment of change of position by a public authority, see *Jazztel Plc v Revenue and Customs Commissioners* [2017] EWHC 677 (Ch), [2017] S.T.C. 1422.

[*Add to note 585, at the end:* page [2168]]
In *Revenue and Customs Commissioners v Investment Trust Companies* [2017] UKSC 29, [2017] 2 W.L.R. 1200 at [81] Lord Reed characterised this as a statutory defence of passing on.

(h) *Compulsion*

Unlawful or illegitimate compulsion

29–095   [*In note 598, update reference to Goff and Jones to:* page [2169]]
Goff and Jones at para.10-12

Extortion *colore officii*

29–100   [*In note 626, update reference to Goff and Jones to:* page [2172]]
Goff and Jones at paras 10-46–10-53

[*In note 629, update reference to Goff and Jones to:* page [2172]]
Goff and Jones at paras 10-42–10-45

Express threat unnecessary

29–101   [*In note 644, update reference to Goff and Jones:* page [2173]]
Goff and Jones at para.10-44

Compulsory payments to a third person

[*Add to note 655, at the end: page* [2175]]
In *Angove's Pty Ltd v Bailey* [2016] UKSC 47, [2016] 1 W.L.R. 3179 at [16(4)] (Lord Sumption) *Moule v Garett* was specifically approved and was explicitly justified by reference to the law of unjust enrichment.

29–105

[*Add to note 658, at the end: page* [2175]]
See also *Angove's Pty Ltd v Bailey* [2016] UKSC 47, [2016] 1 W.L.R. 3179 at [16(4)] (Lord Sumption).

[*Add to paragraph, at the end: page* [2176]]
In *Revenue and Customs Commissioners v Investment Trust Companies*[662a] Lord Reed recognised that where the claimant discharges a debt owed by the defendant to a third party, the defendant can be considered to be directly enriched at the claimant's expense. If the transfer of value to the defendant through the discharge of the debt is defective, rendering the enrichment unjust, the law will reverse it by subrogating the claimant to the rights formerly held by the third party against the defendant. Lord Reed did not consider this to be a restitutionary remedy as such, since it does not restore the parties to their pre-transfer position, although the effect invariably will be to restore to the claimant the value which had been transferred to the third party.

[662a] [2017] UKSC 29, [2017] 2 W.L.R. 1200 at [49]. See also *Lowick Rose LLP v Swynson Ltd* [2017] UKSC 32, [2017] 2 W.L.R. 1161 at [29] (Lord Sumption).

The right to contribution

[*In note 742, update reference to Goff and Jones to: page* [2186]]
Goff and Jones at paras 20-02–20-47

29–127

[*Add to note 743, at the end: page* [2187]]
In New Zealand the award of equitable contribution depends on there being shared liability for the same damage and a judicial assessment of what is just and reasonable: *Hotchin v New Zealand Guardian Trust Co Ltd* [2016] NZSC 24. See Stace (2017) 133 L.Q.R. 20.

(i) *Necessity*

[*Add to note 777, at the end: page* [2191]]
For criticism of necessity as a generalised ground of restitution, see Day [2016] R.L.R. 26.

Necessitous intervention on behalf of the defendant

[*In note 783, update reference to Goff and Jones to: page* [2191]]
Goff and Jones at paras 18-71–18-81

29–137

Salvage

29–142   [*In note 801, update reference to Kennedy and Rose on the Law of Salvage to: page [2193]*]
9th edn (2017)

[*In note 801, update reference to Goff and Jones to: page [2193]*]
Goff and Jones at paras 18-05–18-35

[*In note 813, update reference to Goff and Jones to: page [2194]*]
Goff and Jones at para.18-75

3. RESTITUTION FOR WRONGS

(d) *Equitable Wrongdoing*

Types of equitable wrongdoing

29–163   [*Add to note 952, at the end: page [2211]*]
The fiduciary will be liable to account for a profit made from his position is not dependent on whether the principal had been damaged or benefited from the breach of duty: *Akita Holdings Ltd v Honourable Attorney-General of the Turks and Caicos Islands* [2017] UKPC 7, [2017] 2 W.LR. 1153.

4. PROPRIETARY RESTITUTIONARY CLAIMS

(a) *Establishing Proprietary Rights*

Identifying a proprietary interest

29–167   [*Add to note 976, line 2, after* "decision on unjust enrichment": *page [2213]*]
applied in *Re Hampton Capital Ltd* [2015] EWHC 1905 (Ch), [2016] 1 B.C.L.C. 374.

Constructive trusts

29–168   [*Add to note 980, line 10, after* "(Lord Neuberger MR)": *page [2214]*]
; *Keown v Nahoor* [2015] EWHC 3418 (Ch) at [41] (D Halpern QC).

[*Add to note 981, penultimate line, after* "[2006] 1 B.C.L.C. 66": *page [2214]*]
; *Angove's Pty Ltd v Bailey* [2016] UKSC 47, [2016] 1 W.L.R. 3179 at [30] (Lord Sumption).

[*Add to note 982, at the end: page [2214]*]
See also *Angove's Pty Ltd v Bailey* [2016] UKSC 47, [2016] 1 W.L.R. 3179 at [30] (Lord Sumption) and *Fistar v Riverwood Legion and Community Club Ltd* [2016] NSWCA 81.

[Add to note 984, at the end: page [2214]]
In *Angove's Pty Ltd v Bailey* [2016] UKSC 47, [2016] 1 W.L.R. 3179 the
Supreme Court did not accept that a constructive trust would be recognised
where the recipient of money knew that imminent insolvency would prevent him
from performing the corresponding obligation. In doing so the reasoning in *Nesté
Oy v Lloyd's Bank Plc*, namely that a constructive trust was triggered because a
reasonable and honest person would have repaid the money which had been
received after the directors had concluded that the company was insolvent, was
rejected. The justification for this appears to turn on what good conscience
requires and that, just because a reasonable person would have returned a
payment, it does not follow that it should have been returned. But this misses the
point about the basis for recognising the constructive trust on the ground of
unconscionable retention. The prior question is whether the defendant is liable to
make restitution to the claimant by virtue of unjust enrichment. If there is such
a liability and the defendant is aware of the circumstances which establish the
claim then the money will be held on constructive trust. That is why money paid
by mistake may be held on constructive trust, as was acknowledged by Lord
Sumption, although he described this as a fundamental mistake, thus confusing
mistakes which prevent legal title from passing with mistakes which may trigger
a constructive trust. But if the defendant is liable to make restitution by virtue of
a total failure of consideration and is aware of the circumstances amounting to
this, that should be sufficient to justify the recognition of the constructive trust.
The key question should then be whether a total failure of consideration can be
identified. Despite this, the Supreme Court asserted that neither an actual nor a
potential total failure of consideration will give rise to a proprietary restitutionary
right, but is simply a matter of contractual readjustment. See further Watts (2017)
133 L.Q.R. 11.

[Add to note 986, at the end: page [2215]]
See also *Bainbridge v Bainbridge* [2016] EWHC 898 (Ch), [2016] W.T.L.R.
943.

[Add to note 991, at the end: page [2215]]
; *Angove's Pty Ltd v Bailey* [2016] UKSC 47, [2016] 1 W.L.R. 3179 at [27] (Lord
Sumption).

(b) *Following and Tracing*

Tracing in Equity

[Add to note 1016, line 2, after "(Lord Parker)": page [2218]] **29–172**
; *Clegg v Pache (deceased)* [2017] EWCA Civ 256 at [87] (Briggs L.J.).

(c) *Proprietary Restitutionary Claims*

Subrogation

[Delete the text of the first sub-paragraph (ending at note 1078) and substitute: page **29–180**
[2224]]
By virtue of "subrogation" a person may, in certain situations, "step into the
shoes" of another so as to enjoy the latter's legal position or his rights against a

third person. Subrogation may arise from the express or implied agreement of the parties or by operation of law. In the latter situation subrogation may be triggered by the defendant's unjust enrichment.[1074] It follows that it will be necessary to establish that the defendant was enriched at the expense of the claimant and that a ground of restitution can be identified.[1075] In *Bank of Cyprus UK Ltd v Menelaou*[1076] a bank was subrogated to a vendor's unpaid lien where the bank had released charges on one property which enabled funds to become available to purchase another property, with the bank incorrectly assuming that it would have a valid charge over the second property. The majority in the Supreme Court justified the award of subrogation on the basis that the owner of the second property was unjustly enriched at the Bank's expense. Lord Neuberger considered that it would be hard to find a more appropriate remedy to award in this case,[1077] since it would give to the bank what it should have had if the charge over the second property had been valid. The Supreme Court's recognition of the award of subrogation to reverse the defendant's unjust enrichment involves the award of a proprietary remedy as a response to unjust enrichment, since the effect of subrogation is to give the claimant the benefit of a security interest to gain priority over the defendant's unsecured creditors, even though, as Lord Clarke said, "a claim in unjust enrichment does not need to show a property right".[1078] But, where it is possible to establish that the claimant's value has been used to discharge a secured debt, it is preferable to analyse the award of the remedy of subrogation without necessary recourse to the unjust enrichment principle but with reference to the vindication of equitable property rights, such that the identification of a recognised ground of restitution need not be considered.[1078a] Indeed, this was how Lord Carnwath in *Menelaou* justified the award of the subrogation remedy,[1078b] with the bank being able to establish the necessary proprietary interest in the money which had been used to discharge the unpaid vendor's lien by virtue of a *Quistclose* resulting trust.[1078c] Crucially, subrogation will only be available where the defendant can be considered to have been enriched as the result of a defective transaction. It was for this reason that subrogation was not available in *Lowick Rose LLP v Swynson Ltd*.[1078d] In that case the claimant intentionally discharged a debt owed by one company to another company, which was controlled by the claimant, in order to reduce the latter company's tax liability. Since there was no defect in the transaction involving the discharge of the debt the claimant could not be subrogated to the company's claim against a third party firm of accountants in professional negligence, it having been argued that the accountants had been enriched by the discharge of the debt since the company had no longer suffered any loss as a result of the negligence such that the accountants were relieved of a substantial liability. In fact, unjust enrichment could not have been established anyway because the benefit to the third party was incidental.[1078e] It was also indirect.[1078f]

[1074] *Bank of Cyprus UK Ltd v Menelaou* [2015] UKSC 66, [2016] A.C. 176; *Lowick Rose LLP v Swynson Ltd* [2017] UKSC 32, [2017] 2 W.L.R. 1161. See also *Banque Financière de la Cité SA v Parc (Battersea) Ltd* [1999] 1 A.C. 221, where the claimant sought a personal remedy against a third party by means of subrogation; *Cheltenham & Gloucester Plc v Appleyard* [2004] EWCA Civ 291; *Anfield (UK) Ltd v Bank of Scotland* [2010] EWHC 2374 (Ch), [2011] 1 W.L.R. 2414 at [10] (Proudman J.); *Sandher v Pearson* [2013] EWCA Civ 1822; *Re Beppler & Jacobson Ltd* [2016] EWHC 20 (Ch) at [122] (Hildyard J.). In *Niru Battery Manufacturing Co v Milestone Trading Ltd (No.2)* [2004] EWCA Civ 487, [2004] 2 All E.R. (Comm) 289, the remedy of subrogation was ordered to prevent the defendant's unjust enrichment arising from the discharge of a liability owed by the defendant. It is unclear, however, why this remedy was sought or obtained since the claimant had a direct restitutionary claim to recover the value of the benefit obtained by the defendant and did not need to step into the shoes of any other party to bring such a claim. The High Court of Australia rejected unjust enrichment as the doctrinal foundation of subrogation in Australia: *Bofinger v Kingsway Group Ltd* [2009] HCA 44; Ridge (2010) 126 L.Q.R. 188.

[1075] See *Adams v Moore* Unreported, May 12, 2016 QBD where subrogation was awarded as a remedy to reverse the defendant's unjust enrichment where the claimants had paid money to discharge the defendant's mortgage in circumstances where the claimants understood that they had lent the money to the defendant. Subrogation was justified on the ground that it would be unjust for the claimants not to recover their money, although it is not obvious what the ground of restitution would be. cf. *Re Beppler & Jacobson Ltd* [2016] EWHC 20 (Ch) where it was recognised that subrogation to reverse unjust enrichment will not lie if there is a subsisting contract between the parties. In *Lowick Rose LLP v Swynson Ltd* [2017] UKSC 32, [2017] 2 W.L.R. 1161 at [29], Lord Sumption did warn against trying to fit subrogation into "any broader category of unjust enrichment" and characterised it as *sui generis*. He identified various differences between unjust enrichment generally and unjust enrichment triggering subrogation, including that subrogation is not a restitutionary remedy as such, since it does not restore the parties to their pre-transfer position, but specifically enforces a defeated expectation, and the ground of failure of basis can be established even if the basis is not shared by the parties.

[1076] [2015] UKSC 66, [2016] A.C. 176. See further *Menelaou v Bank of Cyprus UK Ltd* [2016] EWHC 2656 (Ch), where judicial discretion was exercised to sell the property.

[1077] [2015] UKSC 66 at [79].

[1078] [2015] UKSC 66 at [38].

[1078a] See also *Lehman Commercial Mortgage Conduit Ltd v Gatedale Ltd* [2012] EWHC 848 (Ch).

[1078b] [2015] UKSC 66, [2016] A.C. 176 at [107]. Lord Neuberger acknowledged that this route to subrogation was also available, and he considered this would have been simpler and less controversial: [100].

[1078c] *Barclays Bank Ltd v Quistclose Investments Ltd* [1970] A.C. 567.

[1078d] [2017] UKSC 32, [2017] 2 W.L.R. 1161.

[1078e] [2017] UKSC 32 at [88] (Lord Mance) and [113] (Lord Neuberger). See above, para.29–029.

[1078f] [2017] UKSC 32, [2017] 2 W.L.R. 1161 at [86] (Lord Mance) and [115] (Lord Neuberger). See above, para.29–028.

[Add to paragraph, after note 1090: page [2226]]

Subrogation has also been awarded in cases where the payer of money expected to obtain a charge and this expectation was defeated, regardless of whether this expectation was shared by the payee.[1090a]

[1090a] *Chetwyn v Allen* [1899] 1 Ch. 353; *Butler v Rice* [1910] 2 Ch. 277; *Ghana Commercial Bank v Chadiram* [1960] A.C. 732; *Cheltenham and Gloucester Plc v Appleyard* [2004] EWCA Civ 291.

[In note 1094, line 7, delete reference to the Swynson case and substitute: page [2226]]

Lowick Rose LLP v Swynson Ltd [2017] UKSC 32, [2017] 2 W.L.R. 1161.

Personal restitutionary remedies

[Add to note 1101, at the end: page [2227]]

29–181

In *Fistar v Riverwood Legion and Community Club Ltd* [2016] NSWCA 81 the New South Wales Court of Appeal recognised that a strict liability claim in unjust enrichment for money had and received relating to stolen money lay even though the claimant alternatively had a claim in unconscionable receipt which required proof of fault.

Bona fide purchase defence

29–182   [*In note 1108, update reference to Goff and Jones to: page* [2228]]
Goff and Jones, paras 29-03–29-16

5. Defences

(b) *Change of Position*

Key requirements of change of position

29–187   [*Add to note 1152, at the end: page* [2233]]
See also *Dexia Crediop SpA v Comune di Prato* [2016] EWHC 2824 (Comm) at
[75], where it followed from the recognition of the but for test of causation that
the defence would not be applicable if the defendant would have incurred the
expenditure in the ordinary course of events.

Bad faith

29–191   [*Add to paragraph, at the end: page* [2237]]
In *Re Hampton Capital Ltd*[1182a] George Bompas Q.C. sitting as a Deputy High
Court Judge acknowledged that the test of bad faith for change of position was
the same as the test of knowledge for the claim in knowing receipt, namely
whether what was known to the defendant was sufficient to make it unconscionable for the defendant to refuse to repay the money. In that case it was held that
the defendant knew enough to have reasonable grounds to suspect that the money
he had received had been stolen.

[1182a] [2015] EWHC 1905 (Ch), [2016] 1 B.C.L.C. 374.

Similar defences

29–195   [*Add to note 1198, at the end: page* [2239]]
The defence of ministerial receipt was considered by Teare J. in *Marsfield
Automotive Inc v Siddiqi* [2017] EWHC 187 (Comm), where a distinction was
tentatively drawn between a strong and a weak version of the defence. The
former version applies the defence wherever an agent receives a benefit on behalf
of the principal, because the agent should not be considered to be enriched;
rather, it is the principal who is enriched and who should be sued. The weak
version gives the agent a defence only where the agent has transferred the benefit
received in accordance with the principal's instructions and before the agent has
notice of the claimant's right to restitution. This distinction was also acknowledged by Henderson J. in *High Commissioner for Pakistan in the United
Kingdom v Prince Mukkuram Jah* [2016] EWHC 1465 (Ch), [2016] W.T.L.R.
1763 at [150], who noted that both versions were supported by authority. In
Marsfield Automotive Teare J. indicated, (at [34]), that the weak interpretation of
the defence applied where the payment to the agent was made by mistake or as
the result of a wrongful act, whereas the stronger version applied in all other
cases. This is a sensible way of rationalising a confused body of cases.

Part Ten

CONFLICT OF LAWS

CHAPTER 30

CONFLICT OF LAWS

1. PRELIMINARY CONSIDERATIONS

[*Add new paragraph 30–002A: page* [2248]]

"Brexit". As noted above,[6a] the future legal relationship of the UK to the EU remains to be determined. In the absence of any arrangements which include the UK remaining bound by EU law, the impact on conflict of laws is potentially very significant. Key European private international law instruments, notably the Brussels I Regulation (recast) (which governs jurisdiction in European cases) and   **30–002A**

the Rome II Regulation (which governs choice of law in non-contractual cases) would cease to have effect. Most significantly for the purposes of this chapter, the Rome I Regulation, which applies to all contracts entered into on or after December 17, 2009, and whose rules form the main subject matter of this chapter, would no longer be directly effective EU law. One possibility is that the UK would return to the position under the Contracts (Applicable Law) Act 1990, which implemented the Rome Convention into English law. However, the status of those rules following the UK's exit from the EU raises difficult issues of international law and UK statutory law. Alternatively, as choice of law rules are unilateral (not requiring reciprocity, unlike rules of jurisdiction) it would be possible for the UK to enact national legislation which substantially mirrors the Rome I Regulation. All of these issues remain to be determined and this Supplement to Chapter 30, and particularly the discussion of conflict of laws, remains written on the premise that the status of EU law in UK law remains unchanged.[6b]

[6a] See above, paras 1–013A—1–013E.

[6b] For a discussion see A. Dickinson, "Back to the future: the UK's EU exit and the conflict of laws" [2016] JPIL 195; P. Rogerson, "Litigation post-Brexit" [2017] N.L.J. 2016; J. Harris "How will Brexit impact on cross-border litigation?" [2016] S.J. 160; "Brexit & cross-border dispute resolution" [2016] N.L.J. 166; The General Council of the Bar, Brexit Working Group, *Brexit Papers* (December 2016); Commercial Bar Association (COMBAR) *Brexit Report* Conflict of Laws Sub-Group (January 5, 2017); The Law Society of England and Wales, *Brexit and the Law* (January 2017); Final Report of the House of Lords European Union Justice Sub-Committee "Implications of Brexit for the justice system" (March 14, 2017).

3. THE ROME CONVENTION

(a) *In General*

Interpretation: the European Court

30–018   [*Add to note 109, at the end: page* [2261]]
; *ERGO Insurance SE v If P&C Insurance AS* (Joined cases C-359/14 and C-475/14).

"Laws of different countries"

30–021   [*Delete text of note 116 and substitute: page* [2262]]
The relationship between this requirement and art.3(3) is discussed by the Court of Appeal in *Banco Santander Totta SA v Cia de Carris de Ferro de Lisboa SA* [2016] EWCA Civ 1267.

(b) *Exclusions*

Meaning of "contractual obligations"

30–030   [*Add to note 144, at the end: page* [2266]]
In *Verein für Konsumenteninformation v Amazon EU Sarl* (C-191/15) the CJEU held that a claim for an injunction against the use of unfair means in consumer

cases came within the Rome II Regulation whereas the assessment of a particular term of a contract came under the Rome I Regulation.

Wills, succession, etc.

[*Add to note 165, at the end: page* [2268]]   **30–036**
Following the failure to reach a political agreement on these proposals, on March 2, 2016, the European Commission adopted a proposal for a Council decision authorising enhanced cooperation in the area of jurisdiction, applicable law and the recognition and enforcement of decisions on the property regimes of international couples, covering both matters of matrimonial property regimes and the property consequences of registered partnerships (COM(2016) 108 final). The Commission also published proposals for two new Regulations, a Council Regulation on jurisdiction, applicable law and the recognition and enforcement of decisions in matters of matrimonial property regimes (COM(2016) 106 final) and a proposal for a Council Regulation on jurisdiction, applicable law and the recognition and enforcement of decisions in matters of the property consequences of registered partnerships (COM(2016) 107 final). Council Regulation 2016/1103 of 24 June 2016 ([2016] O.J. L183/1) will apply in Member States which participate in advanced cooperation from January 29, 2019 in the context of matrimonial property and the property consequences of registered partnerships.

Arbitration agreements and agreements on the choice of court

[*Add to note 184, at the end: page* [2270]]   **30–039**
In *BCY v BCZ* [2016] SGHC 249 the High Court of Singapore applied such a presumption.

Insurance

[*In note 214, delete from* "However, the implementation date" *in last line to the end*   **30–044**
and substitute: page [2274]]
The Solvency II Directive came into force on January 1, 2016. The UK has implemented the Directive through the Solvency 2 Regulations 2015 (SI 2015/575) making only minor changes to the pre-existing statutory instruments.

(c) Choice of Law by the Parties

Mandatory rules

[*Add to note 296, at the end: page* [2284]]   **30–060**
There is no need to show evasiveness or bad faith*: Banco Santander Totta SA v Cia de Carris de Ferro de Lisboa SA* [2016] EWHC 465 (Comm) at [373], affirmed [2016] EWCA Civ 1267.

[*Add to note 299, at the end: page* [2284]]
In *Banco Santander Totta SA v Cia de Carris de Ferro de Lisboa SA* [2016] EWHC 465 (Comm) the judge confirmed that the test was "deliberately general"

(at [390]) and that it was enough that the case involved "international elements" (at [411]). This decision was affirmed by the Court of Appeal [2016] EWCA Civ 1267. The starting point must be that art.3(3) was an exception to party autonomy and so should be construed narrowly. The only question was whether the situation is "purely domestic". The *Banco Santander Totta* case was followed in *Dexia Crediop SpA v Comune di Prato* [2017] EWCA Civ 428.

"Mandatory rules"

30–062   *[Add to note 308, at the end: page* [2286]]
In *Banco Santander Totta SA v Cia de Carris de Ferro de Lisboa SA* [2016] EWHC 465 (Comm) the judge said that in his view it was sufficient to take a rule outside the scope of art.3(3) if the rule could be disapplied by agreement between the parties whether *ex ante* or *ex post* (at [506]). Although the Court of Appeal upheld the decision of the judge that art.3(3) did not apply, so that any comments on this point were obiter, the majority disagreed and would have held that an *ex post* agreement not to rely on a provision did not mean that it was derogable and so outside art.3(3): [2016] EWCA Civ 1267 (at [73]).

(d) *Applicable Law in the Absence of Choice by the Parties*

Specific applications

30–076   *[Add to note 368, at the end: page* [2294]]
By analogy, the supplier of bunkers in the type of *sui generis* supply contract identified by the Supreme Court in *PST Energy 7 Shipping LLC v OW Bunker Malta Ltd (The Res Cogitans)* [2016] UKSC 23 (see para.44–174A) will also be the characteristic performer.

"Other contracts" involving carriage of goods

30–085   *[In note 434, update the reference to Scrutton on Charterparties to: page* [2302]]
23rd edition (2015), paras 1.013 et seq.

Rebutting the presumptions

30–089   *[Add to paragraph, at the end: page* [2305]]
In *Haeger & Schmidt GmbH v MMA IARD*[459a] the CJEU provided further guidance and held that in order to decide whether to apply art.4(5) the national court must compare the connections existing between the contract and, on the one hand, the country in which the party who effects the characteristic performance has his or its habitual residence at the time of the conclusion of the contract, and, on the other hand, another country with which the contract is closely connected. The CJEU continued by stating that the court:

> " . . . must conduct an overall assessment of all the objective factors characterising the contractual relationship and determine which of these factors are, in its view, most significant . . . Significant connecting factors to be taken into account include the presence of a close connection between the contract in question with another

contract or contracts which are, as the case may be, part of the same chain of contracts, and the place of delivery of the goods."[459b]

[459a] C-305/13, [2015] Q.B. 319. Like the *ICF* case, this case also concerned art.4(4) but again the same principles apply when the question relates to rebutting the otherwise presumed applicable law.

[459b] C-305/13 [2015] Q.B. 319 at [49].

(e) *Certain Consumer Contracts and Individual Employment Contracts*

Article 5(2): first condition: advertising

[*Add to note 503, line 6, after* "within the scope of those activities"": *page* [2312]] **30–096**
and also with art.17(1)(c) of the recast Regulation, which is identical

EU consumer protection legislation

[*Add to note 519, at the end: page* [2315]] **30–102**
For contracts entered into after October 1, 2015, the Unfair Terms in Consumer Contracts Regulations 1999 are replaced by the Consumer Rights Act 2015,

"Employment": autonomous meaning

[*Add to note 550, line 10, after* "[2007] I.L.Pr. 706": *page* [2319]] **30–109**
; *Petter v EMC Europe Ltd* [2015] EWCA Civ 828; [2016] I.L.Pr. 3

[*Add to note 550, at the end: page* [2319]]
In *Holterman Ferho Exploitatie BV v Spies von Büllesheim* (C-47/14) [2015] I.L.Pr. 44 the Court of Justice of the EU adopted an autonomous meaning in the context of Section 5 of the Judgments Regulation.

Territorial limitations

[*Add to note 573, at the end: page* [2322]] **30–114**
; *Olsen v Gearbulk Services Ltd* [2015] I.R.L.R. 818 (EAT); Merrett (2015) I.L.J. 53.

4. THE ROME I REGULATION

(a) *In General*

History

[*Add to note 634, at the end: page* [2330]] **30–129**
A contract entered into before December 17, 2009 is not brought within the scope of the Rome I Regulation because it is amended or varied after that date unless it is a variation of such magnitude that a new contract must be regarded as having been concluded: *Greece v Nikiforidis* (C-135/15) [2017] I.C.R. 147 at [39].

Meaning of "contractual obligations"

30–146   [*Add to note 690, at the end: page* [2337]]
See, for example, in the context of an "implied in law" obligation *Pan Oceanic Chartering Inc v UNIPEC UK Co Ltd* [2016] EWHC 2774 (Comm) and, in the context of a claim made under the French tourism code, *Committeri v Club Mediterranee SA* [2016] EWHC 1510 (QB).

(b) *Exclusions*

Matrimonial property regimes, etc.

30–154   [*Add to note 708, at the end: page* [2339]]
Following the failure to reach a political agreement on these proposals, on March 2, 2016, the European Commission adopted a proposal for a Council decision authorising enhanced cooperation in the area of jurisdiction, applicable law and the recognition and enforcement of decisions on the property regimes of international couples, covering both matters of matrimonial property regimes and the property consequences of registered partnerships (COM(2016) 108 final). The Commission also published proposals for two new Regulations, a Council Regulation on jurisdiction, applicable law and the recognition and enforcement of decisions in matters of matrimonial property regimes (COM(2016) 106 final) and a proposal for a Council Regulation on jurisdiction, applicable law and the recognition and enforcement of decisions in matters of the property consequences of registered partnerships (COM(2016) 107 final). Council Regulation 2016/1103 of 24 June 2016 ([2016] O.J. L183/1) will apply in Member States which participate in advanced cooperation from January 29, 2019 in the context of matrimonial property and the property consequences of registered partners.

(e) *Applicable Law in the Absence of Choice*

Principles

30–187   [*Add to note 783, at the end: page* [2349]]
See generally on choice of law governing commercial disputes in the absence of express choice Arzandeh [2015] L.M.C.L.Q. 525

Sale of goods

30–189   [*Add to note 786, at the end: page* [2349]]
The autonomous Community meaning of "sale of goods" is likely to be broad enough to encompass the *sui generis* supply contracts of the sort considered in *PST Energy Shipping LLC v OW Bunker Malta Ltd (The Res Cogitans)* [2016] UKSC 23, given that such contracts are "in commercial terms" regarded as contracts for the sale of goods ([2015] EWCA Civ 1058 at [33], [2016] 2 W.L.R. 1072). In *Molton Street Capital LLP v Shooters Hill Capital Partners LLP* [2015] EWHC 3419 (Comm) it was disputed whether a sale of junk bonds was a sale of "goods" within the meaning of art.4(1)(a) but it was unnecessary to decide the

point as the seller of the bonds was also the characteristic performer under the default in art.4(2).

Contract concluded within multilateral system

[*Add to note 803, at the end: page* [2351]]   **30–196**
The original Directive has been replaced by Directive 2014/65/EU (MiFID 2) although the deadline for compliance with the new Directive has been extended to January 2018 (COM(2016) 56 final).

Rule of displacement

[*Add to note 826, line 4, after* "displace the primary rule")": *page* [2354]]   **30–203**
; *Molton Street Capital LLP v Shooters Hill Capital Partners LLP* [2015] EWHC 3419 (Comm) at [94] ("The new language and structure suggests a higher threshold, which requires that the cumulative weight of the factors connecting the contract to another country must clearly and decisively outweigh the desideratum of certainty in applying the relevant test in Article 4.1 or 4.2")

Relevant factors

[*Add to note 828, penultimate line, after* "[2012] EWCA Civ 265": *page* [2354]]   **30–204**
; *Aquavita International SA v Ashapura Minechem Ltd* [2015] EWHC 2807 (QB) and Enonchong [2015] L.M.C.L.Q. 194

(f) *Contracts of Carriage*

[*Add to note 832, at the end: page* [2355]]
; Okoli [2015] L.M.C.L.Q. 512.

(g) *Consumer Contracts*

Contract of carriage

[*Add to note 899, at the end; page* [2363]]   **30–235**
A new Package Travel Directive (2015/2302/EU) entered into force on December 31, 2015 and must be implemented by July 1, 2018.

Rights and obligations constituting a financial instrument, etc.

[*Add to note 906, at the end: page* [2364]]   **30–237**
The original Directive has been replaced by Directive 2014/65/EU (MiFID 2) although the deadline for compliance with the new Directive has been extended to January 2018 (COM(2016) 56 final).

[*Add to note 907, at the end: page* [2364]]
In July 2012, the European Commission formally adopted a reform of the UCITS Directive, commonly referred to as UCITS V, which was enacted and published

in July 2014. UCITS V (Directive 2014/91/EU) amends the previous version of the UCITS Directive, known as UCITS IV (Directive 2009/65/EC). The UCITS V Directive has an implementation deadline of March 18, 2016. Unlike the UCITS IV Directive, the UCITS V Directive does not recast the UCITS Directive. Instead, it amends and stands alongside the UCITS IV Directive.

Choice of law by the parties

30–249   [*Add to note 961, at the end: page* [2371]]
On click-wrapping and jurisdiction agreements under the Judgments Regulation see *El Majdoub v CarsOnTheWeb.Deutschland GmbH* (C-322/14) [2015] 1 W.L.R. 3986, and see *Verein für Konsumenteninformation v Amazon EU Sarl* (C-191/15) on standard terms.

(i) *Individual Employment Contracts*

[*Add to note 1028, line 5, after* "Merrett (2010) I.L.J. 355"*: page* [2381]] ; Merrett (2015) I.L.J. 53.

Meaning of individual employment contract

30–279   [*Add to note 1040, at the end; page* [2382]]
In *Holterman Ferho Exploitatie BV v Spies von Büllesheim* (C-47/14) [2015] I.L.Pr. 44, the Court of Justice of the EU adopted an autonomous meaning in the context of Section 5 of the Judgments Regulation.

[*Add new note 1042a, after* "framework of the counterparty" *in line 13: page* [2382]]
1042a Each of these three criteria was referred to by the Court of Justice in *Holterman Ferho Exploitatie BV v Spies von Büllesheim* (C-47/14) [2015] I.L.Pr. 44 when considering the meaning of employment contract under the Judgments Regulation.

(j) *Voluntary Assignment and Contractual Subrogation*

Background

30–289   [*In note 1065, penultimate line, after* "Mollman [2011] L.M.C.L.Q. 262" *add: page* [2385]]
; Goode [2015] L.M.C.L.Q. 289.

(k) *Legal Subrogation*

Background

30–294   [*Add to note 1080, at the end: page* [2388]]
Article 15 is discussed in *ERGO Insurance SE v If P&C Insurance AS* (Joined Cases C-359/14 and C-475/14).

(m) *Set-off*

Set-off in insolvency proceedings

[*Add to note 1099, at the end: page* [2390]]   **30–302**
The Insolvency Regulation is to be replaced by Regulation (EU) 2015/848 of the
European Parliament and of the Council of 20 May 2015 on insolvency proceedings (recast) (Recast Insolvency Regulation). The Recast Insolvency Regulation
will apply to insolvency proceedings commencing on or after June 26, 2017.

5. SCOPE OF THE APPLICABLE LAW

(e) *Burden of proof*

Burden of proof and presumptions

[*Add to note 1329, line 4, after* "negotiated to show that it was)": *page* [2419]]   **30–354**
(for contracts entered into after October 1, 2015, the Unfair Terms in Consumer
Contracts Regulations 1999 are replaced by the Consumer Rights Act 2015).

[*Add to note 1334, at the end: page* [2420]]   **30–355**
For contracts entered into after October 1, 2015, the Unfair Terms in Consumer
Contracts Regulations 1999 are replaced by the Consumer Rights Act 2015.

(f) *Illegality and Public Policy*

Ralli Bros and The Rome Convention

[*Add new note 1357a, line 9, after* "the applicable law of the contract.": *page*   **30–361**
[2423]]
[1357a] See *Eurobank Ergasias SA v Kallirio Navigation Co Ltd* [2015] EWHC 2377 (Comm),
approving this reasoning as expressed in the previous edition of this book.

Effect of Rome I Regulation

[*Add new note 1361a, line 5, after* "the law applicable to the contract": *page*   **30–362**
[2424]]
[1361a] See *Eurobank Ergasias SA v Kallirio Navigation Co Ltd* [2015] EWHC 2377 (Comm),
approving this reasoning as expressed in the previous edition of this book.

"Overriding mandatory provisions"

[*Add to note 1365, at the end: page* [2424]]   **30–363**
As a derogating measure, art.9 must be interpreted strictly: *Greece v Nikiforidis*
(C-135/15) [2017] I.C.R. 147 at [44].

Relevant country

[*Add to paragraph, at the end: page* [2425]]   **30–364**
The list of the overriding mandatory provisions to which the court of the forum
may give effect in art.9 of the Rome I Regulation is exhaustive and must

accordingly be interpreted as precluding the court of the forum from applying, as legal rules, overriding mandatory provisions other than those of the State of the forum or of the State where the obligations arising out of the contract have to be or have been performed.[1371a]

[1371a] *Greece v Nikiforidis* (C-135/15) [2017] I.C.R. 147 at [49].

(g) *Foreign Currency Obligations*

Scope of discussion

30–371   [*In note 1398, update the reference to Mann on the Legal Aspect of Money to: page [2429]*]
7th edn (2012)

CHAPTER 31

AGENCY

1. Agency in General

Foreign law

31–004 [*Add to note 15, at the end: page* [4]]
; Kortmann and Kortmann, "Undisclosed Indirect Representation—Protecting the Principal, the Third Party, or Both?", Ch.6 in Busch, Macgregor and Watts (eds), *Agency Law in Commercial Practice* (OUP, 2016).

Relationship of principal and agent

31–006 [*Add to note 30, at the end: page* [6]]
In *Plevin v Paragon Personal Finance Ltd* [2014] UKSC 61, [2014] 1 W.L.R. 4222, Lord Sumption said, in the context of s.140A of the Consumer Credit Act 1974, that "In their ordinary and natural meaning the words 'on behalf of' import agency": at [30]. The effect was to narrow the broad protective discretion in respect of liability of a lender for acts of others given by s.140A. See comment by McMeel, "Agency and the Retail Distribution of Financial Products", Ch.10 in Busch, Macgregor and Watts (eds), *Agency Law in Commercial Practice* (2016) paras 10.25 et seq.

2. Examples of Types of Agent

Solicitors

31–013 [*Add new note 77a, after* "be easily inferred today" *in line 13: page* [10]]
[77a] The modern position regarding solicitor's authority to bind his or her client, at any rate in Australia, is discussed at length in *Pavlovic v Universal Music Australia Pty Ltd* [2015] NSWCA 313.

3. Commercial Agents

Commercial agents

31–017 [*In note 93, update reference to Singleton, Commercial Agency Agreements: Law and Practice to: page* [12]]
4th edn (2015).

[*Add to note 99, at the end: page* [13]]
See also *Software Incubator Ltd v Computer Associates Ltd* [2016] EWHC 1587 (QB).

[*Add to note 104, at the end: page* [13]]
The commodity exception is considered in *W Nagel v Pluczenik Diamond Co NV* [2017] EWHC 1750 (Comm), when it was held that the activities of a diamond

broker were in the commodity market, some particular operations outside the
exception ranking as secondary.

The Commercial Agents Regulations: conflict of laws

[*Add to note 120, at the end: page* [15]]   **31–020**
; Carruthers, Ch.13 in Busch, Macgregor and Watts (eds), *Agency Law in
Commercial Practice* (2016).

4. CREATION OF AGENCY

(a) *Express Agreement*

Powers of attorney

[*Add to note 141, at the end*: *page* [18]]   **31–025**
Guidance as to wording to be used for execution in the attorney's name is given
in *Yu Hing Tong Ltd v Fung Hing Chiu Cyril* [2016] 5 H.K.L.R.D. 567.

(c) *Ratification*

General rule

[*Add to note 148, at the end: page* [18]]   **31–027**
See in general Krebs, "Ratification", Ch.2 in Busch, Macgregor and Watts (eds),
Agency Law in Commercial Practice (2016).

Proof of ratification

[*Add to note 152, at the end: page* [19]]   **31–028**
See also *Sino Channel Asia Ltd v Dana Shipping and Trading Pte Singapore*
[2016] EWHC 1118 (Comm) (no ratification of arbitration held without valid
service (because of lack of authority to receive it), and hence without participation, by inactivity after award made).

(d) *Agency of Necessity*

Agency of necessity

[*In note 197, update reference to Scrutton on Charterparties to: page* [24]]   **31–035**
23rd edn (2015), Arts 139–142.

Second type of case

[*In note 216, update the reference to Goff and Jones to*: *page* [25]]   **31–037**
9th edn (2016), Ch.18

[In note 218, update the reference to Goff and Jones to: page [26]]
9th edn (2016), Ch.17

6. PRINCIPAL'S RELATIONS WITH THIRD PARTIES

(a) *General Rule*

General rule: identified and unidentified principal

31–054   *[Add to note 313, at the end: page* [36]]
These dicta are doubted by Leggatt J. in *Magellan Spirit ApS v Vitol SA* [2016]
EWHC 454 (Comm) at [19], but no reasons are given.

Cases where contract required to be in writing

31–055   *[Add to note 320, at the end: page* [37]]
In *Rabiu v Marlbray Ltd* [2016] EWCA Civ 476 a husband signed a land contract
on behalf of himself and his wife but without her authority. He was held severally
liable on the contract.

(b) *Apparent Authority*

Apparent authority

31–056   *[In note 329, line 1, delete* "to others": *page* [38]]

*[In note 329, update reference to Handley, Estoppel by Conduct and Election to:
page* [38]]
2nd edn (2016), p.30.

[Add to note 338, at the end: page [39]]
In *Galaxy Aviation v Sayegh Group Aviation* [2015] EWHC 3478 (Comm) it is
said that "in practice this is I think relatively unusual". But that may not be so:
see McMeel, "Agency and the Retail Distribution of Financial Products", Ch.10
in Busch, Macgregor and Watts (eds), *Agency Law in Commercial Practice*
(2016), paras 10.28 et seq.

"True" estoppel

31–057   *[Add to note 358, at the end: page* [41]]
See also the further discussion in *The Bunga Melati 5* [2016] SGCA 20.

Agents of companies

31–058   *[Add to note 361, at the end: page* [42]]
See also Watts, "Directors as Agents—Some Aspects of Disputed Territory",
Ch.7 in Busch, Macgregor and Watts (eds), *Agency Law in Commercial Practice*
(2016).

(c) *Undisclosed Principal*

Doctrine of the undisclosed principal

[*Add to note 396, at the end: page* [45]]   **31–063**
cf. Kortmann and Kortmann, above, para.31–004, n.15; Fridman, "Undisclosed
Principals and the Sale of Goods", Ch.5 in Busch, Macgregor and Watts (eds),
Agency Law in Commercial Practice (2016).

Meaning of "undisclosed principal"

[*Add to note 403, at the end: page* [46]]   **31–065**
In *Magellan Spirit ApS v Vitol SA* [2016] EWHC 454 (Comm) such a proposition
appears to be doubted by Leggatt J., but he may be referring to the initial creation
of the agency (which obviously cannot be created by mere subjective intention)
rather than the intention to act for the principal in a particular instance, which
when the principal is not named is certainly required over and above the basic
authority. The matter is considered at more length in the *Bowstead and Reynolds
on Agency*, 1st Supplement of the 20th edition, para.8–072 (modifying the text
and adding to a footnote).

[*Add to note 404, at the end: page* [46]]
The *Yukong* case is considered by Leggatt J. in *Magellan Spirit ApS v Vitol SA*
[2016] EWHC 454 (Comm) at [27], [28].

(d) *Principals and Third Parties: Further Rules*

Effect of judgment against agent

[*Add to note 446, at the end: page* [50]]   **31–070**
The matter is briefly referred to in *Adams v Atlas International Property Services
Ltd* [2016] EWHC 2680 (QB), [2017] Bus. L.R. 287.

(e) *Agent Bribed*

Effect of bribery of agent

[*Add to note 487, at the end: page* [53]]   **31–073**
In *Chancery Client Partners Ltd v MRC 957 Ltd* [2016] EWHC 2142 (Ch) it was
held that purchasers of tax savings schemes purchased from a third party who had
bribed their agent could not rescind the schemes, as opposed to the contract
between them and the third party scheme provider.

(f) *Agent's Torts*

Agent's torts

[*Add to note 503, at the end: page* [55]]   **31–075**
For a recent example see *Mohamud v Wm Morrison Supermarkets Plc* [2016]
UKSC 11, [2016] A.C. 677 (assault by employee).

7. AGENT'S RELATIONS WITH THIRD PARTIES

(a) *On the Main Contract*

When agent liable and entitled

31–084   [*Add to note 560, at the end: page* [61]]
; *Savills (UK) Ltd v Blacker* [2017] EWCA Civ 68 (a case having similarities
with *The Swan*, above).

Where principal is company not yet in existence

31–097   [*Add to note 623, line 4, after* "(1979) 11 U. Queensland L.J. 53.": *page* [68]]
For a more recent example in respect of an unincorporated association see *Davies
v Barnes Webster & Sons* [2011] EWHC 2560 (Ch), [2012] B.P.I.R. 97 (service
on President of Rugby Club valid).

(c) *Breach of Warranty of Authority*

Implied representation of authority

31–101   [*In note 644, delete text of note and substitute: page* [70]]
Fernée v Gorlitz [1915] 1 Ch. 177; *Yonge v Toynbee*, above; *Simmons v Liberal
Opinion Ltd* [1911] 1 K.B. 966; *Nelson v Nelson* [1997] 1 W.L.R. 233 (bankrupt
could authorise action). These are actually cases on the court's jurisdiction over
solicitors. For a recent discussion of the interaction between this jurisdiction and
the action for breach of warranty of authority see *Aidiniantz v Sherlock Holmes
International Society Ltd* [2016] EWHC 1392 (Ch), [2016] 4 W.L.R. 173 at [20]
onwards.

[*Add to note 644, at the end: page* [70]]
A complicated situation in which the matter arose in connection with other
proceedings concerning whether the agent had been validly appointed as a
director is considered in *Zoya Ltd v Ahmed* [2016] EWHC 2249 (Ch), [2016] 4
W.L.R. 174.

Representation must be of fact and relied on

31–102   [*Add to note 647, at the end: page* [71]]
In *Aidiniantz v Sherlock Holmes International Society Ltd* [2016] EWHC 1392
(Ch), [2016] 4 W.L.R. 173 it was held that the claimant was as well placed as the
agent to inquire whether the agent's authority had come to an end: see esp. at
[29].

Description of principal

31–103   [*Add to note 652, at the end: page* [71]]
The same view is adopted and justified in a long and careful judgment by Mr
Robin Dicker Q.C. in *P&P Property Ltd v Owen White & Catlin LLP* [2016]

EWHC 2276 (Ch), [2016] Bus. L.R. 1337; though a different view was taken in Singapore in *Chu Said Thong v Vision Law LLC* [2014] SGHC 160.

Damages

[*Add to note 664, line 2, after* "[2002] EWCA Civ 1706": *page* [72]]
; *Aidiniantz v Sherlock Holmes International Society Ltd* [2016] EWHC 1392 (Ch), [2016] 4 W.L.R. 173.

31–106

[*Add to note 665, at the end: page* [73]]
In *Aidiniantz v Sherlock Holmes International Society Ltd* [2016] EWHC 1392 (Ch), [2016] 4 W.L.R. 173 this result was attributed to the principle that an award of damages for breach of warranty of authority should not put the claimant in a better position than that in which he would have been had the agent had authority, as in the case of the insolvent principal, see at [17] onwards.

(d) *Restitution*

Repayment of money

[*Add to note 681, at the end: page* [74]]
; *Marsfield Automotive Inc v Siddiqi* [2017] EWHC 187 (Comm) (useful discussion).

31–110

8. OBLIGATIONS OF PRINCIPAL AND AGENT INTER SE

(a) *Duties of Agents*

(i) *Common Law: Carrying Out Instructions*

Authority

[*Add to note 703, at the end: page* [77]]
See further for wider discussion DeMott, "The Poseur as Agent", Ch.3 in Busch, Macgregor and Watts (eds), *Agency Law in Commercial Practice* (2016).

31–113

(ii) *Common Law: Exercise of Care and Skill*

Exercise of care and skill

[*Add to note 704, at the end: page* [77]]
And it has recently been held that where the action is in substance one for breach of contract the contractual rules for the calculation of damages apply: *Wellesley Partners LLP v Withers LLP* [2015] EWCA Civ 1146, [2016] 2 W.L.R. 1351.

31–114

Due care for principal's interests

31–115 *[Add to note 710, at the end: page [78]]*
; *Khouj v Acropolis Capital Partners Ltd* [2016] EWHC 2120 (Comm) (right to inspect agent's documents).

(iii) *Equity: Fiduciary Duties and Duties of Loyalty*

Fiduciary duties and duties of loyalty

31–118 *[Add to note 724, line 8, after "[2003] Eu. L.R. 874": page [79]]*
See in general Tosato, "Commercial Agency and the Duty to Act in Good Faith" [2016] O.J.L.S. 661.

[Add to note 729, at the end: page [80]]
For a recent example see *Vernon v Public Trust* [2016] NZCA 388 (improper use of power of attorney).

Self-dealing

31–124 *[In note 756, update the reference to Goff and Jones to: page [82]]:9th edn (2016), paras 8-175 et seq.

Exclusion of liability

31–126 *[Add to note 775, at the end: page [84]]*
; *Barnsley v Noble* [2016] EWCA Civ 799 (trustee under will).

[Add to note 777, at the end: page [85]]
See discussion of the general topic by McMeel, "Agency and the Retail Distribution of Financial Products", Ch.10 in Busch, Macgregor and Watts (eds), *Agency Law in Commercial Practice* (2016), paras 10.25 et seq., paras 10.19 et seq.

(iv) *Remedies*

Common law

31–127 *[Add to paragraph, at the end: page [86]]*
An agent may be required to permit inspection of documents related to his principal.[787a]

[787a] *Khouj v Acropolis Capital Partners Ltd* [2016] EWHC 2120 (Comm), [2017] W.T.L.R. 83 (order in favour of principal's administrators).

Equity: duty to account and restitution of the trust estate

31–129 *[Add to note 792a, at the end: page [86]]*
; Gummow (2015) 41 Aust. Bar Rev. 5; Millett (2015) *UK Supreme Court Yearbook* 193; Turner [2015] C.L.J. 188; Davies (2015) 78 M.L.R. 681.

[Add new note 792b, at the end of paragraph: page [87]]
^{792b} A recent example is *Main v Giambrone & Law* [2017] EWCA Civ 1193 (wrongful payment out of deposits held by solicitors), though the judgment also considers common law damages.

(vi) *Agent Holding Money for Principal*

Trustee or debtor?

[Add to note 822, at the end: page [90]]   **31–133**
It was said that *Neste Oy v Lloyds Bank Plc* [1983] 2 Lloyd's Rep. 658 (see Main Work, Vol.II, para.31–133 n.821) "cannot be justified", in *Angove's Pty Ltd v Bailey* [2016] UKSC 47, [2016] 1 W.L.R. 3179 at [31].

(b) *Rights of Agents*

General

[Add to note 833, at the end: page [91]]   **31–136**
; Tosato, "Commercial Agency and the Duty to Act in Good Faith" [2016] O.J.L.S. 661. In *Monk v Largo Foods Ltd* [2016] EWHC 1837 (Comm) it was held that reg.4 did not affect the power of a principal to terminate at will when the contract was "subject to successful review".

(i) *Remuneration*

Other types of estate agent's agreement

[Add to note 880, at the end: page [96]]   **31–144**
In *Savill's (UK) Ltd v Blacker* [2017] EWCA Civ 68 estate agents were on the basis of interpretation held entitled to commission although the property had been sold without planning permission, whereas the agents had initially recommended obtaining such permission before sale.

Commercial agents

[In note 916, delete the last sentence, "It seems clear" to the end and substitute: **31–149**
page [100]]
In *ERGO Poist'ovňa a.s.* (C-48/16) the CJEU held that the words "to blame" did not merely refer to the legal reasons which led directly to the termination of the contract, but to the reasons which led up to that termination, taking into account all the facts of the case. In the case itself, dealing with marketing of insurance (which would not be within the English regulations) the principal had treated clients improperly, asking for responses to questions and sending demands for payment which had already been made. The court also decided that reg.11(1) covers not only cases of complete non-execution of the contract but also partial non-execution, for example by reason of non-compliance with the volume of

transactions or the duration envisaged by the contract. A clause in effect providing for pro rata refund on such a basis was held not to be a derogation from the
agent's right.

Termination of contract

31–151   [*Add to note 929, line 5, after "[2007] 3 N.Z.L.R.169": page* [102]]
; *W Nagel v Pluczenik Diamond Co NV* [2017] EWHC 1750 (Comm).

Termination: where Commercial Agents Regulations applicable

31–152   [*Add to note 941, at the end: page* [103]]
For a case where the principal did not accept the agent's breach see *Alan Ramsay
Sales and Marketing Ltd v Typhoo Tea Ltd* [2016] EWHC 486 (Comm), [2016]
4 W.L.R. 59.

[*Add to note 946, at the end: page* [104]]
This is so also where the agent's agreement is terminated during a trial period
agreed at first appointment: *Fadin Habitat (Société) v Constructions Tradi-
tionnelles du Val de Loire* [2015] E.C.C. 27 (Cour de Cassation, France); *Monk
v Largo Foods Ltd* [2016] EWHC 1837 (Comm) (similar facts: duty of good faith
does not impact on absolute right to terminate irrespective of breach).

Indemnity and compensation: indemnity

31–153   [*Add new note 954a, after "the cessation of the contract." in line 5: page* [104]]
      954a "New customers" includes persons brought in by the agent, notwithstanding that the customers
      had already had relations with the principal in relation to other goods: *Marchon Germany GmbH v
      Karaszkiewicz* (C-315/14) [2016] Bus. L.R. 694.

[*Add to note 960, at the end: page* [105]]
In *Quenon K SPRL v Beobank SA* (C-338/14) [2016] Bus. L.R. 264 the CJEU
held that the Directive permitted Member States who had chosen the indemnity
option to provide for recovery of additional loss, provided that "the award of
damages may not result in double recovery by combining the indemnity for
customers with the compensation for loss resulting, in particular, for the loss of
commission following termination of the contract": at [32].

Compensation

31–154   [*Add to note 962, at the end: page* [105]]
In the result, the normal compensation regime applied by default: contrast *Brand
Studio Ltd v St John Knits Inc* [2015] EWHC 3143 (QB), [2015] Bus. L.R. 1421,
where a similar clause was held severable from a choice of indemnity, which
therefore remained valid.

[*Add to note 968, at the end: page* [105]]
; *Alan Ramsay Sales and Marketing Ltd v Typhoo Tea Ltd* [2016] EWHC 486
(Comm), [2016] 4 W.L.R. 59; *Software Incubator Ltd v Computer Associates Ltd*
[2016] EWHC 1587 (QB).

[*Add new note 969a, at end of paragraph: page* [106]]
[969a] For an example of the two methods operating together see *Software Incubator Ltd v Computer Associates Ltd* [2016] EWHC 1587 (QB).

Calculation of compensation

[*Add to note 982, at the end: page* [107]]   **31–155**
; *Alan Ramsay Sales and Marketing Ltd v Typhoo Tea Ltd* [2016] EWHC 486
(Comm), [2016] 4 W.L.R. 59 (food sector, especially cash and carry and wholesale); *Software Incubator Ltd v Computer Associates Ltd* [2016] EWHC 1587
(QB); *Monk v Largo Foods Ltd* [2016] EWHC 1837 (Comm) (consultant to food
manufacturer; contract likely to have been terminated: not decisive on compensation but uncertainties taken into account); *W Nagel v Pluczenik Diamond Co NV*
[2017] EWHC 1750 (Comm).

Commercial agents

[*Add to note 992, line 2, after* "[2003] Eu.L.R. 189": *page* [108]]   **31–157**
; *Monk v Largo Foods Ltd* [2016] EWHC 1837 (Comm).

Loss of commission by default or misconduct

[*Add to note 1011, at the end: page* [110]]   **31–161**
; *Hosking v Marathon Asset Management LLP* [2016] EWHC 2418 (Ch), [2017]
Ch. 157 (applied in the context of partnership).

[*Add to note 1016, at the end: page* [110]]
; *Bank of Ireland v Jaffery* [2012] EWHC 1377 (Ch); *Gamatronic (UK) Ltd v
Hamilton* [2016] EWHC 2225 (QB).

[*Add to note 1017, at the end: page* [110]]
; as to which see also *Wright Hassall LLP v Horton* [2015] EWHC 3716
(QB).

[*Before paragraph 31–162, delete sub-heading* "(ii) Indemnity" *and substitute: page*
110]]
(ii) Common Law Indemnity

Indemnity of agent

[*In note 1022, update the reference to Goff and Jones to: page* [110]]   **31–162**
9th edn (2016), paras 19-16 et seq.

9. Termination of Authority

How authority terminated

[*Add to note 1053, at the end: page* [113]]   **31–166**
See in general Wee and Tan, "The Agency of Liquidators and Receivers", Ch.8
in Busch, Macgregor and Watts (eds), *Agency Law in Commercial Practice*

(2016), stressing that it must be understood that agency notions, as often, apply in flexible ways in this area.

Irrevocable authority

31–167   *[Delete text of paragraph and substitute: pages* [114]–[115]]
Though an agent's authority is, as stated above, normally revocable at will (without prejudice to his right, if any, to damages for breach of contract), there are some cases where this is not so. These are cases where

> "the agent has a relevant interest of his own in the exercise of his authority. This requires first, an agreement that the agent's authority shall be irrevocable, and secondly that the authority is given to secure an interest of the agent, being a proprietary interest (for example a power of attorney given to enable the holder of an equitable interest to perfect it[1065]) or a liability (generally in debt) owed him personally. In these cases, the agent's authority is irrevocable while the interest subsists."[1066]

This involves use of the format of agency at least in part to enable the agent to act in his own interest. But it has been said that it is not necessary that the sole purpose of the arrangement is to secure the agent's financial interest: an agent can remain an agent owing the fiduciary and other duties to act in the principal's interest, while having a personal interest in the exercise of his authority sufficient to make it irrevocable.[1067] The authority to sell goods is not irrevocable merely because the agent has made advances to his principal; but it would be if the arrangement was specifically made to secure such advances.[1068] The mere right to commission is not sufficient to create irrevocable authority,[1069] but an interest in recovering a debt in respect of commission already earned may be. By an extension of this reasoning it has been held that in a sub-underwriting contract, the authority given by a sub-underwriter to apply for shares such as he is bound by his contract to take up is an authority coupled with an interest and as such irrevocable.[1070] The scope of this extension, which may depend also on the fact that other sub-underwriters are involved who may be prejudiced by revocation by one, is still not clear.[1070a]

[1065] *Walsh v Whitcomb* (1797) 2 Esp. 565, 566; *Gaussen v Morton* (1830) 10 B. & C. 731 (powers of attorney to sell to satisfy existing debt).

[1066] *Bailey v Angove's Pty Ltd* [2016] UKSC 47 at [7] per Lord Sumption. See also *Frith v Frith* [1906] A.C. 254, 261; *Restatement, Third, Agency* (2006), para.3.12; Powers of Attorney Act 1971 s.4(1), below, para.31–168.

[1067] *Bailey v Angove's Pty Ltd* [2016] UKSC 47 at [9]. See on this case Watts (2017) 133 L.Q.R.11.

[1068] *Smart v Sandars* (1848) 5 C.B. 895, 917.

[1069] *Doward, Dickson & Co v Williams & Co* (1890) 6 T.L.R. 316.

[1070] *Re Olympic Fire & General Reinsurance Co Ltd* [1920] 2 Ch. 341. See also *Re Hartt Group and Land Securities Ltd* (1984) 7 D.L.R. (4th) 89 (power of landlord to re-enter as agent of tenant); *Slatter v Railway Commissioners for New South Wales* (1931) 45 C.L.R. 68 (power to apply for licence for premises); *Schindler v Brie* [2003] EWHC 1804 (Ch), [2003] W.T.L.R. 1361 (no intention to make authority irrevocable); *Temple Legal Protection Ltd v QBE Insurance (Europe) Ltd* [2009] EWCA Civ 453, [2010] 1 All E.R. (Comm) 903 at [79]; *Despot v Registrar-General of New South Wales* [2013] NSWCA 313. In *Bailey v Angove's Pty Ltd* [2016] UKSC 47 no view was expressed about the basis of these and related cases beyond saying that their results were "undoubtedly convenient": see at [10].

[1070a] The general principle of revocability of authority can cause difficulty when applied to arrangements at Lloyd's, which to a considerable extent depend on irrevocable agency and passivity

of the principal. See Reynolds in Cranston (ed.), *Making Commercial Law* (1997), Ch.10. In *Society of Lloyd's v Leigh* [1997] C.L.C. 759 Colman J. was prepared to uphold irrevocability of authority outside the context of security: but the Court of Appeal decided the case on grounds connected with the Lloyd's Act 1982 and Bylaws made thereunder: sub nom. *Society of Lloyd's v Lyon* [1997] C.L.C. 1398. In *Temple Legal Protection Ltd v QBE Insurance (Europe) Ltd* [2009] EWCA Civ 453, [2010] 1 All E.R. (Comm) 703 it was held that a broker's interest in maintaining and developing his business was not sufficient to render the authority to conduct a run-off irrevocable.

Apparent authority

[*Add to note 1075, at the end: page* [116]]   **31–169**
; and *DVB Bank SE v Isim Amin Ltd* [2014] EWHC 2156 (Comm) (valid service on agent after actual authority had expired).

CHAPTER 32

ARBITRATION

1. STATUTORY REGULATION

Human Rights Act 1998

32–017 [*Add to note 67, at the end: page* [127]]
See also *Yegiazaryan v Smagin* [2016] EWCA Civ 1290, [2017] 1 Lloyd's Rep. 102 at [26].

2. THE ARBITRATION AGREEMENT

Definition of "arbitration agreement" and arbitrability

32–020 [*Add to note 78, at the end: page* [128]]
In *Yegiazaryan v Smagin* [2016] EWCA Civ 1290, [2017] 1 Lloyd's Rep. 102 at [43], the Court of Appeal held that the contractual provision under review was an arbitration agreement because it was a mechanism by which a contracting party could be compelled through arbitration to ensure that it complies with its obligations.

Agreements to be in writing

[Add to note 99, at the end: page [130]]   **32–023**
; *Barrier Ltd v Redhall Marine Ltd* [2016] EWHC 381 (QB)

Separability of arbitration agreement

[Add new note 115a, after "that, unless otherwise agreed," *in line 7: page* [133]]   **32–028**
[115a] In *National Iranian Oil Co v Crescent Petroleum Co International Ltd* [2016] EWHC 510
(Comm), [2016] 2 Lloyd's Rep. 146, at [7]–[14], the Court held that a contractual choice of law
clause, on its own, will not operate as an agreement to the contrary for the purposes of s.7.

[Add to note 116, at the end: page [133]]
See also *Associated British Ports v Tata Steel UK Ltd* [2017] EWHC 694 (Ch),
[2017] 2 Lloyd's Rep. 11.

Scope of the arbitration agreement

[Add to note 144, at the end: page [137]]   **32–030**
See also *Yegiazaryan v Smagin* [2016] EWCA Civ 1290, [2017] 1 Lloyd's Rep.
102 at [44]. cf. *Microsoft Mobile Oy (Ltd) v Sony Europe Ltd* [2017] EWHC 374
(Ch), [2017] 5 C.M.L.R. 5 at [43]–[54].

Pre-conditions

[Add to note 151, at the end: page [137]]   **32–035**
See, e.g. *Ruby Roz Agricol LLP v Republic of Kazakhstan* [2017] EWHC 439
(Comm).

Companies

[Add to note 164, at the end: page [139]]   **32–038**
As to a case where there is an issue whether a foreign company has been
dissolved, see *Silver Dry Bulk Co Ltd v Homer Hulbert Maritime Co Ltd* [2017]
EWHC 44 (Comm), [2017] 1 Lloyd's Rep. 154 at [25]–[31].

[Add to paragraph, at the end: page [139]]
If the rights and obligations of a party to the arbitration agreement are transferred
to another company before or at the time of the original party's dissolution, by
a doctrine of universal succession or a similar mechanism, the successor may rely
on and enforce the arbitration agreement.[166a]

[166a] *A v B* [2016] EWHC 3003 (Comm), [2017] 1 W.L.R. 2030.

Assignees

[Add to note 172, at the end: page [140]]   **32–042**
See also *A v B* [2016] EWHC 3003 (Comm), [2017] 1 W.L.R. 2030.

3. STAY OF LEGAL PROCEEDINGS

Foreign proceedings outside the EU

32–053   [*Add to note 214, at the end: page* [144]]
For the view that the jurisdiction resides only in s.37, see *Southport Success SA v Tsingshan Holding Group Co Ltd* [2015] EWHC 1974 (Comm), [2015] 2 Lloyd's Rep. 578.

[*Add to note 219, line 6, after* "[2013] 1 Lloyd's Rep. 285."*: page* [145]]
; *Crescendo Maritime Co v Bank of Communications Co Ltd* [2015] EWHC 3364 (Comm), [2016] 1 Lloyd's Rep. 414. In *ADM Asia-Pacific Trading Pte Ltd v PT Budi Semesta Satria* [2016] EWHC 1427 (Comm) the Court declined to grant an anti-suit injunction because of the delay in making the application. See also *Essar Shipping Ltd v Bank of China Ltd* [2015] EWHC 3266 (Comm), [2016] 1 Lloyd's Rep. 427; *Ecobank Transnational Inc v Tanoh* [2015] EWCA Civ 1309, [2016] 1 W.L.R. 2231 (anti-enforcement injunction).

[*Add to note 219, at the end: page* [145]]
Where a third party seeks to exercise rights under a contract containing an arbitration clause, see *Shipowners' Mutual Protection and Indemnity Association (Luxembourg) v Containerships Denizcilik Nakliyat ve Ticaret AS* [2016] EWCA Civ 386, [2016] 1 Lloyd's Rep. 641.

Mandatory stay

32–067   [*Add to note 264, at the end: page* [153]]
See also *Associated British Ports v Tata Steel UK Ltd* [2017] EWHC 694 (Ch), [2017] 2 Lloyd's Rep. 11 at [20] (the issue in this case was whether the arbitration agreement was void for uncertainty).

[*Add to note 265, at the end: page* [153]]
An arbitration agreement may be inoperative, if it has been abandoned or repudiated or if a party to the agreement is estopped from relying on it: *Costain Ltd v Tarmac Holdings Ltd* [2017] EWHC 319 (TCC), [2017] 1 Lloyd's Rep. 331 at [81]–[127].

[*Add to note 267, at the end: page* [153]]
See also *Associated British Ports v Tata Steel UK Ltd* [2017] EWHC 694 (Ch), [2017] 2 Lloyd's Rep. 11 at [20].

32–068   [*Add to note 270, at the end: page* [154]]
; [2015] EWCA Civ 1171, (2015) 163 Con. L.R. 259 at [31]–[34] (reversing the judge's decision in exercising his discretion to order a stay).

[*Add to paragraph, at the end: page* [154]]
Indeed, the Court has said that referring the issue to the arbitral tribunal would be contrary to s.9.[272a] The Court has held that in order that the Court determine that there is an applicable arbitration agreement in accordance with s.9(1), the Court must be satisfied that such an agreement exists; it is not sufficient for the

applicant to show merely that it has an arguable case that it is a party to an arbitration agreement.[272b] If the respondent to the application for a stay wishes to rely on s.9(4) in order to prevent the stay, the Court must come to a clear conclusion that the agreement is null and void, inoperative or incapable of performance; a mere arguable case to the contrary would not be sufficient for the Court to give effect to the arbitration agreement.[272c]

[272a] *Joint Stock Company "Aeroflot Russian Airlines" v Berezovsky* [2013] EWCA Civ 784, [2013] 2 Lloyd's Rep. 242 at [76]–[79]; *Costain Ltd v Tarmac Holdings Ltd* [2017] EWHC 319 (TCC), [2017] 1 Lloyd's Rep. 331 at [80]; *Microsoft Mobile Oy (Ltd) v Sony Europe Ltd* [2017] EWHC 374 (Ch), [2017] 5 C.M.L.R. 5 at [41] and [82]–[84].
[272b] *Associated British Ports v Tata Steel UK Ltd* [2017] EWHC 694 (Ch), [2017] 2 Lloyd's Rep. 11 at [20].
[272c] *Golden Ocean Group Ltd v Humpuss Intermoda Transportasi TBK Ltd (The Barito)* [2013] EWHC 1240 (Comm); [2013] 2 Lloyd's Rep. 421 at [73].

4. Commencement of Arbitral Proceedings

Power of court to extend time for beginning arbitral proceedings

[*Add to note 304, at the end: page* [158]]   **32–076**
; *Expofrut SA v Melville Services Inc* [2015] EWHC 1950 (Comm) at [12]–[14]

Commencement of arbitral proceedings

[*Add to note 319, at the end: page* [160]]   **32–081**
; *Glencore International AG v PT Tera Logistic Indonesia* [2016] EWHC 82 (Comm), [2016] 1 Lloyd's Rep. 527 (arbitral proceedings were held to have been commenced in respect of counterclaims by reason of the reference to "*claims*" and "*all disputes arising under the contract*" in the arbitration notices).

5. The Arbitral Tribunal

Procedures for appointment when parties do not agree

[*Add to note 328, at the end: page* [161]]   **32–085**
Where there is a failure by one party to appoint an arbitrator and the arbitration agreement provides for the constitution of the arbitral tribunal in default of that appointment, the Court has no power to act under s.18: *Silver Dry Bulk Co Ltd v Homer Hulbert Maritime Co Ltd* [2017] EWHC 44 (Comm), [2017] 1 Lloyd's Rep. 154 at [32]–[33].

Failure of appointment procedure

[*Add to note 342, line 10, after* "[2014] 1 Lloyd's Rep. 217"*: page* [163]]   **32–087**
; *Silver Dry Bulk Co Ltd v Homer Hulbert Maritime Co Ltd* [2017] EWHC 44 (Comm), [2017] 1 Lloyd's Rep. 154 at [25]–[29].

Removal of arbitrator

32–096   [*Add to note 378, line 22, after* "s.68(2)(a) application failed)": *page* [167]]
; *Cofely Ltd v Bingham* [2016] EWHC 240 (Comm); [2016] 2 All E.R. (Comm) 129 at [98]–[116] (arbitrator removed on the ground of apparent bias where 18 per cent of his appointments and 25 per cent of his arbitrator/adjudicator income over the previous three years had come from cases involving the defendant as a party or as a claims consultant and where the Chartered Institute of Arbitrators acceptance of nomination form calls for disclosure of "*any involvement, however remote, with either party over the last five years*"); *W Ltd v M Sdn Bhd* [2016] EWHC 422 (Comm), [2016] 1 Lloyd's Rep. 552 at [27]–[44] (the IBA Guidelines 2014 are of assistance to the Court, but they are not a statement of English law; the Court noted some "*weaknesses*" in the IBA Guidelines 2014).

[*Add to note 378, line 28, after* "above, at [39]": *page* [167]]
; *Cofely Ltd v Bingham* [2016] EWHC 240 (Comm), [2016] 2 All E.R. (Comm) 129 at [72]; *H v L* [2017] EWHC 137 (Comm), [2017] 1 Lloyd's Rep. 553 at [16].

[*Add to note 378, at the end: page* 167]]
As to the validity of a rule in the Arbitrators' Code of Conduct of the International Cotton Association, see *Aldcroft v International Cotton Association Ltd* [2017] EWHC 642 (Comm), [2017] 1 Lloyd's Rep. 635.

6. JURISDICTION OF THE ARBITRAL TRIBUNAL

Tribunal can rule on its own jurisdiction

32–101   [*Add to note 412, at the end: page* [171]]
In *C v D1* [2015] EWHC 2126 (Comm) at [135] the Court said that s.30 is likely to contain an exhaustive definition of jurisdictional matters.

Objection to substantive jurisdiction of tribunal

32–102   [*Add to note 423, line 7, after* "[2005] 1 Lloyd's Rep. 192 at [66]": *page* [172]]
; *Frontier Agriculture Ltd v Bratt Bros* [2015] EWCA Civ 611, [2015] 2 Lloyd's Rep. 500; *A v B* [2016] EWHC 3003 (Comm), [2017] 1 W.L.R. 2030 at [50]–[63].

32–103   [*Add to paragraph, at the end: page* [172]]
By contrast, a party asserting the existence of an arbitration agreement will not be able to seek a declaration from the Court that the arbitration exists other than pursuant to the procedures laid down in the Arbitration Act 1996 (unless the declaration is sought in support of other relief, such as an anti-suit injunction).[429a]

[429a] *HC Trading Malta Ltd v Tradeland Commodities SL* [2016] EWHC 1279 (Comm), [2016] 1 W.L.R. 3120 at [16]–[20], [40].

7. THE ARBITRAL PROCEEDINGS

Peremptory orders

[*Add new note 504a, after* "with that peremptory order." *in line 8: page* [180]]   **32–121**
504a There is no obligation on the arbitral tribunal to exercise these powers: *Enterprise Insurance Co Plc v U-Drive Solutions (Gibraltar) Ltd* [2016] EWHC 1301 (QB) at [47]–[59].

[*Add to note 510, line 1, after* "the parties: s.42(1)": *page* [180]]   **32–122**
; *Pearl Petroleum Co Ltd v Kurdistan Regional Government of Iraq* [2015] EWHC 3361 (Comm), [2016] 4 W.L.R. 2 at [17]–[27].

8. POWERS OF THE COURT

Court powers in support of arbitral proceedings

[*Add to note 520, line 4, after* "production of documents)": *page* [181]]   **32–123**
; *Silver Dry Bulk Co Ltd v Homer Hulbert Maritime Co Ltd* [2017] EWHC 44 (Comm), [2017] 1 Lloyd's Rep. 154 at [39]–[46] (witness summons for production of documents).

[*Add to note 525, line 9, after* "disclosure refused)": *page* [182]]   **32–124**
; *Silver Dry Bulk Co Ltd v Homer Hulbert Maritime Co Ltd* [2017] EWHC 44 (Comm), [2017] 1 Lloyd's Rep. 154 at [47]–[53] (order for letters of request to a foreign court refused).

[*Add to paragraph, at the end: page* [183]]
It has been held that orders under s.44 cannot be made against non-parties to the arbitration agreement.533a

533a *DTEK Trading SA v Morozov* [2017] EWHC 94 (Comm), [2017] 1 Lloyd's Rep. 126.

Power of court to extend time limits

[*Add to note 546, line 5, after* "[2011] 2 Lloyd's Rep. 159": *page* [185]]   **32–129**
; *Xstrata Coal Queensland Pty Ltd v Benxi Iron & Steel (Group) International Economic & Trading Co Ltd* [2016] EWHC 2022 (Comm).

Anti-arbitration injunction

[*Add to note 552, at the end: page* [186]]   **32–130**
; *AmTrust Europe Ltd v Trust Risk Group SpA* [2015] EWHC 1927 (Comm), [2015] 2 Lloyd's Rep. 231.

9. THE AWARD

Correction of award or additional award: the "slip rule"

32–143   [*Add to note 622, at the end: page* [192]]
; *Union Marine Classification Services LLC v Government of the Union of Comoros* [2016] EWCA Civ 239, [2016] 2 Lloyd's Rep. 193.

[*Add to note 624, line 2, after "Naval Gijon SA, above": page* [192]]
; *Xstrata Coal Queensland Pty Ltd v Benxi Iron & Steel (Group) International Economic & Trading Co Ltd* [2016] EWHC 2022 (Comm).

Award as a defence

32–147   [*Add to note 639, at the end: page* [194]]
In *Michael Wilson & Partners Ltd v Sinclair* [2017] EWCA Civ 3, [2017] 1 W.L.R. 2646 the Court of Appeal held that it would be a rare case where legal proceedings against a person who was not a party to an earlier arbitration would be struck out by reason of the award in that earlier arbitration.

10. COSTS OF THE ARBITRATION

Costs

32–148   [*Add to note 643, at the end: page* [194]]
In *Essar Oilfield Services Ltd v Norscot Rig Management Pvt Ltd* [2016] EWHC 2361 (Comm), [2016] 2 Lloyd's Rep. 481 at [68]–[72], the Court held that "*other costs*" in s.59 can include the costs of obtaining litigation funding.

11. POWERS OF THE COURT IN RELATION TO THE AWARD

[*Insert new paragraph 32–155A before para.32–156: page* [197]]

32–155A   **Introduction.** The Court's powers to review an arbitration award are set out in ss.67–69 of the Arbitration Act 1996. An application under ss.67–69 must conform to the requirements of those provisions and the procedural requirements set out in s.70. The mere fact that the parties agree that the Court should hear a challenge or appeal against an award will not confer jurisdiction on the Court unless the requirements of the Act are satisfied.[677a] In order that ss.67–69 may apply, there must have been an "*award*" made by the arbitral tribunal.[677b] An "*award*" is a formal written record of the arbitral tribunal's decision, in an arbitral reference made pursuant to an arbitration agreement,[677c] which disposes of or resolves an issue or dispute between the parties.[677d]

[677a] *Enterprise Insurance Co Plc v U-Drive Solutions (Gibraltar) Ltd* [2016] EWHC 1301 (QB) at [34].

^{677b} In *Enterprise Insurance Co Plc v U-Drive Solutions (Gibraltar) Ltd* [2016] EWHC 1301 (QB) at [39]–[40], [116] the Court held that an order refusing to strike out a claim and an order for security for costs were not *"awards"* for the purposes of ss.68 and 69.
^{677c} s.5 of the Arbitration Act 1996. A decision by the secretariat of the arbitral institution, as opposed to the tribunal, will not be an award unless the arbitral institution's rules provide otherwise.
^{677d} s.52 of the Arbitration Act 1996 makes provision for the form of the award. See above, para.32–139.

Challenging the award: substantive jurisdiction

[*Add to note 682, at the end: page* [197]]   **32–156**
See *Yegiazaryan v Smagin* [2016] EWCA Civ 1290, [2017] 1 Lloyd's Rep. 102 at [27]–[28].

[*Add to note 684, at the end: page* [198]]
; *Emirates Trading Agency LLC v Sociedade de Fomento Industrial Private Ltd* [2015] EWHC 1452 (Comm), [2015] 2 Lloyd's Rep. 487.

[*Add to note 690, at the end: page* [198]]   **32–157**
In *Sino Channel Asia Ltd v Dana Shipping and Trading Pte Singapore* [2016] EWHC 1118 (Comm), [2016] 2 Lloyd's Rep. 97 at [4]–[5], the Court said that there was no time limit applicable to proceedings under s.72 and such an action may be brought after the making of an arbitration award.

[*Add to note 691, line 9, after* "[2014] 1 Lloyd's Rep. 479": *page* [199]]   **32–158**
; *Frontier Agriculture Ltd v Bratt Bros* [2015] EWCA Civ 611, [2015] 2 Lloyd's Rep. 500; *A v B* [2016] EWHC 3003 (Comm), [2017] 1 W.L.R. 2030 at [50]–[63]

Challenging the award: serious irregularity

[*Add to note 706, at the end: page* [200]]   **32–161**
; *Essar Oilfield Services Ltd v Norscot Rig Management Pvt Ltd* [2016] EWHC 2361 (Comm), [2016] 2 Lloyd's Rep. 481 at [8]–[11].

[*Add to note 708, penultimate line, after* "[2015] 1 Lloyd's Rep. 67": *page* [201]]   **32–162**
; *BV Scheepswerf Damen Gorinchem v Marine Institute* [2015] EWHC 1810 (Comm), [2015] 2 Lloyd's Rep. 351; *W Ltd v M Sdn Bhd* [2016] EWHC 422 (Comm), [2016] 1 Lloyd's Rep. 552.

[*Add to note 709, at the end: page* [202]]
; *C v D1* [2015] EWHC 2126 (Comm) at [136]–[147]; *Essar Oilfield Services Ltd v Norscot Rig Management Pvt Ltd* [2016] EWHC 2361 (Comm), [2016] 2 Lloyd's Rep. 481 at [41]–[47]; *PT Transportasi Gas Indonesia v ConocoPhillips (Grissik) Ltd* [2016] EWHC 2834 (Comm), [2016] 2 Lloyd's Rep. 600 at [53]–[56].

[*Add to note 711, at the end: page* [202]]
; *PT Transportasi Gas Indonesia v ConocoPhillips (Grissik) Ltd* [2016] EWHC 2834 (Comm), [2016] 2 Lloyd's Rep. 600 at [57]–[64]; *A v B* [2017] EWHC 596 (Comm), [2017] 2 Lloyd's Rep. 1 at [35]–[39].

[*Add to note 713, at the end: page* [203]]
; *Celtic Bioenergy Ltd v Knowles* [2017] EWHC 472 (TCC), [2017] 1 Lloyd's Rep. 495 (fraud in a party's deliberate failure to draw the tribunal's attention to relevant correspondence). As to relevance of the public policy of a foreign State, see *PT Transportasi Gas Indonesia v ConocoPhillips (Grissik) Ltd* [2016] EWHC 2834 (Comm), [2016] 2 Lloyd's Rep. 600 at [66]–[72].

[*Add to note 715, at the end: page* [203]]
An admission by a member of the tribunal who is in the minority or who dissents would not be sufficient for this purpose: *A v B* [2017] EWHC 596 (Comm), [2017] 2 Lloyd's Rep. 1 at [53]–[56].

32–163   [*Add to note 719, at the end: page* [204]]
; *BV Scheepswerf Damen Gorinchem v Marine Institute* [2015] EWHC 1810 (Comm), [2015] 2 Lloyd's Rep. 351.

[*Add to note 722, at the end: page* [205]]
Maass v Musion Events Ltd [2015] EWHC 1346 (Comm), [2015] 2 Lloyd's Rep. 383 at [40]–[42]

32–164   [*Add to note 727, at the end: page* [205]]
See also *Essar Oilfield Services Ltd v Norscot Rig Management Pvt Ltd* [2016] EWHC 2361 (Comm), [2016] 2 Lloyd's Rep. 481 at [78]–[85].

Appeal on point of law

32–167   [*Add to note 738, line 3, after* "(consent in advance).": *page* [207]]
cf. *ST Shipping and Transport Pte Ltd v Space Shipping Ltd* [2016] EWHC 880 (Comm), [2016] 2 Lloyd's Rep. 17.

32–169   [*Add to note 757, at the end: page* [210]]
There is no reason why the judge who granted permission to appeal on a point of law cannot hear the substantive appeal: *L v A* [2016] EWHC 1789 (Comm) at [4]–[8].

Challenge or appeal: restrictions and time limits

32–175   [*Add to note 778, line 8, before the final sentence: page* [212]]
In *Essar Oilfield Services Ltd v Norscot Rig Management Pvt Ltd* [2016] EWHC 2361 (Comm), [2016] 2 Lloyd's Rep. 481 at [90]–[93] the Court held that if the award is corrected pursuant to s.57, the 28 day time period runs from the date of the corrected award, provided that the application to correct is material to the issue being raised by the application to the Court. An application is material if it is necessary to enable the party to know whether he or she has grounds to challenge the award or not. It is unclear when time would start running if the application to correct the award is refused. See also *K v S* [2015] EWHC 1945 (Comm), [2015] 2 Lloyd's Rep. 363.

[*Add to note 780, at the end: page* [213]]
In *S v A* [2016] EWHC 846 (Comm), [2016] 1 Lloyd's Rep. 604, at [26], the Court applied the test laid down in *Terna Bahrain Holding Company WLL v Al*

Shamsi, because it was common ground that it should do so, but questioned whether such a test should continue to apply in light of the Court's more recent decision in *Denton v TH White Ltd* [2014] EWCA Civ 906, [2014] 1 W.L.R. 3926.

[Add to note 782, at the end: page [213]]   **32–176**
; *Essar Oilfield Services Ltd v Norscot Rig Management Pvt Ltd* [2016] EWHC 2361 (Comm), [2016] 2 Lloyd's Rep. 481 at [78]–[85].

[Update note 783: page [213]]
Frontier Agriculture Ltd v Bratt Bros [2015] EWCA Civ 611 is reported at [2015] 2 Lloyd's Rep. 500

[Add to note 783, at the end: page [213]]
; *A v B* [2016] EWHC 3003 (Comm), [2017] 1 W.L.R. 2030 at [50]–[63].

Challenge or appeal: supplementary orders

[Add to note 786, at the end: page [214]]   **32–177**
; *Erdenet Mining Corp LLC v ICBC Standard Bank Plc* [2017] EWHC 1090 (Comm), [2017] 2 Lloyd's Rep. 25.

Challenge or appeal: appeals to the Court of Appeal

[Add to note 796, penultimate line, after "[2007] 2 Lloyd's Rep. 548"*: page [215]]*   **32–181**
; *Integral Petroleum Ltd v Melars Group Ltd* [2016] EWCA Civ 108, [2016] 2 Lloyd's Rep. 141.

[Add to note 808, at the end: page [216]]   **32–184**
In *Michael Wilson & Partners Ltd v Emmott* [2015] EWCA Civ 1285, [2016] 1 W.L.R. 857 the Court explained the nature of the Court's jurisdiction. See also *Integral Petroleum Ltd v Melars Group Ltd* [2016] EWCA Civ 108, [2016] 2 Lloyd's Rep. 141 at [25]–[31].

[Add to note 809, at the end: page [216]]
See also *Yegiazaryan v Smagin* [2016] EWCA Civ 1290, [2017] 1 Lloyd's Rep. 102 at [26].

Foreign awards

[Add to note 843, line 8, after "CPR r.62.18."*: page [219]]*   **32–189**
In *Pencil Hill Ltd v US Citta Di Palermo SpA* Unreported, January 19, 2016 at [30], the Court said that there is a strong leaning towards the enforcement of foreign arbitral awards and the circumstances in which the English Court may refuse enforcement are narrow. In this case, the Court allowed the enforcement of an award which included a penalty.

[Add to note 848, at the end: page [219]]
See also *LR Avionics Technologies Ltd v Federal Republic of Nigeria* [2016] EWHC 1761 (Comm), [2016] 4 W.L.R. 120 at [24]–[27].

[*In note 850, lines 24–25 and 35–36, delete* "[2014] EWHC 576 (Comm), [2014] 1
Lloyd's Rep. 625" *(both instances) and substitute: page* [220]]
[2015] EWCA Civ 1144, [2016] 1 Lloyd's Rep. 5; [2015] EWCA Civ 1145,
[2016] 1 Lloyd's Rep. 36 (supplementary judgment)

[*Add to note 850, line 28, after* "[2015] 1 Lloyd's Rep. 423": *page* [220]]
; *Sinocore International Co Ltd v RBRG Trading (UK) Ltd* [2017] EWHC 251
(Comm), [2017] 1 Lloyd's Rep. 375; *Stati v Republic of Kazakhstan* [2017]
EWHC 1348 (Comm).

[*Add to note 850, at the end: page* [220]]
In *IPCO (Nigeria) Ltd v Nigerian National Petroleum Corp* [2017] UKSC 16,
[2017] 1 W.L.R. 970 the Supreme Court held that there was nothing in s.103(2)
or (3) which provided that an enforcing court could make the decision of an issue
raised under that subsection conditional on the provision of security in respect of
the award (unlike s.103(5)).

32–191   [*Add to note 853, line 6, after* "[2014] 1 All E.R. (Comm) 942": *page* [221]]
; *Gold Reserve Inc v Bolivarian Republic of Venezuela* [2016] EWHC 153
(Comm), [2016] 1 W.L.R. 2829; *LR Avionics Technologies Ltd v Federal Repub-
lic of Nigeria* [2016] EWHC 1761 (Comm), [2016] 4 W.L.R. 120.

[*Add to note 853, at the end: page* [221]]:See above para.12–021.

12. MISCELLANEOUS

Adjudication

32–199   [*Add to note 880, at the end: page* [224]]
In *RMC Building & Civil Engineering Ltd v UK Construction Ltd* [2016] EWHC
241 (TCC), [2016] B.L.R. 264 at [56], the Court said that the provisions
introduced by the 1996 Act and the Scheme are all about maintaining cash
flow.

CHAPTER 33

BAILMENT

2. POSSESSION AND RELATED MATTERS

Conversion of the chattel by the bailee

[*Add to note 75, line 4, after* "(2002) 118 L.Q.R. 544)": *page* [236]]   **33–014**
; *Sang Stone Hamoon Jonoub Co Ltd v Baoyue Shipping Co Ltd (The Bao Yue)*
[2015] EWHC 2288 (Comm), [2016] 1 Lloyd's Rep. 320 (although goods may
be converted by a person who creates a lien without the authority of the owner,
an owner who authorises a bailee to deliver goods into storage must be taken to
authorise the creation of a lien where that is a reasonable and foreseeable incident
of the storage contract which the bailee is authorised to conclude).

3. Gratuitous Bailment

(a) Deposit

Deposit

33–032   [*Add to note 159, line 2, after "Chief Constable of West Yorkshire,* above"*: page* [246]]
; *Pennington v De Wan* [2017] EWHC 4 (Ch) at [22].

4. Bailments for Valuable Consideration

(b) Custody for Reward

(i) In General

Custody for reward

33–049   [*Add to note 261, at the end: page* [255]]
; *Rana v Tears of Sutton Bridge* [2015] EWHC 2597 (QB).

The onus of proof and the scope of the duty

33–050   [*Add to note 269, at the end: page* [256]]
and *Rana v Tears of Sutton Bridge* [2015] EWHC 2597 (QB).

(f) Pledge

(i) Pledge at Common Law

Delivery essential for pledge

33–123   [*Add to note 766, at the end: page* [297]]
However, the delivery of a pin code may not suffice to constitute delivery: *MSC Mediterranean Shipping Co SA v Glencore International AG* [2017] EWCA Civ 365 at [25]–[42].

[*Add to note 768, line 1, after* "[1935] A.C. 53, 58–59"*: page* [297]]
; *Impala Warehousing and Logistics (Shanghai) Co Ltd v Wanxiang Resources (Singapore) Pte Ltd* [2015] EWHC 811 (Comm), [2015] 2 All E.R. (Comm) 234 at [54]–[59].

CHAPTER 34

BILLS OF EXCHANGE AND BANKING

1. Negotiable Instruments

(a) *The Nature of Negotiable Instruments*

Promissory notes

34–004 *[Add to note 12, at the beginning: page [312]]*
See, e.g. *Banque Cantonale de Genève v Sanomi* [2016] EWHC 3353 (Comm), where two promissory notes, payable on demand, were used as security for short-term trade finance ("they played the same functional role as guarantees": at [61]).

(b) *Bills of Exchange*

(i) *Definitions and Requirements*

Unconditional order in writing

34–010 *[Add to note 40, at the end: page [316]]*
In *Banque Cantonale de Genève v Sanomi* [2016] EWHC 3353 (Comm), where there were two promissory notes payable on demand, Blair J. (at [32]–[36]), having been referred to the requirement in s.83(1) of the Act that a promissory note must be in writing (the same requirement is found in s.3(1) of the Act for bills of exchange), held that there is a principle (admittedly, of uncertain scope) to the effect that oral evidence is not admissible to contradict the terms of the written instrument (in this case, the maker of the promissory notes alleged that immediately prior to him signing the notes a representative of the promisee bank had told him that the bank would make no demand under the notes).

[Add to note 41, line 10, after "December 2001, para.9.5": page [316]]
; cf. Practice Note on Execution of Documents Using an Electronic Signature (July 21, 2016) issued by a joint working party of the Law Society Company Law Committee and the City of London Law Society Company Law and Financial Law Committees, which suggests (at para.4.2) that an "electronic" promissory

note can be "in writing" and "signed by the maker" for the purposes of s.83(1) of the Bills of Exchange Act 1882 (but without any mention of bills of exchange)

Destruction of negotiability

[Add to note 117, at the end: page [325]]   **34–026**
See, e.g. *Banque Cantonale de Genève v Sanomi* [2016] EWHC 3353 (Comm) at [29] (a promissory note case).

Authorised delivery

[Add to note 147, at the end: page [328]]   **34–034**
; applied in *Banque Cantonale de Genève v Sanomi* [2016] EWHC 3353 (Comm) at [36] (discussed further in n.40 above, and n.587a below).

(ii) *Capacity and Authority of Parties*

Sufficient signature

[Add to note 172, at the end: page [332]]   **34–042**
See also Practice Note on Execution of Documents Using an Electronic Signature (July 21, 2016) issued by a joint working party of the Law Society Company Law Committee and the City of London Law Society Company Law and Financial Law Committees which, inter alia, considers Regulation (EU) No.910/2014 (the eIDAS Regulation) that has direct effect in EU Member States from July 1, 2016 (and see above, para.34–010, n.41).

(iii) *The Consideration for a Bill*

Need to move from promisee

[Add to note 221, at the end: page [340]]   **34–061**
See also *Banque Cantonale de Genève v Sanomi* [2016] EWHC 3353 (Comm) at [47], a promissory note case, where the promisee bank did not rely on s.27(1)(b) because the prior indebtedness owed to the bank at the time the notes were made was that of a third party company (of which the maker of the notes was the founder). However, Blair J. went on to hold (at 48]–[62]) that the promisee bank had provided consideration for the notes by promising and actually forbearing to sue the third party as part of a short-term trade finance transaction.

(iv) *Transfer of Bills*

Negotiation of a bill

[Add to note 290, line 1, after "s.31(2).": page [352]]   **34–085**
"Delivery" is defined in s.2 as the "transfer of possession, actual or constructive, from one person to another". Contrast the narrower definition of delivery in

s.61(1) of the Sale of Goods Act 1979: "*voluntary* transfer of possession from one person to another . . . ".

Rights of mere holder

34–094   [*Add to note 333, at the end: page* [357]]
, distinguished in *Cassa di Risparmio di Parma e Piacenza SpA v Rals International Pte Ltd* [2015] SGHC 264.

(vii) *Discharge of Bill*

Attempt to reconcile

34–129   [*Add to note 445, at the end: page* [375]]
For a recent example of Goff J.'s exception (2)(a), see *Leslie v Farrar Construction Ltd* [2016] EWCA Civ 1041 at [51]–[56].

Assessment

34–134   [*Add to note 457, line 24, after* "commercially unacceptable conduct)"*: page* [378]]
; *T & L Sugars Ltd v Tate & Lyle Industries Ltd* [2015] EWHC 2696 (Comm) at [137] (on anticipatory reliance); *Dexia Crediop SpA v Comune di Prato* [2016] EWHC 2824 (Comm) at [75] (on need for "but for" causal connection between the receipt and any change of position)—but see also [2017] EWCA Civ 428, where the Court of Appeal reversed an earlier, related judgment on a key conflict of law issue in this case, and also held (at [213]) that there was no basis for restitutionary claims by either party

Tracing order

34–135   [*Add to note 461, line 6, after* "[1997] Q.B. 85"*: page* [379]]
; *FHR European Ventures LLP v Mankarious* [2016] EWHC 359 (Ch); *Bainbridge v Bainbridge* [2016] EWHC 898 (Ch)

(d) *Promissory Notes*

Application of provisions regarding bills of exchange to promissory notes

34–182   [*Add new note 587a, line 3, after* " to promissory notes."*: page* [398]]
      [587a] See, e.g. *Banque Cantonale de Genève v Sanomi* [2016] EWHC 3353 (Comm), where Blair J., applying s.8(1) of the Act, held (at [29]) that the promissory notes in question were negotiable because they lacked any words prohibiting transfer or indicating an intention that they should not be transferable and that, in any event, a promissory note which is not negotiable is valid between the parties. Blair J. also (i) applied (at [31]) the well-established principle in English law that the holder of bills and notes is usually entitled to summary judgment because, in principle, a bill or note is to be treated as cash; (ii) held (at [32]–[36]), having been referred to the requirement in s.83(1) of the Act that a promissory note must be in writing, that there is a principle (admittedly, of uncertain scope) to the effect that oral evidence is not admissible to contradict the terms of the written instrument; and

(iii) held (at [46]–[62]) that the promisee bank in the present case had provided consideration to support the maker's promise on the notes in question by promising and actually forbearing to sue a third party company (of which the maker of the notes was the founder) for its existing indebtedness owed to the bank.

2. ASPECTS OF BANKING LAW

(a) *Bank Regulation*

(i) *Overview*

Financial Services Act 2012

[Add to note 650, penultimate line, after "2014/3329)": page [410]]   **34–216**
; see also SI 2014/3348 and SI 2016/1239

The Prudential Regulation Authority (PRA) and the Financial Conduct Authority (FCA)

[In note 654, line 1, delete "is set to replace" and substitute: page [410]]   **34–217**
has now replaced

Banking Conduct of Business Sourcebook (BCOBS)

[Add to note 656, at the end: page [411]]   **34–219**
The Revised Payment Services Directive 2015/2366/EU ("PSD2") repeals and replaces Directive 2007/64/EC. EU Member States have until January 13, 2018 to implement the requirements of PSD2. The Payment Services Regulations 2017 (SI 2017/752) ("PSRs 2017"), implement in part PSD2 in the UK. The PSRs 2017 revoke and replace the Payment Services Regulations 2009. With certain exceptions as set out in reg.1, which include where the implementation period is linked to the coming into force of the secure communication and authentication requirements adopted under art.98 of PSD2, the PSRs 2017 come into force on January 13, 2018 (PSRs 2017 reg.1(6)). See, generally, para.34–223, n.676 below.

[In note 660, line 2, delete "with the current revision published in October 2014" and substitute: page [411]]
with revisions published in October 2014 and September 2015

[Add to note 660, at the end: page [411]]
On July 21, 2016, the Lending Standards Board published a new Standards of Lending Practice for Personal Customers, which come into force on October 1, 2016. The Standards of Lending Practice will replace the Lending Code. The Standards of Lending Practice apply to personal customers and cover loans, credit cards and current account overdrafts. The new Standards represent a move away from the Lending Code, which was focused more on compliance with provisions than customer outcomes. It is anticipated that new standards for

business lending, which will include small and medium-sized businesses (SMEs), will be published in 2017. In the interim the existing protections of the Lending Code will continue to apply to micro-enterprises (Standards of Lending Practice, p.3).

The new Standards of Lending Practice for Business Customers were published on March 28, 2017 and became effective on July 1, 2017. They replace the micro-enterprise provisions of the Lending Code. The protections of the new Standards of Lending Practice for Business Customers apply to businesses/organisations, which at the point of lending (a) have an annual turnover of up to £6.5 million and (b) do not have a complex ownership structure (e.g. businesses with overseas, multiple, or layered ownership structures).

34–220   [*Add new note 662a, line 6, after* "Regulations 2009 apply.".: *page* [412]]
662a Revised versions of Pts 5 and 6 of the Payment Services Regulations 2009 are to be found in Pts 6 and 7 of the Payment Services Regulations 2017. See, generally, n.676 to para.34–223 below.

[*Add new note 662b, line 9, after* "Regulations 2009 apply.".: *page* [412]]
662b Revised versions of Pts 5 and 6 of the Payment Services Regulations 2009 are to be found in Pts 6 and 7 of the Payment Services Regulations 2017. See, generally, n.676 to para.34–223 below.

34–221   [*Add to note 672, line 5, after* "[2014] EWHC 2882 (QB) at [44]".: *page* [412]]
; *Thornbridge Ltd v Barclays Bank Plc* [2015] EWHC 3430 (QB) at [138]–[141]

[*Add to note 672, at the end: page* [412]]
In *Sivagnanam v Barclays Bank Plc* [2015] EWHC 3985 (Comm), it was held (at [8]–[15]) that the claimant, the sole director/shareholder of a company that entered into an interest rate hedging product with the defendant bank, could not bring a claim for loss said to have been suffered as a private person as a result of breach of the conduct of business rules under FSMA 2000 s.138D(2), as he did not fall within the category of person intended to be protected by the FSMA 2000 or the relevant conduct of business rules. It was also held (at [16]–[21]) that his loss, as a shareholder, was irrecoverable due to the rule against reflective loss.

The Lending Code

34–222   [*In note 673, line 2, delete* "with the current revision published in October 2014" *and substitute: page* [413]]
with revisions published in October 2014 and September 2015

[*Add to note 673, at the end: page* [413]]
On July 21, 2016, the Lending Standards Board published a new Standards of Lending Practice for Personal Customers, which come into force on October 1, 2016. The Standards of Lending Practice will replace the Lending Code. The Standards of Lending Practice apply to personal customers and cover loans, credit cards and current account overdrafts. The new Standards represent a move away from the Lending Code, which was focused more on compliance with provisions than customer outcomes. It is anticipated that new standards for business lending, which will include small and medium-sized businesses (SMEs), will be published in 2017. In the interim the existing protections of the

Lending Code will continue to apply to micro-enterprises (Standards of Lending Practice, p.3).

The new Standards of Lending Practice for Business Customers were published on March 28, 2017 and became effective on July 1, 2017. They replace the micro-enterprise provisions of the Lending Code. The protections of the new Standards of Lending Practice for Business Customers apply to businesses/ organisations, which at the point of lending (a) have an annual turnover of up to £6.5 million and (b) do not have a complex ownership structure (e.g. businesses with overseas, multiple, or layered ownership structures).

[In note 674 delete "2nd edn" and substitute: page [413]]
September 28, 2015

Payment Services Regulations

[In note 676, delete from "On July 24, 2013 . . . " in line 2 to the end and   **34–223**
substitute: page [413]]
The Revised Payment Services Directive 2015/2366/EU ("PSD2") repeals and replaces Directive 2007/64/EC. EU Member States have until January 13, 2018 to implement the requirements of PSD2 (see J Chertow, J. Patient and V. Montgomery, "New Payment Services Regime: Preparing for a Revised Landscape" [2016] PLC (August) 21). The Payment Services Regulations 2017, SI 2017/752 ("PSRs 2017"), implement in part PSD2 in the UK. The PSRs 2017 revoke and replace the Payment Services Regulations 2009 ("PSRs 2009"). With certain exceptions as set out in reg.1, which include where the implementation period is linked to the coming into force of the secure communication and authentication requirements adopted under art.98 of PSD2, the PSRs 2017 come into force on January 13, 2018 (PSRs 2017, reg.1(6)).

The PSRs 2017 build on the PSRs 2009. The main differences between them, which relate to matters considered in this section of *Chitty*, include the following:

(1) The PSRs 2017 are of wider scope than the PSRs 2009. Pts 5 and 6 of the PSRs 2009, with some exceptions, only apply if the payment service providers of both the payer and the payee are within the EEA, and the transaction is in euro, sterling or another non-euro Member State currency. This changes with the PSRs 2017. So long as the payment services are provided from an establishment maintained by a service provider or its agent in the UK (PSRs 2017 regs 40(1)(a), 63(1)(a)), Pts 6 (informational requirements) and 7 (rights and obligations) of the PSRs 2017 extend, with some exceptions, to services relating to transactions in non-EEA currencies where both the payer and the payee are located in EEA countries (PSRs 2017 regs 40(1)(b)(ii), 63(1)(b)(ii)), and to services relating to transactions where the payment service provider of either the payer or the payee, but not both, is in the EEA (PSRs 2017 regs 40(1)(b)(iii), 63(1)(b)(iii)). Where the payment service relates to a transaction in a non-EEA currency and both payer and payee are located in the EEA (i.e. it falls within PSRs 2017 regs 40(1)(b)(ii), 63(1)(b)(ii)), or one of the payment service providers is not in the EEA (i.e. it falls within

PSRs 2017 regs 40(1)(b)(iii), 63(1)(b)(iii)), Pts 6 and 7 apply only in respect of those parts of the transaction which are carried out in the EEA (PSRs 2017 regs 40(2)(a),(3)(a), 63(2)(a), (3)(a)). Payment service providers are still able to opt out of all the informational requirements in Pt 6, and certain conduct requirements in Pt 7, when dealing with business customers, unless they are "micro-enterprises" (PSRs 2017 regs 40(7), 63(5)).

(2) The PSRs 2017 retain most of the exemptions contained in the PSRs 2009. For example, cheques and other paper-based transactions are outside the scope of the new regulations (PSRs 2017 Sch.1 Pt 2(g)), as are payment transactions contained within a payment or a securities settlement system (PSRs 2017 Sch.1 Pt 2(h)). A number of the exemptions have been clarified, such as where specific payment instruments can only be used in a limited way (PSRs 2017 Sch.1 Pt 2(k)), and where providers of electronic communication networks provide additional services and those services are the purchase of digital content and voice-based services, or the purchase of tickets and donations to charities, within certain monetary limits (PSRs 2017 Sch.1 Pt 2(l)).

(3) The PSRs 2017 cover the activities of "payment initiation services" and "account information services" (PSRs 2017 Sch.1 Pt 1(g), (h)). A payment initiation service is an online service to initiate a payment order at the request of the payment service user with respect to a payment account held at another payment service provider (PSRs 2017 reg.2). An account information service is an online service to provide consolidated information on one or more payment accounts held by a payment service user with another payment service provider or with more than one payment service provider, and includes such a service whether the information is provided (a) in its original form or after processing; and (b) only to the payment service user or to the payment service user and to another person in accordance with the payment service user's instructions (PSRs 2017 reg.2). This would cover account aggregation services which provide customers with a consolidated view of their bank accounts and enable them to access their accounts online. The PSRs 2017 allow for access to payment accounts which are accessible online by payment initiation service providers (reg.69) and by account information services (reg.70), although access may be denied by an account servicing payment service provider (i.e. a payment service provider providing and maintaining a payment account for a payer) in certain circumstances (i.e. "reasonably justified and duly evidenced reasons relating to unauthorised or fraudulent access to the payment account") (reg.71(7)–(10)).

(4) The PSRs 2017 introduce changes to the way payment service providers authenticate payments. Save for exceptions permitted by the European Banking Authority (EBA), PSD2 requires all payment service providers to use "strong customer authentication" when a payer: (a) accesses a payment account online, (b) initiates an electronic payment transaction, and (c) carries out any action through a remote channel that may imply a risk of payment fraud or other abuses (art.97(1)). In addition, where a payer initiates an electronic remote payment transaction, payment service

providers must apply strong customer authentication that includes elements which dynamically link the transaction to a specific amount and a specific payee (art.97(2)). Strong customer authentication means authentication based on two or more elements categorised as knowledge (i.e. something only the user knows, e.g. a password, code or PIN), possession (i.e. something only the user possesses, e.g. a token, smartcard or mobile phone) and inherence (i.e. something the user is, e.g. a biometric characteristic like a fingerprint or retina scan) that are independent in that breach of one does not compromise the reliability of the others (PSD2 art.4(30); PSRs 2017 reg.2). PSD2 mandates the EBA, in close co-operation with the European Central Bank, with development of regulatory technical standards, including those for strong customer authentication (art.98). This means that regs 68(3)(c), 69(2)(a) and (3)(d), 70(2)(a) and (3)(c) and (6) and 100 of PSRs 2017 (which deal with secure communication and authentication) only come into force 18 months after the date on which the EBA's regulatory technical standards, as adopted by the European Commission, come into force (PSRs 2017 reg.1(6)).

The PSRs 2017 contain similar (but not identical) conduct of business requirements to those found in Pts 5 and 6 of the PSRs 2009: Pt 6 of the PSRs 2017 sets out information requirements for payment services, and Pt 7 of the PSRs 2017 sets out rights and obligations in relation to payment services. Like reg.120 of the PSRs 2009, reg.148 of the PSRs 2017 makes any breach of the requirements of Pts 6 or 7 actionable by a "private person" who suffers loss as a result of the contravention, subject to defences and other incidents applying to actions for breach of statutory duty. However, and new to the PSRs 2017, it is provided, in reg.148(4), that where there is a contravention of a requirement under regs 76(5)(b), 77(6), 93(4) or 95 for a payment service provider to compensate another service provider, the payment service provider to which compensation is required to be paid is to be treated for the purposes of reg.148 as if it were a "private person".

[*Insert new note 682a, line 3, after* "of particular transactions.": *page* [414]]   **34–225**
682a See *BAWAG PSK Bank für Arbeit und Wirtschaft und Österreichische Postsparkasse AG v Verein für Konsumenteninformation* (C-375/15) January 25, 2017, EU:C:2017:38 CJEU for meaning of requirement that payment service provider must "provide" information on a "durable medium" for purposes of arts 36(1) and 41(1) of the Payment Services Directive 2007/64/EC. See also Revised Payment Services Directive 2015/2366/EU arts 44(1) and 54(1).

(iii) *EU Harmonisation Measures*

Single payment market

[*Delete text of note 732 and substitute: page* [420]]   **34–243**
The Revised Payment Services Directive 2015/2366/EU ("PSD2") repeals and replaces Directive 2007/64/EC. EU Member States have until January 13, 2018 to implement the requirements of PSD2. The Payment Services Regulations 2017 (SI 2017/752) ("PSRs 2017"), implement in part PSD2 in the UK. The Payment Services Regulations 2017 revoke and replace the Payment Services Regulations 2009. With certain exceptions as set out in reg.1, which include where the

implementation period is linked to the coming into force of the secure communication and authentication requirements adopted under art.98 of PSD2, the PSRs
2017 come into force on January 13, 2018 (PSRs 2017 reg.1(6)). See, generally,
para.34–223, n.676 above.

(b) *The Relationship of Banker and Customer*

(i) *Definition of a Bank*

Who is a banker: scope of problem

34–245   [*Add to note 738, at the end: page* [421]]
But the term "bank" has not been excised entirely from the "UK regulatory
lexicon", see D.A. Sabalot (2016) 11 J.I.B.F.L. 631.

(ii) *Definition of a Customer*

Account in nominee's name

34–252   [*Add to note 755, at the end: page* [425]]
EU Member States had to implement the Fourth Money Laundering Directive
2015/849/EU by June 26, 2017. The UK did this through the Money Laundering,
Terrorist Financing and Transfer of Funds (Information on the Payer) Regulations 2017 (SI 2017/692), which replace the Money Laundering Regulations
2007 (SI 2007/ 2157) and the Transfer of Funds (Information on the Payer)
Regulations 2007 (SI 2007/ 3298). The new regime places increased emphasis on
a risk-based approach to combating money laundering terrorist financing, and
includes (inter alia) enhanced due diligence for certain types of customers (e.g.
politically exposed persons and correspondent relationships) and increased
emphasis on beneficial ownership of funds.

(iv) *Fiduciary Relationship and Duty of Care*

Limitations of general principle defined

34–257   [*In note 766, line 4, delete* "2nd edn (2014)" *and substitute: page* [428]]
September 28, 2015

[*Add to note 766, at the end: page* [428]]
See also the *Standards of Lending Practice* (above, para.34–222, n.673) at pp.4
(Principles for lending), 6 (Product sale) and 8 (Money Management).

Effect of contractual documents on duty of care

34–260   [*Add to note 778, line 23, after* "a form of estoppel at all)": *page* [431]]
; *Thornbridge Ltd v Barclays Bank Plc* [2015] EWHC 3430 (QB) at [111]

[*Add to note 778, line 30, after* "[2015] EWHC 871 (Comm) at [120]": *page* [431]]
; reversed on appeal [2016] EWCA Civ 1262, where Court of Appeal held at [19]–[20] that a non-contractual "duty-negating" clause fell outside s.3 of the Misrepresentation Act 1967 because it was found in the very document that was said to contain the misrepresentation.

[*Add to note 778, five lines from the end, after* "[2012] 1 B.C.L.C. 317 at [54]": *page* [432]]
; *Thornbridge Ltd v Barclays Bank Plc* [2015] EWHC 3430 (QB) at [96]; *Finch v Lloyds TSB Bank Plc* [2016] EWHC 1236 (QB) at [52]–[58]

[*Add to note 779, line 21, after* "at [115]–[117], [119]–[121]": *page* [432]]
; *Thornbridge Ltd v Barclays Bank Plc* [2015] EWHC 3430 (QB) at [97]–[121] (HH Judge Moulder, sitting as a judge of the High Court, said "the test is not whether the clause attempts to rewrite history or parts company with reality. The first step is to determine as a matter of construction whether the terms define the basis upon which the parties were transacting business or whether they were clauses inserted as a means of evading liability" [105]); *Sears v Minco Plc* [2016] EWHC 433 (Ch) at [74]–[84] (HH Judge Hodge, sitting as a judge of the High Court, said "I respectfully agree with Judge Moulder's analysis and conclusions [in *Thornbridge*]": at [80]); *Taberna Europe CDO II Plc v Selskabet AF 1 September 2008 A/S (formerly Roskilde Bank A/S) (In Bankruptcy)* [2016] EWCA Civ 1262, where Court of Appeal held at [19]–[20] that a non-contractual "duty-negating" (i.e. basis) clause fell outside s.3 of the Misrepresentation Act 1967 because it was found in the very document that was said to contain the misrepresentation.

(v) *Banks and Undue Influence*

Undue influence and suretyship transactions

[*Add to note 792, at the end: page* [433]]   **34–262**
; *Libyan Investment Authority v Goldman Sachs International* [2016] EWHC 2530 (Ch) illustrates just how hard it is for a claim based on undue influence (or unconscionable bargain) to succeed where commercial parties transact with each other and each side can be expected to negotiate their own terms without regard to the other side's interests.

O'Brien guidelines in practice

[*In note 807, line 5, delete* "2nd edn (2014)" *and substitute: page* [436]]   **34–268**
September 28, 2015

[*Add to note 807, at the end: page* [436]]
See the *Standards of Lending Practice for Personal Customers* (above, para.34–222, n.673) at pp.7 (Account maintenance and servicing) and 11 (Customer vulnerability).
See also the *Standards of Lending Practice for Business Customers* (above, para.34–222, n.673) at pp.6–7 (Product sale):

"13. If an individual or a business agrees to be a guarantor or to provide an indemnity, the Firm should make the individual/business aware of their obligations under the agreement and that they have the option to seek legal advice, should they wish to do so.
14. Firms should not accept unlimited guarantees from an individual/business unless it is to support a customer's liabilities under a merchant agreement; however other forms of unlimited third party security may be taken, if available."

and also at pp.9–10 (Product execution):

"6. Firms should ensure that where an individual provides a guarantee/indemnity or other security, they are able to request information regarding their current level of liability, as long as the customer gives their permission and confidentiality is not breached."

as well as the section on "vulnerability" (pp.14–15).

Relationship between surety and debtor

34–271   [*In note 814, update reference to Treitel on The Law of Contract to: page* [437]]
14th edn (2015), paras 10–026 and 10–039

[*Add to note 818, at the end: page* [438]]
But the *O'Brien* principle only applies to suretyship transactions, i.e. tripartite transactions as described by Lord Nicholls in *Etridge* at [43]: *Chancery Client Partners Ltd v MRC 957 Ltd* [2016] EWHC 2142 (Ch) at [28]–[29].

Nature of the transaction

34–272   [*Add to note 819, line 2, after* "loan to mother and son)"*: page* [438]]
; *Bradley v Governor of the Bank of Ireland* [2016] NICh 11 (joint loan to mother and son)

[*Add to note 821, at the end: page* [438]]
For loan made to family partnership, see *O'Neill v Ulster Bank Ltd* [2015] NICA 64, [2016] B.P.I.R. 126 at [17] (arguable that situation analogous to where wife stands surety for loan made to company in which she is a shareholder).

Future transactions

34–274   [*In note 832, line 1, delete* "2nd edn (2014)" *and substitute: page* [440]]
September 28, 2015

[*Add to note 832, at the end: page* [440]]
See the *Standards of Lending Practice for Personal Customers* (above, para.34–222, n.673) at p.7 (Account maintenance and servicing).
   See also the *Standards of Lending Practice for Business Customers* (above, para.34–222, n.673) at pp.9–10 (Product execution), point 6: see para.34–268, n.807 above.

(vi) *Banks as Constructive Trustees*

(ii) Misfeasance or other breach of trust

[*Add to note 885a, at the end: page* [448]]   34–288
See also *Schenk v Cook* [2017] EWHC 144 (QB) at [85].

(iv) Dishonesty

[*Add to note 892, at the end: page* [449]]   34–291
Recklessness is not equivalent to dishonesty but it can be a sign of dishonesty:
see Lord Nicholls at 389–391, as interpreted by Lewison L.J. in *Clydesdale Bank
Plc v Workman* [2016] EWCA Civ 73, [2016] P.N.L.R. 18 at [48]–[53].

Lord Nicholls said that "[c]arelessness is not dishonesty" (above). This is also
reflected in the recent statement of Rose J. in *Singularis Holdings Ltd (In
Liquidation) v Daiwa Capital Markets Europe Ltd* [2017] EWHC 257 (Ch) at
[147]: "There is an important difference between being incompetent—even
grossly incompetent—and being dishonest".

Knowing receipt

[*Add to note 908, at the beginning: page* [453]]   34–297
Arthur v Att-Gen of the Turks and Caicos Islands [2012] UKPC 30 at [37].

Unconscionability as the test of liability

[*Add to note 923, at the end: page* [456]]   34–306
; and, following agreement of the parties, by the Privy Council in *Arthur v Att-
Gen of the Turks and Caicos Islands* [2012] UKPC 30 at [33]–[36] (stressing the
difference between proprietary and personal remedies)

[*Add to note 929, at the end: page* [457]]   34–307
In *Arthur v Att-Gen of the Turks and Caicos Islands* [2012] UKPC 30 at [40], Sir
Terence Etherton, delivering the advice of the Privy Council, said "Knowing
receipt in the *Akindele* sense is . . . not merely absence of notice but unconscionable conduct amounting to equitable fraud. It is a classic example of lack of *bona
fides*".

Strict liability

[*Add to note 933, at the end: page* [458]]   34–308
, and see also D. Salmons [2017] C.L.J. 399.

(vii) *Duty of Secrecy*

Duty of secrecy

[*In note 937, line 9, delete* "2nd edn (2014)" *and substitute: page* [459]]   34–310
September 28, 2015

[*Add to note 937, line 10, after* "treated as private and confidential)"*: page* [459]]
; the *Standards of Lending Practice for Personal Customers* (above, para.34–222, n.673) at pp.7 (Account maintenance and servicing: "Firms will maintain the security of customers' data but may share information about the day-to-day running of a customer's account(s), including positive data, with credit reference agencies where the firm has agreed to follow the principles of reciprocity. [CONC 5]"), and for the same guidance with regard to business customers, see the *Standards of Lending Practice for Business Customers* (above, para.34–222, n.673) at pp.9–10 (Product execution), point 5.

[*Add to note 940, at the end: page* [460]]
; *Santander UK Plc v Royal Bank of Scotland Plc* [2015] EWHC 2560 (Ch) at [11]–[17], but with criticism of the ruling in *Santander UK Plc v National Westminster Bank Plc*, above, that a claim in unjust enrichment was a wrong capable of justifying a *Norwich Pharmacal* order (noted by M. Campbell [2016] L.M.C.L.Q. 42).

[*Add to note 943, at the end: page* [460]]
For examples where legislation allows disclosure but only with customer consent, see the Small and Medium Sized Business (Credit Information) Regulations 2015 (SI 2015/1945) regs 3(2), 6(1)(b); the Small and Medium Sized Business (Finance Platforms) Regulations 2015 (SI 2015/1946) regs 3(4), 6(3)(b).

[*Add to note 945, line 10, after* "of giving banker's references."*: page* [461]]
(See also the *Standards of Lending Practice* (above, para.34–222, n.673) at p.7 (Account maintenance and servicing), with the relevant paragraph set out in n.937 above; and for the same guidance with regard to business customers, see the *Standards of Lending Practice for Business Customers* (above, para.34–222, n.673) at pp.9–10 (Product execution), point 5.)

[*Add to note 945, at the end: page* [461]]
For the duty imposed on designated banks to provide information about their small and medium-sized business customers to designated credit reference agencies ("CRAs"), and the duty on designated CRAs to provide credit information about small and medium-sized businesses to finance providers, see the Small and Medium Sized Business (Credit Information) Regulations 2015 (SI 2015/1945).

(viii) *Termination of Relationship*

Termination of relationship by consent

34–314   [*Add to note 954, at the end: page* [463]]
The Revised Payment Services Directive 2015/2366/EU ("PSD2") repeals and replaces Directive 2007/64/EC. EU Member States have until January 13, 2018 to implement the requirements of PSD2. The Payment Services Regulations 2017 (SI 2017/752) ("PSRs 2017"), implement in part PSD2 in the UK. The PSRs 2017 revoke and replace the Payment Services Regulations 2009. With certain exceptions as set out in reg.1, which include where the implementation period is

linked to the coming into force of the secure communication and authentication requirements adopted under art.98 of PSD2, the PSRs 2017 come into force on January 13, 2018 (PSRs 2017 reg.1(6)). See, generally, para.34–223, n.676 above.

[Delete text of note 955 and substitute: page [463]]
Termination of a "framework contract", such as one for a current account or easy access savings account, including the bank's right to charge for closing the account, is provided for in the Payment Services Regulations 2009 reg.43 (see also PSRs 2017 reg.51). A framework contract is defined in reg.2 (see also PSRs 2017 reg.2) to mean "a contract for payment services which govern the future execution of individual and successive payment transactions and which may contain the obligation and conditions for setting up a payment account". The regulation does not affect the parties' rights to treat the framework contract, in accordance with the general law of contract, as unenforceable, void or discharged (reg.43(7); see also PSRs 2017 reg.51(7)). Where the framework contract is also a regulated agreement under the Consumer Credit Act 1974 reg.43 does not apply (reg.34; see also PSRs 2017 reg.41(2)).

[Add to note 957, at the end: page [463]]
cf. *N v S* [2015] EWHC 3248 (Comm) at [12]–[13], where Burton J. held that the customer had an arguable case that the bank was not entitled to terminate the banking relationship without notice under its contractual terms, and went on to grant an interim mandatory injunction requiring the bank to comply with the customer's instructions in relation to existing transactions, while the customer sought to move its account to a new bank. For reversal of Burton J.'s decision by the Court of Appeal ([2017] EWCA Civ 253), and for the money-laundering aspects of this case, see below, para.34–325A).

[Add to note 958, at the end: page [463]]
See also PSRs 2017 reg.51(4).

(c) *The Current Account*

(i) *Rights and Duties of the Banker*

Nature of relationship

[Add to note 959, at the end: page [464]]   **34–315**
The Revised Payment Services Directive 2015/2366/EU ("PSD2") repeals and replaces Directive 2007/64/EC. EU Member States have until January 13, 2018 to implement the requirements of PSD2. The Payment Services Regulations 2017 (SI 2017/752) ("PSRs 2017"), implement in part PSD2 in the UK. The PSRs 2017 revoke and replace the Payment Services Regulations 2009. With certain exceptions as set out in reg.1, which include where the implementation period is linked to the coming into force of the secure communication and authentication requirements adopted under art.98 of PSD2, the PSRs 2017 come into force on January 13, 2018 (PSRs 2017 reg.1(6)). See, generally, para.34–223 n.676 above.

EU Member States had to implement the Fourth Money Laundering Directive (2015/849/EU) by June 26, 2017. The UK did this through the Money Laundering, Terrorist Financing and Transfer of Funds (Information on the Payer) Regulations 2017 (SI 2017/692), which replace the Money Laundering Regulations 2007 (SI 2007/ 2157) and the Transfer of Funds (Information on the Payer) Regulations 2007 (SI 2007/ 3298). The new regime contains (inter alia) detailed provisions dealing with customer due diligence.

[Add to note 964, at the end: page [464]]
In *Singularis Holdings Ltd (In Liquidation) v Daiwa Capital Markets Europe Ltd* [2017] EWHC 257 (Ch) at [192], Rose J. held that the defendant stockbroker (Daiwa) had made payments from a segregated client account held for the benefit of the claimant company (Singularis), in breach of its *Quincecare* duty of care, because any reasonable banker would have realised that there were many obvious signs that AS, a director and sole shareholder of Singularis, who had instructed Daiwa to make the payments, was perpetrating a fraud on Singularis and was clearly using the funds for his own purposes. In making the disputed payments without proper or any inquiry, Daiwa was negligent and liable to repay the money to the claimant company. The judge (at [184]) rejected Daiwa's defence that AS's fraud was to attributed to Singularis as a "one man company" because this "would denude the [*Quincecare*] duty of any value in cases where it was needed most". She also rejected a defence of illegality, holding (at [215]) that the wrongdoing of AS was not to be attributed to Singularis. However, Rose J. (at [250]) reduced the damages awarded to Singularis by 25 per cent because of its contributory negligence.

The mandate to pay: electronic means of payment

34–316   [Add to note 965, at the end: page [464]]
On its true construction, a "one signature" mandate expressed to authorise payment by cheques or other written instructions and 'for all other purposes' has been held to bind a partnership in respect of loan agreements signed by only one of the partners (*Kotak v Kotak* [2017] EWHC 1821 (Ch)).

[Add to note 967, at the end: page [465]]
The Revised Payment Services Directive 2015/2366/EU ("PSD2") repeals and replaces Directive 2007/64/EC. EU Member States have until January 13, 2018 to implement the requirements of PSD2. The Payment Services Regulations 2017 (SI 2017/752) ("PSRs 2017"), implement in part PSD2 in the UK. The PSRs 2017 revoke and replace the Payment Services Regulations 2009. With certain exceptions as set out in reg.1, which include where the implementation period is linked to the coming into force of the secure communication and authentication requirements adopted under art.98 of PSD2, the PSRs 2017 come into force on January 13, 2018 (PSRs 2017 reg.1(6)). See, generally, para.34–223, n.676 above. Note that PSRs 2017 regs 41 and 64, deal with the application of Pts 6 and 7 respectively in the case of consumer credit agreements.

[Add to note 968, at the end: page [465]]
(see also PSRs 2017 Pt 7).

[*Add new note 968a, line 16, after* "of the PSRs": *page* [465]]
968a See also PSRs 2017 reg.82(5), and note that the obligation to execute is placed on the "account servicing payment service provider" irrespective of whether the payment order is initiated by the payer, through a "payment initiation service provider", or by or thorough a payee, unless execution is otherwise unlawful.

[*Delete text of note 969 and substitute: page* [465]]
For definition of a "framework contract", see reg.2 and n.955 above (see also PSRs 2017 reg.2). But note the "force majeure" provision set out in reg.79 (see also PSRs 2017 reg.96).

[*Add to note 971, at the end: page* [465]]
See also PSRs 2017 Sch.1 Pt 2(g).

Overdrafts

[*Add to note 981, three lines from the end, after* "Mason [2013] L.M.C.L.Q. 233).": **34–319**
page [466]]
The Supreme Court of the UK reviewed the law relating to penalty clauses in *Cavendish Square Holding BV v Makdessi* [2015] UKSC 67, [2016] A.C. 1172, which is now the leading authority on the subject (see above, paras 26–178 et seq.). The Supreme Court (at [40]–[43]) declined to follow the approach taken in Australia and retained the requirement the penalty doctrine is only triggered by breach. The different approaches to the breach requirement in the two jurisdictions has been confirmed by the High Court of Australia in *Paciocco v ANZ Banking Group Ltd* [2016] HCA 28 at [7]–[10] and [119]–[127], which is now the leading authority in relation to the test to be applied in Australia in determining where a clause is penal.

Combining accounts

[*In note 985, penultimate line, delete* "2nd edn (2014)" *and substitute: page* [467]] **34–320**
September 28, 2015

[*Add to note 985, at the end: page* [467]]
Neither the *Standards of Lending Practice for Personal Customers* nor the *Standards of Lending Practice for Business Customers* (above, para.34–222, n.673) have detailed provisions about the use of the right of set off.

[*Add to note 987, at the end: page* [468]]
Mutual dealings and set-off rules are now to be found in r.14.24 (administration) and r.14.25 (winding up) of the Insolvency (England and Wales) Rules 2016 (SI 2016/1024).

Proceeds of Crime Act 2002

[*Add to note 1015, at the end: page* [471]] **34–325**
But see also *National Crime Agency v N* [2017] EWCA Civ 253 at [71], where Hamblen L.J. said that *Bank of Scotland v A*, a tipping-off case, had to be "considered with caution and cannot be regarded as providing general guidance" in the context of the statutory consent regime contained in POCA 2002.

[Add to note 1018, at the end: page [471]]

The court will be given power to extend the moratorium period up to 186 days when amendments to Pt 7 of the 2002 Act, introduced by the Criminal Finances Act 2017 s.10, come into force.

EU Member States had to implement the Fourth Money Laundering Directive (2015/849/EU) by June 26, 2017. The UK did this through the Money Laundering, Terrorist Financing and Transfer of Funds (Information on the Payer) Regulations 2017 (SI 2017/692), which replace the Money Laundering Regulations 2007 (SI 2007/ 2157) and the Transfer of Funds (Information on the Payer) Regulations 2007 (SI 2007/ 3298). The new regime does not change the principal offences under the POCA 2002, nor the regime for reporting money laundering suspicions, but it does introduce a number of changes due to greater emphasis on a risk-based approach to tackling money laundering and terrorist financing.

[Insert new para.34–325A: page [472]]

34–325A   In *N v S*,[1020a] the defendant bank, suspicious about eight accounts held by the claimant foreign exchange dealer (an authorised payment institution), which related to particular customers of the claimant, froze all 160 of the claimant's accounts and gave notice to close all of its accounts with immediate effect. This left 476 individual transactions in limbo and the claimant in danger of going out of business. Burton J., recognising the exceptional nature of the case, granted an interim mandatory injunction requiring the bank to comply with the customer's instructions in relation to the 476 transactions, and made an interim declaration protecting the defendant bank against any related criminal liability that might arise under the Proceeds of Crime Act 2002. The judge held that the claimant had an arguable case that the bank had no contractual right to terminate the banking relationship without notice and that the balance of convenience and justice required the claimant be given this protection. No express consent had been sought from the NCA by the bank in respect of the transactions and the judge accepted that if consent was now sought the resultant moratorium period would almost certainly have disastrous consequences for the claimant. The judge stated that "[t]he significant fact" was that there was no evidence known to the NCA that the monies being transferred were criminal property or suspected of being so.[1020b]

However, Burton J. was reversed in the Court of Appeal.[1020c] Hamblen L.J., delivering a judgment with which Simon and Hickinbottom L.JJ. agreed, confirmed (at [59]–[60]) that the court had jurisdiction to override the compulsory statutory consent procedure under POCA 2002 by granting interim relief, but stated that, as the balance of convenience is likely to lie in favour of the public interest in the prevention of money laundering in most cases, such intervention was likely to be exceptional, e.g. where a bank acted in bad faith. He added (at [61]) that the balance of convenience would generally favour the bank in that the inconvenience to the customer would be outweighed by the potential prejudice to the bank of being compelled by the order to commit, or risk committing, a criminal offence. Hamblen L.J. stated (at [62]) that this prejudice could be overcome if the court could be satisfied at the interim application stage that there was a real prospect of such criminal liability, but considered (at [63]–[64]) that the court would be unlikely to have sufficient evidence to reach a conclusion on the issue at the interim stage. The Court of Appeal ruled (at [88]–[91]) that this case was not sufficiently exceptional to justify the grant of an interim declaration and that (at [92]–[96]), if it was inappropriate to grant an interim declaration to provide the bank with protection, it was inappropriate to grant a mandatory interim injunction.

[1020a] [2015] EWHC 3248 (Comm).
[1020b] At [17].
[1020c] 2017] EWCA Civ 253.

(ii) *Termination of Duty to Pay*

Payment Services Regulations 2009

[*Add new note 1026a, line 1, after paragraph title: page* [473]] **34–328**
[1026a] The Revised Payment Services Directive 2015/2366/EU ("PSD2") repeals and replaces Directive 2007/64/EC. EU Member States have until January 13, 2018 to implement the requirements of PSD2. The Payment Services Regulations 2017 (SI 2017/752) ("PSRs 2017"), implement in part PSD2 in the UK. The PSRs 2017 revoke and replace the Payment Services Regulations 2009. With certain exceptions as set out in reg.1, which include where the implementation period is linked to the coming into force of the secure communication and authentication requirements adopted under art.98 of PSD2, the PSRs 2017 come into force on January 13, 2018 (PSRs 2017 reg.1(6)). See, generally, para.34–223, n.676 above.

[*Delete text of paragraph and substitute: page* [473]]
The Payment Services Regulations 2009 (SI 2009/209) reg.55(3) (see also PSRs 2017 reg.67(3)), provide that the payer's consent to a payment transaction can be withdrawn at any time before the point at which the payment order can no longer be revoked under reg.67 (see also PSRs 2017 reg.83).[1027] Regulation 67(1) (see also PSRs 2017 reg.83(1)), restricts the ability of a payment service user to revoke a payment order by providing that, subject to certain exceptions, the payment service user may not revoke a payment order after it has been received by the payer's payment service provider.[1028] In the case of a payment transaction initiated by or through the payee, the payer may not revoke the payment order after transmitting the payment order or giving consent to execute the payment transaction to the payee (reg.67(2); see also PSRs 2017 reg.83(2), but note the change in wording to include a payment transaction initiated by a "payment initiation service provider", and making the payer's "consent" alone the point at which the payer may not revoke the payment order). In the case of a direct debit, the payer may not revoke the payment order after the end of the business day preceding the day agreed for the debiting of funds (reg.67(3); see also PSRs 2017 reg.83(3)).[1029]

[1027] See also reg.55(4) for withdrawal of consent to the execution of a series of payment transactions (see also PSRs 2017 reg.67(4)). For application of the PSRs in general, see above, paras 34–223 et seq. The PSRs focus only on electronic means of payment, so that cheques fall outside their scope. For application of PSRs 2017 in general, see para.34–223, n.676 above.
[1028] For time of receipt of a payment order, see PSRs reg.65. See also PSRs 2017 reg.81.
[1029] For further provisions relating to revocation, see PSRs reg.67(4)–(6). See also PSRs 2017 reg. 83(4)–(6).

Winding up

[*Add to note 1038, at the end: page* [474]] **34–331**
But in *Officeserve Technologies Ltd (In Liquidation) v Anthony-Mike* [2017] EWHC 1920 (Ch), H.H.J. Paul Matthews, sitting as Judge of the High Court,

stated obiter (at [88]) that whilst he agreed with Lightman J. that there is no disposition of the company's property to the bank on the facts of *Coutts & Co v Stock*, where the account was overdrawn, he considered that there is a disposition caught by s.127 where the account is in credit because the bank's liability to the company has been reduced. The judge (at [88]) preferred the reasoning of Blackburne J. at first instance in *Hollicourt (Contracts) Ltd v Bank of Ireland* [2000] 1 W.L.R. 895, although he did not refer to the Court of Appeal's reasoning when reversing Blackburne J. on appeal at [2001] Ch. 555, and (at [97]) relied on dicta of Lord Neuberger in *Akers v Samba Financial Group* [2017] UKSC 6, [2017] A.C. 424 at [74] to the effect that the giving up of contractual rights by a company would be a "disposition" within s.127.

[Add to note 1039, at the end: page [474]]
; *Re Gray's Inn Construction Ltd* was explained and amplified by the Court of Appeal in *Express Electrical Distributors Ltd v Beavis* [2016] EWCA Civ 765, [2016] 1 W.L.R. 4783, where Sales L.J. (at [56]) said validation would ordinarily only be granted "if there is some special circumstance which shows that the disposition in question ... has been ... for the benefit of the general body of unsecured creditors".

Bankruptcy

34–332   *[Add to note 1042, at the end: page [475]]*
See also *Thomas v D'Eye* [2016] B.P.I.R. 883 at [49], per Baister R., who said of s.284, "we are not dealing with unjust enrichment generally but a particular statutory regime which gives rise to an account for money had and received to which there are limited defences".

Period of limitation

34–336   *[Add to note 1060, at the end: page [478]]*
The Revised Payment Services Directive 2015/2366/EU ("PSD2") repeals and replaces Directive 2007/64/EC. EU Member States have until January 13, 2018 to implement the requirements of PSD2. The Payment Services Regulations 2017 (SI 2017/752) ("PSRs 2017"), implement in part PSD2 in the UK. The PSRs 2017 revoke and replace the Payment Services Regulations 2009. With certain exceptions as set out in reg.1, which include where the implementation period is linked to the coming into force of the secure communication and authentication requirements adopted under art.98 of PSD2, the PSRs 2017 come into force on January 13, 2018 (PSRs 2017 reg.1(6)). See, generally, para.34–223, n676 above.

[Add to note 1061, at the end: page [478]]
PSRs 2017 reg.74(1), makes the payment service user's reporting obligation a condition for redress under regs 76, 91, 92, 93 or 94. Regulation 74(2) relieves the user of this obligation if the user's bank has failed to comply with the various information requirements set out in Pt 6.

(iii) *Protection of Paying Banker in Cases of Unauthorised Payment*

Payment Services Regulations 2009

[*Add to note 1067, at the end: page* [480]] **34–341**
The Revised Payment Services Directive 2015/2366/EU ("PSD2") repeals and
replaces Directive 2007/64/EC. EU Member States have until January 13, 2018
to implement the requirements of PSD2. The Payment Services Regulations 2017
(SI 2017/752) ("PSRs 2017"), implement in part PSD2 in the UK. The PSRs
2017 revoke and replace the Payment Services Regulations 2009. With certain
exceptions as set out in reg.1, which include where the implementation period is
linked to the coming into force of the secure communication and authentication
requirements adopted under art.98 of PSD2, the PSRs 2017 come into force on
January 13, 2018 (PSRs 2017 reg.1(6)). See, generally, para.34–223, n.676
above.

[*Add to note 1068, line 1, after* "Sch.1 Pt 2.": *page* [480]]
See also PSRs 2017, Sch. 1, Pt 2.

[*Add to note 1070, line 2, after* "above, n.955.": *page* [480]]
See also PSRs 2017 reg.51(7).

Tai Hing

[*In note 1097, line 5, delete* "62(2)(a)." *and substitute: page* [486]] **34–350**
62(2). See also PSRs 2017 regs 72(3), 77(3).

(iv) *Special Types of Current Accounts*

Partnership accounts

[*Add to note 1132, at the end: page* [492]] **34–361**
See also *Kotak v Kotak* [2017] EWHC 1821 (Ch) at [118] et seq. (obiter) on
whether a partner who signed a number of loan agreements had done "any act for
carrying on in the usual way business of the kind carried on by the firm of which
he is a member" within the second limb of s.5 of the 1890 Act. It was held in
Kotak v Kotak that, on its true construction, a "one signature" mandate expressed
to authorise payment by cheques or other written instructions and "for all other
purposes" bound the partnership in respect of loan agreements signed by only
one of the partners.

(e) *The Giro System and Electronic Transfer of Funds*

Paper-based and electronic system

[*In paragraph, line 11, delete* "and VocaLink ("BACS") and" *and substitute: page*
[507]] **34–387**
, called BACS,

[*Add to paragraph, line 12, after* "and the Faster Payments Service": *page* [507]]
operated by the Faster Payments Scheme Ltd

Clearing house rules

34–392   [*In paragraph, lines 2–4, delete from* "that operate with the administrative support"
to "of the Payments Council,": *page* [508]]

[*Delete text of note 1223 and substitute: page* [508]]
The Financial Services (Banking Reform) Act 2013 creates a new competition-focused, economic regulator of retail payment systems in the UK: the new Payment Systems Regulator became fully operational on April 1, 2015. In 2015 the Payments Council was replaced by Payments UK, which is the trade association representing the UK payments industry. From July 1, 2017, Payments UK was integrated into a new finance and banking industry trade association called UK Finance (*https://www.ukfinance.org.uk*).

[*Add to note 1226, at the end: page* [508]]
(the judgments, even of the majority, are not easy to reconcile, but all three Lord Justices appear to agree that there can be reliance on banking practice for the purposes of interpretation where the practice is known or reasonably available to both the bank and its customer).

[*Delete text of note 1228 and substitute: page* [509]]
See, e.g. CHAPS Reference Manual (version: July 31, 2017), p.12.

UK clearing systems

34–393   [*In paragraph, lines 2–4, delete from* "operating with the administrative" *to* "of the Payments Council." *and substitute: page* [509]]
supported by Payments UK, which is the trade association representing the UK payments industry. From July 1, 2017, Payments UK was integrated into a new finance and banking industry trade association called UK Finance (*https://www.ukfinance.org.uk*).

[*In paragraph, line 8, delete* "and VocaLink Ltd": *page* [509]]

[*In paragraph, lines 14–15, delete* "also operated by the CHAPS . . . " *to* "Faster Payment System" *and substitute: page* [509]]
operated by Faster Payments Scheme Ltd, is called the Faster Payments Service

[*Add to note 1231, line 3, after* "throughout the EU.": *page* [509]]
The Bank of England decided not to participate in TARGET2, accordingly UK banks have made individual arrangements for cross-border euro payments, using TARGET2 via other Member States.

[*Add to note 1232, at the end: page* [509]]
It is now possible to send individual payments of up to £250,000 using the Faster Payments Service, but individual banks and building societies set their own

limits depending on how the payment is sent and the type of account their customer is sending from (*www.fasterpayments.org.uk*).

Direct debiting

[*Add to note 1239, at the end: page* [511]]   **34–400**
The Payment Services Regulations 2017 (SI 2017/752) reg.79 provides for refunds of payment transactions initiated by or through a payee, and reg.80 provides for requests for refunds for payment transactions initiated by or through a payee. For application of the PSRs 2017, see para.34–223, n.676 above.

Cancellation of a direct debit

[*Add to note 1246, at the end: page* [513]]   **34–402**
In some cases there may be an issue as to whether the 1977 Act is engaged in the first place, see *African Export-Import Bank v Shebah Exploration and Production Co Ltd* [2017] EWCA Civ 845 (no set-off clause in facilities agreement based on industry standard form).

Statutory controls

[*In note 1252, delete from* "On July 24, 2013 . . . " *to the end and substitute: page*   **34–404**
[514]]
The Revised Payment Services Directive 2015/2366/EU ("PSD2") repeals and replaces Directive 2007/64/EC. EU Member States have until January 13, 2018 to implement the requirements of PSD2. The Payment Services Regulations 2017 (SI 2017/752) ("PSRs 2017"), implement in part PSD2 in the UK. The PSRs 2017 revoke and replace the Payment Services Regulations 2009. With certain exceptions as set out in reg.1, which include where the implementation period is linked to the coming into force of the secure communication and authentication requirements adopted under art.98 of PSD2, the PSRs 2017 come into force on January 13, 2018 (PSRs 2017 reg.1(6)). See, generally, para.34–223 n.676 above.

Position of payer's bank under the Payment Services Regulations 2009

[*Delete text of note 1263 and substitute: page* [515]]   **34–406**
For a single payment service contract (defined in reg.2(1) of PSRs 2009 and 2017: essentially, a one-off transaction) information requirements of payer's bank and payee's bank are to be found in regs 36–39 and Sch.4 (see also PSRs 2017 regs 43–47 and Sch.4). For "framework contracts" (defined in n.955 above) information requirements relating to both banks are contained in regs 40–46 and Sch.4 (see also PSRs 2017 regs 48–54 and Sch.4). For provisions common to both types of contract, see regs 47–50 (see also PSRs 2017 regs 55–59). For other information requirements, see PSRs 2017 regs 60 (information requirements for account information service providers), 61 (information on ATM withdrawal charges) and 62 (provision of information leaflet). Also note dispplications in relation to regulated contracts falling within the scope of the Consumer Credit

Act 1974 (reg.34) (see also PSRs 2017 reg.41), and for low-value payment instruments (reg.35) (see also PSRs 2017 reg.42). Part 6 of the PSRs 2017 does not apply to registered account information service providers or EEA registered account information service providers, except for regs 59 and 60 (PSRs 2017 reg.40(4)). The "corporate opt-out" (see above, para.34–404) applies to the information requirements of Pt 5 (reg.33(4)) (the "corporate opt-out" of the information requirements of Pt 6 of the PSRs 2017 is found in reg.40(7) of those Regulations).

[*Add to note 1264, at the end: page* [515]]
Key same terms defined in reg.2(1) of the PSRs 2017. Note the slightly wider definition of "payment transaction" in the PSRs 2017 ("or on behalf of the payer").

Non-execution or defective execution

34–407   [*In paragraph, line 13, delete* "Where the payment transaction is initiated" *and substitute: page* [516]]
Where the payment order is initiated

[*Delete text of note 1266 and substitute: page* [516]]
reg.75(2) (see also PSRs 2017 reg.91(2), but note that reg.91 only applies where a payment order is initiated *directly* by the payer (reg.91(1)): for non-execution or defective execution of a payment order initiated by the payer through a payment initiation service, see PSRs 2017 reg.93, which includes, in reg.93(2), (4), a requirement that a payment initiation service provider, on request, must immediately compensate an account servicing payment service provider for losses incurred or sums paid as a result of the refund to the payer). The general rule is that the payer's bank must ensure that the amount of the payment transaction is credited to the account of the payee's bank by the end of the business day following receipt of the payment order: reg.70(1) (see also PSRs 2017 reg.86(1)); but subject to exceptions in the case of payment instructions initiated by way of a paper payment order, and certain payment transactions (e.g. not in euro or sterling) executed wholly within the EEA: reg.70(3), (4) (see also PSRs 2017 reg.86(2), (3)). See also *Tidal Energy Ltd v Bank of Scotland Plc* [2013] EWHC 2780 (QB), [2013] 2 Lloyd's Rep. 605 at [22] (affirmed [2014] EWCA Civ 1107 without reference to this point), where H.H.J. Havelock-Allan Q.C. said (obiter) that if reg.75 had applied to the transfer (it did not because the PSRs had been expressly excluded by the bank's terms and conditions), the unique identifier given by the payer would have been incorrect because there was a mismatch between the payee's name, on the one hand, and the account number and sort code, on the other, in which case reg.74(2) would have applied. Regulation 74(2) provides: "Where the unique identifier provided by the payment service user is incorrect, the payment service provider is not liable under regulation 75 or 76 for non-execution or defective execution of the payment transaction, but the payment service provider—(a) must make reasonable efforts to recover the funds involved in the payment transaction; and (b) may, if agreed in the framework contract, charge the payment service user for any such recovery". For equivalent provision to reg.74(2), see PSRs 2017 reg.90(2).

[*Delete text of note 1267 and substitute: page* [516]]
reg.75(4) (see also PSRs 2017 reg.91(3)). Liability under reg.75 does not apply if reg.79 (force majeure) applies (see also PSRs 2017 reg.96). The "corporate opt-out" (see above, para.34–404) applies to reg.75 (reg.51(3)) (and also to reg.91 of the PSRs 2017: PSRs 2017 reg.63(5)(a)).

[*Delete text of note 1268 and substitute: page* [516]]
reg.76(5) (see also PSRs 2017 reg.92(6)). Liability under reg.76 does not apply if reg.79 (force majeure) applies (see also PSRs 2017 reg.96). The "corporate opt-out" (see above, para.34–404) applies to reg.76 (see reg.51(3)) (and also to reg.92 of the PSRs 2017: PSRs 2017 reg.63(5)(a)).

[*Add to note 1269, at the end: page* [516]]
(for "corporate opt-out", see reg.51(3)). See also PSRs 2017 reg.94 (for "corporate opt-out", see PSRs 2017 reg.63(5)(a)).

[*Delete text of note 1270 and substitute: page* [516]]
reg.59(1), which makes the payment service user's reporting obligation a condition for redress under regs 61, 75, 76 or 77 (see also PSRs 2017 reg.74(1), which relates to redress under regs 76, 91, 92, 93 or 94). Regulation 59(2) relieves the payment service user of this obligation if his bank has failed to comply with various information requirements in Pt 5 of the PSRs (see also PSRs 2017 reg.74(2)).

[*Add to note 1271, line 1, after* "reg.78": *page* [517]]
(see also PSRs 2017 reg.95)

Unauthorised transactions

[*Add to note 1272, at the end: page* [517]]   **34–408**
(see also PSRs 2017 reg.67(1)).

[*Delete text of note 1273 and substitute: page* [517]]
reg.55(2) (see also PSRs 2017 reg.67(2), which, in (c), extends to consent given via the payee or a payment initiation service provider). For withdrawal of consent, see reg.55(3)–(4) (and above, para.34–328) (see also PSRs 2017 reg.67(3)–(4)). A framework contract may give the payment service provider the right to stop the use of the payment instrument on reasonable grounds relating to (a) security of the payment instrument; (b) the suspected unauthorised or fraudulent use of the payment instrument or (c) in the case of a payment instrument with a credit line, a significantly increased risk that the payer may be unable to fulfil its liability to pay (reg.56(2)) (see also PSRs 2017 reg.71(2)).

[*Add to note 1274, at the end: page* [517]]
(see also PSRs 2017 reg.76(1)).

[*Add to note 1275, at the end: page* [517]]
(see also PSRs 2017 reg.76(1)).

[*Delete text of note 1276 and substitute: page* [517]]
reg.59(1), which makes the payment service user's reporting obligation a condition for redress under regs 61, 75, 76 or 77 (see also PSRs 2017 reg.74(1), which

relates to redress under regs. 76, 91, 92, 93 or 94). Regulation 59(2) relieves the payment service user of this obligation if his bank has failed to comply with various information requirements in Pt 5 of the PSRs (see also PSRs 2017 reg.74(2)).

[Add to note 1277, at the end: page [517]]
For PSRs 2017, see reg.75(1), and also reg.75(2) which deals with the burden of proof where a transaction is initiated through a payment initiation service provider (failure to do so may result in a payment initiation service provider having to compensate an account servicing payment service provider that has had to refund the payer, or restore his account, following an unauthorised payment: reg.76(5)).

[Add to note 1278, at the end: page [517]]
"Authentication" is defined in reg.2 of the PSRs 2017 as "a procedure which allows a payment service provider to verify the identity of a payment service user or the validity of the use of a specific payment instrument, including the use of the user's personalised security credentials". "Personalised security credentials" are defined in reg.2 to mean "personalised features provided by a payment service provider to a payment service user for the purposes of authentication".

[Add to note 1279, at the end: page [517]]
For PSRs 2017, see reg.75(3). The payment service user's obligations in relation to payment instruments and personalised security credentials are set out in PSRs 2017 reg.72: the user must only use the instrument in accordance with its terms and conditions (so long as those terms and conditions are "objective, non-discriminatory and proportionate"), he must notify the payment service provider in the agreed manner and without undue delay on becoming aware of the loss, theft, misappropriation or unauthorised use of the payment instrument, and he must take all reasonable steps to keep safe personalised security credentials relating to the payment instrument or an account information service. If a payment service provider, including a payment initiation service provider, claims that a payer acted fraudulently or failed with intent or gross negligence to comply with reg.72, the payment service provider must provide supporting evidence to the payer (PSRs 2017 reg.75(4)).

[Add to note 1280, at the end: page [518]]
PSRs 2017 reg.73, sets out obligations of the payment service provider in relation to payment instruments.

[Add to note 1281, at the beginning: page [518]]
See also PSRs 2017 reg.77(3) (note that reg.72 sets out the obligations of the payment service user in relation to payment instruments and personalised security credentials).

[Add to note 1282, at the end: page [518]]
Under reg.77(1) of the PSRs 2017, the payer's liability is restricted to £35 at most. However, under PSRs 2017 reg.77(2), the payer will not be liable for any losses if (a) the loss theft or misappropriation of the payment instrument was not detectable by the payer prior to the payment, unless the payer acted fraudulently, or (b) the loss was caused by acts or omissions of an employee, agent or branch

of a payment service provider or of an entity which carried out activities on behalf of the payment service provider.

[*Add to note 1283, at the end: page* [518]]
See also PSRs 2017 reg.77(4)(a).

[*Add to note 1284, at the end: page* [518]]
See also PSRs 2017 reg.77(4)(b).

[*Add to note 1285, at the end: page* [518]]
See also PSRs 2017 reg.77(4)(d). The non-fraudulent payer will also not be liable for any losses where reg.100 requires the application of "strong customer authentication" (see para.34–223, n.676 above), but the payer's payment service provider does not require strong customer authentication (PSRs 2017 reg.77(4)(c)). Where the payer's payment service provider had to make a refund to the payer/restore the debited payment account as the result of an unauthorised payment transaction (reg.76(1)), the payer's payment service provider would be entitled to compensation from the payee or the payee's payment service provider (or both) where reg.100 required the application of strong customer authentication, but the payee or the payee's payment service provider did not accept strong customer authentication (reg.77(6)).

[*Insert new note 1285a, line 42, after* "as with a direct debit"*: page* [518]]
[1285a] reg.63(1).

[*Delete text of note 1286 and substitute: page* [518]]
reg.63(2) (see also PSRs 2017 reg.79(1), (2), but note restrictions in paras (5), (6). Regulation 79(3), sets out the payer's entitlement to an unconditional refund of the full amount of any direct debit transactions denominated in euro which comply with art.1 of Regulation (EU) 260/2012. The payer must make the request for a refund to his bank within eight weeks from the date on which the funds were debited (reg.54(1)) (see also PSRs 2017 reg.80(1)). The bank then has 10 business days in which to make the refund or justify its refusal to do so (reg.54(5)) (see also PSRs 2017 reg.80(4)).

Position of the paying banker at common law

[*In note 1288, lines 1–2, delete* "[2014] EWCA Civ 2780 (QB)" *and substitute: page* [518]]   **34–409**
[2014] 2 Lloyd's Rep. 549

Position of the payee's bank under the Payment Services Regulations 2009

[*Add to note 1293, at the end: page* [519]]   **34–410**
The Revised Payment Services Directive 2015/2366/EU ("PSD2") repeals and replaces Directive 2007/64/EC. EU Member States have until January 13, 2018 to implement the requirements of PSD2. The Payment Services Regulations 2017 (SI 2017/752) ("PSRs 2017"), implement in part PSD2 in the UK. The PSRs 2017 revoke and replace the Payment Services Regulations 2009. With certain

exceptions as set out in reg.1, which include where the implementation period is linked to the coming into force of the secure communication and authentication requirements adopted under art.98 of PSD2, the PSRs 2017 come into force on January 13, 2018 (PSRs 2017 reg.1(6)). See, generally, para.34–223, n.676 below.

[*Add to note 1294, at the end: page* [519]]
See also PSRs 2017 Pt 6.

[*Add to note 1295, at the end: page* [519]]
See also PSRs 2017 Pt 7.

34–411   [*Add to note 1296, at the end: page* [519]]
See also PSRs 2017 reg.86(5).

[*Add to note 1297, at the end: page* [519]]
See also PSRs 2017 reg.86(4), which is not restricted only to payment orders initiate by or through the payee.

[*Delete text of note 1298 and substitute: page* [520]]
reg.73(2) (see also PSRs 2017 reg.89(2), (3), which is not restricted only to payments received as a result of direct debits); and see also reg.71(2) (see also PSRs 2017 reg.87(2)), which applies where the payee has no account at the bank (reg.71(1)) (see also PSRs 2017 reg.87(1)).

[*Add to note 1299, at the end: page* [520]]
See also PSRs 2017, reg. 89(1) and, with specific reference to payment orders initiated by the payee, reg. 92(4).

34–412   [*Add to note 1300, at the end: page* [520]]
See also PSRs 2017 reg.84(1).

[*Add to note 1301, at the end: page* [520]]
See also PSRs 2017 reg.66.

[*Add to note 1302, at the end: page* [520]]
See also PSRs 2017 reg.84(2).

[*Delete text of note 1303 and substitute: page* [520]]
reg.68(3)(b) (see also PSRs reg.84(3)(b)). The payer's bank is responsible for reimbursing the payee for unauthorised deductions where the payer initiates the payment transaction (reg.68(3)(a)) (see also PSRs reg.84(3)(a)).

34–413   [*Add to note 1304, at the end: page* [520]]
See also PSRs 2017 reg.91(2) (for relevant time limits, see reg.86). Regulation 91 only applies where a payment order is initiated *directly* by the payer (reg.91(1)). For non-execution of defective execution of a payment order initiated by the payer through a payment initiation service, see reg.93.

[*Add to note 1305, at the end: page* [520]]
See also PSRs 2017 reg.91(5), (6) and, for late execution, (7). Regulation 91 only applies where a payment order is initiated *directly* by the payer (reg.91(1)). For non-execution or defective execution of a payment order initiated by the payer through a payment initiation service, see PSRs 2017 reg.93.

[Delete text of note 1306 and substitute: page [520]]
reg.76(2) (see also PSRs 2017 reg.92(2)). The payee's bank must transmit the
relevant payment order within the time-limits agreed between the payee and his
bank: reg.70(6) (see also PSRs 2017 reg.86(5).

[Add to note 1307, at the end: page [520]]
See also PSRs 2017 reg.92(3).

[Add to note 1308, at the end: page [520]]
See also PSRs 2017 reg.92(5); note that the payee's payment service provider
must act free of charge.

[Add to note 1309, at the end: page [520]]
See also PSRs 2017 reg.92(6), (7), but if the payer's payment service provider
proves that the payee's service provider has received the amount of the payment
transaction, para.(6) does not apply and the payee's payment service provider
must value date the amount on the payee's payment account no later than the date
the amount would have been value dated if the transaction had been executed
correctly (reg.92(8)).

[Add to note 1310, at the end: page [521]]
See also PSRs 2017 reg.94 (which includes charges and interest incurred as a
result of late execution of the payment transaction).

[Delete text of note 1311 and substitute: page [521]]
reg.59(1), which makes the payment service user's reporting obligation a condition for redress under regs 61, 75, 76 or 77 (see also PSRs 2017 reg.74(1), which
relates to redress under regs 76, 91, 92, 93 or 94). Regulation 59(2) relieves the
payment service user of this obligation if his bank has failed to comply with
various information requirements in Pt 5 of the PSRs (see also PSRs 2017
reg.74(2)).

[Add to note 1312, line 1, after "reg.74(2)"*: page* [521]]
(see also PSRs 2017 reg.90(2))

[Add to note 1313, at the end: page [521]]
See also PSRs 2017 reg.96.

[Add to note 1314, after "reg.78"*: page* [521]]
(see also PSRs 2017 reg.95)

Position of correspondent (intermediary) bank under the Payment Services Regulations 2009

[Add to note 1319, at the end: page [523]]   **34–419**
The Revised Payment Services Directive 2015/2366/EU ("PSD2") repeals and
replaces Directive 2007/64/EC. EU Member States have until January 13, 2018
to implement the requirements of PSD2. The Payment Services Regulations 2017
(SI 2017/752) ("PSRs 2017"), implement in part PSD2 in the UK. The PSRs
2017 revoke and replace the Payment Services Regulations 2009. With certain

exceptions as set out in reg.1, which include where the implementation period is linked to the coming into force of the secure communication and authentication requirements adopted under art.98 of PSD2, the PSRs 2017 come into force on January 13, 2018 (PSRs 2017 reg.1(6)). See, generally, para.34–223, n.676 above.

[*Add to note 1320, at the end: page* [523]]
See also PSRs 2017 reg.95, and note that this also extends to non-execution or defective or late execution of payment transactions initiated through a payment initiation service.

[*Add to note 1321, at the end: page* [523]]
See also PSRs 2017 reg.90.

[*Add to note 1322, at the end: page* [523]]
See also PSRs 2017 reg.96.

Revocation of payment order under Payment Services Regulations 2009

34–421 [*Delete text of paragraph and substitute: page* [524]]
The Payment Services Regulations 2009,[1329] reg.55(3) (see also PSRs 2017 reg.67(3)), provide that the payer's consent to a payment transaction can be withdrawn at any time before the point at which the payment order can no longer be revoked under reg.67 (see also PSRs 2017 reg.83).[1330] Regulation 67(1) (see also PSRs 2017 reg.83(1)) restricts the ability of a payment service user to revoke a payment order by providing that, subject to certain exceptions, the payment service user may not revoke a payment order after it has been received by the payer's payment service provider.[1331] In the case of a payment transaction initiated by or through the payee, the payer may not revoke the payment order after transmitting the payment order or giving consent to execute the payment transaction to the payee (reg.67(2); see also PSRs 2017 reg.83(2), but note change in wording to include a payment transaction initiated by a "payment initiation service provider", and making the payer's "consent" alone the point at which the payer may not revoke the payment order). In the case of a direct debit, the payer may not revoke the payment order after the end of the business day preceding the day agreed for the debiting of funds (reg.67(3)) (see also PSRs 2017 reg.83(3)).[1332]

[1329] SI 2009/209, as amended. For application of the PSRs in general, see above, paras 34–223 et seq., and also para.34–404. See also E.P. Ellinger, E. Lomnicka and C.V.M. Hare, *Ellinger's Modern Banking Law*, 5th edn (2011), pp.607 et seq. The Revised Payment Services Directive 2015/2366/EU ("PSD2") repeals and replaces Directive 2007/64/EC. EU Member States have until January 13, 2018 to implement the requirements of PSD2. The Payment Services Regulations 2017 (SI 2017/752) ("PSRs 2017"), implement in part PSD2 in the UK. The PSRs 2017 revoke and replace the Payment Services Regulations 2009. With certain exceptions as set out in reg.1, which include where the implementation period is linked to the coming into force of the secure communication and authentication requirements adopted under art.98 of PSD2, the PSRs 2017 come into force on January 13, 2018 (PSRs 2017 reg.1(6)). See, generally, para.34–223, n.676 above.
[1330] See also reg.55(4) for withdrawal of consent to the execution of a series of payment transactions. See also PSRs 2017 reg.67(4).
[1331] For time of receipt of a payment order, see PSRs reg.65. See also PSRs 2017 reg.81.

¹³³² For further provisions relating to revocation, see PSRs reg.67(4)–(6). See also PSRs 2017 reg.83(4)–(6).

(f) *The Deposit Account*

Its nature

[*Add to note 1353, at the end: page* [530]]   **34–435**
The Revised Payment Services Directive 2015/2366/EU ("PSD2") repeals and replaces Directive 2007/64/EC. EU Member States have until January 13, 2018 to implement the requirements of PSD2. The Payment Services Regulations 2017 (SI 2017/752) ("PSRs 2017"), implement in part PSD2 in the UK. The PSRs 2017 revoke and replace the Payment Services Regulations 2009. With certain exceptions as set out in reg.1, which include where the implementation period is linked to the coming into force of the secure communication and authentication requirements adopted under art.98 of PSD2, the PSRs 2017 come into force on January 13, 2018 (PSRs 2017 reg.1(6)). See, generally, para.34–223, n.676 above.

(g) *Giving Information on Financial Transactions*

Scope

[*Add to note 1361, line 10, after* "person", see n.672 above.": *page* [532]]   **34–438**
In *Sivagnanam v Barclays Bank Plc* [2015] EWHC 3985 (Comm), it was held (at [8]–[15]) that the claimant, the sole director/shareholder of a company that entered into an interest rate hedging product with the defendant bank, could not bring a claim for loss said to have been suffered as a private person as a result of breach of the conduct of business rules under FSMA 2000 s.138D(2), as he did not fall within the category of person intended to be protected by the FSMA 2000 or the relevant conduct of business rules. It was also held (at [16]–[21]) that his loss, as a shareholder, was irrecoverable due to the rule against reflective loss.

[*Add to note 1361, at the end: page* [532]]
In *Suremime Ltd v Barclays Bank Plc* [2015] EWHC 2277 (QB) the judge, when granting the claimant permission to amend its particulars of claim, held (at [31]–[37]) that it was sufficiently arguable that the claimant had a claim in the tort of negligence against the defendant bank for its conduct of a review of swaps it had agreed with the FCA. However, the judge in *Suremime* did not have *Green & Rowley* cited to him. This omission was noted by the Court of Appeal in *CGL Group Ltd v Royal Bank of Scotland* [2017] EWCA Civ 1073, which held (at [103]) that banks do not owe a duty of care in tort to customers when carrying out a regulatory review of potential swaps mis-selling cases which was required as a result of agreement between the FCA and various banks. In *Flex-E-Vouchers Ltd v Royal Bank of Scotland* [2016] EWHC 2604 (QB) at [53] and [67], it was held that there was no implied term in a swap sale contract that the bank would comply with the requirements of the FSA/FCA's Handbook, including when it conducted a regulatory review.

Advising on investments

34–439   [*Add to paragraph, at the beginning: page* [532]]
In general a bank is not under a legal obligation to provide advice but if it gives
advice then it must do so using reasonable care and skill.[1361a]

> [1361a] *Finch v Lloyds TSB Bank Plc* [2016] EWHC 1236 (QB) at [52].

[*In paragraph, lines 4–5, delete* "The duty is based on the" *to* "banker and the
customer." *and substitute: page* [532]]
The duty will be contractual where the claimant can prove a contract under which
the defendant bank has agreed to provide a service including the provision of
advice,[1362a] otherwise the claimant must establish a tortious duty to advise, and
such a duty will arise only in exceptional circumstances.

> [1362a] Supply of Goods and Services Act 1982 s.13; Consumer Rights Act 2015 s.49.

[*Add to note 1363, at the beginning: page* [532]]
See *Finch v Lloyds TSB Bank Plc* [2016] EWHC 1236 (QB) at [47]–[59]
(borrower's claim that lender owed a contractual or tortious duty to advise it
about a potentially onerous clause in a loan agreement failed because there was
no contract whereby the lender was to provide advice and there was nothing
exceptional about the relationship to justify the imposition of a tortious duty to
advise, especially where borrower represented by professional advisers and
giving of advice might have been contrary to lender's best interests). See also
Worthing v Lloyds Bank Plc [2015] EWHC 2836 (QB) (investors' claim that
bank was in breach of a strict obligation to correct an error in its original
investment advice failed because the original advice had not been given in error
and, even if it had been, there was no strict contractual obligation to correct that
advice).

[*Add to end of note 1363: page* [532]]
In *Finch v Lloyds TSB Bank Plc* [2016] EWHC 1236 (QB), above, at [58], the
judge saw no significance in the fact that the defendant lender had used the
phrase "trusted advisor" in its marketing and training material, finding that the
phrase was merely part of a marketing strategy to differentiate the lender from its
competitors.

[*Add to note 1368, line 7, after* "[13], [22]–[25]": *page* [533]]
; *O'Hare v Coutts & Co* [2016] EWHC 2224 (QB) at [206]–[208], where Kerr
J. adopted the test in *Montgomery v Lanarkshire Health Board* [2015] A.C. 1430,
a medical negligence case, to define the standard of care to be applied in the
explanation of risk as part of the provision of investment advice, and considered
that compliance with COBS rules "is ordinarily enough to comply with a
common law duty to inform, forming part of the duty to exercise reasonable skill
and care; while breach of them will ordinarily also amount to a breach of that
common law duty" (see also *Thomas v Triodos Bank NV* [2017] EWHC 314
(QB) at [89] for application of the test of materiality in the *Montgomery*
case).

[*Add to note 1369, at the end: page* [533]]

But contrast the doubts as to the existence of such an intermediate duty expressed by the judge in *Thornbridge Ltd v Barclays Bank Plc* [2015] EWHC 3430 (QB) at [118]–[131]; and see also the restrictive interpretation of *Crestsign* adopted by Asplin J. in *Property Alliance Group Ltd v Royal Bank of Scotland Plc* [2016] EWHC 3342 (Ch) at [195]–[196]. In *Thomas v Triodos Bank NV* [2017] EWHC 314 (QB), where there was no advisory relationship and no advice was given, the defendant bank, which advertised that it subscribed to the voluntary Business Banking Code (which includes a fairness commitment), was held (at [81]) to owe an "intermediate" duty of care to the claimant customers when providing information in response to their inquiries about the financial consequences of switching from variable to fixed rate loans (there were no disclaimers, "basis" clauses or contractual exclusions to contradict the imposition of the duty).

Banking references

[*In note 1375, lines 4–6, delete from* "[2014] EWHC 2613 (QB) . . . " *to* **34–441**
"contributory negligence and loss)." *and substitute: page* [534]]

[2016] EWCA Civ 457, [2016] 1 W.L.R. 3169 (defendant bank did not owe a duty of care to casino for negligent misstatement as to gambler's creditworthiness when request for reference came from associated company of casino: there was no assumption of responsibility or proximity, because neither the true purpose of the reference nor the existence of the casino was revealed and the reference was "given in strict confidence", and it was not fair, just and reasonable to impose liability on the bank).

(i) *Bankers Commercial Credits*

(i) *The UCP*

Modern practice

[*In paragraph, lines 6–7, delete from* "conditional undertaking to pay given from **34–446**
one bank to another." *and substitute: page* [537]]

undertaking given by an obligor bank (usually the buyer's bank) to a recipient bank (which must be the seller's bank) to pay a specified sum under the condition of a successful electronic matching of data or acceptance of mismatches.

[*Add to note 1391, at the end: page* [537]]

See also *The ICC Guide to the Uniform Rules for Bank Payment Obligations* (ICC Publication No.751E).

[*Add to paragraph, line 13, after* "SWIFT Trade Services Utility": *page* [537]]

; and, unlike the beneficiary of a letter of credit, the seller does not receive a payment undertaking directly from the obligor bank (the seller's claim is against the recipient bank, i.e. the seller's bank, according to the terms of any separate contractual agreement that the seller will usually have entered into with that bank, but this bilateral agreement is not part of the BPO itself).

[*Add to note 1392, at the end: page* [537]]
See also K. Vorpeil, "Bank payment obligations: alternative means of settlement in international trade" [2014] I.B.L.J. 41.

Main changes in the 2007 revision

34–450 [*Add to note 1404, at the end: page* [539]]
See also, R.K. Chhina, "The Uniform Customs and Practice for Documentary Credit (the USP): Are they merely a set of contractual terms?" (2016) 30 B.F.L.R. 245.

Construction of the UCP

34–452 [*In note 1409, line 2, delete* "arbitration awards" *and substitute: page* [541]]
decisions

[*Add to note 1410, line 4, after* "interpretation and implication is": *page* [541]]
Marks & Spencer Plc v BNP Paribas Securities Services Trust Co (Jersey) Ltd [2015] UKSC 72, [2016] A.C. 742, commenting upon

[*Add to note 1410, at the end: page* [541]]
In the context of performance bonds, the courts have consistently emphasised that it will be rare for a term to be implied into such a contract, see below, para.34–548, n.1611.

[*Add to note 1411, at the end: page* [541]]
; cited with evident approval by Blair J. in *Deutsche Bank AG, London v CIMB Bank Berhad* [2017] EWHC 1264 (Comm) at [37].

(ii) *Types of Documentary Credits*

Negotiation credits

34–483 [*Delete paragraph, including heading and footnotes, and substitute: pages* [551]–[552]]
Credits "available by negotiation" and negotiation credits. The credit may be available by negotiation with a bank nominated in the credit (or with any bank if the credit so provides). UCP 600 art.2 defines "negotiation" to mean the purchase by the nominated bank of bills of exchange ("drafts") drawn on a bank other than the nominated bank (e.g. the issuing bank), and/or documents under a complying presentation, by advancing or agreeing to advance funds to the beneficiary on or before the banking day on which reimbursement is due to the nominated bank. This enables the beneficiary to obtain funds without delay by selling the documents to the nominated bank (and so it is only of practical use to the beneficiary where payment under the credit is not immediate). A nominated bank that has honoured or negotiated a complying presentation and forwarded the documents to the issuing bank is entitled to reimbursement from the issuing bank under UCP 600 art.7(c).[1445] In *Société Générale SA v Saad Trading*,[1446] Teare J.

held that (i) if the documents forwarded to the issuing bank are not compliant, the issuing bank is not obliged to reimburse the confirming bank under art.7(c) (and that the issuing bank is not bound by the view of the confirming bank that the documents are compliant)[1447]; and (ii) under art.7(c) the documents to be forwarded to the issuing bank must be the documents presented to the confirming bank under the credit (discretion on the part of the confirming bank as to which documents to forward would be contrary to the principle of strict compliance).[1448] In this case the confirming bank did not forward bills of exchange required to be presented under the letter of credit to the issuing bank, but as there was no dispute that the documents presented by the beneficiary to the confirming bank were compliant, the judge held that the issuing bank was not entitled to refuse to reimburse the confirming bank.[1449]

[1445] In the case of reimbursement of a nominated bank for having "honoured" a complying presentation, the issuing bank's obligation to reimburse arises only where the nominated bank has actually made the payment (*Deutsche Bank AG, London v CIMB Bank Berhad* [2017] EWHC 1264 (Comm) at [38]–[39]). UCP 600 art.7(c), adds that "[r]eimbursement for the amount of a complying presentation under a credit available by acceptance or deferred payment is due at maturity, whether or not the nominated bank prepaid or purchased before maturity". See UCP 600 art.8(c) for a similar undertaking of a confirming bank to reimburse another nominated bank that has honoured or negotiated a complying presentation and forwarded the documents to the confirming bank.

[1446] [2011] EWHC 2424 (Comm), [2011] 2 C.L.C. 629.

[1447] At [44].

[1448] At [45]–[46].

[1449] At [47].

[*Insert new paragraph 38–483A: page* [552]]

"Negotiation credits". The term "negotiation" is sometimes used in a different sense, namely where the undertaking contained in the credit is extended to third parties (including a negotiating bank) as well as the beneficiary, so that the third party may purchase the documents and present them to the issuing bank in its own right. Credits of this type are called "negotiation credits" and should be contrasted with credits "available by negotiation" in the sense described above (and also contrasted with "straight credits" where the issuing bank's payment undertaking is directed solely to the seller). UCP 600 has made the practice of using "negotiation credits" virtually redundant for if, under a credit incorporating UCP 600, it is intended that the beneficiary should be able to obtain payment by selling the documents to any bank, then the credit should be made freely available by negotiation.[1449a]   **34–483A**

[1449a] A. Malek and D. Quest, *Jack: Documentary Credits*, 4th edn (2009), para.2.19.

(iv) *The Relationship of Issuing Banker and Buyer*

Deposit of security

[*Add new note 1503a, after* "recoverable in full by the buyer." *in line 5: page* [563]]   **34–502**

[1503a] See also S. Connelly, "Bank recovery and resolution: the case of contingent letters of credit under bail-in" (2016) 2 J.I.B.F.L. 78.

(v) *The Relationship of Banker and Seller*

The autonomy of an irrevocable credit

34–507   [*Add to note 1523, line 1, after* "[1981] 2 Lloyd's Rep. 394": *page* [567]]
; see also *National Infrastructure Development Co Ltd v Banco Santander SA* [2017] EWCA Civ 27 at [45], and *National Infrastructure Development Co Ltd v BNP Paribas* [2016] EWHC 2508 (Comm) at [17].

[*In note 1524, line 20, delete* "where Wuhan/Paget principles applied." *and substitute: page* [567]]
, and in *South Lanarkshire Council v Aviva Insurance Ltd* [2016] CSOH 83 at [26] (Outer House of Court of Session) and *Bitumen Invest AS v Richmond Mercantile Ltd FZC* [2016] EWHC 2957 (Comm) at [31]. The presumption that an instrument gives rise to independent, primary liability seems to apply "[w]here . . . the granter is a bank or other financial institution whose business includes the granting of financial instruments for a fee", e.g. an insurance company: *South Lanarkshire Council v Aviva Insurance Ltd*, above, at [25], per Lord Doherty, citing *Meritz Fire & Marine Insurance Co Ltd v Jan de Nul NV* [2010] EWHC 3362 (Comm), [2011] 1 All E.R. (Comm) 1049 at [65]–[66], per Beatson J.; *Caterpillar Motoren GmbH & Co KG v Mutual Benefits Assurance Co*, above, at [20], per Teare J.; *Spliethoff's Bevrachtingskantoor BV v Bank of China Ltd*, above, at [83], per Carr J.

[*Add to note 1524, line 36, after* "[2015] EWHC 2304 (Comm)": *page* [567]]
; *Bitumen Invest AS v Richmond Mercantile Ltd FZC* [2016] EWHC 2957 (Comm)

The fraud rule

34–509   [*Add to note 1531, at the end: page* [568]]
It has been held by Phillips J. in *Sinocore International Co Ltd v RBRG Ltd* [2017] EWHC 251 (Comm) at [46] that the authorities do not support a much wider proposition that a party who presents forged documents cannot obtain relief from the court in the transaction more generally, e.g. a claim for damages for a prior breach of the underlying contract.

Obtaining an injunction against a bank

34–510   [*Add to note 1533, line 15, after* "the validity of its demand)": *page* [569]]
, and *National Infrastructure Development Co Ltd v Banco Santander SA* [2017] EWCA Civ 27 at [20]–[24], where *Enka* was said to provide the "correct approach" where the beneficiary of a letter of credit seeks summary judgment against the bank, and that the position was different from those cases where the bank's own customer was seeking an interlocutory injunction against the bank (as in *Solo Industries UK Ltd v Canara Bank* [2001] 1 W.L.R. 1800 and *Alternative Power Solution Ltd v Central Electricity Board* [2014] UKPC 31, [2015] 1 W.L.R. 697: see this paragraph in the Main Work).

[*Add to note 1533, at the end: page* [569]]

In *Petrosaudi Oil Services (Venezuela) Ltd v Novo Banco SA* [2017] EWCA Civ 9, the Court of Appeal, reversing the first instance judge at [2016] EWHC 2456 (Comm), held that the general counsel of the beneficiary had not been fraudulent and had been entitled to sign a demand made on a standby letter of credit certifying that the applicant was "obligated to pay" the beneficiary. Christopher Clarke L.J., delivering a judgment with which Lewison L.J. agreed, construed the meaning of the words used and held (at [80]–[81]) that the statement that there was an obligation to pay was true. Obiter, he expressed some disquiet (at [88]) that the judge had held the general counsel to be fraudulent when the statement in the certificate was, in essence, a representation of law, which turned on a question of construction upon which different people might take different views.

[*In note 1539, line 7, delete* "[2001] EWCA Civ 1041" *and substitute: page* [570]]

[2001] EWCA Civ 1059

Restrictions on beneficiary's right to call for payment

[*Add to note 1555, at the end: page* [573]]   **34–514**

See also Chhina [2016] L.M.C.L.Q. 412. In *National Infrastructure Development Co Ltd v Banco Santander SA* [2016] EWHC 2990 (Comm) (affirmed [2017] EWCA Civ 27), Knowles J. (at [26]–[27]) refused an invitation to develop the law to recognise a different approach to standby letters of credit used to settle performance obligations, as opposed to letters of credit used to settle primary payment obligations, and noted that the position under Singaporean law appeared to be different.

The measure of damages

[*Add to note 1590, at the end: page* [579]]   **34–522**

For position on insolvency of issuing bank or confirming bank, see S. Connelly, "Bank recovery and resolution: the case of contingent letters of credit under bail-in" (2016) 2 J.I.B.F.L. 78.

(vii) *The Tender of Documents*

Construction of terms of credit

[*Add to note 1608, at the end: page* [582]]   **34–528**

Whether the strict compliance rule applies to performance bonds and demand guarantees has been the subject of some uncertainty: but see *IE Contractors Ltd v Lloyds Bank Plc* [1990] 2 Lloyd's Rep. 496 at 500–501, per Staughton L.J. ("[i]t is a question of construction of the bond"), applied in *Sea-Cargo Skips AS v State Bank of India* [2013] EWHC 177 (Comm), [2013] 2 Lloyd's Rep. 477 at [30], *Lukoil Mid-East Ltd v Barclays Bank Plc* [2016] EWHC 166 (TCC) at [17]; *South Lanarkshire Council v Coface SA* [2016] CSIH 15 at [12]; *MUR Joint*

Ventures BV v Compagnie Monegasque de Banque [2016] EWHC 3107 (Comm) at [26]–[28].

> [*In note 1611, lines 1–2, delete from* ", which, through dealing . . . " *to* "letters of credit." *and substitute: page* [582]]

; *Uzinterimpex JSC v Standard Bank Plc* [2007] EWHC 1151 (Comm), [2007] 2 Lloyd's Rep. 187 at [157]–[158]; *South Lanarkshire Council v Aviva Insurance Ltd* [2016] CSOH 83 at [29], which cases, although dealing with performance bonds, ought to apply also to letters of credit.

The ISBP

34–534   [*Add to paragraph, line 3, after "Examination of Documents": page* [585]] *under UCP 600*

CHAPTER 35

CARRIAGE BY AIR

3. Scope and Application of the Conventions

Scope of the Conventions

[In note 24, delete the second sentence and substitute: page [599]]   **35–008**
"Air transport undertaking" is not defined in the Conventions or in the United
Kingdom implementing legislation; however, it is defined in s.95(5) of the
Transport Act 2000, for the purposes of that Act, as meaning "an undertaking
... which includes the provision of services for the carriage by air of passengers
or cargo for hire or reward".

4. European Legislation

European Parliament and Council Regulation 889/2002

An EU carrier, still referred to in the legislation as a "Community air carrier", is   **35–018**
one holding an air operating certificate issued by the authorities of a Member
State. Pre-requisites for the issue of a licence include the carrier having a
principal place of business in the Member State and that nationals of a Member
State own or effectively control the carrier. On the UK withdrawing from the EU,
and subject to any contrary provision in the withdrawal agreement, Regulation
889/2002 will cease to apply to carriers based in and owned by nationals of the

UK. The Montreal Convention will continue to apply on the basis of the UK's earlier ratification. For the effect of the Regulation on non-international carriage, see below, para.35–074).

[*Add to note 82, at the end: page* [607]]
; *Air Baltic Corp AS v Lietuvos Respublikos specialiųjų tyrimų tarnyba* (C-429/14) [2016] 1 Lloyd's Rep. 407 at [23].

Insurance requirements

35–021   [*In note 98, lines 2–3, delete* "arts 138 or 140 of the Air Navigation Order 2005 (SI 2005/1790)" *and substitute: page* [609]]
arts 250 or 252 of the Air Navigation Order 2016 (SI 2016/765)

5. Liability of the Carrier

(a) *Passengers*

Information for passengers

35–026   [*Add to paragraph, at the end: page* [611]]
There are further requirements as to the publication of air fares which must show separately any taxes, airport charges, and other charges, surcharges or fees, such as those related to security or fuel that have been added to the basic fare. Optional price supplements must be communicated in a clear, transparent and unambiguous way at the start of any booking process and their acceptance by the customer must be on an "opt-in" basis.[118a]

[118a] European Parliament and Council Regulation 1008/2008 of 24 September 2008 on common rules for the operation of air services in the Community art.23(1); *Air Berlin Plc & Co Luftverkehrs KG v Bundesverband der Verbraucherzentralen und Verbraucherverbande—Verbraucherzentrale Bundesverband eV* (C-290/16). For enforcement in the UK, see Pt 2 of the Operation of Air Services in the Community (Pricing etc.) Regulations 2013 (SI 2013/486).

Disabled persons and persons with reduced mobility

35–048   [*In paragraph, lines 10–12, delete sentence beginning* "In the United Kingdom" *and note 207, and substitute: page* [624]]
In the United Kingdom enforcement of Regulation 1107/2006 is by means of a civil procedure which replaced the earlier criminal offences.[207]

[207] Civil Aviation (Access to Air Travel for Disabled Persons and Persons with Reduced Mobility) Regulations 2014 (SI 2014/2833), as amended by SI 2016/729 (which designates dispute resolution bodies).

(d) *Delay to Passengers, Baggage or Cargo*

Liability for delay

35–069   There can be liability to persons other than the delayed passenger. The CJEU held (*Air Baltic Corp AS v Lietuvos Respublikos specialiųjų tyrimų tarnyba*

(C-429/14) [2016] 1 Lloyd's Rep. 407) that art.19 of the Montreal Convention applies not only to the damage suffered by a passenger but also to the damage suffered by a person in its capacity as an employer who had concluded a contract of international carriage with an air carrier for the purpose of carriage of passengers who were its employees.

Delay is to be distinguished from "non-performance", the latter falling outside the scope of the Montreal Convention (see *Shawcross and Beaumont on Air Law*, para.VII1003.1 and the very full judgment in *Chaing v Air Canada* Unreported, January 22, 2016 (Cty Ct at Kingston-upon-Thames)).

European Parliament and Council Regulation 261/2004

For commentary on many aspects of the Regulation, see Bobek and Prassl (eds), **35–071** *Air Passenger Rights: Ten Years On* (2016).

Regulation 261/2004 only applies (Regulation 261/2004 art.3) to passengers who have a confirmed reservation on the flight concerned (*Kupeli v Sirketti* [2016] EWHC 930 (QB)) and, except in the case of cancellation, present themselves for check-in by a time specified by the air carrier, the tour operator or an authorised travel agent, or, if no time is indicated, not later than 45 minutes before the published departure (see *Caldwell v easyJet Airline Co Ltd*, 2015 GWD 34-546 (Sheriff Court (Lothian and Borders) (Edinburgh)) (arrival two hours before scheduled departure but unable to check-in before 45 minute deadline owing to slow-moving queues; held within the Regulation).

Difficult issues have arisen in cases involving connecting flights. The European Commission has proposed a new provision that where a passenger misses a connecting flight as a result of a delay to a preceding connecting flight, the passenger is to have a right to compensation by the Community air carrier operating that preceding flight; for this purpose, the delay would be calculated by reference to the scheduled time of arrival at the final destination (COM/ 2013/0130 final).

Remedies

[Add to note 333, at the end; page [638]] **35–072**
The Civil Aviation Authority is responsible for enforcement in the UK: Civil Aviation (Denied Boarding, Compensation and Assistance) Regulations 2005 (SI 2005/975) reg.5(1). Dispute resolution bodies are specified in reg.5(2) as substituted by SI 2016/729.

[Add to note 335, at the end: page [639]]
; *Van der Lans v Koninklijke Luchtvaartmaatschappij NV* (C-257/14); *Pešková v Travel Service a.s.* (C-315/15) (bird strike held to be an extraordinary circumstance; reasonable measures include control measures preventing the presence of birds provided that those measures do not require the carrier to make intolerable sacrifices in the light of the capacities of its undertaking).

[Add to note 340, at the end: page [639]]
and, for a defence of the decision by Judge Malinovský, Bobek and Prassl (eds), *Air Passenger Rights: Ten Years On* (2016), p.25. "Arrival time" is the time at

which at least one of the aircraft doors is opened to allow passengers to disembark: *Germanwings GmbH v Henning* (C-452/13) [2015] C.E.C. 661.

6. NON-INTERNATIONAL CARRIAGE

Applicable rules

35–074   Regulation 889/2002 applies only to "air carriers" defined by art.2(1)(a) to mean air transport undertakings with valid operating licences, and to "Community air carriers" defined by art.2(1)(b) to mean air carriers with valid operating licences granted by a Member State; carriage within a single Member State to view a property from the air by a carrier not required to have a valid operating licence was held not to be within the Regulation or (as it was not international carriage; see Main Work, Vol.II, para.35–012) the Montreal Convention (see *Pruller-Frey v Brodnig* (C-240/14)).

CARRIAGE BY LAND

3. INTERNATIONAL CARRIAGE

(a) *Introduction*

Multi-modal or combined transport

[*Add to note 459, at the end: page* [693]]   **36–084**
As to defining the modes of carriage, see Clarke, "The Shape of the Conventions on the Carriage of Goods" (2015) 50 E.T.L. 371, 375–376.

(b) *Goods by Rail*

Loss, damage and delay

[*Add to note 500, at the end: page* [697]]   **36–093**
As to the possibility of liability beyond that provided for under CIM where it is

contractually incorporated, see *DSM Acrylonitrile BV e.a. v DB Schenker Rail Nederland* (2016) 51 E.T.L. 335 (Rechtbank te Rotterdam).

Claims

36–097   [*Add to note 527, at the end: page* [700]]
Where there is an inconsistency with EU rules on jurisdiction, see *Anon.*, Cour de Cassation de France, November 29, 2016, (2016) 51 E.T.L. 684.

Limitation of actions

36–099   [*Add to note 534, at the end: page* [700]]
Where CIM is contractually incorporated without limitation of the scope of its application, art.48 may not apply to all claims governed by the CIM: *Anon.*, Oberster Gerichtshof Österreich, April 6, 2016, (2016) 51 E.T.L. 443.

(c) *Passengers, Luggage and Vehicles by Rail*

(ii) *Passengers and Hand Luggage*

The ticket

36–105   [*Add to note 551, at the end: page* [702]]
See *Nationale Maatschappij der Belgische Spoorwegen NV v Demey* (C-261/15), EU:C:2016:709 September 21, 2016 (preliminary ruling of ECJ as to passenger not in possession of a ticket).

(d) *Goods by Road*

Loss, damage and delay

36–126   [*Add to note 684, at the end: page* [716]]
Anon., Rechtbank te Rotterdam, March 30, 2016, (2016) 52 E.T.L. 101.

The carrier's exemptions from liability: art.17(4)

36–128   [*Add to note 706, at the end: page* [719]]
See also *Anon.*, Oberster Gerichtshof Österreich, April 27, 2016, (2016) 51 E.T.L. 560.

[*Add to note 707, line 4 after* "loading and stowage"*: page* [719]]
unless the parties agree contractually otherwise (*Anon.*, Oberster Gerichtshof Österreich, July 6, 2016, (2016) 51 E.T.L. 565).

[*Add to note 707, line 6, after* "by the sender."*: page* [720]]
See, e.g. *Anon.*, Bundesgerichtshof, March 19, 2015, (2016) 51 E.T.L. 99.

Upper financial limits of liability and measure of damages

36–130   [*Add to note 724, line 1, after* "and Road Act 1979 s.4(2)."*: page* [722]]
See *Topdanmark Forsikring A/S v DSV Road A/S* (2016) 51 E.T.L. 93 (SC Denmark).

Wilful misconduct: an exception to limitation

[*Add to note 740, at the end: page* [725]]   **36–131**
See also *Topdanmark Forsikring A/S v DSV Road A/S* (2016) 51 E.T.L. 93 (SC
Denmark).

Successive carriers

[*Add new note 759a, after* "takes possession of the goods." *in line 10: page* [728]]   **36–136**
^{759a} See *Anon.*, Hoge Raad der Nederlanden, September 11, 2015, (2016) 51 E.T.L. 109; Laurijssen
(2016) 51 E.T.L. 121.

Contribution proceedings

[*Add to note 784, line 3, after* "exclusive jurisdiction in disputes."*: page* [732]]   **36–141**
See *British American Tobacco Switzerland SA v Exel Europe Ltd* [2015] UKSC
65, [2016] A.C. 262 at [36]–[37], [68].

Jurisdiction

[*In note 814, lines 1–8, delete* "A carrier who did not agree . . . " *to* "at [97]   **36–146**
(subject to appeal)." *and substitute: page* [736]]
A carrier who did not agree to a particular jurisdiction, and had no notice of a
particular jurisdiction agreement, would not be bound by that agreement: *British
American Tobacco Switzerland SA v Exel Europe Ltd* [2012] EWHC 694
(Comm), [2012] 2 Lloyd's Rep. 1 at [46]–[51]; [2015] UKSC 65, [2016] A.C.
262 at [26]. Accordingly, a successive carrier cannot be sued in proceedings
brought against the primary carrier pursuant to a jurisdiction agreement between
the claimant and the primary carrier, if the successive carrier did not agree to that
clause and if the jurisdiction agreement is not in the consignment note, subject to
the other heads of jurisdiction in CMR: *British American Tobacco Switzerland
SA v Exel Europe Ltd* [2015] UKSC 65, [2016] A.C. 262.

[*Add to note 814, line 9, after* "extends to extra-contractual claims."*: page* [736]]
See also *Anon.*, Oberster Gerichtshof Österreich, February 25, 2015, (2015) 50
E.T.L. 700.

[*In note 816, lines 3–6, delete from* "British American Tobacco Switzerland SA v
Exel Europe Ltd" *to* "(subject to appeal to the Supreme Court)" *and substitute:
page* [737]]
British American Tobacco Switzerland SA v Exel Europe Ltd [2015] UKSC 65,
[2016] A.C. 262

[*In note 817, lines 2–4, delete from* "See British American Tobacco Switzerland SA
v Exel Europe Ltd" *to* "(subject to appeal to the Supreme Court)." *and substitute:
page* [737]]
See *British American Tobacco Switzerland SA v Exel Europe Ltd* [2015] UKSC
65, [2016] A.C. 262, at [48]–[58].

[Delete text of note 819 and substitute: page [738]]

Sch. art.36. However, art.36 is not a provision stipulating in which jurisdiction proceedings by cargo claimants may be brought; that is a matter for art.31. See *British American Tobacco Switzerland SA v Exel Europe Ltd* [2015] UKSC 65, [2016] A.C. 262 at [19]–[20], [34]–[47], [67], [69].

[In paragraph, lines 22–29, delete from "Article 31(1) is to be construed" *to* "against the primary carrier.822" *and substitute: page* [738]]

Article 39(2) is concerned only with actions among carriers and not claims by cargo interests (whose claims are governed by art.31).821–822

821–822 *British American Tobacco Switzerland SA v Exel Europe Ltd* [2015] UKSC 65, [2016] A.C. 262 at [36]–[37], [62], [68].

Chapter 37

CONSTRUCTION CONTRACTS

2. Formation of Contract

(c) *Tenders*

Good faith and partnering

37–058 [*Add to note 155, at the end: page* [775]]
See also *Monde Petroleum SA v WesternZagros Ltd* [2016] EWHC 1472 (Comm), [2017] 1 All E.R. (Comm) 1009.

3. Contract Terms

(c) *Implied Terms*

General principles

37–072 [*Add to note 198, at the end: page* [782]]
In *Marks & Spencer Plc v BNP Paribas Securities Services Trust Co (Jersey) Ltd* [2015] UKSC 72, the Supreme Court reaffirmed the applicability of these five principles and provided further guidance as to their usage: see above, para.14–007.

[*Add to note 200, at the end: page* [782]]
In *Walter Lilly & Co Ltd v Clin* [2016] EWHC 357(TCC), [2016] B.L.R. 247 it was held that in order to make a Design Portion JCT Contract work effectively the employer, who had the responsibility for obtaining planning permission, should provide in good time to the local authority the information that its planning officers require and are lawfully entitled to expect in order to grant the necessary consents.

Fitness of works

[Add to paragraph, at the end: page [786]]   **37–079**
However, the decision of the first instance Court was re-instated by the Supreme
Court[241a] which stated that where a contract requires an item to be produced in
accordance prescribed criteria and in accordance with a prescribed design which
will inevitably result in the product falling short of that criteria, the contractor
will often be obliged to improve upon the aspects of the prescribed design
contained in the contract. Whether this is true in any given case is likely to turn
upon the nature of the inconsistency in the contract and the relative expertise of
the contractor and the employer, or its designing architect.

[241a] [2017] UKSC 59.

(d) *Statutes Relevant to Construction*

Unfair Contract Terms Act 1977

[Add new note 260a, line 15, after "written standard terms of business.": *page*   **37–084**
[789]]
[260a] It is not necessary for a party's terms and condition to be incorporated in their entirety to
trigger the application of this section. A single incorporated clause taken from a party's standard
terms and condition may, on the right facts, be sufficient. See *Commercial Management (Investments)
Ltd v Mitchell Design & Construct Ltd* [2016] EWHC 76 (TCC).

(e) *Tort in Construction*

Tort and contract

[Add new note 303a, at the end of paragraph: page [793]]   **37–094**
[303a] Following the Court of Appeal decision in *Wellesley Partners LLP v Withers LLP* [2015]
EWCA Civ 1146 the contractual rules on remoteness, and possibly also causation, would continue to
apply even where there are concurrent duties of care in contract and tort. See above,
para.1–195A.

4. Particular Features

(a) *Variations*

What constitutes a variation

[Add to paragraph, at the end: page [796]]   **37–097**
Variations under a contract are to be distinguished from variations *of* the contract
itself. The wording of the particular contract may be relevant to whether a
variation under or of the contract is recognised. However, in *MWB Business
Exchange Centres Ltd v Rock Advertising Ltd*[330a] it was held by the Court of
Appeal that where a contract contained an anti-oral variation clause and one party
alleged a variation to the same was agreed orally, the anti-oral variation clause
did not necessarily preclude a variation of the contract as the most important
consideration was party autonomy and freedom of contract which entitles the

parties to agree whatever terms they chose, even as variations in such circumstances, subject to certain limits imposed by public policy.

330a [2016] EWCA Civ 553, [2016] 3 W.L.R. 1519.

(d) *Extension of Time and Liquidated Damages*

Relevant delay

37–117   [*Add to paragraph, at the end; page* [807]]
Any extension of time awarded will invariably be added by reference to the period immediately following the contractual completion date, even if the delaying event in fact occurred at some other point in time, such as substantially after the original completion date.[420a] This could produce incongruous results in terms of liability for damages arising from late completion or claims for loss and expense, but it is submitted that such problems can be reduced or eliminated entirely by correctly applying the causation requirements of such subsequent claims rather than focussing too strictly on the period in respect of which an extension of time has been granted.

420a *Carillion Construction Ltd v Emcor Engineering Services Ltd* [2017] EWCA Civ 65 where this was described as an extension being awarded on a "contiguous" basis.

Concurrent delay

37–120   [*Add to note 428, at the end: page* [808]]
; and also approved in *Saga Cruises BDF Ltd v Fincantieri SpA* [2016] EWHC 1875 (Comm) at 249–251.

[*Add new paragraph 37–121A: page* [809]]
37–121A **Revised rule on penalty clauses.** In *Cavendish Square Holding BV v Makdessi* the Supreme Court held that the true test for a penalty is whether the impugned provision is a secondary obligation which imposes a detriment on the contract-breaker out of all proportion to any legitimate interest of the innocent party in the enforcement of the primary obligation.[439a] This test is likely to be more permissive of liquidated damages clauses and any cases pre-dating this decision must be treated with care.

439a [2015] UKSC 67 at [32], [255] and [291]. See above, paras 26–178 et seq.

5. Payment

(b) *Interim Payment and Milestones*

Right to interim payment

37–145   [*Add new note 511a, after* "performed, or to the contract sum." *in line 22: page* [819]]
511a *Grove Developments Ltd v Balfour Beatty Regional Construction Ltd* [2016] EWHC 168 (TCC) at [33]; approved by the Court of Appeal at [2016] EWCA Civ 990.

9. Remedies by Enforcement

(b) *Claims*

Claims for loss and expense

[*Add to paragraph, at the end: page* [863]]   **37–242**
A party seeking to prove a claim on a global or total costs basis carries a greater
burden than a party seeking to prove the same claim on a particularised or
itemised basis.[801a]

 [801a] *Walter Lilly & Co Ltd v Mackay, DMW Developments Ltd* [2012] EWHC 1773 (TCC), [2012]
B.L.R. 503 per Akenhead J. at [486]*; John Sisk & Son Ltd v Carmel Building Services Ltd* [2016]
EWHC 806 (TCC), [2016] B.L.R. 283, per Carr J. at [55]–[56].

10. Disputes

(e) *Adjudication*

The enforcement of adjudicator's awards

[*Add to paragraph, at the end: page* [878]]   **37–267**
Whilst adjudicators' decisions are binding until finally determined, it is possible
and sometimes permissible for the losing party to seek final determination of
legal issues in Court prior to, or at the same time as, any enforcement steps are
taken by the successful party.[896a] This can have the effect that the outcome of the
adjudication is overturned before it can be enforced. However, more recently the
Courts have sought to limit the availability of such a process by making it
available only in cases where the adjudicator's decision is unconscionably wrong
or beyond any rational justification.[896b]

 [896a] *Caledonian Modular Ltd v Mar City Developments Ltd* [2015] EWHC 1855 (TCC) at [13].
 [896b] *Hutton Construction Ltd v Wilson Properties (London) Ltd* [2017] EWHC 517 (TCC) at
[18].

Some procedural aspects of adjudication

[*Add to note 901, at the end: page* [879]]   **37–268**
It had become popular to argue that, in cases where statutory interest runs,
s.5A(2A) of the Late Payment of Commercial Debts (Interest) Act 1998 would
permit a party to recover its reasonable legal costs of pursing a debt claim by
adjudication. In practice, this argument was accepted by a number of adjudicators
but it appears that this approach is incorrect and that on the issue of party
adjudication costs s.108A of the Housing Grants Act takes precedence over
s.5A(2A) of the Late Payment Act 1998; see *Enviroflow Management Ltd v
Redhill Works (Nottingham) Ltd* [2017] EWHC 2159 (TCC).

[*Add to note 906, at the end: page* [879]]
cf. *Paice v Harding (t/a MJ Harding Contractors)* [2015] EWHC 661 (TCC)

[*Add to note 907, at the end: page* [879]]

See also *Cofely Ltd v Bingham* [2016] EWHC 240 (Comm), [2016] B.L.R. 187, where it was held by Hamblen J. that an arbitrator's scale of prior appointments as an adjudicator and arbitrator in disputes involving the claimant, either as a party or party representative, together with his conduct of the arbitration and his reaction to questions concerning his relationship with the claimant, generated the required basis for a finding of apparent bias.

Effect of an adjudicator's decision

37–270   [*Add to note 913, at the end: page* [880]]:
; approved by the Supreme Court at [2015] UKSC 38.

CHAPTER 38

CONSUMER CONTRACTS

[371]

1. Introduction

Legislative protection for consumer contractors

[*In notes 10, 11 and 12 delete "1979" and substitute: page* [886]]   **38–002**
1893

The growing importance of European law

[*Add new note 16a, at end of paragraph title: page* [887]]   **38–003**
[16a] See general note on the significance of the decision that the United Kingdom will leave the European Union, above, para.1–013A.

[*Add to note 22, at the end: page* [887]]
The 1990 Directive is repealed by Directive (EU) 2015/2302 on package travel and linked travel arrangements [2015] O.J. L326/1.

2. The Relationship of EU And UK Consumer Contract Law

(a) *The Continuing Interpretative Significance of EU Directives*

EU regulations and directives

[*Add new note 77a, at end of paragraph title: page* [887]]   **38–012**
[77a] See general note on the announcement that the United Kingdom will leave the European Union, above, para.1–013A.

Significance of EU source of English consumer contract law for its interpretation

[*Add to note 87, at the end: page* [896]]   **38–013**
; *United States of America v Nolan* [2015] UKSC 63, [2016] A.C. 463 where Lord Mance J.S.C. (with whom Lord Neuberger of Abbotsbury P.S.C., Baroness

Hale of Richmond D.P.S.C. and Lord Reed J.S.C. agreed) at [14] described the principle of conforming interpretation as "a cardinal principle of European Union and domestic law".

"Autonomous" and national interpretations

38–014   [*Add to note 99, at the end: page* [898]]
Identical provision to art.3(5) of the 2011 Directive is found in Directive (EU) 2015/2302 on package travel and linked travel arrangements [2015] O.J. L326/1 art.2(3) (this Directive repeals and replaces Directive 90/314/EEC on package travel, package holidays and package tours [1990] O.J. L158/59).

The duty of national courts to intervene of their own motion to protect EU consumer rights

38–018   [*Add to note 121, at the end: page* [901]]
; *Bucura v SC Bancpost SA* (C-348/14) July 9, 2015 para.44. On the possibility that a Member State may incur liability for a court's failure to protect a consumer's EU law rights see *Tomášová v Republic of Slovakia* (C-168/15) July 28, 2016, below, para.38–304.

[*Add to note 127, at the end: page* [901]]
; *Radlinger v Finway a.s.* (C-377/14) April 21, 2016 at paras 62–74 (information duties) and see below, para.38–063A.

[*Add to note 134, at the end: page* [902]]
See also *Margarit Panicello v Hernández Martinez* (C-503/15) A.G. Opinion of September 15, 2016 at [127]–[128] (The CJEU judgment of February 16, 2017 did not comment on these issues).

[*Add to note 135, at the end: page* [902]]
cf. *Radlinger v Finway a.s.* (C-377/14) April 21, 2016 at paras 62–74 where the CJEU recognised an obligation on the national court to consider whether the information duties of the trader under the Consumer Credit Directive 2008 had been complied with simply by reference to the need to ensure the protection of the consumer and to its earlier case-law.

(b) *The Intensity of Harmonisation Required by EU Legislation*

Examples of "minimum harmonisation" directives

38–022   [*Add to note 158, at the end: page* [906]]
The 1990 Directive is repealed by Directive (EU) 2015/2302 on package travel and linked travel arrangements [2015] O.J. L326/1, art.4 of which sets a general principle of full harmonisation. The Directive must be implemented by the UK by January 1, 2018.

Examples of "full harmonisation" and "partial full harmonisation": Unfair Commercial Practices Directive 2005

[Add new note 166a, at end of paragraph title: page [907]] **38–024**
[166a] Directive (EU) 2015/2302 on package travel and linked travel arrangements [2015] O.J. L326/1 art.4 sets a general principle of full harmonisation, with certain exceptions which the Directive itself sets out.

3. DEFINITIONS OF CONSUMER CONTRACT

(b) *"Consumer"*

"Consumer" in EU law

[Add to note 197, at the end: page [911]] **38–030**
However, the 1990 Directive is repealed (as of January 1, 2018) by Directive (EU) 2015/2302 on package travel and linked travel arrangements [2015] O.J. L326/1 which substitutes for "consumer" a new category of "traveller" which "means any person who is seeking to conclude a contract, or is entitled to travel on the basis of a contract concluded, within the scope of [the] Directive": art.3(6). As recital 7 explains, the majority of travellers buying packages or linked travel arrangements are "consumers within the meaning of Union consumer law", but the Directive's protections should extend to "business travellers including members of liberal professions, or self-employed or other natural persons where they do not make travel arrangements on the basis of a general agreement".

European case-law

[Add to paragraph, at the end: page [913]] **38–032**
The Court of Justice has recently held that, in order to determine whether a person was acting as a consumer for the purposes of the Directive on unfair terms in consumer contracts, a national court should take into account "all the circumstances of the case, particularly the nature of the goods or service covered by the contract in question, capable of showing the purpose for which those goods or that service is being acquired",[214a] this being a "functional criterion".[214b] However, the concept of "consumer" is "objective in nature and is distinct from the concrete knowledge the person in question may have, or from the information that person actually has".[214c] As a result, while lawyers may constitute "traders" in their contracts with their own clients,[214d] they may, even if they are technically knowledgeable, nonetheless act as consumers in other transactions as they may be weaker parties compared to the traders with whom they deal.[214e]

[214a] *Costea v SC Volksbank România SA* (C-110/14) April 23, 2015 at para.23.
[214b] *Tarcău v Banca Comercială Intesa Sanpaolo România SA* (C-74/15) Order of CJEU November 19, 2015 at para.27.
[214c] *Costea v SC Volksbank România SA* (C-110/14) April 23, 2015 at para.21. See similarly, *Tarcău v Banca Comercială Intesa Sanpaolo România SA* (C-74/15) Order of CJEU November 19, 2015 para.27 on which see below, paras 38–207 and 45–156.

²¹⁴ᵈ *Šiba v Devėnas* (C-537/13) January 15, 2015 [2015] Bus. L.R. 291 paras 23 and 24.
²¹⁴ᵉ *Costea v SC Volksbank România SA* (C-110/14) April 23, 2015 at paras 20–27.

The Consumer Rights Directive and its possible wider influence

38–034   [*Add to note 225, line 6, after* "2011 Directive recital 17": *page* [915]]
A similar pattern is found in Directive 2014/17/EU of 4 February 2014 on credit
agreements for consumers relating to immovable property [2014] O.J. L60/34
(the "Mortgage Credit Directive") recital 12 and art.4(1), referring to the definition of "consumer" in Directive 2008/48/EC of 23 April 2008 on credit agreements for consumers [2008] O.J. L133/66 art.3(1).

[*In note 227, delete* "The CJEU . . . " *to* "time of writing" *and substitute: page*
[915]]
The CJEU in its judgment of September 3, 2015 did not address this issue.

United Kingdom case-law on earlier definition

38–037   [*Add to note 238, line 4, after* "Brussels I *bis* Regulation") art.17.": *page* [917]]
In commenting on the contrast between the *Apostolakis* and *Rouvroy* decisions,
the HC in *AMT Futures Ltd v Mazillier, Dr Meier & Dr Guntner Rechtsanwalts-
gesellschaft mbH* [2014] EWHC 1085 (Comm), [2015] 2 W.L.R. 187 at [58]
considered that the dividing line between investors who count as "consumers"
and those who do not "is likely to be heavily dependent on the circumstances of
each individual and the nature and pattern of investment". (This point was not
discussed on appeal to the CA or the SC: [2015] EWCA Civ 143, [2015] Q.B.
699; [2017] UKSC 13, [2017] 2 W.L.R. 853).

[*In note 238, lines 18 and 19, delete text* "Chesterton Global . . . as a
'consumer')": *page* [917]]

[*Add to note 238, line 22, after* "Regulations 2008 (SI 2008/1816)": *page* [917]]
; *R. (on the application of Bluefin Insurance Services Ltd) v Financial Ombudsman Service Ltd* [2014] EWHC 3413 at [121]–[128] (director of company taking
out a Directors and Officers Insurance Policy was not a "consumer" for the
purposes of the Financial Ombudsman Service's jurisdiction (which was defined
by reference, inter alia, to the definition of "consumer" in the 1993 Directive) as
the insurance concerned his liability for acts in the course of his trade, business,
or profession).

[*Add to paragraph, at the end: page* [918]]
In *Ashfaq v International Insurance Co of Hannover Plc* the Court of Appeal
applied the approach of the High Court in *Overy v Paypal (Europe) Ltd* to the
context of an individual who had concluded a contract of insurance on a house
which he let to tenants at a profit.²⁴⁶ᵃ In these circumstances, the individual did
not contract as a "consumer" within the meaning of the 1999 Regulations as the
contract was a business insurance even though the individual may also carry on
some unrelated business activity.²⁴⁶ᵇ

²⁴⁶ᵃ [2017] EWCA Civ 357.

[246b] [2017] EWCA Civ 357 at [45]–[57]. cf. *Chesterton Global Ltd v Finney* Unreported, April 30, 2010, Lambeth County Ct where an individual who leased a "buy-to-let" property was held to have done so as a "consumer".

The new UK standard legislative definition of "consumer"

[*Add to note 259, at the end: page* [919]]   **38–038**
See *Christopher Linnett Ltd v Harding (t/a MJ Harding Contractors)* [2017] EWHC 1781 (TCC) at [84] (sole trader not a "consumer" for the purposes of the 2013 Regulations when contracting with an adjudicator for services at least mainly part of his business).

The "average consumer"

[*Add to note 267, at the end: page* [920]]   **38–041**
See also *Konsumentombudsmannen v Ving Sverige AB* (C-122/10) of May 12, 2011.

Consumers as the supplier of goods or services?

[*In note 277, update reference to Treitel on The Law of Contract to: page* [922]]   **38–044**
14th edn (2015), para.7–054

[*In paragraph, lines 41–46, delete from* "On the other hand, . . . " *to* "traders is more arguable.[292]" *and substitute: page* [923]]
And while the wording of the Unfair Terms in Consumer Contracts Directive 1993 (formerly implemented in UK law by the Unfair Terms in Consumer Contracts Regulations 1999 and now by the Consumer Rights Act 2015)[292] is not completely clear, the Court of Justice has recently held that there is no requirement that the "consumer" be the recipient of goods or services and so may apply to a contract under which a natural person acting other than in the course of business guarantees a loan made by a creditor to a commercial company.[292a]

[292] See Main Work, Vol.II, paras 38–192 et seq.
[292a] *Tarcău v Banca Comercială Intesa Sanpaolo România SA* (C-74/15) Order of CJEU November 19, 2015, on which see below, para.38–207.

(c) *The Other Party to Consumer Contracts—"Traders"*

EU legislation

[*Add to note 319, line 4, after* "("organizer" and "retailer")"*: page* [926]]   **38–048**
(this approach is amended by Directive (EU) 2015/2302 on package travel and linked travel arrangements [2015] O.J. L326/1, which revokes and replaces the 1990 Directive. Article 3 of the new Directive defines "organiser" and "retailer" as categories of "trader", which is itself defined and which extends to persons facilitating a "linked travel arrangement")

[Add new paragraph 38–052A: page [930]]

38–052A   **Traders as "intermediaries" of non-traders.** In *Wathelet v Garage Bietheres & Fils SPRL*[342b] a consumer had bought a second-hand car from a garage, the car in fact being owned by a private individual on behalf of whom the garage sold the car. Although the issue was disputed, the national court held that there was "strong, specific and circumstantial evidence indicating that [the private individual] was not informed that it was a private sale".[342c] The question arose as to whether a trader who acts as intermediary on behalf of a non-professional seller counts as a "seller" within the meaning of the Consumer Sales Directive 1999 so as to bear the liabilities which that directive imposes on "sellers", whether or not the trader is remunerated and whether or not the trader informed the prospective buyer that the seller is a private individual.[342d] The Court of Justice of the EU held in this respect, first, that the sale was a "private sale" as the owner of the vehicle was a private individual, the garage acting as a trader as authorised intermediary.[342e] For this purpose, the concept of "seller" must be given an autonomous interpretation for the purposes of the 1999 Directive and, while the definition in the Directive does not cover intermediaries, it should be interpreted as covering "a trader acting as intermediary on behalf of a private individual who has not duly informed the consumer of the fact that the owner of the goods sold is a private individual", which is for the national court to decide on the facts,[342f] taking into account the degree of participation and the amount of effort employed by the intermediary in the sale, the circumstances in which the goods were presented to the consumer, and the latter's behaviour.[342g] This decision does not depend on whether or not the intermediary is remunerated for so acting.[342h] This result was justified by the Court of Justice by the need to ensure the high level of consumer protection required by the 1999 Directive which would be put at risk if the consumer's ignorance concerning the capacity in which the trader acts were allowed to deprive him of the rights provided by the Directive.[342i] In English law, it would seem that in these circumstances the trader would be considered to be the agent of an undisclosed principal,[342j] and so could be sued on the contract of sale as "seller" on this basis.[342k]

[342b] C-149/15 [2017] 1 W.L.R. 865.

[342c] C-149/15 at para.22.

[342d] C-149/15 at para.23. 1999 Directive art.1(1)(c) (*"seller*: shall mean any natural or legal person who, under a contract, sells consumer goods in the course of his trade, business or profession"). On the significance of the 1999 Directive and its implementation in English law see Main Work, Vol.II, paras 38–400 et seq.

[342e] C-149/15 at paras 24–26.

[342f] C-149/15 at paras 28–30 and 45.

[342g] C-149/15 at para.44.

[342h] C-149/15 at para.45. Remuneration was seen as part of the contractual relationship between the individual owner of the goods and the intermediary and therefore outside the scope of the Directive: C-149/15 at para.43.

[342i] C-149/15 at paras 36–42.

[342j] There is a degree of uncertainty here as the A.G.'s Opinion refers to an intermediary acting *in the name of* as well as on behalf of the individual and the former suggests that the agency is disclosed, whereas the CJEU states the facts as being that the consumer was told that her apparent seller acted as an intermediary only after the contract had been concluded: C-149/15 at para.14.

[342k] See Main Work, Vol.I, para.31–063. The general law of agency applies to contracts for the sale of goods: Sale of Goods Act 1979 s.62(2); *Benjamin's Sale of Goods* 10th edn (2017), para.3–002.

4. Information Requirements and Consumers' Rights of Cancellation

(a) *Introduction*

Rationale

[*Add to note 359, at the end: page* [932]]:Directive (EU) 2015/2302 on package   **38–055**
travel and linked travel arrangements [2015] O.J. L326/1 repeals and replaces the
1990 Directive: see below, para.38–132.

The Consumer Rights Directive 2011

[*Add to note 368, at the end: page* [933]]   **38–056**
See also European Commission, *Report from the Commission to the European
Parliament and the Council on the application of Directive 2011/83/EU* [etc.],
COM(2017) 259 final.

[*Add to note 373, at the end: page* [934]]
(Section 90 of the 2015 Act is amended by the Digital Economy Act 2017 s.105
as from a date to be appointed).

Consumer Contracts (Information, Cancellation and Additional Charges) Regulations 2013

[*In paragraph, line 5, delete* "revoked and"*: page* [934]]   **38–057**

[*Add to note 376, line 1, after* "SI 2013/3134"*: page* [934]]
(in force June 13, 2014)

[*Add to note 377, at the end: page* [934]]
The 2008 Regulations (SI 2008/1816) therefore do not apply to contracts entered
into on or after June 13, 2014, being the date of coming into force of the 2013
Regulations: 2013 Regulations reg.2(b).

[*Add to note 378, at the end: page* [934]]
The 2000 Regulations (SI 2000/2334) therefore do not apply to contracts entered
into on or after June 13, 2014, being the date of coming into force of the 2013
Regulations: 2013 Regulations reg.2(a).

[*Add new paragraph 38–063A: page* [939]]
Duty of court in relation to compliance with information duties. The Court of   **38–063A**
Justice of the EU has held that the purpose of consumer protection pursued by a
number of directives requires national courts to raise of their own motion issues
relating to possible rights for the consumer under national laws implementing
those directives.[408a] In *Radlinger v Finway a.s.*[408b] the Court of Justice of the EU
followed this case-law in the context of the information requirements imposed on
traders to consumers by the Consumer Credit Directive 2008. The particular
justification for such a duty as regards information requirements was that the
consumer is in "a weak position vis-à-vis the seller or supplier, as regards both

his bargaining power and his level of knowledge, which leads to the consumer agreeing to terms drawn up in advance by the seller or supplier without being able to influence the content of those terms".[408c] The Court of Justice continued:

> "In that regard, information, before and at the time of concluding a contract, on the terms of the contract and the consequences of concluding it is of fundamental importance for a consumer. It is, in particular, on the basis of that information that the consumer decides whether he wishes to be bound by the conditions drafted in advance by the seller or supplier."[408d]

There is a real risk, moreover, that the consumer may not rely on a legal rule protecting him owing to lack of awareness.[408e] Effective consumer protection therefore requires national courts to consider whether the information duties in the 2008 Directive have been complied with and, if that have not, they must draw all the consequences provided by national law, in the context, as regards penalties imposed as required by that directive.[408f] It is submitted that this reasoning applies by analogy to other information requirements imposed on traders by EU directives for the benefit of consumers and, therefore, that the Court of Justice would equally require national courts to raise the question whether these other information requirements have been fulfilled and, if not, with what effect. This special role of the court in relation to information duties must be borne in mind when considering the range of legal consequences of non-compliance with the information requirements under the 2013 Regulations.[408g]

[408a] See Main Work, Vol.II, paras 38–018—38–019.
[408b] C-377/14, April 21, 2016 ("*Radlinger* (C-377/14)").
[408c] *Radlinger* (C-377/14) at para.63, referring to *ERSTE Bank Hungary Zrt v Sugár* (C-32/14) October 1, 2015 at para.39 (which concerned the 1993 Directive).
[408d] *Radlinger* (C-377/14) at para.64, referring to *Constructora Principado SA v Menéndez Álvarez* (C-226/12) January 16, 2014 at para.25 (which concerned the 1993 Directive).
[408e] *Radlinger* (C-377/14) at paras 65, 70 and 74 (an obligation and not merely a power).
[408f] *Radlinger* (C-377/14) at para.73.
[408g] See Main Work, Vol.II, paras 38–099 et seq.

(b) Contracts Covered by the 2013 Regulations

Distinctions according to the subject matter of the contract

38–067   [*Add to note 418, at the end: page* [940]]
cf. *Software Incubator Ltd v Computer Associates UK Ltd* [2016] EWHC 1587 (QB) at [35]–[69] (contract for the supply of software may constitute a "sale of goods" for the purposes of the Commercial Agents (Council Directive) Regulations 1993 (SI 1993/3053), the court distinguishing the position in the law of sale of goods).

Exclusions from the scope of the 2013 Regulations

38–071   [*Add to note 449, line 2, after* "reg.6(1)(g)": *page* [945]]
(as amended by the Consumer Contracts (Amendment) Regulations 2015 (SI 2015/1629) art.3)

[Add to note 449, at the end: page [945]]
The scope of this exclusion will change on implementation of Directive (EU)
2015/2302 on package travel and linked travel arrangements [2015] O.J. L326/1,
which repeals and replaces the 1990 Directive (see below, para.38–132) and
which excludes only the provisions in the 2015 Directive governing "packages"
(and not therefore "linked travel arrangements") from the scope of the 2011
Directive: 2015 Directive art.3(2), (3) and (5) and art.27(2) (amending the 2011
Directive art.3(3)).

(ii) *Distance Contracts*

"A contract concluded ... under an organised distance sales or service-provision scheme"

[Add to paragraph, line 19, after "with a hair-dresser.": *page* [952]]   **38–082**
And it has been held that a scheme whereby, for a fee, the Royal Institute of
Chartered Surveyors nominates adjudicators as part of its statutory function as an
adjudicator nomination body is not an "organised distance sales scheme" so that
a contract concluded with the adjudicator does not count as a "distance contract"
for the purposes of the 2013 Regulations.[501a]

[501a] *Christopher Linnett Ltd v Harding (t/a MJ Harding Contractors)* [2017] EWHC 1781 (TCC)
at [86].

(c) *Information Requirements*
(iv) *The Effects of the Information Requirements*

General

[Add to paragraph, at the end: page [962]]   **38–099**
As has earlier been noted, the Court of Justice has held that the effectiveness of
the protection provided by information requirements for consumers in the Consumer Credit Directive 2008 means that a national court must raise the issue
whether these requirements have been fulfilled and, if not, must "draw all the
consequences provided for under national law".[577a]

[577a] *Radlinger v Finway a.s.* (C-377/14) April 21, 2016 at paras 62–74 and see above,
para.38–063A.

The contractual significance of information supplied

[In paragraph, line 3, delete "2013 Regulations provide" *and substitute: page*   **38–100**
[962]]
2013 Regulations (as made) provided

[Add to paragraph, at the end: page [963]]
After the enactment of these provisions in the 2015 Act, the 2013 Regulations
were amended so that their own broad provisions governing the contractual
significance of information are replaced with a residual provision to similar effect

but applicable only to contracts for the supply of digital content *other than* for a price paid by the consumer.[585a]

[585a] Consumer Contracts (Amendment) Regulations 2015 (SI 2015/1629) arts 4–6 (replacing 2013 Regulations reg.9(3) (on-premises contracts), reg.10(5) (off-premises contracts) and reg.13(6) (distance contracts)). The intention was that the 2013 Regulations should still apply to contracts under which digital content is supplied which do not fall within the definition of "digital content contracts" in the 2015 Act: Explanatory Note to SI 2015/1629, which states that the amendments are "in consequence of the Act and revoke provisions of the 2013 Regulations to the extent they are replicated in the Act". The retention of the residual category of contracts for the supply of digital content in the 2013 Regulations as amended is required by their broad scope following in this respect the Consumer Rights Directive 2011: see Main Work, Vol.II, para.38–067. However, under the 2015 Act Pt 1 Ch.3, "a contract for a trader to supply digital content to a consumer" is of two types: where digital content "is supplied for a price paid by the consumer" (s.33(1)) and where "(a) it is supplied free with goods or services or other digital content for which the consumer pays a price, and (b) it is not generally available to consumers unless they have paid a price for it or for goods or services or other digital content" (s.33(2)). This being the case, it would appear that the second type of digital content contract defined by s.33(2) would also count as a "contract for the supply of digital content other than for a price paid by the consumer" under the new 2013 Regulations (regs 9(3), 10(5) and 13(6), thus retaining (apparently by mistake) a degree of regulatory overlap. (The amendments to the 2013 Regulations apply to contracts entered into on or after October 1, 2015: SI 2015/1629 art.1).

Effect on the contract of failure to provide information

38–101   [*Add to note 587, at the end: page* [963]]
; *Allproperty Claims Ltd v Tang* [2015] EWHC 2198 (QB) at [45] and cf. *Kell v Department of Energy and Climate Change* (Newcastle upon Tyne County Ct, July 23, 2015).

Criminal law: off-premises contracts

38–102   [*Delete text of note 596 and substitute: page* [964]].
2013 Regulations regs 20–23; regs 24–26 (powers of investigation, obstruction of authorised officers, and freedom from self-incrimination, respectively) were revoked by the Consumer Rights Act 2015 (Consequential Amendments) Order 2015 (SI 2015/1726) art.2, Sch. Pt 2, para.7; the 2015 Act is amended so as to include the 2013 Regulations in the list of legislation to which the investigatory powers in that Act (Sch.5) applies: SI 2015/1726 art.2, Sch. Pt 1 para.6.

Misleading omissions

38–105   [*Add to note 601, line 5, after* "2013 Regulations regs 13 and 14.".*: page* [965]]
For the "complementary nature" of information obligations under specific EU legislation and the provision in art.7(5) of the 2005 Directive (implemented by reg.6(3)(b) of the 2013 Regulations), see *Abcur AB v Apoteket Farmaci, Apoteket AB and Apoteket Farmaci AB* (C-544/13 and C-545/13) July 16, 2015 at paras 78–82 (medicinal products for human use).

Misleading actions

38–106   [*Add to note 609, at the end: page* [966]]
In *Abcur AB v Apoteket Farmaci, Apoteket AB and Apoteket Farmaci AB* (C-544/13 and C-545/13) July 16, 2015 the CJEU held that art.3(4) of the 2005

Directive "applies only in so far as there are no specific EU law provisions regulating specific aspects of unfair commercial practices, such as information requirements and rules on the way the information is presented to the consumer" in relation to medical products for human use (at para.79) and that, where the specific provisions conflict with the provisions in the 2005 Directive, the former "take precedence and apply to those specific aspects of unfair commercial practices" (at para.81), but in the result, this allowed advertising practices relating to such medical products to fall within the scope of the 2005 Directive "provided that the conditions for the application of that directive are satisfied" (at para.83). Moreover, it is submitted that the line of argument in the Main Work is not contradicted by the later judgment in *Citroën Commerce GmbH v Zentralvereinigung des Kraftfahrzeuggewerbes zur Aufrechterhaltung lauteren Wettbewerbs eV (ZLW)* (C-476/14) July 7, 2016 at paras 44–46. There, the CJEU held that the provision in the 2005 Directive regarding the materiality of certain information in invitations to purchase for the purposes of misleading omissions (which included "the price inclusive of taxes" (art.7(4)(c))) could not apply to the case before them "as the aspect relating to the selling price referred to in an advertisement", as that issue was governed by Directive 98/6/EC on consumer protection in the indication of the prices of products offered to customers [1998] O.J. L80/27 art.3(1)'s provision on "selling price": the 1998 Directive governed this "specific aspect" within the meaning of art.3(4) of the 2005 Directive, which therefore "cannot apply as regards that aspect": (C-476/14 judgment at para.45). This case therefore provides an example of where the "special provision" must prevail, as explained in the Main Work.

(d) *The Consumer's Right of Cancellation or Withdrawal*

(i) *The Situations in Which the Right Arises and its Duration*

No effective waiver of right by consumer

[*Add to note 670, at the end: page* [973]]   **38–115**
cf. *Salat v Barutis* [2013] EWCA Civ 1499, [2014] E.C.C. 2 at [22] (CA "inclined to agree" that under the Cancellation of Contracts made in a Consumer's Home or Place of Work etc. Regulations 2008 (SI 2008/1816) (which were replaced by the 2013 Regulations) a consumer cannot affirm a contract that would otherwise be unenforceable against him).

(ii) *The Effects of Cancellation or Withdrawal*

Reimbursement by the trader of payments received from the consumer

[*In note 689, delete from* ". Regulation 34(6) refers" *in line 1 to the end and*   **38–118**
substitute: page [975]]
(as amended by SI 2015/1629 art.7).

(e) *Enforcement*

"Enhanced consumer measures"

38–129 *[Add to note 753, at the end: page* [982]]
See Department for Business, Innovation and Skills, *Enhanced Consumer Measures, Guidance for enforcers of consumer law* (May 2015).

(f) *Special Rules for Financial Services Contracts, Timeshare Contracts, Package Travel Contracts, Contracts Concluded by Electronic Means and ADR*

(i) *Introduction*

Special rules governing particular contracts in EU law

38–130 *[Add to note 764, at the end: page* [983]]
The 1990 Directive is repealed and replaced by Directive (EU) 2015/2302 on package travel and linked travel arrangements [2015] O.J. L326/1. At the time of writing, this directive has not been implemented in UK law.

(ii) *Package Travel, Package Holidays and Package Tours*

Introduction

38–132 *[Add to note 788, at the end: page* [986]]
The 1990 Directive is repealed and replaced by Directive (EU) 2015/2302 on package travel and linked travel arrangements [2015] O.J. L326/1, which must be implemented by January 1, 2018. (At the time of writing, it has not been implemented in UK law.) The 2015 Directive requires significant changes to the law governing package travel, creating a new category of "linked travel arrangements" and in principle requiring "full harmonisation".

Liability for proper performance of the contract

38–134 *[Add to note 806, at the end: page* [988]]
, applied in *Evans v Kosmar Villa Holidays Plc* [2007] EWCA Civ 1003, [2008] 1 W.L.R. 297 at [21] and *Committeri v Club Mediterranee SA* [2016] EWHC 1510 (QB) at [29], where it was also held (at [49]–[53]) that liability arising from national law implementing the 1990 Directive and therefore arising in respect of "the proper performance of the obligations arising from the contract" is contractual rather than non-contractual for the purposes of the EU private law instruments on applicable law, i.e. Regulation 593/2008 on the law applicable to contractual obligations ("Rome I") [2008] O.J. L177/6 (on which see Main Work, Vol.I, paras 30–129 et seq.) and Regulation 864/2007 of the European Parliament and of the Council law applicable to non-contractual obligations ("Rome II Regulation") [2007] O.J. L199/40. See also *X v Kuoni Travel Ltd* [2016] EWHC 3090 (QB) at [43]–[44] (appeal pending).

(iii) *Timeshare and Related Contracts*

Exclusion by agreement or choice of law

[*Add to paragraph, at the end: page* [994]]
38–141

Finally, it would appear that an express choice of law clause in a contract falling within the scope of the 2010 Regulations may be assessed for its fairness under the general controls on unfair contract terms implementing the Unfair Terms in Consumer Contracts Directive 1993, i.e. the Unfair Terms in Consumer Contracts Regulations 1999 or the Consumer Rights Act 2015 Pt 2.[876a]

[876a] cf. *Verein für Konsumenteninformation v Amazon EU Sàrl* (C-191/15) July 28, 2016, see below, para.38–295A. For the relevant controls, see Main Work, Vol.II, paras 38–192 et seq.

(iv) *Trader's Information Duties in Relation to ADR*

EU law and ADR

[*Add to note 886, at the end: page* [995]]
38–143

, "provided that such legislation does not prevent the parties from exercising their right of access to the judicial system". See further *Menini and Rampanelli v Banco Populare Società Cooperativa* (C-75/16) of June 14, 2017 at paras 45 et seq.

[*In note 891, lines 2–3, delete* "(in force July 9, 2015)" *and substitute: page* [995]]
(the amendment came into force on July 9, 2015 but could not take effect until the commencement of SI 2015/542 reg.19 on October 1, 2015).

5. UNFAIR COMMERCIAL PRACTICES AND THE CONSUMER'S RIGHTS TO REDRESS

(b) *The Unfair Commercial Practices Directive 2005*

General

[*Add to note 921, line 5, after* "E.C.R. I-5835 at [33]": *page* [999]]
38–147

; *Europamur Alimentación SA v Dirección General de Commercio y Protección del Consumidor de la Comunidad Autónoma de la Región de Murcia* (C-295/16) Opinion of A.G. Saugmandsgaard Øe of June 29, 2017 at paras 57–59.

Scope of the 2005 Directive

[*Delete text of note 924 and substitute: page* [999]]
38–148

2005 Directive art.2(d). The CJEU has held, therefore, that a "commercial practice" covers "any measure taken in relation not only to the to the conclusion of a contract but also to its performance, and in particular the measures taken in order to obtain payment for the product": *UAB 'Gelvora' v Valstybinė vartotojų teisių apsaugos tarnyba* (C-357/16) of July 20, 2017 at para.21. It therefore further held that where the claims assigned to a debt collection agency originated in the supply of a service (the provision of credit at interest), its debt recovery activities may be regarded as a "product" within the meaning of art.2(c) of the 2005 Directive and may constitute an unfair "commercial practice" as the measures which it adopts are liable to influence the consumer's decision in respect of payment of the product: C-357/16 at paras 21–25. For this purpose, the fact that the existence of the debt was confirmed by a court decision and that that decision was passed for enforcement to a bailiff is without consequence: C-357/16 at para.31.

[*Add to note 925, at the end: page* [999]]
On the CJEU's interpretation of "product" to include practices in which a debt collection agency engages to recover the debt, see *UAB 'Gelvora' v Valstybinė vartotojų teisių apsaugos tarnyba* (C-357/16) of July 20, 2017 noted above, n.924.

Relationship with other EU legislation

38–149   [*Add to note 932, at the end: page* [1000]]
See also above, para.38–106, discussing *Citroën Commerce GmbH v Zentralvereinigung des Kraftfahrzeuggewerbes zur Aufrechterhaltung lauteren Wettbewerbs eV (ZLW)* (C-476/14) July 7, 2016 at paras 44–46.

(c) *The General Scheme of the 2008 Regulations*

Faithful implementation of the 2005 Directive

38–153   [*Add to note 950, at the end: page* [1003]]
On this general test see *Deroo-Blanquart v Sony Europe Ltd* (C-310/15) of September 7, 2016, referring to art.5 of the 2005 Directive.

[*Add to note 951, at the end: page* [1003]]
Schedule 1 of the 2008 Regulations lists 31 "commercial practices which are in all circumstances considered unfair". For the interpretation of one example of these prohibited practices by the CJEU see *'4finance' UAB v Valstybinė vartotojų teisių apsaugos tarnyba* (C-515/12) of April 3, 2014; *Loterie Nationale— National Loterij NV van publiek recht v Adriaensen, De Kesel and The Right Frequency VZW* (C-667/15) of December 15, 2016 (concerning 2005 Directive Annex I, point 14 implemented by 2008 Regulations Sch.1 para.14 (pyramid promotional schemes)).

"Average consumer"

38–157   [*Add to paragraph, at the end: page* [1007]]
Although this is not set out in the 2008 Regulations, recital 18 of the 2005 Directive states that the Directive "takes as a benchmark the average consumer, who is reasonably well-informed and reasonably observant and circumspect, *taking into account social, cultural and linguistic factors*".[987a] Moreover, recital 18 adds that

"[t]he average consumer test is not a statistical test. National courts and authorities will have to exercise their own faculty of judgement, having regard to the case-law of the Court of Justice, to determine the typical reaction of the average consumer in a given case."[987b]

[987a] Emphasis added. See also *Konsumentombudsmannen v Ving Sverige AB* (C-122/10) of May 12, 2011 ("*Canal Digital Denmark A/S* (C-611/14)") at paras 22–23.
[987b] And see *Canal Digital Denmark A/S* (C-611/14) at para.39.

Enforcement by authorities

[Add to note 1000, at the end: page [1008]] **38–159**
From that date, the enforcement authorities instead enjoy the investigatory powers set out under the general regime in the 2015 Act, Sch.5 (as specified by Pt 2 para.10 referring to the 2008 Regulations reg.19(1) and (1A)): SI 2015/1630 art.3(h).

(d) *The New Rights to Civil Redress for Consumers*

(ii) *General Conditions for the Availability of the Rights to Redress*

False or deceptive information

[Add new paragraph 38–168A: page [1015]] **38–168A**
In *Canal Digital Denmark A/S*[1055a] the Court of Justice of the EU was asked whether art.6(1) of the 2005 Directive governing misleading actions (implemented in UK law by art.5(2) of the 2008 Regulations) applies to a case where a trader has chosen to charge for a television subscription both a monthly and a six-monthly charge, but has particularly highlighted the monthly charge in its marketing, while the six-monthly charge is omitted entirely or presented only in a less conspicuous way.[1055b] Having noted the significance of the "average consumer" to whom the practice is addressed,[1055c] the Court of Justice held that in determining whether commercial practices of this sort "deceive or are likely to deceive the average consumer in relation to the price" the national court must "determine, having regard to all the relevant circumstances, whether the commercial communication concerned has the effect of suggesting to the average consumer an attractive price which, ultimately, is proven to be misleading".[1055d] For this purpose,

"consideration may be given, where relevant, to the fact that offers for TV channels are characterised by a wide variety of proposals and combinations that are generally highly structured, both in terms of cost and content, resulting in a significant asymmetry of information that is likely to confuse consumers."[1055e]

On the other hand, the Court of Justice noted that, unlike art.7's provisions governing misleading *omissions*, art.6(1) "contains no reference to limitations of space or time related to the communication medium used", so that "time constraints that may apply to certain communication media, such as television commercials, cannot be taken into account when assessing whether a commercial practice is misleading under art.6(1)".[1055f] However, where the price of a "product"[1055g] is divided into several components, one of which is emphasised in the marketing, while the other is omitted or presented less prominently, the average consumer may be lead to a mistaken perception of the overall offer, particularly in that he is being offered a particularly advantageous price.[1055h] This guidance on the proper approach to the interpretation and application of art.6(1) of the 2005 Directive makes clear that the *omission* of some information regarding an aspect of the "product" (there, its price) may form part of a misleading action rather than constituting only a misleading omission, thereby taking a broad interpretation of "misleading action" for this purpose.[1055i] For this purpose, the Court of Justice also identified an important difference between the two categories of misleading commercial practices (actions and omissions) as a matter of EU law, in that, where "the medium used to communicate the commercial practice imposes limitations of space or time, these limitations and any measures taken by the trader to make the information available to consumers by other means shall be taken into account in deciding whether information has been omitted" whereas no such allowance for the medium used is to be made as regards a misleading action.[1055j] On the other hand, art.7(4) of the Directive makes special provision regarding certain categories of information (including as to price) in "invitations to purchase" whose omission "shall be regarded as material", whereas art.6 makes no similar provision regarding invitations to purchase.[1055k] Overall, therefore, the Court of Justice accepted that a particular commercial practice may constitute at the same time a misleading action *and* a misleading omission, subject to the particular conditions and taking account of the particular considerations set out by arts 6 and 7 of the 2005 Directive respectively.

[1055a] *Criminal Proceedings against Canal Digital Denmark A/S* (C-611/14) of October 26, 2016. ("*Canal Digital Denmark A/S* (C-611/14)").

[1055b] *Canal Digital Denmark A/S* (C-611/14) at para.36.

[1055c] See Main Work, Vol.I, para.38-157.

[1055d] *Canal Digital Denmark A/S* (C-611/14) at para.40.

[1055e] *Canal Digital Denmark A/S* (C-611/14) at para.41.

[1055f] *Canal Digital Denmark A/S* (C-611/14) at para.42.

[1055g] On the definition of "product" see art.2(c) of the 2005 Directive; 2008 Regulations reg.2(1) and Main Work, Vol.II, para.38–156.

[1055h] *Canal Digital Denmark A/S* (C-611/14) at paras 43–44. The CJEU also explained that "the price is, in principle, a determining factor in the mind of the average consumer, when he has to make a transactional decision" (para.46), this being relevant to the requirement in art.6(1) that the relevant commercial practice must cause or be likely to cause the average consumer "to take a transactional decision that he would not have taken otherwise" (and see 2008 Regulations reg.5(2)(b), though note that in the Regulations the definition of "transactional decision" is defined specially for the purposes of the consumers rights to redress under Pt 4A: 2008 Regulations reg.27B(2) and see Main Work, Vol.II, para.38–170).

[1055i] For the significance of this for the availability for the consumer of a "right to redress" under Pt 4A of the 2008 Regulations, see Main Work, Vol.II, para.38–172.

[1055j] *Canal Digital Denmark A/S* (C-611/14) at paras 42 and 58–63.

[1055k] *Canal Digital Denmark A/S* (C-611/14) at paras 52–58.

Misleading omissions

38–172   [*Delete text to note 1077 and substitute: page* [1017]]
2008 Regulations reg.6(3) and see *Carrefour Hypermarchés SAS v ITM Alimentaire International SASU* (C-562/15) of February 8, 2017. Further provision is made for information to be supplied where a commercial practice is an invitation to purchase: 2008 Regulations reg.6(4). On "invitation to purchase"

see 2005 Directive art.2(i) and *Konsumentombudsmannen v Ving Sverige AB* (C-122/10) of May 12, 2011 paras 27–33 and esp. at para.28 ("an invitation to purchase is a specific form of advertising to which is attached a stricter obligation to provide information"), where it was held that the list of information deemed material by art.7(4) (implemented by art.6(4) of the 2008 Regulations) is an exhaustive one: C-122/10 at paras 68–72.

[*Add to note 1079, at the end: page* [1018]]
; *Deroo-Blanquart v Sony Europe Ltd* (C-310/15) of September 7, 2016 esp. at paras 48–49 ("material information" refers to "key items of information which the consumer needs to make an informed transactional decision" , assessed in all the circumstances).

[*Delete last sentence of paragraph,* "Unfortunately, . . . "misleading practices"." *and substitute: pages* [1018]–[1019]]
On the other hand, after the Law Commission's recommendations and the resulting amendments to the 2008 Regulations were made in 2014, the Court of Justice of the EU in *Canal Digital Denmark A/S*[1088] provided guidance on the interpretation and application of arts 6 and 7 of the 2005 Directive on misleading actions and misleading omissions respectively, making clear, first, that the provision of incomplete information may constitute a misleading action, and that, secondly, the same commercial practice may constitute both a misleading action and a misleading omission, subject in either case to its satisfying the particular conditions and taking into account the particular factors which are required by the 2005 Directive.

[1088] *Criminal Proceedings against Canal Digital Denmark A/S* (C-611/14) of October 26, 2016 and see further the note to para.38–168.

Aggressive practice

[*Add new note 1091a, at the end of paragraph: page* [1019]]   **38–173**
[1091a] For examples of "aggressive commercial practices" see *R. v Waters* [2016] EWCA Crim 1112, [2017] E.C.C. 5 (high-pressured sale of furniture to elderly person); *R v Jackson* [2017] EWCA Crim 78 (pressurising elderly and vulnerable person to agree to pay for work trader said he had carried out).

6. The Control of Unfair Contract Terms

(a) *Introduction*

Consumer Rights Act 2015

[*Add to note 1238, at the end: page* [1037]]   **38–196**
See also Conway, *Consumer Rights Act, Briefing Paper* (House of Commons Library, SN 6588, October 1, 2015).

[*Delete text of note 1248 and substitute: page* [1038]]
2015 Act ss.31(7), 47(5), 57(7), 70 and Sch.3, on which see Main Work, Vol.II, para.38–343. In addition, the provisions in Pt 2 of the 2015 Act which implement

the 1993 Directive have been designated as a specified UK law for the purposes of s.212 of the Enterprise Act 2002 ("Community infringements"), and acts or omissions in respect of any provision in Pt 2 of the 2015 Act are specified as possible "domestic infringements" for the purposes of s.211 of the Enterprise Act 2002. For the details and more general discussion of these powers see Main Work, Vol.II, paras 38–388—38–394 (as amended by this Supplement).

Temporal application of the 2015 Act's provisions on unfair terms

38–197   [*In note 1249, line 4, delete* "April 6, 2015: 2015 Order art.4)." *and substitute: page* [1038]]
October 1, 2016: 2015 Order arts 4 and 6(2) as amended by the Consumer Rights Act 2015 (Commencement No.3, Transitional Provisions, Savings and Consequential Amendments) (Amendment) Order 2016 (SI 2016/484) art.2). But see further below, para.38–403.

[*Add to paragraph, line 7, after* "Parts 1 and 2 of the Act were brought into force"*: page* [1039]]
generally

[*Add to note 1250a, penultimate line, after* "Regulations by the 2015 Act."*: page* [1039]]
Similarly, the provisions brought into force on October 1, 2016 in Pt 1 of the 2015 Act in relation to any "contract to supply a consumer transport service" do not apply to contracts entered before that date and the provisions in the Unfair Contract Terms Act 1977 therefore still apply to those contracts until that date: SI 2015/1630 arts 4 and 6(2) (as amended by SI 2016/484 art.2(3)).

(c) *The Old Law: the Unfair Terms in Consumer Contracts Regulations 1999*

Summary of impact of the 1999 Regulations

38–202   [*Add to note 1270, at the end: page* [1042]]
See also CMA, *Consumer law compliance review: cloud storage, Findings report* (May 27, 2016), esp. Ch.5, available at *https://www.gov.uk/government/ uploads/system/uploads/attachment_data/file/526447/cloud-storage-findings-report.pdf.*

(i) *The Types of Contracts Governed by the 1999 Regulations*

All types of consumer contracts

38–203   [*Add to paragraph, after note 1285: page* [1044]]
In *Tarcău v Banca Comercială Intesa Sanpaolo România SA*, the Court of Justice followed this earlier case-law and therefore held that the 1993 Directive could apply to a contract of guarantee undertaken by a natural person acting other than in the course of business under which he or she guaranteed the obligations of a debtor company to a commercial lender.[1285a] According to the Court of Justice "[t]he purpose of the contract is . . . subject to the exceptions listed in the recital

10 of the Directive . . . , irrelevant in determining the scope of the directive".[1285b]

[1285a] C-74/15 Order of CJEU November 19, 2015 ("*Tarcău* (C-74/15)") (an "order" is made by the CJEU where it considers that the question for a preliminary ruling admits of no reasonable doubt). See similarly *Bucura v SC Bancpost SA* (C-348/14) July 9, 2015 (available only in French) paras 35–38 (1993 Directive may apply where the alleged "consumer" contracted as "co-debtor" to a person concluding a contract of consumer credit). See also *Air Berlin Plc & Co. Luftverkehrs KG v Bundesverband der Verbraucherzentralen und Verbracherverbände—Verbracherzentrale Bundesverband eV* (C-290/16) of July 6, 2017 at para.44 (1993 Directive is a "general directive for consumer protection, intended to apply to all sectors of economic activity"). National legislation implementing the 1993 Directive could therefore apply to the contracts of air transport falling within the scope of Regulation (EC) 1008/2008 of the European Parliament and of the Council on common rules for the operation of air services in the Community the absence of express provision in the Regulation (which there is not).

[1285b] *Tarcău* (C-74/15) at para.22. On the status of these "exceptions" see Main Work, para.38–203 n.1280.

"Consumers" as "suppliers"?

[*In note 1308, update reference to Treitel on The Law of Contract to: page* [1046]]   **38–207**
14th edn (2015), para.7–054

[*Delete text of note 1314 and substitute: page* [1047]]
The view taken by this paragraph that the 1993 Directive can apply to contracts under which "consumers" supply persons acting in the course of business was recently confirmed explicitly by the Court of Justice in its decision in *Tarcău v Banca Comercială Intesa Sanpaolo România SA* (C-74/15) Order of CJEU November 19, 2015 ("*Tarcău* (C-74/15)"). In that case, the national court had considered that the 1993 Directive applied only to contracts for the supply of goods or services to consumers, but the Court of Justice held the Directive applies to "all contracts" between consumers and sellers or suppliers and that "[t]he purpose of the contract is thus, subject to the exceptions listed in the recital 10 of the Directive . . . , irrelevant in determining the scope of the directive": *Tarcău* (C-74/15) at para.22 and on the status of these "exceptions" see Main Work, para.38–203 n.1280. According to the Court of Justice:

> "It is therefore by reference to the capacity of the contracting parties, according to whether or not they are acting for purposes relating to their trade, business or profession, that the directive defines the contracts to which it applies" (*Tarcău v Banca Comercială* (C-74/15) at para.23).

The Court therefore further held that whether a natural person who agrees to secure the contractual obligations owed by a commercial company to a banking institution under a credit agreement is to be regarded as a "consumer" depends on whether he "acted for purposes relating to his trade, business or profession or because of functional links he has with that company, such as a directorship or non-negligible shareholding" or whether instead "he acted for purposes of a private nature": *Tarcău* (C-74/15) at para.29.

[*Delete text of note 1316 and substitute: page* [1047]]
See *Tarcău v Banca Comercială Intesa Sanpaolo România SA* (C-74/15) Order of CJEU November 19, 2015 (discussed above, para.38–207, n.1314).

Third parties and consumers

38–209   *[Add to note 1322, at the end: page* [1048]*]*
For the position of a third party assignee of the consumer's rights in relation to contract terms "not binding" on the consumer as unfair, see below, para.38–315.

An autonomous view of "contract"?

38–211   *[Add new note 1327a, after* "considered non-contractual." *in line 5: page* [1049]*]*
    [1327a] On the other hand, some legal relationships which involve elements of agreement in one or both parties may nevertheless be properly characterised as "non-contractual" owing to the nature or extent of their regulation: e.g. the relationship between a student on the Bar Professional Training Course and the Bar Council: *R. (on the application of Prescott) v General Council of the Bar* [2015] EWHC 1919 (Admin) at [79].

[Add to note 1335, at the end: page [1050]*]*
cf. *Roundlistic Ltd v Jones* [2016] UKUT 325 (LC) at [100], where it was held that a lease of residential premises granted by a landlord to its tenant was a contract concluded between those parties, despite the fact that it was concluded within the context of the obligation on the landlord to grant a new lease pursuant to the Leasehold Reform, Housing and Development Act 1993, though it was further held that these terms of the new lease were excluded from the scope of the 1999 Regulations on the basis that they reflected "mandatory statutory provisions" within the meaning of reg.4(2), on which see below, para.38–217A.

(ii) *Contract Terms Excluded From the 1999 Regulations*

[Add new paragraph 38–217A: page [1056]*]*
38–217A   **Statutory obligation to grant contract on same terms.** In *Roundlistic Ltd v Jones*,[1377a] a new lease had been granted to a tenant by her landlord under its obligation imposed by the Leasehold Reform, Housing and Development Act 1993.[1377b] The Upper Tribunal (Lands Chamber) noted that the terms upon which the landlord was obliged to grant the new lease were provided by the Act and that, while there was scope for some alternations in the terms, the Act's starting-point was that the new lease was to be on the same terms as the existing lease subject to certain limited modifications.[1377c] In these circumstances, the Upper Tribunal concluded that the 1999 Regulations did not apply to the terms of the new lease as they fell within the exclusion in reg.4(2) concerning "mandatory statutory provisions".[1377d] It is submitted, however, that this decision extends the scope of application of reg.4(2) beyond the likely interpretation by the Court of Justice of the EU of art.1(2) of the 1993 Directive which reg.4(2) implements[1377e]: art.1(2) is to be strictly construed[1377f] and there is a difference between contract terms required by legislation itself (where "it may legitimately be supposed that the national legislature struck a balance between all the rights and obligations of the parties to certain contracts"[1377g]) and contract terms which reflect an earlier contract between the parties whose content has not been the object of any legislative consideration or imposition.

[1377a] [2016] UKUT 325 (LC).

[1377b] i.e. ss.43, 56 and 57.

[1377c] [2016] UKUT 325 (LC) at [101].

[1377d] [2016] UKUT 325 (LC) at [101]. It had been held that the new lease was a "contract" for the purposes of the 1999 Regulations despite its compulsory elements: see above, para.38–321.

[1377e] See notably *RWE Vertrieb AG v Verbraucherzentrale Nordrhein-Westfalen eV* (C-92/11) March 21, 2013 ("*RWE Vertrieb AG* (C-92/11)") discussed in the Main Work, Vol.II, para.38–215.

[1377f] *Kušionová v SMART Capital a.s.* (C-34/13) September 10, 2014 para.77.

[1377g] *RWE Vertrieb AG* (C-92/11) at para.29. See also the explanation of the exclusion in art.1(2) in recital 13 of the 1993 Directive that "the statutory or regulatory provisions of the Member States which directly or indirectly determine the terms of consumer contracts are presumed not to contain unfair terms".

Terms which reflect "the provisions of international conventions"

[*Add new note 1380a, at the end of the paragraph: page* [1056]]   **38–218**

[1380a] On the other hand, a term of a contract which is governed by an international convention but which does not reflect the provisions of that convention remains subject to the controls in the 1993 Directive: cf. *Air Berlin Plc & Co Luftverkehrs KG v Bundesverband der Verbraucherzentralen und Verbraucherverbände—Verbracherzentrale Bundesverband eV* (C-290/16) of July 6, 2017 at paras 44–45 (emphasising the applicability of the 1993 Directive to international contracts of carriage of passengers by air, though not addressing this point).

(iii) *The Requirement of Fairness*

(bb) *The "Core Exclusion"*

The condition that the "terms are in plain intelligible language"

[*Add to note 1484, at the end: page* [1072]]   **38–239**
See similarly *Bucura v SC Bancpost SA* (C-348/14) July 9, 2015 at paras 57–63.

(cc) *The Composite Test of Unfairness*

[*Add new paragraph 38–251A: page* [1085]]

ParkingEye Ltd v Beavis. In *ParkingEye Ltd v Beavis*[1571a] the Supreme Court   **38–251A**
considered how the test of unfairness in the 1999 Regulations would apply to a term in a contract under which a consumer could park for free in a car park for up to two hours, but would incur a charge of £85 for overstaying this permitted period or for breaking other rules set by the management company of the car park, such as parking only within marked bays.[1571b] A notice to this effect in "large, prominent and legible" print was displayed on signs at the entrance of the car park and around it.[1571c] A user of the car park (the "consumer") overstayed the two-hour limit by nearly an hour and the management company sought to recover the charge from him. The Supreme Court considered that contract was a licence to park cars on the terms posted at its entrance, that the charge was not a charge for the right to park or even to overstay at the car park, but arose only on certain breaches of the contract by the user.[1571d] The car park was operated in this way as its owner was concerned to ensure that motorists should park for free to attract customers for the retailers to which it had leased other parts of its site,

but that these customers should not overstay their parking period so as to increase the potential number of customers. The purposes of the charge were therefore to manage the efficient use of parking spaces in the interests of the owner, the retailers and other would-be customers and to provide an income stream for the car park's managers to meet its costs and make a profit.[1571e] In considering the fairness of the term imposing the charge under the 1999 Regulations, the Supreme Court followed the guidance of the Court of Justice of the EU in *Aziz*,[1571f] which it saw as the "leading case on the topic" provided by that court.[1571g] It noted Advocate General Kokott's advice in *Aziz*, which was followed by the Court of Justice, that the requirement that the "significant imbalance" in the contracting parties' rights and obligations to the detriment of the consumer should be contrary to good faith allows account to be taken of the legitimate interests of the parties to organise their own legal relationship even in a way which derogates from national legal rules otherwise applicable.[1571h] In this respect, the Supreme Court noted the formula used by the Court of Justice to assess good faith by reference to the hypothetical test of whether the seller or supplier "could reasonably assume that the consumer would have agreed to such a term in individual negotiations" and the views of Advocate General Kokott on the relevant circumstances for this purpose, such as whether or not the term would be surprising.[1571i] A majority of the Supreme Court therefore held that the contract term on which the £85 charge was based was fair within the meaning of the Regulations. While the term did create an imbalance in the parties' rights and obligations to the detriment to the consumer, both the management company and the owners of the car park had a legitimate interest in imposing a liability on consumers in excess of any damages recoverable in inducing them to observe the two-hour time limit: indeed "charging overstayers £85 underpinned the business model which enabled members of the public to park free of charge for two hours" and was "fundamental to the contractual relationship created by [consumers'] acceptance of the terms of the notice, whose whole object was the efficient management of the car park".[1571j] In the view of the majority of the Supreme Court, the hypothetical test was objective:

> "the question is not whether [the defendant consumer] himself would in fact have agreed to the term imposing the £85 charge in a negotiation, but whether a reasonable motorist in his position would have done so. In [its] view, a reasonable motorist would have agreed."[1571k]

Motorists generally and the defendant in particular *did* accept the term and while this would not usually have much weight as regards standard terms, the term in question "could not have been briefer, simpler or more prominently proclaimed".[1571l] Moreover, objectively, they had every reason to accept the terms, as they were allowed to park free for two hours in return for the risk of the £85 charge if they overstayed.[1571m] The terms were beneficial to motorists themselves as they freed up parking spaces, as well as being beneficial to the management company, the site owner and the retailers and the level of the charge was not exorbitant: the terms were therefore "objectively reasonable".[1571n] In this respect, Lord Mance's view was more nuanced, considering that the Court of Justice of the EU in *Aziz* could not be taken to have identified the hypothetical test as conclusive, but rather relevant to the assessment of fairness of a term, given that the Directive requires a court to take into account all circumstances for these purposes.[1571o] Lord Mance found the argument that the management company could not reasonably have assumed that customers in the defendant's position would have agreed to the scheme in individual contractual negotiation "less easy to address", as such a customer, if asked, would have been satisfied with the proposal of two hours of free parking, but would probably have asked for "some form of gradated payment in the event of overstaying".[1571p] Nevertheless, Lord Mance concluded that the term was not unfair within the meaning of the Regulations, as a term of this sort is simple and familiar and clear notice was given; there is no significant imbalance in the parties' rights and obligations given that the consumer is given a valuable privilege (the free parking) in return for a promise to pay a sum in the event of overstaying; and, finally, the charge is not disproportionately high.[1571q] By contrast, Lord Toulson dissented on this issue, and would have held the term unfair under the 1999 Regulations. In his view, the term on which the charge was based did create a significant imbalance in the parties' rights and obligations to the detriment of the consumer as the charge far exceeded any amount which was otherwise likely to be recoverable as damages.[1571r] Moreover, he considered that the hypothetical test which *Aziz* used to explain the requirement of good faith is "significantly more favourable to the consumer" than is the general common law governing penalty clauses, as its starting point is the special protection of consumers rather than that parties should be kept to their bargains.[1571s] In his view, no assumption can fairly be made that a consumer would have agreed to the term in individual negotiations and the burden of proof is on the trader to establish that he or she would have done as it makes no allowance for circumstances, allows period of grace and provides no room for adjustment.[1571t] He therefore concluded that the term was unfair.[1571u]

[1571a] [2015] UKSC 67, [2015] 3 W.L.R. 1373. Subsequent to the decision of the SC (but without reference to it) it has been said that a term of a new lease granted pursuant to the landlord's obligation under the Leasehold Reform, Housing and Development Act 1993 and therefore replicating a term in an earlier lease not subject to the 1999 Regulations, was not "contrary to the requirement of good faith", though it had earlier been held that that the 1999 Regulations did not apply to the term as it fell within the exclusion in reg.4(2): *Roundlistic Ltd v Jones* [2016] UKUT 325 (LC) at [101] and [104]; see above, para.38–217A.
[1571b] [2015] UKSC 67 at [90] and [123].
[1571c] [2015] UKSC 67 at [91].
[1571d] [2015] UKSC 67 at [94].
[1571e] [2015] UKSC 67 at [97]–[98].
[1571f] *Aziz v Caixa d'Estalvis de Catalunya, Tarragona i Manresa* (C-415/11) March 14, 2013 discussed in the Main Work, Vol.II, para.38–247.
[1571g] [2015] UKSC 67 at [105] (Lord Neuberger of Abbotsbury P.S.C., Lord Sumption and Lord Carnwath JJ.S.C.) (with whom Lord Hodge J.S.C. (at [289]) and Lord Clarke of Stone-cum-Ebony J.S.C. (at [291]) agreed on these points); [204] and [208] (Lord Mance J.S.C.); Lord Toulson J.S.C. agreed on the importance of the *Aziz* decision (at [306]–[308]), but dissented on its significance on the facts of *ParkingEye Ltd*: see below. The SC also held that the term imposing the charge was not a penalty clause at common law as the management company had a legitimate interest in imposing these charges which could not be satisfied by damages even though the amount did not represent any loss caused to them by the breaches by the user and, secondly, the sum was *not* out of all proportion to its interest or the owner's interests: [2015] UKSC 67 at [99]–[101] (Lord Neuberger, Lord Sumption and Lord Carnwath); [197]–[199] (Lord Mance); Lord Toulson did not express a decided view on this issue: at [316]. *ParkingEye Ltd v Beavis* was joined with *Cavendish Square Holding BV v Makdessi* which concerned the common law regarding contractual penalty clauses in a commercial context, on which see above, paras 26–178 et seq.

[1571h] [2015] UKSC 67 at [106], referring to A.G. Kokott's Opinion at paras 73 and 87. Recital 16 of the 1993 Directive itself explains the requirement of good faith as allowing "an overall evaluation of the different interests involved" as noted in the Main Work, Vol.II, para.38–244.

[1571i] [2015] UKSC 67 at [106]; A.G. Kokott's Opinion, *Aziz v Caixa d'Estalvis de Catalunya, Tarragona i Manresa* (C-415/11) at para.75 quoted in Main Work, Vol.II, para.38–247.

[1571j] [2015] UKSC 67 at [106] (Lord Neuberger, Lord Sumption and Lord Carnwath, with whom Lord Hodge (at [289]) and Lord Clarke (at [291]) agreed on this point).

[1571k] [2015] UKSC 67 at [108] (referring for this purpose to A.G. Kokott's Opinion in *Aziz* at para.75, though her reference was to "an objective reason for the term" rather than specifically an objective approach to the hypothetical test).

[1571l] [2015] UKSC 67 at [108].

[1571m] [2015] UKSC 67 at [109].

[1571n] [2015] UKSC 67 at [109]. See also at [111]–[113] rejecting further arguments as to the unfairness of the term.

[1571o] [2015] UKSC 67 at [208], having noted (at [202]–[203]), the 1999 Regulations reg.6(1) and the 1993 Directive recital 16 to this effect.

[1571p] [2015] UKSC 67 at [209].

[1571q] [2015] UKSC 67 at [212], adopting the conclusions of Judge Maloney Q.C. at trial.

[1571r] [2015] UKSC 67 at [307].

[1571s] [2015] UKSC 67 at [308].

[1571t] [2015] UKSC 67 at [309]–[310].

[1571u] [2015] UKSC 67 at [314].

"Unfairness" under the 1993 Directive and "unfair commercial practices"

38–252   [*Add to note 1585, at the end: page* [1086]]

A.G. Kokott has argued that, where relevant to the fairness of a term of a consumer contract under the Unfair Terms in Consumer Contracts Directive 1993, a national court has an obligation to raise the unfairness of any relevant *commercial practice* within the meaning of the Unfair Commercial Practices Directive 2005: *Margarit Panicello v Hernández Martinez* (C-503/15) A.G. Opinion of September 15, 2016 at [127]–[128]. The CJEU (judgment of February 16, 2017) did not comment on these issues as it ruled that it had no jurisdiction to hear the request for a preliminary ruling.

Potential for unfairness

38–255   [*Add to note 1592a, penultimate line, after* "binding" *on the consumer": page* [1088]]

See similarly *Radlinger v Finway a.s.* (C-377/14) April 21, 2016 at para.95 (potential cumulative effect of all penalty clauses on consumer the basis for assessment of fairness).

[*Add to paragraph, at the end: page* [1088]]

And, as Advocate General Szpunar has observed, reasonable behaviour on the part of the trader under an unfair contract cannot deprive a term of its unfair character.[1592b] On the other hand, as Advocate General Wahl has observed, the significant imbalance in the rights and obligations of the parties should be assessed by reference to the circumstances and information available at the date of conclusion of the contract, so that changes occurring after its conclusion which make the contract excessively onerous to the consumer are irrelevant to the fairness of a contract term.[1592c]

1592b *Banco Primus SA v Gutiérrez Garcia* (C-421/14) A.G. Opinion February 2, 2016 para.85 (paraphrase from the French by the editor) (judgment of the CJEU pending at the time of writing).
1592c *Andriciuc v Banca Românească* (C-186/16) Opinion of A.G. Wahl of April 26, 2016, paras 73–90 (the judgment of the CJEU pending).

The significance of imbalance

[*Add to note 1597, at the end: page* [1089]]   **38–256**
cf. *Roundlistic Ltd v Jones* [2016] UKUT 325 (LC) at [103] where it was held that the fact that the terms of a new long lease (subject to the 1999 Regulations) granted on the same terms as a lease for which it was substituted (which had 80 years remaining and which was not subject to the 1999 Regulations) meant that a term of the new lease could not be said to "cause" a significant imbalance in the rights and obligations of the contracting parties: "[i]f there was a significant imbalance it already existed". See also *Abbott v RCI Europe* [2016] EWHC 2602 (Ch) at [45]–[47] (term of a contract under which consumers "deposited" their own timeshare rights with a company so as to enable them to exchange those rights for access to other properties held fair as creating no significant imbalance given the fetters imposed by law on the company's exercise of its discretion under the term and the power in the consumers to cancel the contract without penalty).

"All the circumstances attending the conclusion of the contract"

[*Add to note 1603, at the end: page* [1090]]   **38–259**
The CJEU has held that national legislation cannot therefore apply a restricted legal standard for the assessment of a contract term, such as a restriction on the rate of default interest to three times the interest otherwise owed under the contract: *Ibercaja Banco SAU v Cortés González* (C-613/15) March 17, 2016 (available only in French) at para.33.

[*Add new note 1603a, after* "conclusion of the contract" *in line 4: page* [1090]]
1603a In *Banco Primus SA v Gutiérrez Garcia* (C-421/14), A.G. Szpunar in his Opinion of February 2, 2016 at para.70 advised the CJEU that the "circumstances attending the conclusion of the contract" can include circumstances that were easily foreseeable by the parties at the time of its conclusion even though they occur afterwards and circumstances already existing but known only to one of the contracting parties (for example, likely market changes known to the trader but unknown to the consumer). At the time of writing, the CJEU had not given judgment in this case.

[*In note 1610, update reference to Treitel on The Law of Contract to: page* [1090]]
14th edn (2015), paras 7–004—7–010.

Lack of plainness or intelligibility sufficient?

[*Add to paragraph, at the end: page* [1092]]   **38–260**
On the other hand, in *Verein für Konsumenteninformation v Amazon EU Sàrl*,1624a the Court of Justice of the EU came close to saying that an express choice of law clause in a consumer contract *will* be unfair if the trader does not explain that its effect is limited by the restrictions imposed by art.6(2) of the Rome I Regulation

on the law applicable to contractual obligations, on the basis that this means that the term fails the requirement of plain intelligible language.[1624b]

[1624a] C-191/15, July 28, 2016 ("*Amazon EU Sàrl* (C-191/15)").
[1624b] *Amazon EU Sàrl* (C-191/15) at para.68 and see further below, para.38–295A.

Procedural issues

38–272   [*Add to note 1663, at the end: page* [1098]]
See also below, para.38–306A in relation to *Sales Sinués v Caixabank SA, Drame Ba v Catalunja Caixa SA* (Joined Cases C-381/14 and C-385/14) April 14, 2016 concerning stays of individual claims by consumers.

(dd) *The "Indicative List" of Terms*

Exclusion or limitation clauses

38–275   [*Add to note 1674, at the end: page* [1100]]
See also CMA, *Consumer law compliance review: cloud storage, Findings report* (May 27, 2016), paras 5.59–5.66 (on exclusions or limitations of liability in contract for the provision of "cloud computing" services), available at *https://www.gov.uk/government/uploads/system/uploads/attachment_data/file/526447/cloud-storage-findings-report.pdf*.

Choice of jurisdiction clauses

38–277   [*Add new note 1693a at end of paragraph title: page* [1103]]
[1693a] cf. the position as regards choice of law clauses discussed below, para.38–395A.

[*Add to paragraph, at the end: page* [1104]]
However, the decision in *Apostolakis (No.2)* was distinguished in *Chopra v Bank of Singapore Ltd* on the basis that the clause in the latter case conferred only non-exclusive jurisdiction, the contract was in a language (English) known to the consumers and was "fairly simple and straightforward": there was, moreover, no evidence that if they had known about the clause they would not have entered the contract.[1697a]

[1697a] [2015] EWHC 1549 (Ch) at [139]–[140].

Penalty clauses

38–280   [*Add new note 1701a, line 7, after* "(valid) liquidated damages clause"*: page* [1105]]
[1701a] See, however, the reformulation of the common law of penalty clauses in *Cavendish Square Holding BV v Makdessi, ParkingEye Ltd v Beavis* [2015] UKSC 67, [2015] 3 W.L.R. 1373, discussed above, para.26–197. The decision of the SC in *ParkingEye Ltd* in relation to the 1999 Regulations is noted below, para.38–281 and also above, para.38–251A.

38–281   [*Add to note 1708, at the end: page* [1106]]
The CJEU has held that where more than one term in a consumer contract requires the consumer to pay sums in compensation for failure to perform his obligation, the national court should assess the cumulative effect of all such terms

in assessing their disproportionate effect, whether or not the trader actually insists on their enforcement: *Radlinger v Finway a.s.* (C-377/14) April 21, 2016 at paras 92–95.

[*In paragraph, delete text and notes after note 1710a to the end and substitute: pages* [1106]–[1107]]

For example, as earlier noted, in *ParkingEye Ltd v Beavis*[1710b] the Supreme Court held that a term in a contract under which a consumer parked for free in a car park for up to two hours, but who incurred a charge of £85 for overstaying this permitted period was not unfair even though this amount did not reflect the potential loss caused by its breach to the managers of the car park,[1710c] as the amount was not disproportionate to the legitimate interest of the managers of the car park, its owners and its other users in the efficient management of the car park.[1710d]

[1710b] [2015] UKSC 67, [2015] 3 W.L.R. 1373 on which see above, para.38–251A.
[1710c] [2015] UKSC 67, [2015] 3 W.L.R. 1373 at [97] (concession by the car park's managers).
[1710d] See above, para.38–251A.

"Automatic extension clauses"

[*Add to note 1717, at the end: page* [1108]]   **38–284**
See also CMA, *Consumer law compliance review: cloud storage, Findings report* (May 27, 2016), paras 5.50–5.58 (on terms which automatically renew fixed-term contract for the provision of "cloud computing" services), available at *https://www.gov.uk/government/uploads/system/uploads/attachment_data/file/526447/cloud-storage-findings-report.pdf.*

Variation clauses

[*Delete text of note 1721 and substitute: page* [1109]]   **38–286**
cf. the position under the Consumer Rights Act 2015, which provides that certain categories of information provided by the trader about goods or digital content are to be treated as included as a term of the relevant contract and that "any change to any of that information, made before entering into the contract or later, is not effective unless expressly agreed between the consumer and the trader" (2015 Act ss.11(4)–(5) and 12(2)–(3) (goods contracts); ss.36(3)–(4) and 37(2)–(3) (digital content contracts)) and which makes similar provision in respect of information provided by the trader in respect of a services contract (2015 Act s.50(2) and (3)). On these provisions see Main Work, Vol.II, para.38–100.

[*Add to note 1722, at the beginning: page* [1109]]
The CMA has expressed concern as to the fairness of contract terms under which the provider of "cloud computer" services reserves to itself broad powers of unilateral variation of the terms of the contract or the characteristics of the services: see CMA, *Consumer law compliance review: cloud storage, Findings*

report (May 27, 2016), paras 5.24–5.38, available at *https://www.gov.uk/government/uploads/system/uploads/attachment_data/file/526447/cloud-storage-findings-report.pdf*.

"Unequal opt out clauses"

38–293   [*Add to note 1762, at the end: page* [1115]]
cf. CMA, *Consumer law compliance review: cloud storage, Findings report* (May 27, 2016), paras 5.39–5.49 available at *https://www.gov.uk/government/uploads/system/uploads/attachment_data/file/526447/cloud-storage-findings-report.pdf* (terms allowing the trader to suspend or terminate the service in the context of cloud computing).

[*Add new paragraph 38–296A: page* [1118]]

38–296A   **Choice of law clauses.** In *Verein für Konsumenteninformation v Amazon EU Sàrl* the question arose as to the fairness under the 1993 Directive of a standard contract term in an online trader's contracts which designated the law of Luxembourg (which was the place of the trader's "seat") as "applicable to the exclusion of the United Nations Convention on the international sale of goods".[1782a] While arts 3(1) and 6(1) of the Rome I Regulation recognise that in principle the parties to a consumer contract may choose the law applicable to it, art.6(2) provides that, subject to certain conditions, any such choice of law does not "have the result of depriving the consumer of the protection afforded to him by provisions that cannot be derogated from by agreement" under the law of his habitual residence[1782b] and this may include national law implementing the 1993 Directive even where they ensure a higher level of protection for the consumer than the Directive requires.[1782c] In *Amazon EU Sàrl*, the Court of Justice of the EU noted the position governing choice of law clauses in consumer contracts under the Rome I Regulation, and that therefore:

> "a pre-formulated term on the choice of the applicable law designating the law of the Member State in which the seller or supplier is established is unfair only in so far as it displays certain specific characteristics inherent in its wording or context which cause a significant imbalance in the rights and obligations of the parties."[1782d]

For this purpose, the Court noticed that the unfairness of a such a term may result from its failure to conform to the requirement of plain and intelligible language by the trader failing to inform the consumer that the effects of a term are affected by mandatory statutory provisions for the consumer's protection (as in the case of art.6(2) of the Rome I Regulation).[1782e] And if the national court finds that the trader has failed to do so and "so leads the consumer into error by giving him the impression that only the law of [the Member State chosen] applies to the contract", then the choice of law clause would itself be an unfair term.[1782f]

[1782a] C-191/15, July 28, 2016 ("*Amazon EU Sàrl* (C-191/15)").
[1782b] Regulation (EC) 593/2008 on the law applicable to contractual obligations ("Rome I") [2008] O.J. L177/6.
[1782c] *Amazon EU Sàrl* (C-191/15) at para.59 (noting art.8 of the Directive).
[1782d] *Amazon EU Sàrl* (C-191/15) at para.67.
[1782e] *Amazon EU Sàrl* (C-191/15) at paras 68–70.
[1782f] *Amazon EU Sàrl* (C-191/15) at para.71.

(ff) *The Relative Roles of the Court of Justice of the EU, National Courts and the Parties*

Judicial discretion and domestic appeals

[*In note 1813, update reference to Treitel on The Law of Contract to: page* [1122]] **38–303**
14th edn (2015), para.7–082

The power and duty of national courts to intervene of their own initiative

[*Add to note 1823, at the end: page* [1123]] **38–304**
; *Bucura v SC Bancpost SA* (C-348/14) July 9, 2015 para.44. In *Tomášová v Republic of Slovakia* (C-168/15) July 28, 2016 at paras 33–34 (available only in French), the CJEU held that only on its decision in *Pannon* had it made clear that national courts have an *obligation* to consider the fairness of terms in consumer contracts and that therefore before the date of this decision a national court could not be said to have committed a sufficiently serious breach of EU law by its failure to do so for the purpose of State liability under the *Francovich* principle (on which see Craig and de Búrca, *EU Law*, 6th edn (2015) pp.251 et seq.).

"National procedural autonomy" and its limits

[*Add to note 1839, line 10, after* "credit: C-618/10 at paras 45, 49–57)": *page* **38–306**
[1126]]
; see similarly, *Finanmadrid EFC SA v Albán Zambrano* (C-49/14) February 18, 2016.

[*Add to note 1839, line 12, delete* "(both" *and substitute: page* [1126]]
; *Banco Santander SA v Sánchez López* (C-598/15) Opinion of A.G. Wahl of June 29, 2017 (all three

[*Add to note 1839, at the end: page* [1126]]
; *ERSTE Bank Hungary Zrt v Sugár* (C-32/14) October 1, 2015 (effectiveness of the protection of consumers in context of national law governing notaries); *BBVA SA v Peñalva López* (C-8/14) October 29, 2015 (time-limit for relying on unfairness of terms specified by transitional legislation); *Radlinger v Finway a.s.* (C-377/14) April 21, 2016 at paras 51–59 (court's duty applies to insolvency proceedings).

[*Add to note 1846a, at the end: page* [1128]]
cf. A.G. Kokott's argument that, where relevant to the fairness of a term of a consumer contract under the Unfair Terms in Consumer Contracts Directive 1993, a national court has an obligation to raise the unfairness of any *commercial practice* within the meaning of the Unfair Commercial Practices Directive 2005: *Margarit Panicello v Hernández Martinez* (C-503/15) A.G. Opinion of September 15, 2016 at [127]–[128]. The CJEU (judgment of February 16, 2017) did not comment on these issues.

[*Add new paragraph 38–306A: page* [1128]]
Collective actions and stays of proceedings. Under the Civil Procedure Rules, **38–306A**
the courts possess a power to stay the whole or part of any proceedings or

judgment either generally or until a specified date or event.[1846b] This power was used to stay the many thousands of proceedings relating to "bank charges" which had been brought by consumers against their banks until the general legal issues relating to the contract terms on the basis of which these charges were imposed were resolved by the courts in proceedings between the OFT against eight major banks for a declaration as to the ambit of the "core exclusion" allowed by art.4(2) of the 1993 Directive.[1846c] However, in *Sales Sinués and Drame Ba*[1846d] the Court of Justice of the EU considered the lawfulness of the staying of individual actions brought by consumers pending the outcome of "collective proceedings" on a preliminary reference from a Spanish court. There, individual proceedings had been brought by consumers for the annulment of a particular category of allegedly unfair terms ("interest rate floor clauses") in their contracts of consumer credit with banks, and the latter had asked the courts seized of these proceedings to stay them under a national provision allowing the staying of proceedings with the same subject-matter pending the outcome of "collective proceedings" brought by a consumers' association under art.7 of the 1993 Directive. Under Spanish law, the individual consumers could join the collective proceedings, but only subject to various constraints not imposed in respect of the individual proceedings. The Court of Justice explained the different purposes and legal effects of individual actions by consumers and collective actions under art.7, and that the principle of procedural autonomy allows national laws to establish the rules applicable to those collective actions subject to the principles of equivalence and effectiveness.[1846e] As regards the latter, the Court held that it was clear from the national court's reference that the provision of national law under which the consumers' individual actions may be stayed would lead to the consumer no longer being able individually to assert the rights which the 1993 Directive recognises other than by joining the collective proceedings.[1846f] This

> "is liable to undermine the effectiveness of the protection intended by that directive, in view of the differences in the purpose and nature of the consumer-protection mechanisms given specific expression by those actions."[1846g]

For if the consumer joins the collective proceedings, national civil procedure rules would prevent the court hearing them from considering the circumstances relating to the individual consumer contract, the individual consumer would be dependent on the period set for the collective proceedings without consideration of his particular circumstances and he or she would be subject to further procedural constraints: these rules therefore do not constitute an adequate or effective means of bringing the continued use of unfair terms to an end contrary to art.7[1846h]; and as regards the consumer's individual proceedings that would be stayed,

> "the need to ensure consistency between judicial decisions cannot justify such a lack of effectiveness since . . . the difference in nature between judicial control exercised in the context of a collective action and that exercised in the context of an individual action should, in principle, prevent the risk of incompatible judicial decisions."[1846i]

Moreover, the "need to avoid overburdening the courts" cannot justify the effective exercise of a consumer's own individual ("subjective") rights.[1846j] While the decision in *Sales Sinués and Drame Ba* has no direct application in the English context, it does emphasise that any power under the English Civil

Procedure Rules to stay consumers' individual proceedings must not be exercised in a way which undermines the practical exercise of their own individual rights under the UK legislation implementing the 1993 Directive.

[1846b] CPR r.3.1(f).

[1846c] *Office of Fair Trading v Abbey National Plc* [2009] UKSC 6, [2010] 1 A.C. 696 at [17] and [61]. For general discussion of this case, see Main Work, Vol.II, paras 38–226—38–227 and 38–241.

[1846d] *Sales Sinués v Caixabank SA, Drame Ba v Catalunja Caixa SA* (Joined Cases C-381/14 and C-385/14) April 14, 2016.

[1846e] Joined Cases C-381/14 and C-385/14 at paras 30–32.

[1846f] Joined Cases C-381/14 and C-385/14 at para.35.

[1846g] Joined Cases C-381/14 and C-385/14 at para.36.

[1846h] Joined Cases C-381/14 and C-385/14 at paras 37–39.

[1846i] Joined Cases C-381/14 and C-385/14 at para.41.

[1846j] Joined Cases C-381/14 and C-385/14 at para.42. The judgment of the Court of Justice is expressed in terms of the precluding of a national provision which *requires* the national court *automatically* to suspend the consumer's individual action without considering its effect on the protection of the consumer and without that consumer being able to dissociate himself from the collective proceedings, even though (as A.G. Szpunar made clear at paras 29, 45 and 74) the national provision itself appears to provide a discretion rather than impose a duty. This is apparently explained by the existence of uncertainty at the national level of the proper force of the provision in question.

(gg) *The Effects of a Finding That a Term is Unfair*

"The contract shall continue to bind the parties upon those terms if it is capable of continuing in existence without the unfair terms"

[*In note 1880a, update reference to Treitel on The Law of Contract to: page* [1133]] **38–313**
14th edn (2015), para.7–120

No application of national "supplementary rules" more generally

[*Add to note 1880n, at the end: page* [1135]] **38–313A**
And see *Cavendish Square Holding BV v Makdessi, ParkingEye Ltd v Beavis* [2015] UKSC 67, [2015] 3 W.L.R. 1373 at [9].

Restitution of money paid by the consumer

[*Replace text and notes of paragraph and substitute: pages* [1135] and [1136]] **38–314**
Neither the 1993 Directive nor the 1999 Regulations make express provision regarding any possible restitutionary consequences of a finding that a term is "not binding" on the consumer on the ground of its unfairness. In this respect, art.6(1) of the Directive refers to an unfair term not binding the consumer "as provided for under their national law" and this neutrality as between the conceptual mechanisms of "non-bindingness" (such as invalidity or nullity) could suggest that other possible consequential effects of "non-bindingness" (notably, as to the availability of restitution and its incidents) are similarly a matter for national law. However, in *Gutiérrez Naranjo* the Court of Justice of the EU made clear that the restitutionary consequences of non-bindingness are, in principle, a matter for EU law.[1881] The background to judgment case was that in 2013 the Spanish Supreme Court had held contract terms providing that the variable

interest rate in a mortgage loan would not go below a certain threshold ("floor clauses") were not transparent and were unfair under Spanish legislation implementing the 1993 Directive, but the same court later held that while the effect of this unfairness was to render the terms invalid, this did not affect claims for restitution in respect of which a judgment with the force of *res judicata* had been given nor claims in respect of monies paid under the clauses *after* the date of its judgment on unfairness, the latter on the basis of "considerations of legal certainty, good faith and risk of serious economic difficulties".[1882] Advocate General Mengozzi had advised the Court that this limitation on the temporal effect of its judgment was a matter for Spanish law subject to the principles of equivalence and effectiveness, the latter of which was not infringed as the national court was entitled (exceptionally) to balance the purposes of the 1993 Directive (including its deterrent effect) and "the macroeconomic challenges to the already weakened banking system of a Member State".[1883] However, the Court of Justice disagreed. Taking into account, in particular, that art.6(1) of the 1993 Directive is a "mandatory provision that is intended to replace the formal balance established by the contract between the rights and obligations of the parties with an effective balance that re-establishes equality between them",[1884] art.6(1)

> "must be interpreted as meaning that a contractual term held to be unfair must be regarded, in principle, as never having existed, so that it cannot have any effect on the consumer. Therefore, the determination by a court that such a term is unfair must, in principle, have the consequence of restoring the consumer to the legal and factual situation that he would have been in if that term had not existed.
>
> It follows that the obligation for the national court to exclude an unfair contract term imposing the payment of amounts that prove not to be due entails, in principle, a corresponding restitutory [sic] effect in respect of those same amounts."[1885]

The Court of Justice therefore considered that while the reference to national law in art.6(1) means that Member States may define "the detailed rules under which the unfairness of a contractual clause is established and the actual legal effects of that finding are produced", the consumer must be allowed "a right of restitution of advantages wrongly obtained".[1886] While exceptions to this position may be made in respect of claims subject to *res judicata* and while reasonable time-limits may be imposed for the bringing of proceedings, only the Court of Justice of the EU itself is entitled to decide upon temporal limitations to be placed on its own interpretations of a rule of EU law.[1887] By contrast, the Spanish Supreme Court's restriction of claims by consumers to payments made before its own decision on the unfairness of the relevant terms was tantamount to depriving the consumers affected of their rights to obtain repayment in full of the amounts overpaid.[1888] The national court therefore had failed to provide the adequate and effective means of preventing the continued use of the relevant unfair terms as required by art.7(1) of the 1993 Directive.[1889]

38–314A The particular issues presented to the Court of Justice in *Gutiérrez Naranjo* are not directly relevant to the context of the interpretation and application of the 1999 Regulations (nor indeed the Consumer Rights Act Pt 2[1889a]) by the English courts. However, the decision of the Court of Justice in *Gutiérrez Naranjo* makes clear that EU law requires in principle that a consumer who has paid money under a contract term found unfair has a right to recovery of that money, as in the case of penalty clause, an unfair variation of price clause or an unintelligible[1889b] and unfair price clause. However, the exact legal nature of this recovery and its incidents (for example, as regards limitation period or even any defence of change of position by the seller or supplier or contributory fault in the consumer) could still be thought to be a matter for national (and therefore English) law, as being "detailed rules" governing the effect of the non-bindingness of the term in question, subject to the qualification that the practical effect of the nature and incidents of the recovery must not prejudice the effectiveness of the consumer's protection.[1889c] In this respect, in *Chesterton Global Ltd v Finney* the court held that a consumer who had paid sums under a term later found unfair within the meaning of the 1999 Regulations could recover these sums under *Kleinwort Benson Ltd v Lincoln City Council*[1889d] that is, under a mistake of law.[1889e]

[1881] *Gutiérrez Naranjo v Cajasur Banco SAU, Palacios Martinez v Banco Bilbao Vizcaya Argentaria SA (BBVA), Banco Popular Español, SA v Irles López* (Joined Cases C-154/15, C-307/15 and C-308/15) of December 21, 2016 ("*Gutiérrez Naranjo* (Joined Cases C-154/15, C-307/15 and C-308/15)").

[1882] Opinion of A.G. Mengozzi, *Gutiérrez Naranjo* (Joined Cases C-154/15, C-307/15 and C-308/15) at para.21 and see also decision of CJEU in *Gutiérrez Naranjo* (Joined Cases C-154/15, C-307/15 and C-308/15) paras 18–26.

[1883] Opinion, *Gutiérrez Naranjo* (Joined Cases C-154/15, C-307/15 and C-308/15) at para.72.

[1884] *Gutiérrez Naranjo* (Joined Cases C-154/15, C-307/15 and C-308/15) at para.55.

[1885] *Gutiérrez Naranjo* (Joined Cases C-154/15, C-307/15 and C-308/15) at paras 61–62.

[1886] *Gutiérrez Naranjo* (Joined Cases C-154/15, C-307/15 and C-308/15) at paras 64–66.

[1887] *Gutiérrez Naranjo* (Joined Cases C-154/15, C-307/15 and C-308/15) at paras 67–71.

[1888] *Gutiérrez Naranjo* (Joined Cases C-154/15, C-307/15 and C-308/15) at para.72.

[1889] *Gutiérrez Naranjo* (Joined Cases C-154/15, C-307/15 and C-308/15) at para.73.

[1889a] On which see Main Work, Vol.II paras 38–334 et seq.

[1889b] This further requirement stems from the condition of the "core exclusion" from the test of unfairness: see Main Work, Vol.I, para.38–239.

[1889c] *Gutiérrez Naranjo* (Joined Cases C-154/15, C-307/15 and C-308/15) at paras 66 and 69. On limitation of actions cf. *Cofidis CA v Fredout* (C-473/00) [2002] E.C.R. I-10875 (national limitation period held unable to prevent court intervening as regards the fairness of a contract term) and *Hamilton v Volksbank Filder eG* (C-412/06) [2008] E.C.R. I-2383 especially A.G. Maduro's Opinion at para.24 ("The existence of a general principle of limitation should therefore be recognised, while leaving the Member States the necessary discretion to implement it in their respective legal systems").

[1889d] [1992] 2 A.C. 349 and see further Main Work, Vol.I, paras 29–047—29–049.

[1889e] *Chesterton Global Ltd v Finney* Unreported, April 30, 2010 (Lambeth County Ct) and on this ground of restitutionary recovery see Main Work, Vol.I, paras 29–044—29–049. See also *Re Welcome Financial Services Ltd* [2015] EWHC 815 (Ch) at [106], where the court accepted (in the context a scheme of arrangement under Pt 26 of the Companies Act 2006) that a consumer who had paid money under a contract term held unfair under the 1999 Regulations could recover it.

Terms "not binding" on consumer and third parties

[*In note 1890, last line, delete* "(not in force at the time of writing)" *and substitute: page* [1137]]   **38–315**

(in force on May 26, 2015: 2015 Act s.100(4) and see the Consumer Rights Act 2015 (Consequential Amendments) Order 2015 (SI 2015/1726) arts 2–4; Sch. paras 2–5).

[*In paragraph, lines 18 and 19, delete* "which provides for a success fee" *and substitute: page* [1137]]

(including one which provides for a success fee)

[*Add to paragraph, at the end: page* [1137]]
Finally, more difficult is the position of a person who, while not party to the original contract, enjoys rights under the contract by way of assignment or grant. For example, a landlord (the "trader") may grant a long lease to a tenant (the "consumer"), the contract of tenancy constituting a "consumer contract" for the purposes of the 1999 Regulations.[1895a] If the tenant sells the lease to a third party, the question could arise as to whether that third party can claim the benefit of the controls of the 1999 Regulations on the fairness of its terms, even though not party to the original contract and, in some situations, even though not himself a "consumer".[1895b] It could be argued that the protections which the 1993 Directive (and therefore the 1999 Regulations) provide are personal to the consumer party to the contract with the trader and therefore cannot be enjoyed by a third party. However, it is submitted that in principle where under the contract of transfer the third party enjoys the *contractual* rights of the consumer, then he should also be able to claim the benefit of the protections of the 1999 Regulations which his own transferor would have enjoyed: the purpose of the requirement of fairness under the 1999 Regulations is to "re-balance" the parties' rights and obligations under the consumer contract and it is these "rebalanced" rights which the third party acquires.[1895c]

[1895a] *London Borough of Newham v Khatun* [2004] EWCA Civ 55, [2005] Q.B. 37 and see Main Work, Vol.II, paras 38–203—38–204.
[1895b] cf. the position in *Roundlistic Ltd v Jones* [2016] UKUT 325 (LC) where, however, these points were not raised: on this case, see above, para.38–211.
[1895c] On the idea that the purpose of the requirement of fairness is to re-balance the parties' rights, see *Aziz v Caixa d'Estalvis de Catalunya, Tarragona i Manresa* (C-415/11) March 14, 2013 at paras 44–45, on which see Main Work, Vol.II, para.38–247.

(iv) *The Requirement of Plain and Intelligible Language*

The place of the requirement in the Regulations

38–319   [*Add to note 1904, at the end: page* [1139]]
; *Allproperty Claims Ltd v Tang* [2015] EWHC 2198 QB) at [45].

Broad approach to the requirement of transparency in the CJEU

38–320   [*Add to note 1915, at the end: page* [1140]]
See also *Verein für Konsumenteninformation v Amazon EU Sàrl* (C-191/15) July 28, 2016 at paras 67–71 and above, para.38–260.

(v) *Choice of Law Clauses*

Choice of law clauses ineffective

38–322   [*In paragraph, line 10, delete* "allows" *and substitute: page* [1141]]
does not control

[*Add to paragraph, at the end: page* [1141]]
However, an express choice of law clause may be held unfair under the national law applicable to its assessment under the Rome I Regulation, as explained earlier.[1924a]

[1924a] See above, para.38–295A.

(vi) *The Prevention of Unfair Terms*

Nature of relief: injunctions and declarations

[*Add to note 1965, at the end: page* [1147]]
cf. *Biuro podróży 'Partner' sp. z o.o. sp.k. w Dąbrowie Górniczej v Prezes Urzędu Ochrony Konkurencji i Konsumentów* (C-119/15) of December 25, 2016 at para.40 (trader fined for use of terms *equivalent to* a standard condition of business declared unlawful in other proceedings and placed on a national register must have a right to challenge the assessment of unfairness and the penalty as a result of the right to an effective judicial remedy under art.47 of the Charter of Fundamental Rights of the European Union).

38–327

(d) *The New Law: The Consumer Rights Act 2015*

(i) *Introduction and Overview*

Temporal application of the 2015 Act's provisions on unfair terms

[*Add to paragraph, line 3, after* "contract terms were brought into force"*: page* [1152]]
generally

38–335

[*Add to note 2005a, line 3, after* "arts 3(a)–(c), 6(1), (3) and (4)"*: page* [1152]]
The exception to this general position is found in relation to "consumer transport services" where the relevant provisions in the Act apply only from October 1, 2016: 2015 Order arts 4 and 6(2) as amended by the Consumer Rights Act 2015 (Commencement No.3, Transitional Provisions, Savings and Consequential Amendments) (Amendment) Order 2016 (SI 2016/484) art.2; and for further likely future qualifications, see above, para.38–403.

The strategies of the 2015 Act in relation to contract terms

[*Add new note 2014a, at the end of paragraph: page* [1153]]
[2014a] The CMA has published guidance on the unfair contract terms provisions in the 2015 Act: *Unfair contract terms guidance, Guidance on the unfair terms provisions in the Consumer Rights Act 2015* (CMA37, July 2015).

38–339

[*In note 2035, lines 1–6, delete* "The question whether . . . " *to* "under s.212 of the Enterprise Act 2002." *and substitute: page* [1156]]
In addition, acts or omissions in respect of any provision in Pts 1 and 2 of the 2015 Act are specified as possible "domestic infringements" for the purposes of

38–343

s.212 of the Enterprise Act 2002: Enterprise Act 2002 (Part 8 Domestic Infringements) Order 2015 (SI 2015/1727) art.2.

(iv) *Contract Terms and Notices Not Binding on the Consumer Where Assessed as Unfair*

(aa) *Terms of Consumer Contracts*

General test of unfairness

38–359   [*In paragraph, replace final full stop with comma after* "found in the Consumer Rights Act" *and before note 2123 in line 21: page* [1165]]

[*Add to paragraph, after note 2123: page* [1165]]
with the following qualification. As explained in the Main Work, the Court of Justice in *Aziz* advised that, under the requirement of good faith, the national court must assess whether the trader "dealing fairly and equitably with the consumer, could reasonably assume that the consumer would have agreed to such a term in individual contract negotiations".[2123a] However, there is a particular difficulty in applying this approach to the test of unfairness in the Consumer Rights Act 2015, as the latter can apply to terms which *have been* individually negotiated as well as to terms which have not.[2123b] Where it does, explaining the requirement of good faith by reference to a hypothetical test of what the trader could objectively have assumed the (reasonable) consumer would have agreed in individual negotiations would make little sense, given that, ex hypothesi, the consumer had in fact agreed to the term in question.[2123c] It is submitted that this difficulty disappears if the hypothetical test is treated as *relevant* to the assessment of good faith but not conclusive of it,[2123d] as this allows a court to be able to interpret the requirement of good faith in the context of an individually negotiated term on other and broader grounds, as is indeed suggested by recital 16 of the 1993 Directive itself.[2123e] This is apparently the view taken by the CMA, which has observed that the "requirement of good faith . . . allows for proper account to be taken of the significance of any real negotiation that has actually taken place", but considers that

> "any contention that a particular consumer has actually influenced the substance of a term has to be tested against a detailed consideration of the circumstances existing at the time the contract was concluded. In [the CMA's] view, individual consumers rarely in practice have the required knowledge and bargaining power to ensure that contractual negotiations involving them are effectively conducted on equal terms."[2123f]

[2123a] *Aziz v Caixa d'Estalvis de Catalunya, Tarragona i Manresa* (C-415/11) March 14, 2013 at para.69, and see Main Work, para.38–247.

[2123b] 2015 Act s.62 and see Main Work, para.38–358.

[2123c] cf. the discussion of the hypothetical test in *Aziz* in *ParkingEye Ltd v Beavis* [2015] UKSC 67, [2015] 3 W.L.R. 1373 above, para.38–251A.

[2123d] This view was taken by Lord Mance in *ParkingEye Ltd v Beavis* [2015] UKSC 67 at [208].

[2123e] See Main Work, Vol.II, paras 38–244—38–245.

[2123f] CMA, *Unfair contract terms guidance, Guidance on the unfair terms provisions in the Consumer Rights Act 2015* (CMA37, July 2015), para.2.30.

The "indicative list of terms"

[*Add to note 2126, at the end: page* [1166]]   **38–360**
While the list of terms in Sch.2 applies to "contract terms" rather than to
"consumer notices", the CMA's view is that its "indicative list" also serves to
illustrate the forms that unfairness can take in non-contractual notices: CMA,
*Unfair contract terms guidance, Guidance on the unfair terms provisions in the
Consumer Rights Act 2015* (CMA37, July 2015), para.1.25 and Pt 5 (which
considers the practical significance of the examples in the list more generally).

[*Add to note 2128, at the end: page* [1166]]
For discussion of these new examples of terms in the list see CMA, *Unfair
contract terms guidance, Guidance on the unfair terms provisions in the Consumer Rights Act 2015* (CMA37, July 2015), paras 5.15.1–5.15.7,
5.22.11–5.22.12 and 5.23.1–5.23.7.

Comments; relationship to recent case-law of the CJEU

[*Add to note 2175, at the end: page* [1172]]   **38–368**
In the view of A.G. Wahl, the requirement of plain intelligible language "implies
that *the consumer acquires actual knowledge* of all the terms": *Andriciuc v
Banca Românească* (C-186/16) A.G. Opinion of April 26, 2016 at para.62.

[*Add to note 2178, at the end: page* [1172]]
; *Andriciuc v Banca Românească* (C-186/16) Opinion of A.G. Wahl of April 26,
2016 paras 60–72.

[*Add to note 2179, at the end: page* [1172]]
See also the guidance in CMA, *Unfair contract terms guidance, Guidance on the
unfair terms provisions in the Consumer Rights Act 2015* (CMA37, July 2015),
paras 3.20–3.32.

(bb) *Certain Types of Term of "Secondary Contracts"*

Extending the controls of Pt 2 to certain types of term in "secondary contracts"

[*In note 2203, update reference to Treitel on The Law of Contract to: page* [1175]]   **38–370**
14th edn (2015), para.7–084

[*In note 2208, update reference to Treitel on The Law of Contract to: page* [1176]]
14th edn (2015), para.7–084

(vii) *Choice of Law*

Special rule governing choice of law

[*Add to paragraph, after note 2275: page* [1185]]   **38–386**
Be that as it may, the Court of Justice of the EU has held that where a consumer
contract contains a choice of law clause which designates the law of another

Member State, that term may itself be an unfair term within the meaning of the 1993 Directive.[2275a]

[2275a] *Verein für Konsumenteninformation v Amazon EU Sàrl* (C-191/15) July 28, 2016, above, para.38–295A.

(viii) *Enforcement*

Summary of position before enactment of the Consumer Rights Act 2015

38–387 [*Add to note 2281, line 1, after* "paras 38–323—38–333"*: page* [1185]]
(where the qualifications on this general position are noted)

[*Add to note 2284, at the end: page* [1186]]
cf. the position as regards "domestic infringements" under Pt 8 of the 2002 Act, which extend, inter alia, to the Unfair Contract Terms Act 1977: Enterprise Act 2002 (Part 8 Domestic Infringements) Order 2003 (SI 2003/1593) art.2 and Sch. Pt 1.

Enforcement measures under the Consumer Rights Act 2015

38–388 [*In paragraph, after note 2303, delete* "The Act" *and substitute: page* [1187]]
For this purpose, the relevant provisions in Pt 2 of the 2015 Act which implement the 1993 Directive have been designated as a specified UK law for the purposes of s.212 of the 2002 Act[2303a] and in addition, acts or omissions in respect of any provision in Pt 2 of the 2015 Act are specified as possible "domestic infringements" for the purposes of s.211 of the Enterprise Act 2002.[2303b] The 2015 Act

[2303a] Enterprise Act 2002 s.212(3); Enterprise Act 2002 (Part 8 Community Infringements Specified UK Laws) Order 2003 art.3; Sch., as amended by the Enterprise Act 2002 (Part 8 Community Infringements and Specified UK Laws) (Amendment) Order 2015 (SI 2015/1628) art.2(2)(a), listing 2015 Act ss.2, 61–64, 67–70, 72–74, Schs 2 and 3 and Sch.5 Pt 3.
[2303b] Enterprise Act 2002 s.211(2); Enterprise Act 2002 (Part 8 Domestic Infringements) Order 2015 (SI 2015/1727) art.2.

The impact of "full harmonisation" under the Unfair Commercial Practices Directive 2005

38–390 [*Add to note 2311, at the end: page* [1188]]
The 1990 Directive is repealed and replaced by Directive (EU) 2015/2302 on package travel and linked travel arrangements [2015] O.J. L326/1.

[*Add to note 2312, at the end: page* [1188]]
And see *Citroën Commerce GmbH v Zentralvereinigung des Kraftfahrzeuggewerbes zur Aufrechterhaltung lauteren Wettbewerbs eV (ZLW)* (C-476/14) July 7, 2016 at paras 44–46, noted above, para.38–106.

(e) *Special Rules Governing Consumer Payments*

Payment surcharges

[*Add to note 2339, line 1, after* "(the "2012 Regulations")": *page* [1193]]   **38–396**
(as amended by the 2013 Regulations (SI 2013/3134))

[*Add new paragraph 38–396A: page* [1194]]
Abolition of charges for use of payment instruments by consumers. However,   **38–396A**
the law governing payment surcharges set out in para.38–396 of the Main Work
is set to change on the coming into force of amendments to the Consumer Rights
(Payment Surcharges) Regulations 2012 by the Payment Services Regulations
2017.[2343a] These amendments implement (but go further than) a requirement
imposed by the Second Payment Services Directive 2015.[2343b] Under the 2015
Directive, a payee, such as a retailer, "shall not request charges for the use of
payment instruments" where their interchange fees are capped under the Interchange Fees Regulation 2015,[2343c] and this includes the majority of consumer
debit and credit cards.[2343d] However, as just noted, the UK's implementation goes
further than this requirement, as is permitted by the 2015 Directive where a
Member State considers that this is needed to encourage competition and pro-
mote the use of efficient payment instruments.[2343e] As a result, under reg.6A(1)
of the 2012 Regulations (as inserted by the 2017 Regulations), "a payee must not
charge a payer any fee in respect of payment by means of a payment instrument"
as long as it is not a commercial card or other payment instrument,[2343f] whether
or not it is a card-based payment instrument within the meaning of the Interchange Fees Regulation 2015; nor must a payee charge in respect of a payment
service (such as a direct debit) in euro.[2343g] As a result (and subject to territorial
limitations[2343h]), reg.6A(1) imposes a ban on surcharging applicable to all non-
commercial retail payment instruments.[2343i] According to the Explanatory Memorandum to the 2017 Regulations, "this is intended to level the playing field
across all non-commercial retail payment instruments and create a clearer picture
for consumers in which they know the full price of the product/service they are
purchasing upfront and are confident that there will be no additional charges
when they come to pay using a particular payment instrument".[2343j] The 2017
Regulations make further consequential amendments of the 2012 Regulations,
including as regards the consumer's rights to redress.[2343k] These amendments to
the 2012 Regulations come into force as regards contracts entered into on
January 13, 2018.[2343l]

[2343a] SI 2017/752 ("2017 Regulations") reg.156; Sch.8 Pt 3 para.12.

[2343b] Directive (EU) 2015/2366 of the European Parliament and of the Council of 25 November
2015 on payment services in the internal market [2015] O.J. L337/35 ("2015 Directive"),
art.62(3)–(4).

[2343c] Regulation (EU) 2015/251 of the European Parliament and of the Council of 29 April 2015
on interchange fees for card-based payment transactions [2015] O.J. L123/1 ("Interchange Fees
Regulation 2015").

[2343d] Explanatory Memorandum to the 2017 Regulations, para.7.16.

[2343e] 2015 Directive art.62(5).

[2343f] 2012 Regulations reg.6A(1)(a)(ii) and (b)(ii). "Commercial card" is defined by art.2(6) of the
Interchange Fees Regulation 2015 as "any card-based payment instrument issued to undertakings or
public sector entities or self-employed natural persons which is limited in use for business expenses
where the payments made with such cards are charged directly to the account of the undertaking or
public sector entity or self-employed natural person".

^{2343g} "Payment service" is defined by reference to Regulation (EU) 260/2012 of the European Parliament and of the Council of March 14, 2012 establishing technical and business requirements for credit transfers and direct debits in euro [2012] O.J. L95/22.

^{2343h} These are contained in the 2012 Regulations reg.6B.

²³⁴³ⁱ Explanatory Memorandum to the 2017 Regulations, para.7.16.

^{2343j} Explanatory Memorandum to the 2017 Regulations, para.7.16.

^{2343k} 2012 Regulations reg.10 as amended by 2017 Regulations Sch.3 Pt 3 para.12(8).

^{2343l} 2017 Regulations reg.2(6), although confusingly reg.1(3) of the 2012 Regulations (as inserted on January 13, 2018) provides that reg.6A "applies in relation to contracts entered into after the date on which the Payment Services Regulations 2017 were *made*" (emphasis added) and the 2017 Regulations were made on July 18, 2017.

Helpline charges over basic rate

38–398   [*Add to paragraph, line 6, after* "than the basic rate.".: *page* [1195]]

Although "basic rate" is not defined by the Directive nor the Regulations for this purpose, the Court of Justice of the EU has held that it refers to "an ordinary rate for a telephone call at no additional cost for the consumer" i.e. the cost of a call to a standard geographic landline or mobile telephone line and that this means that traders are not allowed to charge consumers premium rates even where they do not make a profit in doing so.^{2349a}

^{2349a} *Zentrale zur Bekämpfung unlauteren Wettbewerbs Frankfurt am Main eV v comtech GmbH* (C-568/15) of March 2, 2017 at paras 27–32.

7. Contracts for the Supply of Goods, Digital Content or Services

(a) *Introduction*

Temporal application of Pt 1 of the 2015 Act

38–403   [*In note 2395, lines 3–4, delete* "do not apply to . . . " *to* "2015 Order art.4." *and substitute: page* [1199]]

do not apply to certain "consumer transport services" (certain rail passenger services, carriage by air, and sea and inland waterway transport, all as specially defined by the 2015 Order art.2) until October 1, 2016: 2015 Order arts 4 and 6(2) as amended by the Consumer Rights Act 2015 (Commencement No.3, Transitional Provisions, Savings and Consequential Amendments) (Amendment) Order 2016 (SI 2016/484) art.2. The main reason for this delay in the bringing into force of the provisions of the 2015 Act in this area was a concern that the Act's provisions (especially s.57's controls on the exclusion or restriction of liability in the carrier) would risk complexity and duplication with sectoral transport schemes: Department of Transport, *Applying the Consumer Rights Act 2015 to the rail, aviation and maritime sectors, Response to Consultation, Moving Britain Ahead* (July, 2016). Although the Department of Transport (para.2.4) had earlier announced that the exemption from the application of s.57(3) of the 2015 Act (governing *restrictions* on liability, as noted by the Main Work, Vol.II, para.38–546) would continue to apply to passenger services operated by EU licensed rail passenger operators until October 1, 2017 (see *draft Consumer Rights (Rail Passenger Service Exemption, Enforcement and Amendments) Order 2016 (laid before Parliament, July 7, 2016)*) on September 6, 2016 it was announced that the 2015 Act would apply in full to all passenger transport services, including mainline rail passenger services as from October 1, 2016: *https://www.gov.uk/government/publications/consumer-rights-act-application-to-transport-services.*

[*Add new paragraph 38–403A: page* [1199]]

Proposed EU directives on distance contracts for the sale of goods and on contracts for the supply of digital content. The EU Commission has published two proposals for directives which would, if enacted and implemented in UK law, require the amendment of the 2015 Act's provisions governing contracts of sale of goods and contracts for the supply of digital content. Both proposed directives would require "full harmonization"[2395a] and this would make their implementation within the existing frameworks of English law particularly difficult. The first is a proposal for a directive on aspects of the law governing "distance contracts" for the sale of goods[2395b]: if enacted, this directive would disapply the Consumer Sales Directive 1999 from distance contracts for the sale of goods[2395c] and could require the UK either to amend Ch.2 of Pt 1 of the 2015 Act so as to follow the scheme of the new directive even beyond its scope of "distance contracts" or to disapply Ch.2 from distance contracts of sale of goods and enact a dedicated regime for this purpose. The second is a proposal for a directive on aspects of the law governing the distance supply of digital content.[2395d] If enacted, this could require the amendment of Ch.3 of Pt 1 of the 2015 Act.[2395e]

38–403A

[2395a] Distance sales directive proposal 2015 art.3; Digital content directive proposal 2015 art.4.
[2395b] Proposal for a Directive of the European Parliament and of the Council on certain aspects concerning contracts for the online and other distance sales of goods COM(2015) 635 final ("Distance sales directive proposal 2015").
[2395c] Distance sales directive proposal 2015 art.19.
[2395d] Proposal for a Directive of the European Parliament and of the Council on certain aspects concerning contracts for the supply of digital content COM(2015) 634 final ("Digital content directive proposal 2015").
[2395e] On this law, see Main Work, Vol.II, paras 38–496—38–526.

(b) *The Old Law: Special Rules for Buyers and Hirer in Consumer Cases*

(iii) *Special Remedies for Buyers Dealing as Consumers*

Fixed time limits

[*Add to note 2469, at the end: page* [1210]]
On the distinction between time-limits on liability in the seller and on the period during which the consumer can exercise the rights arising in respect of that liability see *Ferenschild v JPC Motor SA* (C-133/16) of July 13, 2017.

38–425

(c) *The New Law: Consumer Rights in Respect of Goods Contracts, Digital Content Contracts and Services Contracts*

(ii) *"Goods Contracts"*

(aa) *The Four Types of "Goods Contracts"*

"Sales contracts"

38–452   [*Add to note 2593, at the end: page* [1221]]
cf. *Software Incubator Ltd v Computer Associates UK Ltd* [2016] EWHC 1587 (QB) at [35]–[69] where it was held that a contract for the supply of software could constitute a "sale of goods" for the purposes of the Commercial Agents (Council Directive) Regulations 1993 (SI 1993/3053), distinguishing (at [47]) the position under the Consumer Rights Act 2015.

[*Add to note 2594, at the end: page* [1221]]
And see above, para.38–052A, which discusses *Wathelet v Garage Bietheres & Fils SPRL* (C-149/15) [2017] 1 W.L.R. 865 on the question when a trader who acts on behalf of a private individual is to be treated as a "seller" of goods under the Consumer Sales Directive 1999.

[*Add to end of note 2595: page* [1221]]
In *PST Energy 7 Shipping LLC v OW Bunker Malta (The Res Cogitans)* [2016] UKSC 23, [2016] 2 W.L.R. 1193 (decided in a commercial context), the Supreme Court held that if a contract provides for possession of goods to be given, coupled with a legal entitlement to use or consume them before the property in them is transferred upon payment, then the contract is not one of sale of goods within the meaning of the Sale of Goods Act 1979 as the transferor does not undertake to transfer property in the goods, but is instead sui generis, a bailment coupled with a licence to use or consume the goods, and that this is the case even where it is agreed that the property is to pass in any goods still in existence at the time of payment. On the complex legal issues arising if such a contract were concluded between a trader and a consumer within the meanings of the 2015 Act, see *Benjamin's Sale of Goods*, 10th edn (2017) paras 14-062–14-065.

"Contracts for the transfer of goods"

38–457   [*Add new note 2620a, at the end of paragraph: page* [1224]]
[2620a] In *Wood v TUI Travel PLC (t/a First Choice)* [2017] EWCA Civ 11, [2017] 1 Lloyd's Rep. 322 esp. at [27] it was held that where a contract for a holiday for consumers under which a hotel is to provide food and drink, in the absence of express agreement to the contrary, the property in the meal transfers to them when it is served, whether or not that meal is accompanied with a service. As a result, such a contract is a "contract for the transfer of property in goods" under s.4 of the Supply of Goods of Services Act 1982 (The decision related to a contract made before the coming into force of the 2015 Act on October 1, 2015.)

(cc) *The Scheme of Remedies for the Consumer*

The right to reject: general provisions

38–478   [*In note 2757, update reference to Treitel on The Law of Contract to: page* [1240]]
14th edn (2015), para.18–001

[Add new paragraph 38-484A: page [1245]]

Limitation of actions. Article 5(1) of the Consumer Sales Directive 1999 **38–484A**
provides that:

> "The seller shall be held liable under Article 3 where the lack of conformity becomes
> apparent within two years as from delivery of the goods. If, under national legisla-
> tion, the rights laid down in Article 3(2) are subject to a limitation period, that period
> shall not expire within a period of two years from the time of delivery."

In *Ferenschild*[2794a] the Court of Justice of the EU held that art.5(1) distinguishes
between two types of time-limits: the first governing the period of *liability* of the
seller where non-conformity of the goods becomes apparent and which is set in
principle as two years from the time of delivery of the goods[2794b]; the second
governing the "period of time during which the consumer can actually exercise
the rights that arose in the period of liability of the seller, with regard to the
latter".[2794c] Under the Directive, Member States may choose whether or not to
impose a time-limit of the second type[2794d] and the UK in its implementation of
the 1999 Directive did not choose to do so. As regards the period of liability of
the seller, following the position under the 1979 Act,[2794e] the 2015 Act has not
retained the relatively short period for liability in the seller and instead generally
allows consumers to bring their claims under the 2015 Act within the general
limitation period of six years provided by the Limitation Act 1980.[2794f] While an
exception to this pattern is of course found in the "short-term right to reject"
which has a time-limit of 30 days,[2794g] this rule is compatible with the 1999
Directive as the short-term right to reject is not required by the Directive but is
additional to (and therefore more protective than) the Directive's own scheme of
consumer rights, as permitted by its minimum harmonisation character.[2794h]

[2794a] *Ferenschild v JPC Motor SA* (C-133/16) of July 13, 2017 ("*Ferenschild* (C-133/16)").
[2794b] *Ferenschild* (C-133/16) at paras 33–34.
[2794c] *Ferenschild* (C-133/16) at para.35.
[2794d] *Ferenschild* (C-133/16) at para.36.
[2794e] See Main Work, Vol.I, para.38–425.
[2794f] Limitation Act 1980 s.5 (six years from accrual of the cause of action). The general rule in
contract is that the cause of action accrues when the breach takes place rather than when any damage
may have been suffered: Main Work, Vol.I, paras 28–032 et seq. While art.5(1) of the 1999 Directive
requires liability in the seller for two years from the date of delivery, it is submitted that breach will
not precede delivery in this context. The UK equally chose not to exercise the option provided by
art.7(2) of the 1999 Directive which allows Member States to provide that in the case of second-hand
goods, the seller and the consumer buyer may agree contract terms which have a time period of
liability shorter than the two years set by art.5(1) first sentence as long as it is not less than one
year.
[2794g] 2015 Act s.22 and above, para.38–481 (which explain the starting-points for this period).
[2794h] 1999 Directive arts 3 and 8(2) and cf. *Ferenschild* (C-133/16) at para.48.

Discretion as to appropriate remedy

[In paragraph, line 13, delete "These powers" *and substitute: page* [1245]] **38–485**
It is submitted, though, that in the case of contracts for the *sale* of goods ("sales
contracts"), the consumer's right to repair or replacement of goods in the Act
reflects requirements of the Consumer Sales Directive 1999 and so the provisions
of the Act relating to them must be interpreted with this in mind and in the light
of the principle of effectiveness, here, of the consumer's protection.[2799a] For this
purpose, in *Weber and Putz* the Court of Justice of the EU assumed that the

consumer's specific rights under the Directive were enforceable in kind against the seller, holding that national law must not allow replacement to be refused by a trader on the ground of disproportionality with regard to the value of the goods as conforming and the significance of the non-conformity, even though in the circumstances this meant that the trader had to bear the costs of the removal of goods installed by the consumer and the reinstallation of the replacement goods.[2799b] This suggests that an English court should not refuse specific performance in support of the consumer's right to repair or replacement of goods sold on the ground that damages would be an adequate remedy, as this would to this extent replace the consumer's "European rights" with damages and so render them ineffective and that the court should not take into account other traditional elements governing the availability of specific performance stemming from its equitable nature on the basis that the Directive itself provides only two circumstances (impossibility and disproportionality compared to the other specific remedy) where the trader is entitled to refuse to repair or replace.[2799c] It also suggests that, in the case of "sales contracts", the court's powers to substitute another "appropriate right" under s.58 is incompatible with the 1999 Directive. Finally, on their terms, the court's powers under s.58

[2799a] See Whittaker (2017) 133 L.Q.R. 47. On the Consumer Sales Directive 1999 generally, see Main Work, Vol.II, para.38–400. On "sales contracts" see Main Work, Vol.II, paras 38–452—38–454.

[2799b] *Gebr Weber GmbH v Wittmer, Putz v Medianess Electronics GmbH* (C-65/09 and C-87/09) [2011] 3 C.M.L.R. 27 at [63]–[78].

[2799c] 1999 Directive art.3(3), reflected in 2015 Act s.23(3)–(4) and see Main Work, Vol.II, para.38–482.

(dd) *Other Rules About Goods Contracts*

Delivery of goods in sales contracts

38–489   [*Add to note 2833, at the end: page* [1249]]
(revoked by SI 2015/1629 art.8).

Passing of risk

38–490   [*Add to note 2858, at the end: page* [1251]]
The 2015 Act s.29 implements the Consumer Rights Directive 2011 art.20 and replaces its earlier implementation by the 2013 Regulations reg.43 (which was itself revoked by the Consumer Contracts (Amendment) Regulations 2015 (SI 2015/1629) art.8 as regards contracts entered into on or after October 1, 2015).

(ee) *Exclusion of Liability and Choice of Law*

Enforcement of Pt 1 more generally

38–495   [*In paragraph, delete from* "However, what is less clear . . . " *in line 7 to the end and substitute: page* [1255]]
As a result, the relevant provisions in Ch.2 of the 2015 Act, which implement the 1999 Directive or the 2011 Directive or which "provide additional permitted

protections",²⁸⁹⁴ have been designated as specified UK laws for the purposes of s.212 of the 2002 Act.²⁸⁹⁴ᵃ In addition, acts or omissions in respect of any provision in Pt 1 of the 2015 Act are specified as possible "domestic infringements" for the purposes of s.211 of the Enterprise Act 2002.²⁸⁹⁴ᵇ

²⁸⁹⁴ Enterprise Act 2002 s.212(1)(b).
²⁸⁹⁴ᵃ Enterprise Act 2002 s.212(3); Enterprise Act 2002 (Part 8 Community Infringements Specified UK Laws) Order 2003 art.3; Sch., as amended by the Enterprise Act 2002 (Part 8 Community Infringements and Specified UK Laws) (Amendment) Order 2015 (SI 2015/1628) art.2(2)(b) listing 2015 Act ss.2, 3, 9–11, 13–15, 19, 23, 24, 30–32, 58 and 59 (1999 Directive); art.3(2) listing 2015 Act ss.5, 11(4)–(6), 12, 19, 28, 29, 36(3)–(4), 37, 38, 42, 50 and 54 (2011 Directive).
²⁸⁹⁴ᵇ Enterprise Act 2002 s.211(2); Enterprise Act 2002 (Part 8 Domestic Infringements) Order 2015 (SI 2015/1727) art.2.

(iv) *Digital Content Contracts*

Introduction

[*Add new note 2894c, after* "defines for these purposes." *in line 3: note* [1255]]   **38–496**
²⁸⁹⁴ᶜ On the Proposal for a Directive of the European Parliament and of the Council on certain aspects concerning contracts for the supply of digital content COM(2015) 634 final, see above, para.38–403A.

[*Add to note 2895, at the end: page* [1256]]
cf. *Software Incubator Ltd v Computer Associates UK Ltd* [2016] EWHC 1587 (QB) at [35]–[69] (a contract for the supply of software could constitute a "sale of goods" for the purposes of the Commercial Agents (Council Directive) Regulations 1993 (SI 1993/3053), distinguishing (at [47]) the position under the Consumer Rights Act 2015).

(aa) *"Digital Content Contracts"*

"Digital content contracts" and other contracts in Pt 1 of the Act

[*Add to note 2924, at the end: page* [1259]]   **38–503**
cf. *Software Incubator Ltd v Computer Associates UK Ltd* [2016] EWHC 1587 (QB), [2017] Bus. L.R. 245 at [35]–[69] (a contract for the supply of software may constitute a "sale of goods" for the purposes of the Commercial Agents (Council Directive) Regulations 1993 (SI 1993/3053), distinguishing the position under the law of sale of goods).

(bb) *The Statutory Terms*

Time of supply by transmission

[*Add to note 2989, at the end: page* [1267]]   **38–512**
See further Krebs (2017) J.B.L. 376.

(ee) *Exclusion of Liability*

Enforcement

38–526   [*Add to paragraph, at the end: page* [1277]]
As a result, the relevant provisions in Ch.3 of Pt 1 of the 2015 Act which implement the 2011 Directive or which "provide additional permitted protections"[3066a] have been designated as specified UK laws for the purposes of s.212 of the 2002 Act.[3066b] In addition, acts or omissions in respect of any provision in Pt 1 of the 2015 Act are specified as possible "domestic infringements" for the purposes of s.211 of the Enterprise Act 2002.[3066c]

[3066a] Enterprise Act 2002 s.212(1)(b).
[3066b] Enterprise Act 2002 s.212(3); Enterprise Act 2002 (Part 8 EU Infringements) Order 2014 (SI 2014/2908) art.4; Schedule (as amended by the Enterprise Act 2002 (Part 8 Community Infringements and Specified UK Laws) (Amendment) Order 2015 (SI 2015/1628) art.3(2)) listing, inter alia, 2015 Act ss.36(3)–(4), 37, 38 and 42.
[3066c] Enterprise Act 2002 s.211(2); Enterprise Act 2002 (Part 8 Domestic Infringements) Order 2015 (SI 2015/1727) art.2.

(v) *Services Contracts*

(aa) *Introduction*

Background

38–527   [*Add new note 3066d, after* "governing "services contracts"" *in line 2: page* [1278]]
[3066d] The 2015 Act's substantive provisions on "services contracts" generally came into force on October 1, 2015, but exceptions have been made as regards certain categories of "consumer transport service" as explained in the Main Work, Vol.II, para.38–403, esp. at n.2395 as amended by this Supplement.

(bb) *The statutory terms*

Express terms; relation of statutory terms to other law on contract terms

38–539   [*Add to note 3112, at the end: page* [1284]]
An example may be found in relation to contracts of services governed by the carriage of air conventions (notably, the Warsaw Convention and the Montreal Convention, on which see Main Work, Vol.II, paras 35–002 et seq.) which, in the view of the UK government, will remain the exclusive basis of liability on the routes to which they apply even after the 2015 Act applies to them: Department of Transport, *Applying the Consumer Rights Act 2015 to the rail, aviation and maritime sectors, Response to Consultation, Moving Britain Ahead* (July 2016), para.2.8.

(ee) *Enforcement*

Enforcement of provisions on exclusion of trader's liabilities

38–547   [*Add to paragraph, at the end: page* [1290]]
Secondly, the relevant provisions in Ch.4 of the 2015 Act which implement the 2011 Directive or which "provide additional permitted protections"[3153] (notably,

the provisions in s.50 giving contractual effect to certain categories of information provided by the trader to the consumer) have been designated as specified UK laws for the purposes of s.212 of the 2002 Act.[3154] And, thirdly, acts or omissions in respect of any provision in Pt 1 of the 2015 Act are specified as possible "domestic infringements" for the purposes of s.211 of the Enterprise Act 2002.[3155]

[3153] Enterprise Act 2002 s.212(1)(b).
[3154] Enterprise Act 2002 s.212(3); Enterprise Act 2002 (Part 8 Community Infringements Specified UK Laws) Order 2003, art.3; Sch., as amended by the Enterprise Act 2002 (Part 8 Community Infringements and Specified UK Laws) (Amendment) Order 2015 (SI 2015/1628) art.3, listing 2015 Act ss.50 and 54.
[3155] Enterprise Act 2002 s.211(2); Enterprise Act 2002 (Part 8 Domestic Infringements) Order 2015 (SI 2015/1727) art.2.

Chapter 39

CREDIT AND SECURITY

1. The Regulation of Consumer Credit

The Mortgage Credit Directive

This Directive came into force on March 21, 2016 and hence most residential **39–003**
mortgages (and so called "MCD art.3(1)(b) agreements", see n.11, below) are
now no longer regulated under the Consumer Credit Act 1974 (being "exempt
agreements", see para.39–038, below) but are within the FSMA 2000 regime.

The future of consumer credit regulation

[*Add new note 14a, at the end of the paragraph: page* [1293]] **39–004**
14a The FCA has begun the review process: see *Call for Input: Review of retained provisions of the
Consumer Credit Act*, February 2016, but this has been delayed due to uncertainties over Brexit.

Consumer Credit Directive

[*Note 46: page* [1296]] **39–011**
The Mortgage Credit Directive (and hence the relevant amendment) came into
force on March 21, 2016.

Banks and investment firms authorised in other EEA states

The expected impact of "Brexit" on the operation of the "single market pass- **39–012**
port" is presently uncertain.

Lending Code

[*Replace title, text and notes and substitute: page* [1297]] **39–013**
The Standards of Lending Practice These "Standards", which set the benchmark of good lending practices, are issued by the Lending Standards Board and
replace the old "Lending Code" (which itself replaced, in part, the provisions of
the old Banking Code[56]). Like the Code, they are voluntary "soft law" in the
sense that lending institutions agree to be bound by them in their dealings with
both personal and (small) business customers. The scope and content of the
Standards differs from that of the consumer credit regulatory regime but there is
a considerable degree of overlap. In some respects the protection is more
extensive than that of the statutory regime and in other respects it is less
extensive. But nothing in the Standards can detract from the statutory
regime.[57–60]

56 The other parts of the old Banking Code are replaced by the BCOBS Module of the FCA
Handbook.
57–60 See CCA1974 s.173, above, para.39–009

Other EU Directives

The Mortgage Credit Directive came into force on March 21, 2016 and hence the **39–014**
relevant changes were effected then.

English law, as altered by the implementation of these directives, it not expected to be amended as a result of Brexit, at least in the near future.

[In note 65, delete "Ch.37" *and substitute: page* [1298]]
paras 38–334 et seq.

(a) *Terminology*

"Regulated" consumer credit agreement

39–017   *[Note 85: page* [1300]]
The Mortgage Credit Directive (and hence the relevant amendment) came into force on March 21, 2016.

"Credit"

39–019   *[Add to note 98, at the end: page* [1301]]
; *Burrell v Helical (Bramshott Place) Ltd* [2015] EWHC 3727 (Ch) (no deferment of any obligation to pay hence no credit).

The Consumer Credit Directive: "credit exceeding £60,260"

39–022   *[Note 113: page* [1302]]
The Mortgage Credit Directive (and hence the relevant amendment) came into force on March 21, 2016.

"Debtor-creditor agreement"/"borrower-lender agreement"

39–033   *[In note 168, line 1, delete* "16(2),": *page* [1308]]

"Exempt agreements": general

39–038   *[Note 214: page* [1312]]
The Mortgage Credit Directive (and hence the relevant amendments) came into force on March 21, 2016.

Exempt land mortgages

39–039   The Mortgage Credit Directive (and hence the relevant amendments noted in the footnotes) came into force on March 21, 2016 and resulted in significant changes to the three types of mortgages that are exempt from the 1974 Act. In relation to the first type of exempt mortgage mentioned, this now results in most residential land mortgages (as well as any loans to acquire or retain property rights in residential property (so called "MCD art.3(1)(b) agreements": see CCA 1974 s.8(3)(b), added on March 21, 2016 by the Mortgage Credit Directive Order 2015 (SI 2015/910) art.3 and Sch.1 para.2(2)) being "exempt agreements", the majority of residential mortgages now being regulated under the Financial Services and Markets Act 2000. And note that none of the three types of exemption mentioned apply in so far as they are incompatible with that Directive (see the list of mortgage contracts that are not "regulated mortgage contracts" in the new RAO art.60HA, added by the Mortgage Credit Directive Order 2015 (SI 2015/910) art.3 and Sch.1 para.4(19), mentioned in nn.223 and 228 in relation to the second and third types of exempt mortgages).

"Investment mortgages" exemption

The Mortgage Credit Directive (and hence the relevant amendments noted in the footnotes) came into force on March 21, 2016.   **39–040**

[*Add to note 234, at the end: page* [1314]]
But such so-called "MCD art.3(1)(b) agreements" (see para.39–039, above) are not regulated by the CCA 1974 by reason of CCA 1974 s.8(3)(b), added on March 21, 2016 by the Mortgage Credit Directive Order 2015 (SI 2015/910) art.3 and Sch.1 para.2(2).

Exempt credit agreements: number of payments

[*Note 238: page* [1314]]   **39–041**
The Mortgage Credit Directive (and hence the relevant amendment) came into force on March 21, 2016.

[*Add to note 244, line 1, after* "RAO art.60F(4)": *page* [1315]]
Note (see n.238) that art.60F(4) does not apply in so far as it is incompatible with the Mortgage Credit Directive.

Exempt credit agreements: low-cost of credit

[*Note 246: page* [1315]]   **39–042**
The Mortgage Credit Directive (and hence the relevant amendment) came into force on March 21, 2016.

High net worth "opt-out" exemption

[*Note 259: page* [1316]]   **39–045**
The Mortgage Credit Directive (and hence the relevant amendment) came into force on March 21, 2016.

[*Note 260: page* [1316]]
The Mortgage Credit Directive (and hence the relevant amendment) came into force on March 21, 2016.

"Business purpose" exemption

[*Add to note 262, at the end: page* [1316]]   **39–046**
See also, on art.60C(3)–(7), *Newmafruit Farms Ltd v Pither* [2016] EWHC 2205 (QB), [2017] C.C.L.R. 8.

"Linked transaction"

39–055   *[Add to note 330, line 4, before* "Linked transactions": *page* [1322]]
In *Townson v FCE Bank Plc (t/a Ford Credit)*, Unreported, June 23, 2016 (Birmingham Cty Ct) a PPI policy that was a "linked transaction" (within s.19(1)(c), see below, para.39–057) was held to be a "related transaction" in the context of the "unfair relationship" provisions.

39–057   *[Add at end of note 341: page* [1324]]
See *Townson v FCE Bank Plc (t/a Ford Credit)*, Unreported, June 23, 2016 (Birmingham Cty Ct): PPI policy within s.19(1)(c).

(b) *Authorisation of Credit and Hire Businesses*

"Business"

39–062   *[Add to note 384, line 3, after* "in FSMA 2000 s.22": *page* [1327]]
(confirmed in *Newmafruit Farms Ltd v Pither* [2016] EWHC 2205 (QB), [2017] C.C.L.R. 8)

Authorisation and regulatory control

39–063   *[Add note 396, at the end: page* [1328]]
But see Main Work, Vol.II, para.39–063, n.388 and accompanying text (civil liability).

Trading whilst unauthorised

39–064   *[Add to note 400, at the end: page* [1328]]
Special provision for the specific funding of teams detecting illegal money lenders (so-called "loan sharks") has been made in the Bank of England and Financial Services Act 2016 (new Pt XXB added to the Financial Services and Markets Act 2000, in force July 16, 2016).

(c) *Seeking Business*

Canvassing

39–068   *[In note 426, line 4, delete* "para.39–247" *and substitute: page* [1330]]
para.39–252

(e) *The Agreement*

Pre-contract disclosure

39–076   *[Note 460: page* [1333]]
The Mortgage Credit Directive (and hence the relevant amendments) came into force on March 21, 2016.

Copy of draft agreement

[Note 478: page [1335]]   **39–079**
The Mortgage Credit Directive (and hence the relevant amendment) came into
force on March 21, 2016.

Form and content of agreement: general

[Note 488: page [1336]]   **39–080**
The Mortgage Credit Directive (and hence the relevant amendment) came into
force on March 21, 2016.

Form and content of agreement: the 2010 Agreements Regulations

[Note 500: page [1337]]   **39–082**
The Mortgage Credit Directive (and hence the relevant amendment) came into
force on March 21, 2016.

Supply of copies: two regimes

[Note 524: page [1339]]   **39–085**
The Mortgage Credit Directive (and hence the relevant amendment) came into
force on March 21, 2016.

(f) *Withdrawal and Cancellation*

14-day "right of withdrawal"

[Note 607: page [1345]]   **39–101**
The Mortgage Credit Directive (and hence the relevant amendment) came into
force on March 21, 2016.

Consumer Contracts (Information, Cancellation and Additional Charges) Regulations 2013

[Add to note 764, at the end: page [1357]]   **39–125**
and *Allproperty Claims v Tang* [2015] EWHC 2198 (lack of notification of
cancellation right rendered agreement unenforceable).

(g) *Supply of Information*

Statement of account to debtor under fixed-sum credit agreement on request

[Note 816: page [1361]]   **39–130**
The Mortgage Credit Directive (and hence the relevant amendment) came into
force on March 21, 2016.

[In note 817, line 2, delete "s.16B(2)–(5)" and substitute: page [1361]]
RAO art.60(3)–(7)

(h) *Variation of Agreements*

Unilateral variation under a power in agreement: the general rule

39–146   *[In note 947, line 5, delete "para.38–201" and substitute: page* [1371]]
para.39–201

(l) *Judicial Control*

Enforcement orders in cases of infringement

39–200   *[Add to note 1211, at the end: page* [1395]]
Given the "multifactorial assessment" that must be made by the court, summary
judgment is unlikely to be available: *Newmafruit Farms Ltd v Pither* [2016]
EWHC 2205 (QB), [2017] C.C.L.R. 8.

(m) *Unfair Relationships*

[Add to note 1295, at the end: page [1401]]
Brown (2016) 36(2) L.S. 230-257.

Extortionate credit bargains

39–212   *[Add to note 1304, line 7, after* "consumer 'exploited'))": *page* [1402]]
; *Nelmes v NRAM Plc* [2016] EWCA Civ 491 (in business context, payment by
the lender of a "procurement fee" (being half the arrangement fee charged by the
lender to the borrower) to the borrower's broker deprived the borrower of the
disinterested advice of his broker and hence rendered the credit relationship
"unfair"; lender accountable to borrower for all the undisclosed "procurement
fee" plus interest from the date of payment); *Townson v FCE Bank Plc (t/a Ford
Credit),* Unreported, June 23, 2016, (Birmingham Cty Ct) ("unfair relationship"
found where PPI (of which the debtor was unaware and by implication did not
want) was sold by car dealer to a debtor under a hire-purchase agreement).

[Add to note 1304, at the end: page [1403]]
; *Barclays Bank Plc v McMillan* [2015] EWHC 1596 (Comm) (loan to finance
US law firm's partner's capital subscription on usual terms); *Bluestone Mortgages Ltd v Momoh* [2015] EW Misc B4 (CC) (refusal of permission to appeal
the decision of the county court that failure to notify in advance that mortgagee
would invoke usual clause in buy-to-let mortgage permitting him to pay outstanding lease charges if mortgagor failed to do so, did not give rise to an unfair
relationship); *Commercial First Business Ltd v Pickup* [2017] C.T.L.C. 1, [2017]
C.C.L.R. 15 (although only the fact (and not the amount) of commission was
disclosed by the brokers, as the debtors were experienced property investors and
knew all the relevant facts; *Deutsche Bank (Suisse) SA v Khan* [2013] EWHC

482 (Comm), see this footnote in Main Work, Vol.II, was applied to deny that the relationship was "unfair").

Wide application of "unfair relationship" provisions

[*Add to note 1305, line 9, after* "did not provide 'credit')": *page* [1403]]
; *Bank of Ireland (UK) Plc v McLaughlin* [2016] NICA 33; [2017] C.C.L.R. 5 (refusal of appeal from the lower court ([2014] NIQB 104) that a guarantor of a corporate debtor could not invoke the unfair relationship provisions); *Newmafruit Farms Ltd v Pither* [2016] EWHC 2205 (QB), [2017] C.C.L.R. 8 (corporate debtor could not invoke the unfair relationship provisions).

39–213

[*Add to note 1306, at the end: page* [1403]]
And note the "buy-to-let" loans considered in *Paragon Mortgages Ltd v McEwan-Peters* [2011] EWHC 2491 (Comm); *Graves v Capital Home Loans Ltd* [2014] EWCA Civ 1297; *Bluestone Mortgages Ltd v Momoh* [2015] EW Misc B4 (CC) and *Nelmes v NRAM Plc* [2016] EWCA Civ 491.

[*Note 1310: page* [1403]]
The Mortgage Credit Directive came into force on March 21, 2016 and hence the relevant protection has been lost.

[*Add to note 1310, line 1, after* "s.140A(5).": *page* [1403]]
See *AIB v Donnelly* [2015] NI Master 13 (Master Hardstaff) (confirmation that unfair relationship provisions do not apply to FCA regulated mortgage contracts).

"Any related agreement"

[*Add to note 1315, at the end: page* [1404]]
See *Townson v FCE Bank Plc (t/a Ford Credit)*, Unreported, June 23, 2016 (Birmingham Cty Ct), (PPI policy held to be a "linked transaction" within s.19(1)(c) in relation to the credit agreement (and hence a "related transaction"); "unfair relationship" found where that PPI (of which the debtor was unaware and by implication did not want) was sold by car dealer to a debtor under a hire-purchase agreement).

39–214

Exercise or enforcement of rights by creditor

[*Add to note 1360, at the end: page* [1408]]
See also *Bluestone Mortgages Ltd v Faith Momoh* [2015] EW Misc B4 (CC) (refusal of permission to appeal the decision of the county court that failure to notify in advance that mortgagee would invoke usual clause in buy-to-let mortgage permitting him to pay outstanding lease charges if mortgagor failed to do so, did not give rise to an unfair relationship).

39–221

[*In note 1363, line 2, delete* "Lending Code" *and substitute: page* [1408]]
Standards of Lending Practice (financial difficulties sections)

Any other action by creditor

39–222 *[In paragraph, line 13, delete "Harrison v Black Horse Ltd" and substitute: page [1409]]*
Plevin v Paragon Personal Finance Ltd

[Add to note 1378, line 1, after "[2012] J.B.L. 713 at 727": page [1409]]
and Lomnicka, "The impact of rule-making by financial services regulators on the common law: the lessons of PPI", in Gullifer and Vogenauer (eds) *English and European Perspectives on Contract and Commercial Law: Essays in Honour of Hugh Beale* (Hart, 2014), Ch.4.

[Add to note 1381, at the end: page [1409]]
The FCA has intervened in relation to PPI (see FCA PS 17/3: Payment protection insurance complaints: Feedback on CP16/20 and final rules and guidance (March 2017)) and has set a single 50 per cent commission "tipping point" (with undisclosed profit-share (as defined) being treated in the same way as undisclosed commission) at which it states that firms should presume, for the purposes of handling PPI complaints and making recompense (the excess over 50 per cent together with interest), that the failure to disclose commission gives rise to an unfair relationship under s.140A.

Onus of proof

39–224 *[Add to note 1400, at the end: page [1411]]*
Bevin v Datum Finance Ltd was noted in *Bluestone Mortgages Ltd v Momoh* [2015] EW Misc B4 (CC) but the Court of Appeal nevertheless refused permission to appeal a summary judgment that the relationship was not unfair even though no evidence was adduced by the creditor to discharge the burden of proof.

[Add to note 1401, line 3, after "prospects of success)": page [1411]]
as was the case in *Bluestone Mortgages Ltd v Momoh* [2015] EW Misc B4 (CC), see previous note.

Nature of relief

39–225 *[In note 1407, delete from "For orders to repay . . . " in line 3 to the end and substitute: page [1412]]*
For orders to repay premiums of mis-sold PPI policies see *Scotland v British Credit Trust Ltd* [2014] EWCA Civ 790 and *Plevin v Paragon Personal Finance Ltd* [2016] C.C.L.R. 5, March 2, 2015, Manchester Cty Ct (the sequel to *Plevin v Paragon Personal Finance Ltd* [2014] UKSC 61), where the amount of commission received by the PPI seller was, on the facts, regarded as the appropriate remediation. In *Nelmes v NRAM Plc* [2016] EWCA Civ 491 the court ordered the repayment of a secret commission paid by the lender to the borrower's broker, plus interest.

(n) *Ancillary Credit Businesses*

Credit broking: exclusions

[Note 1451: page [1415]]   **39–233**
The Mortgage Credit Directive (and hence the relevant new version of art.36E) came into force on March 21, 2016.

Debt-counselling: exclusions

[In note 1470, delete "art.39K" *and substitute: page* [1417]]   **39–237**
art.39KA

Seeking business: promotion

[Add new note 1529a, at the end of the paragraph: page [1422]]   **39–251**
1529a See above, paras 38–153 et seq.

Right to recover brokerage fees

[Add to note 1543, at the end: page [1423]]   **39–253**
For similar obligations, see now the FCA Handbook, CONC 4.4.1R(2) and (4).

(o) *Operating an electronic system in relation to lending*

Operating an electronic system in relation to lending

[Add to note 1553, at the end: page [1424]]   **39–256**
See the exclusions in arts 36I and 36IA.

[Add to note 1557, at the end: page [1424]]
For special P2P regulatory provisions, see FCA Handbook, CONC 3.7A (financial promotion); CONC 4.3 (pre-contractual requirements); CONC 5.5 (creditworthiness assessment); CONC 7.17–7.19 (NOSIAs etc.); CONC 11.2 (cancellation).

2. LOANS AND INTEREST

(a) *Loans of Money*

Breach of executory contract: remedies of borrower

[Add new note 1594a, after paragraph title: page [1428]]   **39–265**
1594a For a discussion in the context of the model contract of the Loan Markets Association, Multicurrency Term and Revolving Facilities Agreement (April 2009), see Rawlings, (2012) J.B.L. 89.

Term loans

39–268   *[Add to note 1610, at the end: page* [1430]*]*
Note *Alexander v West Bromwich Mortgage Co Ltd* [2016] EWCA Civ 496.

"No set-off" clauses

39–271   *[Add to note 1624, line 1, after* "para.15–104 n.541.".*: page* [1432]*]*
As noted above at para.38–334, for consumer contracts made on or after October 1, 2015, the 1977 Act is replaced by provisions in the Consumer Rights Act 2015 Pt 2, see above paras 38–334 et seq.

[Add to note 1624, at the end: page [1432]*]*
See the unsuccessful attempt to invoke that Act in *African Export-Import Bank v Shebah Exploration and Product Co Ltd* [2016] EWHC 311 (Comm) (syndicated loan).

(b) Interest

Variation of interest rate

39–293   *[In paragraph, last sentence, delete* "Lending Code" *and substitute: page* [1442]*]*
Standards of Lending Practice

[Add to note 1721, at the end: page [1441]*]*
See *Alexander v West Bromwich Mortgage Co Ltd* [2016] EWCA Civ 496 (power to vary interest inconsistent with mortgage offered as "tracker mortgage").

Default interest

39–294   *[In note 1734, line 2, delete* "Vol.I, para.26–182" *and substitute : page* [1443]*]*
; *Cavendish Square Holdings BV v Makdessi* [2015] UKSC 67, see above, paras 26–178 et seq.

[Add to note 1735, line 1, after "[1996] Q.B. 752"*: page* [1443]*]*
(approved in *Cavendish Square Holdings BV v Makdessi* [2015] UKSC 67 at [26]–[28], [146]–[148], [222] and [239]–[241])

(c) Effect of Consumer Credit Regulation

Unfair relationships

39–301   *[Add to note 1782, at the end: page* [1446]*]*
; *Barclays Bank Plc v McMillan* [2015] EWHC 1596 (Comm).

Additional "connected lender liability"

39–305   *[Note 1809: page* [1448]*]*
The Mortgage Credit Directive (and hence the relevant amendment) came into force on March 21, 2016.

3. Hire-Purchase Agreements

(b) *At Common Law*

Sums paid by hirer

[*Add to note 1952, at the end: page* [1463]]
See also *Cadogan Petroleum Holdings Ltd v Global Process Systems LLC* [2013] 2 Lloyd's Rep. 26 (*Stockloser v Johnson* considered when availability of jurisdiction conceded but not applied in relation to repayments towards acquisition of gas plants). The relationship between the doctrines of "penalties" and "relief against forfeiture" was inconclusively discussed by the Supreme Court in *Cavendish Square Holdings BV v Makdessi* [2015] UKSC 67, approving *BICC Plc v Bundy Corp* [1985] Ch. 232. See above, paras 26–216X et seq.

39–344

[*Add to paragraph, at the end: page* [1464]]
In *Cavendish Square Holdings BV v Makdessi*[1954a] the Supreme Court declined to opine at length on forfeiture clauses (as the allegation was that the relevant clauses were penalty not forfeiture clauses) and hence only referred to *Stockloser v Johnson* in passing.

[1954a] [2015] UKSC 67. See above, paras 26–216S et seq.

Operative on events other than breach

[*Add to paragraph, at the end: page* [1466]]
Moreover, in *Cavendish Square Holdings BV v Makdessi*[1981a] the Supreme Court declined to follow Australian authority extending the doctrine of penalties to clauses operative on events other than breach.[1981b]

39–350

[1981a] [2015] UKSC 67 at [41]–[43], [129]–[130], [163]–[165].
[1981b] See above, para.26–216C.

Bridge v Campbell Discount Co Ltd

See now the new the Supreme Court decision on penalties in *Cavendish Square Holdings BV v Makdessi* [2015] UKSC 67, in particular that the general test is not whether the clause is not a genuine estimate of the respondents' loss (a liquidated damages clause) but whether it comprises "a secondary obligation which imposes a detriment on the contract breaker out of all proportion to any legitimate interest of the innocent party in the enforcement of the primary obligation" (per Lord Neuberger J.S.C. at [32]; see also Lord Mance J.S.C. at [152] and Lord Hodge J.S.C. at [255]). Hence where the legitimate interest is in performance (and hence compensation) the approach in *Dunlop Pneumatic Tyre Co Ltd v New Garage and Motor Co Ltd* was regarded as "usually . . . perfectly adequate to determine [the clause's] validity" (at [32]).

39–351

[*Add to note 2002, at the end: page* [1469]]
And see the confirmation that the penalty jurisdiction does not apply in non-breach cases by the Supreme Court in *Cavendish Square Holdings BV v Makdessi* [2015] UKSC 67, noted above, para.39–351 and see above, para.26–216C.

39–354

6. CREDIT AND OTHER PAYMENT CARDS, AND CHECKS

The consumer credit regulatory regime

39–485   [*Add to note 2453, line 1, after* "Supply of Goods and Services Act 1982,": *page* [1512]]
or under the Consumer Rights Act 2015,

Misuse of credit-token

39–508   [*In note 2545, line 2, delete* "Lending Code" *and substitute: page* [1518]]
Standards of Lending Practice

7. MORTGAGES OF PERSONAL PROPERTY

Bills of Sale Act 1882

39–519   It is expected that the Bills of Sale Acts will be replaced with a new Goods
Mortgages Act which is expected to introduce protection measures for borrowers
mortgaging their personal property (e.g. their cars under so-called "log-book
loans") similar to those available under the Consumer Credit Act 1974 in relation
to hire purchase and conditional sale (see Main Work, Vol.II, paras 39–356 and
39–443).

8. MORTGAGES OF LAND

Consumer credit regulation

39–529   [*Add to note 2647, at the end: page* [1526]]
Article 61 was further amended on March 21, 2016 by the Mortgage Credit
Directive Order 2015 (SI 2015/910) art.3 and Sch.1 para.4(21) so as to include
second charge residential mortgages previously regulated by the CCA 1974.

[*Note 2651: page* [1527]]
The Mortgage Credit Directive (and hence the relevant amendments) came into
force on March 21, 2016.

[*Note 2652: page* [1527]]
The Mortgage Credit Directive (and hence the relevant amendments) came into
force on March 21, 2016.

[*Note 2653: page* [1527]]
The Mortgage Credit Directive (and hence the relevant amendments) came into
force on March 21, 2016.

The Mortgage Credit Directive

The Mortgage Credit Directive came into force on March 21, 2016 and hence the **39–531** proposed changes noted in this paragraph have come into force, reducing the number of CCA-regulated mortgages. As a result (and see above, para.39–529) the Consumer Credit Act 1974 provisions considered below only apply to a small number of land mortgages.

CHAPTER 40

EMPLOYMENT

[*Add to note 1, at the beginning: page* [1533]]
Freedland (Gen. ed.) *The Contract of Employment* (2016).

1. INTRODUCTION

The contract of service or personally to execute any work or labour: "workers" and "persons employed"

[*Add to note 53, at the end: page* [1540]]   **40–009**
, and *Pimlico Plumbers v Smith* [2017] EWCA Civ 51, [2017] I.C.R. 657 which found self-employed plumbers to be workers. A recent string of cases arising from intermittent work arrangements in the so-called "on-demand economy" has similarly found individuals to be workers: see, for example, *Aslam v Uber BV* [2017] I.R.L.R. 4 (ET).

[*Add to note 57, at the end: page* [1541]]
cf. also now *Unite the Union v Nailard* [2016] I.R.L.R. 906.

[*In note 58, update reference to Windle v Secretary of State for Justice to: page* [1541]]
[2016] EWCA Civ 459; [2016] I.R.L.R. 628.

[*Add to note 58, at the end: page* [1541]]
In the case of personal service companies, another avenue for recourse could be found in *EAD Solicitors LLP v Abrams* [2015] I.R.L.R. 978 (EAT).

2. THE FACTORS IDENTIFYING A CONTRACT OF EMPLOYMENT

The intention of the parties

[*Add to note 164, at the end: page* [1552]]   **40–025**
Compare now also *Farmer v Heart of Birmingham Teaching Primary Care Trust* [2016] I.C.R. 1088 (EAT), where the employment judge found that a written agreement identifying a "legal employer" did not reflect the reality of the situation.

Special cases: (2) agency workers

[*Add to note 188, at the end: page* [1554]]   **40–027**
Compare now also *Smith v Carillion (JM) Ltd* [2015] EWCA Civ 209, [2015] I.R.L.R. 467.

[Add to paragraph, line 34, after "filled only by legislation.": page [1554]]
The fact that an individual has a contract of employment with one employer does not preclude their being a worker in the extended agency work sense under s.43K of the Employment Rights Act 1996.[188a]

[188a] *Day v Lewisham and Greenwich NHS Trust* [2017] EWCA Civ 329, [2017] I.R.L.R. 623; see also *McTigue v University Hospital Bristol NHS Foundation Trust* [2016] I.R.L.R. 742 (EAT).

[Add to note 190, at the end: page [1555]]
See now also the Conduct of Employment Agencies and Employment Businesses (Amendment) Regulations 2016 (SI 2016/510).

[Add to note 192, at the end: page [1555]]
In *Coles v Ministry of Defence* [2015] I.R.L.R. 872 (EAT) the confinement of the equal treatment obligation to basic working and employment conditions was emphasised in the context of recruitment to jobs.

40–031 *[Add to note 207, at the end: page [1557]]*
See now also The Exclusivity Terms in Zero Hours Contracts (Redress) Regulations 2015 (SI 2015/2021).

3. FORMATION OF THE CONTRACT

Formation and variation of the contract

40–032 *[Add to note 212, at the end: page [1157]]*
or the contractual check-off mechanism which was held not to be derogable in *Cavanagh v Secretary of State for Work and Pensions* [2016] EWHC 1136, [2016] I.R.L.R. 591.

[Add to paragraph, at the end: page [1557]]
In *Sparks v Department for Transport*,[213a] the High Court held that in the absence of an explicit agreement, the employer could only make unilateral changes to terms and conditions if they were not detrimental to employees. Moreover, any explicit contractual power to vary must be stated in express and clear terms.[213b]

[213a] [2015] EWHC 181, [2015] I.R.L.R. 641,
[213b] *Norman v National Audit Office* [2015] I.R.L.R. 634 (EAT).

Effect of illegality on statutory rights

40–037 *[In note 237, delete the words "Addey and Stanhope School Governing Body v Vakante" and substitute: page [1560]]*
V v Addey & Stanhope School Governing Body

[In note 245, delete the words "Vakante v Addey & Stanhope School Governing Body" and substitute: page [1561]]
V v Addey & Stanhope School Governing Body

5. Rights and Duties Under and Associated with a Contract of Employment

(b) *Duties of the Employer*

(i) *Remuneration*

The national minimum wage

[*Add to note 535, at the end: page* [1591]]   **40–080**
Different considerations may apply where the worker's home was her place of work: *Shannon v Rampersad (t/a Clifton House Residential Home)* [2015] I.R.L.R. 982 (EAT).

Holidays and holiday pay

[*In note 548, delete* "[2015] I.R.L.R. 438 EAT" *and substitute: page* [1592]] **40–081**
[2016] EWCA Civ 983, [2016] I.R.L.R. 946

Opportunity to earn and the right of lay-off

[*Add to note 613, at the end: page* [1598]]   **40–089**
Compare, however, *Craig v Bob Lindfield & Son Ltd* [2016] I.C.R. 527 (EAT).

(ii) *Other Duties*

The Working Time Regulations

[*Add to paragraph, after note 820: page* [1616]]   **40–112**
"Working Time" is to be interpreted widely and purposively, including for example travel from a worker's place of residence to customer premises,[820a] or the attendance of meetings as a trade union or health and safety representative.[820b]

[820a] *Federacion de Servicios Privados del sindicato Comisiones obreras (CC OO) v Tyco Integrated Security SL* (C-266/14) EU:C:2015:578; [2016] 1 C.M.L.R. 22.
[820b] *Edwards v Encirc Ltd* [2015] I.R.L.R. 528 (EAT).

[*Add to paragraph, after note 828: page* [1617]]
It is incumbent on the employer proactively to ensure that working arrangements allow for workers to take their due rest breaks.[828a]

[828a] *Grange v Abellio London Ltd* [2017] I.R.L.R. 108 (EAT).

Further applications and extensions of the implied obligation of trust and confidence

40–152   [*Add to note 1014, at the end: page* [1637]]
and *Patural v DB Services (UK) Ltd* [2015] EWHC 3659 (QB), [2016] I.R.L.R. 286.

[*Add to note 1016, at the end: page* [1637]]
Compare now also *Hills v Niksun Inc* [2016] EWCA Civ 115, [2016] I.R.L.R. 715, as well as *Stevens v University of Birmingham* [2015] EWHC 2300 (QB), [2015] I.R.L.R. 899 and *Simpkin v Berkeley Group Holdings Plc* [2016] EWHC 1619 (QB), [2017] 1 Costs L.O. 13.

[*Add to paragraph, at the end: page* [1637]]
The Court opined in *Bradbury v BBC*[1016a] that an employer's several actions might cumulatively amount to a breach of the implied term.

[1016a] [2015] EWHC 1368 (Ch), [2015] Pens. L.R. 457.

Disclosures of information in the public interest

40–154   [*Add to note 1030, at the end: page* [1639]]
Though cf. *Day v Lewisham and Greenwich NHS Trust* [2016] I.R.L.R. 415 (EAT).

[*Add to paragraph, after note 1030: page* [1639]]
Claims can be brought both against a worker's employer, an end-user of agency services, or both if the exercise of employer functions is shared.[1030a]

[1030a] *McTigue v University Hospital Bristol NHS Foundation Trust* [2016] UKEAT/0354/15/JOJ , [2016] I.R.L.R. 742.

Duties to avoid less favourable treatment of part-time work and fixed-term work

40–155   [*Add to note 1040, at the end: page* [1640]]
O'Brien was distinguished in *Gilham v Ministry of Justice* [2017] I.R.L.R. 23 (EAT), where a narrower interpretation was favoured in the context of purely domestic employment rights.

6. TERMINATION OF THE CONTRACT

(f) *Summary Dismissal*

Illustration of misconduct

40–185   [*Add to paragraph, at the end: page* [1664]]
In *Adesokan v Sainsbury's Supermarkets Ltd*, the Court of Appeal held that an act of gross negligence might in an appropriate case amount to gross misconduct

justifying dismissal where it inflicted grave damage upon the relationship between the parties.[1276a]

[1276a] [2017] EWCA Civ 22, [2017] I.R.L.R. 346.

7. REMEDIES, AND RIGHTS INCIDENTAL TO THE TERMINATION OF EMPLOYMENT

(b) *Recovery of Remuneration*

Apportionment of wages or salary.

[*Add to note 1373, at the end: page* [1674]]   **40–196**
A similar approach was followed in *Hartley v King Edward VI College* [2015] EWCA Civ 455, [2015] I.R.L.R. 650, but that decision was subsequently overturned by the Supreme Court [2017] UKSC 39, [2017] 1 W.L.R. 2110, where the statutory principle of equal daily apportionment was held to apply and not to have been excluded by the particular contract.

8. UNFAIR AND DISCRIMINATORY DISMISSAL

(a) *Unfair Dismissal*

(ii) *Dismissal and Effective Date of Termination*

The effective date of termination

[*Add to note 1579, at the end: page* [1694]]   **40–221**
See now also *Sandle v Adecco UK Ltd* [2016] I.R.L.R. 941 (EAT).

(iv) *Remedies*

Introduction

[*Add to note 1690, after "ss.112–117": page* [1704]]   **40–236**
See now generally *McBride v Scottish Police Authority* [2016] UKSC 27, [2016] I.R.L.R. 633.

Orders for reinstatement

[*Add to note 1701, at the end: page* [1705]]   **40–237**
See *McBride v Scottish Police Authority* [2016] UKSC 27, [2016] I.R.L.R. 633.

9. Redundancy Payments and Procedure

(b) *Redundancy Procedure*

Consultation with the representatives of recognised trade unions or of employees

40–260   [*In note 1893, delete from* "The restriction to . . . " *to the end and substitute: page* [1722]]

The restriction to "at one establishment" had been placed in doubt by *USDAW v Ethel Austin Ltd (In Administration)* [2014] EWCA Civ 142, [2014] 2 C.M.L.R. 45, but was subsequently confirmed by the CJEU in *USDAW v Ethel Austin Ltd* (C-80/14) EU:C:2015:291, [2015] 3 C.M.L.R. 32.

CHAPTER 41

GAMBLING CONTRACTS

1. INTRODUCTION

"Gambling" and "wagering"

41–006

[Add to note 35, at the end: page [1729]*]*
See also the Contracts for Difference (Standard Terms) Regulations 2014, SI 2014/2012 as amended by Contracts for Difference (Standard Terms) (Amendment) Regulations 2017, SI 2017/112.

[Add to note 36, at the end: page [1729]*]*
cf. WW Properties Investments Ltd v National Westminster Bank plc [2016] EWCA Civ 1142, [2017] 1 Lloyd's Rep. 87, where an entity which had borrowed money from a bank entered into four "interest rate hedging contracts" with the bank; the first three of these were called "Collars" while the fourth "was a Swap Agreement" ([2016] EWCA Civ 1142 at [2]). The purpose of these agreements was to hedge the borrower's liabilities which, under the contract of loan, could

rise in line with increases in Base Rate (at [23]). Although these four agreements were "contracts for difference" (at [24]), it was held that they were not wagers: contracts for differences would not be wagers: if they were entered into (as these contracts were) "for a commercial purpose such as hedging" (see at [28], citing Leggatt L.J. in *City Index Ltd v Leslie* [1992] 2 Q.B. 98, which had in turn been cited by Hobhouse J. in *Morgan Grenfell and Co Ltd v Welwyn Hatfield District Council* [1995] 1 All E.R. 1 (a decision that was approved in the *WW Property* case [2016] EWCA Civ 1142 at [42]); and relying on Financial Services Act 1986 s.63 and Sch.1 Pt 1 para.8 note 1). In *Banco Santander Totta SA v Companjia de Carris de Ferro de Lisboa SA* [2016] EWHC 465 (Comm), [2016] 4 W.L.R. 49 interest rate swaps were likewise found not to be void under Portuguese law as "games of chance", though that finding was not strictly necessary to the outcome in that case. The sentence in the Main Work ending with this footnote was quoted with apparent approval by Vos L.J. in *Nextia Properties Ltd v Royal Bank of Scotland plc* [2014] EWCA Civ 740 at [24] (refusing leave to appeal from the decision of H.H.J. Behrens [2013] EWHC 3167 (QB)).

2. ENFORCEABILITY OF GAMBLING CONTRACTS

(b) *Enforceability under the Gambling Act 2005*

Contracts relating to gambling generally enforceable: s.335(1)

41–011   [*Add to note 81, at the end: page* [1733]]

In *WW Property Investments Ltd v National Westminster Bank PLC* [2016] EWCA Civ 1142, [2017] 1 Lloyd's Rep. 87 the Court of Appeal held that the "Collar" and "Swap" agreements were not wagers; the reasons for this conclusion are stated in para.41–006 above. But the Court went on to consider what the position would have been, if it had held that those agreements *had* been wagers, and in particular whether in that case whether they would then have been legally enforceable under the general rule of common law stated in para.41–010 of Vol.II of the Main Work, having regard also to common law exceptions to that general rule. The Court gave a negative answer to this question on the ground that the Collar and Swap Agreements were contracts for differences and that, in the light of the "comprehensive regime established by the Gambling Act [2005] and the FMSA [*i.e.* the Financial Services and Markets Act] 2000 there was in such a case no room for any common law rule" limiting the validity of gambling contracts by way of exception to the common law rule that such contracts were valid: see at [66]; and at [67] referring to the judgment of Vos L.J. in *Nextia Properties Ltd v Royal Bank of Scotland plc* [2014] EWCA Civ 740, especially at [22], refusing leave to appeal from the decision of H.H.J. Behrens [2013] EWHC 3167 (QB); for earlier proceedings in which Christopher Clarke J. had likewise refused leave to appeal from that decision, see the *Nextia* case [2014] EWCA Civ 740 at [1] to [4] and the *WW Property* case [2016] EWCA Civ 1142 at [20]. The judgment in the latter case also refers at [67] to "the Regulations made thereunder", i.e. to the Financial Services and Markets 2000 (Regulated

Activities) Order 2001 (SI 2001/544, the relevant parts of which are cited in the *WW Property* case at [64]; Art.85 refers to "Contracts for differences"). It should be noted that this part of the judgment refers only to contracts subject to the "comprehensive regime" established by all this legislation. The same point is also reflected in the use of words such as "financial contracts", "a contract of the kind in question" and "contracts such as the present" (at [66], where "section 35" is a misprint for "section 335"), all of which indicate that this part of the judgment has a restricted scope. It would not, for example, apply to a wager on the outcome of a sporting competition or of an election. In such cases there might still be room for common law rules recognising or limiting the validity of gambling contracts in ways considered in paras 41–011 and 41–020 (at n.117) of the Main Work. It remains true that even in such cases the repeal of the Gambling Act 1845 would not "revive the [common law] rule" (at [68]) which had existed before the repeal but it would not preclude the court from developing new rules which, as a matter of common law, restricted the legal validity of gambling contracts.

Legal effects other than enforceability

[*Add new note 85a, line 7, after* "or depositor merely": *page* [1734]]   **41–014**
[85a] The above assumption seems to underlie the claim for the return of money paid under the contracts in *WW Property Investments Ltd v National Westminster Bank PLC* [2016] EWCA Civ 1142, [2017] 1 Lloyd's Rep. 87, as described in paras [18] and [19] of the report. That claim was based on the argument that the claim was *invalid* at common law; but the argument that the outcome continued to be governed by the common law as it stood before the legislation that was repealed by the Gambling Act 2005 (see Main Work, Vol.II, paras 41–001, 41–010) was rejected for the reasons given in para.41–011, n.81 above.

(c) *Exceptions to Enforceability under the Gambling Act 2005*

(i) *"Unlawfulness"*

Failure to comply with other provisions of the Act

[*Add to note 102, at the end: page* [1736]]   **41–019**
See also *Ritz Hotel Casino Ltd v Al Geabury* [2015] EWHC 2294 (QB), [2015] L.L.R. 860 where an action on a dishonoured cheque given by a gambler in exchange for chips (which he gambled away) succeeded as there had been *no* breach of the casino's licence condition or of the Gambling Commission's Code of Practice, and hence no illegality by reason of any violation of s.33 or 82 of the Gambling Act 2005.

Scope of s.335(2)

[*Add to note 122a, at the end: page* [1739]]   **41–021**
Ivey v Genting Casinos UK Ltd [2014] EWHC 3394 (QB) has been affirmed by a majority of the Court of Appeal: [2016] EWCA Civ 1093, [2017] 1 W.L.R. 679, where Arden and Tomlinson L.JJ., Sharp L.J. dissenting, also held that dishonesty was not a requirement of "cheating" for the purpose of s.42 of the Gambling Act 2005: see at [37], [40], [48] and [97].

(e) *Related Transactions*

(ii) *Enforceability*

Related transactions in general enforceable

41–026   [*Add to paragraph, at the end: page* [1744]]

This provision can, of course, only apply if the transaction relied upon by the person seeking enforcement has contractual force; and this requirement was held not to have been satisfied in *Ritz Hotel Casino Ltd v Al Geabury*[172a] where a persistent gambler had entered into a "voluntary self-exclusion agreement" (VSE) with the casino by which he had excluded himself for life from gambling at the casino. In an action by the casino against him on a cheque which had had given to the casino in payment for chips,[172b] he counterclaimed for damages for breach of the contract alleged to have been contained in the VSE. The claim was rejected by Simler J. on the ground that the VSE did not amount to a contract since the requirement of consideration was not satisfied. Her reason for this conclusion was that "nothing moved from the Defendant to the Claimant"[172c] and that it was "difficult to see what consideration flows from the defendant when he enters a self exclusion agreement providing nothing in return".[172d] This reasoning, with respect, gives rise to some difficulty since it makes no reference to the generally accepted principle that, though consideration must move from the promisee, it need not move to the promisor.[172e] Evidently the gambler was regarded as the promisee and the casino as the promisor, though it is not altogether clear what promise was made to the gambler by the promisor; presumably it was one to deny him the gambling facilities from which he had asked to be excluded. The loss of those facilities, even if only for a limited time,[172f] can plausibly be regarded as a detriment to the gambler (just as is the case where a promisee has, in response to the promise, given up smoking or drinking). The doctrine of consideration does not impose any further requirement that anything should "move to the Claimant"[172g] (i.e. to the casino). It could perhaps be argued that the gambler's self-exclusion did not amount to consideration because the gambler's signature of the VES form had not been requested by the casino; but that is not the ground given in the judgment in its short discussion of the consideration point.[172h]

[172a] [2015] EWHC 2294 (QB), [2015] L.L.R. 860.

[172b] *cf.* above, para.41–018 n.102.

[172c] [2015] EWHC 2294(QB) at [137].

[172d] *ibid.*

[172e] See Main Work, Vol.I, para.4–040.

[172f] The self-exclusion form signed by the gambler was expressed to be "for life" but the VSE agreement was in fact revoked by mutual consent (see at [125]) of the parties to it less than a year after it had been made: see at [2(iii)], [3(ii)], [137].

[172g] See above at n.172c.

[172h] In the passage quoted at n.172c above, Simler J. relies on statements by Briggs J. in *Calvert v William Hill Credit Ltd* [2008] EWHC 454 (Ch), [2008] L.L.R. 583 at [175], [178], [180] to the effect that a voluntary self-exclusion agreement was "without consideration"; the decision was affirmed [2008] EWCA Civ 1427 where the same view is stated at [26]. No reason is given for this view either by Briggs J. or by the Court of Appeal but it should be pointed out that the judgments in the *Calvert* case dealt with a transaction concluded before the Gaming Act 2005 had come into force: (see [2008] EWCA Civ 1427 at [2], [13]) and when the earlier gambling (or gaming and wagering) legislation referred to in Main Work, Vol.II, para.41–001 was still in force. The gambler

would therefore be excluding himself from making bets that were void in law, while in the *Al Geabury* case he had excluded himself from transactions which, in general, were legally enforceable. This difference makes the argument that the gambler had provided consideration in the *Al Geabury* case more plausible (for the reason given in the *Calvert* case). This would not be the only situation in which the change in the law, making gambling contracts enforceable in law, could affect issues of consideration arising from gambling contracts or related transactions: see, for example, the discussions of *Lipkin Gorman v Karpnale Ltd* [1991] 2 A.C. 548 in Main Work, Vol.II, paras 41–047 and 41–048 and also in Main Work, Vol.I, para.4–190.

"Unlawfulness"

[*Add to note 176, line 4, after* "904, 928 (synallagmatic)"*: page* [1744]]   **41–027**
; *Arnold v Britton* [2015] UKSC 36, [2015] A.C. 1619 at [21] ("Given that a contract is a bilateral, or synallagmatic, arrangement . . . ")

CHAPTER 42

INSURANCE

1. THE NATURE OF INSURANCE

[*In note 1, update reference to MacGillivray on Insurance Law to: page* [1763]]
13th edn (2015)

Indemnity insurance

42–003   [*Add to paragraph, at the end: page* [1766]]
However, this third consequence changed upon the entry into force of ss.13A and
16A of the Insurance Act 2015 on May 4, 2017.[18a] This new legislation introduced into every insurance contract an implied term that the insurer must pay

insurance claims within a reasonable time (allowing for investigation and assessment of the claim). If there is a breach of this implied term, the assured will have remedies (e.g. damages) available at common law (and otherwise) in addition to the payment of the claim under the policy and statutory interest.[18b]

[18a] These provisions of the Insurance Act 2015 were introduced by the Enterprise Act 2016 ss.28–30.
[18b] s.13A. See Parliament's Explanatory Notes, para.264. See below para.42–111A.

2. Insurable Interest

Types of insurable interest

[*In note 51, update reference to MacGillivray on Insurance Law to: page* [1769]]   **42–008**
13th edn (2015), para.1–161

Impact of the Gambling Act 2005

[*In note 123, update reference to MacGillivray on Insurance Law to: page* [1776]]   **42–016**
13th edn (2015), paras 1–027, 1–039

3. The Event Insured Against

Event insured against

[*Add to note 137, line 9 after* "Lloyd's Rep. I.R. 258": *page* [1778]]   **42–018**
; *Spire Healthcare Ltd v Royal & Sun Alliance Insurance Plc* [2016] EWHC 3278 (Comm), [2017] Lloyd's Rep. I.R. 118. In *Simmonds v Gammell* [2016] EWHC 2515 (Comm), [2016] 2 Lloyd's Rep. 631 at [22]–[27], Sir Jeremy Cooke confirmed that in identifying an aggregating "event", it should be appropriate to the aggregating function, it should be a common factor which could properly be described as an event, and it should be causative of the losses claimed under the policy, which need not be proximate, but must not be too remote.

[*Add to note 137, at the end: page* [1778]]
See also *AIG Europe Ltd v Woodman* [2017] UKSC 18, [2017] 1 W.L.R. 1168.

(a) *The Nature of the Event*

Uncertainty

[*Add to note 140, at the end: page* [1778]]   **42–020**
In *Quek Kwee Kee v American International Assurance Co Ltd* [2016] SGHC 47, [2016] Lloyd's Rep. I.R. 660 at [42]–[54], the Singapore High Court confirmed

that the unexpected consequences of a voluntary act may constitute an "accident" under an insurance contract, i.e. a fortuity. See also *Leeds Beckett University v Travelers Insurance Co Ltd* [2017] EWHC 558 (TCC) at [199]–[208].

[*Add to note 141, line 7, after* "risks, not certainties."*: page* [1779]]
See also *Leeds Beckett University v Travelers Insurance Co Ltd* [2017] EWHC 558 (TCC) at [199]–[208].

Public policy

42–023   [*In note 166, update reference to MacGillivray on Insurance Law to: page* [1781]]:13th edn (2015), para.30–010

[*Add to note 167, at the end: page* [1782]]
In *Les Laboratoires Servier v Apotex Inc* [2014] UKSC 55, [2015] A.C. 430 at [23]–[29], the Supreme Court said that generally the conduct should be criminal or quasi-criminal before public policy might be engaged.

[*Add to paragraph, at the end: page* [1783]]
The principles of public policy as they apply to insurance contracts have been cast into some doubt by the recent decision of the majority of the Supreme Court in *Patel v Mirza*,[175a] where it was held that a claim will not be enforced if it is contrary to the public interest, meaning that it would be harmful to the integrity of the legal system (or, possibly, certain aspects of public morality). The Supreme Court decided not to follow the reliance test adopted by the House of Lords in *Tinsley v Milligan*.[175b]

[175a] [2016] UKSC 42, [2016] 3 W.L.R. 399 at [101], [120], [174], [186].
[175b] [1994] 1 A.C. 340. See above, paras 16–014A et seq.

4. UTMOST GOOD FAITH AND FAIR PRESENTATION OF THE RISK

(a) *Existing law applicable to non-consumer insurance contracts*

Utmost good faith

42–033   [*In note 222, update reference to MacGillivray on Insurance Law to: page* [1788]]
13th edn (2015), Chs 16–17

[*Add to note 223, at the end: page* [1788]]
; *Dalecroft Properties Ltd v Underwriters* [2017] EWHC 1263 (Comm) at [80].

Exceptions to the duty of disclosure

42–036   [*Add to note 256, line 5, after* "at [16]–[20]"*: page* [1792]]
; *Aldridge v Liberty Mutual Insurance Europe Ltd* [2016] EWHC 3037 (Comm) at [33]–[38].

[In note 264, update reference to MacGillivray on Insurance Law to: page [1794]]
13th edn (2015), paras 17–063—17–067

Inducement

[Add to note 294, line 2, after "Lloyd's Rep. I.R. 131 at [62]"*: page* [1797]]   **42–041**
; *AXA Versicherung AG v Arab Insurance Group (BSC)* [2017] EWCA Civ 96,
[2017] Lloyd's Rep. I.R. 216 at [138].

[Add to note 298, at the end: page [1797]]
; *Aldridge v Liberty Mutual Insurance Europe Ltd* [2016] EWHC 3037 (Comm)
at [28].

[Add to note 300, at the end: page [1798]]
; *Aldridge v Liberty Mutual Insurance Europe Ltd* [2016] EWHC 3037 (Comm)
at [29].

Effect of non-disclosure or misrepresentation

[Add to note 301, line 1, "para.42–033 n.223."*: page* [1798]]   **42–042**
If the contract is separable into distinct parts such that they represent separate
insurances, the insurer's remedy of avoidance is likely to relate to that divisible
part rather than the entire contract: *Dalecroft Properties Ltd v Underwriters*
[2017] EWHC 1263 (Comm) at [99]–[100].

Affirmation and waiver by estoppel

[Add to note 320, at the end: page [1800]]   **42–043**
As to the requirement of knowledge of the legal right to avoid in circumstances
where the insurer is being advised by solicitors, see *Moore Large & Co Ltd v
Hermes Credit and Guarantee Plc* [2003] EWHC 26 (Comm), [2003] Lloyd's
Rep. I.R. 315 at [92]–[100]; *Involnert Management Inc v Aprilgrange Ltd* [2015]
EWHC 2225 (Comm), [2015] 2 Lloyd's Rep. 289 at [157]–[161].

Modification of the duty by contract

[Add to paragraph, after note 327: page [1801]]   **42–044**
or that the policy is voidable only if the assured is guilty of a fraudulent non-
disclosure or misrepresentation,[327a]

[327a] *Mutual Energy Ltd v Starr Underwriting Agents Ltd* [2016] EWHC 590 (TCC), [2016] B.L.R.
312.

FCA Insurance Conduct of Business Sourcebook (ICOBS)

[Add to note 337, at the end: page [1802]]   **42–045**
; *Ashfaq v International Insurance Co of Hannover Plc* [2017] EWCA Civ 357,
[2017] H.L.R. 29.

(b) *Existing law applicable to consumer insurance contracts*

Consumer Insurance (Disclosure and Representations) Act 2012

42–046   [*Add to note 339, at the end: page* [1803]]
cf. *Ashfaq v International Insurance Co of Hannover Plc* [2017] EWCA Civ 357, [2017] H.L.R. 29 at [45]–[58]. The 2012 Act did not apply to the insurance contract in this case: at [15].

The insurer's remedies

42–049   [*Add to paragraph, line 8, after* "relevant to the insurer) or careless": *page* [1804]]
The finding that an assured's breach of duty was deliberate or reckless may be supported by the presumptions allowed under s.5(5), in particular that the consumer knew that a matter about which the insurer asked a clear and specific question was relevant to the insurer.[346a]

[346a] *Tesco Underwriting Ltd v Achunche*, Unreported, July 7, 2016.

(c) *Insurance Act 2015*

The insurer's remedies for unfair presentation of the risk

42–057   [*Add to note 387, at the end: page* [1809]]
As to what constitutes a deliberate non-disclosure, see *Mutual Energy Ltd v Starr Underwriting Agents Ltd* [2016] EWHC 590 (TCC), [2016] B.L.R. 312.

(d) *Post-contractual duty of utmost good faith*

The post-contractual duty of utmost good faith: existing law

42–061   [*Add to paragraph, at the end: page* [1811]]
There may be circumstances where, having regard to the duty of utmost good faith, the insurer will assume a duty to warn the assured that it is not complying with the relevant terms of the insurance contract in respect of claims.[408a]

[408a] *Ted Baker Plc v Axa Insurance UK Plc* [2017] EWCA Civ 4097 at [69]–[90].

5. THE PARTIES

Agents of the insurer

42–065   [*Add new note 419a, after* "agents to solicit business." *in line 2: page* [1813]]
[419a] As to the regulatory requirements for the authorisation of agents and representatives, see s.39 of the Financial Services and Markets Act 2000 and art.25 of the Financial Services and Markets Act 2000 (Regulated Activities) Order 2001 (SI 2001/544). See *Personal Touch Financial Services Ltd v Simplysure Ltd* [2016] EWCA Civ 461 (private medical insurance).

[Add to paragraph, at the end: page [1813]]
The insurer's agent is not, by reason of the agency alone, a party to the insurance contract.[427a]

[427a] *Temple Legal Protection Ltd v QBE Insurance (Europe) Ltd* [2009] EWCA Civ 453, [2009] Lloyd's Rep. I.R. 544; *PM Law Ltd v Motorplus Ltd* [2016] EWHC 193 (QB), [2016] 1 Costs L.R. 143 at [58]

Broker

[Add to note 433, line 12, after "225 at [86]"*: page* [1814]]   **42–066**
; *RR Securities Ltd v Towergate Underwriting Group Ltd* [2016] EWHC 2653 (QB)

[Add to note 433, line 19, after "[1996] 2 Lloyd's Rep. 619"*: page* [1814]]
; *Involnert Management Inc v Aprilgrange Ltd* [2015] EWHC 2225 (Comm), [2015] 2 Lloyd's Rep. 289 at [288]–[292]

Lloyd's

[In note 440, update reference to MacGillivray on Insurance Law to: page [1816]]   **42–067**
13th edn (2015), Ch.37

6. The Contract of Insurance

Renewal

[Add to note 477, at the end: page [1820]]   **42–073**
See *Dalecroft Properties Ltd v Underwriters* [2017] EWHC 1263 (Comm) at [85.2].

[In note 475, update reference to MacGillivray on Insurance Law to: page [1820]]
13th edn (2015), paras 7–038—7–039

Payment of premium

[In note 481, update reference to MacGillivray on Insurance Law to: page [1821]]   **42–075**
13th edn (2015), paras 7–019—7–021

Return of premium

[In note 505, update reference to MacGillivray on Insurance Law to: page [1823]]   **42–076**
13th edn (2015), para.8–030

Construction of insurance contracts

[Add to paragraph, after note 513: page [1824]]   **42–077**
The commercial purpose of the insurance contract, however, should not be lightly invoked to undermine the importance of the contractual language which the parties have chosen to embody their agreement.[513a]

⁵¹³ᵃ *Spire Healthcare Ltd v Royal & Sun Alliance Insurance Plc* [2016] EWHC 3278 (Comm), [2017] Lloyd's Rep. I.R. 118 at [11].

[Add to paragraph, after note 516: page [1824]]
If the insurance contract is based on a standard form of contract to which the parties have added special clauses, greater weight will be given to the special provisions, and, in the event of conflict or inconsistency between the general and special provisions, the latter will prevail.⁵¹⁶ᵃ

⁵¹⁶ᵃ *Milton Furniture Ltd v Brit Insurance Ltd* [2015] EWCA Civ 671, [2016] Lloyd's Rep. I.R. 192 at [24].

[In paragraph, lines 19–20, delete "such as a condition precedent, warranty or possibly an exclusion" *and substitute: page* [1824]]
such as a condition precedent or warranty

[Add to paragraph, at the end: page [1824]]
Having regard to the decision of the Supreme Court in *Impact Funding Solutions Ltd v AIG Europe Insurance Ltd*,⁵¹⁸ᵃ the fact that a provision in an insurance contract is expressed as an exception or exclusion does not necessarily mean that it should be approached with a pre-disposition to construe it narrowly or restrictively, at least insofar as it delineates the scope of the insurer's primary obligation of indemnity, as opposed to excluding a liability or a remedy where the primary obligation would otherwise have rendered the insurer liable.

⁵¹⁸ᵃ [2016] UKSC 57, [2017] A.C. 73 at [35].

7. The Terms of the Insurance Contract

Conditions precedent

42–079   *[Add to note 522, at the end: page* [1825]]
See also *Denso Manufacturing UK Ltd v Great Lakes Reinsurance (UK) Plc* [2017] EWHC 391 (Comm), [2017] Lloyd's Rep. I.R. 240 at [22]–[40].

[In note 524, update reference to MacGillivray on Insurance Law to: page [1825]]
13th edn (2015), paras 10–010—10–011

Promissory warranties and their effect: existing law

42–080   *[In note 531, update reference to MacGillivray on Insurance Law to: page* [1827]]
13th edn (2015), paras 10–026—10–027

[Add to note 532, at the end: page [1827]]
; *Aldridge v Liberty Mutual Insurance Europe Ltd* [2016] EWHC 3037 (Comm) at [119]; *Ashfaq v International Insurance Co of Hannover Plc* [2017] EWCA Civ 357, [2017] H.L.R. 29 at [58]–[59].

FCA Insurance: Conduct of Business Sourcebook (ICOBS)

[*Add to note 572, at the end: page* [1831]]   **42–085**
See also *Ashfaq v International Insurance Co of Hannover Plc* [2017] EWCA
Civ 357, [2017] H.L.R. 29.

Waiver

[*In note 573, update reference to MacGillivray on Insurance Law to: page* [1831]]   **42–086**
13th edn (2015), paras 10–103—10–126

Unfair Terms in Consumer Contracts Regulations 1999

[*Add to note 586, at the end: page* [1833]]   **42–087**
See *Ashfaq v International Insurance Co of Hannover Plc* [2017] EWCA Civ
357, [2017] H.L.R. 29 at [45]–[58].

Consumer Rights Act 2015

[*Add to note 597, at the end: page* [1834]]   **42–088**
As to the meaning of "consumer", cf. *Ashfaq v International Insurance Co of
Hannover Plc* [2017] EWCA Civ 357, [2017] H.L.R. 29 at [45]–[58].

[*Add new note 599a, after* "the services provided," *in line 13: page* [1834]]
599a See *Van Hove v CNP Assurances SA* (C-96/14) [2015] 3 C.M.L.R. 31 at [34]–[35].

8. ASSIGNMENT

Assignment of the policy

[*In note 603, update reference to MacGillivray on Insurance Law to: page* [1834]]   **42–089**
13th edn (2015), paras 26–070—26–113

9. CLAIMS

Notice of loss

[*In note 632, lines 5–6, delete* "*Maccaferri Ltd v Zurich Insurance Plc* [2015]   **42–093**
EWHC 1708 (Comm)" *and substitute: page* [1837]]
Zurich Insurance Plc v Maccaferri Ltd [2016] EWCA Civ 1302, [2017] Lloyd's
Rep. I.R. 200.

[*Add to note 635, line 2, after* "[2009] 1 Lloyd's Rep. 8": *page* [1838]]
; *Involnert Management Inc v Aprilgrange Ltd* [2015] EWHC 2225 (Comm),
[2015] 2 Lloyd's Rep. 289 at [225]–[243].

[Add to note 637, line 1, after "(1902) 51 W.R. 222.": page [1838]]
In *Zurich Insurance Plc v Maccaferri Ltd* [2016] EWCA Civ 1302, [2017] Lloyd's Rep. I.R. 200 at [31]–[32], the Court of Appeal held that "'*Immediately*' itself does not mean instantaneously but '*with all reasonable speed considering the circumstances of the case*'".

[Add to note 637, at the end: page [1838]]
In *Denso Manufacturing UK Ltd v Great Lakes Reinsurance (UK) Plc* [2017] EWHC 391 (Comm), [2017] Lloyd's Rep. I.R. 240 at [55]–[56], the Court considered the meaning of "*as soon as*" and "*without delay*" in a different context.

[In note 638, delete the final sentence and substitute: page [1838]]
Under the Third Parties (Rights against Insurers) Act 2010 s.9(2), it is provided that anything done by the third party which, if done by the insured, would have amounted to or contributed to fulfilment of the condition is to be treated as if done by the insured. This would include notification obligations. However, under ss.9(3) and (4), any condition requiring the insured to provide information or assistance to the insurer—other than notification of the existence of a claim—need not be fulfilled if the insured no longer exists.

Details of loss

42–094   *[Add to note 643, line 5, after "[2010] Lloyd's Rep. I.R. 373 at [124]–[130].": page* [1839]]
See also *Ted Baker Plc v Axa Insurance UK Plc* [2017] EWCA Civ 4097.

Fraudulent claims

42–098   *[Delete text of paragraph and substitute: page* [1842]]
There appear to be three species of "fraudulent claim",[669] namely: (a) a fraudulent claim for a loss, which is non-existent; (b) a fraudulent claim for a loss, which is itself genuine, but which is excluded or not covered by the insurance policy; (c) a fraudulent claim for a loss which is otherwise genuine and covered by the policy but which is exaggerated.[670] Each of these will attract the same remedy. The precise definition of a fraudulent claim has not been authoritatively stated, although it is likely to require proof of the elements of deceit (other than inducement).[671] In order to be fraudulent, the claim must be substantially fraudulent, that is if the fraudulent element of the claim was de minimis, the assured would not bear the legal consequences of a fraudulent claim.[672] Mere exaggeration is not conclusive evidence of fraud,[673] though it affords strong evidence of fraud if the claim is out of all proportion to the true loss,[674] as does gross negligence.[675] The availability of the remedy for a fraudulent claim does not depend on actual inducement of the insurer, so that the fraud does not have to be successful; the mere making of the fraudulent claim is sufficient to engage the appropriate remedy.[676] In order for the fraudulent claim rule to apply, the fraud must be material to the recoverability of the claim under the insurance policy or, in other words, to the insurer's liability under the policy. That is, if the insurer would be liable to indemnify the assured in respect of the claim, absent any lie,

the making of such a lie is necessarily collateral and will not constitute a fraudulent claim in itself. This was the finding of the Supreme Court in *Versloot Dredging BV v HDI Gerling Industrie Versicherung AG*,[677] overriding earlier authorities.[678] The fraud of the assured will preclude his trustee in bankruptcy,[679] and any joint assured, from recovering, and the same appears to be true for an assignee of the policy.[680] Where, however, the contract is a composite one insuring several parties for their different interests, an innocent assured is not prejudiced by another's fraud.[681] The assured, although himself innocent, may be affected by a claim presented fraudulently by his agent insofar as the latter was acting within the scope of his authority.[682] The duty of utmost good faith does not impose any duty to disclose or not to misrepresent material facts in connection with a claim wider than the duty not to present a fraudulent claim.[682a]

[669] In *Agapitos v Agnew (The Aegeon)* [2002] EWCA Civ 247, [2002] 2 Lloyd's Rep. 42 at [15]–[18] the Court of Appeal considered that an originally honest claim which was subsequently appreciated as unfounded or exaggerated would be a fraudulent claim and that the deliberate suppression of a valid defence would render a claim fraudulent. See also *Versloot Dredging BV v HDI Gerling Industrie Versicherung AG* [2016] UKSC 45, [2016] 3 W.L.R. 543 at [96]. A fraud committed in performance of a contract of compromise of an insurance claim will not be a fraudulent claim attracting the remedies discussed in this paragraph: *Direct Line Insurance Plc v Fox* [2009] EWHC 386 (QB), [2009] 1 All E.R. (Comm) 1017.

[670] As to exaggerated claims, see *Versloot Dredging BV v HDI Gerling Industrie Versicherung AG* [2016] UKSC 45, [2016] 3 W.L.R. 543 at [25]–[26], [36], [51], [92]–[93].

[671] *Lek v Mathews* (1927) 29 Ll.L. Rep. 141; *Aviva Insurance Ltd v Brown* [2011] EWHC 362 (QB), [2012] Lloyd's Rep. I.R. 211 at [61]–[73], although in this case it was submitted that there was an additional requirement of dishonesty within the meaning discussed in *Twinsectra Ltd v Yardley* [2002] UKHL 12, [2002] 2 A.C. 164; such an additional requirement would appear to go beyond the bounds of the authorities. There is also a question whether the fraudulent claim can be constituted by a non-disclosure, as well as by a misrepresentation: *Marc Rich Agriculture Trading SA v Fortis Corporate Insurance NV* [2004] EWHC 2632 (Comm), [2005] Lloyd's Rep. I.R. 396; *Aviva Insurance Ltd v Brown* [2011] EWHC 362 (QB), [2012] Lloyd's Rep. I.R. 211 at [64].

[672] *Galloway v Guardian Royal Exchange (UK) Ltd* [1999] Lloyd's Rep. I.R. 209; *Tonkin v UK Insurance Ltd* [2006] EWHC 1120 (TCC), [2007] Lloyd's Rep. I.R. 283 at [176]–[178]; *Aviva Insurance Ltd v Brown* [2011] EWHC 362 (QB), [2012] Lloyd's Rep. I.R. 211 at [76]–[77].

[673] *London Assurance v Clare* (1937) 57 Ll.L. Rep. 254, 268; *Orakpo v Barclays Insurance Services Co Ltd* [1995] L.R.L.R. 443 at 451.

[674] *Chapman v Pole* (1870) 22 L.T. 306; *Herman v Phoenix Assurance Co Ltd* (1924) 18 Ll.L. Rep. 371; *Dome Mining Corp Ltd v Drysdale* (1931) 41 Ll.L. Rep. 109; *Central Bank of India Ltd v Guardian Assurance Co Ltd* (1936) 54 Ll.L. Rep. 247; *Shoot v Hill* (1936) 55 Ll.L. Rep. 29.

[675] *Goodman v Harvey* (1836) 4 Ad. & El. 870.

[676] *Versloot Dredging BV v HDI Gerling Industrie Versicherung AG* [2016] UKSC 45, [2016] 3 W.L.R. 543 at [28]–[36], although Lord Sumption in that case appeared to curtail the principle underlying the fraudulent claim rule to the fact that inducement was not required.

[677] [2016] UKSC 45, [2016] 3 W.L.R. 543, at [36], [39], [92]–[93], [100]–[103], [109]. See also *K/S Merc-Scandia XXXXII v Lloyd's Underwriters* [2001] EWCA Civ 1275, [2001] 2 Lloyd's Rep. 563 at [35].

[678] *Agapitos v Agnew (The Aegeon)* [2002] EWCA Civ 247, [2002] 2 Lloyd's Rep. 42 at [38].

[679] *Re Carr and Sun Insurance* (1897) T.L.R. 186.

[680] *Black King Shipping Corp v Massie (The Litsion Pride)* [1985] 1 Lloyd's Rep. 437, 517–519.

[681] *General Accident, Fire and Life Assurance Corp Ltd v Midland Bank Ltd* [1940] 2 K.B. 388; *Lombard Australia v NRMA Insurance* [1969] 1 Lloyd's Rep. 575. See also *Woolcott v Sun Alliance and London Insurance Ltd* [1978] 1 Lloyd's Rep. 629. *New Hampshire Insurance Co v MGN Ltd* [1997] L.R.L.R. 24; *Arab Bank Plc v Zurich Insurance Co* [1999] 1 Lloyd's Rep. 262.

[682] *Savash v CIS General Insurance Ltd* [2014] EWHC 375 (TCC), [2014] Lloyd's Rep. I.R. 471 at [55]–[59].

[682a] *Royal Boskalis Westminster NV v Mountain* [1997] L.R.L.R. 523; reversed on other grounds [1997] 2 All E.R. 929; *Manifest Shipping & Co Ltd v Uni-Polaris Insurance Co Ltd (The Star Sea)*

[2001] UKHL 1, [2001] 2 W.L.R. 170. See also *Alfred McAlpine Plc v BAI (Run-off) Ltd* [2000] 1 Lloyd's Rep. 437, where it was held that mere negligence in supplying details of claim pursuant to a notice provision in the policy did not constitute a breach of the obligation of utmost good faith.

Remedy for fraudulent claims: existing law

42–099   [*Add to paragraph, line 9, after* "applicable to a fraudulent claim": *page* [1844]]
In *Versloot Dredging BV v HDI Gerling Industrie Versicherung AG*, Lords Sumption and Hughes were similarly sceptical.[685a]

685a [2016] UKSC 45, [2016] 3 W.L.R. 543, at [8], [67].

[*Update note 689, line 3: page* [1844]]
Aviva Insurance Ltd v Brown [2011] EWHC 362 (QB) is reported at [2012] Lloyd's Rep. I.R. 211.

[*In note 690, delete from* "In *Versloot Dredging BV v HDI . . .* " *in line 3 to the end: page* [1844]]

[*Add to paragraph, after note 690: page* [1844]]
In *Versloot Dredging BV v HDI Gerling Industrie Versicherung AG*,[690a] the Supreme Court appeared to assume that forfeiture of the insurance claim (including the genuine parts of the claim)—as opposed to the forfeiture of any other benefit under the policy—was the consequence of a fraudulent claim.

690a [2016] UKSC 45, [2016] 3 W.L.R. 543.

Proof of insured and excepted perils

42–102   [*Add to note 706, at the end: page* [1846]]
; *Leeds Beckett University v Travelers Insurance Co Ltd* [2017] EWHC 558 (TCC) at [199]–[208].

Causation

42–103   [*Add to note 716, at the end: page* [1847]]
; *ARC Capital Partners Ltd v Brit Syndicates Ltd* [2016] EWHC 141 (Comm), [2016] 4 W.L.R. 18.

The amount recoverable

42–105   [*Add to note 730, at the end: page* [1849]]
Upon the entry into force of ss.13A and 16A of the Insurance Act 2015 on May 4, 2017, the assured is entitled to recover damages for the late payment of a claim under an insurance contract in breach of a term implied by s.13A requiring the insurer to pay insurance claims within a reasonable time. In non-consumer insurance contracts, it is open to the parties to agree to a modification of this implied term to the insurer's benefit subject to the restrictions imposed by s.16A of the 2015 Act and the transparency requirements of the Insurance Act 2015. See below, para.42–111A.

[*Add new note 732a, line 14, after* "cost of reinstatement or repair": *page* [1849]]
[732a] *Prattley Enterprises Ltd v Vero Insurance New Zealand Ltd* [2016] NZSC 158, [2017] Lloyd's Rep. I.R. 175 at [38]–[43].

[*Add to note 738, at the end: page* [1850]]
In *Great Lakes Reinsurance (UK) SE v Western Trading Ltd* [2016] EWCA Civ 1003, [2016] Lloyd's Rep. I.R. 643 at [40], the Court of Appeal held that where real property is destroyed the measure of indemnity to which the insured is entitled will depend on: (i) the terms of the policy; (ii) the interest of the insured in, or its obligations in respect of, the property insured; and (iii) the facts of the case including, in particular, the intention of the insured at the time of the loss. If the insured has a limited interest in the property it will be material to consider whether the subject matter of the insurance is the whole interest in the property insured and not solely that of the insured himself and, if it is the whole interest, whether the insured is accountable to others for any sum received in excess of his interest. At [67]–[75], the Court held that where no reinstatement costs had yet been incurred, whether or not the cost of reinstatement was the correct measure of indemnity depended on whether the insured had a fixed, settled and genuine intention to reinstate. See also *Prattley Enterprises Ltd v Vero Insurance New Zealand Ltd* [2016] NZSC 158, [2017] Lloyd's Rep. I.R. 175 at [38]–[43].

[*Add to note 741, at the beginning: page* [1850]]
Prattley Enterprises Ltd v Vero Insurance New Zealand Ltd [2016] NZSC 158, [2017] Lloyd's Rep. I.R. 175 at [38]–[43].

Reinstatement

[*Add new note 769a, line 3, after* "or damaged property.": *page* [1853]]   **42–111**
[769a] *Prattley Enterprises Ltd v Vero Insurance New Zealand Ltd* [2016] NZSC 158, [2017] Lloyd's Rep. I.R. 175 at [38].

[*Add new paragraph 42–111A: page* [1853]]
Late payment of insurance claims. At common law, if the insurer unreasonably   **42–111A** failed to pay an insurance claim within a reasonable time, the assured had no remedy over and above the entitlement to an insurance indemnity and statutory interest.[777a] This was the result of a peculiarity of insurance law in that the claim for an indemnity is, as a legal fiction, a claim for unliquidated damages for breach of contract by the insurer (the breach being constituted by the assured's suffering an insured loss),[777b] and in that a contracting party is not entitled to recover damages for the late payment of damages.[777c] In addition, the Court held that there was no implied term in the insurance contract obliging the insurer to assess and pay an insurance claim with reasonable diligence and due expedition.[777d] In order to address the perceived unfairness with this state of the law, the Enterprise Act 2016 ss.28–30 were passed so as to amend the Insurance Act 2015 (by the addition of ss.13A and 16A). This legislation entered into force on May 4, 2017 and introduces into every insurance contract an implied term that the insurer must pay insurance claims within a reasonable time (allowing for investigation and assessment of the claim).[777e] If there is a breach of this implied term, the assured will have remedies (e.g. damages) available at common law (and otherwise) in addition to the payment of the claim under the policy and statutory interest.[777f] By s.13A(4), if the insurer shows there are reasonable grounds for disputing the

claim, there is no breach of the implied term while the dispute is continuing. Insofar as any term of the insurance contract puts the assured in a worse position as regards the implied term provided for in s.13A, such term is invalid insofar as consumer insurances are concerned and insofar as any breach of the implied term by the insurer is deliberate or reckless. Otherwise, such a term is valid if it satisfies the transparency requirements of the Insurance Act 2015.[777g]

[777a] *The Italia Express* [1992] 2 Lloyd's Rep. 281; *Sprung v Royal Insurance (UK) Ltd* [1999] Lloyd's Rep. I.R. 111; *Callaghan v Dominion Insurance Co Ltd* [1997] 2 Lloyd's Rep. 541; *Tonkin v UK Insurance Ltd* [2006] EWHC 1120 (TCC), [2007] Lloyd's Rep. I.R. 283 at [34]–[38]; *Turville Heath Inc v Chartis Insurance UK Ltd* [2012] EWHC 3019 (TCC), (2012) 145 Con L.R. 163 at [36].

[777b] *Grant v Royal Exchange Assurance Co* (1816) 5 M. & S. 439, 442; *Swan and Cleland's Graving Dock and Slipway Co v Maritime Insurance Co* [1907] 1 K.B. 116, 123–124; *William Pickersgill & Sons Ltd v London and Provincial Marine & General Insurance Co Ltd* [1912] 3 K.B. 614, 622; *Seele Austria GmbH & Co KG v Tokio Marine Europe Insurance Ltd* [2009] EWHC 2066 (TCC) at [50]–[52].

[777c] *President of India v Lips Maritime Corp* [1988] 1 A.C. 395, 424–425.

[777d] *Insurance Corp of the Channel Islands Ltd v McHugh* [1997] L.R.L.R. 94, 136–138.

[777e] What constitutes a reasonable time depends on all of the circumstances of the case, including the type, size and complexity of the claim, compliance with statutory or regulatory rules or guidance and factors beyond the control of the insurer (s.13A(3)).

[777f] Parliament's Explanatory Notes, para.264. See also s.13A(5) of the 2015 Act. By amendment to the Limitation Act 1980 s.5, introduced by the Enterprise Act 2016 s.30, a claim for breach of the implied term may not be brought after the expiration of one year from the date on which the insurer has paid all the sums due under the insurance contract.

[777g] Insurance Act 2015 s.16A. As to the transparency requirements, see Main Work, Vol.II, para.42–060.

10. The Rights of the Insurer upon Payment

Salvage

42–113   [*In note 781, update reference to MacGillivray on Insurance Law to: page* [1854]] 13th edn (2015), paras 24–006—24–010

Subrogation

42–114   [*In note 789, update reference to MacGillivray on Insurance Law to: page* [1855]] 13th edn (2015), para.24–032

Subrogation: rights of action

42–115   [*Add to note 805, line 6, after* "(1999) 20 W.A.R. 380 Full Ct, WA": *page* [1856]] ; *Cape Distribution Ltd v Cape Intermediate Holdings Plc* [2016] EWHC 1786 (QB).

[*Add to note 805, at the end: page* [1857]]
See also *Gard Marine & Energy Ltd v China National Chartering Co Ltd* [2017] UKSC 35, [2017] 1 W.L.R. 1793 at [109]–[126], [131]–[146]; *contra* at [48]–[57], [89], [99]–[103].

[Add to note 807, line 1, after "[1986] Q.B. 211"*: page* [1857]]
; *Fresca-Judd v Golovina* [2016] EWHC 497 (QB), [2016] 4 W.L.R. 107.

11. SPECIFIC TYPES OF INSURANCE CONTRACT

(a) *Liability Insurance*

[In note 834, update reference to MacGillivray on Insurance Law to: page [1860]]
13th edn (2015), Ch.30

General characteristics

[Add to note 839, at the end: page [1861]]   **42–119**
In *Cape Distribution Ltd v Cape Intermediate Holdings Plc* [2016] EWHC 1786
(QB), [2017] Lloyd's Rep. I.R. 1, at [161]–[163] the Court held that the contractual liability exclusion applied only to claims which could be made only in
contract.

Employers' liability

[Add to paragraph, line 4, after note 846: page [1862]]   **42–120**
The 1969 Act requires employers to take out an "*approved policy*" against such
liability.

[Add to paragraph, line 7, after "only temporarily in this country."*: page* [1862]]
The Regulations prohibit certain conditions being included in the policy which
would otherwise entitle the insurer to be discharged from liability in the event of
breach.[847a]

[847a] reg.2. See *Amlin UK Ltd v Geo-Rope Ltd* [2016] CSOH 165, [2017] Lloyd's Rep. I.R. 277.

[Add to note 848, line 1, after "[1995] Q.B. 123"*: page* [1862]]
; *Campbell v Gordon* [2016] UKSC 38, [2016] Lloyd's Rep. I.R. 591.

[Add to note 848, at the end: page [1862]]
See *Amlin UK Ltd v Geo-Rope Ltd* [2016] CSOH 165, [2017] Lloyd's Rep. I.R.
277 at [25]–[27].

Statutory assignment

[Add to note 852, line 10, after "437, 451"*: page* [1863]]   **42–121**
; *Denso Manufacturing UK Ltd v Great Lakes Reinsurance (UK) Plc* [2017]
EWHC 391 (Comm), [2017] Lloyd's Rep. I.R. 240 at [142]–[152].

The Third Parties (Rights against Insurers) Act 2010

42–122   *[In paragraph, lines 3–4, delete* "Although the 2010 Act has . . . " *to* "of this new Act." *and substitute: page* [1864]]
The 2010 Act entered into force on August 1, 2016.[856a]

> [856a] Third Parties (Rights against Insurers) Act 2010 (Commencement) Order 2016 (SI 2016/550). See also Third Parties (Rights against Insurers) Regulations 2016 (SI 2016/570).

[Add to paragraph, line 23, after "judgment, award or agreement"*: page* [1864]]
even if there is a dispute as to whether the third party claim, if proved and established, falls within the scope of cover afforded by the policy.[861a]

> [861a] *BAE Systems Pension Funds Trustees Ltd v Royal & Sun Alliance Insurance Plc* [2017] EWHC 2082 (TCC) at [15]–[24].

(b) *Motor insurance*

[In note 864, update reference to MacGillivray on Insurance Law to: page [1865]]
13th edn (2015), Ch.31

Road Traffic Act 1988

42–123   *[Add to note 867, line 4, after* "[1986] R.T.R. 1."*: page* [1865]]
In *UK Insurance Ltd v Holden* [2017] EWCA Civ 259, [2017] 3 W.L.R. 450 at [68]–[69], the Court of Appeal held that the repair of a car, which the owner was driving but due to disrepair could not be lawfully and safely driven, and which the owner wished to effect as soon as possible in order to be able to drive the car lawfully and safely, was "*use*" of the car.

[Add to note 867, at the end: page [1865]]
See *Vnuk v Zavarovalnica Triglav dd* (C-162/13) [2015] Lloyd's Rep. I.R. 142. In *Sahin v Havard* [2016] EWCA Civ 1202, [2017] 1 W.L.R. 1853 at [20], the Court of Appeal held that permitting the use of a vehicle is not the same as using the vehicle such that the liability of someone who permits another to use a vehicle without an insurance policy is not a liability which is itself required to be insured under s.145 and is not therefore a liability which an insurer is obliged to satisfy under s.151.

[Add to note 868, at the end: page [1865]]
In *UK Insurance Ltd v Holden* [2016] EWHC 264 (QB), [2016] 4 W.L.R. 38; [2017] EWCA Civ 259, [2017] 3 W.L.R. 450 at [44], the Court held that a motor insurance policy might extend beyond roads, if there was no express limitation in the policy to use on roads. The Court also discussed whether "*roads*" under the Road Traffic Act 1988 s.145(3) meant "*public roads*".

Rights of third parties

42–124   *[Add new note 880a, line 2, after* "against the person insured,"*: page* [1866]]
> [880a] This is so, even if the third party claimant has obtained judgment against the insured as an "unknown" or "unnamed" driver: *Cameron v Hussain* [2017] EWCA Civ 366, [2017] R.T.R. 23.

Third parties and uninsured drivers

[*Delete text of note 895 and substitute: page* [1868]]
In *Moreno v Motor Insurers' Bureau* [2016] UKSC 52, [2017] Lloyd's Rep. I.R. 99 at [39], the Supreme Court held that the Motor Vehicles (Compulsory Insurance) (Information Centre and Compensation Body) Regulations 2003 (SI 2003/37) proceed on the basis that a victim's entitlement to compensation will be measured on a consistent basis, by reference to the law of the state of the accident, whichever of the routes to recovery provided by the Directives he or she invokes. In so doing, the Court overruled *Jacobs v Motor Insurers' Bureau* [2010] EWCA Civ 1208, [2011] 1 All E.R. 844. See also *Wigley-Foster v Wilson* [2016] EWCA Civ 454, [2016] 1 W.L.R. 4769.

(c) *Reinsurance*

[*In note 901, update reference to MacGillivray on Insurance Law to: page* [1869]]
13th edn (2015), Ch.35

General characteristics

[*Add to note 906, at the end: page* [1870]]
See also *Metlife Insurance Ltd v RGA Reinsurance Company of Australia Ltd* [2016] NSWSC 980; [2017] Lloyd's Rep. I.R. 160 at [57] (NSWSC).

(d) *Insurance against Financial Loss*

[*In note 922, update reference to MacGillivray on Insurance Law to: page* [1873]]
13th edn (2015), Ch.33

(e) *Fire Insurance*

[*In note 932, update reference to MacGillivray on Insurance Law to: page* [1874]]
13th edn (2015), Ch.28

Special features

[*In note 933, update reference to MacGillivray on Insurance Law to: page* [1874]]
13th edn (2015), Ch.28

(f) *Life Insurance*

[*In note 936, update reference to MacGillivray on Insurance Law to: page* [1874]]
13th edn (2015), Ch.26

CHAPTER 43

RESTRICTIVE AGREEMENTS AND COMPETITION

1. INTRODUCTION

Relationship between the EU competition rules and the provisions of domestic law

43–003   *[Add to paragraph, at the end: page* [1879]]
Clearly the substance of this paragraph may require fundamental change following withdrawal by the United Kingdom from the European Union pursuant to the referendum of June 23, 2016.[9a]

   [9a] For a general note on "Brexit", see above, paras 1–013A et seq.

2. Competition Rules Under the TFEU

(a) *In General*

Principal sources of law

[*In note 22 update reference to Butterworths Competition Law Handbook to: page* [1880]]
22nd edn (2016)

43–008

(c) *Article 101(3)*

Block exemptions currently in force

Note that the block exemption regulation for certain insurance agreements, Regulation 267/2010, expired on March 31, 2017.

43–034

(d) *Application of Art.101 to Specific Agreements*

Typical horizontal agreements

[*Add to note 124, at the end: page* [1892]]
The Commission's decision in *Lundbeck* was upheld on appeal to the General Court, *H Lundbeck A/S v Commission* (T-472/13) EU:T:2016:449; the case is on further appeal to the Court of Justice, *P Lundbeck A/S v Commission* (C-591/16), not yet decided.

43–035

(e) *Article 102*

Examples of abusive contractual provisions

[*Add to note 185, at the end: page* [1903]]
On September 6, 2017, the Court of Justice referred the case back to the General Court for further consideration of whether the rebates violated art.102.

43–063

(f) *Enforcement at the National Level*

Breaches of arts 101 or 102 as a cause of action

[*Add to paragraph, at the end: page* [1906]]
The private enforcement of EU competition law was given added impetus by the adoption in November 2014 of the EU Damages Directive,[205a] which entered into force on December 27, 2016. Most Member States failed to implement by that date, although most have now done so. It was implemented in UK law by the Claims in Respect of Loss or Damage Arising from Competition Infringements (Competition Act 1998 and Other Enactments (Amendment)) Regulations 2017.[205b]

43–070

[205a] Directive 2014/14/EU of the European Parliament and of the Council on certain rules governing actions for damages under national law for infringements of the competition law provisions of the Member States and of the European Union [2014] O.J. L349/1.
[205b] SI 2017/385.

3. United Kingdom Competition Law

(a) *Introduction*

Reform of the law

43–077   [*Add to paragraph, at the end: page* [1909]]
The withdrawal by the United Kingdom from the European Union pursuant to the referendum of June 23, 2016 is likely to lead to significant changes to the domestic competition law of the UK in due course.[225a]

[225a] For a general note on "Brexit", see above, paras 1–013A et seq.

(g) *The Competition Appeal Tribunal*

The Competition Appeal Tribunal

43–139   [*Add to paragraph, at the end: page* [1926]]
It is also now possible for the Competition Appeal Tribunal to hear so-called "standalone" actions for an injunction and/or damages as a result of changes introduced with effect from October 1, 2015; that is to say it can now hear cases where there has been no prior decision by a competition authority in the UK or the EU.

CHAPTER 44

SALE OF GOODS

1. In General

(a) *Introduction*

Vienna Convention of 1980

44–014   [*Add to note 79, at the end: page* [1936]]
In December 2015, the Commission proposed a directive on contracts for online and other distance sales of goods (the Online Sale of Goods Directive COM(2015) 635 final). This would partly replace the existing Consumer Sales Directive with regard to distance sales (both online and offline). The proposed Online Sale of Goods Directive is part of the Digital Single Market Strategy and comes alongside several other proposed legal instruments, notably in connection with digital content supply and the portability of digital content. On May 25, 2016, the Commission published an E-commerce package (COM(2016) 320 final) aimed at three particular aspects of ecommerce: unjustified geo-blocking, transparency of parcel delivery prices and enforcement of consumer rights.

(b) *Definitions*

Definitions

44–015   [*Add to note 85, line 19, after* "[2010] NSWSC 267."*: page* [1938]]
In *Software Incubator Ltd v Computer Associates UK Ltd* [2016] EWHC 1587 (QB) HH Judge Waxman (sitting as a Judge of the High Court) held that the sale of computer software was a sale of goods for the purposes of the Commercial Agents (Council Directive) Regulations 1993. Although he stressed that context was all and that it was possible that there could be a different answer under the

Sale of Goods Act, he reviewed the authorities on the Act (at [47] et seq.) and concluded that the case law was scarce and limited in effect.

2. FORMATION OF THE CONTRACT

(a) *Contract of Sale*

Sale and agreement to sell

[*Add to note 103, at the end*: *page* [1940]]   **44–020**
; and the transfer of property must be the essence of the contract: see *PST Energy 7 Shipping LLC v OW Bunker Malta Ltd (The Res Cogitans)* [2016] UKSC 23. The Supreme Court, upholding the decision of the Court of Appeal ([2015] EWCA Civ 1058; see L. Shmilovits [2016] L.M.C.L.Q. 20 and A. Tettenborn [2016] L.M.C.L.Q. 24 and, in relation to the decision of the Supreme Court, L. Gullifer [2017] L.Q.R. 244), held that a contract for the supply of fuel bunkers, which contained a retention of title clause and permitted the purchasing vessel owners to consume the bunkers during the credit period, was not a contract for the sale of goods within the meaning of s.2(1). See below, para.44–174A.

[*Add to note 104, line 3, after* "connection with future goods": *page* [1940]]
. In *Hughes v Pendragon Sabre Ltd (t/a Porsche Centre Bolton)* [2016] EWCA Civ 18 there was a contract to sell if the seller was allocated one of a new model of car by the manufacturer. The contract was construed as an agreement to sell future goods to be acquired by the seller which depended on a contingency:

Conditional sale agreements

[*In note 145, delete* "[2015] EWHC 2022 (Comm)" *and substitute*: *page* [1944]]   **44–028**
[2016] UKSC 23

(b) *Capacity of Parties*

Capacity of parties

[*In note 170, update the reference to Treitel, The Law of Contract to*: *page* [1947]]   **44–033**
14th edn (2015), para.12–008

[*In note 170, update the reference to Goff and Jones, The Law of Unjust Enrichment to*: *page* [1947]]
9th edn (2016), para.24-018

(d) *Subject Matter*

Future goods

[*Add to note 175, at the end*: *page* [1948]]   **44–037**
, applied in *Hughes v Pendragon Sabre Ltd (t/a Porsche Centre Bolton)* [2016] EWCA Civ 18 (at [42]).

Contracts for the sale of future goods

44–038   [*Add to note 178, at the end: page* [1948]]
See *Hughes v Pendragon Sabre Ltd (t/a Porsche Centre Bolton)* [2016] EWCA Civ 18.

Sale of goods already perished

44–045   [*In note 199, update the reference to Atiyah to: page* [1950]]
Twigg-Flessner, Canavan and MacQueen (eds), *Atiyah and Adams' Sale of Goods*, p.77

Operation of s.7

44–050   [*In note 218, update the reference to Atiyah to: page* [1952]]
Twigg-Flessner, Canavan and MacQueen (eds), *Atiyah and Adams' Sale of Goods*, p.293

3. Terms of the Contract

(a) *Conditions, Warranties, Misrepresentations and Puffs*

Measure of damages

44–061   [*Add in note 266, line 3, after* "This is, however, arguable.": *page* [1958]]
The Singapore Court of Appeal doubted the correctness of *Royscot* in *RBC Properties v Defu Furniture Pte Ltd* [2014] SGCA 62, [2015] 1 S.L.R. 997; see Liau [2015] L.M.C.L.Q. 464.

(b) *Implied Terms*

(i) *Implied Terms about Title*

Breaches of s.12

44–077   [*Add to note 330, at the end: page* [1965]]
; in the context of retention of title clauses, see *PST Energy 7 Shipping LLC v OW Bunker Malta Ltd* [2015] EWCA Civ 1058 (noted Tettenborn [2016] L.M.C.L.Q. 24), affirmed [2016] UKSC 23 and see L. Gullifer [2017] L.Q.R. 244.

(iii) *Implied Terms about Quality and Fitness for Purpose*

Guidelines

44–100   [*Add to note 450, at the end: page* [1979]]
; see also *Peebles v Rembrand Builders Merchants Ltd* Unreported, April 18, 2017 Sherriff Court (Tayside, Central and Fife) (Dundee) (roof tiles which became patchy and discoloured were not of satisfactory quality).

Reasonably fit for purpose

[*Add to note 484, at the end: page* [1983]]   **44–109**
; *Fluor Ltd v Shanghai Zhenhua Heavy Industries Ltd* [2016] EWHC 2062 (TCC)
(if a buyer knows of goods' true condition but is unable to discover without
lengthy investigation whether or not that condition affects use of the goods, they
are not fit for purpose).

4. EFFECTS OF THE CONTRACT

(a) *Transfer of Property as between Seller and Buyer*

"Romalpa" clauses: retention of title

[*Add to note 741, at the end: page* [2015]]   **44–174**
However, where the buyer is at liberty to consume the goods before the price
becomes due, such that the transfer of the property in the goods may never
happen, the contract may not be a contract of sale at all: see *PST Energy 7
Shipping LLC v OW Bunker Malta Ltd* [2016] UKSC 23 where the Supreme
Court characterised a bunker contract with these characteristics as a sui generis
supply contract. See below, para.44–174A.

[*Add new paragraphs 44–174A and 44–174B: page* [2015]]
Right to consume before property has passed. If the contract provides for   **44–174A**
possession of goods to be given, coupled with a legal entitlement to consume
them before the property in them is transferred upon payment, then, according to
the Supreme Court in *PST Energy 7 Shipping LLC v OW Bunker Malta Ltd*[747a]
the contract is not one of sale but is sui generis as a bailment coupled with a
licence to consume the goods. Since almost all retention of title clauses allow the
buyer to use or resell the goods before property in them has passed, this means
that a very large number of contracts with reservation of title clauses will no
longer be contracts of sale within the meaning of the Sale of Goods Act.

[747a] [2016] UKSC 23, [2016] 2 W.L.R. 1193, [2016] 1 Lloyd's Rep. 589. For a critical review of
this decision see L. Gullifer [2017] L.Q.R. 244. The Court of Appeal in *Wood v TUI Travel Plc (t/a
First Choice)* [2017] EWCA Civ 11, [2017] 1 Lloyd's Rep. 322 held that *PST Energy 7 Shipping LLC*
was not authority for the proposition that there was no intention that property in any food or drink
served by a hotel to guests would pass to them. The conclusion in *PST Energy 7 Shipping LLC*
depended upon the relationship between a retention of title clause and the liberty to consume fuel in
which property had not already passed and was accordingly distinguishable.

Sui generis supply contracts analogous to contracts for the sale of goods. A   **44–174B**
consequence of the conclusion in *PST Energy 7 Shipping LLC* is that a body of
common law parallel to the Sale of Goods Act will have to be elaborated to deal
with sui generis supply contracts. Although the Court of Appeal was clear that
the incidents of the sui generis contract should track those of a sale of goods
contract,[747b] it cannot be assumed that the entire Sale of Goods Act can be
applied by analogy to sui generis contracts.[747ba] The Supreme Court gave consideration to an obligation comparable to the right to sell goods that is the

equivalent of s.12 of the Act. However, the judge at first instance saw no need for a warranty of quiet possession akin to the one that exists for sale of goods contracts in s.12(2)(b).[747c] The first reason given was that the recipient of the goods obtained sufficient protection from the implied term of lawful permission to use or consume. The second reason was that the warranty of quiet possession in sale of goods contracts was concerned with events after the passing of property. However, neither reason seems compelling and there may be a practical need for such a warranty. It is likely that equivalent common law rules should apply to such sui generis contracts in relation to matters such as delivery (including time and quantity of delivery and delivery by instalments) payment and quality (although, on a strict view, the statutory provisions which modify the common law rules on merchantable quality, etc. would not apply). The potential applicability of the statutory exceptions to the *nemo dat* rule is complex. The supplier of goods under a sui generis contract is not a "seller" for the purposes of s.24, nor is the recipient a "buyer" of goods for the purpose of s.25. However, it is likely that the receipt of goods with a licence to use or consume them should be regarded as a disposition for the purposes of these sections. The definition of a mercantile agent in s.1(1) of the Factors Act 1889 may be broad enough to capture a person who buys and resells under a sui generis supply contract, given that such contracts are "in commercial terms" regarded as contracts for the sale of goods[747d] and that the Factors Act is not confined to sale of goods contracts as these are defined in the Sale of Goods Act. Thus the provisions of s.2(1) of the Factors Act may apply. By contrast, certain provisions of the Sale of Goods Act are statutory inventions and did not codify existing common law. Such sections cannot apply by analogy at common law. For example, it is possible, though perhaps unlikely, that a bulk may consist of goods supplied to two or more recipients under sui generis supply contracts and that the bulk has not been exhausted by the time that one or more recipients has paid in full. Section 20A, which is not declaratory of the common law, cannot apply to such contracts by analogy. Similarly, ss.15A and 30(2A) cannot apply.

[747b] "There is no reason why the incidents of a contract of sale of goods for which the Act provides should not apply equally to such a contract at common law": Moore-Bick L.J., [2015] EWCA Civ 1058 at [33].

[747ba] See L. Gullifer [2017] L.Q.R. 244, 258 and *Benjamin's Sale of Goods* (2016) 2nd Supplement, paras 4-001, 4-025 and 4-030.

[747c] [2015] EWHC 2022 (Comm) at [63].

[747d] [2015] EWCA Civ 1058 at [33].

Disadvantages of "Romalpa" clauses

44–183   [*In paragraph, lines 4–5, delete* ", the seller will ordinarily not . . . action for the price and" *including n.813: page* [2021]]

[*Add to paragraph, after note 814: page* [2021]]
It had been held[814a] that an action for the price would not be available unless either s.49(1) or s.49(2) were satisfied and that accordingly the presence of a "Romalpa" clause, which prevented property from passing to the buyer, would ordinarily mean that the seller could not maintain an action for the price. In *PST Energy 7 Shipping LLC v OW Bunker Malta Ltd*[814b] the Supreme Court held that the bunker supply contract fell outside the Sale of Goods Act and accordingly it was not necessary to decide whether an action for the price under the Act would

have been maintainable in the circumstances. However, the Supreme Court indicated, obiter, that the price would have been recoverable on the date stated by virtue of the contract's express terms providing the goods had been delivered, indicating that they would have overruled the decision of the Court of Appeal in *Caterpillar* on this point.[814c]

[814a] *Caterpillar (NI) Ltd (formerly FG Wilson (Engineering) Ltd) v John Holt & Co (Liverpool) Ltd* [2013] EWCA Civ 1232, [2014] 1 All E.R. (Comm) 393 at [60], [61] and [75]–[76].
[814b] [2016] UKSC 23.
[814c] See further below, para.44–365.

(c) *Transfer of Title*

(i) *Sale by Person not the Owner*

(aa) *Estoppel*

Estoppel by representation

[*Add to note 867, at the end: page* [2027]]   **44–197**
; *Chatfields-Martin Walter Ltd v Lombard North Central Plc* [2014] EWHC 1222 (QB) (representation via the Hire Purchase Register that the owner had no legitimate interest in a vehicle).

Estoppel by negligent conduct

[*Add to note 873, at the end: page* [2027]]   **44–198**
However, if the owner of a vehicle changes the register to represent that it no longer has an interest it will be estopped from going back on that representation (*Chatfields-Martin Walter Ltd v Lombard North Central Plc* [2014] EWHC 1222 (QB)).

(gg) *Disposition by Buyer in Possession*

Possession of buyer

[*Add to note 952, at the beginning: page* [2035]]   **44–221**
See for example *Carlos Soto SAV v AP Moller-Maersk AS* [2015] EWHC 458 (Comm), where the buyer had obtained a bill of lading in good faith and without notice.

5. PERFORMANCE OF THE CONTRACT

(b) *Rules Governing Delivery*

(vi) *Instalment Deliveries*

Anticipatory breach: repudiation accepted

[*Add to note 1103, at the end: page* [2053]]   **44–267**
On whether damages should be assessed in a different way in commodity sales see P. Todd [2017] L.M.C.L.Q. 122.

6. REMEDIES OF THE SELLER

(a) *Rights of Unpaid Seller against the Goods*

(ii) *Stoppage in Transit*

Other provisions as to transit

44–334   [*In note 1452, update the reference to Scrutton on Charterparties and Bills of Lading to: page* [2085]]
23rd edn (2015), paras 1.013 et seq.

[*In note 1452, delete "Scrutton, above": page* [2085]]

(b) *Action for the Price*

Claim for price due on "a day certain"

44–364   [*Add to note 1643, penultimate line, after* "within a fixed period after delivery.": *page* [2103]]
This point was not considered in detail by the Court of Appeal [2015] EWCA Civ 1058 or Supreme Court [2016] UKSC 23. In *Caterpillar (NI) Ltd (formerly FG Wilson (Engineering) Ltd) v John Holt & Co (Liverpool) Ltd* [2013] EWCA Civ 1232, [2014] 1 All E.R. (Comm) 393 Longmore L.J. (at [44]) indicated that a term for payment 30 days after invoice would have fallen within s.49(2), but as the sending of an invoice itself depended on delivery, it seems questionable whether this is a term for payment on a day certain "irrespective of delivery".

Action for the price outside s.49

44–365   [*Add to paragraph, after note 1654: page* [2104]]
In *PST Energy 7 Shipping LLC v OW Bunker Malta Ltd*[1654a] the Supreme Court held that the bunker supply contract fell outside the Sale of Goods Act and accordingly it was not necessary to decide whether an action for the price under the Act would have been maintainable in the circumstances. However, Lord Mance, delivering the unanimous judgment of the Court, said that he would have overruled the decision of the Court of Appeal in *Caterpillar* on this point. Section 49 was not a complete code of situations in which the price may be recoverable under a contract of sale. There was room for claims for the price in other circumstances, including the present case, where the bunkers remained the seller's property but were at the buyer's risk and where under the contract the buyer was permitted to use the goods before payment.

[1654a] [2016] UKSC 23 at [40]–[58].

[*Add to note 1655, at the end: page* [2104]]
While noting the artificiality, Lord Mance, delivering the unanimous judgment of the Supreme Court in *PST Energy 7 Shipping LLC v OW Bunker Malta Ltd* [2016] UKSC 23, saw no reason why a claim for damages for non-payment should not in principle be available (at [48]–[49]).

[472]

(c) *Action for Damages*

An available market

[*Add to note 1672, at the beginning: page* [2106]]   **44–368**
For a discussion of the market price rule generally and how it interacts with the
compensation principle, see M. Bridge [2016] L.Q.R. 405.

[*Add to note 1682, at the end: page* [2107]]
In *Hughes v Pendragon Sabre Ltd (t/a Porsche Centre Bolton)* [2016] EWCA
Civ 18 a rare new limited edition Porsche was sufficiently specialised for there
to be insufficient activity to evidence a market.

[*In note 1683, update the reference to McGregor on Damages to: page* [2107]]
19th edn (2015), paras 23–118 et seq.

7. REMEDIES OF THE BUYER

(a) *Damages for Non-Delivery*

Damages where there is an available market

[*Add in note 1816, penultimate line, after* "9th edn (2014), para.17–009": *page*   **44–388**
[2120]]
; Peel [2016] L.Q.R. 177 and Yip and Goh [2016] J.B.L. 335.

Damages for non-delivery in the absence of an available market

[*Add new note 1880a, after* "the cost of the nearest equivalent," *in line 8: page*   **44–397**
[2127]]
1880a *Hughes v Pendragon Sabre Ltd (t/a Porsche Centre Bolton)* [2016] EWCA Civ 18.

(c) *Damages for Defective Quality*

(i) *Diminution in Value*

Damages for diminution in market value

[*Add to note 1977, at the end: page* [2138]]   **44–412**
See, applying the market price rule, *Amira G Foods Ltd v RS Foods Ltd* [2016]
EWHC 76 (QB).

Damages for the cost of adaptations, or of substitute goods

[*Add to note 1993, at the end: page* [2139]]   **44–414**
However, in *Peebles v Rembrand Builders Merchants Ltd* Unreported, April 18,
2017, Sheriff Court (Tayside, Central and Fife) (Dundee), the court refused to
award the full cost of replacing defective roof tiles because the expense was
unreasonable and the claimant had failed to mitigate its loss.

(ii) *Losses other than Diminution in Value*

Compensation paid by the buyer to a sub-buyer

44–433   [*Add to note 2089, line 1, after* "[1951] 2 K.B. 314, 320": *page* [2150]]
(applied in *Meadowbank Vac Alloys Ltd v Eurokey Recycling Ltd*, Unreported,
May 16, 2016 (QBD Manchester District Registry))

(d) *Other Remedies of the Buyer*

Restitution: recovery of money paid to the seller

44–439   [*In note 2120, update the reference to Goff and Jones, The Law of Unjust
Enrichment to: page* [2153]]
9th edn (2016)

8. CONSUMER PROTECTION ACT 1987

Meaning of "defect"

44–451   [*Add to note 2195, at the end: page* [2161]]
; *Wilkes v Depuy International Ltd* [2016] EWHC 3096 (QB) (failed hip replacement not defective).

SURETYSHIP

1. IN GENERAL

Performance guarantees

[Add to note 44, line 4, after "[2002] 1 Lloyd's Rep. 617 at [16]"*: page* [2173]]   **45–009**
; *Caterpillar Motoren GmbH & Co KG v Mutual Benefits Assurance Co* [2015] EWHC 2304 (Comm), [2016] 2 All E.R. (Comm) 322 at [13]–[15], [19]–[22] and [25]–[27]; *Spliethoff's Bevrachtingskantoor BV v Bank of China Ltd* [2015] EWHC 999 (Comm), [2015] 2 Lloyd's Rep. 123 at [69]–[85]. But where a contract contains a clause as is mentioned in (iv) of "*Paget's* presumption" (quoted in the Main Work) this may be explicable as inserted so as to put beyond doubt that the rule applicable to true guarantees does not apply: [2015] EWHC 2304 (Comm) at [21], referring to *Caja de Ahorros v Gold Coast Ltd del Mediterraneo* [2001] EWCA Civ 1806, [2002] 1 Lloyd's Rep. 617 at [25].

[Add to note 45, at the end: page [2173]]
cf. *Caterpillar Motoren GmbH & Co KG v Mutual Benefits Assurance Co* [2015] EWHC 2304 (Comm), [2016] 2 All E.R. (Comm) 322 at [20] (no material distinction between bank and other financial institution, such as an insurance company engaged in the business of providing bonds to its customers).

[Add to note 46, at the end: page [2173]]
Where the main contract is in the nature of a financing transaction (even though in the form of a sale and demise charter with a "deed of guarantee" as part of it), any presumption generally applicable to non-banking cases will more readily give way to language to the contrary: *Bitumen Invest AS v Richmond Mercantile Ltd FZC* [2016] EWHC 2957 (Comm), [2017] 1 Lloyd's Rep. 219 at [17] (where the fact that the trigger for payment was the issue of a demand for an amount certified by the beneficiary of the guarantee provided the key feature in finding it to be an "on demand guarantee" ([2016] EWHC 2957 (Comm) esp. at [21]–[26])).

New tenancies: breaking privity of contract

45–016   *[Add to note 85, at the end: page [2179]]*
An assignment by a tenant of the lease to the guarantor of that tenant's covenants (the guarantee being expressed as imposing the same liability as if principal debtor) has been held void under the 1995 Act: *EMI Group Ltd v O & H Q1 Ltd* [2016] EWHC 529 (Ch), [2016] Ch. 586 at [77]–[91]. This is because on such an assignment the provisions of the Act would apply as follows: (i) the original tenant (T1) is released from the tenant covenants (s.5(2)(a)); (ii) the guarantor is released from the tenant covenants as from T1's release (s.24(2)); (iii) the effect of s.24(2) is that as from the release of T1 (i.e. as from the assignment to the guarantor/second tenant (T2)), the guarantor should be released from its liabilities as guarantor; however, (iv) as from the assignment to T2/the guarantor, T2 becomes bound by the tenant covenants (s.3(2)(a)). As a result, the assignment releases the guarantor from the tenant covenants but at the same moment binds the guarantor to them as T2, the liability under the guarantee being the same or essentially the same as the liability of T1. Such an assignment "frustrates" the operation of s.24(2)(b) and is therefore rendered void by s.25(1)(a): [2016] EWHC 529 (Ch) at [79]–[80]. Given that the assignment is void, the lease remains vested in the original tenant and the purported assignee remains bound as guarantor of that tenant's covenants: [2016] EWHC 529 (Ch) at [89]–[91].

2. FORMATION OF THE CONTRACT

(b) *Consideration*

Guarantee of past and future transactions

45–024   *[Add to note 121, at the end: page [2183]]*
cf. *Tailby v HSBC Bank Plc* [2015] B.P.I.R. 143 Ch D (earlier provision of a continuing facility to principal debtor was a "real commercial benefit" to the guarantor and this constituted consideration).

3. Formalities

A question of substance rather than of form

[Add to note 232, at the end: page [2196]]   **45–045**
See also *Erith Holdings Ltd v Murphy* [2017] EWHC 1364 (TCC) at [88] and [90].

4. Construction of the Contract

The role of "business common sense"

[Add to note 340, at the end: page [2210]]   **45–068**
See also (though not in the context of suretyship) *Arnold v Britton* [2015] UKSC 36, [2015] A.C. 1619 at [15]–[23], [66] and [76]–[77]; *Wood v Capita Insurance Services Ltd* [2017] UKSC 24, [2017] 2 W.L.R. 1095 at [8]–[15].

Guarantee and penalty clause in main contract

[Add to note 376, at the end: page [2214]]   **45–074**
On the general common law governing penalty clauses see Main Work, Vol.I, paras 26–178 et seq.

Conditional guarantees

[Add to note 381, at the end: page [2214]]   **45–075**
And if A (a bank) requires B (the director of C Co) to provide both real security and his own personal guarantee for a loan to C Co, but executes only the guarantee, A may enforce the guarantee against B as A may waive the condition designed to protect its position: *Barclays Bank Plc v Sutton* [2015] EWHC 3192 (QB) at [21] and [26].

6. Discharge of Surety

(b) *Discharge of Surety through Discharge of Principal Debtor*

Discharge of debtor by bankruptcy

[In paragraph, line 27, delete "s.260(1)(b) of the Insolvency Act 1986" *and*   **45–098**
  substitute: page [2228]]
s.260(2)(b) of the Insolvency Act 1986

[Add new note 488a, after "these arrangements on sureties." *in line 31: page*
  [2228]]
[488a] [1999] Ch.117 at 129–130. (The wording of s.260(2) of the 1986 Act has been amended, but without relevant substantive change.)

Discharge of debtor through creditor's breach of contract

45–099   [*Add note 496, at the end: page* [2229]]
; *Spliethoff's Bevrachtingskantoor BV v Bank of China Ltd* [2015] EWHC 999
(Comm), [2015] 2 Lloyd's Rep. 123 at [183]–[199].

[*Delete text of note 497 and substitute: page* [2229]]
National Westminster Bank Plc v Riley [1986] B.C.L.C. 268, 275–276 (referring
to *Holme v Brunskill* (1878) 3 Q.B.D. 495 (on which see Main Work, Vol.II,
para.45–104) Cf. *Spliethoff's Bevrachtingskantoor BV v Bank of China Ltd*
[2015] EWHC 999 (Comm), [2015] 2 Lloyd's Rep. 123 at [185]–[186], which
distinguished between discharge of the guarantor on the ground of not unsub-
stantial non-repudiatory breach by the creditor and on the ground of variation by
reference to *Wardens and Commonality of the Mystery of the Mercers of the City
of London v New Hampshire Insurance Co* [1992] 2 Lloyd's Rep. 365 (though
the contract there was held not to be a guarantee at least in the ordinary sense (at
369, 371, 374 and 375) and the distinction between discharge by variation and
discharge by breach by the creditor reflected a concession by counsel (at
367)).

[*Add text at the end of note 502: page* [2230]]
cf. *Spliethoff's Bevrachtingskantoor BV v Bank of China Ltd* [2015] EWHC 999
(Comm), [2015] 2 Lloyd's Rep. 123 at [172]–[181] (a term in a contract
(assumed to be a true guarantee for this purpose, though held to be a performance
bond) whereby the guarantor's obligations "shall not be affected or prejudiced by
any dispute" between the creditor and principal debtor held to cover disputes
involving an allegation of fraud in the creditor so that guarantor not discharged).

(d) *Discharge of Surety on Other Grounds*

Release or surrender of securities

45–119   [*In note 592, delete* "Insolvency Rules 1986 ... r.6.109(2)" *and substitute: page*
[2240]]
; Insolvency (England and Wales) Rules 2016 (SI 2016/1024) r.14.19(2) (in force
April 6, 2017).

Neglect of creditor in relation to securities

45–120   [*Add to note 597, at the end: page* [2241]]
; *Alpstream AG v PK Airfinance Sarl* [2015] EWCA Civ 1318, [2016] 2 P. & C.R.
2 at [115]–[118].

Creditor free to decide whether to realise security

45–121   [*Add to note 603, at the end: page* [2241]]
; *Alpstream AG v PK Airfinance Sarl* [2015] EWCA Civ 1318, [2016] 2 P. & C.R.
2 at [121]–[124].

Implied term

> [*In paragraph, lines 9–11, delete* "(although it may . . . *Belize Telecom Ltd*).".: *page* [2243]]

45–122

> [*Delete text of note 617 and substitute: page* [2243]]

On the general approach to the implication of terms, see Main Work, Vol.I, Ch.14. See also *General Mediterranean Holding SA.SPF (aka General Mediterranean Holding SA) v Qucomhaps Holdings Ltd* [2017] EWHC 1409 (QB) (no implied term in principal contract that creditor should take a particular step in foreign court proceedings to protect security).

Statutory demands under Insolvency Act against guarantor

> [*Add to note 624, at the end: page* [2244]]

45–123

; applied in *Inbakumar v United Trust Bank Ltd* [2012] EWHC 845 (Ch), [2012] B.P.I.R. 758.

> [*Add to paragraph, at the end: page* [2244]]

With effect from April 6, 2017, the Insolvency Rules 1986 are replaced by the Insolvency (England and Wales) Rules 2016,[627a] but the provisions formerly contained in the 1986 Rules r.6.5(4) which are the subject of the cases discussed in this paragraph are re-enacted without substantive change in r.10.5(5) of the 2016 Rules.[627b]

[627a] SI 2016/1024.
[627b] The equivalent provisions are: 2016 Rules rr.10.5(5)(a), 10.5(5)(c) and 10.5(5)(d) replacing 1986 Rules rr.6.5(4)(a), 6.5(4)(c) and 6.5(4)(d) respectively.

> [*Add new paragraph 45–124A: page* [2245]]

Creditor estopped from enforcing guarantee. In principle, a creditor may be estopped from enforcing a guarantee under the doctrine of promissory estoppel (sometimes known as forbearance in equity).[636a] However, where, for example, a creditor promises not to enforce a guarantee "indefinitely" while the guarantor works (unpaid) for the principal debtor, such a promise to postpone enforcement is likely to be interpreted as applying only where the creditor agrees to the continuation of the work rather than so as to allow the guarantor unilaterally to prevent the enforcement of the guarantee by continuing to undertake the work.[636b]

45–124A

[636a] *Dunbar Assets Plc v Butler* [2015] EWHC 2546 (Ch), [2015] B.P.I.R. 1358. On this doctrine generally see Main Work, Vol.I, paras 3–085 et seq.
[636b] *Dunbar Assets Plc v Butler* [2015] EWHC 2546 (Ch) at [49]–[50].

7. Surety's Right to Indemnity and Contribution

Surety's right to indemnity against principal debtor

> [*In note 637, update reference to Goff and Jones, The Law of Unjust Enrichment to: page* [2245]]

45–125

9th edn (2016), paras 19-16–19-21

Payment without request

45–126 [In note 649, delete "(this point not being addressed by the 8th edn)" *and substitute: page* [2246]]
(this point not being addressed by the 9th edn)

[In note 650, update reference to Goff and Jones, The Law of Unjust Enrichment to: page [2246]]

9th edn (2016), para.20-02

Surety's right to contribution from co-sureties

45–135 [*In note 686, update reference to Goff and Jones, The Law of Unjust Enrichment to: page* [2251]]
9th edn (2016), paras 19-9–19.13

[*In paragraph, lines 16–17 of, delete* "Civil Liability (Contribution) Act 1978" *and substitute: page* [2251]]
Limitation Act 1980

8. Legislative Protection of Sureties

Introduction

45–146 [*Add to note 736, line 1, after* "above, para.38–335": *page* [2256]]
(as amended by this Supplement).

(a) *Consumer Protection from Unfair Trading Regulations 2008*

No "rights of redress" for consumer sureties

45–148 [*In note 761, line 3, delete* "s.2(3)" *and substitute: page* [2259]]
s.2(4)

(c) *Unfair Contract Terms Act 1977*

Unfair Contract Terms Act 1977 and Consumer Rights Act 2015

45–150 [*Add to note 768, line 2, after* "contracts made on or": *page* [2259]]
after

Exclusion of surety's rights to be discharged

45–153 [*In note 785, update reference to Treitel on The Law of Contract to: page* [2261]]
14th edn (2015), paras 7–074—7–075

(d) *Unfair Terms in Consumer Contracts*

h4s Application of these controls to contracts of suretyship; and English
decisions

45–156 to
45–158

[*Delete the text of paragraphs 45–156 to 45–158 and substitute: pages*
[2263]–[2266]]

45–156–
158

Application of these controls to contracts of suretyship. The question whether
the 1999 Regulations and, for contracts made on or after October 1, 2015, the
Consumer Rights Act 2015 Pt 2, apply to contracts of suretyship received no
definitive answer until the recent decision of the Court of Justice of the EU in
Tarcău v Banca Comercială Intesa Sanpaolo România SA.[800] The 1999 Regulations (following the 1993 Directive itself) did not specify the types of contract to
which they applied beyond defining their parties; and these parties were referred
to as the "seller and supplier" (the person contracting in the course of business)
and "consumer" (the individual not contracting in the course of business), this
reflecting closely the terminology used by the English language version of the
1993 Directive.[801] This terminology suggested that the business sells goods (or
other property) or supplies services (including financial services) *to* the consumer,[802] and this in turn suggested that the 1993 Directive (and therefore also
the 1999 Regulations) applied to contracts of suretyship only in the rare situation
where the *creditor* is a consumer, and the surety the person acting in the course
of business.[803] However, other language versions of the 1993 Directive instead
refer more openly to a "professional" or "tradesman" defined in a similar
manner,[804] and, noting this, the Court of Justice of the EU has clarified that the
1993 Directive applies to *all types* of consumer contract, defined merely by
reference to their parties: persons contracting in the course of business on the one
hand, and consumers, viz, natural persons contracting other than in the course of
business, on the other.[805] According to the Court of Justice, this interpretation
gives effect to the purpose of the Directive in the protection of consumers as
"weaker parties" as regards both their bargaining power and their level of
knowledge.[806] This general view was then applied to the context of contracts of
suretyship by the Court of Justice in *Tarcău*.[807] There, the parents of the director
and sole shareholder of a commercial company had guaranteed and provided real
security for the payment of sums owed by that company to a bank. The national
court making the preliminary reference considered that the 1993 Directive (and
therefore its national implementing legislation) applied only to contracts for the
supply of goods or services *to* consumers,[808] but the Court of Justice confirmed
that the Directive applies to "all contracts" between consumers and sellers or
suppliers and that "[t]he purpose of the contract is thus, subject to the exceptions
listed in the recital 10 of the Directive[809] . . . irrelevant in determining the scope
of the directive".[810] As a result, the 1993 Directive could apply to a contract of
guarantee undertaken by a "consumer" or to another contract under which a
"consumer" provides security for the performance of an obligation by another
person, even if that other person is a commercial company rather than another
consumer.[811] Indeed, in the view of the Court of Justice, the protection provided
by the 1993 Directive for consumers as "weaker parties"

"is particularly important in the case of a contract providing security or a contract of guarantee concluded between a banking institution and a consumer. Such a contract is based on a personal commitment of the surety or guarantor to pay a contractual debt owed by a third party. That commitment involves onerous obligations for the person entering into it, the effect of which is to subject that person's own property to a financial risk which is often difficult to quantify."[812]

For this purpose, "consumer" is an "objective" concept (and therefore does not depend on the knowledge or bargaining power of the individual) and is to be assessed by reference to the "functional criterion" of whether the contract arose in the course of activities outside his trade, business or profession.[813] The question whether a particular person is to be categorised as a "consumer" in this way remains for the national court to determine taking into account of all the circumstances,[814] but in the case of security being provided for performance of the obligations of a commercial company, this would turn on whether he "acted for purposes relating to his trade, business or profession or because of functional links he has with that company, such as a directorship or non-negligible share-holding" or whether instead "he acted for purposes of a private nature".[815] Earlier English decisions on the application of the 1999 Regulations to contracts of suretyship must now be read subject to this very clear ruling by the Court of Justice on the application of the 1993 Directive.[816] Similarly, the provisions of the Consumer Rights Act 2015 which implement the 1993 Directive by subjecting the terms of a consumer contract to a test of unfairness must also be interpreted as applying to contracts by which a "consumer" guarantees the debt or other obligation of a third party.[817] This interpretation fits more naturally the terminology used by the 2015 Act, as it calls the business party the "trader" rather than the seller or supplier.[818] It should also be noted that the 2015 Act extends (or appears to extend) the definition of "consumer" to an individual contracting "wholly or *mainly*" for purposes outside that individual's trade, etc.[819]

[800] C-74/15 (Order of CJEU) November 19, 2015 ("*Tarcău* (C-74/15)"). Main Work, Vol.II, para.45–156 and corresponding paragraphs in earlier editions have argued that the 1993 Directive (and, therefore, its UK implementing legislation, the 1999 Regulations) apply to contracts of suretyship where the surety is a "consumer" by reference to the same textual and teleological grounds as formed the basis of the reasoning of the CJEU in *Brusse v Jahani BV* (C-488/11) May 30, 2013 and *Šiba v Devėnas* (C-537/13) January 15, 2015, on which its decision in *Tarcău* (C-74/15) was based.

[801] See Main Work, Vol.II, para.38–207.

[802] See Main Work, Vol.II, para.38–207.

[803] An example of a contract covered in this way would be a loan by a private individual to another person, whether for that person's business or not, which is guaranteed by a bank or other financial institution. Here, the guarantor (the bank) would be acting in the course of a business and the creditor (the lender of the money) could fall within the definition of a "consumer".

[804] The non-consumer party to the contract is termed *professionnel* in the French and *Gewerbetreibender* in the German versions of Directive 93/13/EEC art.2(c).

[805] *Brusse v Jahani BV* (C-488/11) May 30, 2013; *Šiba v Devėnas* (C-537/13) January 15, 2015, on which see Main Work, Vol.II, para.38–203.

[806] *Brusse v Jahani BV* (C-488/11) at para.31.

[807] C-74/15 (Order of CJEU) November 19, 2015.

[808] *Tarcău* (C-74/15) at para.14.

[809] On these "exceptions" see Main Work, Vol.II, para.38–203 n.1280.

[810] *Tarcău* (C-74/15) at para.22. On the status of these "exceptions" see Main Work, para.1280 n.1280. The CJEU contrasted the position under the former Council Directive 87/102/EEC of 22 December 1986 concerning consumer credit (itself repealed by Directive 2008/48/EC of the European Parliament and of the Council of 23 April 2008 on credit agreements for consumers) which

applied only to "contracts whereby a creditor grants or promises to grant a consumer a credit" which has led the Court to exclude contracts of guarantee from its scope: *Tarcău* (C-74/15) at para.22, citing *Berliner Kindl Brauerie AG v Siepert* (C-208/98) [2000] E.C.R. I-1741 at paras 17–23.

⁸¹¹ *Tarcău* (C-74/15) paras 24–25. The CJEU therefore confirmed the view taken by the Main Work, para.45–156 that the 1993 Directive clearly applies to contracts of suretyship. It is submitted that no distinction is to be made for this purpose between contracts of guarantee and contracts of indemnity as this distinction is understood by English law and as explained in the Main Work, Vol.II, paras 45–006—45–008. Indeed, in *Bucura v SC Bancpost SA* (C-348/14) July 9, 2015 (available only in French) at paras 35–38 the CJEU held that the 1993 Directive could apply to a contract under which the alleged "consumer" contracted as "co-debtor" to a person concluding a contract of consumer credit.

⁸¹² *Tarcău* (C-74/15) at para.25.

⁸¹³ *Tarcău* (C-74/15) at para.27 citing *Costea v SC Volksbank România SA* (C-110/14) April 23, 2015 para.21, on which see above, para.38–032.

⁸¹⁴ *Tarcău* (C-74/15) at para.28.

⁸¹⁵ *Tarcău* (C-74/15) at para.29.

⁸¹⁶ *Governor and Co of the Bank of Scotland v Singh*, Unreported June 17, 2005 (QB, Mercantile Ct, Manchester); *Manches LLP v Freer* [2006] EWHC 991 (QB) at [25]; *Williamson v Governor of the Bank of Scotland* [2006] EWHC 1289 (Ch) (1999 Regulations cannot apply to contracts of guarantee undertaken by a natural person acting other than in the course of business). cf. *Barclays Bank Plc v Kufner*; *Royal Bank of Scotland v Chandra* [2010] EWHC 105 (Ch), [2010] 1 Lloyd's Rep. 677 at [102] (affirmed [2011] EWCA Civ 192, [2011] Bus. L.R. D149 on other grounds); *United Trust Bank Ltd v Dohil* [2011] EWHC 3302 (QB) at [73] (1999 Regulations can apply to contracts of guarantee undertaken by a natural person acting other than in the course of business).

⁸¹⁷ The 2015 Act sets out the general scheme of controls of unfair contract terms in Pt 2: see Main Work, Vol.II, paras 38–334 et seq.

⁸¹⁸ Consumer Rights Act 2015 s.2(2), above, para.38–352.

⁸¹⁹ 2015 Act s.2(3); s.76(2).

Vulnerable types of clause

[*In paragraph, lines 1–4, delete* "If the Directive (and, . . . " *to* "fairness may be significant." *and substitute: page* [2266]]   **45–159**

There are a number of areas where the terms of a contract of suretyship by a consumer surety and a creditor acting in the course of business (and therefore a "trader") may be open to the charge of unfairness within the meaning of the 1999 Regulations or Pt 2 of the Consumer Rights Act 2015.

[*Add to paragraph, line 21, after* "creditor (the "supplier"": *page* [2267]]   **45–160**
or "trader"

[*Delete text of note 837 and substitute: page* [2267]]
See above, para.45–156.